Strategic Management

Theory and Practice

Third Edition

By the Same Author

HUSSEY, D.E. and LANGHAM, M.J.
Corporate Planning—The Human Factor

HUSSEY, D.E.
Introducing Corporate Planning, 4th Edition

HUSSEY, D.E.
Management Training and Corporate Strategy

TAYLOR, B. & HUSSEY, D.E.
The Realities of Planning

Other Titles of Interest

DOZ, Y.
Strategic Management in Multinational Companies

FRIEND, J. AND HICKLING, A.
Planning under Pressure

McNAMEE, P.
Developing Strategies for Competitive Advantage
Tools and Techniques for Strategic Management

THE BEST OF LONG RANGE PLANNING—FIRST SERIES

Strategic Planning—The Chief Executive and the Board. Bernard Taylor (ed.)
Entrepreneurship. Bruce Lloyd (ed.)
Making Strategic Planning Work in Practice. Basil Denning (ed.)
Planning for Information as a Corporate Resource. Alfred Collins (ed.)
Developing Strategies for Competitive Advantage. Patrick McNamee (ed.)
Strategic Planning for Human Resources. Sheila Rothwell (ed.)
Strategic Service Management. Denis Boyle (ed.)
Strategic Management in Major Multinational Companies. Nigel Freedman (ed.)
Turning Strategy into Action. Ken Irons (ed.)
Shareholder Value: Key to Corporate Development. Christopher Clarke (ed.)
Strategic Management in Japanese Companies. Toyohiro Kono (ed.)
Strategic Planning for Public Service and Non-Profit Organizations. John M.
   Bryson (ed.)

Strategic Management

Theory and Practice

Previously titled Corporate Planning: Theory and Practice

D. E. HUSSEY

Managing Director

Harbridge Consulting Group Ltd

THIRD EDITION

PERGAMON

U.K.	Elsevier Science Ltd, The Boulevard, Langford Lane, Kidlington, Oxford OX5 1GB, U.K
U.S.A.	Elsevier Science Inc., 660 White Plains Road, Tarrytown, New York 10591-5153, U.S.A.
JAPAN	Elsevier Science Japan, Tsunashima Building Annex, 3-20-12 Yushima, Bunkyo-ku, Tokyo 113, Japan

Copyright © 1994 David E. Hussey

First Edition 1974
Second Edition 1982
Reprinted 1984
Third Edition 1994

Library of Congress Cataloging in Publication Data

Hussey, D. E. (David E.)
    Strategic management: theory and practice/by D. E. Hussey.
    p. cm.
    Includes bibliographical references (p.   ).
    1. Strategic planning. I. Title.
    HD30.28.H882 1993
    658.4'012–dc20   93–48265

British Library Cataloguing in Publication Data

A catalogue record for this book is available from the British Library

ISBN 0 08 041394 3 (Hardcover)
ISBN 0 08 042562 3 (Flexicover)

Printed and bound in Great Britain by The Alden Press, Oxford

Acknowledgements

Acknowledgement of quotations is made in the text with a detailed reference at the end of each chapter. As the quotations I have used make an important contribution to this book, I should like to stress this by giving a summary list of the works quoted.

The definition of PLAN from the 5th edition of the *Concise Oxford Dictionary*, © 1964, Oxford University Press, is used by permission of the Clarendon Press, Oxford.

R. C. Ackoff, *A Concept of Corporate Planning*, Wiley Interscience (John Wiley & Sons Inc.), 1970.

E. K. Warren, *Long Range Planning: The Executive Viewpoint*, © 1970, is used by permission of Prentice-Hall, Inc., Englewood Cliffs, New Jersey. The influence of this book on the development of my own philosophies has been far greater than is perhaps suggested by the few extracts quoted.

Quotations from B. W. Denning, *Corporate Planning: Selected Concepts*, © 1971, McGraw-Hill Book Co. (UK) Ltd., are reproduced with permission.

The three useful quotations from B. W. Scott's work are reprinted by permission of the publisher from *Long Range Planning in American Industry*, © 1965, by the American Management Association Inc. The same publisher also gave permission for the reprint of a diagram from J. L. Dooley and J. A. Ciapolla "Guides to screening new product ideas", *Management for the Smaller Company*, © 1959.

P. Irving allowed me to make extensive use of his thesis "Corporate planning in practice".

R. N. Anthony's book *Planning and Control Systems: A Framework for Analysis*, © 1965, Harvard University, was also a source of much inspiration.

The publishers, Elsevier Science Ltd., and authors of the following articles from *Long Range Planning*; also Microfilms International Marketing Corporation gave permission for me to quote from them:

H. F. R. Perrin, "Long Range Planning: the Concept and the Need", September 1968.

D. Smalter, "Anatomy of a Long Range Plan"; A. J. A. Argenti, "Defining corporate objectives"; D. Hargraves, "Corporative Planning—A Chairman's Guide", March 1969.

M. Kami, "Gap Analysis—Key to Super Growth", June 1969.

E. von Allmen, "Setting up Corporate Planning", September 1969.

K. A. Ringbakk, "Organised Planning in Major US Companies"; K. Pavitt, "Technological Innovations in European Industry", December 1969.

J. R. Champion, "Corporate Planning in CPC Europe"; H. I. Ansoff, J. Avner, R. G. Brandenburg, P. E. Portner, and R. Radosevitch, "Does Planning Pay?" The Effect of Planning on Success of Acquisitions in American Firms, December 1970.

J. R. Boulden, "Computerised Corporate Planning"; G. Teeling Smith, "Medicine in the 1990s"; B. Taylor and P. Irving, "Organised Planning in Major UK Companies", June 1971.

M. W. Pennington, "Why Has Planning Failed", March 1972.

R. W. Kashyap, "Management Information Systems for Corporate Planning and Control", December 1972.

Professor Ansoff also gave permission for me to quote from *Planning as a Practical Management Tool*, Bradford University Seminar Manual, 1966. Dr. Ringbakk allowed the use of extracts from "Why Planning Fails", *European Business*, Spring 1971.

Urwick Orr & Partners Ltd. allowed the reproduction of certain corporate planning and M & O diagrams. K. Lander let me quote from his article "Corporate Planning" which appeared in *The Consulting Engineer*, December 1968.

J. D. Bernal, *Science in History*, Pelican, with acknowledgement to C. A. Watts & Co. Ltd., London.

S. Thume and R. J. House, "Where Long-range Planning Pays off", *Business Horizons*, August 1970.

Stanford Research Institute for permission to reproduce the copyright diagram "The System of Plans" from *The Strategic Plan*, and other reports.

A. Saunders and N. J. Smith gave permission for me to use a diagram from their study "Hydraulic Cranes from Armstrong's Elswick Works, 1846–1936: a product life cycle in capital goods", *Journal and Proceedings of the Industrial Market Research Association*, Vol. 6, No. 2, May 1970.

The editors of the *Daily Telegraph* and the *Financial Times* who allowed me to quote from various articles appearing in their newspapers.

G. J. Norwood and M. L. Smith "Market Mortality of New Productions in the Pharmaceutical Industry", *Journal of the American Pharmaceutical Association*, November 1971.

A diagram was reproduced with permission from E. J. McCarthy's *Basic Marketing: A Managerial Approach*, 3rd edn., Homewood, Ill., Richard D. Irwin Inc.

G. A. Steiner, *Top Management Planning*, Macmillan Publishing Co., Inc., New York, © the Trustees of Columbia University in the City of New York, 1969.

A. Marshall, *Principles of Economics*, 8th edn., 1920 (from the 1956 reprint), with the permission of Macmillan, London, Basingstoke, and New York.

B. W. Denning and M. E. Lehr, "The Extent and Nature of Corporate Long Range Planning in the United Kingdom", *Journal of Management Studies*, Vol. 8, 2 May 1971; Vol. 9, 1 February 1972.

Quotations from H. I. Ansoff, *Corporate Strategy*, © 1964, McGraw-Hill; T. Levitt, *Innovation in Marketing*, © 1962, McGraw-Hill; and M. Koontz, *Towards a Unified Theory of Management*, © 1964, are all used with the permission of McGraw-Hill Book Company, New York.

G. G. C. Parker and E. L. Segura, "How to Get a Better Forecast", *Harvard Business Review*, March–April 1971.

A. C. Carr, "Can an Executive Afford a Conscience?" *Harvard Business Review*, July–August 1970.

H. E. Wrapp, "Organisation for Long-range Planning", *Harvard Business Review*, January–February 1957.

Table 14 of the *Annual Abstract of Statistics* 1972 is reproduced with permission of Her Majesty's Stationery Office.

H. Heaton, *Economic History of Europe*, Harper & Row, 1948.

N. Wates, "Social Responsibilities in Industry", (lecture to the Runnymede Trust, 5 October 1971).

P. Drucker, *The Practice of Management*, Wm. Heinemann Ltd., 1955, and *Managing for Results*, Wm. Heinemann Ltd., 1964, are used with the permission of Wm. Heinemann Ltd., London, and Harper & Row Inc., New York.

The extracts from A. J. A. Argenti, *Corporate Planning: A Practical Guide* (George Allen & Unwin, 1968) are used with the permission of George Allen & Unwin Ltd. and Dow-Jones Irwin Inc.

J. B. Quinn and H. Rance, "Technological Strategies for Industrial Companies", "Financing R & D", both from *Management Decision*, Autumn 1968, are used by permission.

A paper by G. H. Doughty, presented at a Society for Long Range Planning Conference in January 1971, is also referred to.

I. Carson, "The Big Leap in Corporate Planning", *International Management*, April 1972. International Computes Ltd., Robin Ramm & Partners, and Baring Brothers & Co. Ltd., all gave me permission to use various examples of the use of computerised corporate models.

A. C. Neilsen Co. Ltd. gave permission for me to quote from the *Neilsen Researcher*. Kraushar Andrews & Eassie Ltd. let me make use of their research findings in *New Products in the Grocery Trade*, 1971.

Tube Industries Ltd., Tate & Lyle Ltd., Union Carbide Europe SA (on behalf of Union Carbide Corporation, New York), Procter & Gamble Ltd., and the Shell-Mex & BP Group all allowed me to use copyright material.

The editor of *The Accountant* gave permission for me to reproduce an article "Corporate Planning—Some Problems and Benefits" which I wrote for the 30 September 1971 issue.

American Heritage for permission to quote from *The Horizon Book of the Elizabethan World*, 1967.

Harbridge Consulting Group Ltd. for permission to use various models and to quote from research publications and other copyright material.

CONTENTS

PART 4. OPERATIONAL PLANNING

PART 5. INTRODUCING PLANNING TO AN ORGANISATION

Introduction to the Third Edition

Planning has come a long way since the first edition of this book—then titled *Corporate Planning: Theory and Practice*—was published in 1974. When I revised it for the second edition in 1982 I added a number of new chapters. This process has continued in this new edition, which is not surprising after a lapse of 12 years.

The intention of the first edition was to produce a book that was comprehensive, and provided a good coverage of the theory and practice of the subject. It was this combined objective, which was new at the time, which probably contributed to the book becoming a winner of the John Player Management Author of the Year Award, an event which still gives me considerable pleasure.

In this new edition I have tried to bring the book up to date, and make it the most comprehensive guide available. Those who have followed the first two editions will notice that the number of chapters on strategic analysis continues to increase. This time I have tried to add to the practicality by providing additional chapters with detailed guidance on the application of two of the major techniques—competitor analysis and portfolio analysis. I hope that this will help those who have to apply these techniques to move more easily from concept to application. The behavioural aspects of planning now take up many more chapters, and the chapter on Human Resource Planning is new, and includes much of the new thinking I have been developing over the past 5 years.

The reader will find many approaches in the book which are original, if not in concept, then at least in the detailed methods of application. Almost every analytical approach described has been used by me personally in a number of situations, either in my career as a planner in industry, or with my experience post 1976 in consultancy. Where this is not the case, I have tried to remember to say so.

A comprehensive book on strategic management has to do more than reflect personal experience. Throughout I have given references to the main authorities on the subject, with descriptions of their views, and comprehensive references to other works. This should be useful for the practitioner, but is essential for academic purposes. References have been made to research, and the book contains many examples and case studies. Again I have been fortunate in being able to draw on the findings of various research studies of my own firm, and of course to add to this as much published work as I could identify.

There is one major change in that I have had to drop the extensive bibliography of books and articles which appeared in the first two editions. This is a matter of practicality, in that the literature is now so vast that it is a major task to record it all, and the resultant bibliography would fill volumes. In its place I have given a guide to resource sources, that is the books that others have compiled that provide extensive references for the subject, and I have restricted my lists to recommendations for further reading.

I am fortunate in that my job helps me to keep up to date on the subject, as well as providing me with a continuous flow of new situations. Through my writing and editing, which include two serial publications I am in regular contact with practitioners and academics from around the world. This is very helpful for staying abreast of new ideas, and ensuring that I read a fair sample of new books and articles. However if there are any key omissions I have to take the blame myself. Keeping a book up to date is more than just modifying its title to fit modern concepts, and I hope readers will notice more changes than this.

The main point is for the book to be useful. I set out to produce a comprehensive, useful guide, and I am sure that my fellow practitioners will soon let me know of any deficiencies.

D. E. Hussey
Horsham
Sussex

PART 1

The Concept and the Need

"If a man take no thought about what is distant, he will find sorrow near at hand"—

CONFUCIUS, 551–497 BC

1

From Planning and the Tasks of Management to Strategic Management

In any aspect of management theory, the enthusiastic practitioner is both a source of strength and a cause of weakness. Strength, because no concept of management can grow and mature unless it has the backing of keen supporters: weakness, because enthusiasm too often leads to an overselling of its benefits. The act of overselling causes a lack of definition about the subject and surrounds it in a hazy vagueness.

Strategic management is no exception. It undoubtedly has a strong body of supporters, many of whom have contributed to the development of the subject. Without them it would have died. But if some of its enthusiasts have never really understood the subject: others have overemphasised its benefits without also pointing out the difficulties. As a result it, too, suffers from conceptual misunderstandings concealed under a semantic smoke screen. Too often it is seen as a universal miracle cure for all corporate ills and ailments: too often its enthusiasts shelter behind platitudes which themselves reveal a lack of knowledge of the underlying concepts.

Blurring of meaning also comes about because the subject develops over time, new terms are coined to explain new nuances of emphasis, old terms are used in a slightly different way, and because there is no standard dictionary of management terms various authors attach different meanings to each of the various terms.

In the mid-1960s the "in" description was long range planning, and this was attached to the first society formed in the UK for those concerned with planning. The emphasis behind this description was getting organisations to plan beyond the annual budget. By the late 1960s, many authorities were using the term corporate planning, on the theory that there should be an integration between the short and the long term. This term still exists, and is used later in this chapter to look at the planning element of our subject.

Most writers on corporate planning talked about the strategic plan as part of what they were about. By the early 1970s many put more emphasis on the strategic

3

role, and strategic planning began to be a more widely used term to describe the whole process. At one point in its history the Society for Long Range Planning changed its name to the Society for Strategic Planning, reflecting the change in thinking that the title suggested.

By the late 1970s the idea of strategic planning was swallowed up in a broader concept of strategic management, which put as much emphasis on implementation as on strategy formulation. This term has lasted until the 1990s, although there is now the beginnings of a hint that the slant may now be shifting to the management of strategic change. But more of this later.

To try to make sense out of what can be semantic jungle I will standardise on corporate planning to relate what is meant here to planning as used in the literature on the tasks of management. Later in the chapter I will discuss the newer terms and what they mean.

Part of the problem lies in understanding what is meant by "planning" and what is meant by "management". A frequent statement of corporate planners is that as planning is part of the task of management, every manager ought to spend a definite percentage of time on planning: just how much is a matter for the whim of the planner. Certainly planning is an important element of management, although the percentage of time that should be spent on it is probably indefinable. At the very least it will vary between function, industry, and company. As a generalisation it is probably true to say that the higher the echelon of management the greater the time that should be devoted to planning. But there is more to it than this, for the type of planning will vary between function. The chief executive stands at one extreme with a concern for strategic decision areas with relatively long time horizons. At the other end of the management scale, the plant foreman will probably be only concerned with planning today's jobs. Tomorrow's plan will be made tomorrow. All this is "planning" and certainly an important part of management activity.

Yet the true corporate planner means much more when talking about planning. Somehow the dictionary definitions do not seem to fit:

"PLAN[1] 1. Drawing, diagram made by projection on flat surfaces, esp. one showing relative position of parts of (one floor of) a building; large-scale detailed map of town or district; table indicating times, places, etc., of intended proceedings etc.; scheme of arrangement; project, design; way of proceeding, as *the better plan is to peel them after boiling*; plan of campaign; (perspective) of any of the imaginary planes, perpendicular to line of vision, passing through objects shown in picture.

"2. Make a plan of (ground, existing building); design (building to be constructed etc.) scheme, arrange beforehand (procedure etc.), as *planned economy; make plans.*"

Some of these meanings in the dictionary appear to be only distant relations of the term planning as used in business. Planners mean much more besides. They mean a continuing process of corporate planning which involves many other aspects of management besides "making plans".

Many writers have written brief definitions of planning, long-range planning, and corporate planning. Some of the numerous examples are quoted to provide something of the broad flavour of meaning which corporate planners give to the term. It is only fair to stress that all the authors explore the meaning in greater depth and the only way to appreciate their full arguments is to read their works.

Ackoff[2] states: "Planning is the design of a desired future and of effective ways of bringing it out".

Long-range planning is held by Perrin[3] to be a "Systematic attempt to increase the rate of profitable growth of an entity in the long run".

For Warren[4] "Planning is essentially a process of preparing for the commitment of resources in the most economical fashion and, by preparing, of allowing this commitment to be made faster and less disruptively".

Denning[5] defines corporate planning as "A formal, systematic, managerial process, organised by responsibility, time and information, to ensure that operational planning, project planning and strategic planning are carried out regularly to enable top management to direct and control the future of the enterprise".

Scott[6] believes "Planning is an analytical process which encompasses an assessment of the future, the determination of desired objectives—the context of that future, the development of alternative courses of action to achieve such objectives; and the selection of a course (or courses) of action from among these alternatives".

Irving[7] defines corporate planning as "1. The formal process of developing objectives for the corporation and its component parts, evolving alternative strategies to achieve these objectives, and doing this against a background of a systematic appraisal of internal strengths and weaknesses and external environmental changes. "2. The process of translating strategy into detailed operational plans and seeing that these plans are carried out".

Although Steiner[8] states bluntly that "Planning without plans is a waste of time" (a statement which I fully support), it is obvious from the various concepts outlined in the quoted definitions that planning is much more than preparing plans. It has been said that plans are the product of planning: if this is true they are an intermediate. The real product is action, for without this plans are also a waste of time.

When corporate planners talk of "planning", or "corporate planning", or "long-range planning", they mean all the things that run through this management process to the final actions. The word "planning" is made to work very hard, and means things which are not covered by the dictionary definition. They also think of a continuous management process: something that goes on in the organisation all the time, although individual parts of that process may also result in occasional plans, e.g. a specific project plan for a new factory.

There is much more to be explored here, but before we do this I should like to widen the issue to the nature of the management tasks or process. This, again, is a subject that has been defined and re-defined by generations of management writers. It is not my intention to plough the furrow again, but rather to look specifically at what a number of writers consider to be the components of the management task. (Those who wish to study this further are referred to the literature survey by Martin V. Sears and Mabel T. Gragg, which appeared in an appendix of a work by Anthony[9] which will be referred to later in this chapter.) I also drew on an article by Osmond.[10]

Most subsequent writers owe some debt to Fayol,[11] who believed that there were six individual activities in the total industrial undertaking: technical (production, manufacture, adaptation); commercial (buying, selling, exchange); financial (sources and use of capital); security (of property and persons); accounting (custodianal and management information); managerial.

Managerial activities, which he considered the most important, consisted of:

1. *Planning:* "examining the future and drawing up a plan of action".
2. *Organising:* establishing a human and physical frame to enable the under-taking to achieve results (he defined sixteen duties of the "organiser" manager).
3. *Commanding:* activating the organisation.
4. *Co-ordinating:* drawing together all activity and effort.
5. *Controlling:* "seeing that everything occurs in conformity with established rules and expressed command".

Urwick[12] suggests that the general management functions are to: forecast; plan; organise; direct; co-ordinate; control; communicate.

Drucker[13] believes that there are five basic operations in the work of a manager: setting objectives; organising; motivating and communicating; measuring perfor-mance; and developing people.

A similar but simpler classification of the management process is suggested by Brech:[14] plan; motivate and co-ordinate; and control.

Neuschel[15] states "The orderly and successful performance of any major undertaking, of whatever character, requires that a definite sequence of steps be followed in its planning and execution". He lists these as: setting objectives, developing policies to achieve objectives, organising, making a plan of action, applying skilled techniques to the task, controlling through the measurement of results.

The work of an administrator is, according to Newman,[16] divided into five basic processes: planning (which he defines as including objectives, policies, mapping of programmes, procedures, and scheduling); organising; assembling resources; supervising; and controlling.

Rathe[17] defines the basic essentials of the "management cycle" as: planning; operations; and control.

Mackenzie[18] suggests that the sequential functions of the process of manage-ment are: planning (forecasting, objectives, strategies, programming, budgeting, setting procedures, policies); organising; staffing; directing; controlling.

Although there are differences in these views, there are also many similarities. There are, of course, many other writers, some of whom have different opinions. My intention has not been to conduct a survey of all views but to prepare a background against which we can continue to examine the meaning of the word "planning".

It is possible to re-classify the various elements of the management tasks into three broad categories.

Deterministic: those tasks concerned with the creative, planning, and arranging functions and including organising, policies, and procedures.

Motivational: tasks which motivate the organisation, including communication, leadership, and personal development.

Directing: implementation, co-ordination, and controlling.

The purpose of this classification is as an aid to the thoughts which follow: it is not postulated as a scheme of analysis which is better than the references.

Certainly the word "planning" appears frequently as one of the fundamental management tasks, and if this word is taken to mean "making plans" we have one aspect of interpretation which can be expected. But "planning" in the sense of "corporate planning" includes many of the other factors which are listed as functions of the management process. A glance back at the reference to "planning" will make some of this clear.

When a manager talks of corporate planning he is referring to a comprehensive business process which involves many types of planning activity. It also includes elements which can be classified under the simple scheme given earlier.

Deterministic: making plans, creating ideas, determining objectives, organising to fulfil plans, setting policies and procedures. Co-ordinating.

Motivational: demonstrating leadership, encouraging others to work for a defined future, motivating through clear communication, participation in certain aspects of the planning process, and through a system of personal objectives. Clarifying what the organisation is trying to do so that people can do it! Co-ordinating. Developing people.

Directing: Monitoring and controlling progress against plans. Referring changed circumstances back to the deterministic stage for re-planning. Issuing instructions so that plans can be implemented. Co-ordinating.

To put it another way, a planner would argue that a corporate planning process could be classified under any one of the analyses of the *complete management task.* One example will suffice, using Drucker's classification.

Corporate planning includes the setting of objectives, organising the work, people, and systems to enable those objectives to be attained, motivating through the planning process and through the plans, measuring performance and so controlling progress of the plan, and developing people through better decision-making, clearer objectives, more involvement, and awareness of progress.

If we look at it this way, we can see quite clearly that corporate planning *is* management. It is not *all* there is to management, for there are other aspects that also run across the whole spectrum. It is fair to say that it is a complete dimension of management, around which can be structured a total approach to the running of a business.

It is also possible to fulfil all the management tasks without having a process of corporate planning. Companies have always planned, even though they may not have used the methods described in this book; they have always fulfilled the other aspects of the management task even though they may have used other methods to do it. Corporate planning had not been "invented" when Fayol propounded his definitions. Much as planners hate to admit it, it is even possible to be successful without undertaking any corporate planning.

When corporate planning is properly applied as a management process it becomes something which unites all parts of the company, all aspects of the management task, into one complete management approach.

Certain things follow from this. Corporate planning must be comprehensive. It embraces all types of actiity and all time horizons within the company. It is also possible for a company to apply beneficially certain selected parts of the corporate planning process and to elect to forego the other elements. As it is a process, it is continuous. It is formally applied: that is, it results in written documents that can be communicated and controlled without distortion. The extent to which documents are formalised is something that may be varied to suit the company.

Much of the process is future oriented. It is designed to fulfil the various tasks of management by giving the company a greater concern for the future, and accepting the fact that even the smallest of today's decisions has some effect on the future.

It is also concerned with short-term plans and programmes, and with the definition of standing policies and procedures. These aspects are subsidiary but fully co-ordinated with the attention which corporate planning pays to the future.

Previously we examined a few descriptions of the management process. Now I should like to refer to two short definitions of "management". Hopf[19] states:

"Management is the direction of an enterprise, through planning, organising, co-ordinating and controlling of its human and material resources, toward the achievement of a predetermined objective."

Koontz[20] refers to "...the establishment of an environment in which people can effectively perform in a formalised group for the attainment of group goals".

It would be possible to substitute corporate planning for management in each of these definitions. However, this would suggest that corporate planning was more than a complete dimension of management. A much more meaningful statement results if we add the phrase "which may be achieved through corporate planning".

The contention that corporate planning is a complete process of management which involves more than just "making plans" is the framework for this book. I believe that it is a viewpoint which many managers overlook, which leads to confusion about what they are trying to achieve through corporate planning. Kirby Warren[4] provides a useful analysis of misconceptions about corporate planning (for which he uses the term long-range planning):

"Where they exist, these misconceptions fall into three basic categories. They are:

1. Confusion between long-range planning and one of its major parts or elements.
2. Confusion between long-range planning and one of the key areas in which it is required.
3. Confusion between long-range planning and one of its common characteristics."

This discussion of corporate planning has not yet ventured below the surface into the maze of semantics which surround other aspects of planning, e.g. strategic, operational, project, and others. These will be fully covered in subsequent chapters. Two points remain to be considered at this time.

The first is the term long-range planning. As mentioned earlier this has largely been superseded, and can generally be treated as synonymous with corporate planning. The process of planning is concerned with all aspects, not just the long range. Although the future orientation is certainly the most important argument in favour of the process, long-range planning without the back up of short-range plans will fail.

The second point is that mention should be made of the work of Anthony[9] in establishing an analytical framework as a basis for future research into the broad area of planning and control systems. Anthony's scheme is not adopted for further analysis in this book, but is relevant because it provides more insight into the terms planning and control.

He divides the concept into three key terms "strategic planning", "management control", and "operational control" (Fig. 1.1) (but note that strategic planning will be discussed in the wider sense in the appropriate chapters which follow).

"*Strategic planning* is the process of deciding on objectives of the organisation, on changes in these objectives, on the resources used to attain these objectives, and on the policies that are to govern the acquisition, use, and disposition of these resources."

"*Management control* is the process by which managers assure that resources are obtained and used effectively in the accomplishment of the organisation's objectives. Management control includes decisions about what to do in the future (i.e.

Strategic planning	Management control	Operational control
Choosing company objectives	Formulating budgets	
Planning the organisation	Planning staff levels	Controlling hiring
Setting personnel policies	Formulating personnel practices	Implementing policies
Setting financial policies	Working capital planning	Controlling credit extension
Setting marketing policies	Formulating advertising programmes	Controlling placement of advertisements
Setting research policies	Deciding on research projects	
Choosing new product lines	Choosing product improvements	
Acquiring a new division	Deciding on plant rearrangement	Scheduling production
Deciding on non-routine capital expenditures	Deciding on routine capital expenditures	
	Formulating decision rules for operational control	Controlling inventory
	Measuring, appraising, and improving management efficiency	Measuring, appraising, and improving workers' efficiency

FIG. 1.1. Example of activities in a business organisation issued in major framework headings. (Quoted from R. N. Anthony, *Planning and Control Systems*, Harvard, 1965.)

planning), but these are carried out within guidelines established by strategic planning."

"*Operational control* is the process of assuming that specific tasks are carried out effectively and efficiently. The focus here is on execution whereas in management control both execution and planning are important."

The foregoing description of corporate planning as embracing much of what is management, and being more than the task of writing plans appeared in the first edition of this book and was written in 1973 and published a year later. It was already a long way along the path to the modern concept of strategic management.

Ansoff, DeClerk and Hayes[21] edited a book in 1976 that launched the new way of thinking about strategy and planning. It derived from a conference at Vanderbilt University, and took account of the increasing complexity of modern business. Where strategic planning emphasised the "hard" analytical aspects and looked mainly externally at the environment and markets, climate, the need for implementation and control, and the social and political aspects of managing strategy.

"Thus strategic management may be seen as a more complete way of managing a business, concerned not only with markets and decision making, but also with social developments, implementation and the 'fit' of strategy with organisational structure and climate" (Hussey[22]).

McNamee[23] defines strategic management as "...that type of management through which an organisation tries to obtain a good fit with its environment". He sees the need to understand the environment in which the organisation operates, understand the organisation, including its strategies, develop appropriate strategies, implement those strategies, and to control, evaluate and amend strategies.

Johnson and Scholes[24] state that "strategic management is concerned with deciding on strategy and planning how that strategy is to be put into effect. It can be thought of as having three main elements within it. ... There is *strategic analysis* in which the strategist seeks to understand the strategic position of the organisation. There is a *strategic choice* stage which is to do with the formulation of possible courses of action, their evaluation and the choice between them. Finally there is a *strategic implementation* stage which is concerned with planning how the choice of strategy can be put into effect".

Ansoff[25] defined the term again in 1992: "Strategic management has been alternatively described as *disciplined entrepreneurship*. Creativity, vision and entrepreneurial risk taking by key managers are essential prerequisites for success. But they are not sufficient. The key management must be supported by an organisational capability which is designed to respond to environmental turbulence. This capability consists of organisational culture; rewards; power structure; information, planning and control systems; and organisational structure which are mutually supportive and tuned to respond to discontinuous and surpriseful events."

The modern concept of planning is one that blends the analytical with the behavioural, and is as concerned with the implementation of strategy and its outcomes, as with the processes of analysis and formulation. It is worth referring to the strategic thinking imperative stressed by Ohmae[26]: "...successful business strategies result not from rigorous analysis but from a particular state of mind. In what I call the mind of the strategist, insight and a consequent drive for achievement, often amounting to a sense of mission, fuel a thought process which is basically creative and intuitive rather than rational. Strategists do not reject analysis. Indeed they can hardly do without it. But they use it only to stimulate the creative process, to test the ideas that emerge, to work out their strategic implications, or to ensure successful execution of high-potential 'wild' ideas that might otherwise never be implemented properly. Great strategies, like great works of art or great scientific discoveries, call for technical mastery in the working out but originate in insights that are beyond the reach of conscious analysis."

The term corporate is still widely used to describe the key staff role in the process of strategy management. This implies an analyst rather than a behaviouralist. Strategic management requires people who combine both sets of skills. This is where the role of the planner will move in the future, with the emphasis on managing strategic change, instead of coordinating the corporate plan.

This chapter has established a base point from which exploration of corporate planning as a way of managing a business may begin. It is an exciting concept, and one which, despite its snags and pitfalls, can bring great benefit to the companies that practise it. But the benefit is something that has to be proved and this is the task of the next chapter.

References

1. *Concise Oxford Dictionary*, 5th ed., Oxford University Press, 1964.
2. Ackoff, R. C. *A Concept of Corporate Planning*, Wiley, Interscience, 1970.
3. Perrin, H. F. R. "Long Range Planning: The Concept and the Need", *Long Range Planning*, September 1968.
4. Warren, E. K. *Long Range Planning: The Executive Viewpoint*, Prentice-Hall, 1966.
5. Denning, B. W. *Corporate Planning: Selected Concepts*, McGraw-Hill, 1971.
6. Scott, B. W. *Long Range Planning in American Industry*, American Management Assocation, 1965.
7. Irving, P. "Corporate Planning in Practice: a study of the development of organised planning in major United Kingdom companies", M.Sc. dissertation, University of Bradford, 1970.
8. Steiner, G. A. *Top Management Planning*, Macmillan, 1969.
9. Anthony, R. N. *Planning and Control Systems: A Framework for Analysis*, Harvard, 1965.
10. Osmond, C. N. "Corporate Planning: its Impact on Management", *Long Range Planning*, April 1971.
11. Fayol, H. *General and Industrial Management*, Pitman, 1949.
12. Urwick, L. F. *The Pattern of Management*, University of Minnesota Press, 1956.
13. Drucker, P. F. *The Practice of Management*, Heinemann, 1955.
14. Brech, E. L. F. *Organisation*, Longmans, 1966.
15. Neuschel, R. F. *Management by System*, McGraw-Hill, 1960.
16. Newman, W. H. *Administrative Action: The Techniques of Organisation and Management*, Prentice-Hall, 1963.
17. Rathe, A. W. "Management Controls", Malcom, D. G. and Rowe, A. J. (eds.) *Business Management Control Systems*, Wiley, 1960.
18. Mackenzie, R. A. "The Management Process in 3D", *Harvard Business Review*, 1969.
19. Hope, M. A. *Office Management: Its Development and Future*, H. A. Hopf & Co., 1942.
20. Koontz, H. *Towards a Unified Theory of Management*, McGraw-Hill, 1964.
21. Ansoff, H. I., DeClerk, R. P. and Hayes, R. L. (eds.) *Strategic Planning to Strategic Management*, Wiley, 1976.

22. Hussey, D. E. "Developments in Strategic Management", Hussey, D. E. (ed.), *International Review of Strategic Management*, Volume 1, Wiley, 1990.
23. McNamee, P. *Management Accounting: Strategic Planning and Marketing*, Heinemann in association with the Chartered Institute of Management Accountants, 1988.
24. Johnson, G. and Scholes, K. *Exploring Corporate Strategy*, Prentice Hall, 1984.
25. Ansoff, H. I. "Strategic Management in a Historical perspective", Hussey, D. E. (ed.), *International Review of Strategic Management*, Vol. 2, No. 1, 1991.
26. Ohmae, K. *The Mind of the Strategist*, Penguin, 1983.

2

Strategic Management: Success or Failure?

There can only be one justification for the introduction of a system of corporate planning into a company—a belief that it can lead to improved results, which for the businessman means increased profits. For a government agency, an educational body, or other similar unit, it may mean increased service at lower costs.

Unless a chief executive has a personal belief in the ability of strategic management, and its accompanying commitment to planning, to improve bottom line results over a sustained period, he or she should not attempt to introduce it to the organisation: indeed without this belief there can be no valid reason why a chief executive should want to indulge in such a style of management.

It is a fact that many companies throughout the world practise some form of strategic management and this provides circumstantial evidence that a body of chief executives have this conviction. In my opinion the fact that hard-headed businessmen use this management style is a very good reason for assuming that they get some benefit from it.

Unfortunately, many of the benefits of a planning process are difficult to prove in absolute terms. This is because once planning is introduced, the company changes, and it is never possible to compare what has happened with what would have happened under different circumstances. It is rather like changes in the economic policy of a government. One can speculate—as the opposition parties usually do—that another and often totally opposite course of action would have led to better results. Such arguments can only rest on logic, economic theory, and idealistic belief. It is never possible to turn the clock back, and neither is it conceivable that two economic solutions could be run in parallel on a test market basis to see which is best.

In addition there is a major problem in identifying the costs of planning. Real benefit can only come if the additional profit earned exceeds the additional costs of planning. Quite apart from the conceptual problem of specifically separating the benefits of planning from those of other causes, it is almost impossible to identify costs. It may be easy to isolate the costs of any specialist planning staff, but this is only a part. It is very difficult to estimate the cost of the participation of other mangers in the process—and an overwhelming task to try to see how the cost of their participation differs from what it would be under some other style of management. Under any circumstances managers will spend some time on planning: how much more (or less) they will spend where a company has a formal planning process can probably never be computed in meaningful terms.

Logical consideration leads to an expectation that planning procedures will bring more in profits than they cost. At one time it would have been necessary to close this chapter at that point—perhaps adding that the worthiness of many other areas of management decision were also incapable of absolute proof—but a number of studies have changed this viewpoint. It is now possible to quote evidence which supports the contention that corporate planning leads to better results. These studies are not always perfect, frequently suffer from problems of sampling, and usually can only try to measure one or two aspects of results. Those quoted in this chapter refer to a formal planning process, which may not necessarily be the same as strategic management under a modern interpretation.

Planning can be carried out well or it can be done badly. Again, there is an increasing body of knowledge on the degree of satisfaction felt by companies with their planning efforts and on the problems that arise in practice.

The findings of some of these serious attempts to measure the results of planning will be woven into the fabric of this chapter. Before this step is taken it is as well to return to the beginning and look critically at the evidence proving that companies actually do planning.

As might be expected, formal corporate planning as a contribution to the science of management arose in the United States and by the early 1960s had reached a high level of management acceptance. It arrived in the United Kingdom a year or two later and attained a high point of management interest by 1967 when the Society of Long Range Planning was formed. By 1970 this society had attracted about 1000 members all concerned in some ways with long-range planning. Numerous case histories have been presented at conferences or written up as articles in the journal of the society, *Long Range Planning*, mainly supplied by companies in the United Kingdom, the United States, or the Continent of Europe. There are now companies which use this style of management in many countries throughout the world—one reason for this spread being through multinational companies applying a planning process throughout all their subsidiaries.

One of the first serious attempts to survey planning in the United Kingdom was undertaken by Denning and Lehr[1] in 1967. It was found that 25% of companies from *The Times* top 300 (excluding financial concerns and nationalised companies) were practising some form of corporate planning. The survey showed that, at that time, that it was only in seven industry groups that 25% or more of the companies in those groups were definitely undertaking corporate planning. This lead to some further analyses which will be referred to later.

Across the Atlantic, evidence that planning was acceptable was provided by the 1966 National Industrial Conference Board Survey of Business Opinions and Experience.[2] This revealed that over 90% of manufacturers sampled practised some form of formal corporate planning. Similar studies in certain other countries have suggested that around 80% of companies sampled have some kind of wide long-range plan. For example, Komo produced evidence of Japanese practise,[3] from 1965 to 1975, the Stanford Research Institute[4] surveyed the European situation in 1971, and Eppink, Keuning and de Jong[5] produced similar figures for Holland in 1976. The Dutch survey suggested that Holland lagged the USA and UK by about five years.

Denning's and Lehr's and subsequent studies in both the United Kingdom and the United States proved that there were companies who had moved into corporate planning as early as the 1950s. Not all the evidence is straightforward. Another survey by Kempner[6] and Hewkins in 1968 found that few British companies had implemented corporate planning, while a number of executives rejected it completely. These results caused a certain amount of surprise because at that time many companies were known to undertake corporate planning: the fact that few of these emerged in the survey was probably partly due to sampling problems and partly to the fact that subsidiaries of external companies were not included. Thus the result did not purport to be typical of all companies operating in Britain. The Denning/Lehr survey also showed the skewed nature of the universe to certain industries, causing sampling problems on a small-scale survey.

A membership survey carried out by the Society for Long Range Planning in 1974[7] gave further confirmation of the differences of timing in the introduction of planning by type of industry. Figure 2.1 illustrates some of the findings.

The median year of introduction would, of course, move if the survey were to be repeated today and if new firms had commenced planning. (Those not planning were organisations who had employees who belong to the Society, and the overall total not planning in the industry would be higher.) In the mid-1960s finding companies that planned in some industries (for example banking) was rather like seeking needles in haystacks.

Industries	Replies	No. not planning	Median yr. of intro. planning
Food, drink, tobacco	30	1	1970
Chemicals, pharmaceuticals	35	4	1969
Oil and energy	10	–	1969
Metals and metal manufacture	17	1	1968
Mechanical engineering	22	2	1969
Electrical engineering, electronics	17	2	1968
Motor vehicles, aircraft, ships	13	3	1969
Textiles, fibres, footwear	8	1	1971
Other manufactures	51	5	1969
Construction	20	4	1969
Transport	16	–	1969
Retailing	13	5	1970
Banking, insurance, finance	39	4	1971

FIG. 2.1. Introduction of planning by industry sectors.

The fact that many companies were undertaking planning is one thing. Whether or not they were satisfied with what they were getting out of it was another. One of the first, and still one of the most useful studies on the implementation of planning, was that by Warren,[8] which was mentioned in the previous chapter.

Ringbakk[9] describes a survey of a sample of forty US companies identified in advance as having planning staffs. This confirmed that most companies had only begun corporate planning in the early 1960s, and established that many companies were disappointed by what they had achieved, and that not all the managements concerned practised planning as vigorously or accepted it as firmly as might have been assumed. A further general conclusion was that in most of the companies, planning was still in an evolutionary stage.

Perhaps one of the important points arising from this study is a reinforcement of a fairly obvious generalisation. Any new process of management can be applied well or badly, and the results achieved are affected by the skill with which the process is applied. To me this suggests that any company considering the introduction of a formal process of planning should take pains to learn how to do it well, and should be sure that it is the type of company that can benefit from such a system. More is made of these issues in Chapter 21 which examines a number of problems of implementation.

Irving[10] made a detailed study in 1969 of twenty-seven British companies (again excluding subsidiaries of overseas companies) which were identified as undertaking a planning process. (I personally feel some affection for this survey as I acted as the guinea-pig on whom his questionnaire was piloted.) He had little difficulty in identifying his sample, but, as in the Ringbakk survey, he found that many companies had only recently undertaken planning and that their systems were still in an evolutionary stage.

Taylor and Irving,[11] in an article based on this survey, stated:

"Corporate Planning in major U.K. companies is neither as well developed nor as fully accepted as one might expect. Less than half the sample companies were found to have complete corporate plans and a further 22 per cent had functional or divisional plans only, with little or no input from the corporate level. In a number of companies there was a heavy bias towards financial projections where objectives or action programmes had not been developed for the time period in question. In others, 'planning' consisted of little more than extended budgeting.

"Since an effort was made to select those companies who were thought to have made substantial progress in the development of corporate planning, one may conclude that industry in general is doing much less.

"These findings therefore support those of Ringbakk and Kempner–Hewkins concerning the present state of development of corporate planning in Britain and America."

In general, the conclusions of the survey evidence to this point was that an increasing number of companies were introducing this system of management, but many had a long way to go before they could be classified as effective planners. Since the mid-1970s, planning has become established in most organisations of any size, in most major countries. However, there has also been almost continuous any size, in most major countries. However, there has also been almost continuous researches that have regularly thrown up the feeling that planning has not worked as well as it should have in many organisations. This theme will be returned to in later chapters.

The Society for Long Range Planning[5] study mentioned earlier provided fascinating evidence of what planning companies did and did not do. While most practised formal financial planning, forecast external events and reviewed performance against plan, only 25% undertook contingency planning, 36% diversification planning and 22% divestiment planning. Equally surprising, only 45% undertook formal organisation planning and 53% formal manpower planning.

Irving also provides some evidence of why companies decide to change to a system of corporate planning. In more than a third of his sample the introduction of planning was a direct result of major changes at board level. (My own personal experience has been that most of the planning appointments I have held have been the result of a change of chief executive. My consulting experience is similar.) In practically all cases, planning was initiated as the result of a perceived need to deliberately meet a factor of change which the company faced or expected to face. Less than a fifth of respondents stated that there was no specific event which caused planning to arrive in their companies.

Denning and Lehr[1] subjected their survey results to a detailed statistical evaluation in order to establish whether there were any particular characteristics of the planning companies when compared with the non-planners:

"If the introduction of formal long-range planning is, in fact, a managerial response to critical strategic or co-ordinative needs, one would expect evidence to that effect in the observed pattern of incidence. Vital strategic needs exist in situations of high financial risk or opportunity, whereas co-ordinative needs increase with the complexity of organizations. The following key parameters were selected for the analysis:

Financial Risk/Opportunity—Rate of technological change
                                    —Growth and variability of turnover/profits
              Complexity—Size
                              —Type of organization structure
                              —Degree of vertical integration."

Each variable was analysed separately and the data were then subjected to a multivariate analysis. The main findings were that there was a strong positive correlation between the introduction of long-range planning and companies with a high rate of technological change and a clear positive relationship between planning and capital intensity. Growth and variability of turnover were found to effect the introduction of planning only marginally.

Only two of the "complexity" factors could be measured, both size and organisational complexity having a strong relationship with the introduction of planning. Futher it was found that there was a tendency for the more complex companies to have introduced planning earlier than the less complex ones.

Two additional facts of interest emerging from the study were variation in the way that companies tackled the planning task and the higher proportion of subsidiaries of foreign companies who were doing corporate planning. While British companies included 23% known "planners", the foreign subsidiaries had 61% of their number engaged in this activity.

It is possible to draw two alternative hypotheses from the Denning/Lehr survey:

—That the complex, high capital, technological companies are the companies most likely to benefit from corporate planning; *or*
—That they are likely to perceive the need for planning before (as did the more complex companies in the sample) other types of company, and that where they lead other industries will follow. In my view the fact that over 40% of companies had introduced planning for the first time in 1967, the year of the survey, lends some support to this hypothesis. This hypothesis seems to be supported by the other research quoted.

A number of case histories of planning activities are now available from companies in Europe and the United States, and many of these provide statements about the benefits of planning. Generally, such testimony tends to fall into three groups: those who judge the system by its efficiency as a system, those who point to short-term results, and those who attempt to describe the real long-term benefits being achieved.

In my opinion, the first type of argument is fallacious. (It is interesting to note that about one half of respondents in the Ringbakk[9] survey gave this sort of argument as demonstrating planning's contribution to corporate performance.) Certainly a planning process which does not produce clear objectives and logically evaluated plans will have little value, and the efficiency of the system is a very important factor in its success. In itself, it can never be an argument for corporate planning as a management activity. British Rail may, for example, run a fast and efficient service between London and Manchester—poor consolation for the person who wants to travel to Cornwall. An efficient planning system must do more than simply be efficient: it must satisfy some economic need in a better way than would otherwise have been the case.

The next group of arguments are valid in an economic sense, but in my opinion do not provide a long-term justification for planning. Certainly, the assessment of strengths and weaknesses may lead to immediate profit improvement opportunities, the co-ordinative ability of planning may bring an immediate improvement in communication, or planning may be the factor which sparks off an organisational change. The results of all this activity can often be quantified and are frequently impressive. What should be realised is that in these cases planning is only one of a number of agencies which could have been used to secure the same results: for example, a firm of management consultants if properly briefed could have achieved the same benefit. I believe that these short-term results are the bonuses of planning, not the ultimate justification. Certainly they can pay for all the planning effort the company is likely to make in the future, so that, in effect, the other benefits are obtained free of charge.

In the third group of reasons there is a genuine effort to identify the real and tangible results of corporate planning. Such writers usually point to sustained growth and profitability, clarity of purpose, better communication, identification of additional opportunities, co-ordination, and better decision-making. The following quotation from a case history by Champion[12] is representative of the type of general belief in the value of corporate planning which numerous writers have expressed:

"As regards the immediate results hoped for from the system, they were basically two. First, top management wanted to transform its European operations from a group of quasi-autonomous affiliates into a smoothly functioning integrated European unit. To do that it was necessary among other things, that the affiliates plan together within the framework of Europe-wide objectives. The planning system has unquestionably contributed to the achievement of this goal. CPC Europe is a solid unity today imbued by a team spirit which is nourished by effective dialogue up and down the management hierarchy and across functional and national boundary lines. Clearly, this major and very difficult achievement cannot be attributed exclusively to the planning system, but the system by establishing requirements and procedures for co-operation and coordination across all boundary lines and by stimulating the frank recognition and examination of common as well as particular business problems has aided importantly.

"Secondly, top management wanted to insure that all affiliates looked at their present and future business in a rational, analytic and systematic way. It is fair to say that CPC/E management has today a thorough and organized understanding, at both the national and European levels of its present and future business potentials and that rational and organized planning has become a habit with the managers. Again, the planning system contributed significantly to the achievement by defining the parts into which a complex business and organization logically break down and by suggesting the means by which the functioning of these parts should be analyzed.

"The second part of the question can be paraphrased into 'Has the planning system contributed indirectly to profits?' It is the most difficult question to answer. Profit-wise CPC Europe has done well since the planning system was installed. It would be ridiculous to assume that the company would not have done well without the planning system. The factors that make for success or failure in business are too numerous and too complex to make it possible to point to one as the determinant factor. But it is difficult to believe that an approach to planning which rationally structures the identification and evaluation of opportunities and the identification and measurement of risks does not in some small way at least contribute to sounder management decisions regarding which opportunities to pursue and which risks to take. This is not a completely satisfactory answer, but the truth is that planning systems, like management in general, must to a certain degree be accepted on the faith that their presence is beneficial."

This belief in the benefits of planning is echoed in Irving's[6] survey. Some of the responses are quoted in the Taylor/Irving[11] article:

"Main Board Director of a large international group: 'I couldn't run the Company without a management planning system. The only way of controlling it is through management by exception. The old fashioned budgeting systems are absolutely worthless—the difference between management planning and budgeting is action. The biggest change is a change in attitude—the difference between saying that's what we expect to happen and that's what we are going to make happen.'

"The General Manager of a Consumer Products Division of a large organisation commented: 'I feel planning is essential—without it, you don't know where you are going, it makes you look at a field in the widest possible sense, and consider alternatives. It makes you appreciate that there is change and the need to plan ahead to meet it. When you are in a fast moving environment, unless you can predict market trends, you will be continually behind.'

"A main Board Director of a textile group said: 'If you have a long-range plan, you have to take a much closer look at the organization to highlight its strengths and weaknesses. It makes a managing director sit down and say "where do I want to be in three or five years' time?" It's a thought provoking process—once you've been provoked into thought, benefits must inevitably follow.'

"The Deputy Chairman of the same group said: 'We've been growing very rapidly as a group, therefore tidy setting down of objectives has been God's gift to us. We now realise how essential it is—we could have saved ourselves a lot of time and trouble had we had it before.'

"The Chairman of the U.K. Division of a multi-national company said: 'I think it is impossible to operate without planning, principally because the size of investment means that you can't afford mistakes and also because of the lead time required to acquire, install and put into operation equipment. If we don't plan in advance, it takes at least two years to change direction, and we may miss opportunities—if you don't plan you cannot operate.'

"A General Manager in the chemical industry said: 'The business and its component parts are all pointing in the same direction. Everyone knows what we are trying to achieve. Only by the process of planning can you really sort out what your objectives should be and apply analytical questioning to those objectives. It is inherently a control system—the chances of success are increased by the planning approach because you've done your homework. It's a way of living rather than a technique.'

"A Senior Line Manager of a national building contractor observed: 'We couldn't exist without it—our resources would be over-stretched or under-utilized. You can't use your resources effectively without planning. It gives a target that must be worked to and indicates the implications of not meeting target. It motivates people all the way down the lines—one is always striving to improve on existing performance.'"

These comments illustrate that planning is seen differently in different situations, but in each situation, if planning is to develop at all, it must satisfy a need.

What the testimony shows is that there are people who have strong personal beliefs in the efficacy of corporate planning. When taken in conjunction with the earlier evidence, the interpretations can only be that a large number of senior managers believe that planning works. This is an important factor, because, as stated earlier, no chief executive should introduce corporate planning unless he has this belief.

We do not have to rely on individual testimony, and there now are a growing number of studies which provide objective evidence in support of this belief.

Levitt[13] states:

"For many years the Stanford Research Institute has been studying the reasons why certain companies have outstanding growth records and others merely drift along at the national rate of economic growth. The major conclusions are as follows:

(1) They systematically seek out, find, and reach for growth products and growth markets.

(2) They characteristically have organized programmes to seek and promote new business opportunities.

(3) They are consistently self-critical about the adequacy of their present operations and therefore consistently demonstrate superior competitive abilities in their present line of business.

(4) Their top management slots are staffed by uniquely courageous, adventurous, high-spirited executives who bubble with dissatisfaction and are driven by an energetic zeal to lead rather than to follow.

(5) The companies almost invariably have established formal systems of discovering opportunities and offsetting extreme risks by 'planning for the unseeable' with the context of clearly defined and growth-inspiring statements of 'company goals'.

(6) The chief executive consciously and continuously, by word and by deed, establish an organizational environment of ruthless self-examination and effervescent high adventure.

"Top management must see that the entire company becomes saturated with the idea of creativity and the merits of self-criticism. It must develop and transmit some guiding philosophy about the creative function—indeed, the creative necessity—of the really effective business enterprise."

A study by Thune and House[14] was carried out in the United States analysing the results of certain companies up to 1965. A sample of matched pairs of formal and informal "planners" was selected from a larger sample drawn from six industry groups: drug, chemical, machinery, oil, food, and steel. Performance of the sample companies was then examined over periods of seven to fifteen years (depending on the date of the introduction of formal planning), in terms of five economic measures.

The significant results of the study were that the formal planning companies outperformed their counterparts on three of the five measures: earnings per share, earning on common equity, and earnings on total capital employed. In fact results for average sales and stock price appreciation were also better for the planners, but these measures were not statistically significant.

This is only a partial indication of results, and a comparison was also made of planning companies' performance before and after the introduction of planning. Again, the finding was that formal planning brought better results and planning companies improved their results on three of the economic measures: sales, earnings per share, and stock-price appreciation. (Data was not available for the other two measures.)

To confirm these findings, the performance of planning companies was compared against the informal planners for a period of time before the introduction of planning. There was no significant difference in results. The authors state:

"Thus the first major conclusion of the study is quite clear: formal planners from the time they initiated long-range planning through 1965 significantly outperformed informal planners with respect to earnings per share, earnings on common equity, and earnings on total capital employed. Furthermore, these companies outperformed their own records based on an equal period of time before they began formal planning. Finally, informal planners did not surpass formal planners on any of the measures of economic performance after long-range planning was introduced."

On an individual industry basis the findings held good for the drug, chemical, and machinery industries. Steel had to be omitted because of the length of time this industry had been planning. While food and oil showed generally better results among planners, there was no clear assocation of these results with the introduction of planning, since these companies also showed better results in the pre-planning era. These findings go some way to supporting the contention of Denning and Lehr[1] that some industries and company types are more likely to benefit than others from planning.

Herold[15] extended and validated part of the Thune and House study in 1972, although it was possible to do this for only five of the original eighteen matched pairs of companies used in the original study. All were in the drug and chemical industries. The conclusion was that those companies that engaged in corporate planning significantly out performed those that did not.

Another study of considerable value, also performed in the United States, was carried out by Ansoff et al.[16] of the Carnegie Mellon University. This examined the effect of planning on the success of acquisitions in American firms, and was limited to companies with a four-year acquisition free period, followed by an acquisition period during which no more than one year elapsed between successive acquisitions, followed by a post-acquisition period of at least two years. The universe for companies which met these criteria was 412 (from the sources used). All 412 companies were approached, resulting in 93 usable replies (22.6%).

The study examined two types of acquisition behaviour: strategic planning (defining corporate objectives and acquisition strategies) and operational planning (identifying the means of acquisition, establishing search criteria, allocation of supporting budgets, and similar activities). Operational planning follows the strategic planning activities.

Corporate performance was measured against thirteen variables: sales, earnings, earnings/share, total assets, earnings/equity, dividends/share, stock price (adjusted), debt/equity, common equity, earnings/total equity, P/E ratio (adjusted), payout (dividends/earnings), and price/equity ratio. Three types of measurement were designed (average of annual percentage change, average percentage change over period, and the simple average value over period). The use, where relevant, of these three measures against the thirteen variables resulted in a total of twenty-one different measures of performance.

The questionnaire established eight characteristics of managerial behaviour during acquisition activity—four were concerned with strategic and four with operational planning. This enabled the sample to be divided into four subgroups: companies with little planning, companies with strategic planning only, those with operational planning only, and those with both types of planning. Overall, the "planners"—that is companies exhibiting at least six of the eight characteristics—comprised 22.7% of the sample.

A comparison of performance between what might be termed as the extensive planning and those with little or no planning revealed that on all the variables with the exception of total assets growth those firms which had extensively planned their acquisition programmes significantly out-performed those that did little or no formal planning. The variables which exhibited the most notable out-performance were sales growth, earnings growth, earnings/share growth, and earnings/common equity growth.

The investigators carried out a second analysis. The performance of twenty-two of the twenty-six "planners" was compared with that of the forty firms which had no more than four of the eight characteristics. This study supported the findings of superior average performance by planning, and also revealed that the planners performed more consistently. The four most notable variables of outstanding performance were the same as those in the first analysis.

Further analysis supported the contention that planners did better mainly because they were able to avoid failure. A number of individual non-planners had performances which exceeded the best of the planners, but a much higher percentage of the non-planners had very poor performances.

The authors[15] conclude:

(1) "Firms which engage in acquisition activity tend to take one of two distinctive approaches to acquisition planning. The first is an unplanned opportunistic approach and the other, a systematic planned approach. If a firm fails to plan any phase of the programme, it is likely to forgo planning altogether. If a firm does plan a phase, it is likely to make a complete strategic and operating plan.

(2) Firms which do plan tend to use these plans and to exhibit deliberate and systematic acquisition behaviour.

(3) Although subjective evaluation of results by management does not differ greatly between planners and non-planners, objective financial measurements show a substantial difference.

(4) On virtually all relevant financial criteria, the planners in our sample significantly outperformed the non-planners.

(5) Not only did the planners do better on the average, they performed more predictably than non-planners. Thus, planners appear to have narrowed the uncertainty in the outcomes of acquisition behaviour."

A further survey by Malik and Karger[17] in 1975 concluded that

"So the answer to the question of whether long range planning is more promising than results seems clear: more results. Hard data suggests long range planning pays. And since studies by others have produced similar results, the weight of evidence is mounting rapidly. Companies engaged in long range planning are using a tool that has demonstrated its worth."

Yet another study, reported by Vancil,[18] is worthy of passing mention. This examined the accuracy of forecasts made by companies of the outcome of their plans and demonstrated that certain company characteristics and planning techniques were associated with more accurate forecasts. In particular the systems design features associated with the accurate forecasts were top-management involvement, association of subordinates in setting their own goals, discipline in linking the plan to the budget, and a philosophy that an important purpose of planning is to provide a frame of reference for the operational budget.

However, the author raised a stimulating question: the possibility that too much emphasis on accuracy could lead to self-fulfilling prophecies and below-optimum performance. If the contention of many planners that planning is a corporate mind stretching exercise is true, it may be that accuracy for its own sake is a less desirable trait than many believe.

There are still many of the benefits of corporate planning which have yet to be proved objectively, and no doubt in the future there will be additional evidence forthcoming which will take the study of corporate planning even further forward. I believe that the combined total of evidence now available proves beyond doubt that corporate planning can be a beneficial style of management. Research since the mid-1970s has tended to concentrate on other aspects of strategic management, but there is enough body of evidence to show that everything is rosy. But is it? While the research was showing that planning was producing results, whole swathes of companies in the UK and USA were sliding into an abyss. In the UK the motor cycle industry had disappeared by the mid-1970s, part of the major decline of the country's manufacturing base. Somehow, while corporate planning was improving results, there seemed to be some degree of strategic failure. I wrote about this in 1988:[19]

"It seems to me that the research proves beyond doubt that corporate planning *can* be beneficial, but does it prove that it *will* always be beneficial in every case. Firstly if it is applied badly it is unlikely to succeed. Secondly, there must be degrees of success and not all organisations allow corporate planning to run to its full potential: my impression in the UK is that many top managers do not set high enough an expectation from their planning work and therefore have a satisfaction level that is too low.

"Perhaps the most important point is that strategic decisions have to be made whether or not the company plans, and these decisions can be good or bad. All managers are prisoners within the boundaries of their own perception, and although corporate planning is supposed to move these boundaries it does not always do so. It is thus possible for a company to achieve better results because of the co-ordination and motivational impact of its planning processes and yet still to be following the wrong strategic path. My argument is that this has certainly happened in the UK, and that in many companies planning has failed to change these perceptual boundaries, through failings of managers and planners.''

We may add to this thinking by remembering that most of the studies either looked at a company's pre and post planning results, or compared matched pairs within an industry within the country. Being better than your peers in a country is not necessarily the same as being best in the world, and many industries were already facing global competition by the early 1970s.

The conclusion is that planning is a good thing, but we have to pay a lot more attention to the principles behind successful strategies, and that for many the only relevant benchmarking is world class performance. These themes will be returned to as we continue to develop the concept of strategic management through the book.

—The fact that companies practise corporate planning does not necessarily mean that they do it well.
—Corporate planning does not mean that a company will never make a bad decision or that an event of low probability will never occur.
—It is possible for companies that do not practise planning to be successful.

The first of these points has already been referred to briefly and is supported by certain of the quoted studies of British and American planning practice. Inferior skills in corporate planning must lead to a lesser benefit than the theoretically possible, and it is my personal belief that in certain circumstances a poorly conceived and implemented system of planning can have a bad effect on company results. Some companies would achieve a higher performance if they scrapped their planning departments as a cost reduction exercise. Failure and disappointment are for the majority of firms avoidable. The lesson to be learnt is that top management must think long and hard about corporate planning before introducing it.

Evidence so far available suggests, as we have seen, that planning leads to better performance. However, it is wise for those studying or practising management to remember that it is a human activity and is therefore fallible. Strategic decisions may, despite all analysis, turn out to be bad ones. All that corporate planning can do in the strategic decision area is to help eliminate some of the worst alternatives and to give the top management a better chance of being right.

Related to this is the matter of probability. A company might conceivably reach a point when every major strategic decision taken had a 99% chance of being a success. But let us be quite clear: the 1% chance can still happen. And not only that, it can happen several times in a row. Everyone must have had the million-to-one chance event in meeting unexpectedly a friend in the street of a town which neither normally visits.

The third point is again supported both by a general knowledge of the business world and from the quoted studies of performance. Success can come to many styles of management, and the primary factors for success are the skill, judgement, and ability of the company's chief executive. It is very easy for a planner to become so engrossed in his subject that he forgets this very important fact. I would go further than this and state that although some successful companies might achieve more if they embraced corporate planning, there are other companies which should not attempt to introduce it. An earlier analysis[17] I made of this still stands:

"In my opinion there are only four types of situation when corporate planning has a high probability of failure:

(i) When the chief executive does not believe in it: more, much more, will be said on this later.

(ii) When the chief executive allows no one else to make decisions. Of course there are many companies like this, and their size is a function of the ability of the one person who runs them. They are unlikely to be of great size, and without some change in policy (or a new chief executive of the same kind) will die with the entrepreneur who leads them. Successful or unsuccessful, they will all be unable to use the discipline of corporate planning—if only because it is a discipline and has a formal approach.

(iii) The small company that simply cannot afford the time needed to write down plans, and which in any case is so straightforward that all the major implications can be carried in the chief executive's head. The very small companies, that do not employ an accountant of their own, would be wasting their money if they moved into a more sophisticated area of management. While small, they can be very successful without formal planning, and of course have a high probability of remaining small.

(iv) The company that is sinking so rapidly that it requires all those on board to man the pumps. Until it can get the holes caulked and the ship floating it has very little prospect of formalising its planning process. Such a company may, of course, wish that it had introduced corporate planning many years ago, and so avoided the situation in which it now finds itself.

"Although these companies may not benefit from the corporate planning methods described in this book, they must still think about their future. Every chief executive has a duty to think ahead, a duty which cannot be avoided. Only in the method used does he or she have a freedom of choice."

References

1. Denning, B. W. and Lehr, M. E. "The Extent and Nature of Corporate Long Range Planning in the United Kingdom, Parts 1 and 2", *Journal of Management Studies*, Vol. 8, May 1971; Vol. 9, February 1972.
2. Brown, J. K., Sands, S. S. and Thompson, G. C. "Long Range Planning in the USA—NICB Survey", *Long Range Planning*, March 1969.
3. Komo, T. "Long Range Planning—Japan—USE—A Comparative Study", *Long Range Planning*, October 1976.
4. Schuller-Gotzburg, V. V. and Dawson, R. W. *Organised Planning in 50 Western European Companies*, Stanford Research Institute, 1971. (Proprietary study.)
5. Eppink, D. J., Keuning, D. and de Jong, K. "Corporate Planning in the Netherlands", *Long Range Planning*, October 1976.
6. Kempner, T. and Hewkins, J. W. M. "Is Corporate Planning Necessary?", *British Institute of Management*, December 1968.

7. Knowlson, P. *Organisation and Membership Survey*, December 1974. Society for Long Range Planning.
8. Warren, E. K. *Long Range Planning: The Executive Viewpoint*, Prentice-Hall, 1966.
9. Ringbakk, K. A. "Organised Planning in Major US Companies", *Long Range Planning*, December 1968.
10. Irving, P. "Corporate Planning in Practice: A Study of the Development of Organised Planning in Major United Kingdom Companies", University of Bradford, M.Sc. dissertation, 1970.
11. Taylor, B. and Irving, P. "Organised Planning in Major UK Companies", *Long Range Planning*, June 1971.
12. Champion, J. R. "Corporate Planning in CPC Europe", *Long Range Planning*, December 1970.
13. Levitt, T. *Innovation in Marketing*, McGraw-Hill, 1962.
14. Thune, S. S. and House, R. J. "Where Long Range Planning Pays Off", *Business Horizons*, August 1970.
15. Herold, D. M. "Long Range Planning and Organisational Performance: A Cross Validation Study", *Academy of Management Journal*, March 1972.
16. Ansoff, H. I., Avner, J., Brandenburg, R. J., Portner, F. E. and Radosevitch, R. "Does Planning Pay? The Effect of Planning of Success of Acquisition in American Firms", *Long Range Planning*, December 1970.
17. Malik, A. and Karger, D. W. "Does Long Range Planning Improve Company Performance?" *Management Review*, September 1975.
18. Vancil, R. F. "The Accuracy of Long Range Planning", *Harvard Business Review*, September/October 1970.
19. Hussey, D. E. *Management Training and Corporate Strategy*, Pergamon, 1988.
20. Hussey, D. E. *Introducing Corporate Planning*, 4th ed., Pergamon, 1991.

3

A Look at the Total Process

Components of Strategic Management

The last chapter demonstrated that planning improves results, but raised concerns over whether even an apparently beneficial planning process always led to appropriate strategies. This chapter will begin to show how the two can go hand in hand, a theme that will be continued in later chapters. The emphasis will be on the management of strategy, although this chapter will also look at models for the completion of plans and of planning processes.

Strategy does not exist in a vacuum, and has both an influence on, and is influenced by the culture of the organisation, its structure and the people it employs. How you want people to act is driven by strategy: how they actually act depends on reward systems, control mechanisms, and the climate of the organisation. Strategy management has to get all these things in harmony, and ensure that the strategy the organisation is following is appropriate.

Leavitt[1] drew attention in 1964 to the interlinking of task, structure, people and technology (tools) and showed how changes to one factor would cause changes to the others. Leavitt's "diamond" was worked on by others, particularly Mckinsey and Company with their 7s model (see Peters and Waterman[2] and Galbraith and Nathanson[3]). These models began to add dimensions such as strategy, culture, and reward systems. Considerable research had been undertaken during the 1960s and 1970s into the relationship of strategy and structure (some details will be given in when we deal with human resource planning in a later chapter).

Figure 3.1 draws on all this thinking to suggest one way of considering the elements that must be considered and put into some degree of equilibrium. Strategy is shown as the driver, interacting with the other organisational components to produce results. Even a poor interaction will lead to results, but to increase chances of getting the results we want. The "organisation" is looked at in terms of eight boxes.

Tasks

A strategy leads to a need for certain things to be done by people. A change in strategy may change those tasks. For example, a strategy to be more customer

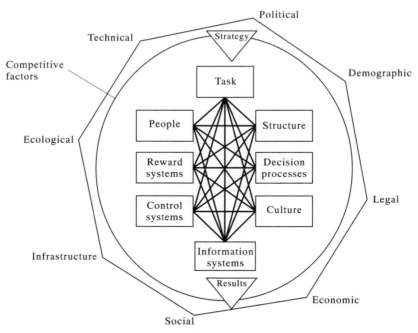

FIG. 3.1. Organisation and the environment.

responsive may require some tasks to be undertaken differently, and new ones to be added.

People

This means the nature, knowledge and skills of the various individuals already in the organisation, or who need to be recruited to the organisation to implement the strategy. The people required are influenced by the tasks, but also can influence the way the organisation looks at those tasks in the first place.

Reward Systems

How people are rewarded will affect whether they perform the tasks in the way the strategy required. Frequently reward structures are out of step with the strategy. For example the company may have an intention to sell the most profitable mix of products, but if the reward system pays sales bonuses in the total value of sales, the sales force are more likely to go for volume than for profit.

Control Systems

How people are controlled will also affect what they actually do. Control mechanisms that emphasise individual effort, particularly if linked to reward, will affect behaviour far more than a management exhortation for teamwork. If team-work is the important thing, then controls need to be designed accordingly. The nature of a control system can also influence, and is related to, the culture of the organisation. Delegated decision making, for example, will only happen if the control mechanisms allow it. In many organisations the exhortation is to take a long term view, while the controls emphasise the short term. Action tends to relate to the control, and not the exhortation.

Information Systems

Organisations are also affected by the way information is collected and dissemi-nated. Empowerment of lower levels of management can only take place if they also receive the information needed to do the job. Information should also be related to the structure of the organisation. In many organisations it lags behind structural changes, making it harder for managers to manage. Strategy can become impossible to implement because of the failure of information systems to meet the needs of organisations. For example there are still insurance companies that can only provide information by policy and not by customer. They cannot find out easily all the types of insurance held with them by a particular client. It is not hard to see how this could frustrate an excellent strategy for selling additional services to existing clients.

Decision Making Systems

Where and how decisions are made, and who is allowed to make them will affect all parts of the model. The airline, SAS, caused a revolution in thinking in its organisation when it empowered the person in contact with the customer to make all reasonable decisions about matters that affected the customer. Previously these were all referred upwards in a bureaucratic process This change had a funda-mental impact on the culture of SAS.

Culture

The culture of an organisation is increasingly seen as one of the most important components to manage. Culture depends on all the other boxes in the model, and is also influenced by the nature of the company's business, its history, and where it operates. If culture does not fit with strategy, something will have to give, and it will probably be the strategy. Take a worldwide organisation, that operates indivi-dual businesses with full local autonomy, in various parts of the world. For good strategic reasons the company decides to integrate its businesses globally, stan-dardising products, and rationalising many of its activities on a world basis. Will this all happen just because someone says it will? Unlikely! The existing culture will get in the way of the changes, so action would also be needed to bring about changes to this culture.

Structure

Finally there is the way the tasks are grouped into jobs, and jobs are grouped into organisational units. Structure like the other components of the model has a two-directional link with every other component, and can help a strategy to be implemented, or can make it totally impossible.

The circle outside the components of organisation represents the competitive arena in which the organisation operates. This has an obvious relationship with strategy, and much of this book will be about that relationship. It also impacts on the other components of the model, for example through the level of salaries paid to people in the industry, or the training provided by the educational system for people in that industry.

Outside is an eight-sided figure, which also will receive more attention later in the book. This represents the external business environment in which the organisation operates. One of the definitions on strategic management referred to earlier in this book stressed that it was about obtaining a good fit with the environment in which it operates. This is partly about strategy analysis and formulation, but it is also about managing the other elements in the model to achieve a harmony between them.

Vision and Leadership

The description given above may strike the reader as little more than an assessment of the main tasks of top management in any organisation. That is exactly what strategic management is. All the interrelationships exist whether or not the organisation uses strategic management as the chosen means to bring about strategic change in the organisation. Under strategic management the driver is strategy, and the tasks of analysis and formulation are supported by a formal approach to planning.

One important element in the whole strategic management process is the development of a vision for the organisation by top management. This does not necessarily have to come out of the head of only one person, although sometimes it may. The vision is the view which goes beyond the life span of the corporate plans, which identifies the future nature and philosophy of the organisation. The quality of the vision is tied in directly with the quality of leadership, and of course a good system of planning cannot compensate for a lack of leadership. We will return to both vision and leadership later. The word "vision" has many meanings. In this context it combines things like "foresight", "a vivid concept or mental picture", "imaginative perception", "a pleasing imaginative plan for, or anticipation of, future events". (All taken from Chambers Twentieth Century Dictionary.)

The dictionary through some of the other meanings also reveals the pitfalls in the concept of vision, such as "a revelation … in sleep", or a visionary "given to reverie or fantasy", and "out of touch with reality, impractical". My own description of visions gone wrong comes through word association: "vision … dream … nightmare". Like so much else in strategic management, the chief executive has to get it right.

When thinking of vision in the context of strategic management we are really beginning to think of leadership, and it is an obvious fact that the success of an organisation is at least as much related to the quality of leadership as it is to the formation of a superior strategy. Much has been written about leadership, and it is a subject in its own right. However it embraces many concepts, and people often mean different things when they think of leadership. John Nicholls[4] draws a useful distinction between micro leadership and macro leadership. Micro is related to the job or task, to the internal organisation, and to efficiency. It is about the here and now. Success comes from adapting one's leadership style to the various situations. The leading authorities on this aspect, which they term situational leadership, are Hersey and Blanchard.[5] Macro is related to the team or organisation, is concerned about how things could be, rather than as they are, is externally focused, and is concerned with long-term effectiveness. Leadership is performed through role in the organisation.

One useful model for thinking about the macro, or transformational aspect of leadership has been developed by management consultants Harbridge House Inc. (see Dinkelspiel and Bailey[6]), and is reproduced in Fig. 3.2.

The outer ring in this model bears a strong relationship to the concepts with which this chapter opened. The inner ring emphasises three elements of personal leadership, vision, commitment and execution.

"Vision consists of three elements that reflect the leader's sense of external opportunities, the ways in which internal resources can be mobilised to capitalise on these opportunities, and the leader's personal role in this process.

"Commitment is the leader's ability to get others dedicated to turning the vision into reality.

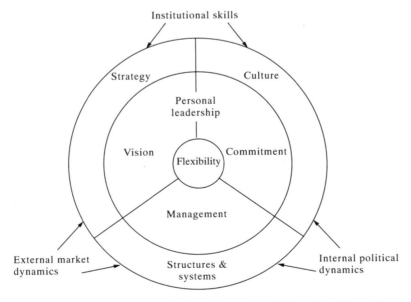

FIG. 3.2. The Effective Organisational Leadership model. © Harbridge House Inc. Used with permission

"Execution is the ability to lay out and implement a road map and a discipline that focuses the organisation's energy to produce tangible results." (Dinkelspiel and Bailey[6].) (Note that they use the word management, but this has been changed to execution to fit the current descriptions of this model provided by Harbridge House.)

If leadership is important to strategic success, we might expect successful approaches to planning to vary with the beliefs and values of the leader. I believe that this is the right interpretation of another study into strategic management.

Styles of Strategic Management

Goold and Campbell[7] published an important research-based study of styles of strategic management. They saw the styles as arising from the attempt by top managers to determine the appropriate role for the corporate office vis-à-vis the business units, during which process trade-offs have to be made. The desire to give strong leadership from the centre conflicts with the desire to encourage entrepreneurial activity at the business unit level. Styles arise as a result of the way in which the group chief executive determines where the trade-offs have to be made.

A number of possible styles were identified on a matrix of planning influence from the corporate level (high, medium and low), and corporate control influence (flexible, tight strategic and tight financial). Of the nine possible positions on that matrix, three were found in the sample of companies studied. These were labelled *strategic planning*, with a high planning influence accompanied by flexible control, *strategic control*, which has medium level planning influence and tight strategic control, and *financial control*, with low planning influence and tight financial control. Figure 3.3 summarises the main differences between the styles.

There are strengths and weaknesses to each style, and the head office can both add and subtract value under each style. The authors conclude that the appropriate style is one that fits the situation of the business, and that appropriate matching is an important determinant of business success. In this way it is akin to situational leadership, where the right style is relevant to the situation in which the leader operates. Business factors fall under two headings, those related to the business situation, and those related to the resources in the organisation. Among the former are issues such as the ferocity of the competitive environment, size and length of payback of investments, and the shape of the corporate portfolio. Among the latter are the financial health of the company, the personality of the chief executive and the skills of senior management.

Although one might expect the situation faced by the companies to be the most important determinant of planning style, and indeed the next concept I will review provides a framework for such a consideration, my belief, fuelled by a close professional association with two of the companies in the Campbell and Goold

	Strategic planning	Strategic control	Financial control
Strategy responsibility	Business level but multiple perspectives	Divisional and business unit	Unit and even profit centre
Review	Extensive to influence proposals and raise quality	Extensive-raise quality	Budget key planning process
Corporate support	For strategic themes	Avoidance of central strategies	Major use of acquisition (centre or unit)
Inter divisional coordination	Central coordination	Little strong div. level coordination	Group level MGRs flow info centre/units
Source of new ideas	Centre or unit	From units (divestment corporate)	Suggestions from centre
Source of goals	From plans	Objectives set	Short term payback criteria
Reporting	Detailed to centre	Detailed	Frequent monitoring
Control	Flexible strategy key	Tight-incentives and sanctions	Budget as contract strong pressure on problem units-management change
Resource allocation	Centre allocates, sets priorities	Centre allocates sets priorities	Centre funds all good projects

FIG. 3.3. Styles of strategic management. (Derived from Goold and Campbell, *Strategies and Styles.*)

sample, is that the individual differences between chief executives were a greater influence than the differences between business situations.

Environmental Turbulence

Igor Ansoff has done much to develop the concepts of strategic management, and might be termed, with considerable justification, the founder of the subject. Beginning in the 1980s, Igor Ansoff and his colleagues have been researching and developing the concept that the way in which an organisation should undertake strategic management should be related to the degree of environmental turbulence in which it has to operate. The concept has been described in a number of publications, particularly Ansoff and McDonnell[8] and Ansoff.[9] A summary of eight years of research supporting the models developed appears in Ansoff et al.[10]

The Ansoff approach sought to identify the different environmental conditions under which different organisations were operating, and sought to match these with appropriate approaches to management and strategy. The starting concept was thus different from that of Goold and Campbell discussed above, where different concepts of strategic management were identified in organisations, but not related specifically to different sets of strategic conditions. The Ansoff approach suggests a scale of turbulence:

Level	State of Turbulence	Strategic Aggressiveness
1	Repetitive	Stable, based on precedents
2	Expanding	Reactive, incremental based on experience
3	Changing	Anticipatory, incremental, based on extrapolation
4	Discontinuous	Entrepreneurial, based on expected futures
5	Surpriseful	Creative, based on creativity

The approach to strategic decision-making is different under each level, as the above description suggests. It follows that the optimum approach to strategic management should also vary with the turbulence level. Ansoff[9] suggests that for level 1 the appropriate system is management by procedures, since nothing is changing, and the best guide to the future is the past. However it is doubtful whether this level of turbulence is currently experienced by many commercial organisations. For level 2, the right approach is what he terms financial control, where the emphasis is on control through budgets, rather than seeking new strategies. At level 3 the approach is extrapolative, and termed long-range planning: the emphasis is on sticking to the historical strategies of success, since the future is a logical extrapolation of the past.

At level 4 it is no longer safe to assume that tomorrow will be a continuation of the trends of yesterday, and the appropriate process is strategic planning. Ansoff[9] defines this as being "...focussed on selecting new strategies for the future and redirecting the firm's energies and resources to follow the logic of the new strategy development... Thus strategic planning repositions the firm for success in the future environment".

Ansoff argues that even before level 5 is reached forward looking strategic planning is not adequate to ensure a speedy response to future events. This is particularly true when future changes are both violent and difficult to foresee. He suggests two "real time" system responses: issue management, which can begin to supplement strategic planning from level 4, and surprise management. Issue management attempts to anticipate and respond to threats and opportunities. There is a link here with the scenario planning approaches which are used by some organisations.

By level 5 an increasing number of issues confront the organisation without prior warning. To cope with these the firm needs to add a further management system to deal with surprises. He suggests an emergency communication network, with a top level strategic task force to cross organisational boundaries to deal with the issue. The key to success is plan the surprise management organisation, and to train people in operating it. In other words, while issue management is a form of contingency planning for a predicted possibility, surprise management is a planned framework to deal with contingencies that cannot be foreseen.

The appropriate approach may vary in different parts of the same organisation. Thus it is quite possible for an organisation to have one strategic business unit operating under level 3 and another under level 5. The approach to strategic management should be varied by strategic business unit to take account of this.

In theory there are organisations operating under all levels of turbulence: there has also been an evolutionary movement from the lower to the higher levels. Thus there are more organisations in levels 4 and 5 now than there were in the 1970s. It is reasonable to suggest that this increase in uncertainty will continue in the future.

Although not a specific part of the Ansoff model, from observation I would suggest that organisations make temporary changes to higher levels of turbulence from time to time, sometimes reverting back to their old position when the period of turbulence is over. It is reasonable to suggest that in severe economic recession even organisations that are normally at level 3 will for a period find themselves operating at level 5.

Evolution of Planning Approaches

Some support for the evolution of approaches to planning is provided by Gluck *et al.*[11] who concluded in a 1980 study that there had been four phases in the evolution of formal strategic planning. The stages are shown in Fig. 3.4. The dates are my own observations and do not appear in the study, but relate to empirical observations of my own and related observations on the evolution of planning approaches (Hussey[12]). Approaches to planning tend to co-exist, which means that it is possible to find all forms in current use. Gluck and his co-authors noted that at the time of their work only a few companies were managing strategically, and that all of these were multi-national and diversified companies.

Phase 1 could also be described as extended budgeting, and the approach is largely based on projecting the figures in the budget out for a few more years. This tends to emphasise the existing aspects of the business, and allows little room for major changes in strategy. In these companies any new strategic thinking occurs outside of the planning system.

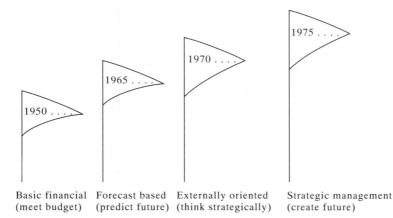

1950 . . . .
1965 . . . .
1970 . . . .
1975 . . . .

Basic financial   Forecast based   Externally oriented   Strategic management
(meet budget)   (predict future)   (think strategically)   (create future)

FIG. 3.4. Phases in the evolution of strategic planning. (Derived from Gluck, Kaufman and Walleck, *Harvard Business Review*, July/August, 1980.)

In phase 2 the approach tries to match the company's strategies to the perversities of the real world. The feeling is that more accurate forecasting would lead to better planning, and the emphasis on this approach is on forecasting techniques and models. Operational research techniques were high on the list of the planner's tools when this approach was at its most popular, and you would be invited to attend seminars with titles such as *Corporate planning, the control of company destiny*. The Gluck study observes that one benefit of this approach was greater attention to resource allocation, and the growing use of portfolio analysis techniques to aid this.

Repeated frustration from the discontinuity of the events in the world in which we operate created a realisation that accurate forecasting was not possible. The figure suggests 1970 as the time when phase 3, externally based planning began to appear, but for the majority of companies the trigger was the 1973 oil crisis, which overnight put the world into a situation of unexpected turbulence. Externally based planning is characterised by more attention to markets, and the dynamic causes of market change, and much closer examination of competitors. Resource allocation takes a more dynamic role, and the approach was accompanied by the formal grouping of businesses with like strategic characteristics into S B Us, or strategic business units. Planners are expected to produce alternative strategies, an action which under the forecast based approach would have been seen as indecisiveness. According to the Gluck study the weakness of externally based planning is that it imposes a burden of choice on top management which is too heavy, with the consequential result that many major decisions by default end up being taken by the planners rather than the managers.

Phase 4 melds strategic planning and management into one process. In their definition of strategic management, Gluck and his co-authors differ a little from the Ansoff and other definitions given in Chapter 1. They define it as "a system of corporate values, planning responsibilities, or organisational responsibilities that couple strategic thinking with operational decision making at all levels and across all functional lines of authority in a corporation". The main difference between phase 3 and 4 is of management philosophy rather than technique, and as the Ansoff view described earlier suggests, more emphasis is placed on the "soft" internal aspects of management such as values and culture. Some of these themes will be picked up later when we look at the main behavioural advances in planning.

Without putting too much weight on the conclusion, I think we can roughly correlate the Gluck and Ansoff conclusions.

Ansoff Turbulence level	Gluck Planning Stage
1	no equivalent
2	1
3	2
4	3 and 4
5	no equivalent

Strategic Management

The stage has now been set for a deeper consideration of strategic management as a complete way of running a business. In the rest of this chapter an outline will be given of the total process of planning, the individual parts of which will be studied in greater detail as the book progresses. The aim is to introduce the components of planning and to relate them to each other. If the book so far has set the stage, the rest of this chapter offers a synopsis for the play, the individual scenes of which will be enacted as the book progresses.

It will have already become clear that there are several ways in which a planning process can be designed. It is important that each company which introduces planning should do so in a way that meets its own particular needs. The various examples examined here should be seen as starting points and should not be read too dogmatically. It will also already be apparent that part of the difference between planning systems in organisations is not the schematics showing what plans are prepared, or what should go into a plan, but where the analysis and decisions are undertaken. This is where all the ideas and research quoted so far in this chapter are particularly useful. A planning system will be examined in some depth, and this will be followed by illustrations of other approaches which although constructed differently arrive at approximately the same place. The chapter will conclude with a generalised model of what should be considered when a plan is prepared, although the detail of this will be considerably expanded in later chapters.

A strategic management process should aim to unleash for the company the benefits which have already been discussed in some detail—better results through better decisions, the identification of more opportunities, the consideration of more factors, improved coordination and communication, strong motivation, and the provision for the company of a means of coping with the pressures of change.

Any total planning process is concerned with plans of differing durations. It will incorporate plans for both the long and the short term. Immediately the words "long term" are used they cause a flurry of concern among those who are newly come to planning. How long is a long-range plan? is a question which is frequently asked at introductory conferences, and it is a question which does not have a simple answer. Many planners believe that although the principles which guide the answer are important, the answer itself is nowhere near as vital as the questioners believe.

This is something of a paradox which deserves explanation. The first principle I would urge is that any plan which looks beyond the time-horizons of the annual budget is taking a major step forward: even if the time-span first chosen turns out to be wrong for the company, the benefits of moving out in time will more than outweigh the temporary disadvantage of having to adjust the period at the next planning cycle.

If plans were prepared on an absolutely rigid time-horizon perhaps it would be more important to get the time right the first time around. In fact most companies work their plans on a "rolling" basis. Every year the first year of the plan drops off and another is added at the end, so that the period provided for is always the three-, five-, ten-, or whatever years' span for which the company is trying to plan.

This method gives the opportunity of regularly revising the plan, so that the company is not trying to follow a rigid path which has been outdated by events. The rolling system gives to planning that degree of flexibility which is essential in a fast-changing world and as has already been seen this degree of flexibility may still be inadequate when organisations are operating at the higher levels of environmental turbulence.

Not all companies use the rolling system. There are some who believe that an *x*-year plan should last *x* years and, upon expiry, be replaced by a further plan which will be followed with the same rigidity. A similar approach is often adopted by the national development plans of governments (e.g. the Indian five-year plan) and regional development authorities (the twenty-five-year general development plan of Rhodesia's Sabi–Limpopo Authority[13]). Those interested in the techniques of governmental economic planning will find Kidel's[14] description of the French fifth plan of value. There are valid reasons for the differences in approach, as the different types of plans are used for different purposes. A government development plan is not required as part of its process of management in quite the same way that corporate planning is used by business. The type of reactions that governments may make to adverse circumstances have little relation to those open to business.

However even here the dangers of trying to plan too far in advance are very real, and are illustrated by one of the examples mentioned above. Rhodesia no longer exists as a country. Long before the 25 years of the plan had expired it became Zimbabwe, with a different style of government, operating under different market conditions. Droughts have dried up many of the dams which irrigated the area under the planning control of the authority, and the authority itself ceased to exist as a result of political changes before the ending of the civil war and the handing over of power to a government elected on a broader electoral franchise.

Each company should try to select a planning period which satisfies its particular and unique needs. There may be an identifiable cycle in a business which should be taken into account or some market or other factor which makes one length of time more appropriate than any other. A mining company might think in terms of the expected economic life of its mines: a company whose mines were expected to be depleted within ten years should be considering at least this time-horizon in its strategies. It takes seven years to bring new plantings of apple trees to an economic orchard: forestry activities are on an even longer cycle. For a fashion business anything more than three years ahead may be groping in the dark because of the particular nature of the market. Other industries may find the question of lead time important: the number of years taken to introduce a new product, or to complete work in progress, or to effect some other change, may be important determinants of the planning period.

All this must be tempered with good sense. A business may have activities equivalent to growing mature oaks from acorns, but this does not necessarily dictate a hundred-year plan. A planning period that is too long will mean that none of the present managers will have much interest in it as they do not expect to be around that long. Warren[15] pointed out that division managers seldom stay at the same job for more than five years, and that the average tenure of office is under four years—which by implication means that many move jobs in an even shorter time-period. When this is coupled to Pennington's[16] statement that a planner's "life expectancy" in a US company is only three-and-a-half years, the extent of the problem of choosing too long a horizon becomes very obvious.

There are thus human reasons why too long a period is not practicable for all parts of the organisation. Perhaps this is why many companies have settled for the five-year plan, which leads the field as the most popular time-span. In fact for many companies five years is a good choice. It is far enough ahead to give the company perspective, yet not so far that it loses management interest or runs into severe forecasting problems (not that a forecast is any more than a building block for a plan). It is long enough for many actions to be implemented and for results to make themselves felt. A lesser period often gives rise to the problem that is shorter than the lead time of its most important projects, which means that their results cannot be included, and the business loses much of the potential benefit of thinking ahead. For this reason three years is generally far too short, and two years is nothing more than an extended budget.

Some companies may find that one time-period meets all their planning needs. Most will almost certainly decide that some things should be treated differently from the period chosen for most of the plans. Thus the appraisal of specific projects might take a fifteen-year period into account, even though the normal planning time scale is five years. Equally necessary for many companies, although perceived less frequently, is the need to take strategic thinking further ahead than the formal five-year plan. This may be done through strategic scenarios which take into account longer term influences, technological forecasts of the future, implications of research and development programmes, and other factors. Such scenarios help give perspective to the strategic plan.

The terms strategic and project plans have been used in this and previous chapters and, along with other types of plans, require definition. Although most writers are in broad agreement on the meanings of many of the terms, there are areas of semantic confusion. My purpose is not to make a comparative study of all the meanings assigned to the terms but to demonstrate how they are used in this book. The exception to this rule will be where alternative approaches to designing a system of plans are illustrated which use the words in a different way.

I see the strategic plan as something which defines the objectives of an organisation, and the means by which those objectives are to be attained. (It may be interesting for the reader to refer back to the definition by Anthony quoted in Chapter 1.) An alternative and more detailed definition, which helps to clarify the meaning of my shorter version, is quoted from Denning:[17]

"...the determination of the future posture of the business with special reference to its product-market posture, its profitability, its size, its rate of innovation, its relationships with executives its employees and certain external undertakings."

The strategic planning may be divided into sub-plans: ways of looking at this problem will be discussed later.

Operating plans are defined here as the plans of an existing area of the business. By virtue of the definition of strategic plans, they must be a spin-off from these, even though in practice the decision to continue in that particular area of business may be implicit rather than explicitly taken at the start of each planning cycle. Denning[17] states operating plans to be "...the forward planning of existing operations in existing markets with existing customers and facilities".

In practical situations it may be more sensible to incorporate part of the strategic task in an operating plan since there are many activities, seen as purely strategic by the implications of Denning's definition of operating plans, which are very closely integrated with existing operations and which can only be isolated from them with difficulty—such as a decision to seek new customers. The fact that, for the more effective running of a system, management may delegate parts of its strategic task, does not invalidate the definitions.

Project plans are plans covering particular capital investments, marketing or other operations. In the words of Denning[17]: "...the generation and appraisal of the commitment to and detailed working out of the detailed execution of an action *outside the scope of the present operations* which is capable of separate analysis and control."

The italics are mine, for I do not agree entirely with this particular phrase and would argue that projects can emerge from both the strategic and operating areas. Techniques of appraisal and control are the same, regardless of the source of a project. This is a good illustration of how differences in viewpoint can lead to considerable semantic confusion unless they are clearly identified.

The term tactical plan is sometimes used to suggest an essentially shorter-term action plan which leads to the implementation of the actions proposed in the strategic plan. Sometimes the term tactical is given a slightly wider meaning, as in the following quotation from Lander:[18]

"Strategic planning is carried out by the Chief Executive and his first line executives. It is concerned with the broad concept of the company in the future and the provision and allocation of total resources to product-market opportunities to realise the company's profit potential through selected strategies— tactical planning which embraces all the detailed plans and actions involved in implementing it can be undertaken by the first line executives and those who report to them."

In addition to its plans, every company practising corporate planning needs defined policies and procedures. Some will derive from specific plans, others will be attempts to bring order into the apparent chaos of the many areas of a modern business which are relatively unchanging and which do not justify any other form of planning. Future plans may alter established policy and procedure at any time.

An example of the derivation of policy and procedure from a plan may help to illustrate the relationships.

1. *Plan.* To reduce travelling expenditure of employees by 10% in the following year by controlling class of travel, reducing frequency of travel, scrutinising expense claims more rigidly, and ensuring that all journeys are appropriately authorised.
2. *Policy.* All employees of the company are to travel second class on the railways unless the journey is of more than three hours (scheduled) duration.

3. *Procedure*. A defined system by which the policy is implemented and control-
    led—ticket-booking rules, expense claim forms and way of obtaining reim-
    bursement, systems of authorisation of expense claims.

In any modern business there are hundreds of policies and procedures which
must be applied if the organisation is to function at all. Definition provides a
measure of uniformity, precision and control, and ensures that they are understood by all those who need to understand them. Where policies and procedures
are of a "permanent" nature they may beneficially be enshrined in books of regulations and standing orders. Every company has a host of these permanent areas:
think for a moment of the areas of personnel, purchasing, office stationery, and
general administration—although in many companies they are often implicitly
rather than explicitly defined.

Careful attention to this area is a useful aid to better corporate planning. Often
definition of a policy will lead to a recognition that it is incompatible with the plans
and needs changing: if it is not defined it may be unknown to the people who
would realise that it is inappropriate. The point should not be laboured, for there
are no new principles involved, but it is nevertheless worth making.

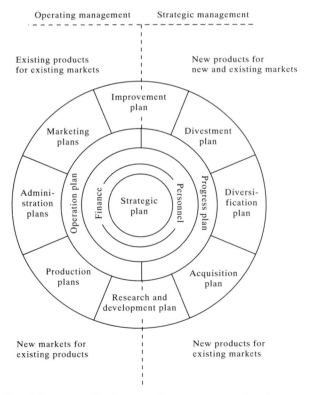

FIG. 3.5. Generalised approach to corporate planning.

An Approach to Corporate Planning

Figure 3.5 shows a generalised approach to a process of corporate planning.

This is conceived as a series of circles and segments of circles. In the centre are the three master plans which deal with the company's strategy: the strategic plan itself, and its interrelated and supporting plans for finance and personnel. These plans *together* fulfil the definitions of strategic plans given earlier in this chapter. Separately they show the main product marketing actions the company is to take in order to attain its defined profit targets and other objectives, the financial resources which will be deployed (and the financial strategies employed) to enable the strategies to come about, and the human resources involved. The personnel plan embraces what is sometimes called manpower planning.

The diagram indicates the important difference between strategic and operating management tasks, both in relation to product-markets and in relation to the types of plans. Operational plans cover marketing, production, and administration and deal with existing products. New markets for existing products are shown under this responsibility although it is also possible for this to be a major decision area.

Strategic management has divestment, diversification, and acquisition as three of its major components. Improvement, and research and development, are areas which may be either strategic or operating and are shown conceptually as coming under both (in reality it may be either) operating and strategic management.

The diagram sets out to illustrate the relationships between the various types of plans.

Figure 3.6 takes these concepts and turns them into a total planning system. Again this is on a generalised basis and is used to illustrate the principles. And, of course, each element of this system is examined in greater depth later in the book.

The circle and the box on which it stands illustrate a simplified view of all the plans in the system, while the other boxes and arrows show stages in the planning system and information flows. Once again, the heart of the system is seen as the strategic, personnel, and finance plans—all briefly described in earlier paragraphs and each the subject of considerable discussion in later chapters. It is fair to claim that a large part of this book is about this problem of planning the company's future strategy.

Strategy does not arise in a vacuum, and one of the first steps in planning is to perform an appraisal of strengths and weaknesses. This is likely to lead to a number of long- and short-term decisions, including many for profit improvement. An immediate spin-off from this stage in the planning process might therefore be projects—symbolised by the box in the bottom left-hand corner.

Most companies which practise strategic management try to achieve predetermined objectives which are related to the vision, and the process of setting these may be considered an integral part of strategic planning. Objectives are influenced by shareholders (although usually not explicitly) and, to some degree, by the assessment of strengths and weaknesses.

The third key stage is to relate the company to its business environment. This has an effect on strategies through the identification of opportunities, the anticipation

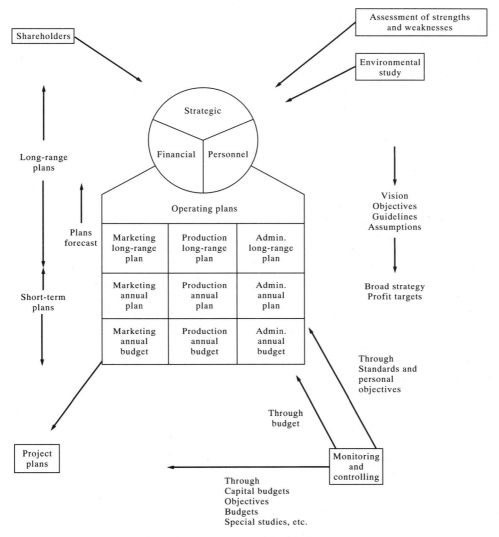

FIG. 3.6. Generalised planning system.

of threats, and the improvement of forecasts. It may help the company to see where it has to take an avoidance action. Environmental study will cover a number of factors including the economy, political events, technology, market forces, legal implications, and social factors. The study of these factors may of itself be a complex operation, and involve the application of a number of management techniques.

The chief executive, the planner, and the top management team consider the various alternatives against the background of the objectives, strengths and weaknesses, and external factors. From this, more projects may spin off (bottom left-hand corner again) for detailed planning.

From the total corporate strategy may be derived objectives and guidelines for the operating plans, and from the environmental study and its consideration in the strategic planning process may come defined planning assumptions. For a simple company, such as that shown in the diagram, the setting of objectives and targets may be easy. Most companies are much more complex, and the multi-divisional, multi-national organisation may find it a very complex matter. These problems receive more treatment later in the book, and a deeper consideration is given to what is meant by objectives.

Long-range operating plans are properly the responsibility of those line managers in charge of the function or area concerned. The diagram shows three functional areas: in practice there may be more, or the company may be organised into subsidiaries or divisions. This additional complication does not change the principle, although it may make much harder the task of designing a planning system and introducing corporate planning. The detailed consideration of these points is also left until later in the book.

Operating planning gives rise to plans and forecasts which flow back to the strategic planning process, where they are considered in the light of the company's objectives and strategy, and may be either accepted or returned to operating managers for refinement. In turn, the considered plans of the operating units may lead to amendments to the thinking at strategic level and to changes in the strategic plans.

In this way there is a link between all the factors which go into the making of strategies and the thoughts of managers down the line. In many instances the managers who, as part of the top management team, work with the chief executive on strategic planning, will be the same people who initiate work on the operating plans of their particular functional areas. This is particularly so in smaller companies. In the large multi-nationals the people who complete operating plans may play little or no part in the formation of corporate strategy except for the influence their plans have on the final plans. It is possible to devise methods so that these managers have more involvement in strategic thinking, and some companies have given a great deal of attention to making this possible.

Projects may be identified at operating level and give rise to further project plans.

The company now has a completely integrated and closely co-ordinated strategic plan covering all its areas of activity. It knows what it intends to achieve, how it intends to do it, and the expected effect on financial and personnel resources of these actions. Its next task is to move to implementation.

One way of doing this is through annual operating plans and the annual budget. The broad strategy and profit targets pass to the annual plans from the long-range operating plan. The annual operating plan shows the strategies and actions which have to be implemented over the forthcoming year if the plan is to be achieved. It takes these a stage further, and develops personal objectives for which named persons are responsible. If wished, this may be part of a complete system of management by objectives.

The annual budget becomes the expression in financial terms of the annual plan. Because this has strong links with the long-range plans, the budget is also closely linked with the long-range plans. It therefore becomes more than an instrument of management control in that it is a part of the implementation process of the total planning system.

Any implementation plan needs a monitoring and controlling mechanism, illustrated by the box in Fig. 3.6 at the bottom right-hand corner. This mechanism ensures that the personal objectives are carried out; it checks the budget through normal methods of budgetary control and through various methods controls the performance of the projects. The outcome of measuring actual results against the plan might be a need to modify plans in some further cycle. Certainly the performance of the company is a factor which is related to its strengths and weaknesses and is then taken into account in the following year.

All this compresses and simplifies and makes little mention of the tools of the corporate planner. These tools include various techniques of management science, some of the more important of which will be discussed in later pages. The point to stress here is that the techniques are not the plan. There is sometimes a tendency for a planning system to be overshadowed by the techniques used in it. Although corporate models, forecasting models, decision trees, and networks may be invaluable tools, although a sophisticated management information system may be of great importance, the fact is that none of these are as important as the philosophy of planning itself.

One of the main difficulties in designing a planning process is to emphasise strategy. If strategic management is a key aim of the process, as it should be, the process should emphasise this. Although this claim can be done through the process illustrated in Fig. 3.6 there is a danger of bottom up operating plans swamping the strategy. All this would mean in the final event was that the "plans" would bear little resemblance to what strategic decisions were taken at the top.

Vancil and Lorange[19] were among the first to suggest a three-stage planning process, consisting of a review of strategy: completion of plan; annual plan budget. This approach has been made into a workable process (see Young and Hussey[20]), following a few simple concepts.

The strategic review process is designed to provide a forum for agreeing the main strategic issues and decisions in discussion between head office and business unit. Its input is a number of working documents at both levels, and a summary of the main strategic points as seen from each viewpoint. Its output is a set of agreed strategic guidelines which are then used as the framework for the detailed planning stage. The main advantage of the extra step is that it allows a free discussion and careful focus on the appropriate strategic issues, with major inputs from corporate level, before business units have become locked into their plans, and before the main issues have been swamped by the volume of the plan. It is easier to change before the plan has been completed than after, if only because the volume of work in completing a detailed plan can prevent easy alteration. My experience is that this method facilitates strategic management. An example is given in Fig. 3.7.

There are numerous other general systems which have been suggested from time to time, all of which have many similarities with and some differences from

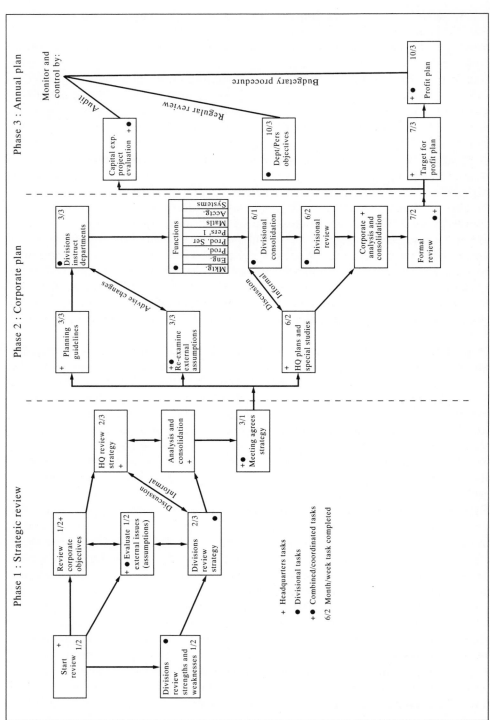

FIG. 3.7. Three stage "strategic review" planning process. (From "Corporate Planning at Rolls Royce Motors" *Long Range Planning*, R. Young and D. E. Hussey, April 1977.)

the outline in the preceding pages. Two brief examples are given here, not because they are any more "correct" than the others but because they may stimulate thought about different approaches. When systems are moved from the concept to a particular company situation they invariably need some modifications to fit that company. The aim should be to design a system that suits the unique needs of the particular business rather than to expect all companies to fit the textbook. Those interested may find numerous case histories, illustrating the way particular companies have solved this problem, in the pages of *Long Range Planning* and the *Journal of Strategic Change* or in Steiner[21] or Baynes.[22] Steiner deals with US experience, while Baynes's examples are from European companies.

Figure 3.8 shows the system of plans suggested by the Stanford Research Institute.[23] This, too, divides the planning task into two blocks (using the term corporate management where in Fig. 3.6 I used strategic management).

It divides the strategic planning task into a number of sub-units. Basically, in the sense of this figure, the strategic plan shows the potential of the company and whether it can be attained from present operations. The development plan looks at the alternative ways in which the gap between potential and present operations may be filled, and moves through the two sub-plans for divestment and diversification. The second sub-plan again divides into acquisition and research and development. (In fact, although not illustrated in either Fig. 3.5 or Fig. 3.8 there are certain other methods of diversification which will be described in the chapters on strategy.)

Although not specifically mentioned, it is possible to make provision for top-level financial and manpower planning within the framework of this system.

The second approach is that developed by Urwick Orr & Partners Ltd., which is illustrated in Fig. 3.9 with the steps which lead up to it. This diagram is thus directly comparable with that in Fig. 3.6. (Urwick Orr was acquired by Price Waterhouse and no longer operates as a separate organisation.)

Here we have a system which, although it highlights certain factors which are different from those emphasised in the two earlier approaches, is still covering the same ground and, at the final analysis, is suggesting much the same thing. The Urwick Orr approach links closely with management by objectives, the process for which is described later. The meanings of "strategic" and "tactical" have been given earlier in the reference from Lander.[18]

The broad issues described in these pages are important because unless the delicate and interdependent relationship between the component parts of a planning system are understood, it becomes difficult to view planning in anything but a fragmented way. A strategic management system and its parts may be compared to a motor-car engine. A few refinements may be added to give an improved performance: an occasional nut or bolt might drop off without making much difference to running. If the water-tank bursts or the fan-belt breaks, the engine will still operate in the short term although ultimately this will lead to severe damage. Most parts, although they may not look very important, will cause complete and immediate failure if removed. To understand any component it must be examined and studied individually—but it can only be used when related back to the total engine.

So it is with strategic management. Some modifications may improve the system; there is latitude in one or two minor areas. The system may appear to work in the short term even if certain key parts are neglected, but in the long term will destroy itself. Ignore most of the parts at your peril, for the system will never

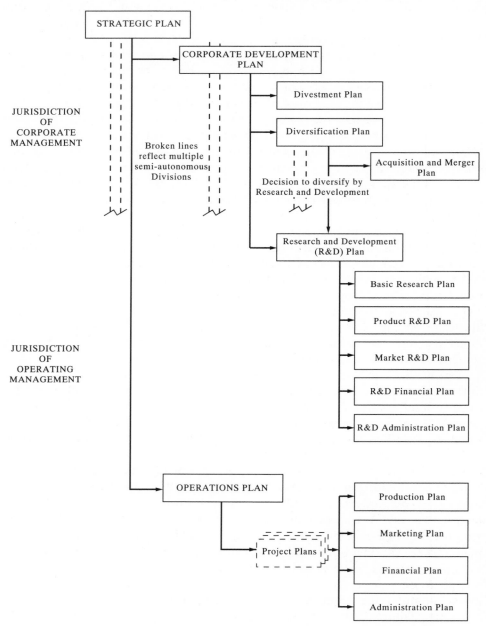

FIG. 3.8. System of plans devised by the Stanford Research Institute (reprinted with permission).

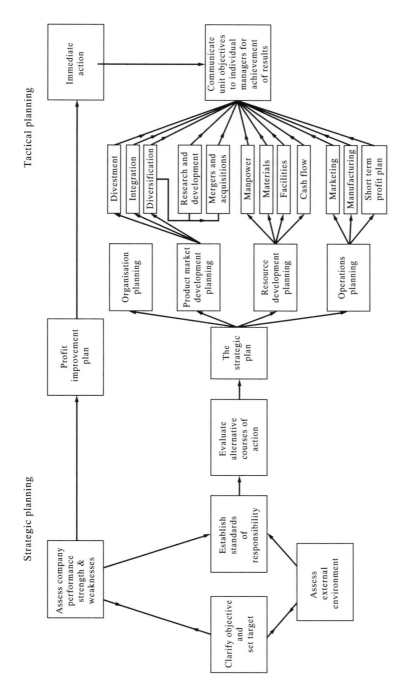

FIG. 3.9. System of plans devised by Urwick Orr & Partners (reprinted with permission). *Note*: Urwick Orr are now absorbed into the Price Waterhouse organization.

get started. Certainly each part of the process may be studied in depth as a separate entity—but its meaning will only emerge when it is considered as an integral part of the whole.

Elements of a Business Plan

The descriptions of planning processes all require the preparation of plans. In addition many managers may from time to time be required to write a business plan, even though their organisation may not operate a continuous process of strategic management. An all purpose business plan framework is offered here in Fig. 3.10. It is suitable for a strategic plan of a business unit, an operating plan, and as a general outline for a project plan. The concepts are appropriate for a complex, multi-divisional organisation, but there will be differences at what is considered to be strategic compared to a simple single division business. These differences will become clearer from the later detailed chapters on strategy and strategic analysis.

There is a strong correlation between Figs 3.10 and 3.6, the main difference

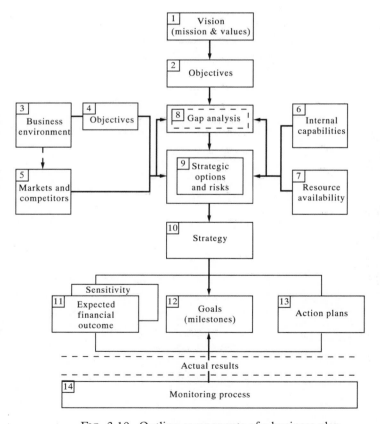

FIG. 3.10. Outline components of a business plan.

being that Fig. 3.6 describes a process, while Fig. 3.10 shows what topics should be covered in a plan. The only new concepts introduced in this model are assumptions, risk, and gap analysis. In addition it separates strengths and weaknesses into two parts, the internal capabilities (or lack of capability), and resource availability. The reason for this is that, although most successful organisations have access to resources of finance, skills and people beyond what is currently within the organisation, there is still a finite limit on resources which can affect what strategies are possible.

Assumptions are the subject of a separate chapter. For present purposes they may be defined as the statements about the environment on which the plan is based. The reason for making them explicit is partly to aid the interpretation of the plan and the risks to which it is subject, and partly to enable them to be monitored so that a fast reaction is facilitated should they prove to be erroneous.

Gap analysis is also described more fully later. It is a simple concept which looks at the expected future gap between objectives and forecasts of current activities, and how that gap might be closed.

Risk is an inherent part of the assessment of strategy. One does not take strategic decisions and then look at the risks involved, but assess the risks as part of the decision making process.

The problem of business plan preparation will be returned to in Chapter 23, when we will look at how to evaluate a plan.

The exploration so far has given us a skeleton for strategic management. Bones by themselves have a useful but limited function. In the next chapters we will put flesh on these bones, to explore the process of strategy formulation in much greater detail. We will also explore how to put the breath of life into our process, so that it becomes a live, dynamic contributor to corporate success.

References

1. Leavitt, H. J. "Applied Organisation Change in Industry: Structural, Technical and Human Approaches", abridged version of a 1964 article, Vroom, V. H. and Deci, E. L. (eds.), *Management and Motivation*, Penguin, Harmondsworth, 1970.
2. Peters, T. J. and Waterman, R. H. *In Search of Excellence*, Harper & Row, New York, 1982.
3. Galbraith, J. R. and Nathason, D. A. *Strategy Implementation: The Role of Strategy and Process*, West, St Paul, 1978.
4. Nicholls, J. "Rescuing Leadership from Humpty Dumpty", *Journal of General Management*, Vol. 16, No. 2, 1990.
5. Hersey, P. and Blanchard, K. *Management of Organisational Behaviour*, Prentice Hall, Englewood Cliffs, 1969.
6. Dinkelspiel, J. and Bailey, J. "High performing Organisations: Aligning Culture and Organisation around Strategy", Hussey, D. E. (ed.), *International Review of Strategic Management*, Vol. 2, No. 1, Wiley, Chichester, 1991.
7. Goold, M. and Campbell, A. *Strategies and Styles*, Blackwell, Oxford, 1987.
8. Ansoff, H. I. and McDonnell, E. *Implanting Strategic Management*, 2nd ed. Prentice Hall, Hemel Hempstead, 1990.
9. Ansoff, H. I. "Strategic Management in a Historical Perspective", Hussey, D. E. (ed.), *International Review of Strategic Management*, Vol. 2, No. 1, Wiley, Chichester, 1991.
10. Ansoff, H. I. and Sullivan, P. A. *et al.* "Empirical Proof of a Paradigmic Theory of Strategic

Success Behaviours of Environment Serving Organisations", Hussey, D. E. (ed.), *International Review of Strategic Management*, Vol. 4, Wiley, Chichester, 1993.

11. Gluck, F. W., Kaufman, S. P. and Walleck, A. S. "Strategic Management for Competitive Advantage", *Harvard Business Review*, July/August 1980.

12. Hussey, D. E. "Evolution of Planning Approaches", *Professional Administration*, April 1979.

13. Stanbridge, P. J. "Long Range Planning in Underdeveloped Countries—A Case History", *Long Range Planning*, December 1969.

14. Kidel, A. K. "Techniques and Methodology of the French Fifth Plan", *Long Range Planning*, March 1969.

15. Warren, E. K. *Long Range Planning: The Executive Viewpoint*, Prentice Hall, 1966.

16. Pennington, M. W. "Why has Planning Failed?", *Long Range Planning*, March 1972.

17. Denning, B. W. (ed.), Introduction in *Corporate Planning: Selected Concepts*, McGraw-Hill, 1971.

18. Lander, K. E. "Corporate Planning", *The Consulting Engineer*, December 1968.

19. Vancil, R. F. and Lorange, P. "Strategic Planning in Diversified Companies", *Harvard Business Review*, January–February 1975.

20. Young, R. and Hussey, D. E. "Corporate Planning at Rolls Royce Motors Ltd", *Long Range Planning*, April 1977.

21. Steiner, G. A. (ed.), *Managerial Long Range Planning*, McGraw-Hill, 1963.

22. Baynes, P. (ed.), *Case Studies in Corporate Planning*, Pitman, 1973.

23. Stewart, R. F., Allen, J. K. and Cavender, J. M., *The Strategic Plan*, Stanford Research Institute, 1963.

PART 2

The Changing Environment

"The only fence against the world is a thorough knowledge of it"—JOHN LOCK, *Some Thoughts on Education*, 1693

4

The Challenge of the Future

One of the justifications given for subjecting a business to a process of strategic management is that it is the only satisfactory way of coming to terms with a changing world. Events in the environment in which the company operates have a direct effect on the success or failure of that company. Strategic management seeks, as one of its aims, to relate the company to its environment, and to identify in advance the threats and opportunities which environmental change brings. At the outset the unique character of each business should be stressed: the effect of change in factors outside the control of the company will vary not only between industries but also between companies in the same industry. What causes the effect to vary are not only the obvious things like the nature of business, countries of operation, and size of organisation: there are also the fundamental differences in the attitudes and abilities of various managements. What one manager views as a threat may be seized as an opportunity by another. Some accept the challenge of change as one of the factors which adds a stimulant to the task of management: others try ostrich-like to ignore it, or sit like Canute on the beach defying the inevitable movements of the tides of the times: still others see the change taking place and, like Nero, expend their energies on what—in the context of their problems—are frivolous activities. The Nero managers are the worst, because it is a management crime to see a threat and not to avoid it, to notice an opportunity yet not to understand it.

There can be few managers who are unaware that the world has changed. Even since the Second World War, revolutionary advances have been made through the impact of technology on the day-to-day life of the common man. In many Western societies the motor-car is now commonplace: just before the Second World War it was the richer man's prerogative (except, perhaps, in the United States where, even then, there was wider ownership). At the turn of the century, still within living memory, the motor-car was a rarity, an innovation. From the horse-and-cart age of the first twenty years of this century to the motorised world of today is one vast turmoil of change.

Similar parallels can be drawn in other areas. The miracle of man's first flight, the acceptance of flight as a normal method of transportation, the introduction of longer-range aeroplanes, and the invention of the jet engine, and—the ultimate master stroke—the development of the manned space ship. In medicine growing knowledge has pushed back the frontiers of disease in every country in the world; the identification of the real cause of many illnesses, the greater understanding of the human body (the science of biochemistry is a relatively new one), and the discovery of new drugs (of which perhaps penicillin is the shining example). Even the food eaten as a part of modern daily life is different. The great growth of the convenience food industry has occurred in the last twenty-five years.

The contrasts are not only in the fields of technology. In Europe and the United States there is a whole new structure of society. The underdeveloped countries may not have the same economic standards of prosperity as the industrial countries, but even here the comparison between every-day life today shows a vastly different quality from that of the primitive world of 1890. The British Empire is no more. Britain's pride of place in world affairs has been yielded to other countries.

This list could go on for ever, but the point has been made. What is of equal importance is not just that the world has changed but that the rate of change has increased. Change in all directions has occurred much more rapidly in the last twenty to thirty years than in the preceding forty to fifty. And the process continues to accelerate.

In addition, on many fronts (although not all) the expense of each technological development increases to the point where in industries such as aerospace it is almost impossible for private enterprise to operate without government support, and where one technological mistake can bring a giant like Rolls-Royce crashing to insolvency.

Throughout history inability to cope has led to extinction. In biological terms there is the example of the dinosaur, of whom the only traces are a few fossilised bones (although it is also relevant to point out that the dinosaur did survive for 140 million years). In business terms the company which makes no adjustments usually disappears with even fewer traces. Its only fossilised remains are its managers. Change in this context has many facets, some of which will be quoted later in this chapter.

Management books frequently refer to the failure of many businesses in the horse-and-cart age (horse-and-buggy in American writings) to come to terms with their changing environment. Many disappeared because of their inability to adapt. It is perhaps interesting to point to a business which did adapt.

In 1970 the London firm of Glover, Webb & Liversidge celebrated its 250th anniversary. The business was originally established as a carriage builder, and soon developed a respectable position in the market for phaetons, gigs, broughams, coaches, and farm and trade vehicles (this was in the pre-Nielson days of 1720). The company are still carriage builders and hold the Royal Warrant for the maintenance of the coaches and carriages of the Royal Mews.

The process of adaption began in the twentieth century when the company introduced motorised goods vehicles ("Gloverley"). In the 1930s it moved its attention to the refuse-vehicle business, building the first all-steel moving-floor dust-carts. Their main product areas are now dust-carts and security vans.

This company must owe much of its success over 250 years to its adaptability.

Not all companies are so adaptable. The inherent inflexibility of many of the larger companies often prevents them from seizing the opportunities that change can offer: lack of resources and sheer lack of ability frequently causes the smaller companies to resist any move which is different. Levitt[1] states:

"The inability or refusal of companies to see the opportunities produced by change often seems to be a peculiar affliction of big, well-organised companies. General Electric turned down the opportunity to get exclusive American rights to manufacture and distribute neon lights, saying there was no market for them. A new small company had to be organised by Europeans to pioneer this big profitable market. Frozen orange juice had to be started by a company not in the food business.

"The big hotel chains fought the motel idea for years, in spite of its greater customer satisfying benefits . . . .

"Why do big companies so often seem to resist some of these changes so rigorously, acting only after the ideas are proved out, even when the companies pridefully promote their impressive slogans of progressiveness? Why is this complacency, this fat cat constipation, so often a big company problem?"

Part of the duty of all managements is to make those strategic moves which ensure that the business grows, prospers, and therefore survives. Although all change is not caused by external events, frequently it is what is going on in the world outside which is its most forceful agency.

Change of any type is anathema to most human beings. There is comfort and a feeling of false security in following the time-worn and well-known rut, often even to the extent that it goes deep enough for the sides to collapse and smother its occupant, killing all drive and initiative. One might also define a natural law of human inertia which can only be overcome by the restlessness and creative urge possessed by men of vision.

Most managers will be aware of the stock responses, the "road-blocks" to new ideas which are produced automatically whenever the *status quo* is threatened (Fig. 4.1). If all men observed these there would be no progress of any kind. In some cases the road-block may show the correct decision—but it is a result arrived at by emotional response rather than reason. In many more cases it is an unthinking reaction which kills initiative and preserves the false security of the known. At one time or another every manager will be guilty of road-blocking. Some do it all the time.

For the individual, change appears too frequently as a threat. A manager that sticks to the old tried and true course of action may be less often at loggerheads with colleagues, and may feel less at risk than if he or she "sticks his/her neck out". An error of omission is frequently less noticeable than one of commission: sometimes the missed opportunity is known only to the manager himself: everybody knows if he/she takes it and fails. Modern management calls for a measure of courage, the willingness to take reasonable (but not reckless) decisions which change the current state of affairs. The company whose managers look always inwards to the "safe" path will never be a leader: in many instances it will already have sown the seeds of its own failure. The challenge of the future with its gauntlet

```
We're too small for that
Our competitors don't do it
We're too big
Shouldn't we do some market research?
The present system works all right
We've never done it before
Let's bring it up again in six months
What would our customers think?
It won't work
I've always done it this way
What about our sunk costs?
The Board would never approve
That's not the way we do things here
You're ahead of your time
The Union wouldn't like it
Why don't you go away and think it out again?
We could never market it
That's not our responsibility
Let them try it first
Too hard to sell
Not really practicable
We tried it before
Why not sleep on it?
Why should we be the first to change?
```

FIG. 4.1. Examples of typical "road-blocks" to new ideas.

of change is faced by every company, large or small. Only those which square up to the situation and pick up the gauntlet can hope to succeed. Those that ignore it, or try to run away, will sooner or later come to grief.

It is by this unique ability to create change that man has become the most successful of all the animals. Where the lesser animals are prisoners of their environment and can change only by the slow process of evolution (with the risk of extinction in the way), Man has freedom to adapt and change the environment. This is part of our heritage.

At the same time it is understandable that change should be resisted since the psychological security of the individual may be threatened. Change may menace learned skills, a lifetime of experience, or a person's place in the community.

The fact that changes may be associated with risk has already been mentioned. Those who propose major changes may have to face the resentment—and sometimes ridicule—of their fellows. They may put at risk their prestige, their capital, and their livelihood.

In addition, the life pattern of each person is based on the present, and from this he or she may make assumptions about the future. Any change which threatens those assumptions may cause confusion. When the well-known landmarks are destroyed, even the most familiar path may become a journey to the unknown—a frightening experience. So we tend to resist.

Coping with a changing world calls for managers who have a measure of dissatisfaction. The restless person will always seek new methods and opportunities: the complacent rarely see a reason for doing things differently. Henry Ford is reported to have said "I'm looking for a lot of men with an infinite capacity for not knowing what can't be done". It is people who refuse to accept that things are impossible, who will not be baulked by difficulties, who strive to overcome obstacles, and see opportunities where others see threats: it is people such as these who possess what is perhaps the essence of real management.

This dissatisfaction, this refusal to bow down to the inevitable, requires another quality, creativity, and frequently both are found within the same person. The creative person is often restless. One of a chief executive's prime duties is to ensure that the company has a supply of creative managers. The organisational systems must encourage flair, initiative, and innovative skills. It is on these that the future success of the business lies. The planning manager has a particular duty to ensure that the planning system also encourages these qualities. All too often an ill-conceived and poorly designed process of formal planning does the opposite: it becomes an empty form filling exercise which merely helps to maintain the existing situation. This is a state of affairs which no chief executive should tolerate and which no planner need allow to happen. Good planning methods, the principles of which are discussed in other chapters, will assist the company to develop those qualities which allow it to meet the challenge of the future.

"Creativity" is an important word. *Chambers's Twentieth Century Dictionary*[2] defines it as the "state or quality of being creative: ability to create". Both "creative" and "create" have meanings which include words like "imagination" and "originality". Two meanings of "create" are "to bring into being or form out of nothing; to bring into being by force of imagination". It is, I think, important to remember that creativity comes from people, although it may be the resources of the business or society which enables the original, imaginative solution to a problem to become something that can be implemented.

It is individual creativity, harnessed to achieve specific corporate objectives, which allows the company to innovate. Innovation is the function which enables a company to grow and profit from opportunities which arise from the changing world. In addition another function which has already been mentioned is required—adaptability. This is the ability to adjust to new circumstances, particularly to avoid threats arising from the changing environment. Creativity must assist this function also, although more important are probably qualities of corporate self-criticism, flexibility, and the courage to change.

Change is an unavoidable factor in modern business life. As Drucker[3] has so aptly observed, tomorrow always arrives and is always different. What will happen in the future can never be certain, and the corporate planning process should take account of this. Change for the sake of change is not a good thing. The chief executive must retain a sense of balance. Just as in many companies it is next to impossible to get anyone to do anything differently, there are others—equally unhealthy—where nothing is constant, and changes are implemented with neither thought nor reason.

The rest of this chapter will examine in outline some of the main environmental factors which cause the challenge of the future. Succeeding chapters will show how these should be treated in the planning process, and some of the techniques of forecasting which the planner may need to use.

The external factors which affect performance and progress are, of course, legion. Not only are there many of them, but there are numerous interrelations: for example, technological change may bring about a different economic performance which in turn may change social attitudes. Although, for analysis purposes, it is necessary to group environmental factors under convenient headings, in practice the divisions are not absolute, other classifications are possible, and the real situation is a good deal more complicated. What this particular analysis tries to do is, through practical illustration, to draw attention to some of the factors which a chief executive should consider in the development of future strategies, and which for this reason should be systematically studied so that they may be adequately treated in the planning process. One of the tasks of the planner is to identify the relevant environmental factors to make the scope of the study manageable.

It is probably as well to try to dispel any illusions that taking account of environmental factors is easy. Although it is by no means difficult to consider factors in general terms, as we are doing here, it is very, very difficult to weave them into the fabric of plans. There are conceptual problems, disagreements, and uncertainties which ensure that the strategic planner's life is a very complicated affair.

The classification system chosen for this analysis is illustrated in Fig. 4.2. Only a general overview is possible: every business must estimate for itself its own individual situation.

The diagram also makes the point that all the factors are to some degree interdependent. Changes in technology can, for example, have a profound effect on many or all of the other factors. Computers, and particularly the arrival of low cost but powerful computing, can be seen to have impacted many other factors:

(i) The economic situation has been altered by automatic trading in the stock market, with sales being triggered when prices fall to a predetermined level.

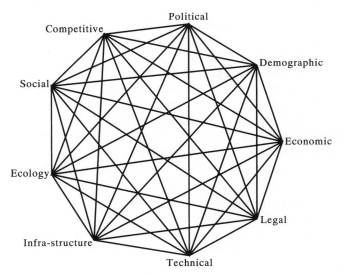

FIG. 4.2. The environment.

This is blamed for stock market crashes and is accused of affecting business confidence and thereby impacting on economic output.

(ii) Social changes have been triggered. For example more people are able to work at home, because information technology means that this is as effective as travelling to an office, although more lonely. The hole in the wall cash dispenser has changed social habits.

(iii) The competitive environment has changed, although there are few examples of permanent advantages being gained from IT. However there are numerous competitive *disadvantages* created for those organisations which do not keep up to date.

(iv) New legislation has come about through the need to protect data, prevent individual rights from being infringed, prevent copyright infringement, and many other areas.

(v) Political events are changed because IT and opinion polls rapidly alter perceptions of what is important to the electorate.

At the same time, some of the lines of force are two way. It is the backlash of social opinion against abuses, or expected abuses, of data by debt control and other firms, that led to the legislation to control the use of data bases (Data Protection Act) in the UK, and also in other countries.

The diagram includes the competitive environment, for completeness at this stage. In analysing this, as we shall see when we look at industry and competitor analysis later, my preference is to remove the factor from the outer perimeter of the diagram, and reposition it within the centre of the diagram, to study in more detail the impact of the other environmental factors on the industry, of which the particular company is a member.

It is also necessary to think of the speed of change, an issue discussed already when we looked at the concept of environmental turbulence.

Demographic Factors

Populations change in many ways which are relevant to the business situation. It is not only the obvious generalisation that larger populations mean larger markets, assuming that economic prosperity continues: the altering structure of that population may be even more important.

A widespread trend in many parts of the world is for an aging population, with fewer young people, and more older ones. In addition, the older people are living longer. The trend holds true in the USA, much of Europe, Japan, and Singapore, and no doubt in many other countries that I have not studied. It is brought about by social changes which have led to falling birth rates, added to the longevity factor already mentioned. Such changes create strategic considerations for organisations, varying from the availability of people for employment to changes in markets because of different life styles. Politically, the retired are becoming a higher proportion of the electorate, and will therefore exercise a greater influence on government policies.

There is another, less obvious aspect of population change which has come to the fore in the USA, and is relevent for other countries. This is the diversity of the population, particularly those who are economically active, with increasing numbers from different ethnic and language groups in particular age bands, and occupations. This brings a need for greater intra-national cultural understanding, while convergence of countries, as in the Economic Community, makes international cultural understanding more important.

All these trends are potentially important in the planning of strategy. Fortunately, demographics are generally less turbulent than many of the other environmental factors. Most developed countries have a history of population censuses which means that the statistics are sound. Birth and death rates can be forecast with reasonable accuracy, and if the life expectancy at various ages is known, the movement of those of us who already exist into progressively higher age bands is close to a certainty. Immigration and emigration may be the greatest unknowns. Underdeveloped countries, and those developed countries such as what was once Yugoslavia, who have blundered into civil war, are a forecaster's nightmare. Disease (particularly AIDS in Africa), famine and war mean that both life expectancy and live birth rates are unknown, and the death, and migrations of refugees meant that there is no statistical base from which to project.

Economic Factors

Virtually all the demographic factors manifest themselves as an influence on another environmental function—the economy. As with all other factors, the effect on each country, each industry, and each business is not necessarily a constant, although every business is in some way under the influence of the economies in which it operates.

A study of all economic factors would be beyond the scope of this book, and would probably be an academic exercise unless carried out with the interests of a particular business in mind. Instead, a few examples are quoted to underline the importance of the economic factors, and it is hoped that these examples will illustrate the need for business to take them into account when preparing its corporate plans.

The problem is compounded by the increasing tendency for companies to become multinational in their scope. Although there are companies which still operate in one country only, many more will either be truly multi-national or have at least an export trade. It follows that for many companies the economic factors to be studied are those applying in not just one but a number of countries.

Relation of Company to the Economy

Perhaps the first step is to try to relate company results to the general progress of the economy. Does the company mirror the ups and downs of the trade cycle or the general direction and rate of economic growth? Not all companies do—in fact some may thrive whatever seems to be going on in the wider economic front. Others may find themselves in a growth situation in times of prosperity, falling back very quickly in the event of a period of stagnation or decline (the situation with many consumer durables, machine tools, and construction).

Many companies straddle a number of industries, and it may be necessary to study each separately. Similarly, it may be desirable to study exports separately: certainly there is not an immediate major correlation to be expected between reflation in the United Kingdom and sales in Japan. These are commonsense qualifications, and others certainly will occur (such as correcting for abnormal patterns caused by a reorganisation). What should arise from a study such as this is a much greater understanding of the business and its economic environment, useful both for strategic planning and for analysing risk.

Inflation

A second economic factor is inflation. This, of course, is closely related to general economic performance. Inflation has its own implications for forward-looking management, and, indeed, is a problem which causes concern to most chief executives.

Inflation is a worldwide problem, but one which varies in intensity between countries. Lietner[4] quotes the example of Indonesia, which considered a national inflation rate in 1968 of 85% a great improvement over a previous figure of 360%. Many South American countries have an inflation rate of between 20 and 50% and the United States has tended to regard 5–6% as a norm. Any increase over the norm can be traumatic and will move quickly to the political arena.

The immediate problem business faces is improving profits in a situation where rising costs are cutting into margins. Profits should increase at least as much as the inflation if the real return to shareholders is not to decrease and if the company is to provide its requirements of capital.

Inflation, like all other economic factors, will not affect all companies the same way. All other things being equal a labour-intensive industry will feel the effect of inflation much more violently than a capital-intensive industry with modern plant and adequate capacity.

Some managers argue that the inflation element should be ignored in long-range planning since price rises will compensate for the inflation effect. There are a number of reasons why this argument is fallacious. Perhaps the most important is that the strategy for dealing with inflation is a matter of top management judgement, is a decision, not an automatic result, and in any case may be something other than a price adjustment. In addition, there are always time-lags between cost and price increases, and even the cost increases do not incur all at once—labour rates may rise this week, raw materials next month, and trasnport costs next quarter; they may not have equal impact on all competitors. A third point, important for the implementation of plans, is that monitoring and controlling plans becomes next to impossible unless they are calculated at current prices.

So inflation, particularly the rates as applicable to the company, rather than the nation, is a key area of external influence. (A method of measuring internal company inflation is described in Hussey[5].)

Exchange Rates

The multi-national company has to take account not only of economic growth and inflation but also variations in exchange rates. Revaluation or devaluation can knock holes in any profit forecast. Some countries, for instance many of those in Africa, are subject to frequent and violent changes in exchange rates. Even those which are relatively stable are subject to change, as is demonstrated by the 1992 European exchange rate crisis.

Governmental Economic Policies

Government policies have a direct effect both on the economy at large, and the individual company. Many of these are self-evident, and changes in fiscal policies have already been mentioned. These are by no means the only policies of concern to the company, as a few other examples will make clear.

In many countries, particularly the underdeveloped, government economic policies play a key part in the encouragement of new industry (e.g. protective customs duties). In the United Kingdom fiscal incentives were used for a long time as one part of a policy to entice industry to particular areas of the country.

At times of economic pressure policies are introduced which have an impact on business. Changes in hire-purchase legislation may be made for economic rather than legal reasons (raising minimum deposits and reducing repayment periods), credit may be restricted or expanded, and the liquidity of importers may be reduced through a system of import deposits.

Legal Factors

Many of the economic policies will have the support of legislation. In addition, there are numerous aspects of the legal environment in which the company operates and which must be taken into account in the planning of strategy. Again, emphasis must be limited to a few specific examples.

The legal environment may be considered as having three parts: the existing pattern of laws under which every company operates, areas which change but where changes are advised in advance, and the unannounced introduction of new regulations or suspended clauses of existing laws.

In planning corporate strategy the pattern of existing laws is only of relevance for detailed consideration in so far as they are unusual, a particular constraint, or affect a type of business venture with which the company has no previous experience. It would be patently silly for a chief executive (or the planner) to list all laws which affect the business. However, the existing legal implications should not be forgotten, as it is possible for opportunities to be lost, or profits reduced, by failure in this area.

An "unusual" legal constraint might be one which affects one industry but not another. For example, in the United Kingdom the pharmaceutical industry has to consider a number of special constraints which it cannot ignore when formulating strategy. It is not possible to market a new drug until clearance has been obtained from a government agency: to obtain clearance, various controlled trials must be performed and other data assembled to prove that the drug does its job and that all harmful side-effects have been identified, and that the problem of side-effects is not greater than the illness cured. To overlook this factor in long-term planning would be foolhardy since it has the effect of increasing the lead time before a new product can be introduced and can add to the risk of pre-launch failure.

On the other hand, I do not believe that better plans would be produced because *all* managers had expert personal knowledge about property laws, laws governing lighting in offices, or the host of day-to-day factors arising from commercial transactions. Each of these legal implications is important, and must be considered by someone in the organisation, but it is only infrequently a factor for strategic planning.

Areas of change in the legal environment are matters of greater concern in planning. Unlike many other environmental factors, changes in the legal situation are often known considerably in advance with a high degree of certainty. For example, British businesses had several years warning of the date on which decimal currency would be introduced. To many this was just a cost-increasing factor, not particularly important to their overall plans. Others found in decimalisation an opportunity—not only the obvious increased market for cash register and calculating machine companies, but an opportunity for printers, publishers, educational, and training concerns. Less obvious, certain distributive concerns were able to offer an explanatory and training service to their customers, thus using decimalisation as an element of marketing strategy to increase sales of their normal products. No doubt many businesses ignored decimalisation, despite the warnings, until they were caught up in it.

This example shows that environmental factors may bring out a different reaction from different businesses. There are numerous other legal changes which fall into this "advanced warning" area, and, indeed, in democratic countries most new legislation will fall under this category. Laws take time to be enacted and can rarely be introduced overnight. The warning may not always be as long as with decimalisation, although it is frequently a matter of years.

The third classification, factors which change without warning, presents business planners with a different sort of problem where plans have to be based on predictions and assessments rather than near certainties.

Technological Factors

The increasing magnitude and rapidity of technological change was discussed at the beginning of this chapter and was positioned as one of the key factors in the environment. It does not stand alone, and is interrelated with all the other factors (the industrial revolution, for example, was noted for economic, social, and legal change in addition to the rapid development of technology).

Bernal[6] maintains that we are currently passing through a new industrial revolution. Whereas the original was characterised by the harnessing of power to perform what were previously heavy manual tasks, the new revolution is the substitution of mechanical or electronic devices for individual skill. The new revolution introduces the speed, control, judgement, and precision of electronic instruments. It is a revolution "...in which planned scientific research is taking the place more and more of individual mechanical ingenuity".

Certainly the company of today which ignores technology in its plans is very shortsighted. Technological change has, for most companies, at least two dimensions. The first is the change brought about for marketing reasons, often involving the creation of entirely new products or new uses for existing products. Thus metal guttering gives way to plastic, clay roofing tiles are replaced by cement, frozen vegetables replace the canned product, man-made fibres take a share of the textile market from natural fibres, and polythene bags cut into an area previously dominated by paper. These examples are all obvious because they have happened: many more problems arise from changes which might happen in the future.

The second dimension is change in processes, production methods, and other technology, which alters the way an established product is made. The basic product offered for sale may change only marginally: the way it is made may be totally new. Houses may be built by industrialised methods, far removed from traditional bricks and mortar with construction by on-site labour. Production lines may be automated and electronically controlled to give fine tolerances. An organic compound may be synthesised and produced from completely different raw materials by new processes. Machines may change in capacity and speed of production, in their efficiency rates, or in general reliability. Technological obsolescence is a factor not because of competition from new products in the market but because the company becomes increasingly uncompetitive in its costs. Extra fast obsolescence can cause problems of under-recovered depreciation, increased capital requirements, and machinery sold for scrap long before its useful life is over.

Technological change may alter market structure without basically changing the product. Many of the requirements of office printing have been basically unchanged for many years. The availability of low-cost, efficient, and relatively simple office printing machines changed the place where printing takes place. It is both practicable and economic for office forms to be internally printed by even the smaller companies—business which has moved from the printing industry itself. Desk top publication has put high quality book and report printing into the hands of the originator of the material.

It would be a mistake to assume that the only important technological changes are big ones. Relatively small changes in technology can have a disproportionate result.

For decades the world banana trade was based on a very simple system. Bananas were shipped in an unripe state on the stem on which nature grew them, usually loosely wrapped in straw (and later plastic). Each bundle was irregular in size and shape and was difficult to handle mechanically. Importing countries ripened the bananas in warehouses and, when this process was complete, the fruit was stripped of the stem in hands, packed into boxes, and delivered to retailers. Processes were generally labour intensive, there were problems over the disposal of quantities of vegetable matter in urban areas, and there was much double handling.

A relatively minor technological advance meant that green bananas could be picked in a standard carton in the exporting country and ripened in the same carton in the importers' warehouses, ultimately reaching the retail trade in the same container. Standard boxes enabled ships to use their cubic capacity to better advantage, and a greater weight could be carried on each voyage. Warehouses, for the same reason, could hold more produce. Mechanical handling became practicable. The amount of waste vegetable matter transported was reduced.

The results of this development have been so far reaching that virtually all the world's leading banana companies have adapted to it. Many of the smaller wholesalers, which did not adapt, have vanished.

Like all environmental change, technological developments can bring both problems and opportunity. Part of management's challenge of the future is to come to grips with technology so that their businesses continue to prosper.

Another example of the balancing of opportunity from various technological development is provided by the British Oxygen Company, although their story is little different from that of other oxygen manufacturers elsewhere in the world.

The manufacture of oxygen is itself a response to technological development. With the expansion of demand, in particular from new processes in the steel industry, there came a greater increase in the volume requirements of individual customers. The company developed its techniques to meet these needs: had they not done so some of the new uses of oxygen would not have developed because transport costs would have made the gas too expensive.

The original type of small gas cylinder is still in use, and meets the needs of many small-volume users. For the larger-volume user there is a tanker delivery service which pumps gas into storage tanks on the customer's own premises.

Very large customers may have an atmospheric gas plant structured on their own premises, so that BOC can supply oxygen without any transport problems. A logical development from this was the installation of oxygen grids—pipelines which connected large users of oxygen with one or more oxygen plants. In this way a back-up service was provided against plant breakdown; customers whose usage did not justify a separate plant could be connected to the grid, and economies of scale could be obtained from the operation of large plants.

The British Oxygen story illustrates the snowballing effect of technological change. Each successive development took place to meet a demand created by the development which preceded it.

Factors Relating to Infrastructure

For most businesses which operate in the developed world, the infrastructure is not a major planning problem. The situation is different in underdeveloped countries, where what is happening to the infrastructure may be the determinant factor in deciding what strategies are viable, or even possible. Many years ago I worked on development planning in what is now Zimbabwe. The importance of infrastructure became clear to me through my experiences: helping to bring rail communications to a remote area of the country; seeing the effect of the lack of a road bridge at a particular point on the River Sabi on the ability of farmers to get their produce quickly and cheaply to market; and of preventing a planned new airfield from being built in a position which would have had the runway leading to a new sugar mill of some height, the foundations of which were about to be laid. At a very personal level, the lack of telephone communications to a remote agricultural research station nearly brought my career to an end. An intricate itinerary was set up at short notice for a government committee of enquiry, which involved many visits, and careful transport planning. I had them arriving by small plane at an airstrip some few miles from the research station, but had still to arrange things with the station itself. My assumption that they were on the phone suddenly became critically wrong. There was no time to write. Fortunately I tracked down a government department that had a radio link with the station, and got the problem resolved. But it left me with a much greater awareness of the importance of the infrastructure, and of the value of not taking things for granted when planning.

Ecological Factors

A few years ago ecology would hardly have been considered as an environmental factor worthy of inclusion in a serious book on corporate planning. Two things have happened in recent years that change this viewpoint. The first is a greater understanding of the balance of nature and of the effect of man's activities on this balance. Science and the growth of human population have long been known to change ecological factors: what is now understood is that many of the changes bring penalties as well as benefits. The coin has two sides. The second factor is a change in social attitudes, at least in Europe and the United States, which has created a certain amount of public awareness and concern for ecological factors. There is now an ever-increasing weight of public opinion against things which threaten the ecological balance; much of this opinion manifesting itself in positive attitudes against pollution. The knowledge and attitudes have been reinforced by major disasters: nuclear power in Russia; oil tankers breaking up in the USA and Europe; poison gas escaping from a chemical plant in India.

There are a number of ecological factors which have implications for business. Part of the world growth in population is caused by upsetting the existing balance. Live birth rates have increased and the average span of life extended because of the benefits of modern medicine. In the Western world rising standards of living have led to social attitudes which have brought about a reduction in the overall birth rate and therefore in family size. In underdeveloped countries economic factors have not improved, the corresponding social attitudes have not developed, and family size continues to remain high. The result is that the poor countries tend to become poorer, while on a total basis the world population threatens to outstrip its resources.

Areas of land are swallowed up under urban developments, or different agricultural patterns which permanently change the natural animal and plant life. The availability of water supplies is a problem which is becoming increasingly acute in many areas; although technology and science can overcome some of the ecological problems (including the purification of sea water), the "cure" often leads to further ills.

For the strategic planner these problems are of interest, but often have little direct effect on the business. Some of the factors influence corporate plans through the change they cause to other environmental areas (e.g. population has already been discussed). Sometimes the effect is specific but localised—a shortage of water in one area may mean that a new factory has to be sited somewhere else. As with all other environmental factors, the answer is to identify what is relevant to the particular business.

The one ecological factor which is becoming of greater concern to many businesses is pollution. The fact that this is a topical issue can be illustrated by a few extracts from newspaper articles:

"The River Mississippi is dying. It has become a sewer for most of Middle America and will soon be capable of only carrying millions of tons of agricultural and municipal waste into the Gulf of Mexico each year. The fish population has already been heavily affected, some water fowl have disappeared and many experts feel its water is already too polluted to be treated for drinking."[7]

"Lake Constance, Germany's biggest inland sea, is becoming increasingly polluted. Its waters are threatening human beings with infection and fish with extermination."[8]

"West Germany and other Rhine countries are shipping about half a million tons of waste chemicals down the river annually for dumping in the North Sea, nearly a fourfold increase since 1968."[9]

The pollution factor may affect the extractive and chemical industries more than any others, but it would be wrong to think that only this type of business should consider problems of this nature. Already large areas in England come under clean-air control, which restricts the right of anyone to burn fuels that discharge sulphurous gases in the air. This applies to all businesses.

Pollution should be considered by the corporate planner in a number of ways. The first is definition of the moral viewpoint taken by the company (see Chapter 7). The next is to consider how legally enforced anti-pollution measures are likely to change production methods and costs in the future, and to make allowance for this (including the required capital) in the plans. The business may decide to form a pressure group to modify the extent to which outside forces dictate which anti-pollution measures take place.

All these possibilities treat pollution as a threat to the company's business and profits. In addition there may be opportunities, e.g. to devise and market machinery and methods which reduce pollution, to produce new products which are pollution free (such as plastic containers which degenerate when thrown away), or simply the public relations opportunity from being able to demonstrate attention to the problems of society.

Sociological Factors

Society is in a continuous process of change. Attitudes rarely alter overnight, but the time span during which they do alter is usually relevant to the corporate strategic plan. Two examples from the UK may help show the fundamental nature of some of the changes.

(i) In the 1960s smoking was the norm, and any non-smoker who complained about the fumes in an office was seen as abnormal. By the 1980s, the non-smokers were in the majority, and non-smoking offices becomig common. By the 1990s it was the person who wished to smoke at a business meeting who was atypical, and smoking was increasingly becoming prohibited on public transport. The smoker is now seen as anti-social, whereas a decade or so previously the non-smoker bore this label.

(ii) Nudity is now common in films and television broadcasts, and causes no offence to the majority of people. What is normal now would have caused an outcry not all that long ago.

Some of the trends are related to different life styles. "Portfolio careers", working from home, high levels of home ownership all result in different patterns of life, and different attitudes to what is acceptable and respectable. In the 1970s a manager who was made redundant carried a stigma. He—and at that time it would have been a he—"could not be any good otherwise someone else would have been chosen". Two major recessions, and a decade of structural changes as companies try to reduce costs to be globally competitive have meant that now no one thinks the worse of someone who has been the victim of these changes.

There are at least three ways in which social trends are important for strategic planning.

(i) Markets are directly affected by social changes, in the design of products, the trends in market size, and the way people make their buying decisions.

(ii) Social changes often lead to legal changes. Thus there is an increasing amount of social and employment legislation in most developed countries.

(iii) Expectations which people hold are important for human resource planning. It would be wrong to claim that in the UK women without exception have equal career opportunities with men. However prospects are better than they were in the past, and are improving as we move into the future. Many men now have a deep belief that women are as equally competent as men in management positions, and many more are willing to think about the issue. Other attitudes that are important for HR planning include work ethics, willingness to accept authority, and identification with the need for economic success. Future plans depend heavily on the view of how attitudes such as these will change over the years.

The results of changes do more than affect markets and our human resource policies. They have a massive impact on how organisations are managed, and how leaders have to behave if they want to have any followers. The impact is on strategic management, and not just on planning.

Political Factors

Close to social changes come politics. In a democracy there is a two-way cause and effect relationship between social attitudes and the policies of the various political parties. Each may change the other. Leadership is required from a prime minister, but woe betide any who lead from the front and are too far ahead. In other societies politics may come from the barrel of a gun, and policies may be determined through other motivations.

For the strategic planner, particularly when involved in global strategy or multi country operations, the key issue is political stability. The prognosis for this will not be the same everywhere, and is an important area for study.

In a domestic situation the concern is the changes in policy, and thereafter legislation and decisions, which would follow a change in political fortunes of the various parties.

The observant reader will have noticed that the competitive environment has not been discussed here. This is because the approach to thinking about and analysing this is somewhat different from the other factors, and is dealt with at some length later when we look at strategy and strategic analysis.

All the above thoughts sketch only briefly the challenge that environmental factors offer to business. The outlines can only faintly be drawn in any generalised description: only the individual company itself can turn the hesitant pencil marks into a drawing that has meaning and value.

This chapter has outlined the challenge of the environment, which still leaves the planner with the practical problem of how to actually use environmental factors in planning. This is an aspect which is taken up in the next chapter.

References

1. Levitt, T., *Innovation in Marketing* , McGraw-Hill, 1962.
2. Macdonald, A. M. (ed.), *Chambers's Twentieth Century Dictionary*, W. & R. Chambers, 1972.
3. Drucker, P. F., *Managing for Results*, Heinemann, 1964.
4. Lietner, B. A. "Prepare Your Company for Inflation", *Harbard Business Review*, September/October 1970.
5. Hussey, D. E., *Corporate Planning in Inflationary Conditions*, Institute of Cost and Management Accountants, 1979.
6. Bernal, J. D., *Science in History*, Pelican, 1969.
7. Riding, A., "The Mississippi, a Vast River of Pollution", *Financial Times*, 7 April 1971.
8. *Daily Telegraph*, "Dangers in Lake Constance", 5 May 1971
9. *Daily Telegraph*, "Rhine Ships Dump Half a Million Tons of Acids in Sea Every Year", 21 April 1971.

5

The Environment: Assumptions in Planning

The importance of the business environment to the company was stressed in some detail in the previous chapter. Strategic planning is about coping with change and uncertainty. As Scott[1] states:

"Planning is a process of groping forward. The future is enveloped in fog which grows denser the further we try to peer. Prediction of future events and circumstances means grappling with the uncertainties looming in this fog, and trying to make incomplete and indirect information as intelligible as possible."

Strategic management's problem is not only demonstrating to managers that they must accept the challenge of the future, but also finding a way of dealing with those half-perceived and moving shadows in the fog. While the challenge has been analysed in depth in many excellent books on corporate planning, marketing, or general management, the way of handling that challenge in a practical and workable fashion has received less attention.

The purpose of this chapter is to try to provide a framework to help the company move from a perception of its future environment to a method whereby this perception can become the basis of all long-range plans. The premiss from which to start is that the future is always uncertain, and that the most talented of planners or managers will never be in a position to foretell all that will affect the company. Planning is not an exercise in clairvoyance, and planners do not have secret arts or psychic knowledge: nor does their portfolio of management techniques include those of the mystic.

Rational plans can only be made from a firm base. If a company's future success depends on the continuance of exports to a certain country, a plan can only be made if the company reaches some sort of conclusion about whether or not that country will continue to allow imports. A marketing manager who sits back and says "I don't know so I won't say anything" and then still expects manufacturing to meet all requirements in any eventuality, is not planning, but trying to opt out.

Refusal to face up to a problem is hardly likely to persuade that problem to go away, and no rational plans can be completed in these circumstances.

Although no manager can predict a future event with guaranteed accuracy, any manager can determine a logical outcome of events if the prediction is correct. It becomes possible to make a sound plan based on *assumptions* about the future which will be valid for as long as the assumptions are valid. If these prove to be wrong, it may be necessary to modify the plans or sometimes to completely restructure them.

Van Dam[2] reports how CP International Inc. looked at the problem of production for Central America. The area was studied in detail and the conclusion was reached that there would be a move towards a Central American Common Market. This conclusion became an assumption on which a strategic plan could be prepared for the area.

An assumption may be defined as a statement of opinion about the occurrence of an event which is outside the control of the planner. This statement is treated as fact during the preparation of plans, although the company must never delude itself into believing that the assumption is an expression of a certainty. Assumptions themselves do not remove any uncertainty although they should be used in subsequent analysis and actions to reduce risk: their task is to enable objective thought to take place about the nature, shape, and size of those shadows in the fog, so actions can take place which have a rational basis.

Assumptions, besides providing a foundation for plans, also have a co-ordinating effect. It is very important for all those involved in the company to base their plan on common assumptions. Failure to do this can only result in chaos. For example, a marketing manager might prepare forecasts of demand for a product based on one set of economic assumptions—those costing the product might be working on another set. Demand and supply calculations are thus on different bases and may be wildly incompatible.

In addition, unless all plans are based on similar assumptions, it becomes impossible for a company to identify the effect on the company if assumptions prove incorrect.

This, then, is one of the first rules in the use of assumptions. They must be common to all areas of the company, even if an individual manager disagrees violently with them. A measure of self-discipline is required, and this is frequently difficult to achieve in practice since managers tend to be individualistic and like to back their own hunches.

The second rule is that only assumptions which really affect the company should be included in the plans. There is always a danger that a company will fall into the elephant trap of corporate self-delusion. Because it lists a hundred and one assumptions on each and every factor in the environment it believes that it is taking account of these factors in its plans. Too often it is dealing in dreams, and too often the assumptions could be completely reversed without making the slightest difference to any of the plans and forecasts. This is a situation to be avoided.

In practical terms this means that not only must various forecasts and predictions be made of the environment, but that some form of screening process must be set up to select those factors which really do have an impact on the company. There are a number of ways in which this can be done. One method is for the planner, or other person charged with preparing the forecasts, to complete an analysis of what is thought likely to be relevant. A second approach is for groups of managers to be drawn together in "think-tank" type meetings, so that a number of minds are brought to bear on the problem. In other companies it may be more appropriate to use a combination of both methods. Whatever the solution chosen, the problem is one which deserves a considerable amount of corporate thought: there can, too, be side benefits which arise from the process, and I have been present at sessions such as this which have led to the identification of new opportunities.

Assumptions are required at both the strategic and operational planning level. For the strategic plan the assumptions are assessments of those events outside of the control of the company itself: many of these will be carried forward to the operating plans. In addition, at operating level, there may be certain assumptions about events which are under the control of the company—that is, as far as any future event can be said to be under the control of anybody—but which are not controlled by the manager of the department completing the plan. For example:

(i) An assumption by individual operational departments that capital will be available to support their plans within the general framework of the guidelines provided. Ultimate analysis and the completion of the strategic plan may prove that this is an untrue assumption, and some modification may be necessary.

(ii) For production the sales forecast may be a basic assumption. The achievement of this is outside of the control of production: their job is to provide for the manufacture of the items specified in the forecast for delivery at the time required. Unless the forecast is taken as a basic assumption, no planning can be undertaken.

(iii) A marketing assumption that a new product will prove to be acceptable even though it is only in an early stage of development.

What is unacceptable is for operating managers to try to evade their responsibilities by defining assumptions about actions which *are* under their control. I have seen plans which included statements like:

—"I assume my forecasts are correct."
—"I assume that I will cut labour costs by 10%."
—"I assume that my new products will be test-marketed on the date stated."

Assumptions have a very important part to play in the analysis of decisions and the avoidance of risk. They have no part to play in the avoidance of responsibility. And even with the basic environmental assumptions their purpose is not to provide an excuse for failure but rather to lead to a complex network of alternative decisions which enable the company to change its strategies quickly so that it remains on course despite adverse circumstances.

So far the discussion on the setting of assumptions is of methods most appropriate for the smaller companies or those which have a relatively narrow span of diversity of operation. Some modification becomes necessary when assumptions are being set by multi-national companies or companies with many subsidiaries in widely diverse operations. Here it is necessary to divide assumptions into those which are required to be set centrally, because of a need to apply a common approach to a number of subsidiaries, and those which should be decentralised, being more properly the concern of the management of the subsidiary. Part of the solution will depend on the degree of autonomy allowed subsidiaries, but even where this is wide there will still remain some planning assumptions which should be standardised internationally.

Exactly what should go into which group of assumptions is a matter for individual decision which will vary from company to company. The criteria should be that assumptions of major significance which are common to more than one subsidiary should be centralised, as should assumptions about the world economy (as opposed to those about a particular country) and assumptions derived from technological forecasts which lead to decisions about the future of research and development activity. Some examples of assumptions relevant to each of these three different sets of circumstances may make the explanation a little clearer:

(i)   If a multi-national company has subsidiaries in both Australia and New Zealand each should work on the same assumption about the future of the New Zealand and Australian Free Trade Agreement. (Similarly, European subsidiaries should have a common assumption about new entrants to the European Community.)

(ii) The total group should operate to one set of assumptions about changes in the relative exchange rates of various international currencies. If this is not done international co-ordination is likely to be a matter of juggling "apples and pears" rather than an examination of real corporate value.

(iii) Basic policy for the future direction of research and development should be a central corporate decision regardless of the location of the research and development unit, although this does not mean that projects which fit within the defined policy have all to be decided centrally. A fundamental assumption on, for example, world food supplies which leads to research into new sources of food—such as biotechnology—should therefore be decided centrally.

In each and every case, provided that the co-ordination of the inputs does not become an overwhelming task, there may be participation by the local subsidiary in setting the assumption. But the final decision should be a central one.

Every company will face another problem area—the varying "quality" of the assumption. In the previous chapter mention was made of environmental factors for which advanced warning was available—as in, for example, changes to the legal environment. Assumptions that these events will come about have a high degree of "quality": they are not certainties, but they are as close to being certain as it is possible to get when considering any future event.

At the other extreme there are assumptions which are necessary although the company may have little or no information on which to base its judgements. This should not prevent assumptions from being made, for every company would make an implicit assumption even if it did not state what this was (usually this is what is happening today will continue to happen tomorrow). There are many advantages in defining this type of assumption explicitly. Even if it is subsequently proved to be wrong, the company knows that it is wrong and that certain changes are overdue in its strategy.

In between there are varying degrees of "quality" in assumptions, stretching from those derived from data that respond well to statistical analysis (e.g. medium-term population changes) to assumptions which can only be a matter of informed judgement. The next chapter will deal with certain techniques which can be used to improve forecasting (and therefore the quality of assumptions), but it must not be forgotten that there will always be many areas where an assumption has to be defined from very scanty data.

The sensible company will look very closely at the type of decisions made on low-quality assumptions. The less certain an event is, the more risk of failure there is likely to be in strategies which depend on it: some decisions might be rejected purely because the company does not have enough confidence on the assumption on which success depends. But there is much more to decision analysis than this, and we are anticipating later sections of this book.

Every company will also have to decide between what environmental studies are possible, and how much it can afford to spend. More and more effort can often be applied to enable more accurate assumptions to be developed, which in turn will lead to more effective decisions. Regular sources of data can be supplemented by special research studies, by complicated forecasting models, or by a massive investment in technological forecasting. For the multi-national company the problem becomes more complex. It may be reasonable to make a comprehensive study of all factors for one or two countries. Is it necessarily reasonable to give the same attention to ten countries, or twenty countries, or to the whole world? Deciding where to sacrifice quality in making assumptions is just one of the many management tasks involved in a process of stragegic management.

In effect, there is a corollary with what was stated earlier. Not only must factors be screened so that the irrelevant is rejected: the key areas must be identified and more attention given to making assumptions about these areas than any of the other possibilities. For example, a company engaged in food manufacture, processing large volumes of commodity raw materials, is likely to need to spend as much effort on making accurate assumptions about these as it does on factors influencing the market for its own products.

At this point it is worth mentioning that there are organisations which regularly publish environmental information, and others make forecasts of future trends. For example, in the United Kingdom the Registrar-General publishes population forecasts; there are a number of commercial organisations, such as the Economist Intelligence Unit Ltd. and Henley Centre for Forecasting; bodies such as the National Institute of Economic and Social Research; and a growing output of technological forecasts from a variety of sources. These may not make the task of setting planning assumptions easy, but they certainly make it easier.

Scott[1] suggests that the process of setting assumptions can be divided into three stages. Firstly, there are the *initial assumptions*. At this stage in planning little may be known about the subject, and educated guesses may be used to form the bases of planning assumptions. These are really on trial, and are imposed so that corporate strategy may develop while further work examines the validity of the assumption.

Initial assumptions next move to the *working assumption* stage. Here further analysis and development takes place, and those assumptions which are still valid and useful are used further in the planning process.

The last classification is *final assumptions*. These are those assumptions which find their way into the final written plan. Along the way their validity may be re-examined, so that what results is the most relevant and valid set of assumptions that the company can prepare. Scott makes the practical point that the written plan should only include those assumptions which are needed to use the plan or to understand the plan as a whole. The myriad of minor assumptions which may have been used at various working stages in the planning process should be omitted from the final document.

So far only one use of assumptions in corporate planning has been discussed: clearly defined assumptions as a prerequisite for any form of logical and rational planning. By itself this use would justify the effort put into this aspect of planning, especially as it carries the side benefit that environmental study also leads to the spotting of new opportunities. In addition to this, assumptions are very important tools which, used with skill and craftmanship, can help the company to weigh the chances of success in its favour. In effect they can be used to bias the corporate dice, so that some of the risk is removed from the throwing of it, that it may more often yield the high numbers.

It is probably fair to say that many companies do not get the maximum benefit out of their use of assumptions, and many still stop at the first and most obvious use. For instance, Ringbakk[3] mentions that many American companies still produce "one-point" plans: that is, plans which contain only one set of strategic forecasts leading to one estimated result. If a fundamental assumption fails, the plan fails. Plans such as this are likely to be somewhat inflexible. This need not be so.

Assumptions should instead be used in a number of positive ways as the basis for understanding the nature of the risks the company faces and for actions which eliminate or reduce those risks. This is not always easy, and in practical terms may be a planning refinement which comes only with the second or third planning cycle, but the methods will repay careful attention.

The subject of risk and sensitivity analysis will appear in more detail later in this book, for there are techniques which are worth using and these have a wider use than in conjunction with assumptions alone. Some things need to be said now because the sensitivity of various strategies based on key assumptions must be considered before it is possible to analyse ways of using assumptions to reduce risk.

Part of the key to risk analysis was given earlier in this chapter when the quality of assumptions was discussed, and in stressing the need to assess the importance of the assumption to the company. Good planning requires management to look closely at the effects a wrong assumption would have on the strategies selected: firstly, to quantify the effect of error, and, secondly, to assess the probability of error. It is always a good idea to look at the best and the worst which might happen. A large adverse effect is patently more worrying than a small one.

In making decisions based on assumptions it is often easy to forget that they are not firm facts. The importance of quantifying the effect of wrong assumptions cannot be overstressed. In general terms a situation where a wrong assumption would bankrupt the company is to be avoided, even when the probability of a wrong assumption is fairly low. At the other end of the scale, a company may tolerate an assumption with a fairly high risk of failure if the total effect of failure on profits is small. (It must not be overlooked that there are alternative strategic choices possible from one assumption, each with its own pattern of risks of success or failure: this point is made use of later.)

Assessing probabilities can be a complex task and is sometimes impossible in any scientific way. However, it is always possible for any manager to assess "betting odds" on any assumption he uses, and for corporate management to reach some measure of agreement on the "betting odds" of the chances of any proving to be true. Although this part of exercise may not be justifiable mathematically, it has the effect of helping managers to accept that part of their difficult task as managers is to make decisions in conditions of uncertainty.

For the time being the difficulties of sensitivity and risk analysis will be passed over and attention focused on other important uses of assumptions—the reduction of risk.

Risk may be positively reduced in three ways:

—Choice of strategies with lower adverse effects if assumptions are wrong.
—Contingency plans.
—Hedging actions.

The first of these is part of the process of strategic decision-making, and is an extension of what has already been said. Where a strategy would bring the risk of the complete collapse of the company should its base assumptions prove incorrect, it is eminently sensible to choose an alternative. Although the alternative may have a lower earning potential, the effect in case of failure may be far less disastrous. It is, of course, this form of reasoning which leads to test-marketing and other forms of experimental marketing research to try alternative strategies before making irreversible decisions to implement them.

Another example is provided in a backwards integration situation. On the basic assumptions sales forecasts may be developed, for the ultimate product, and it is possible to envisage a situation where it appears profitable to integrate backwards and to provide all the necessary raw materials. Closer consideration of risk might indicate that a better decision would be to produce, for example, only 60% of each raw material, buying the rest from other sources. In this way demand can fall heavily before the plant producing the raw materials is in any way affected. The acknowledgement of the risk element inherent in any decision which affects the future may take the company down a completely different strategic path. This path may meander more than any other, but if it avoids the pitfalls and hazards of the direct route, the extra effort expended is well worth while.

This key use of assumptions in strategy has further relevance in another area—contingency planning. However much work a company has put into its assumptions, however much faith it has that the assumptions will prove to be correct, there is still an element of uncertainty. The man who turns up at his railway station to catch his morning train to work does so on the assumption that, even if his train does not run, there will be another train to catch. If he has caught a train at this time every working day for the past twenty-five years, he may reasonably assume that there will be a train today. Yet his assumption may be wrong: there may have been a strike, a train crash, the collapse of a bridge, a landslide, or many other such chance events. If he is a careful man he will have already made his contingency plan for just such an eventuality, and have worked out an alternative way of reaching his destination.

In ideal circumstances every strategy would have a portfolio of alternative or contingency plans which can be swung into action in the event of the failure of an assumption. These may vary from contingency plans which enable the continued pursuit of a basic strategy to complete alternative strategies into which the company may move without losing stride as it follows a new path to its objectives. Circumstances are seldom ideal. Companies can only very rarely afford the work to develop a comprehensive portfolio of alternatives which may never be used, and in practice it is usually necessary to concentrate on a few key areas, where failure would have a significant effect.

A leading British food wholesaler and importer distributed most of its products from the port of importation to its chain of depots by a rail-container system. This was the most economic form of transport for its particular situation. All its forward plans were based on the assumption that the rail service would not be upset by strikes, industrial unrest, or labour disputes. Indeed, the rational planning of marketing activities and depot requirements would have been impossible under any other assumption. At the same time the company was not blind to the fact that the assumption might be wrong, and that rail services might be disrupted on a short-term basis. For this reason it also had a contingency plan—a plan for a complete alternative distribution service which could be put into effect almost instantaneously. This plan was fully documented and attempted to foresee—and plan for—every adverse effect of rail disruption which might occur, including failures in the postal service.

Those British companies which had prepared contingency plans to cope with a failure of postal services generally fared better in the 1971 postal strike than the many firms which gave the matter no thought at all until *after* the strike had begun.

It would, of course, be wrong to imply that contingency plans could be developed for all risks. There are many that have to be faced without any fallback position. It is nevertheless true that many organisations do not give enough attention to this aspect of planning.

The food wholesaler provided a short-term contingency plan to meet an operational difficulty. An example of contingency planning at the strategic level comes from a former Government Agency of what was then called Rhodesia.

The Sabi–Limpopo Authority is a statutory body which was set up to co-ordinate and expand a major irrigation development scheme which would ultimately irrigate 600,000 acres. Much of the development which had already been effected, and much of that planned, was based on sugar, on the assumption that "moderate" prices would obtain. This assumption was made at the time of the 1963/4 situation of unusually high prices. At the same time, although sugar was the key strategy, both private developers and Government had devoted some effort to examine other alternative crops. After UDI, the Rhodesia's export sugar market vanished under the onslaught of United Nations' sanctions. Thus the base assumption proved false. Without any major difficulty the Sabi–Limpopo Authority changed an entire estate, which was being set up for sugar, over to wheat. The alternative strategy was ready and was capable of speedy implementation.

A more recent development of this train of thought has been the use of scenarios for strategic planning.[4] These provide a number of complete views of possible future states combining networks of assumptions, and strategies are developed to meet each. This provides an opportunity to compare different possible strategic paths, to assess the degree of commonality of variance between strategies, and leads to conscious decisions to build in flexibility into the plans.

Hedging actions have been practised since business began, and may often be a legitimate way of avoiding risk when assumptions prove to be incorrect. For example, for many years United Kingdom corporate planners had to forecast whether—and if so when—the United Kingdom would enter the EEC, when not even governments knew the answer. Even where a company planned on the assumption that the United Kingdom would not enter, it frequently made sense to "hedge", to establish business with the EEC countries that would stand the company in good stead even if it were wrong.

Simlarly, the company might assume that a particular source of raw materials will continue without problem into the future. At the same time it may be expedient to develop other contracts and buy some supplies on a regular basis from other sources, even though the price may be a little higher.

Perhaps the last thing that should be said on the subject of assumptions is that it is very, very easy for the expected results to be taken as truth and the underlying assumptions forgotten. An assumed happening very quickly takes on the character of a sacred oath: the fact that it *is* only assumed vanishes with a rapidity which would do credit to any stage magician's sleight of hand. This is something which every manager must beware of, and one of the most effective ways of doing this is to establish a system of monitoring, revision, and control which constantly keeps the company aware of the changing validity of its assumptions. This subject is taken up again in Chapter 19.

The whole process of setting planning assumptions calls for much creative corporate thought. It is a task which should not be skimped, for failure to put adequate effort into planning at this stage may bring all the subsequent plans tumbling down like a house of cards. The key to flexible plans often lies in the assumption stage: it is a key which helps the company open many of the barriers which lie between its present position and its future objectives. Yet it is a key which remains invisible to many of those engaged on the planning task.

References

1. Scott, B. W. *Long Range Planning in American Industry*, American Management Association, 1962.
2. Van Dam, A. "Corporate planning for Asia, Latin America and Africa", paper presented to the International Conference of Corporate Planners, Montreal, 9 December 1971.
3. Ringbakk, K. A. "Organised Planning in Major US Companies", *Long Range Planning*, December 1969.
4. O'Connor, R. *Planning under Uncertainty*, Conference Board (Report 741), 1978.

6

Forecasting

Forecasting is not the same as planning, although a plan may be based on certain forecasts: for example, of some of the environmental factors discussed earlier. One of the by products of a plan may be a forecast of the results that will be attained if it is implemented. So forecasts may be both part of the raw material of planning and a manifestation of its outcome.

All forecasts deal with matters of uncertainty—a point which has already been discussed—and the more this uncertainty can be reduced, the better the chance a company has of planning the right decisions. Although we have already seen (Chapter 2) that too much stress on the accuracy of results may reduce the value of planning, the same cannot be said of environmental forecasts which cause the company to commit resources to achieve a particular plan.

Any person may make a forecast and, indeed, every person does from time to time. The method of forecasting may vary from a blind guess, through informed judgement, to the use of a more scientific approach. Some forecasting techniques are very complicated, and it is easy to fall into the trap of believing that complexity is beneficial for its own sake: simple methods may often be the most cost-effective.

Marshall,[1] the great English economist, had a word of sense to say about an approach to economics when in 1898 he wrote: "It is doubtless true that much of this work has less need of elaborate scientific methods than of a shrewd mother wit, a sound sense of proportion and a large experience of life."

The same might be said about approaches to forecasting.

Some writers on the subject distinguish between a forecast, a prediction, a projection, and an anticipation, but as there is little common agreement on the use of these terms, no attempt is made here to assign particular meanings to the words.

The Product Life Cycle

One concept which is of value in many forecasting situations is that of the product life cycle. This suggests that all products pass through a series of growth curves (the first part of which is S-shaped), until they reach a point when they either level out or begin to decline. The concept is illustrated in Fig. 6.1.

FIG. 6.1. Product life-cycle curve.

The curve begins with a period of low sales and low profits as the new product is introduced to the market. This is followed by a period of take-off associated with rapidly increasing sales and relatively high profits: the period during which the product is gaining acceptance and has little competition. At this stage any competitive activity tends to increase the total market. At the same time unit costs are lower because the benefits of increasing scale of production are achieved.

By the third stage the rate of growth has slowed considerably as more competitors enter the market and as, in any case, it becomes more difficult to increase sales penetration. The additional expenditure to increase sales and to meet competitive activity reduces the profit per unit (although it may still increase in total).

The product moves to maturity, where it has a situation of low or declining sales growth, and a fall off in profitability. Yet another final stage may result, where the product declines rapidly to obscurity.

One forecasting problem can be seen from a study of Fig. 6.1. A statistical projection made at any one of the stages of the life-cycle curve would have resulted in a completely wrong forecast (this can be seen by imaging a trend line at each stage).

The second forecasting problem is that the time-span of the life cycle must be months, years, or decades. This is further complicated by the fact that actions may be taken accidentally or deliberately to extend the product life cycle, and thus distort the expected pattern. Levitt[2] gives an example of various stages in the life cycle of oil:

(a) Crude oil as a medicine.
(b) Paraffin for lighting.
(c) Paraffin for space heating.
(d) Petrol for internal combustion engines.
(e) Oil for central heating.
(f) Petro-chemical industry.

Such actions to alter the shape of the life cycle may be taken by a company: in fact one aspect of strategy might be to do just this. Shape may be altered by the introduction of actions to extend the cycle (e.g. the introduction of a successful ethical pharmaceutical product as an "over-the-counter" product supported by promotion). Alternatively, action may be taken to lengthen each phase of the cycle by changing the rate at which things happen: for example, in the 1960s the British furniture industry had a joint industry-wide promotion "old furniture must go", designed to persuade people to replace their furniture more frequently and thus increase demand.

Figure 6.2 shows a "real" product life cycle from an analysis of the demand for hydraulic cranes over a ninety-year period carried out by Saunders and Smith.[3] This is a good illustration of the fact that the cycle may last many years and that it will show some deviations from the theoretical pattern.

Statistical Projections

There are a number of techniques which provide a projection of a statistical series into the future and which rely entirely on analysis of the series. They are based on the assumption that past performance will be a guide to the future.

Whether such an assumption is correct depends, of course, on many factors, including the age of the product, the point reached in its life cycle, and the length of time for which the forecast is made. There are many methods which are very valuable for short-term forecasts of a few months, but which are rarely accurate beyond this.

One use of these methods is to gain perspective: to see where a trend *might* lead. If this projected position is patently impossible the forecaster will have learnt something about the data.

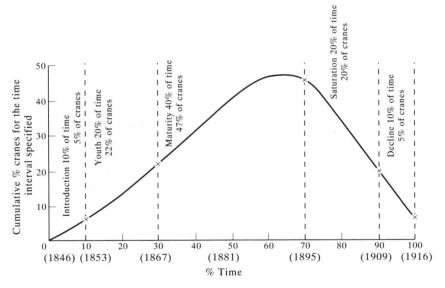

FIG. 6.2. Modified life cycle. Hydraulic cranes from Armstrong's Elswick Works. Reprinted by permission from an article by A. Saunders and N. J. Smith.[3]

(i) Simple Growth Pattern

A commonly used method of forecasting is based on the average annual growth rate calculated over a period, simply worked out by expressing the latest year as an index of the earliest and working out the growth rate from a book of compound interest tables. Variations on this theme include allowing for erratic movements in the data or in a typical year. It may also be postulated that the expected change is a particular percentage of the previous growth rate.

(ii) Moving Averages

A moving average is a method of eliminating regular seasonal or cyclical patterns from the data to indicate the underlying smoothed trend. (Having calculated the trend, it then becomes possible to eliminate it statistically, to enable a study to be made of the seasonal factors.) Each point in the moving average is the mean of a number of consecutive points of the series: the number of data points is chosen by judgement to give the period which best eliminates the seasonal irregularities. The average used may be the arithmetic or geometric means, or the median.

Moving averages are rarely useful for long-term forecasts. One of their disadvantages is that they always fall short of the actual data available: any projection has to cover not only the future but also some of the past.

(iii) Exponential Smoothing

Another technique for short-term forecasting, which has a particular value for inventory and production control systems, is exponential smoothing. The method is based on a moving average which is exponentially weighted so that the more recent data is given a greater weighting, and that the past forecasting error is taken into account in each successive forecast. A full description of the method is given by Coutie et al.[4] Statistical confidence limits may also be calculated.

A more sophisticated variant of exponential smoothing is the Box–Jenkins method, which is even more accurate in short-term forecasting (up to three months).

(iv) Mathematical Trends

A number of mathematical formulae are available for calculating a trend line in a time series and extending this line to some future point.

The simplest, and often a valuable starting position, is to fit a line on a graph by eye, using a ruler so that the area on the graph under the trend line is approximately equal to the area above it.

By eye alone the line of "best fit" is difficult to place exactly, but may be calculated mathematically by the method of least squares. An indication of the likely validity of a least squares trend line as a method for predicting the future trend of a series of data can be obtained using the Cartesian coordinate method. This will reveal whether the data has any correlation or if it is completely dissociated. A full description of these methods will be found in most books on elementary statistics, e.g. Moroney.[5]

There are many other methods, including logarithms, square roots, and ways of fitting a curvilinear trend.

All these methods have value in medium- and long-term forecasting, but give little indication of turning points in the data. Thus in the product life-cycle diagram, it is probable that the methods would be useful during much of the time for each period in the curve, but would lose their validity each time there is a change in shape to a new period of the cycle.

Marketing and Market Research Methods

When thinking about forecasting it is very easy to concentrate on mathematics and operational research and to forget some of the other time-tested methods which are used continuously by practising managers. Many of these methods may be grouped under the heading of marketing and marketing research and include experimental marketing, special surveys, comparative studies, and similar approaches. Even a relatively routine piece of market research is used as a minor forecasting tool: assuming that the information gathered when the fieldwork was carried out a few weeks ago is still valid when decisions are based on the report.

(i) Comparative Studies

A useful forecasting method is to examine the performance of something similar to the item being forecast. For example, a company launching a new proprietary pharmaceutical, say a cough cure, might well study the price, promotion, and progress of other types of proprietary products introduced in the previous five years. An analogy might be derived from the performance of these similar products, which can be of value in predicting the likely results of the new item about to be launched.

Similar analogies may be drawn from studies of promotional expenditures and market performance of competitive or similar products. Methods such as these may be used to give a greater understanding of the forecasting situation, thus enabling forecasts by other methods to be interpreted intelligently.

In some cases the analogy may be drawn against performance in another country.

Many forecasters find it valuable to use past performance in the United States as a guide to future performance in the United Kingdom. It is not only sales and market forecasts which may be compared in this way, but similar events. For example, those forecasting the effects of decimalisation in the United Kingdom learnt from experiences in South Africa and Australia.

(ii) Leading Indicators

The leading indicator should, more correctly, be classified as an economic research method, except that it seems to me to have some similarities with the comparative studies mentioned above. A leading indicator is an event which always precedes an event of another type, thus giving a prior warning of change. Thus an economic output figure for the building industry might be used as an indicator for other economic activity. Forward attendance bookings at management seminars, or figures of executive advertisements, may also give an advanced indication of general movement in the economy. It is essentially a tool for forecasting the short term.

(iii) Experimental Market Research

Under this heading I include all marketing tests designed to yield information that can be used to assess the profitability of the proposed move, and to give quantitative data that may be used for forecasting. If the experiments are well designed and properly controlled, so that they measure what they were intended to measure, valuable information can be yielded which can be extended from the test area to a wider universe. Examples of such experiments are test-market operations, advertising weighting experiments, price experiments, and marketing methods: an example of the last is a telephone-selling operation which could be tested in a small area before a decision was made to change.

The disadvantage of such tests is that a true experiment eliminates all variables except the one being measured: this is not always possible in practice. In addition the experimental area is rarely a replica in miniature of the whole country. Nevertheless, much useful data may be collected: at the worst this enables the company to be more accurate about the probability of success or failure (a product which fails in test market is most unlikely to succeed on a national basis); at the best it provides a means of making simple forecasts and of providing data on causal relationships which can be used for more complex forecasting models.

(iv) Intention-to-buy Surveys

These may be used for both consumer and industrial goods. There are two main uses: firstly for gaining information about proposed new products, and, secondly, to calculate an index for existing products, on a regular basis, which can be related to actual performance, thus providing a predictive index for forecasting future sales. Occasionally, with industrial products where there are few customers, this data may be reliable enough to be used raw.

The use of such surveys in connection with new products is usually part of wider concept work, and leads to the design of market tests rather than firm forecasts.

(v) Marketing Judgement

There are many occasions when little or no data exists on which to base a forecast of a product or environmental event, but where the knowledge and experience of the company's employees can be called upon, or when common-sense can be used to forecast bands of possible results based on some other data.

New products are among the most difficult of forecasting problems. It is frequently possible to keep the forecasts within the bounds of possibility if various likely, reasonable, and impossible parameters are set up in connection with some other data. For example, the total number of households is known. A company planning to launch a new food snack may make initial working forecasts based on:

Likely: each household buys one packet per month.
Reasonable: each household buys one packet per fortnight.
Impossible: each household buys two packets per week.

This sort of exercise depends a great deal on assumptions, many draw heavily on desk research and in-house surveys, and although it suffers from many disadvantages is considerably better than just guessing.

McCarthy[6] provides a further example of quantifying "judgement" in his procedure for building a subjective demand curve. This probes the judgement of key executives by asking what quantity they believe they could sell at various prices, and enables a theoretical demand curve to be derived.

(vi) Other Surveys

Marketing research can also provide much information which can be used in forecasting situations. A consumer usage and attitude survey might well be used to identify the dynamics of demand, which in turn may be used in forecasts or marketing models. Cause and effect are not always easy to identify; for example:

In the United Kingdom cars are polished more frequently where the owners do not have garages. Is this because they have no garages and give extra protection this way—in which case it might be a predictive tool? Or is it that people without garages tend to belong to a grouping who for other reasons polish their cars more frequently?

Analytical Forecasts and Models

Some of the most exciting forecasting techniques require complicated econometric and mathematical skills before they can be applied. They may draw heavily on market surveys, economic research, and desk studies for valid explanations and assumptions which may be incorporated into the forecasting model. Although most of the earlier statistical forecasting techniques can be calculated manually, these more complex models rely heavily on the computer. One forecast may require many thousand calculations: possible in theory without using a computer, but hardly practicable.

(i) Regression Analysis

The advantage of the regression analysis technique is that it explores the mathematical relationships of other variables with the one being studied and relates this data into a joint equation. Variables selected for this analysis must have a causal relationship—completely unrelated data, although it might well fit statistically, cannot yield meaningful results.

Parker and Seguara[7] argue that:

"Regression is more powerful than subjective estimation because it enables the forecaster to measure explicitly the apparent association between variable over time, thus eliminating a large portion of the guesswork. If the user finds a statistical association between the level of growth in sales and the movement of four or five other variables, then this relationship becomes the basis of the forecast itself."

Although variables are examined statistically, their initial identification as possible influence factors is a matter of judgement. Market surveys may help identify related factors although such identification is of most value when it is possible to obtain a number of years history for each variable.

The strength of the regression analysis method is that it provides a rational way of using management judgement. A marketing manager might believe that the market for his product is influenced by changes in, for example, the adult population, disposable income, the building of new houses, industry promotional expenditure, and the average daily temperature. Regression analysis provides the means of identifying and using for forecasting purposes those factors which are statistically significant. As with all forecasts that rely on past data, the implicit assumption is that past relationship will continue: as with all forecasts, this may not be true.

(ii) Economic Models

An economic model is an attempt to represent, in mathematical terms, the interdependent relationships of a number of variables which effect a particular activity. Models may be built to forecast numerous fields of activity, e.g. sales, market performance, the economy, commodity prices.

Such models may be very complex, and may be built to take account of all known factors which have a causal relationship with the item being forecast. Thus a sales forecast would, in addition to the factors causing demand, take account of all the other factors in the distribution system, such as inventory levels.

Apart from the mathematical skills, an econometric model builder needs to be able to identify and understand the causal factors which have a bearing on his forecast. Gathering the necessary data is often of itself a complex task; information is seldom available exactly as the model builder would like it. A decision to build a model can bring a requirement for considerable economic and marketing research.

(iii) Input–Output Analysis

The first national input–output table was published by W. W. Leontieff in 1937. Originally developed on a national basis to show the inter-industry flow of goods and services in the total economy, these tables have now been developed as a means of studying a company or a market.

Every industry appears twice in the table—once as an input and once as an output. The table shows what flows of inputs must occur to produce a certain flow of outputs: thus causal relationships may be explored, provided sufficient care and attention has been given to constructing the table in the first place. A change in output of the motor-vehicle industry would, for example, require inputs from the iron and steel industry. This input is the output of this industry, and, in turn, causes a demand for inputs from other industries.

Most countries now produce input–output tables to reflect past economic performance. A number of agencies have also produced tables relating to the future, which incorporate forecasts from different industries and economic sectors. For the normal company an effective input–output table can be a very expensive tool to develop, and the additional benefit conferred by such a model would need careful study against its cost.

Combination Forecasts

Many forecasts are arrived at by combining forecasts of numerous variables. This is a situation met in many common business situations: for example, a forecast of results to be expected from a capital expenditure project. Such a forecast would be a composite of forecasts of sales of various products, production and distribution costs, and capital expenditure. In addition the analysis would call for a forecast of corporation tax rates.

A similar composite approach may be used in other situations, e.g. forecasting the economy.

Technological Forecasting ("Futures")

The term technological forecasting has come to be applied to a group of techniques which have been developed in recent years. In fact this is something of a misnomer, for the techniques are used in many forecasting situations as well as the future state of technology: they may be as useful for forecasting social patterns and economic activity as for suggesting new products and approaches to their manufacture.

Unfortunately many of the practitioners of technological forecasting have thrown a semantic smokescreen around their subject, coining words that have no meaning to the manager who is expected to base decisions on the results of those forecasts. There is also an aura of mystique around methods which purport to give forecasts of what will happen twenty to thirty years hence. My view is that a technological forecast should be interpreted not so much as a prediction of what *will* happen, but as an indication of what is possible and which can therefore be made to happen. Used in this sense it can be seen as a major contributor to strategic decisions, helping the company to choose its commitments to the future from a more rational base. It has particular relevance in research and development strategies, particularly those with a long time-span, and for major capital investment decisions such as the siting and nature of a new airport.

It is by no means new for an entrepreneur to have a sense of vision which shapes all his strategies, and many of the world's biggest companies started with little more than determination, a willingness to work, and a dream. Simlarly, judgement forecasts about any event have always been (and probably always will be) a feature of the management scene: they have already been discussed in this chapter. Many of the techniques of technological forecasting systemise and improve some of the vision and judgement. They provide a framework for assessing the logical interrelationships of isolated forecasts: they provide a means of combining the judgement of many experts. Frequently they present the decision-makers with a number of alternative futures to give a measure of choice and control over their own future.

There are now a number of techniques grouped under the broad heading of technological forecasting. The use of many of these is becoming more widespread, and there are now a number of institutes and commercial companies in both Europe and the United States which specialise in "futurology". Many of the studies, by bodies such as the Club of Rome, on the future availability of the world's sources have been given wide publicity and are publicly available.

(i) Delphi Technique

Perhaps one of the best-known techniques is Delphi, which has the advantage that it can be organised fairly inexpensively and may be carried out by post.

Essentially the technique is the use of a panel of experts to forecast future events or developments through a sequence of questionnaires. Results of one questionnaire are used to produce the next, and each expert is made aware of any additional information about actual developments which is contributed by any of the other experts. Successive questionnaires also show to each expert the extent to which his opinion differs from the others. He is given the opportunity of modifying or adding to his first statements, and to show how far he agrees with aspects of opinion which are additional to his own.

Many Delphi studies are carried out entirely by postal questionnaire, and the experts never come into contact with each other; all contact is through a co-ordinator. The selection of the panel is a matter of some importance, for the identification of genuine experts is often a matter of difficulty. One approach used in a long-range study of medicine, is reported by Teeling-Smith[8] as an "expanding nucleus" technique. As experts were identified they were invited to suggest other qualified people who could serve on the panel. From a small beginning with "people from different fields of medicine and from the pharmaceutical industry— selected on a personal basis because they were known to have expert knowledge and to be generally forward looking", eighty experts were identified from which a panel of fifty from various parts of the world was constructed.

The advantage of the Delphi technique is that it stimulates creative thinking and corrects the bias of individual personal judgement without swinging to the other extreme of domination by majority opinion. The questionnaire usually is designed in such a way that it forces a quantified answer: for example, the percentage of households with two cars at a certain date or the probability of an event happening by a certain time.

Some Delphi studies invite the chosen expert to consult with other people he knows when formulating his opinions. Others ask the expert to leave blank questions which he feels he is not personally competent to answer. It is also possible to build in a weighting system into the answers, so the opinion of those most competent to judge is given more attention than that of those with less knowledge on that particular question.

The relative ease of conducting a Delphi study, and the current vogue for pronouncements about the future, have led to a large harvest of published Delphi studies about practically every topic under the sun. Unfortunately, it is not always easy to separate the tares from the grain, and many of the studies have little positive value.

(ii) Scenarios

A scenario is an attempt to describe a sequence of events which demonstrate how a particular goal might be reached. For example, a number of exercises have been carried out extrapolating various trends which would lead ultimately to the destruction of the world. The scenario technique might take this as background, postulate an alternative state of affairs which is to be preferred, and identify the various actions which have to be taken over time to reach this preferred goal. Scenario writing is a creative exercise which attempts to correlate various necessary actions and their effect on each other, and to assign a time-scale to these. It is very much a forecast of the possible.

As scenario writing is creative, it benefits from the involvement of several people. It is possible to use the technique in a much narrower area than the future of the world discussed above: for example, a number of alternative developments of a particular technology might be postulated, and experts asked to write scenarios showing what implications the developments will have.

Scenarios may also be used in conjunction with other techniques: for example, to provide the questions which are to be incorporated into a Delphi study.

(iii) Impact Analysis

In many ways only a branch of scenario writing, this technique concentrates on the impact which various forecast technological developments might have on particular industries. Where the scenario shows a route to a goal, impact analysis concentrates on analysing the effects of an expected development which may or may not be desired. The analysis provides the company with the opportunity of spotting opportunities or taking avoidance action where appropriate.

(iv) Extrapolative Techniques

There are a number of extrapolative techniques of technological forecasting which have an obvious link with general economic forecasting. They are based on the study of technological trends and their extrapolation into the future.

For example, it is possible to plot the development of a particular end-use over a span of years, setting up a graph with an efficiency rating on the vertical axis and time on the horizontal. The end-use might result from a number of different technologies. It is possible to imagine such a graph plotting the development of military weapons: the efficiency index might be the weapon's destructive ability.

On this imaginary graph it is possible to plot man's first weapon, stones, and one of his latest, H-bombs. In between are swords, spears, bows and arrows, guns, bombs, and many more. Each successive development showing a great increase in destructive ability, and occurring in an ever-decreasing time-span. Thus the past is established in a series of points through which a trend line may be fitted. The next step is to extrapolate the trend to a likely new technological development and its position on the efficiency scale, although one hesitates to forecast anything more destructive than the H-bomb even as an imaginary exercise.

The technique has many faults, although its validity is improved when applied to a genuine problem. Perhaps the military weapon example is a little unreal, but it is not hard to move from this point to a real problem: for example, energy output, food processing developments or something similar.

It becomes a more real analysis when the forecaster applies a second technique in conjunction with the first. This studies the life-cycle curve of each individual technology, extrapolating the curves so that it becomes possible to see when one technology is reaching its turning point or is being overtaken by another. Some efficiency ceilings are predictable for a particular technology—the maximum energy output of, say, a windmill under the optimum theoretical circumstances is calculable—and if these ceilings are below the requirement of the users of the technology it indicates that a change of technology is imminent.

The life-cycle curve will normally take the typical S-shape discussed earlier in this chapter. Imagine a chart showing bow-and-arrow and gunpowder technologies. Bows and arrows would have a relatively short development time (the bottom of the S), a relatively short climb over a short period as maximum destructive efficiency increased and a long top to the S, lasting centuries, as the technology reached a peak beyond which it could not improve. Gunpowder technology would start with a destructive ability something below the top of the bow-and-arrow curve. For a period both technologies would overlap. For several hundred years destructive efficiency would increase until this technology, too, reached its peak of performance and turned round the top of its S-curve.

Although this technique may give an early warning of the expected onset of a new technology, it will not always enable management to predict exactly what will replace it. However, it may identify a problem which could then be analysed by one of the other techniques covered in this chapter.

There are several other extrapolative techniques of varying complexity, including the consideration of multiple trends and "technology precursors". A description of these will be found in most comprehensive works on technological forecasting.

(v) Morphological Analysis

This technique possesses one of the tongue-twisting names that helps build that semantic barrier between "expert" and manager. Essentially the method consists of an exhaustive analysis to identify all the technological requirements of a product and the relationships between them. The dimensions are plotted in a multi-dimensional matrix so that possible alternatives may be explored.

The technique is useful for considering a multiplicity of technological or environmental options. It is, however, a method which is very difficult to apply in practice, and which is both complex and involved.

Choosing the Best Technique

This wealth of available techniques brings an inevitable problem. How may a company choose the best method? The answer to this question is that selection is a matter of judgement supported by experience. However, there are some principles which can assist.

(i) The purpose of the forecast should be clearly defined and, therefore, the degree of accuracy required. Is it an area where a close approximation is all that is required for decision-making (e.g. for setting salesmen's targets), or is it an issue of key importance on which a whole network of major decisions will be based?

(ii) The ability of the company to use the forecast is also important. Time and time again managers use environmental forecasts in an unsophisticated way, often only partially taking account of them in plans and decisions. A major change in environmental forecast is not always reflected in a change of action by the manager. Where a company is in this state it cannot justify the more complex forecasting methods that it may require at a later stage when it improves its planning ability.

(iii) Cost-effectiveness is one of the most important of criteria. Will the additional cost of a complex technique be re-couped in better decisions? If it will not, a cheaper and simpler method should be prescribed. The cost is not simply that of producing the forecast, and includes the collection of any special data needed. A forecast that can be made from readily available data is likely to be cheaper, regardless of technique, than one which calls for special studies and research surveys.

(iv) The ability of the company to use sophisticated methods is a key factor. Although any company may buy out forecasting skills by using consultants and software packages available from computer manufacturers and bureaux, it is frequently inadvisable to use methods which the management of the company cannot understand and to which key individual managers may be hostile. Every company has at any point in time a threshold of sophistication beyond which it cannot immediately rise: this principle runs through the design of any aspect of a planning system.

(v) The speed at which forecasts are needed is also very important. A forecast needed today cannot be met by the construction of an econometric model taking two months or more to build. In these circumstances the fact that an econometric model may be more accurate is an irrelevance.

(vi) The frequency with which a forecast has to be made will also have an impact, particularly on cost-effectiveness. An econometric model which may be used for successive forecasts at different times as the value of its parameters change is of potentially more value than a model designed to solve a particular isolated problem. Similarly, a forecasting routine which is part of a total company model, using a computer for the analysis of alternatives, will have different requirements again.

Examples of Comprehensive Forecasts

The final part of this chapter will provide examples of forecasts made by different methods. They are drawn from published works. In addition to illustrating an approach, the first provides valuable insight into the changing management trends, brought about by different patterns of competition, technology changes, social and demographic changes.

Management in the 1990s

The first study was undertaken in the UK, although the research base was European. Its conclusions were echoed by a less rigorous but similar study in the USA. Both were based on market research style methods, with interviews conducted with key managers from organisations which had already started to experience the new trends. From these interviews it was possible to present a form of scenario about the main challenges. The UK study claims to provide insight rather than a prescriptive picture of the future.

What results from considering all this evidence is a coherent picture of at least a major element of difference between managing through the 1980s and managing in the 1990s and beyond.

Although comparable research may not be available for other countries, it is reasonable to suggest that results can be extrapolated outside of the research area, although with caution. This is because many of the triggers for change are of a global nature.

The landmark UK study was Barham *et al.*,[13] carried out in 1988. This was later expanded by Barham and Bassam in 1989,[14] and it is from this latter reference that this summary is drawn. The research identified a number of factors or pressures which the respondents saw as critical for the future.

Intensifying of Competition

This was seen as a continuing trend, with pressure coming from two main sources. Firstly there is the continuing trend for many industries to become more global, which not only brings new competitors into play, but also changes the critical success factors of the industries concerned. The second source is the continuing merging of competition, as companies in related industries changed their boundaries: for example building societies moving into retail banking. Both sources cause discontinuities, and neither is expected to abate.

Information Technology

The effective management of IT is seen as an important factor for the 1990s. The authors also cite the problem of managers whose uncertainty is increased because they now have too much information, but insufficient time to enable them to use it.

"City" Pressures

Tension between the short term requirements of investors and the long term needs of the business is seen as an unfortunate reality today and in the future.

Organisations to Become More Dynamic

As a response to competitive pressures, organisations will be more dynamic. Expectations include decentralised structures, managers at all levels to take more responsibility, more entrepreneurial organisations, and mechanisms such as task force management.

Market Focus

Organisations will be more market focused, with segmentation becoming even more critical. In response to pressures, organisations will also become more customer driven. Relationship building is critical, and service will increasingly be seen as part of the product. There will be a greater need for innovation.

Quality

Total quality management becomes obligatory, and is driven as much by customer demands as by the will of the organisation itself.

Speed of Product Development

As product life cycles shorten, the need to speed up product development increases

Acquisitions

Acquisitions continue to be a key element in corporate strategies, now frequently triggered by the need to become more global.

These findings have many similarities with those of Sullivan[15] whose research was undertaken in 1989. The findings related to the USA, and were classified as business forces and the trends in organisational response. In Table 6.1, the findings of the two studies have been combined. As well as illustrating the outcomes of studies of the future, this table offers information which is of interest to any one concerned with strategic management.

Trigger Factor	Organisational response trends
* Intensifying competition/ global competition	* World class manufacturing * More dynamic and flatter organisations * Market focus * More strategic alliances * Continuing acquisition activity * Effective harnessing of IT
* Customer demands for quality and service	* Service becomes part of the product * Customer focused organisations * Total quality management
* Accelerating technological obsolescence	* Innovation given more priority * Reduction of time in product development
* City pressures on short term profits	* Short term/long term tension * Emphasis on shareholder value
* Demographic trends	* Culture/strategy issues * Smaller, flatter structures * Different work practices * People seen as more important * Managing cultural diversity

TABLE 6.1. Trends which affect management.

The next example is something which fits the image of a futures study. It used thematic, trend and impact analysis, and sequential logic, resulting in a number of scenarios showing the new order of nations in the year 2010. Assumptions are clearly stated.

TABLE 6.2. % of world population by stage of development.

	1986	2025
Post industrial	20.1	13.5
Advanced industrial	1.3	1.6
Transitioning industrial	5.5	5.3
Industrial	48.5	45.6
Pre-industrial	24.7	34.0

The study is by C. W. Taylor[16] and was published in 1992, and was written on behalf of the Strategic Studies Institute, US Army War College. Some elements of the study deal with military issues. Of wider interest are the first chapters that deal with world international order, world population, world interdependence and sociopolitical change, and world technological issues. In fact some of the forecasts which support the scenarios go beyond 2010 to 2025. It contains worrying forecasts, such as the proportion of world population in developed countries falling from 23% in 1991 to 16% by 2025.

Taylor provides a view of the world of the future which is of considerable interest, particularly to those following a global strategy. By 2025 he suggests the pattern of population outlined in Table 6.2.

The book provides a coherent scenario against which plans could be made, the above figures being a tiny extract in summary form. There is no guarantee that its predictions will come true, and certainly other scenarios could be developed. Although most organisations are satisfied with strategic plans based on one set of forecasts, there is an approach used by some called scenario planning which develops strategies for more than one likely scenario of the future. This method will be one of the subjects of the next chapter, which explores some of the ways of ensuring that issues from the business environment are identified and incorporated into the strategic planning process.

References

1. Marshall, A. *Principles of Economics*, 8th ed., Macmillan, 1956.
2. Levitt, T. *Innovation in Marketing*, Pan, 1968.
3. Saunders, A. and Smith, N. J. "Hydraulic Cranes from Armstrong's Elswick Works, 18461936: a Product Life Cycle in Capital Goods", *Journal and Proceedings of the Industrial Market Research Association*, Vol. 6, No. 2, May 1970.
4. Coutie, G. A., Davies, O. L., Horsell, C. H., Millar, D. W. G. P. and Morrell A. J. H. *Short-term Forecasting*, ICL Monograph No. 2, Oliver & Boyd, 1964.
5. Moroney, M. J. *Facts from Figures*, Pelican, 1951.
6. McCarthy, E. J. *Basic Marketing: A Managerial Approach*, Irwin, 1964.
7. Parker, G. G. C. and Seguara, E. L. "How to Get a Better Forecast", *Harvard Business Review*, March–April, 1971.
8. Teeling-Smith, G. "Medicines in the 1990s: experiences with a Delphi forecast", *Long Range Planning*, June 1971.
9. Wills, G., Ashton, D. and Taylor, B. (eds.) *Technological Forecasting and Corporate Strategy*, Bradford University Press, Crosby Lockwood, 1969.
10. Wills, G. with Wilson, R., Manning, N. and Hildebrandt, R. *Technological Forecasting*, Pelican, 1972.
11. Majaro, S. Forecasting the future, paper presented at a Conference, "Corporate Strategy", Society for Long Range Planning, 19–20 May 1971.
12. Chambers, J. C., Satindes, K. M. and Smith, D. D. "How to Choose the Right Forecasting Technique", *Harvard Business Review*, July–August 1971.
13. Barham, K. A., Fraser, J. and Heath, L. *Management for the Future*, Ashridge Management College and the Fountain for Management Development, UK, 1988.
14. Barham, K. A. and Bassam, C. *Shaping the Corporate Future*, Unwin/Hyman, London, 1989.
15. Sullivan, P. Managing in the 1990s, unpublished research, Harbridge House Inc, Boston, USA, 1989.
16. Taylor, C. W. *A World 2010: A New Order of Nations*, Strategic Studies Institute, US Army War College, Carlisle Barracks, PA, 1992.

7

Techniques for Assessing the Environment

So far we have explored a model to help the strategist think of the various factors in the business environment, we have seen how the task of formulating strategy is assisted through the setting of assumptions, and we have looked at some of the approaches to forecasting. What we now need to do is to explore ways to help determine what the critical environmental issues are for a particular organisation, and some ways of dealing with uncertainty. On route to these issues we should also give some thought to the setting up of a strategic information unit within the organisation.

The model in Fig. 4.2 has a particular strength in that it draws attention to the inter-related nature of the various factors that make up the business environment. It also illuminates a difficulty that we have as humans: it is very hard for us to consider a large number of variables simultaneously. The approaches in this chapter all try to help with this problem.

Setting up a strategic information unit

It is not impossible to make plans without accessing detailed information about the business environment, but the probability that sound plans will be prepared will increase if attention can be given to the collection and analysis of information on a regular basis. The effort that can be given to this will of course vary with the resources of the organisation, but in these days of data bases that can be accessed at reasonable cost, there is little reason why even the smallest organisation should lack information. Ruth Stanat[1,2] suggests undertaking a strategic information audit, to evaluate what is being provided at present compared with the real needs of the organisation. The audit would also cover the effectiveness of current information sources, and of the means by which information is distributed within the organisation. Although the scheme I am following chooses to treat industry and competitor analysis as a separate subject to be discussed later, any strategic information system should cover these needs as well as those arising from the broader environment.

Figure 7.1, from work by Butcher and Mainelli,[3] relates the role of an external information unit, to information systems and strategic planning units. A key aspect is being aware of the interfaces where more than one of the units has both a need and a responsibility. Successful strategic information management involves managing these to avoid duplication, and making sure that the responsibilities of all three are considered.

Butcher and Mainelli divide information into three types:

"*Information for assumptions*: tends to be trend information for stable assumptions, e.g. average customer size, and discrete events for unstable assumptions, e.g. an assumption of new entrants in a market would be contradicted by news of a major acquisition of a competitor.

"*Information for decisions*: on a strategic level, the information tends to be voluminous and oriented to specific new projects or cancellations, e.g. should a new product be launched.

"*Information for success factors*: measurement tends to be exact for internally supplied information, but base statistical information may be all that is available for external information, e.g. a success factor of press coverage could be measured by column inches multiplied by impact factor of publication."

We will look closer at information requirements for competitor analysis, and ways of compressing information so that management can track the important issues, in later chapters, including a case history which deals with both the task of obtaining relevant in a legal and moral way, and the tracking problem. Any one

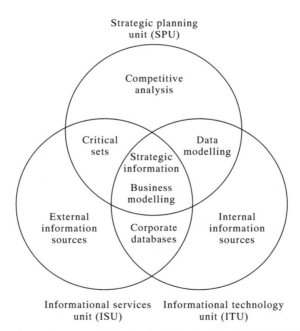

FIG. 7.1. Role of strategic planning unit. (From Butcher, H. and Mainelli, M., 1990. *Strategic Information Management*, in Hussey, D. E. (ed.) *International Review of Strategic Management*, Vol. 1. Wiley. Used with permission.)

who wants to follow a continuity of thought about information could jump to Chapters 10 and 11 now.

In this chapter we will next look at ways of determining what issues are relevant to the strategic management of a particular organisation. However it is worth stressing that none of the techniques illustrated do more than take a photograph, at a given point of time. Some information scanning mechanism is desirable as discussed above, with periodic repeat analysis using one or other of the techniques described here (or other similar approaches which are available) to ensure that there have been no changes in what is important.

Relating to the Environment

There are similarities in a number of the methods available, and many of them seem to have been developed around the same time, in the mid to late 1970s. I have chosen to illustrate two methods in some detail, one developed by my own consulting organisation and the other by Fred Neubauer, who is now a professor at IMD, Lausanne. For the record I should also like to refer the reader to some of the similar approaches, for example Hargreaves and Dauman,[4] Hofer and Schendel[5] and McNamee.[6]

Facing Up To Change

The approach developed by the Harbridge Consulting Group has not been published outside the firm, but has been used widely with clients over a long period. It is capable of use as an analytical check list, but is more often used in small group work to facilitate thinking about the environment among line and other managers who are involved in the strategy formulation process.

The heart of the approach is reproduced in Fig. 7.2. The categories listed on the left hand side are similar to those in Fig. 4.2. Under each heading there are sub headings showing the type of factor that may be important. The aim here is to provide a starting prompt list. It is not the intention to suggest that all items are relevant to a particular organisation, nor that only items on the list should be considered. The analysis really begins with column 1, where respondents identify the issues that appear important. An effective method is to have the questionnaires completed individually by a number of managers, preferably including line people who know the business well, and others who may have access to environmental information. The individuals come together in groups to agree what is important. If done well, one value of this approach is that it encourages a deep consideration of more factors, and forces thinking about their relative importance.

Columns 2 to 4 require respondents to reach a view on the importance of each identified factor to the organisation. This is achieved through a scoring method which converts opinions into numbers. The rules are:

Category	Check list of possible changes (Examples only)	1 Possible changes for your company	2 Impact	3 Probability	4 Overall importance	5 Preparation	6 Who is aware of the change?	7 Whose responsibility?	8 Is effective action likely?	9 Are the resources available?
Demographic	School leaver availability	Demographic								
	Ageing population									
	Minorities									
	Women									
	Graduate availability									
Social	Consumer attitudes	Social								
	Employee attitudes									
	Attitudes to training									
Economic	Inflation	Economic								
	Reflation/recession									
	EEC harmonisation									
	Employment levels									
	International trade									
	Balance of payments									
	Interest rates									
Political	Change of domestic government	Political								
	Changes of government in other countries									
	Privatisation									
Ecological	Pollution	Ecological								
	Waste									
	Climate									
Technological	New materials	Technological								
	Patents									
	Product life									
	Information technology									
	Production methods and processes									
	Machine replacement									
Legal	Equal opportunities legislation	Legal								
	Health/safety/welfare									
	Taxation									
	Competitive interference									
	EEC harmonisation									
	Information disclosure									
	Participation									
Infrastructure	Transport systems	Infrastructure								
	Communications systems									

FIG. 7.2. Extract from facing up to change. (Copyright Harbridge Consulting Group Ltd, 1976, 1990.)

Impact

What impact would it have?	Score
Extremely High Impact	6
	5
High Impact	4
	3
Relatively Low Impact	2
	1
Don't know	7

Probability of it happening

A Certainty	100%	6
Very Likely	84%	5
Quite Possible	67%	4
As Likely as Not	50%	3
Probably Not	33%	2
Highly Unlikely	16%	1
Don't Know		7

Overall importance is calculated by multiplying the impact score by the probability score. "Don't know" scores high so that something important is not overlooked through ignorance. Attention is focused on those factors which have the highest overall scores.

Column 5, headed *preparation* is the response to another question. How ready are you for the important changes? The word "you" refers to the unit for which the strategies are being considered, and could be a total company, a business unit, a department or a product. Again a numerical score is entered:

Completely prepared, including an implementation plan	6
Fairly well prepared, with tentative plans	5
Have decided a general approach	4
Not well prepared, with only a general idea of response	3
Vague awareness	2
Not at all prepared	1

This time attention is focused on the low scores for preparedness, concentrating on those items with a high score for impact.

Columns 6–7 begin to explore the possibilities for action. Firstly who is aware of the threats and opportunities represented by the change? This would be a superfluous question if all the decision makers were working on the questionnaire, but becomes important if the group is of planners or middle managers, or does not include all the appropriate top people. The next column pins down responsibility for dealing with the change. Complex issues may lead to multiple responsibilities, such as changes in the demographic mix affecting Human Resources and Marketing, for different reasons, or being a problem for one division but an opportunity for another.

Columns 8 and 9 both use numerical scales, varying from 6 (the best) to 1 (the worst). One column probes perception of whether effective action will in fact be taken. The other assesses whether the organisation can/will make the appropriate resources available to deal with it.

The rest of the approach consists of a number of other questions and headings which are designed to lead to action. These are not reproduced here.

One should not be trapped by the neat mathematics. The tool is an aid to thinking about the right things, and the numbers are a way of helping focus on the most important. In the end the value of the approach lies in the awareness it creates and the actions stimulated. By themselves the numbers have no value and are merely a means to an end.

An additional technique has been developed around columns 1–5 of Fig. 7.2, and related to methods of portfolio analysis. This is called risk matrix, and will be described in a later chapter, as it is not possible to make sense of it independently of portfolio analysis, a topic in its own right.

The Neubauer/Solomon Approach

This method was published by the authors in 1977,[7] having earlier been proved by them in various situations. It uses a briefer classification of environmental factors: natural/man-made, social/cultural, technological, political, and economic. However the classification postulated in Fig. 4.2 could be substituted if desired. Two types of environmental conditions are considered, Trends and Constituents. Trends are self descriptive. Constituents refer to those individuals and institutions in the environment who may impact the business, such as trade unions and governments.

The method identifies the critical factors and their impact, as will be explained, and studies the threats and opportunities that they create. In turn these are related to the mission and strategies of the organisation. The final part of the exercise examines organisational responsiveness, including constraints and capabilities. Figure 7.3 illustrates the steps that the approach takes to reach a new strategy, if required: shown as a modified strategy in the figure.

For the purpose of this analysis the authors define strategy as the "major decisions and/or action programmes employed by the company to fulfil its mission". Mission in their terms is the answer to the three questions: whose and what needs are the company satisfying, and what value does it provide to those whose needs it is satisfying? The authors suggest restricting the strategies listed to no more than eight, which should all satisfy the criteria of having long term impact, being crucial to the survival and development of the organisation, having breadth of cope, being hard to reverse, and involving the commitment of resources. Similarly they suggest reducing mission to the three answers to the questions posed above.

With this background we can begin to look at Fig. 7.4, which is an enlargement of the matrix within Fig. 7.3, and into which the analyst will enter scores which relate the impact of the environmental factors on the strategies and mission of the organisation. This figure is shown uncompleted, and it will be noted that in addi-

FIG. 7.3. Neubauer/Solomon Method Part A.

tion to restricting the number of strategies considered, the authors also suggest limiting the external factors to eight trends and nine expectations of constituents. A larger number may be examined in the initial stages of analysis, but only the most important will be carried through for this detailed study.

The rating scale is shown in Fig. 7.5. Zero is neutral: a negative score represents a threat and a positive score an opportunity. The larger the number scored, the greater is the impact on the organisation.

Scores are entered into the matrix, as in the example in Fig. 7.6. This gives a great deal of information. Reading across the matrix we can see from the final two columns which trends and constituent expectations impact the organisation most, in either a beneficial or harmful way. Reading down the matrix we can see which strategies and which elements of the mission should be reconsidered, either because of threats or opportunities. An alternative action might be to continue a strategy, but with a better understanding of its risks, which in turn might indicate some hedging strategies, or a modification so that a risky strategy is still followed, but the organisation's involvement reduced: for example through an alliance to share risk, rather than doing everything itself.

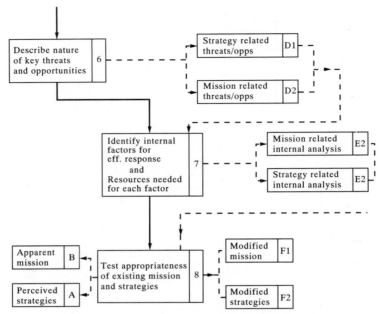

FIG. 7.3. (*cont.*). Neubauer/Solomon Method Part B.

Selection Criteria														
		Strategies								Mission			Impact	
		S1	S2	S3	S4	S5	S6	S7	S8	M1	M2	M3	+	−
External forces for change	Trends	T1												
		T2												
		T3												
		T4												
		T5												
		T6												
		T7												
		T8												
	Const expectations	E1												
		E2												
		E3												
		E4												
		E5												
		E6												
		E7												
		E8												
		E9												
Impact		+												
		−												

M1 = Whose needs   M3 = What value

M2 = What needs

FIG. 7.4. Neubauer/Solomon Scoring Matrix.

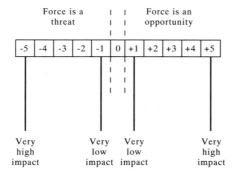

Test each external force for change against
each strategy/mission. Enter number in
appropriate box in matrix.

FIG. 7.5. Neubauer/Solomon Rating Score.

			Selection Criteria												
			Strategies								Mission			Impact	
			S1	S2	S3	S4	S5	S6	S7	S8	M1	M2	M3	+	-
External forces for change	Trends	T1	0	0	0	+5	-3	-5	+3	0	+1	0	0	+9	-8
		T2	0	-5	-4	-4	+1	0	0	0	0	+5	0	+6	-13
		T3	+1	-2	-1	+3	0	-2	+2	0	0	+5	-5	+11	-10
		T4	+1	-1	+3	0	0	-1	+4	0	0	0	-5	+8	-7
		T5	0	0	+2	0	+3	0	+1	0	+2	0	-4	+8	-4
		T6	0	0	0	+3	0	+1	0	0	0	+5	0	+12	-1
		T7	+4	0	0	+2	+2	-3	0	0	0	0	0	+8	-3
		T8	0	0	0	0	+2	0	0	+5	-1	+5	0	+12	-1
	Const expectations	E1	-5	+1	-1	0	0	-5	-2	-2	0	0	-5	+1	-20
		E2	-1	0	0	0	+1	-5	-1	-3	0	0	-5	+1	-14
		E3	-1	0	+1	0	0	0	-2	0	-1	0	0	+1	-4
		E4	0	+2	-2	+2	-3	0	0	0	0	0	+1	+5	-5
		E5	0	0	0	+5	-2	+1	+1	0	+2	-5	+5	+14	-7
		E6	+1	0	+2	-1	-3	-3	+1	0	0	0	+5	+9	-7
		E7	0	0	0	0	0	0	0	0	-1	0	0	0	-1
		E8	-3	-1	0	+2	+1	-4	0	+1	-2	+1	0	+5	-10
		E9	+2	-3	0	0	0	0	-1	0	-1	+5	-3	+7	-8
Impact		+	+9	+3	+8	+22	+10	+2	+12	+6	+5	+26	+11		
		-	-10	-12	-8	-5	-11	-28	-6	-5	-6	-5	-26		

M1 = Whose needs   M3 = What value
M2 = What needs

FIG. 7.6. Neubauer/Solomon Completed Matrix.

Scenario Planning

One way in which organisations try to plan in an uncertain world is through
scenario planning. In a nutshell, this consists of preparing a number of scenarios of
different possible futures the organisation might face, and developing a different

strategic plan for each. Although the approach is well known, and the most open and experienced practitioner is probably Shell, it has not become widely applied. O'Connor[8] maintains that "Despite the purported intent of furnishing alternative assumptions for planning, the importance of scenarios in management lies principally in their ability to answer many other needs that uncertainty creates, many planning executives state. Specifically, scenarios are intended to raise awareness in managers and to avoid surprise. Alternate scenarios broaden the outlook of managers to the external forces that shape the future of the company and sensitize them to their vulnerabilities and to the opportunities that lie within other possible futures".

Chandler and Cockle[9] provide one of the few books specifically devoted to scenario planning, based on experience at Reed International. Although there have been many articles, and article length chapters in planning books, the literature on scenario planning does not appear to be extensive.

Disadvantages are that it uses considerably more management time than does a more traditional approach to planning. It is more staff heavy, both in the development of credible scenarios and in the management of what is a multiple planning process. And there still remains the difficulty that having examined three scenarios, and developed strategies for each, the organisation has to decide what to follow. Some organisations have simplified their use of scenarios by asking managers to look at only two. This would seem to be little better than a good plan based on one scenario with careful risk analysis.

Proponents of scenario planning argue that the examination of the strategies developed for all the scenarios leads to the selection of a best-fit strategy for all scenarios. In other words the "best" strategy for one scenario may not be chosen, because of the possible impact on it of the others. My view is that any approach that helps an organisation to consider the outside world in a coherent manner is worth following. Of all the plans which come to me for comment as a consultant, very few address the impact of the external world in an adequate way, because of the sheer difficulty of handling numerous variables. In organisations subject to considerable uncertainty, it is worth considering scenario planning as an addition to the techniques already discussed. In fact research into scenario planning, such as that by Malasca et al.,[10] suggests that it is indeed these types of companies which lead the way in scenario planning. Some of the conclusions from the Malasca study are of interest:

"Companies operating in the most turbulent environments and companies with long term experience of strategic planning have been pioneers in adopting MSA (*multiple scenario analysis*).

"MSA is able to remove some of the drawbacks of strategic planning and especially to improve control of the uncertainty and unpredictability of the corporate environment....

"There is no uniform method of procedure with MSA, nor is there likely to be in the future...."

Before we leave scenario planning to look at responding to the environment in another way, we should also remember Ansoff's views about environmental turbulence described in Chapter 3. Where turbulence is extreme, perhaps even scenario planning will be too lengthy a process to enable fast response to new circumstances.

Ways of Responding

The implication so far has been that things go on in the outside world, and the organisation can only react. This is only partly true, in that in some circumstances the organisation can change the trend. Figure 7.7 provides four quadrants for thinking about the environment.

One axis deals with the organisation's willingness and ability to influence the direction of the trend. The other is its willingness or ability to change its strategies. The top lefthand quadrant has the organisation in the position of being able to exert some influence on the trend, but not altering its strategy. How successful this will be will depend on how far the trend can be influenced. A minor change may still affect the organisation adversely: a major change may be very favourable. The common methods of influencing the trend consist of lobbying, and the effective use of information to provide a reason why something should be done or not done. Frequently the best approach is through pressure groups, such as industry associations, and through representation, usually through such groups, on advisory bodies, such as those setting standards. For some issues this may be no more than a measure aimed at the civil servants to ensure that regulations are drawn up in a beneficial way, for example standards or labelling. For others it may involve influencing ministers and members of parliament, convincing them that a proposed or expected policy would be bad for the economy, and therefore for votes. Really big issues may involve ways of influencing public opinion through mass public relations and even advertising.

Pressure groups are not restricted to business and one approach to changing the trends might be to provide a counter to the activities of other pressure groups. Of course there are many pressure groups that are not important to the organisation, but those that are should not be ignored. Nestlé experienced massive loss of sales because of the activities of INFACT, an organisation set up in the USA in 1977 to force Nestlé to change its marketing and promotional activities for baby milk in the Third World, where there were many deaths because the product was used inap-

FIG. 7.7. Responses to environmental change.

propriately by many mothers. Among the weapons was an attempt to boycott all Nestlé products until it conformed to INFACT's demands. Hartley,[11] who provides a case study of this event, maintains that the impact on Nestlé was wider than loss of sales and profits, as it also caused action by governments and world bodies.

The top right hand side of the diagram states the situation where action is taken both to affect the trend and to change strategy. In the Nestlé example the company did much through its own public relations activity to combat the power of the pressure group. An alternative, suggested by Hartley, might have been to be seen to cooperate with them, and to ensure that there were no grounds on which accusations could be levelled. What the strategic change might be is very dependent on the circumstances, but might include measures to reduce risk, or to deal with the partial modification of a trend which still left the organisation needing to adjust its actions.

In the bottom half of the matrix we have a situation where either on grounds of practicability or cost, the organisation intends to take no actions to influence trends. This may be a general view that applies to every aspect of the environment, or may be applied only to specific trends: for example no companies are in a position to change the world's demographic trends!

Where the underlying strategy is also not to be changed, the bottom left side of the figure, it may be sensible to take actions that enable the organisation to reduce risk. This may include careful monitoring of trends, and actions inside to reduce lead times for reacting. Lead times before changes can be made to different conditions may involve setting up different decision processes, taking steps to reduce the time needed for new product development, or installing flexible manufacturing methods which make it easier to change what is produced.

The bottom right hand corner can cover an enormous variety of possible changes to strategy. There are also types of strategic decisions which may reduce risk. Among these are shifting risks to others in the chain from first supplier to ultimate buyer, perhaps by changing contract terms so that inflation risks were taken by someone else, or by franchising so that certain risks were avoided. It may be preferable to work through alliances and joint ventures rather than taking on the whole risk oneself (often at the same time increasing the chance of success by neutralising a potential source of competition). There may be major investments to build a different strategic position. For example one of the reasons behind Sony's purchase of film studios in the USA is believed to be to avoid losing a future video configuration battle, if producers do not use it for their products: a reaction to its failure with an earlier video system, which had technical superiority and no cost disadvantage, but failed because there were few videos for rental in that configuration.

There is still another aspect to relating the organisation to the business environment that we have not yet covered. This is the issue of business ethics and social responsibility, and the concept of the social audit which achieved some popularity in the late 1970s and early 1980s. A dimension of the social audit which remains topical is concerned with the physical environment, and the requirement to be "green". These are issues for the next chapter.

References

1. Stanat, R. *The Intelligent Corporation*, Amacom, New York, 1990.
2. Stanat, R. "Trends in Data Collection and Analysis: a New Approach to the Collection of Global Information", Hussey, D. E. (ed.), *International Review of Strategic Management*, Vol. 3, Wiley, Chichester, 1992.
3. Butcher, H. and Mainelli, M. "Strategic Information Management", Hussey, D. E. (ed.), *International Review of Strategic Management*, Vol. 1, Wiley, Chichester, 1990.
4. Hargreaves, J. and Dauman, J. *Business Survival and Social Change*, Associated Business Programmes, London, 1975.
5. Hofer, C. W. and Schendrel, D. *Strategy Formulation: Analytical Concepts*, West, St. Paul, USA, 1978.
6. McNamee, P. *Management Accounting: Strategic Planning and Marketing*, Heinemann in association with CIMA, London, 1988.
7. Neubauer, F-F. and Solomon, N. B. "A Managerial Approach to Environmental Assessment", *Long Range Planning*, Vol. 10, No. 2, 1977.
8. O'Connor, R. *Planning Under Uncertainty*, Conference Board, New York, 1978.
9. Chandler, J. and Cockle, P. *Techniques for Scenario Planning*, McGraw-Hill, London, 1982.
10. Malasca, P. *et al.* "Scenarios in Europe—Who Uses Them And Why?", *Long Range Planning*, Vol. 17, No. 5, 1984.
11. Hartley, R. F. *Marketing Mistakes*, 3rd ed., Chapter 4, Wiley, New York, 1986.

8

Business Philosophy (Ethics and Morality) and Strategic Management

Most managers would accept the statement that every business has to observe certain obligations which modify the way it operates. There would be widespread disagreement over the extent and nature of these obligations and the way in which they should be allowed to influence or interfere with business decisions and actions. In general terms it might be said that every business has obligations towards its shareholders, employees, customers, suppliers, and to the community. Yet the way in which it observes these obligations will vary from staying just on the right side of those which are enforced by law to having so violent a conviction about a particular principle that application of it becomes almost a crusade. There is as much variation in the business philosophies of corporations as there is in the standards of ethics of individual people.

It is no part of the study of strategic management to moralise on what is the "correct" business philosophy. Much more relevant is the appreciation of the need to define the most significant aspects of a company's particular philosophy as one of the stages in the planning process, the understanding of how the philosophy affects the plans of the company, and knowing something of the dynamics of change which mould and alter society's approach to standards of business ethics and behaviour. Perhaps this last point is among the most important because by definition strategic management is concerned with the long term, and the norms of society are under constant and continual pressure from the forces of change. What is sacred to one generation may become profane to the next.

The pattern of development frequently involves government legislation. A pressure group builds up in the society and challenges a particular norm often in the teeth of ferocious opposition from business: certain business men react faster than others (or may, indeed, themselves be members of the pressure group) and adjust their business philosophies accordingly: Government may submit to the pressure by introducing a law which forces all to adhere to the new standards. There are variations to the process, which range from the failure of the pressure group to make any significant impact, to a spontaneous change without the need for government interference. It would be nonsense to suggest that every minority viewpoint eventually becomes the norm, or that no change can take place without government assistance, and, of course, in a democratic community government actions tend to be linked with the wishes of society.

During the medieval period the Church had great influence on business. It had definite views on the charging of interest which, to say the least, were different from those accepted by modern society. The doctrine of the "just price" was a constraint accepted by many Christians. Heaton[1] states:

"In selling, as in lending, greed was anathema. Some church writers inherited the ancient aristocratic contempt for the trader: others condemned some of his methods. To St. Thomas Aquinas (about 1250) trade was an undesirable calling, a badge of man's fall from grace; but since it was a necessary (or inevitable) evil, it might be tolerated if the seller was content with a *just* price. Let him be satisfied with a return which covered his material costs and paid him for his labour; let him meet the needs of a modest living standard and give any surplus to the poor; then his activities would be lawful and Christian.... But all writers agreed that justice was violated when any man monopolised the supply of a commodity and sought to extract exorbitant prices from the consumer."

The Swiss hotel business in the Geneva of Calvin conformed to a different business philosophy from that of today.

"In 1546 the inns of Geneva were re-organised as 'abbeys' and placed under strict government supervision: and a precise code of behaviour for guests and hosts was laid down. Among other items it included the following:

"If any one blasphemes the name of God or says, 'By the body, 'sblood, zounds' or anything like, or who gives himself to the devil or uses similar execrable imprecations, he shall be punished....

"*Item:* The host shall not allow any person of whatever quality he be to drink or eat anything in his house without first having asked a blessing and afterward said grace.

"*Item:* The host shall be obliged to keep in a public place a French Bible, in which anyone who wishes may read....

"*Item:* The host shall not allow any dissoluteness like dancing, dice, or cards, nor shall he receive anyone suspected of being a debauchee or ruffian.

"*Item:* He shall only allow people to play honest games without swearing or blasphemy, and without wasting more time than that allowed for a meal....

"*Item:* Nobody shall be allowed to sit up after nine o'clock at night except spies...."[2]

Not all businessmen have followed the ethics and standards of the day. In the height of the bad period of the industrial revolution, with all the well-known abuses of child labour, long hours, and inhuman working conditions, some employers stood alone. For example, Robert Owen (1771–1858):

"For twenty-three years he experimented in making a model mill and a model village. He gave up using pauper apprentices, forbade children under ten to work and sent them to school instead. He limited hours to twelve a day, less $1\frac{3}{4}$ hours for meals. He established a store to sell food at cost, improved houses, provided medical care, set up a sick fund, and founded a savings bank. Though his plans frightened his partners, he made profits, and New Lanark became one of the seven wonders of Britain."[1]

Many of Robert Owen's actions, advanced though they were for the times, would be considered to demonstrate an antiquated philosophy by the standards of today. So the pattern continually changes and reforms: the *avant-garde* philosophy of today becomes the traditionalist view of tomorrow. Whatever top managements' views on its obligations, business is part of the fabric of the society of the present, and its long-range plans will be implemented in the society of the future. (We have already considered in Chapter 4 some of the sociological trends which should be considered in planning.)

Of the five groups to whom the company has obligations the one which would cause least surprise is the duty owed to shareholders. In general terms we may describe this as a duty to earn the shareholder an adequate return on his investment and to preserve his assets for the future. Chapter 12, dealing in detail with corporate objectives, defines this generalisation in more detail and in a way which can be meaningly quantified for planning purposes. For the present purpose the general concept of profit is sufficient. Other duties to shareholders may be harder to define and cause more differences of opinion—consider, for instance, the paucity of information given to shareholders by many companies: despite improvements by some, many annual company reports are designed to conceal more than they reveal.

What perhaps is of more significance to a study of business philosophy and ethics is the lack of influence that shareholders have on the day-to-day management of the companies they own. The *Financial Times*[3] reports Galbraith as arguing that:

"Some 40 per cent of the Gross National Product of the U.S. is controlled by 2000 giant corporations in manufacturing, merchandising, transport and the utilities. If the great state corporations are included in the 'technostructure', a similar proportion of the national product in Italy, France and Britain is controlled by an equally small number of concerns.

"Their ambitions may not coincide with those of society as a whole. Shareholders, Galbraith maintains, no longer have much influence on the day-to-day management of corporations. As a result managers have become more concerned with growth than with earnings. So long as a corporation makes a reasonable rate of return its managers have virtually complete power and their brief concern is to enlarge the scope of their operations and increase the size of their company."

The enormous size of some of the modern multi-national corporations means that they have the ability, e.g. the sheer power of their investment, to transcend the policies of the governments of their host countries.

In one way the freedom of action of managers is subject to a constraint: at least the reasonable rate of return referred to by Galbraith must be earned if shareholders are to be contented and managers keep their jobs. This definitely has an effect on the development and application of actions resulting from matters of conscience. Carr[4] points out:

"Perhaps there are some executives who are so strongly positioned that they can afford to urge their management to accept a reduced rate of return on investments for the sake of society of which they are a part. But for the large majority of corporate employees who want to keep their jobs and win their superiors' approbation, to propose such a thing would be inviting oneself to the corporate guillotine."

In recent years there has been more attention given to the concept of shareholder value, both in terms of the strategies that create this, and ways of looking at it. The modern concepts apply discounted cash flow approaches to the measurement and selection of strategies. Chapter 12 will explore these concepts in some detail.

To move into this area of business moral and ethical behaviour is to move into an area of double-talk and public-relations puffing. It is an area of platitudes, of noble sounding statements which frequently have no bearing on the real way in which the business operates. Perhaps the best example of this is provided by the "Back Britain" campaign of the late 1960s. This began spontaneously with a voluntary contribution of unpaid overtime by certain people to help set Britain on the path to economic recovery. The idea gained momentum against the background of encouraging news releases from employees (extra work) and employers (price increases held back). Unfortunately it also provided a platform for certain companies to gain public acclaim for announcing they were not going to do something which they had never had any intention of doing anyway. How many of the "delayed" price increases were really the result of the campaign no one will ever know: probably very few.

The matter is complicated further by the fact that in addition to these doubtful areas of public relations opportunism and inept platitudes there is a further confusion between genuine moral restraint and corporate strategy. This difference is not always very easy to identify, and is often known only by the top management of the business concerned—and even here, in the process of time, there may be a merging so that the two are inseparable. This mixture of moral actions caused by personal beliefs, and strategic actions which achieve the same results, is part of the process of development and change which is continually taking place. And, indeed, it may be a tactical move for a manager to position a genuinely held moral conviction to shareholders. In fact Carr[4] suggests that the executive with a conscience should position this sort of problem as a longer-term profit improvement exercise if he is to have an impact on profit-motivated top management.

The confused world of morals and ethics is bemused even further by the incompatibilities of the modern business situation. It is not even necessary for a chief executive to compromise his or her own moral standards to run into circumstances where he or she cannot win. For example, it is a genuine intention of many companies that they be "good citizens" of the countries in which they operate. This is the task which immediately brings a conflict of interest. How can an American parent company be a good citizen of both the United States and the United Kingdom when both countries are facing balance of payment problems (e.g. when the U.K. Government would like dividends of the U.K. subsidiary reduced and the U.S. Government urges that they be increased)? Similarly, actions to direct exports to the cheapest source of supply can result in production switches away from overseas subsidiaries, a strategy which runs contrary to the natural interests of the countries concerned. When governments themselves are in conflict, the ability of the chief executive to live up to a "good citizen" motive becomes even more difficult.

It is important for these problems to be faced seriously and for the chief executive to determine in advance what really is intended and how the organisation will react in the sort of circumstance described above. Honesty of thought is much more important than high-sounding words, for employees in any company react very quickly to double standards. The sort of statement which some chief executives frequently hand out to all employees is often disbelieved on sight: if credibility is wanted the meaning behind the words must be demonstrated. And if a chief executive wishes anyone to act upon his or her words, for the statements to have an impact on the way business activities are performed in the company, for the moral constraints which he or she considers important to be built into the fabric of the corporate plans, he or she must, above all, obtain this necessary measure of credibility.

Setting difficult and sometimes costly standards for operating a business is rarely easy. For most chief executives the avoidance situations like not cheating the customers, not offering bribes, and not breaking their word, may be found relatively easy in a world where honesty in business has gained some acceptance as a welcome ideal. Those philosophies which require a positive action—like investing capital to reduce pollution beyond the requirements of the law—may not be so easy to face. Not every chief executive is a Robert Owen, willing to move ahead of his time. Yet, as we shall see, in addition to the moral issues it is often in industry's own interest that it keeps to the fore of the field because this renders government interference unnecessary.

Many business men would claim that there are standards: the one they use for their private lives, and the one used for business. The stereotype of the regular church-goer and supporter of charities who habitually exploits the employees, gives short measure to the customers, and sends the suppliers into bankruptcy will probably always be with us. If chief executives can live with standards such as these, this is their privilege. A business normally reflects the philosophies, ethics, and morals of the person at the top, and it must be for these qualities as well as the ability to earn profits that a person is selected by the owners to run that business. I believe that it is both right and proper that a chief executive should have definite views on the way in which the corporation should behave.

Wates[5] states:

"... that the proposition that there are values which I endeavour to uphold as a private citizen which I must abjure as an industrialist, is totally untenable .... In academic and in churchy circles one frequently meets the 'two worlds' view of business and the rest of life, which seems to be based on the idea that business consisting as it does of exploiting and manipulating markets in the interests of higher profits, is itself basically immoral and therefore anything goes in that jungle. Indeed in this respect business is its own worst enemy since the shorthand way some business men have of talking about maximising profit as an end in itself, lends colour to this view. Such people stand capitalism on its head and make it indefensible. They certainly provide no answer to those compelling arguments based on 'social justice' with which alternative economic systems appeal with such great effect to the young and to the underdeveloped countries. "These arguments have to be faced; I simply cannot accept that business is by definition immoral; in fact I believe that capitalism both needs and has a moral base."

Personal standards in business are not restricted to chief executives:

One of the larger firms in the UK fruit and vegetable trade operates a "travelling wholesaler" section—the business of selling to the retail greengrocer off a lorry. A driver/salesman employed by the company consistently refused to call on a particular customer on his round because the retailer habitually swore at him and treated him in a degrading way. "I may be only a lorry driver, but I am entitled to be treated as a human being." For this driver his self-respect was more important than the risk of losing his job.

The point that should be emphasised is that chief executives must be true to themselves. This is not always easy, and it must be accepted that it is a simpler task for the chief executive of a family business, or a company in which he or she happens to have a very high shareholding, or the small private company (where the shareholders are known personally) to reconcile a private moral position with a duty to the shareholders.

The remaining obligations listed earlier each bring their own particular moral and ethical problems to the chief executive of a modern company. An attempt is made to examine some of the possible implications, although again it should be stressed that there is no intention to moralise. There is little doubt that philosophies will vary between companies, since not all chief executives share the same beliefs, attitudes, and opinions; and, indeed, it is desirable that there should be differences.

The Community

Obligations to the community (or to society, to put it another way) probably include the most complex, the most contentious, and the most thought-provoking aspects in any chief executive's business philosophy. Perception of the company's obligations will vary from a feeling that as long as the company is growing and making profits the community is well served, to a fundamental belief that business is a sociological process which has numerous obligations to others. Unfortunately, some of the issues faced by modern business make it more and more difficult for any chief executive to take the extreme viewpoints: they are no longer as simple as deciding whether factory premises play a part in local community relations.

Perhaps the most serious issues can be clustered under one word—green. Carr[4] argues that:

"The public shrugs at the company president who conspires with his peers to fix prices. It grins at the vice president in charge of sales who provides call girls for a customer. After we have heard a few such stories they become monotonous.

"We cannot shrug or grin, however, at the refusal of powerful corporations to take vigorous action against great dangers threatening the society, and to which they contribute. Compared with such a corporation or with the executive who is willing to jeopardise the health and well-being of an entire people in order to add something to current earnings, the man who merely embezzles company funds is as insignificant in the annals of morality as Jesse James is compared with Nero."

Pollution of the environment has only recently been recognised as an international problem, threatening the entire ecology of the world and the survival of the human race itself. Business is not the only cause of pollution; government and local authorities are themselves deeply involved. In America and Europe there is some evidence of government concern: on the other hand, other countries appear quite willing to accept a higher degree of atmospheric pollution as part of the price of economic growth. Pollution takes many forms—the poisoning of the air with smoke and gas emission, the discharge of industrial wastes, the pumping of sewage into rivers, canals, and the sea, the uncontrolled use of insecticides and herbicides, the mountains of unrottable rubbish which cities create daily, and the pollution of the countryside with litter, old furniture, and abandoned cars. Ironically some of the companies which purport to exist to improve the health of mankind are among the worst offenders: many of the companies engaged in pharmaceuticals also have interests in chemicals and dyestuffs. A major German firm in this field is reported[6] to discharge 400,000 tons of liquid wastes annually into the sea (although it maintains that this creates no hazard for sea life): but this is only a passing example.

The chief executive's dilemma if the organisation operates in one of the many industries which cause pollution is to decide whether to take a moral attitude on an acute and life-threatening problem or to pretend the problem does not exist and wait until government forces action. The trends make it harder not to notice the problem. Twenty-five years ago it would rarely have been a subject that called for top management action. Today the better understanding of the real issues has led to public protest and pressure groups, as well as attention by the Government and industrial and academic scientists. If, in the 1970s, Ralph Nader's protest movement can shake a giant like General Motors, and if in the 1980s the world can be shocked into action by a nuclear accident in Russia, chemical plant explosions in India, and oil tanker disasters in the USA, it is highly likely that issues of responsibility to the community will loom even larger through the 1990s and beyond.

Another obligation which some companies accept is adopting a positive approach to relations with the government: an attitude which, partly in their own interests and partly for higher motives, requires more than the law-abidingness called for from every citizen. The giant American-based multi-national concern Union Carbide Corporation[7] interpreted this duty by establishing a special high-level department to maintain contact with government offices. Other companies in various parts of the world operate similar departments. Such units, of course, are more often established to fulfil a lobbying role than as an attempt to benefit governments.

Chief executives may, for moral reasons, feel that part of their obligation to the community lies in determining types of business in which they will not participate. The activities prescribed in this way may be within the law but outside of their own code of ethics (in fact we need not concern ourselves with firms which intend to act outside the law since they are unlikely to be involved in the sort of management approach described in this book). Thus for these reasons a company may decide not to enter fields such as gambling, night clubs, alcohol production, or the tobacco industry. The decision is personal to the company: others may quite happily enter these areas without any feeling that they are behaving immorally.

Ethical problems appear in other directions. Another subject of increasing concern is the use of industrial espionage and the differences between this and legitimate marketing research. In considering industrial espionage we are moving away from the more contentious motives into an area related to simple standards of honesty and basic integrity. Yet not all companies are averse to gaining advantage over competitors by means such as these.

Related in some ways with the attitude to industrial espionage is a chief executive's philosophy towards competitors. This may be based on fair dealing and high standards of integrity, or it may be completely the opposite. Keen competition can still exist under conditions of amicable relations, although not all managers believe this.

The manager of one of the divisions of one company operating in the United Kingdom was annoyed when his chief executive agreed to show a major competitor how a system of profit improvement was designed and implemented. "You may help the enemy, but you don't clean their rifles for them", he grumbled.

Some years ago in South Africa one cigarette manufacturer took another to court. Salesmen of the rival company had been spreading the rumour among African consumers that the claimant's cigarettes caused sterility, causing a large decline in sales.

It would be tedious to attempt to analyse all aspects of a company's possible obligations to society. Such topics as race relations, equal opportunity for women, the use of sex and nudity in advertising, and the support of political parties are among the many issues on which a chief executive might be expected to take an attitude which may make the task of fulfilling duties to shareholders that much harder.

Employees

Obligations to employees may seem, at first glance, to be an area of little difficulty. Of course most modern companies, in whatever country they operate, recognise that Victorian attitudes are no longer acceptable and that they have a certain responsibility for the health and well-being of those they employ. On the other hand, few chief executives would be wise to give every employee a life-long guarantee of continuity of employment.

Many companies which practise corporate planning build some form of policy statement about their attitude to people into their plans.

Union Carbide UK Ltd.[8] stated that one of its goals was "To ensure that the company obtains the human resources necessary for growth". When read in conjunction with its objectives it is apparent that there is much more significance to these words than it might be thought at first sight.

The chief executive of another British group with widespread interests stated:

"I sincerely accept the statement that human beings are always more important than machines, systems or organisation, and that all decisions should therefore adequately reflect this understanding.

"...I believe it to be imperative that due regard be given to the motivation of individuals and that consistent with the basic purpose of the Group we must seek to meet these needs."

The "basic purpose" of this company refers to profit objectives.

Another British company with a number of overseas subsidiaries and operating mainly in the grocery field, defined its broad obligations to employees.

"The Company exists for the benefit of all its owners and will operate in such a way that it holds the net profit returned to its owners as the prime consideration in all decisions: subject to the constraints that the Company will endeavour to be a 'good citizen' of each country in which it operates, that it will always conduct its business in an ethical manner, and that it will have the regard of a 'good employer' for the health and well-being of its employees.

"In its own long-term interests the Company will act in such a way that it is regarded internally and externally as a progressive and dynamic concern, giving fair treatment to customers and to employees."

These are typical examples of what companies say. How they live up to the statements is another matter, and only those inside the company know whether what it says bears any relation to what it does. For many companies this sort of statement is more than a platitude and really does influence day-to-day behaviour.

The well-known British firm of building and civil engineering contractors, Wates Ltd., have definite objectives for their relations with employees which they express as "to grow people". This is further stated as a policy of "optimising individual and the company goals". Implementation of this objective was a little unusual in that it led Wates to a decision that "the idea of doing business in South Africa is totally unacceptable" on the grounds that conditions in that country would prevent the company from fulfilling this objective. It was against all the moral and moralistic idealistic beliefs of the Board that they should voluntarily begin business in a country where they were prevented by law from offering equal opportunity to all employees, regardless of race.

This example is important in that it demonstrates how a particular philosophy can shape a company's attitude to its opportunities for profit. Not everyone would agree with Wates' decisions: the significant factor is not *what* was decided, but *why*.

Another insight is given by the philosophy of the chief executive of the pharmaceutical and foods interests of the well-known Sandoz of Basle, Switzerland:[9]

"...modern business management is oriented towards the individual and sets out to place his potential and his need for self-fulfilment at the service of the company in a co-ordinated way."

Many US companies have problems in relating to one aspect considered important by many employees, recognition of trade unions in overseas subsidiaries. Failures here have contributed to the growth of the international trade unionism and have been one element leading to international controls in multinationals. Although these controls, through OECD, ILO and potentially the United Nations, are at present not very onerous, they could well become so in the future.

Social responsibility issues in employment have been increasingly the subject of legislation in all developed countries, and the trend to replacing choices freely made by the organisation with legal obligations is likely to continue.

Customers

Obligations to customers appear at first sight to present few philosophical problems: how a business treats its customers is on the surface a matter of commercial self-interest, bound up with its marketing strategy and the desire to retain and expand its customer lists. Few companies adopt the "selling refrigerators to Eskimos approach" (at least without an after-sales service!), and, for most, cheating or misleading the customer would be a matter of economic suicide.

Moral issues can, in this area too, run deep below the surface, and the company may accept obligations which are more far-reaching than those dictated by commercial prudence or enforced by legislation. On the other hand, it may not.

In 1969 the American Government banned as harmful the use of cyclamates (a sugar substitute) in the manufacture of food. Following this ban products containing these chemicals disappeared from the U.S. market. Despite the evidence and government action, many American companies continued to export these products to countries where no legal ban had been imposed. In these companies the obligation felt towards overseas customers was obviously minimal.

The world's pharmaceutical companies have generally had a high standard of moral behaviour to consumers long before governments began to legislate for the control of new drugs. This was undoubtedly partly through self-interest (claims for damages—such as in the thalidomide cases—can be expensive both in terms of compensation and adverse publicity) and partly through association with the medical profession, which itself is renowned for its high ethical standards: in addition many managers in the pharmaceutical industry have a pride in their moral obligations to their consumers which transcend the bare minimum.

Safety of the health and well-being of customers is not just a moral issue which faces the food and pharmaceutical industries. Many other businesses have to decide on the extent to which they accept similar obligations which avoid harming the customer: examples are toy manufacturers (and many potentially harmful toys are made, particularly in South East Asia), the motor-car industry, clothing (many deaths have been caused through the use of inflammable acrylic fibres in children's nightdresses), toiletries, and electrical appliances. Printing a warning on their plastic bags about danger to young children probably did not gain the British retail giants Marks & Spencer a single extra sale, and certainly would have involved them in thought, if not cost.

Chief executives might well have differing views over pricing policies. Is it immoral to make abnormally high profits on a transaction if an opportunity arises? Attitudes to price policies and competition vary between individuals, between groups in the society, between government and industry, and often the government attitude to different industries. Government may take a very lofty attitude if it discovers two competing consumer goods companies have had "discussions" on price rises: yet it will consider a rate-fixing cartel like IATA, or one of the shipping conferences, as something which is completely justified. Is there really any difference? While many chief executives would agree that forming a ring to frustrate normal tendering procedures would be immoral, I suspect that many would not be quite so concerned about "suggesting" to a competitor that rising costs justified price increases. As society and government have different standards, it must be equally difficult for a chief executive to decide what is ethically right or wrong. This ambivalence carried through public attitudes to business. Much of society will congratulate a company for its efficiency in gaining profit growth, and at the same time pillorise it for increasing its margins. The borderline between profit and profiteering is a fine one.

Suppliers

Various philosophies are possible in relation to a chief executive's obligations to suppliers. On the one hand, there is the chain store which sets out to ensnare small suppliers in such a tight web that eventually they face the choice of bankruptcy or selling their businesses, to what has become their only customer, at only a fraction of their real value. At the other extreme there is the company which goes out of its way to assist its suppliers, and gives its creditors better treatment than it receives from its debtors. Somewhere in the middle there is the company who elects that its only obligation is to pursue a path of commercial probity, giving neither more nor less to a supplier than he is legally entitled to have.

Again, the choice falls on the chief executive: it is philosophy and outlook from the top which will condition a company's behaviour to its suppliers.

An interesting example of how a business may go out of its way to help its suppliers is provided by Marks & Spencer, who have already been mentioned in another connection in this chapter. This company operates a production engineering unit at its London headquarters which provides a service to its smaller suppliers to help them become more efficient. In addition, with the help of Urwick Orr (management consultants), it arranged a series of training courses for the production staffs of its food and garment suppliers. No doubt there is a commercial benefit, as well as a feeling of ethical satisfaction, from these moves—yet the position of the company in relation to its suppliers could not be further from the type of chain store which is prepared to trample its suppliers underfoot in its search for additional profit.

There is also room for ethical considerations in considering price attitudes. Obtaining supplies at the lowest possible cost is, of course, an essential aspect of efficient management. Many chief executives would consider it unethical to band together with competitors in order to create a monopsonistic situation. However it is not unknown for "rings" of antique dealers to be exposed from time to time in the UK, and no doubt other countries. The ring rigs auctions in such a way that they are able to buy at low prices and share the profits among ring members. A ring such as this has featured in the BBC's longest running soap, *The Archers*, so no one can have any doubts that they really exist!

Modern concepts of continuous improvement, or total quality management, stress that suppliers should be treated more as alliance partners than adversaries. Those that follow this concept are moving into a different pattern of supplier relationships, where there may be preferred suppliers with whom there is a long-term relationship, with both contributing to the continuous improvement of quality. This changes what might previously have been an ethical choice into enlightened self interest.

Business Ethics and Planning

Earlier in this chapter it was mentioned that much of the pattern of changing ethical standards is conditioned by society, and frequently government plays a part by legislating to change standards to conform to the norms of the age. In all countries there are laws governing certain aspects of conduct towards employees, and in most there are complex legal safeguards of fostering the interest of customers and the community.

Often it is in the interests of business to keep ahead of legislation, since governments frequently tend to over-react. Godden[10] maintains that government interference in the pharmaceutical industry (particularly in the United Kingdom and the United States) to reduce the price of prescription medicines has diminished the effort of research and development which will in turn reduce the incidence of discovery of new drugs. He also considers that government controls over the introduction of new drugs can delay their introduction and therefore the saving of thousands of lives.

Governments, of course, will always err on the side of the event which is most visible and of most public concern. It will legislate to prevent a reoccurrence of a thalidomide type of disaster rather than consider the virtually unidentifiable lives which might be saved from a less time-consuming system of control.

Similarly, governments throughout the world will begin to react more stringently—and frequently overreact—to the pollution menace. In these circumstances industry could be penalised to a greater degree than if it had acted independently. The fact that an industry can exercise a self-control which obviates the need for legal enforcement has frequently been demonstrated. For example, advertising ethics are controlled by the industries concerned.

The advent of government interference is one of the factors which changes social values and is, therefore, important. It departs a little from the main theme of the chapter, which is concerned more with the constraints chief executives voluntarily observe, rather than the ones to which they are compelled to surrender. The difference between the two is not always easy to define, and is of minor significance in planning treatment.

Some attention should now be given to relating moral and ethical philosophies to a concept of modern management and strategic planning. The point has been made, and must be stressed, that the decisions made in this area are personal to the chief executive. In planning terms there is no difference in treatment between the company whose chief executive has low standards of integrity and is happy for the entire company to cheat, lie, and defraud without the slightest twinge of conscience, and the company whose affairs are conducted on a higher plane. The chief executive of the former company will have less to consider or define than that of his or her counterpart. The freedom of each executive to decide these things for himself is a very important point of principle. Drucker[11] states: "No one but the management of each particular business can decide what the objectives in the area of *public responsibility* should be."

Many writers on corporate planning suggest that ethical or moral obligations should be called constraints to distinguish them from objectives of profit. Constraints may be defined as:

Things which for moral or ethical reasons the company will not do, despite the fact that to do them would put the company a long way towards the achievement of its profit objectives. Ansoff[12] uses a simpler definition: "constraints are decision rules, which exclude certain options from the firm's freedom actions." Argenti[13] provides a basically similar approach.

Ansoff[12] makes a distinction between constraints and responsibilities. Under his classification a responsibility is something which a company accepts and which adds to its expense without in any way reducing its freedom of strategic action. Thus a company may, as many companies do, accept a liability to support a particular charitable foundation, or an employee's pension fund, but these actions in no way exclude any options from its strategy. The difference between a responsibility and a constraint is that a constraint does inhibit a company's freedom of action.

An important principle is that constraints must be defined and written down as part of the planning process (and, of course, this also includes certain of the major constraints imposed by law). Only when they are clearly defined can the chief executive be sure that they are clearly communicated through the organisation. The fact that this sort of policy action is called a constraint does not mean that it is in any way negative. The negative "Thou shalt not steal" can be interpreted as the very positive "be honest".

It must be stressed that it is as important to define the constraints as to define any other element in a corporate plan. Only after this act is it possible for the organisation to be sure that its plans and day-to-day actions truly reflect the philosophies of the chief executive.

The defined constraints become an integral part of the company's corporate plans, and should be one of the criteria against which the plans and strategies are measured. The reason for clearly stating the constraints is practical, not academic. It is so that they can be used in the running of the business. In their application in planning constraints stand next to objectives, which means that most of the discussion on this subject (Chapter 12) also has a bearing on the subject.

In an ideal world more attention would perhaps be given to defining the constraints caused by ethical and moral considerations than is usually customary in modern business. Argenti[14] is perhaps a little idealistic in his views:

"Unfortunately, however, it was found to be only too easy to run a company so that it satisfied the shareholders—but failed to satisfy—indeed bitterly dissatisfied—other groups. Gradually, therefore, over the past few decades the shareholder has dropped from first beneficiary to the last—or so it would appear at first sight. In fact, he has always been last, he had always been the residual beneficiary after all other expenses of running the company have been met; the difference is only that most companies now recognise what some did not before, that it is not morally acceptable to take advantage of one's employees, suppliers, or customers even if it were possible (and in modern conditions, with full employment and vigorous competition, it seldom is). Thus the shareholder received, and still receives, whatever profit was left over from the company's operations; the distinction being that nowadays there is less left over because companies in general meet their social obligations instead of neglecting them."

Drucker's[11] view of what should happen is perhaps a useful note on which to summarise the debate so far.

"But what is most important is that management realise it must consider the impact of every business policy and business action upon society. It has to consider whether the action is likely to promote the public good, to advance the basic beliefs of our society, to contribute to its stability, strength and harmony."

How pleasant life would be if all chief executives of all businesses approached their problems in this way!

Cadbury[15] should have the last words on ethical issues, from his article that won the Harvard Business Review 1986 Annual Ethics in Business Prize. Among his many practical and thoughtful comments are two statements. One is that "shelving hard decisions is the least ethical course" of action for a chief executive, and of course many ethical decisions are neither easy to take, nor pleasant to implement. My own interpretation of this is that the golden glow of righteousness over a no bribes policy in the Third World is easier to maintain when it does not mean making a large number of people redundant in the home country through lack of work. Moral decisions with no consequences are not the ones that cause sleepless nights!

The second is that "actions are unethical if they won't stand scrutiny". He argues that openness and ethics go together. "Openness is also, I believe, the best way to disarm outside suspicion of companies' motives and actions. Disclosure is not a panacea for improving the relations between business and society, but the willingness to operate an open system is the foundation of those relations. Business needs to be open to the views of society and open in return about its own activities; this is essential for the establishment of trust".

Social Audit

Hargreaves and Dauman,[16] whose book (published in 1975) unfortunately is now out of print, state:

"The idea of a social audit for organisations, particularly in business, is new. Indeed the term 'social audit' itself is still interpreted differently by different people. To some it means the public disclosure of a company's social performance. To others it means the internal (confidential) evaluation of a company's social responsibility performance. Others go further and define the social audit as a comprehensive evaluation of the way a company discharges all its responsibilities, to shareholders, customers, employees and suppliers, to the wider community, indeed to all its stakeholders."

They suggest a number of reasons why organisations should conduct a social audit. Firstly, social responsibility is becoming an issue which is important to the growth and survival of the organisation. Secondly, like it or not, many organisations, without giving consent, are subject to social audits by external organisations. Many of these have a particular political axe to grind. Reports have been published on a number of companies by the Public Interest Research Centre, and Social Audits Ltd of the UK and by the Project on Corporate Responsibility in the USA. Companies such as General Motors, Tube Investments and Avon Rubber have been the targets. A third reason advanced by the authors is the ever increasing requirement for disclosure in various countries, and their belief that industry is better off moving in advance of legislation, and thereby setting the pace and the rules that follow. They see as a fourth reason the pressure by shareholders for more information. Since they wrote their book there have been developments on all fronts, including the setting up of a number of ethical unit trusts which will only invest in companies that make acceptable products and behave in an ethical way, as defined by the unit trust.

There is no one acceptable way of conducting a social audit. One school of thought moves into social accounting, the idea that all social actions, negative and positive can be quantified and presented either as a broad numerical statement, or even more precisely as a form of balance sheet. This concept is very difficult to make workable. There are enough problems over the judgement areas in normal accounting, to show the problems that could arise when almost every statement was a judgement.

If the intention is to use the social audit as one element in the formulation of strategy within a company, and the purpose is totally internal, the resultant report should become another way of helping to relate the internal elements of the organisation to the external environment. Such an audit might be approached by listing the critical issues, some of which may also be partially covered by legislation, and the constituents who have a concern with the firm. Against these lists it is then possible to evaluate every strategy, policy and operating practice of the organisation. It would probably be necessary to repeat this exercise at various organisational levels: by business unit, by functional area, by geographical location, and by department. Immediately one can see that this is not a small task, while those that have been involved in quality audits for BS 5750 (ISO 9000) accreditation will be aware of the work involved in a much narrower aspect of policy and performance audit.

The types of issue that might be considered will vary over time, as what is considered socially important changes over time, as we have seen. However they might include consumer responsiveness, health and safety, environmental pollution, use of scarce raw materials, third world actions, employment of women or of ethnic minorities, energy utilisation and many more. Constituents have been defined in the preceding chapter when we looked at the Neubauer/Solomon method of analysing the environment. Indeed, one can visualise the construction of matrices with scoring systems to help identify the success and problem areas.

In periods of recession, pressure on organisations to conduct social audits tends to alleviate, as organisations grapple with the more immediate task of staying solvent. *Green* issues have now become the most pressing, and some authorities now urge organisations to undertake audits of green issues. Vandermerwe and Oliff,[17,18] (a shortened version of the same material) argue that consumers are willing to buy *green*. They argue the need for a green audit, and the development of strategies across all functions. Most organisations have given some thought to green issues, and my experience is that they are even more complicated than other social issues. An organisation may clean up its own act, and be convinced that it creates no pollution, but unless it looks right across the chain of supply through to the ultimate consumer, it may simply be shifting the problem elsewhere. Perhaps it uses a raw material which is in itself safe and non polluting, but the supplier who makes it has to create a toxic waste. Maybe the packaging used is beautifully clean and hygienic, but will not bio-degrade after use. Any audit needs to be very broad, and conducted with action in mind.

Vandermerwe and Oliff argue that organisations should set green goals. They list:

—Identifying benchmarks for green performance.
—Determining the opportunities and risks from the "green wave".
—Extend strategic planning to cover a broad range of green scenarios.
—Undertake a careful assessment of the costs and benefits of being a green company.

References

1. Heaton, H. *Economic History of Europe*, Harper & Bros., 1948.
2. Smith, L. N. *The Horizon Book of the Elizabethan World*, Paul Hamlyn, 1967.
3. *Financial Times*, 7 April 1971.
4. Carr, A. C. "Can an Executive Afford a Conscience?", *Harvard Business Review*, July–August, 1970.
5. Wates, N. Social Responsibilities in Industry, Lecture to the Runnymede Trust, Oct 15th, 1971.
6. *Daily Telegraph*, 21 April 1971.
7. Rush, K. "Business Planning at Union Carbide", *Long Range Planning*, December 1968.
8. Wilson, R. The First Five Years as Managing Director, *Proceedings of the Society for Long Range Planning*, May 1968–May 1969.

9. Dunant, Y. "Some Aspects of Management in the Sandoz Group of Companies", address to the ordinary general meeting of shareholders, 9 April 1969.
10. Godden, E. P. The implication of environmental change on consumer demand, papers presented at a conference "Corporate Planning and the Environment" of the Society for Long Range Planning, December 1970.
11. Drucker, P. *The Practice of Management*, Heinemann, 1955.
12. Ansoff, H. I. *Corporate Strategy*, McGraw-Hill, 1965.
13. Argenti, A. J. A. *Corporate Planning: A Practical Guide*, Allen & Unwin, 1968.
14. Argenti, A. J. A. "Defining Corporate Objectives", *Long Range Planning*, March 1969.
15. Cadbury, Sir Adrian, "Ethical Managers Make Their Own Rules", *Harvard Business Review*, September/October, 1987.
16. Hargreaves, J. and Dauman, J. *Business Survival and Social Change*, Associated Business Programmes, London, 1975.
17. Vandermerwe, S. and Oliff, M. D. "Customers Drive Corporations Green", *Long Range Planning*, December, Vol. 23, No. 6, 1990.
18. Vandermerwe, S. and Oliff, M. D. "Strategies For The '90s Mean Full Green Ahead Say Top Executives", *Strategic Management Review* (Tokyo), Vol. 16, No. 2, 1991.

PART 3

The Making of Strategy

"Where there is no vision the people perish"—*PROVERBS*, 29:18

9

The Corporate Appraisal—Assessing Strengths and Weaknesses

So far this book has examined the broader aspects of corporate planning and has looked at the process of planning in relation to a changing environment. It is now time to concentrate on a very specific step in the process—the assessment of corporate strengths and weaknesses. Planning literature refers to this important stage under various headings: the corporate appraisal, the position audit, and assessing the present position. The particular terminology used is not important: the action itself is vital.

The corporate appraisal should be one of the first steps in the process of preparing strategic plans, and should provide both the platform from which the corporate objectives are established and the baseline of the strategic plan. Attempting to plan without carrying out this fundamental step is rather like trying to reach the top floor of a building without using the stairs or lift: the ascent is possible, but is highly dangerous and calls for much more effort. Omission of the basic step may lead the company to adopt the wrong strategy, to take decisions which at best restrict its achievement of its highest potential, and at worst lead it on the road to ruin.

In many ways the corporate appraisal may be one of the most difficult stages the planner has to face. It sometimes means striking at the established practices and business areas of the company. It means facing up to unpleasant facts, an action which tends to destroy the wall of false security behind which it is so easy for even good managers to take complacent shelter. It can easily be considered as criticism by managers and accordingly resented. This is the area in which emotional responses may easily be roused. It is probably for these reasons that most companies which have a process of strategic planning—except when they have installed it with the aid of an outside management consultant—will confess to have either omitted this step entirely or glossed over it so brusquely that they pay only lip service to the concepts.

It is by no means unknown for a company to take stock of itself without practising any form of formal planning. Cost reduction areas and productivity increases are frequently sought by companies which are pointed much more to the present than to the future. General consultancy assignments are carried out in many companies by management consultants. It is perhaps because so many of the elements of the corporate appraisal are long-established management procedures that many books on planning do not dwell very much on the process of the corporate appraisal. Nearly all stress the need to assess strengths and weaknesses, but few give any indication how to set about it. The word "strategy" conjures up visions of daring action on the corporate battlefield: the driving off of competitors; the subjugation of another company through acquisition—perhaps it even becomes the prize for winning a duel with other competing bidders; the conquest of new markets; and the deployment of massive resources of men and finance in gigantic projects. These emotive phrases may describe where strategy will eventually evolve. They are certainly not the starting point. And it is perfectly possible for a company to produce a sound strategy that is based almost entirely on opportunities uncovered during the corporate appraisal.

I like to think of the corporate appraisal as a process of establishing the corporate identity. There is a direct comparison between the guidance offered by a career counsellor to an individual person, and the use of the corporate appraisal by a forward-thinking management. No good career counsellor would consider the job well done if he or she simply provided the applicant with a list of situations vacant. What the counsellor tries to do is find out a great deal about the aspirations, ambitions, education, general intelligence, abilities, experience, and personality of the person being helped. Instead of a name he or she begins to deal with an identity; a real person who can be matched to a career which will complement his or her own individual and personal characteristics. So it is with the company. A superficial list of "opportunities" can be produced in five minutes for any company. And it will probably be worth less than the time spent thinking about it. Instead the corporate identity should be established, and this unique combination of skills and experience, faults and abilities, matched to opportunities which exploit the strong points and correct the weak ones.

Ansoff[1] makes an invaluable contribution to corporate planning by demonstrating how the company can relate itself to the alternatives open to it, seeking "synergy" in all its decisions. Synergy is the process by which the effect of putting two parts together is greater than the sum of their individual parts: the two-plus-two-equals-five effect.

Denning[2] suggests that a function of a corporate appraisal is not of itself a long-range plan, it should be conducted with the future in mind. Much of it will, of necessity, be equivalent to a photograph of the current position, but there will be many areas where it is possible to extend this static picture into the future. The appraisal should be designed to help solve the problems of tomorrow and, wherever possible, should be made dynamic rather than static. The fact that a particular product *today* contributes 80% of profit is interesting: it becomes much more interesting when linked to information about competitive activity, and whether it is in a declining or growth market. Although at this stage in planning it may not be possible to be too specific about the future, the general indications should be given wherever the appraisal can identify them. Drucker[3] stresses that it is as important to identify "tomorrow's breadwinners" as it is to identify today's. It is because of this future-oriented outlook that I believe the term appraising the company's present position to be a bad description of what should happen.

No company in the world, however profitable, can afford to neglect opportunities for cost reduction and profit improvement. (It may deliberately opt to implement them, but this is decision, not neglect.) Although the main purpose of the appraisal has to do with the future, the immediate profit potential which arises is a strong additional reason for not ignoring this step in the planning process. It is possible to argue that taking any cost reduction opportunity is a positive way of removing a weakness and avoiding the perpetuation of an unsatisfactory situation, and any additional contribution to cash flow reinforces the company's ability to exploit new opportunities.

There can be few properly conducted corporate appraisals which have not given a bonus in immediate profit improvements, frequently of a sufficient size to repay the costs of introducing planning and leave a worth-while surplus.

Woodhall[4] reports how Laporte Industries Ltd. carried out a corporate appraisal with one of its subsidiaries. A few major actions significantly improved profits: the competitive and market position had been misinterpreted in many export markets, and many cost reduction areas were identified. These improvement areas alone added £100,000 per annum to profits.

A British food manufacturer, during a similar appraisal, uncovered many cost reduction opportunities. One illustration may be provided. An aluminium foil "tagger" acted as a seal in every tin of dried food product sold. The need for the seal which was inserted immediately under the lever lid was not in dispute. What was raised was a question no one had thought of before: why was the "tagger" printed with the product name? It was invisible to the housewife before purchase, and was immediately discarded once the tin was opened. A decision to use unprinted taggers in future brought an immediate profit improvement of £5000 to £7000 per year: small by itself, but significant when added to the numerous other improvement areas discovered.

Another example is provided by a furniture company with premises in Greater London which took stock of itself because events forced it to. It had many problems, one being the vast area of warehouse space needed to store finished stock. A serious attempt to standardise measurements (e.g. drawer sizes) and the introduction of new machinery which enabled manufacture to precise sizes, meant that it became possible to store "finished stock" in a knocked down condition with assembly just before shipment. The effect on warehouse space was dramatic—the whole factory was able to move into what used to be the finished stock warehouse, enabling much of the company's land and buildings to be sold to realise capital for growth and new developments.

Any company that decides to undertake a corporate appraisal must first establish how to set about it. One method might be to put the whole thing in the hands of consultants: but this is really begging the question since the consultants themselves would apply a certain methodology. The second approach might be to put the study in the hands of one person—the chief executive personally, or the planner. On an individual basis, the ability of any one person to probe deeply must be limited by the size of the group: a vast multinational giant would have to decentralise its approach if it were ever to finish.

The third approach uses a series of teams on a part-time basis, led by—depending on size—a number of people who had been allocated full time to the appraisal, with all the work being co-ordinated and controlled by one person. This method has the merit that it really works and, provided the co-ordinator gets the teams working in the right areas and seeking answers to the right questions, it goes a long way to ensuring that the results are objective and emotionally detached. The areas which should be covered in such an approach will be discussed later.

There are several variants of a self-analysis approach which provide other ways of looking at the problem. Present operations are studied in a future-oriented manner and are classified under headings such as "satisfactory", "weakness", "strength", "opportunity", "threat"—the company can easily set its own system of classification.

Under this approach an attempt is made to establish what has to be done to maintain the satisfactory things and correct the faults, to ensure that opportunities are exploited, and threats avoided or reduced in impact.

There is nothing really new so far because this is what all the methods of conducting a corporate appraisal aim to do. Where this approach does differ is that it is basically a self-appraisal scheme. Managers are asked to comment under this classification on aspects of their own operations: to record their own opinions, which may often not be the same as current company policy. As analyses may be obtained from various levels in the organisation, a variety of opinions and ideas may be forthcoming. These are analysed and discussed, and eventually refined to working lists.

One problem I have found in practice is stimulating managers to take a balanced view of strengths and weaknesses. Often all that results from a self appraisal is a shopping list which is often painfully inadequate. To help managers be more objective I often use what I call the equilibrium approach in group discussions. This is illustrated in Fig. 9.1 , and is probably the simplest technique ever designed. It consists of a scale and a line.

The line represents the current state of something—anything—that is to be considered. Examples are current market share, state of labour turnover, present profitability.

Above the line the group are asked to identify the factors which keep it as *low* as it is. Below the line they are asked to say what keeps it as *high* as it is. In practice it helps to switch to and from with remarks like "You've identified so much that holds it down that I'm surprised you have any business at all! Why is it that you are doing as well as you are?".

Arrows can be drawn from each key item identified, using the scale to provide a judgmental view of the importance of the factor. Longer lines are more important than short ones. The final stage is to identify what issues (a) can and (b) should be addressed, to remove negative factors or strengthen positive ones. This simple approach is very effective in achieving balance and consensus.

It is perfectly feasible to use this approach as well as one of the other methods.

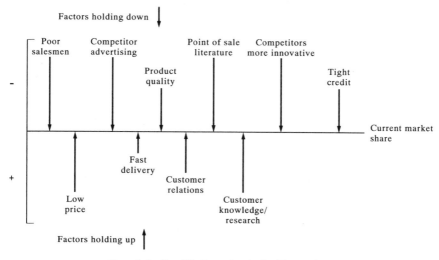

FIG. 9.1. Equilibrium Analysis (Example).

For example, a teamwork appraisal might be made on the introduction of the planning system; the self-analyses method might be used for the next three or four planning cycles until it becomes practical to consider mounting another team study.

One of the most difficult things to encourage is a *continual* inward-looking approach. It is very easy to regard a corporate appraisal as a once and for all exercise, which of course it should never be. While the process of studying environmental opportunities, which are readily perceived to be always changing, is a planning tool which becomes sharpened with use, the internal self-criticism of the company's affairs, which do not always appear to be altering, can easily become a very blunt probe.

Self-analysis methods help to keep the point sharp.

The corporate appraisal should not be seen as being completely isolated from the studies of the environment. There are interrelationships, and although the two stages are conceptually separate, each impinges on the other. Thus the first appreciation of the appraisal may be modified by what is learned about environmental trends and expectations. Turning the microscope inwards also involves a measure of peering outwards. Market share and the performance of competitors are but two examples of external factors which properly form part of the corporate appraisal. There is no hard and fast line where it is possible to say that the corporate appraisal ends and environmental trends begin, just as on a hazy day it is not possible to be precise about the exact spot on the horizon where the sky disappears and the sea is seen. This does not mean that the appraisal is not different from the environmental study—and no one would argue that sea and sky are the same, even though their extremes are confused.

What factors should be considered in the appraisal? The answer will vary between organisations, and although a generalised view can be given, a real situation would call for some critical selection. So the items which follow should only be treated as indicative.

There is another problem. The written word gives the impression that events follow in logical sequence, like loops in a chain. Life is not like this because there are few events in real situations which are completely divorced from every other event. In a real situation the factors studied hang together like a spider's web. Strands are linked to other strands directly and indirectly.

A number of basic concepts should be carried in mind as the appraisal progresses, and performance rated against these.

(i) It should always be assumed that there might be a better way of doing anything until the contrary is proved.

(ii) It is usually a relatively small amount of effort which produces most of the return. Actual figures will vary, but will generally prove that a large amount of profit, say 80%, comes from, say, 20% of effort. The remaining 20% of profit comes from 80% of effort. Unfortunately, it is rarely possible to be specific about the *exact* point when effort could profitably be curtailed, although any action which reduces the amount of less profitable action should lead to corporate improvement.

(iii) Often knowledge of what is being done is not as perfect as managers within a company believe. One of the tasks of the corporate appraisal should be to ascertain the facts. This can often be a very difficult exercise. Incorrect answers are often supplied to the investigators' questions out of ignorance, and in good faith.

(iv) When *what* is being done has been established, the question Why? should be asked.

(v) The future is more important than the present, where the trends and effects on the aspects studied can be foreseen.

(vi) The appraisal should cover all aspects of the company.

Trends of Results

An obvious starting point is the company's historical pattern of performance: trends in profit, sales, capital employed, and then all the various ratios which may be derived from these to measure efficiency. To make sense the analysis should be broken down by subsidiary companies, departments, or areas of performance (such as home and export sales). Practical difficulties may arise in the detailed analysis because of lack of information: for example, capital employed may be difficult to calculate for divisions using common facilities for even the current year, quite apart from any past data. The whole basis of accounting may have changed over the period, so that definitions are not strictly comparable. Accounting systems may even vary between subsidiaries—even more probable with companies operating in several countries.

All this means that there may be gaps and imperfections in the data collected.

The examination of these historical figures will show whether the company is improving or worsening its position; it becomes possible to see the broad activity areas contributing to the results and—even at this early stage—to isolate poor performances for further thought. At this point it may be possible to add a few question marks to the data which take account of some of the future aspects— perhaps indicating a market area which is likely to change radically, or a major change that might be expected in a subsidiary because of economic trends in a particular country.

Sources of Profits

Analysis by broad department or subsidiary can only be regarded as a starting point. The next stage should be a detailed examination of profitability and prospects on a product basis, in terms of geographical sales, where relevant (e.g. by export market), and by distribution method.

This is one of the many stages when the accounting methods of the firm should be queried. Although most companies have detailed costs by product, the exercise should question the bases on which these are calculated. This usually means looking at the way in which certain costs are allocated.

Queries of this nature do not necessarily mean that the cost accounting system is "wrong". In fact workable alternatives to the allocations used by the cost accountants may be difficult to establish for *regular* reporting purposes, although they may be ascertainable for an *ad hoc* exercise such as the corporate appraisal. The cost accountant's job is to ensure that all costs are apportioned somewhere, so that at the end of the day the company does not find items it has not recovered. The planner is more interested in the dynamics of change: he wishes to see what would be left if a particular product or activity were carried out in a different way.

Many costs which are allocated to products or activities are apportioned on some form of percentage basis, spread evenly across the activity. Thus it is quite common to find transportation costs charged at a flat percentage of sales value: order processing costs, sales force costs, and various other variable overheads may be allocated in the same way. The assumption is that all these costs fall on products in a normal distribution.

In fact this is an erroneous assumption because these costs fall unevenly in a highly skewed distribution. Transport costs will vary with order size and distance from depot. Order processing costs will vary with the number of lines on the invoice: it costs no more to process an order for £1000 than for an order of £1 of the same product.

Drucker[3] indicates the value of allocating costs like this on a "transaction" basis—making an attempt to re-examine product and activity profitability when costs are allocated in a way which is much closer to the way in which they really fall. This part of the exercise may require the support of work study or O & M specialists, but can repay the effort handsomely, often bringing a completely new perception of the business.

A food manufacturer found that after re-allocating its transport and order processing costs by number of orders instead of by percentage of sales value, a whole class of distributive outlet was shown to be unprofitable. These outlets accounted for some 55% of orders but under 7% of sales. Within the class of outlet there was some profitable business, and it was possible to lay down broad parameters showing activities that should either be eliminated or changed to improve margins. This was a completely new perspective for the company.

In another part of the same exercise it was noted that an identical product with different labels (government contract and normal trade) was sold at a lower price to one type of distribution outlet than to another. The product costings showed that the cheaper priced label cost less to produce than the more expensive one. Common sense indicated an error somewhere and investigation showed that certain overheads had been allocated *pro rata* to selling price. On the same assumption, if the product had been given away, it would have incurred no overheads.

Fyffes Group Ltd. have documented[5] how by applying a "transaction" view to physical distribution problems they were able to reduce their lorry fleet of over 300 vehicles by 20% during an eighteen-month period of increasing turnover.

It is studies such as these which enable the appraisal to identify the real "breadwinners" in the organisation. At the same time they also indicate changes which should be made to various levels of strategy within the company. One of the most frequent strategic decisions which emerges is the reduction of variety, the elimination of certain products, or a pricing or order size change which effectively eliminates certain classes of customer. Many firms take pride in the length of their product list: many would make much more profit if they eliminated those which did not adequately contribute to profits.

Even where products do make a positive contribution, this may sometimes be increased if the number of varieties can be reduced, or greater standardisation introduced, of raw materials, packaging, or product.

Wander Ltd.,* food and pharmaceutical manufacturers, found that they had fifty-three varieties of their main product, Ovaltine. Immediate action reduced this to below 50, and by careful thought, leading to the combination of various exports labels, within two years the number of label and size variations had been further reduced to about two dozen. As many of the export tins were of lithographed metal, these moves brought inventory savings all the way through the production line.

Risk

The investigators now have a clear indication of the company's main sources of profits. The next stage is to examine some of the risks attached to these products.

Firstly, there is the obvious situation where a company is very dependent on one product for its profit. There have been many companies in this position, and they can carry on for decades making good returns and seemingly giving little cause for

---

*This and certain other improvements, were documented in a lecture I gave at Bradford University in December 1971, and later published under the title "Physical distribution A. Wander Ltd.—a case history of a decision", *Journal of Physical Distribution*, June 1972.

concern. Yet there is a problem, and over-dependence on one product—or indeed, to a lesser degree one market—carries a high probability of future problems.

Secondly, a similar type of risk is where the bulk of a company's business is tied up with a few customers. This is often the case with certain industrial products, and is an increasing tendency in certain types of retailing. Again the business may be quite safe, although there is a strong indication for strategic development elsewhere. In some cases the strategic implication may mean a new approach in the same market, widening the pattern of distribution: in others it may indicate different products or completely new types of business.

Thirdly, there is raw material risk which may vary from a world difficulty of supply to over-dependence on one supplier.

Market risk should also be examined. The market position of each main product should be established. It is equally important for the firm to understand the areas in which it has leadership. What is it that makes its products unique so that people are willing to purchase them? A product does not have to be a brand leader to have uniqueness or particular attributes in which it has a leadership position. This is the point in the study when market research reports should be linked with the internally derived data and supplemented with informed judgement from people inside the company. Market risks are an important consideration in the study of which of the products will develop as future breadwinners and which are likely to decline or die.

Finally, technological risk should be considered, not only the possibility of product obsolescence but also the likely changes in production processes which are likely to cause the company problems in the area of plant and machinery. Anything which affects the company's future competitive position is a risk which should be carefully considered.

Manufacturing Activity

With this developing profile of its products in mind, the company should turn its attention to the processes by which these are made, looking for areas of potential cost reduction, alternative production methods, alternative formulae or composition of products, and technological developments which could improve costs. To aid this study, it may be useful to use work-study techniques or value analysis.

There is frequently a general assumption in companies that its production processes are efficient. This they may be. The question to be answered is whether they can be more efficient, or is it possible to achieve the same end product by cheaper alternatives. This is the point in time when the company should examine make-or-buy situations for its components, and should look at the prices of outside services in comparison with its own costs.

The graph in Fig. 9.2 provides an answer to those who argue that production is a sacrosanct area. This shows efficiency ratings on a theoretical yield basis for the processing of a basic commodity in a food plant. For years the plant had had an average efficiency of about 94–95%. Suddenly it slumped dangerously. Corrective action brought a modest improvement. At this stage a process engineering team was brought in—not as part of a corporate appraisal but as an operational neces-

FIG. 9.2. Improvement in the efficiency of a food process.

sity. Successive actions gradually increased the yield, which soon passed the old average of 94–95%. Improvement continued, and at one point a yield greater than the theoretical maximum was obtained. The point of the story is that after the study the plant was operated more efficiently than it had ever been, although earlier in the year management would have argued that it was already efficient. In this case it took what proved to be a happy accident to bring about improvements.

Consideration of the process should include the raw materials, the standards set for their purchase, and the efficiency of the company as buyers.

Rationalisation of Resources

Another aspect of the study, particularly in companies with many sites, is whether facilities of plant or buildings can be rationalised or re-located. Where two plants or two office buildings can be amalgamated into one, considerable cost savings may frequently be obtained. A similar approach should be applied to distribution depots: many companies have made a substantial impact on their profit position by drastically reducing the number of depots operated.

A company with plants located in different countries should re-examine its supply and demand patterns. Perhaps a particular plant should be closed or the source of supply to a particular importing country changed. International studies such as this are invariably complex and involve more than factory cost comparisons. Marginal costs should be considered, the effect of change on fixed overheads, investment requirements, and differing tax liabilities. There may also be legal problems to be considered where profits are, in effect, transferred from one legal entity to another.

Organisation and Management Structure

Facilities are important, but they are not the only resources a company has to deploy. Even more important are people. The corporate appraisal should look at the people resource from a number of viewpoints.

A good place to start is the basic organisational structure. What is the company's organisational structure? A simple question that a surprisingly large number of companies are unable to answer because no one has ever set down the structure on paper.

Once the structure has been identified it becomes possible to look at impending management problems such as succession and the strengths and weaknesses of the key managers and their teams. In many family businesses succession to the top management slots is often a problem, recognition of which does not always come until the death, illness, or retirement of a key manager. The assessment of managerial capability is a very delicate task, yet it is one which is most important. There is very little point in deciding to launch a range of new products if it is known that the marketing manager is incapable of making a success of the venture. Assessments such as this can only be made at the highest level in the organisation, which is one reason why the chief executive must be very closely involved in the appraisal.

In a very large company, organisational and managerial capability assessment may be a complex problem—and particularly complex where the company is also multi-national and the appraisal is complicated by the need to make examinations across a very wide front.

Organisational problems may exist at every level in the company, as may the question of the quality of individual performance, and it is sensible to also examine other aspects of the people resource. What are the company's labour relations like—are these a strength or a weakness? How does productivity compare with that in other industries?

In one study of a small warehouse depot of a large organisation, I found that the company was paying a very high overtime bill, with employees working very late on certain days of the week. However, on other days they were finishing their work by lunch time and either carrying out unnecessary tasks (like sweeping a floor twice) or were actually going home before closing time. Overall, they were working less than the normal weekly number of hours, yet at the same time were drawing considerable sums in overtime payments. Simple re-scheduling of the work load removed all the overtime. (However, it should be noted that in most circumstances other problems will arise if take-home pay is reduced.)

The appraisal should also consider the company's relation with its trade unions, and whether anything should be done to improve or maintain these. What, indeed, is the company's policy to trade unions?

Perhaps most important of all is the general morale of employees (which may vary by sector) and their attitudes to the company. There is also often a sort of "corporate motivation" which may be important: thus sometimes whole companies think only in terms of their major product. In other companies there may be absolutely no feeling for profit. Still others may think only of profit and never of people. If "judgement" assessments backed by overt evidence, such as a number of labour disputes, are distrusted, it is possible to use a more scientific approach to establish these factors using opinion research techniques.

Financial Resources

At this stage an assessment should be made of the company's liquid resources and probable future cash-flow position. A company with a very high debt must take a different view of its future strategic options from one with a surplus of cash. This aspect of the appraisal should also consider the effects on cash flow that could result from internal changes, such as a reduction of inventories or debtors, or the disposal of certain fixed assets. Even at this early stage thought should be given to the future, and the company's financial potential identified in some detail.

Corporate Capability

In addition to the corporate motivation discussed earlier, every company has—often for no easily discernible reason—a number of things it is good at and a number at which it is mediocre or poor. On paper the individual people frequently appear no different or no better than those in other companies: yet collectively they often obtain a level of synergy which is difficult to explain. So one company may be particularly effective in its customer service, another may be excellent at physical distribution. It may be possible for one company to utilise design skills more skilfully than its competitors. Another may have a particular and unique marketing flair.

These strong and weak points should be identified where possible—again using marketing research, internal opinion, and company results as the sources of data.

Systems

The corporate appraisal should also look at the systems used within the company, attempting to identify areas of strength and areas of weakness. Again a future oriented examination is called for: it is not only a question of current effectiveness, but also how the system could stand up to expected changes. Can the order processing department cope with a dramatic increase in the number of new products? How efficient is the costing system—and will it creak under the strain of new requirements? Does the budgetary control process really work—is it dynamic enough for modern business? Are there any written policies in existence in the form of "standing orders", or is everything always decided on an *ad hoc* basis? What are the systems of decision-taking? How effective is the inventory control procedure? Have the warehouse routines ever been subjected to work study? What methods are used for the evaluation of capital expenditure projects?

The inquiry should probe into every corner of the company, seeking information which will help to provide colour, form, and shape to some of the blank pieces which contribute to the total jigsaw which is the corporate identity.

Use of Resources

One of the objects of the study is to produce a pattern from the jumble of facts that has been collected—to put some of the pieces of the puzzle together so that tentative conclusions may be made about the form the whole picture will take.

An important step is to examine the allocation of resources between products and to compare this with their real profit contribution. "Resources" means not only money, buildings, and plant, but also what are probably the scarcer resources of management talent, capability, and technical skills.

Analysis of this nature usually is imperfect because it has to attempt to divide what is often the indivisible, and may bring particular problems of management when dealing with the less-specific data. Nevertheless, sensible conclusions can be drawn. What so often happens is that the study shows where emphasis is misplaced. Too frequently a declining product area is given to the best managers to "put on its feet". Corporate pride will not allow the company to let the product die—or to deliberately kill it—and resources of time, money, and effort are squandered when they could be spent wisely if used on a successful product area that can be made more successful.

Divisions that can boast of past glories frequently obtain the lion's share of all the available resources, even though other business areas offer more potential. Research & Development effort may be misdirected; perhaps trying to breathe new life into a dying product when the company should be practising euthanasia.

Out of this aspect of the appraisal should come an understanding of which products are what Drucker[3] calls an investment in management ego—projects carried on through feelings of personal or corporate pride, which greedily swallow resources and contribute neither to present nor future profits.

If nothing more than a change of emphasis emerges, this aspect of the appraisal will have contributed much, and occasionally it may result in a complete reorientation of the company.

The next two chapters will deal in detail with industry and competitor analysis, both of which contribute to the corporate appraisal, the formulation of strategy, and the monitoring of the outcome of that strategy. There is one extension to industry analysis which should be mentioned here. It is related to the modern trend for many organisations to find that the competitive arena has moved from a multi-country operation, where each country could be seen as an almost independent strategic decision unit, to a global market. When an organisation has a global strategy it has to think of all country markets at once, and develop an approach that takes the maximum advantage from size without losing all its ability to respond to local needs. Global strategy will feature in a later chapter. It is an area where most of the writing is new, and much is still evolving. The point for the appraisal is to check that the organisation is managing in the best way for the situation it is in. Head on competition with a global marketer by an organisation that manages on a multi country basis (that is, all decisions taken locally and independently) will in almost all cases lead to ultimate failure. Therefore, if the company is running its business in a way which is a mis-match with the competitive arena in which it operates, this should be a point of debate from the appraisal. The words competitive bench-marking might be mentioned here, as a further trailer to matters germane to the appraisal, but which will be expanded in the next chapter.

Reporting on the Appraisal

By this stage in the investigation those engaged in the appraisal will be ready to complete the final report. What they should have is a mass of data, some already partly assembled, some in the form of detailed reports which have to be summarised and integrated, and the rest in the form of brief notes. The final report will draw on data generated in the study as well as information and reports which are already existing.

In theory the report will cover all areas of the company with equal efficiency, and will contain all relevant data to enable immediate profit improvements to be made and to provide a foundation stone for every future strategic decision. In practice things will be somewhat different. The report should bring improvements; it should help in the formation of strategy, but it will be neither complete nor perfect. Some of the data will be more reliable than the rest; there may be complete gaps where it has been impossible to make any analysis. In other areas tentative estimates may be all that is possible, yet—despite these imperfections—the final report can be a document of great value to the company.

In practice, too, there may have been an implementation of some of the recommendations as the sub-reports are completed, and some action may have been taken before the formal unveiling of the final report. This is, indeed, what should happen, and it is a mistake to see the report as something which has no part in the management of the company until the final dramatic moment when it is dropped on the chief executive's desk. Yet although the appraisal will have unearthed many things on which immediate action can be taken, it should—if it has done its job well—draw many conclusions which are a surprise to the company. It may make recommendations which bring out a strong emotional reaction from individual members in the company.

Such a reaction should not take the investigators unawares. Frequently, appraisals of this nature challenge the established order of things and bring the company face to face with the impact of change. Often, the factual information can lead to a number of different actions, and there may be strong differences of opinion over what these may be. The report may shake the existing power structure within the company, and aspects of it may be resented by those whose positions are challenged. And often, what appears to be the firm rocky ground on which the company's past and therefore its future is based, is revealed as about to turn to a quivering quicksand: this can be hard to accept.

It is possible to argue that, unless some differences of opinion occur within the company, either the appraisal has not got to the root of the situation or the company is one of the lucky few that is doing everything well. In order that he may be sure that he will obtain a really effective corporate appraisal, the chief executive must choose the investigators wisely. It must be possible to rely on their objectivity and professional integrity, and they must be mature and senior enough not to bend their conclusions to suit personalities in the company.

At the same time the team must be given a measure of protection and the chief executive must ensure that effective use is made of the report and that it is not shelved merely because it is unpleasant. There must be a willingness to accept that certain conclusions might even be construed as criticisms of his or her own present or past actions. Indeed, the chief executive should try to get his management team to view the document not as criticism of the past but rather as an objective analysis of what the company must now do. This is often more difficult in practice than in theory, since it is very hard for most managers to forget their personal involvement and view the recommendations and conclusions with objectivity.

Normally, a corporate appraisal such as this should be available to the whole of the senior management team, while some of the sub-reports and extracts may be shown to managers of lower levels. There may be some aspects of the report which the chief executive wishes to keep confidential—e.g. the appraisal of individual management abilities: the chief executive may well have carried out these parts of the exercise personally, and even the investigators may be unaware of the chief executive's conclusions in these areas.

Because the corporate appraisal is so important, a great deal of thought should go into the writing of the final report—not only in the quality of the content but in the format and presentation of the report. There are many "right" ways of writing this, and it is an area about which it is dangerous to be dogmatic.

My own approach has been to prepare a brief summary report showing the main strengths and weaknesses of the company and the strategic implications of these. Each statement is backed up by a more detailed report and analysis, examining the subject in considerable depth. Significant figures and charts may be attached as appendices. The method is not perfect but it enables the conclusions and recommendations to be presented in a way that has considerable dramatic impact and which forces the main issues to the attention. The volume and variety of the appendices will depend very much on the individual circumstances.

A simplified, abbreviated example of this style of presentation is given in Fig. 9.3.

The example is not meant to illustrate a real company, and certainly an organisation in as bad a way as this might well have to consider closing down. In this particular appraisal the reader is asked to assume that the aspects not shown provide the management with grounds for believing that improvement is possible. But no wonder morale in marketing is reported to be low.

An additional, and for some companies a very helpful way of presenting a part of the data, might be to prepare a capability profile. This has already been mentioned, and no better example can be quoted than that of Denning,[2] which is reproduced in Fig. 9.4. Another way of using this type of critical skills profile will be discussed in the next chapter.

However the corporate appraisal is tackled, whether by any of the methods

PART 1: Weaknesses/Limiting Factors

Factor	Strategic Implications
1. Management	1. Management
(a) Chief executive age 65, no obvious successor.	(a) Recruitment, merger, or sale of business. Main priority for action.
(b) Middle management can be graded as:	(b) (i) Recruitment in weak areas.

% of Managers

Weak	50
Mediocre	10
Good	40

(ii) Management development and training.

(iii) Reorganisation.

(c) The company undertakes no management development or training of any kind.

(c) Investigate feasibility of systematic approach to management development.

(d) Organisational lines and relationships are undefined. No organisation chart exists.

(d) Implementation of the reorganisation proposals (recommended in separate report).

(e) Marketing manager 60, has been seriously ill and is unlikely to be able to cope with change or expansion.

(e) See reorganisational proposals. Problem must be solved if company to develop.

2. Marketing

(a) 75% of profits emanate from product A. Market declining at 10% per year. Market share under attack from competitors with superior product.

2. Marketing

(a) (i) Reduce dependence on this one product – see separate report.

(ii) Examine market strategy to seek improvement (see also 2b).

(iii) Improve product.

(iv) Cost reduction – value analysis, process development.

(b) Advertising and promotional expenditure is haphazard, dispersed over various types of media and methods, and is without any form of follow up to measure impact or effect.

(b) (i) Relate to new marketing strategy.

(ii) Cease promotion through sponsorship – saving £50,000 per year.

(iii) Market research to measure impact of current advertising.

(c) Fifty-six variations of pack or label of product A.

(c) Reduce variety to ten, saving £30,000 per year in packaging, warehousing, finance, and production costs.

(d) Fifteen products(one hundred variations) account for 12% of sales and contribute no profit. Ten of these are in a loss situation (two make a loss on variable costs).

(d) (i) Cease production, re-deploy resources on twelve products.

(ii) Develop marketing plan to exploit three products in growth markets.

(e) 45% of order transactions account for $2^{1}/_{2}$% of sales. There is a loss on these transactions.

(e) Review minimum order sizes, price structures, and physical distribution methods.

PART 2: Strengths

Factor	Strategic Implications
1. Management	
(a) Skilful and competent production management.	(a) Exploit in managing new product production and costs reduction on existing products.
2. People	
(a) Strong sense of loyalty to company, and morale high in factories (although not high in marketing).	(a) (i) Make best use of this in reorganising for change.
	(ii) Ensure that managerial style encourages these feelings.
3. Marketing	
(a) Strong image among consumers for service. Quality image remains although suffering from impact of competitors' better product.	(a) Transfer to other products.

FIG. 9.3. Example of one method of summarising strengths and weaknesses.

Product	Current annual sales (£000)	% of total sales	Sales growth past 5 years	Market prospects	Competitors	Brand share	True profit contr. (£000)	% Total profit contr.	Utilisation of resources					Remarks
									% fixed assets	% working capital	% R%D time	% Prod. capacity	% sales force time	
A (56 variations)	3000	50	2% p.a.	-10% p.a.	Strong and strengthening	40%	300	75	60	45	5	40	95	Present bread-winner, doubtful future
B (3 variations)	600	10	15% p.a.	+25% p.a.	Weak—new competition probable	75%	4	1	5	10	25	12	1	Future bread-winner. Profit can be improved by new process just developed
C (1 variation)	300	5	New product	+10% p.a.	Nil—will change within two years	100%	60	15	2	4	30	10	3	High profitability will not continue once product under competitive attack
D (30 variations)	30	1	Nil	+25% p.a.	Many competitors	10%	-4	-1	10	1	12	10	Nil	No future for this product
E (10 variations)	30	1	+2½% p.a.	Not known	No information	Not known	4	1	1	1	Nil	1	Nil	

FIG. 9.3: APPENDIX A. Product Contribution and Resources.

	Customers	Channels	Servicing	Promotional skills	Export skills	Selling skills
Marketing						
Production	Process skills	Assembly skills	Batch / Mass / Process } production skills	Quality control	Cost control skills	Transportation skills
Finance	Investment skills	Consumer financing	Credit control	Fund-raising skills	Working capital management	International financial skills
Organisation	Type of administration skills	International management skills	Management of new enterprises	Joint venture	Contract negotiation	
Development	Types of research		e.g. process-new product development skills Project teams work		Model change skills	

- - - - - = Key skills for an international oil company

———— = Key skills for an automobile manufacturer

FIG. 9.4. Capability profile and key skills. (From *Corporate Planning: Selected Concepts*, by Basil W. Denning, © 1971 McGraw-Hill Book Co. (UK) Ltd. Reproduced with permission.)

outlined in this chapter, or by a different approach altogether, there is no doubt that it is an essential first step in the process of strategic planning. It is the springboard from which the great leap may be made into the mists of the future.

References

1. Ansoff, H. I. *Corporate Strategy*, McGraw-Hill, 1965.
2. Denning, B. W. *Corporate Planning: Selected Concepts*, McGraw-Hill, 1971.
3. Drucker, P. F. *Managing for Results*, Heinemann, 1964.
4. Woodhall, W. Laporte Industries Ltd.: business results at Fullers Earth Union Ltd., in *Improving Business Results*, Humble, J. W. (ed.), McGraw-Hill, 1967.
5. Anon, *Modern Management in a Traditional Trade*, Fyffes Group Ltd.

10

Analysing the Industry and Competitors

An Approach to Competitor Analysis

In the next two chapters we will explore some ideas about industry and competitor analysis. The concepts are discussed in this chapter, to be followed in Chapter 11 with a case history showing some of the applications. Industry analysis is a sort of half way house between strengths and weakness analysis and strategy formulation. It provides another way of measuring the internal elements of the organisation against what is going on in the wider world, but it is also an essential to the formulation of sound future oriented strategies. As we will see there can also be a connection between industry analysis and portfolio analysis. The questionnaire in this chapter can be used both for industry analysis and to collect information for the directional policy matrix, which is described in more detail in a later chapter.

It is useful to think of the various components of industry and competitor analysis as a linked series of steps leading to the building of competitive advantage. Figure 10.1 shows this approach as one overall process, as a series of eight steps built around sources of strategic information. It may not be essential for every organisation to go through every step each time, but it makes sense to make what to do or what not to do a matter of rational decision.

The heart of the diagram is the strategic information system, which has been shown broken down into four very different sources of information. Information was discussed in an earlier chapter, so what will be covered here will be only those aspects which are peculiar to competitor analysis.

The outer ring follows a logical sequence. It is recommended that the sequence is maintained, even if some steps are omitted, because each step provides information which is useful to the steps that follow.

Industry analysis is a way of looking at the relative power of all the players in the chain of supply through to consumer. The purpose is not just diagnosis, but should lead to strategies to improve the position of the company. A large part of this chapter will be spent on the principles of industry analysis.

Industry mapping is a way of presenting the results of industry analysis, so that

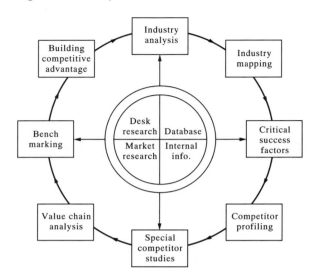

FIG. 10.1. Approach to competitor analysis.

the information is accessible, and conflicts between different pieces of information are forced into the limelight.

We have already met critical success factors. Here we will look more closely at how they might be derived from industry analysis, and used as one element of competitor analysis.

Competitor profiling is a way of compressing the strategic information about a competitor so that it can be used more effectively. The method can be extended to customers and suppliers, where the strategies that they are following are important for your own organisation's success. It is a small jump to use these profiles to generate a series of different scenarios about where strategic change might be triggered, and who by.

Special competitor studies are needed sometimes to look at particular aspects of strategy. They may be narrowly focused into, say, one product, activities in specific countries, or particular issues, such as production methods.

Value chain analysis is an approach to help the organisation identify its sources of competitive advantages. It is thus as much about identifying differentiation compared to competitors, although not restricted to market differentiation, as about the company in relation to its markets.

Benchmarking is one of those activities that need not be restricted to competitors. It may be desirable for a bank, for example, to compare its counter service with that of competitors. More frequently benchmarking may be used to lift a level of activity to the best it can be compared with, inside and outside the industry. Thus a study of customer service by one type of retailer might cover many non competing retailers. Total quality management might be benchmarked against the leaders in the field regardless of industry. An aim of benchmarking is usually to seek excellence in performance by reaching world class performance in any area of activity which is relevant.

The final box in the diagram is about bringing all the components together to develop strategies that create sustainable competitive advantage. Unfortunately sustainable advantage needs continual improvement, as others seek to emulate. Part of the strategic task is therefore to find ways of keeping ahead.

Industry Analysis

The person most associated with competitor analysis is Michael Porter,[1] who did an excellent job in drawing together the threads of analytical thought about industry analysis, and then went on to develop the value chain concept. The basic ideas of industry analysis have been around for many years. Entry barriers have been described in economic textbooks almost since economics became a subject. The idea of studying suppliers as well as competitors can be found in many books which pre-dated those of Porter, for example Farmer and Taylor,[2] while the earliest of marketing books talked about studying customers. Porter's contribution to industry analysis was firstly to take these random threads and turn them into a rope, and secondly to write about his concept in such a way as to make it the main thrust of strategic thinking during the 1980s. This was no mean achievement.

The basic model appears in Fig. 10.2. This version is a little different from Porter's original in that it is set within the environmental diagram, which was described in full in earlier chapters. In addition his original five forces have been expanded to show that substitutes are a force between the industry and its suppliers, and between the industry and its buyers. A third difference is that exit barriers

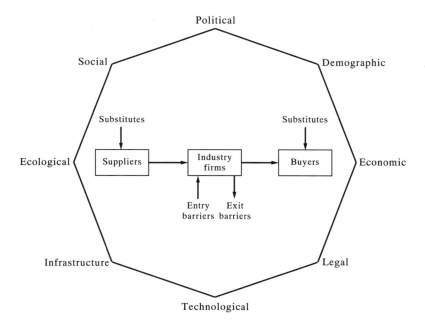

FIG. 10.2. Basic elements affecting industry profitability.

have been separated from entry barriers. To be strictly correct another force should be shown on the figure, although this is based on my own experience and is not mentioned in the original Porter concept. This is the role of influencers, who also may operate between the industry and its suppliers or buyers. By influencers I mean individuals or firms who may determine the purchase, but are not themselves buyers. A doctor for example prescribes drugs, which the customer buys from the chemist. However even this is a simplification in a welfare state, where all or part of the purchase may also be influenced by the national equivalent to the UK's Ministry of Health. An architect may specify the lift that is installed in a new building. It may be a consulting engineer that determines the specifications of a new sewage treatment plant, and by so doing may change the number of competitors who are able to bid. No study of the industry can afford to ignore any influencers who might operate within the industry.

A second problem with industry analysis which Porter does deal with is the need to determine the appropriate competitive arena. This has two dimensions, one of geography and the other of product. Anyone who analyses an industry has to decide whether the right basis of analysis is the world, a region such as the Economic Community, a country, or a local area within a country. If the picture is too broad, it becomes impossible to undertake a meaningful analysis. If it is too narrow, it is likely that the wrong signals will be read, and that what appears to be a powerful position is in fact very weak. A later chapter will deal at length with global strategy and the forces which drive organisations to take a global view. However for present purposes the guidance that can be offered is to decide what is relevant by studying the customers and the competitors. An individual company may be the driver that turns an industry global, but the company that refuses to acknowledge that an industry is global is hardly likely to change it back. To analyse a global industry there is a need to cascade down from a global overview, through regions, to key countries.

At the product level it is an easy trap to take a market segment as the industry. In my time with the food company that markets *Ovaltine*, I remember the claims that we were the market leaders. In beverages including tea and coffee? In food type drinks like *Horlicks* and drinking chocolate? In malted milk beverages, of which our product was one? No, in brown malted milk products. This might be a useful classification for marketing purposes, and might indeed have been the product that served particular segments of the market. It would have been useless as a basis for industry analysis.

It is important to remember that industry definitions change over time, and that there may be strong overlaps with other industries so that the industry becomes different, although all sectors are not necessarily in competition. Not so long ago there was a typewriter industry, a telephone industry, a computer industry, and a video industry. What we have seen over the last decade or so is a merging of these so that it becomes possible to argue that they are now all parts of the same industry, or if they are not they soon will be. It would clearly be a nonsense for any one to analyse the typewriter industry without also including computers. Would it make sense to look at telex in isolation from computers, electronic mail, and fax? In this particular set of product categories the boundaries are still changing.

There are a number of general principles that can be determined for each box in Fig. 10.2, and it is possible to say that if a certain condition occurs, it is likely to lead to more or less aggressive behaviour between competitors, or to move the balance of advantage from the industry to a buyer or a supplier. The check list approach is useful, but the skill in interpretation comes from looking at the inter-action of all the factors. What gives the buyer an advantage may be offset by another factor that favours the industry firm. An example is management consul-tancy, where the product is perishable (yesterday's unused time has no value) and entry barriers are low. These factors put bargaining power in the hands of the buyer. However, the better firms in the industry do not suffer continual erosion of margins, because they may offer scarce skills, large potential benefits, proprietary approaches, and have reputations that allay fears present among buyers of intan-gibles. There are thus offsetting factors which neutralise or reduce some of the adverse factors. However, competitive positions in what is a highly fragmented industry are variable, there are many segments to the market, with competition strong in some and weak in others. Some firms offer a clearly differentiated service: others are at the commodity end. Setting a competitive strategy in this industry is not a simple matter of plucking a couple of issues from a check list and devising actions in response. It is a matter of applying human ingenuity to the composite impact of all the factors taken in conjunction with each other. And so it would be if we were to use another industry as an example.

With this caution in mind, it is possible to make more sense from a study of the individual elements of industry analysis.

Industry firms

It is traditional for analysts to examine such factors as market shares and to pay some attention to the different positioning of each firm in the market-place. Industry analysis tries to identify all the factors which affect the intensity of competitive behaviour. The competitiveness of the industry is not revealed by brand shares alone, although these are important. Competitive behaviour is also influenced by many other factors, including:

Growth Rates of the Industry

Competitive behaviour tends to be less aggressive if industry growth rates are relatively high, because each firm can increase its sales without necessarily increasing its market share. This statement is considerably modified by the firm's position on the life-cycle curve. In a new industry high growth rates may bring in new competitors, which will tend to lead to aggressive behaviour. In almost all industries, a fall in the growth rate will tend to intensify competition. Often it is the change that causes new patterns, rather than the growth rate itself. Other things being equal, one would expect to find more aggressive behaviour in an industry whose annual growth rate has fallen suddenly from 10 to 3% than in an industry whose growth has stabilised at 3%.

General Level of Profits

Lack of profits among the industry (or significant firms in the industry) will tend to make competitive behaviour less predictable. Where profits are high for all, there may be a measure of tolerance of competitors. A change to lower profits may trigger a more aggressive attitude.

Level of Fixed Costs

Where investment is large, highly specialised and fixed costs are a relatively high proportion of total costs; competitors tend to 'hang on', selling at less than full costs, when the market slumps or there is over-capacity for some other reason. Shipping, oil refinery and petrochemicals all provide examples where competitive behaviour may lead to low profits or losses over a very long period of time, because the alternative is plant closure at a time when assets cannot be realised.

Economies of Scale–Experience Curve

Competitive behaviour is likely to be more aggressive when there are clear advantages in being big. This may happen when cost levels are dependent on high volumes, or when the experience curve effect means that progressively higher volumes will lead to progressively lower costs. Lower costs mean prices can be reduced, which in turn means that even higher volumes can be gained. In a growth market, where demand is elastic and the product subject to mass production (e.g. motor cycles, calculating machines, electronic components) the experience curve effect can bring dominance to the firm that gets far enough ahead. Competitive behaviour is likely to be very aggressive during this period.

Degree of Differentiation

Market imperfections give a degree of protection to individual firms and reduce the impact of competition. Thus it is reasonable to expect the fiercest competition when all firms are offering products of commodity status, and the most peaceful behaviour when each firm offers such a highly differentiated product that it is almost unique.

Number of Firms and Market Shares

A fragmented industry, with no one firm having a significant market share, tends to be more competitive than one which has a clear market leader who is in a dominant position. To some degree, these tendencies may be modified by the position on the product life cycle. It is unwise to assume that mature markets will all have gone through the shakeout period. Some are highly fragmented because the economic circumstances do not favour large firms (e.g. many service industries).

New Entrant

In long established industries, firms often reach unspoken forms of accommodation with each other, softening aggressiveness of competition. This will often change with the entry of a new firm who either does not know or chooses to ignore these implicit 'rules' (e.g. the impact of Laker on the Atlantic air routes). A similar effect may occur if one of the companies appoints a new chief executive from outside the industry.

Nature of Product

A perishable product (e.g. airline tickets, fresh produce) is likely to be more susceptible to random price-cutting than one which can be stored easily and cheaply.

Buyers

There are two reasons for studying the structure of the industry along the channel to the ultimate consumer. The first is to ensure that the whole of the present structure is known, as this may reveal new strategic options, including the all important one of changing the "rules of the game" by finding another way to get the product to the consumer.

A second reason is to determine the relative influence on profits exercised by the various stages in the chain, and the way power is likely to shift in the future. It is not necessarily the industry itself which determines its own margins and profitability; sometimes the greater power is in the hands of the buyers. Factors which influence the relative location of this power and influence include:

Relative Size

If the industry includes firms which are considerably larger than their customers, sheer weight of resources may put them in the dominant position. The opposite may apply when the buying organisations are the larger. This is not a universal truth, as other factors may outweigh size in importance. For example, UK grocery products are largely controlled by supermarket chains, who not only have most of the retail outlets, but have also developed their own label products that they can adjust in volume and price if the brand manufacturers do not toe the line. In this way they may determine the profitability of manufacturers whose organisations may be considerably larger than those of the supermarkets.

Dependencies

Bargaining strength may lie with the least dependent of the two parties. This is a composite of the number of industry firms contrasted with the number of buying firms (what flexibility does each have?), and the importance of the product to the profits of each party.

Profitability of the Buying Industry

The industry firms are likely to be in a healthier position when they are selling to a profitable industry. Where buyers are unprofitable or have low profits, there is likely to be stronger resistance against price increases. This resistance will increase when the buyer is facing an elastic demand curve, and cannot easily pass on his or her extra costs.

Experience of Buyers

Buyers purchasing from a mature industry are likely to have more experience than those dealing with a new industry. Thus, the more mature the industry, the weaker its bargaining position may become (subject, of course, to other factors). Where the buying industry is also mature, there may be a tendency for the degree of product differentiation to fall, making it more difficult for the industry to sustain high margins.

Threat of Integration

The industry firm that patently has the capability and strength to integrate into its buying industry possesses a key bargaining point. If the buying industry thwarts its profit aims, it has the potential to remove the blockage. The opposite applies when the buying industry can offer a credible threat of backwards integration. In either case the credibility of the threat is enhanced when both parties are aware that such a move would be economically viable. Do not forget that the actions of *your* customer may be affected by the power of *their* customer.

The key factor in successfully analysing the customers in a particular industry is segmenting them into groups and distinguishing them either by the reason they buy or how they buy. Criteria for segmenting customer groups include:

—Industry or market segment.
—Geographic location.
—Size of purchase.
—Frequency of purchase.

Suppliers

It is traditional for an industry to believe that it holds the edge over both its buyers and suppliers, a statement that patently cannot always be true since the industry itself is a buyer to its supplier. Relations with the supplying industry are rarely studied as a matter of strategic importance. In reality the analysis of suppliers is the converse of the analysis of buyers. The factors to consider are therefore the same: industry or market segment, product application, geographic location, size of purchase, and frequency of purchase.

Suppliers exercise power in an industry in a number of ways: by lowering the quality of goods for a given purchase price, by tightening payment and service terms, and so on, to the extent that suppliers in general, or particular supplier groups, exercise significant power; as a result, industry costs increase and profitability diminishes.

Substitutes

The availability of substitutes may have a dramatic effect on the prospects for an industry, and will unleash a further set of competitive relationships. Emergence of a new substitute may bring new firms with different cost structures into the competitive arena. A substitute will often increase the power of the buyer and reduce the power of the seller. The emergence of potential new substitutes is therefore a possibility that should be studied for each industry.

Where the number of existing substitutes is large, the possibility that the industry has been ill-defined should be considered. It may be that a production view has been taken rather than a marketing view. In any event, the substitute industry should be studied as rigorously as the firm's own industry.

Entry and Exit Barriers

The entry and exit barriers will affect the profitability of an industry and the way in which competitors behave.

Entry barriers can only be interpreted in relation to the attractiveness of the industry. Relatively low barriers will deter firms from entering low profit/low growth industries. The barriers may have to be very high to keep a new entrant out of a highly attractive industry.

Examples of entry barriers which *raise the costs* of a new entrant are:

(i) Economies of scale/the experience curve factor may raise the capital costs of entry to a very high level (e.g. electronic calculators).
(ii) *Highly differentiated products* may require extensive advertising support before a newcomer can break in (e.g. household detergents). This may raise costs to prohibitive levels.
(iii) *The nature of distribution* may require entry at a high level of output (e.g. supermarkets will not stock brands which are slow-moving and have low market shares).

Other entry barriers may create a legal restriction to entry, or in some way deny access to a critical part of the market:

—Patents.
—Legal controls (e.g. auditors, television broadcasting companies).
—Control of distribution outlets (e.g. British film industry until recently).
—Contracts with key customers or suppliers.

Where entry barriers are very low the industry may become fragmented and competition fierce, with new competitors regularly coming into the market. Industry profitability is to a large extent dependent on market imperfections, and one element of corporate strategy might be to find ways of raising the entry barriers.

Exit barriers are the factors which tie a firm to the industry and make it difficult or impossible for it to leave. Where they occur, the firm will hang on, trading as best it can, and depressing profits in the industry.

Exit barriers may be around the need to write off specialised assets for which there is no buyer, particular contracts, or legal requirements which make it costly to meet severance payments to employees. There may also be government pressure on the firm to stay in the business.

Industry Mapping

So far the discussion of industry analysis has been to illustrate the principles. It is possible to move straight from concept to practical application. However this is rarely easy, so I should like to suggest an approach which I have developed over numerous studies of different industries, and which I know to be helpful. I call this industry mapping.

One of the considerations in a real life study is that the headings used so far are too broad. Buyers, for example, are of many types and may perform many different functions. Some of the products of a components company, for example, may go to original equipment manufacturers. The sale of spares and replacements may take quite different channels. Really we are interested in all stages to the final consumer. A related issue is that the components company cited above would be classed as a supplier if we had been looking through the eyes of an OEM company. However it was the "industry" in my study. However if the industry studied was one stage back I could have looked at the electronic components that my component factory buys to put into their product. If I had done this my stream of analysis would have covered only one of the buying channels for these electronic supplies.

In industry mapping an attempt is made to plot the whole chain from first supplier through to final consumer, examining the relationships of each link in the chain. We still have to define what we are doing. If we took the view of my components company we should probably not want to study in detail all that happened to the rest of the output of the electronics supplier, but we would want to study any other industries we supplied to, apart from the one mentioned. The OEM company might take an even narrower focus than us. But even they may have different ways of reaching their customers: direct sale, distributors and agents. They may feel a need to study the second-hand and retrofit markets, since these may have a direct bearing on their prospects.

All these examples add up to a need to think very clearly about the industry. The industry mapping approach starts by drawing an outline diagram showing all the links in the chain. Figures 10.3–10.6 give some examples of outline maps for a number of industries. It should be stressed that at this stage the need is to look at the industry and not just the firm. This may not seem a profound statement, but I have seen many businesses which can draw such a map for what they themselves do, but have no knowledge of channels which they do not use.

One way of developing the outline is to define the industry in diagram form by thinking of the logical ways in which business might flow through the channels. This provides a hypothesis for discussion with those inside the company who have appropriate knowledge. The next step is to relate the draft diagram to company market research and any external published information.

When drawing the boxes, keep in mind the next part of the analysis, when all the key information about the industry will be recorded on the diagram.

Notes on Figures 10.3–10.6

Fig. 10.3: Note that the two main product areas are shown, which in reality may have different sets of competitors. Also included are consulting engineers who influence the buying decisions but are not themselves buyers. Note that, as with the other examples, it might be desirable to group buyers by their characteristics, and in some industries it may be worth looking beyond the buyers to their customers. Similarly it is sometimes useful to explore the chain of supply into those links that support the suppliers.

Fig. 10.4: In this sort of industry there are often two different supply channels for the OEM and after market. There may even be different competitors in each. OEM companies may influence the replacement market to a greater degree than the diagram suggests.

Fig. 10.5: We may want to break retailers down into several boxes, particularly if there are wholesalers that specialise in different outlets (e.g. chemists). If we were looking at household detergents we might want to break the competitors down into product headings, and take the supply chain back several stages. The example makes it clear that competitors have several main routes to the end consumer.

Fig. 10.6: This is an initial model for a complex industry which handles many unrelated products. Every stage illustrated is capable of being analysed further.

In the next stage of analysis the key information that enables the industry to be interpreted is recorded on the block diagram.

Figure 10.7 provides a summary of the nature of the information that we will want to record. The points are all directly related to the concepts of industry analysis discussed earlier, except that we will want to change the data requirements slightly to fit the nature of each box we have identified on the block diagram. Thus the buyers' headings would be different if we were looking at a manufacturer, retailer or end consumer.

The industry map becomes complex once the information is added. For this reason, the examples shown are incomplete—they are given to show how the map is built up.

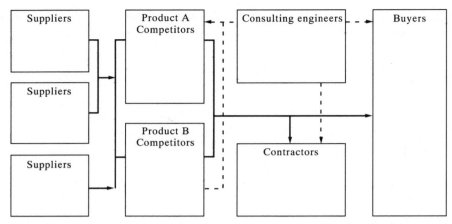

FIG. 10.3. Example industry map outline. Plant such as water purification, power generation,

Figure 10.8 is a very rudimentary outline of what must have been (*c.* 1969), and probably still is, one of the most convoluted industry structures imaginable. On the map we have started to record information about the number of firms in each box. How we complete the rest of the map would depend on our business interest. If for example we were an importer, we would probably be interested in the whole structure, and the really critical information would be who controlled the retail outlets, and the percentage of our type of product that passed through the various channels. We would probably want to plot some of the integrated players like Fyffes and Geest on the map, and some of the main importers like

FIG. 10.4. Components for original equipment.

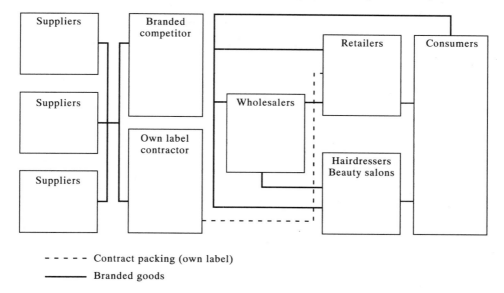

- - - - - Contract packing (own label)
————— Branded goods

FIG. 10.5. Products such as toiletries (e.g. hair care).

Jaffa. We would probably group many of the other players, rather than trying to study them individually.

Figure 10.9 shows a more complex map. Again it is simplified and represents the metal container industry in the USA as it was in 1962. Before looking at the data, note that the map ends at the buying industries. In a real situation we might have a need to examine the customers of these industries—in most cases the consumer, but sometimes another manufacturer. If the product had been chicken

FIG. 10.6. Generalised outline model—general insurance.

FIG. 10.7. Summary of factors in Industry analysis.

killing equipment, for example, we would have an incomplete analysis if we stopped at poultry processors, since the main forces in this industry are the supermarkets on the one hand and the fast food firms on the other.

On the map in Fig. 10.9 you will notice that, although there are obvious gaps in information that could have been plotted, we have a very clear summary picture emerging from the forces which will affect competitive behaviour among can manufacturers. There are two dominant competitors in an industry squeezed by suppliers and customers and subject to both backwards and forwards integration. Further inspection shows markets such as brewing, soft drinks and aerosols where the needs are more specialised, the buyers more profitable, and markets growing. Had we taken this analysis to the competitor profiling, we should have found that one competitor, Crown Cork, had spotted this and had a strategy aimed particularly at these segments, lifting it a step above the commodity nature of the industry.

Just by reading the information on the map, we can gain a picture that would have taken about 20 pages of narrative description. And we can also see the obvious important gaps in the information that we would need to plug.

Figure 10.10 comes from an article by Crawshaw[3] which describes a case history of an industry mapping exercise. In all these examples, information has been recorded in note form. A practical point is that a dossier of information in a more detailed format should be built up by those preparing the map. This becomes a reference book of source material, which of course should include the sources of all information.

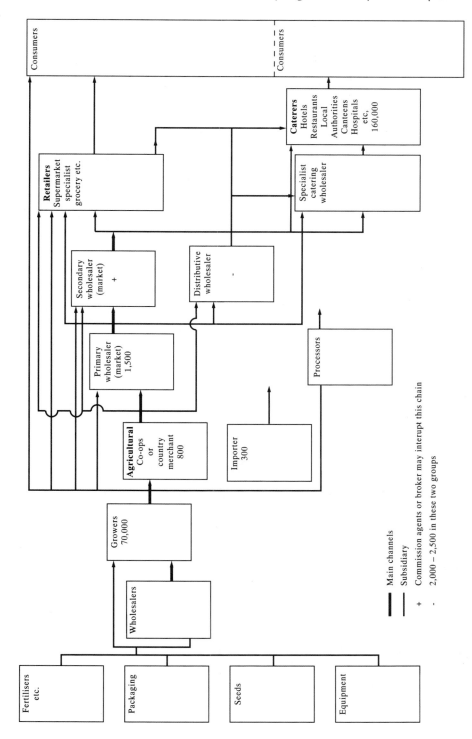

FIG. 10.8. Fruit and vegetable distribution. [From D. E. Hussey, *Introducing Corporate Planning*, Pergamon, 1991 (4th edition)].

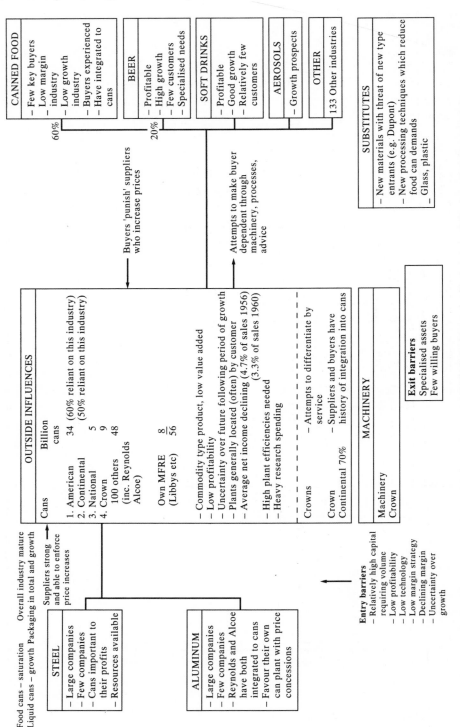

Fig. 10.9. Metal container industry—1962—U.S.A. (From *Introducing Corporate Planning* by D. E. Hussey.)

PRODUCERS/PUBLISHERS   'RETAILERS'   MARKETS/SECTORS

© INFORMAT 1989

FIG. 10.10. Outline map of the information industry. (S. Crawshaw: Strategic analysis for an information business—a case study. *Journal of Strategic Change*, Jan–Feb 1992. Used with permission.)

Typical problems observed in building up these maps offer a very good reason why for most companies this is a useful approach:

(i) Perceptions of the competitive arena often differ from the reality, resulting in suppression of options when competitive strategies are formulated.

(ii) Often only one part of the problem has been perceived. Acrow, a once great, scaffolding pole company with a hire or sale strategy ignored the growing hire and erect competitors who eventually took over most of the market. This contributed to the demise of the company.

(iii) Market segmentation is often confused with strategic segmentation. The former may be achieved by product positioning and promotion but has few entry barriers. The latter offers a longer term position because it is defensible. The ultra luxury car is a strategic segment of the car market: the upmarket versions of, say, the Ford Escort represent a market segmentation.

(iv) Data used by the company is often incorrect, mainly because it has been used functionally and goes unchecked against other sources (e.g. manufacturing people using capacity information about the industry, and not relating this to the market share data used by marketing).

(v) Information is often missing, leading to the need to decide its potential importance and whether action should be taken. This is a straight cost–benefit decision. Few of us need perfection.

Critical Success Factors

In the previous chapter we touched briefly on the idea of critical success factors. Industry analysis provides one way through which these can be derived, and the analyst has a rich vein of information to mine from the industry map and the date that lies behind it.

Critical success factors may be defined as the things that have to be done well if the companies in the industry are to be successful. There may be additional factors to add which are unique to the competitive positioning for which the organisation is striving, but the core factors will apply to all competitors operating in the same sector of the industry. They therefore provide a useful standard for measuring both one's own performance against them, and that of key competitors.

In doing this analysis, it is important not to overlook the fact that the same industry may contain sectors with widely differing critical success factors. A good example is the own label contractor and the branded competitor classifications of Fig. 10.5. Both produce virtually identical products, but the critical success factors of the two sectors have little in common.

Thus we might expect those for the contractor to include:

—Flexible manufacture, with the ability to change lines quickly.
—Low cost manufacture.
—Ability to formulate quickly copies of branded products.
—Negotiation ability, since there are relatively few buyers and these are supplied on contract.

The branded competitors' critical success factors might not include any of the above, but would cover:

—Segmentation and promotional skills; the ability to create markets.
—Marketing research skills to identify new marketing needs.
—R&D skills to invent new products.
—Distribution skills.
—Pricing skills to ensure the right margins.

Strategic Implications

Tentative strategic conclusions can begin to be drawn as the industry mapping analysis progresses. I have found it helpful to present maps on A3 paper, organised so that when opened out there is a map on one side and a narrative sheet on the other. The narrative highlights all the strategic issues arising. Some of the headings I have used in the past include:

—Key points observed in the analysis
—Concerns over the availability or accuracy of some of the information
—Trends which may change the map
—Problems in competitive positioning
—Critical success factors
—Strategic issues and points for consideration.

This should not be undertaken in isolation from other elements of strategic analysis, particularly the impact of trends from the business environment, as these can change the shape and structure of an industry.

One of the exciting things about this type of analysis is that we are taking a photograph of what exists today. Often strategies can be derived which when implemented will change the shape and structure of the industry. Figure 10.11 shows in matrix form some of the strategic options which may emerge from an industry mapping exercise.

Cell 1: Same Activity, Same Structure

Here the strategic options are about improving position. This may be gaining advantage through a changed cost structure (for example the complete relocation of the Vickers Armoured Fighting Vehicle plant in the early 1980s from multiple Victorian buildings to a one-building, green field site). It may include careful segmentation, or other marketing strategies which beat the competition.

Cell 2: New Activity, Same Structure

This is the group of strategies which deals with the introduction of an alternative, better product (not merely an improved copy of an old product). For example the lightweight, self-propelled booms to give access on construction sites both found a new market and removed a major share from the previous heavy, cumbersome telescopic booms that were previously used. The firm that introduced the self-propelled booms gained a considerable advantage over the companies that had been market leaders in this area.

Cell 3: Same Activity, Changed Structure

This is the strategy followed by companies that have tried to achieve leadership in a fragmented industry through acquisition of competitors.

		Activity	
		Same	Novel
Structure of Industry	Same	• Niches/segmentation • Improvement strategies	Niches/segmentation
	Changed	• Acquire competitors • Create new channels	Create new opportunity

FIG. 10.11. Strategy matrix. (Copyright Harbridge Consulting Group Ltd. Used with permission)

Cell 4: New Activity, Changed Structure

An old example is the supermarkets who began by offering a different approach to grocery retailing, and went on to change the structure of the industry through increasing buyer power as they gained control of the channels. A more recent example is Sears Roebuck in the USA, which brought together its insurance company, Allstate, and several new financial service company acquisitions, a new general credit card (launched on the back of the store card), and its retail network to offer a new way of marketing consumer financial services.

Competitor Profiling

Industry mapping helps us to understand the forces which determine competitive behaviour in general, and also to identify which competitors should be studied at an individual level. The next stages of competitor analysis are designed to achieve a number of aims, which include:

  (i) Formulation of an appropriate strategy in the reality of the competition. An appropriate strategy might be one which chooses those areas for the industry analysis that avoid ferocious competition. Or, for a dominant competitor, it may mean ensuring that it retains this position.
 (ii) Finding a superior strategy that gives competitive advantage.
(iii) Being prepared for competitor actions and expected reactions to your strategies.
 (iv) Influencing competitor reactions, by trying to get the competitor to do what you want.
  (v) Developing an alliance strategy with competitors. Relations with competitors do not always have to be hostile, and in some industries there are opportunities which can best be exploited as a joint venture or alliance.
 (vi) Identifying the true competitors. Not all the players in an industry are necessarily all competing against each other. The case study in the next chapter gives an example of an industry where there are so many segments and so much fragmentation that many players in the industry are neither offering similar products, nor selling them to the same buyers.

Competitor profiling provides a way of looking at competitors, and presenting the results in an easy to read form, again on one A3 sheet of paper. Sometimes more pages are needed, particularly when a competitor has to be studied at different levels (product or geographic), but the principle of reducing the analysis to summary statements can be preserved. This process increases understanding of the competitor, focuses attention on the appropriate issues, and provides a format which eases internal communication and can be stored in a database.

Financial Results

	Group					Division					Unit				
	YR	YR	YR	YR	YR	YR	YR	YR	YR	YR	YR	YR	YR	YR	YR
Sales															
PBT															
PAT															
ROA															
ROS															
Sales Growth															
EPS															

Product Analysis

Product	Sales		Direct Costs		Contribution		Market Share	
	YR	YR	YR	YR	YR	YR	YR	YR
1								
2								
3								
4								
5								
6								
7								
8								

Marketing and Sales Activity

Sources of Competitive Advantage

SOURCE	NOTES
Infra Structure	
R & D	
Logistics In	
Operations	
Logistics Out	
Marketing	
Sales	
Services	

Importance of Activity to Group

Scope of International Operations

Key Factors

Strengths   Weaknesses

Implications   Implications

CSF Ratings

Factor	Comp-titor	Own	Index

Notes
Assess each factor 0–10 index is
COMPETITIOR SCORE
OWN SCORE

Apparent Strategy

Organisation Philosophy

Personnel Policies

FIG. 10.12. Outline competitor profile. (Copyright Harbridge Consulting Group Ltd. Used with permission.)

A pro-forma competitor profile is provided in Fig. 10.12. In practice this will require modification to suit the types of competitor in the industry. Each block of information is discussed below.

Financial Results

Choose the key figures that mean the most to you. Typically these would include sales, profits, and key ratios such as earnings per share, return on assets, return on sales and growth rates. The example shows that there may be a need to repeat this information at various levels, such as the total group, the division and the business unit. These headings will change with the objectives of the analysis, and the structure of the competitor. What can be recorded is of course limited by the information that can be legitimately obtained, and the special knowledge of the analyst which may allow certain estimates to be made. At the broadest levels, the information will probably come from annual reports: at the lowest levels it may be necessary to estimate sales and profit figures from market research and other sources.

Product Analysis

This is another breakdown of the information into products or product categories. Data may come from annual reports, but will invariably have to be supplemented by market research information, and possibly analysis of the competitive product so that cost structures can be estimated. The ability to complete every cell will vary with the information that can be obtained, and the justification of the effort that should be put on this will vary with the importance of the competitor. Very often the analyst will have to be satisfied with a less than complete answer. This section incorporates market shares. It could also be extended if appropriate to show segment shares: again a judgement has to be made on the value of this information and whether it can be obtained.

Marketing and Sales Activity

This is a note pad to record key information about how the competitor influences the market. It may include information on advertising spends, the size of the sales force, direct mail activity, or whatever else is strategically important.

Importance of Activity to Group

This part of the form assesses the significance of the industry being analysed to the total operations of the competitor. The reason for this is to establish whether the activity is core to the competitor, in which case more resources might be made available to fight off a competitive threat. Something which is peripheral may not receive the same management time, nor have additional resources made available. One complex way of showing this is to draw a portfolio chart of all the competitor's activities.

This is always difficult, and particularly so if the competitor operates in a number of industries on which the analyst has little real knowledge. Just how difficult will become clearer in a later chapter which deals with portfolio analysis. An alternative method is illustrated in Fig. 10.13, which immediately shows the importance of an activity to a competitor as a source of turnover, profits and growth.

Sources of Competitive Advantage

This box begins to tie into value chain analysis, and is an attempt to identify just what it is which is giving a competitor an edge. Are they a particularly efficient manufacturer? Is the edge in their ability to develop continuous product innova-

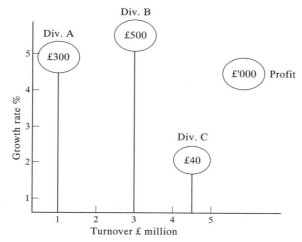

FIG. 10.13. Importance of corporate activities.

tions? Is it a superior after sales service? An extension or alternative to this box could be to try to identify the core competence of the competitor. Prahalad and Doz[4] stress the importance of studying the core technologies and competencies of organisations as well as their particular product market attributes. They quote, as one example, Honda and argue that its competitive strength comes from engines, a core technology, as well as brand recognition.

Scope of International Operations

This box provides a note pad to record information about the operations of a competitor outside of any particular country which may be being studied. The two main aspects which should not be ignored are any marketing advantage given by international operations, and the way in which the competitor runs its international operations. The competitive reactions to your strategy will be very different if the competitor operates on an individual country basis, what has been termed "multi-local", than if it manages globally through an integrated strategy. One European wide grocery products company I studied operated at a competitive disadvantage because each country operation was treated as a separate business, and had to achieve its return on investment targets as its main priority. Its major competitor, who was winning all the battles in every country, treated Europe as one strategic area and would put resources into any country to beat off a competitive threat, regardless of the short-term impact on that subsidiary's bottom line. The virtually uncoordinated country strategies of my client meant that it could rarely win against the superior strategy of the competitor. Knowing how your competitor views global operations is a critical first step to understanding and predicting how it will behave in different circumstances.

Key Factors

This is another note pad to record any major points about the competitor which do not fit under the other headings.

Apparent Strategy

This box records what the competitor's strategy appears to be. I use the word apparent, because it can only be a deduction, based on the analysis of all the information (the factual situation drawn from the market research and hard data, and the assessments made from statements in annual reports, press announcements, interviews, and company literature). This is one of the most important pieces of information on the profile and should be discussed at some length within the company that is doing the analysis.

Strengths and Weaknesses

The purpose of this box is self evident. It will be easier to complete if hard data and specific market research into the view from the customer is used, as well as the impressions of your own managers. It is very easy to attribute to competitors strengths and weaknesses that they do not possess, or which are of trivial importance in the market place.

Critical Success Factor Ratings

The critical success factors discussed earlier can be used as one way of comparing competitors against one's own operations. I have found it useful to score the competitor and the company on whose behalf the analysis is undertaken against each critical factor. If possible I have this exercise undertaken by a number of informed managers individually, argue out the extreme views, and average the final answers. What usually becomes apparent is a series of strengths that may not have emerged from the first exercise.

Organisation Philosophy

This matters because how a company organises itself will affect how it behaves in the market place. One dimension of philosophy was discussed when we looked at the international operations box. There are many others, including the degree of centralisation/decentralisation, where strategic decisions are taken, and whether organised into strategic business units or subsidiaries. Is the main owning organisation a holding company, perhaps operating like a Hansen, or an integrated part of the overall business, like British Petroleum? Goold and Campbell[5] provide useful insight into the various philosophies for the organisation of strategic decision making.

Personnel Policies

The final box records those personnel policies which impact on strategy. For example, the type of people recruited, how they are developed, the reward policies applied, and the importance placed on people are all aspects which have potential strategic importance.

The next chapter provides a case history of the application of competitor analysis, using the methods described in this chapter. It includes an example of a completed profile.

The process of profiling is beneficial in itself, as it forces systematic consideration of competitors. It also offers a way in which masses of information can be sifted and reduced to something that the human mind can handle. I have used such profiles as the foundation of a data base enabling electronic storage and retrieval.

The compression of lots of data into a one page information sheet is very helpful when a number of managers are working together to formulate strategy. It is at least possible to get everyone reading the same information at the same time!

Such profiles can also be completed on any key players on the industry map, and it may be of equal value to study the strategies of key industry customers in a similar way.

Competitor Groupings (Strategic Groups)

Unfortunately competitor profiling cannot deal with all the competitive situations we may meet. In a fragmented market, for example, there may be hundreds of relatively small competitors, many of whom may never be met in a competitive situation. Studying each individually may add little insight. This is one reason why we have to find another way of looking at competitors. Porter[1] argues that competitors can be studied on the basis of strategic groups. His definition is:

"A strategic group is the group of firms in an industry following the same or a similar strategy (...portion omitted...). An industry could have only one strategy group if all the firms followed essentially the same strategy. At the other extreme, each firm could be a different strategic group."

One solution to the fragmented industry would be to identify strategic groups and study these. Some authorities, including Porter would recommend this for all industries. The identification of criteria for strategic groups has exercised many minds. McGee and Thomas[6] provide an excellent review of many of the research studies into strategic group identification. McNamee and McHugh[7] give a case study of defining strategic groups in the Northern Ireland clothing industry. A number of matrix classifications have been used to identify groups. Porter[1] suggests specialisation and vertical integration as the two axes of a matrix for plotting the strategic groups. In his example of the US chain saw industry, he uses quality branded image as one axis and the mix of channels used as another. The McNamee and McHugh[7] argument is that such diagrams need also to display the intensity of competition in each group plotted.

McGee and Thomas should be left with the last word on the usefulness of the strategic group concept in competitor analysis:

"By occupying an intermediate level of analysis between firms and industry, strategic groups are helpful for identifying issues about an organisation's competitive position (e.g. Who are the direct competitors? What are the competitive forces? What are the distinct competitive assets?) Indeed the key to understanding industry evolution lies in the way in which firms change their asset structures, in other words, the ways in which mobility barriers change and redefine the strategic groups thus enabling predictions about future industry evolution to be advanced... (portion omitted...)."

"(1) Groups can be used to preserve information characterising individual firms which is typically lost in industry studies using averaged and aggregated data."

"(2) Because groups allow us to investigate multiple firms concurrently, they allow us to assess the effectiveness of their strategic actions over a wide range of variations than a single firm's experience affords."

"(3) Group analysis can be used to summarise information to bring key dimensions into high relief, for example to facilitate an assessment of the consequences of a collective movement by many firms into similar competitive postures, or to verify similarities of strategic direction across an industry."

Special Competitor Studies

The profiling approach will cover most competitor analysis needs most of the time. However, from time to time there may be a requirement to undertake a special study of one competitor, or of several competitors in a comparative study. The latter comes close to benchmarking which will be discussed later.

There is little difference in concept between undertaking a special study of a competitor to build competitive advantage, or of a competitor or other organisation as an acquisition candidate. The sources of information are the same, although the purposes may be different.

A special study of a competitor may be more focused. It may be restricted to a functional area, such as their use of information systems, or a country (are they doing anything in Poland?), or to an attempt to predict the direction of their research and development. Such reports have to be designed to fit the purpose, so very little guidance can be given on their shape. Perhaps more interesting is an idea of some of the legitimate sources of information that can be tapped. This will be left until the end of the chapter, as it applies to every aspect of competitor analysis.

Value Chain Analysis

The concept of value chain analysis was another innovation from Michael Porter.[8] Hussey[9] defined value chains as:

"A method for separating the activities the firm performs in order to identify the underlying areas of competitive advantage. All broad stages of the process from *in-bound logistics* to after sales service are identified. They are then broken down into more detailed chains of activity, so that areas where the firm has advantages can be studied. Similar analysis is undertaken on competitors, leading to more effective competitive strategies and a fuller understanding of how each competitor is achieving differentiation.''

Porter argues that *value activities* are those which are technologically and strategically distinct. They are rarely the same as accounting definitions, and one of the first tasks is re-assess costs by the value chain classifications rather than those traditionally chosen by the cost accountant. Competitive advantage can be gained by performing an activity in the value chain at a lower cost than competitors. It can also be gained by giving a service to the customer which is valued and more advantageous than that offered by competitors. It is also possible to gain advantage from the application of improved technologies to various components of the value chain. One point to emphasise when undertaking such an analysis is that value must be looked at through the eyes of the customer. The fact that you feel something is beneficial does not automatically mean that there are customers who share your view.

Porter's generic model divides the firm first into broad value categories. The primary activities include:

Physical distribution, in-bound. All the activities concerned with the receipt, storage, handling and recording of the raw materials and supplies obtained by the company.

Operations. The activities performed by the organisation to transform the inputs into final finished form.

Physical distribution, out-bound. Activities from warehousing the finished product to getting it to the customer.

Marketing and Sales. The provision of a means through which the buyer can purchase the product.

Service. The activities which enhance the value of the product, such as after sales service, spare parts availability, installation and training.

The support activities are grouped into purchasing, technology development, human resource management and the firm's infrastructure.

Value can be provided through any of these links in the chain. In addition each link should be further broken down into smaller chains. Thus sales and marketing might be broken down into such activities as order receipt, selling, advertising, telephone sales, and enquiry handling.

Value chain analysis is not easy, and there is as yet not a great deal that has been written about its practical application.

Benchmarking

Benchmarking is a process through which the organisation seeks to identify the best practices that are relevant to the industry. It is thus different from a study that merely seeks to identify what a competitor does, because firstly our interest is only with the best, and secondly good practice is not necessarily restricted to those in the industry.

I am grateful to Bengt Karlöff[10] for giving me sight of the manuscript of the English translation of one of his Swedish books, and thus drawing my attention to the two concepts of Best Internal Practice and Best External Practice.

Best internal practice is a benchmarking concept that can be applied by any organisation that has replicated activity within a country, or across the world. This may be duplicated factories, branch operations, or service operations. He recommends breaking down the operations to comparable value chain activities. If this sort of analysis is to be meaningful, it has to cluster activities by relevant differences. If we take as an example the service operations of a European elevator company, there may not be much to be gained from comparing one country with another. There may be a great deal to be learned by sorting service centres into groups with similar characteristics, and seeking best practice within each group, regardless of which country it falls within. The advantages of the best internal practice approach is that data can be obtained on whatever parameters are determined to be appropriate for the study, and it is possible to find out the reasons for variances, thus enabling action to be taken. The disadvantages are that the organisation's best may only equate to competitor's worst, that such comparisons often become bogged down by company politics, leading to defensive behaviour and manipulation of the figures.

Best external practice is easier for support activities across industries than it is for detailed cost analysis between competitors. Occasionally it is possible to get support from all competitors for an honest broker to collect and analyse the figures, and to present them in a meaningful but non confidential way. The non confidential data are helpful in putting a particular organisation on a league table, but does not necessarily help in identifying what it is that contributes to the best performer's figures.

Some things can be benchmarked relatively easily. Service levels can usually be measured through market research studies. Productivity levels, or manufacturing processes are a much tougher proposition. As always in this book I am only referring to information that can be obtained by legitimate means. My own standard is that if I would feel uncomfortable telling a competitor how I obtained my information, I should not use that source.

Inter industry benchmarking studies can yield valuable information. My own organisation has found little difficulty in undertaking some of these studies for clients, for example in particular aspects of human resource management (in one case the policies and approaches used by organisations in the USA and the UK to manage cultural diversity in the work force), and in policies for customer service. These sorts of studies really fall outside of the analysis of competitors, but may lead to ways of building competitive advantage.

Building Competitive Advantage

Competitor analysis can be used in an avoidance sort of way. By being aware of what competitors are doing, it becomes possible to avoid activities which would lead to a head-on battle on ground which was not of your own choosing.

Building competitive advantage is a high sounding aim. In reality, much of the competitor analysis is about removing competitive disadvantage rather than creating a permanent gap between your activities and those of competitors. There are comparatively few actions that cannot be copied by competitors. However, it is usually much harder for a competitor to regain ground that has been lost, so even a temporary advantage may be beneficial, particularly if accompanied by an intention to take the next set of actions that enables the organisation to stay ahead.

Porter[1] argues that there are only three generic strategies that can be followed. He provides a matrix with "industry wide" and "particular segment only" as the two positions on one axis, and "uniqueness perceived by the customer" and "low cost position" as the two positions on the other axis. This results in either an industry wide differentiation strategy, or an overall cost leadership strategy, or a focus strategy. In a later work[8] he modified these conclusions to accept that a focus strategy could be differentiated or cost based. He used the phrase stuck in the middle to describe firms which failed to make a clear choice between one of the three strategies. I find it hard to agree with such a simple view of the choices, and believe that they are too stark and uncompromising. Within a cost leadership strategy there is room for differentiation. It is possible to argue that all supermarket chains follow a cost leadership strategy, but there are also key elements of differentiation. Few people would see Tesco, Sainsbury, Waitrose and ASDA in the UK as being identical companies. Differentiation is created by image, by the range of products stocked, originality in own label brands, location and layout of stores, and no doubt many other factors.

What I do believe is important is clarity over what it is that the organisation is trying to do, and the implications of the various options, compared to the offerings and approaches of competitors. However, the strategies themselves must emerge from a study of the market opportunities, tempered by the sort of analysis suggested in this chapter. It would be naive to suggest that competitor analysis is all that matters. It is the mechanism which helps to fine tune a strategic idea, a way of avoiding expensive errors, a method for ensuring that customers are provided with reasons to buy your product rather than that of someone else. However, if there is no market, or the advantages you offer are not valued by the market, there will be no success. Industry and competitor analysis are important, they help in understanding markets, and in strategic positioning, but they are only one of the elements needed to create a sound strategy.

Information for Competitor Analysis

The need for strategic information was discussed in an earlier chapter, and competitor information is only a subset of this. In addition, as already mentioned, there may be little difference between information for competitor analysis and for acquisition or alliance purposes.

The lengths that should be gone to are a matter for cost–benefit analysis. How important is that missing piece of information that may be very costly to obtain? Is it worth commissioning a special piece of market research only to assess the strengths and weaknesses of competitors as seen through the eyes of customers?

These sorts of decisions require careful judgement on a case by case basis. Will the information be likely to lead to different decisions? How critical are these decisions? Will the costs of getting the information exceed the benefits?

An example of what can be involved is provided by Gulliver,[11] the former chief executive of Argyll Group, writing about the impact on Argyll of the Guinness affair and the battle to acquire Distillers.

"My team went back 15 years with the Distillers accounts and up to ten years with the principal trading subsidiaries. With a total of about 80 trading subsidiaries we were able to prepare a group consolidation which gave us a good feel for the contribution of individual profit centres. In addition, we scrutinised analysts' reports and trade and financial press cuttings back to the 1960s. Drink industry reports were obtained, and independent market research on Distillers' products were commissioned on the pretext of Argyll examining new market opportunities. We also looked at its industrial relations.

"Finally we made a pavement inspection of Distillers' properties. After checking trade directories and *Yellow Pages*, a small team photographed and produced a report on every Distillers' property we could find."

Legitimate sources of information are summarised in Fig. 10.14. Many of these are self evident, but there are one or two less obvious sources which are worth special mention.

Types of Initiative	Examples
1. Library research	Annual reports Press/journal material Investment analysts' reports Government reports Published market intelligence Company literature Company history Academic case studies Computer-based information services Competitor advertising
2. Interviews–secondary sources	Investment analysis Journalists Academics Others with special knowledge
3. Direct contact	Visits to plants Trade associations
4. Conferences, etc.	Industry associations Industry conferences and seminars
5. Primary market research	Consumer surveys Trade(retail/wholesale) surveys Industrial market research Retail audits Diary panels
6. Sales analysis	Bids loss/gain analysis
7. Engineering/R & D	Product comparison
8. Soft information	Own managers Own sales staff

FIG. 10.14. Sources of information. (Reproduced from Hussey, D.E., *Introducing Corporate Planning*, 4th edition. Pergamon Press, Oxford, 1991.)

The thing to remember is that every organisation has to communicate: to shareholders, customers, employees and prospective employees, to certain officials, and in some cases to special interest groups that can affect its business. I find it worthwhile to think through the various ways in which a particular company may be doing this. If we take prospective employees the immediate and obvious source is recruitment advertisements. These may give information on new activities, through different skills being sort, new locations, expansion strategies, and in a few instances hard facts like "join our team of 25 applied psychologists", "all of the main UK banks use our systems", or "we manufacture in five locations round the world". Small snippets often help the jigsaw of miscellaneous information to fall into a pattern. Many companies also produce recruitment brochures, particularly if they recruit graduates. These brochures often provide information and insights that may not be published elsewhere, as do speeches to professional bodies or business schools.

The company newspaper or journal is often a very good source of information, and there are libraries which keep collections of this type of material. Of course it depends on the publication, and if it serves a purely social purpose, little will be gained. Often it provides explanations of policies, details of new ventures, and many other insights.

Shareholders receive information directly through annual reports, which can be a mine of good information. There is also indirect communication through press statements, speeches, and statements to investment analysts and journalists. To obtain the support of shareholders, it is often necessary for organisations to explain their strategies, and library searches or data base services are a good source of such information. The data bases may be particularly useful because they may include world wide reports. A company chairman may be called upon to give explanations in one country which are not reported in his or her home base.

Customers receive communication through sales literature, trade press announcements, advertisements and sales calls. The hard aspects of communication are usually easy to obtain: few companies will refuse to give a copy of their brochures when requested by a competitor, because they could easily be obtained by other means. Often original research is the only way to identify what the image is among customers of key competitors. In a bid situation much can be learned from failures as well as successes. I know of one organisation, who bid for about 80% of contracts in their market segments. By constructing a data base, which included information about who won the contract, and in most cases the price in which it was let, they had a source of hard information, capable of being analysed by geographical region, competitor, customer, influencers, and type and size of installation. The value of this in competitor analysis is self evident.

Patents have to be filed and may be a rich source of information, although they need to be scanned by appropriately qualified people. Information moves into the public domain as a result of special government enquiries.

Reverse engineering of products is often valuable to determine technical or other advantages, and also to calculate the costs of production.

Fuld[12] provides a number of examples of such sources of competitor analysis and how to make use of them.

There is always more information available than might at first be expected. Often the missing elements can be deducted from the parts of the picture that can be seen. One of my clients analysed their competitors. They then had somebody analyse their own organisation from published sources, and were amazed how much, of what was thought of as a confidential strategy, could be deduced by an intelligent analyst. But remember that strategy is not just what people say: it is what they do. For the most part actions such as a new product, concentration on a particular segment, or a geographical expansion produce evidence that can be observed, and measured in a way that is independent of any statements by competitors.

In the next chapter there is a case history of the application of industry and competitor analysis. This should help show the practical advantages of this type of analysis, and also the limitations that occur in any real-life situation.

References

1. Porter, M. E. *Competitive Strategy*, Free Press, New York, 1980.
2. Farmer, D. H. and Taylor, B. *Corporate Planning and Procurement*, Heinemann, London, 1975.
3. Crawshaw, H. S. "Strategic Analysis for the Information Industry", *Journal of Strategic Change*, Vol. 1, No. 1, 1992.
4. Prahalad, C. K. and Doz, Y. *The Multinational Mission*, Free Press, New York, 1987.
5. Goold, M. and Campbell, A. *Strategies and Styles*, Blackwell, Oxford, 1987.
6. McGee, J. and Thomas, H. "Strategic Groups and Intra-Industry competition", Hussey, D. E. (ed.), *International Review of Strategic Management*, Vol. 3, Wiley, Chichester, 1992.
7. McNamee, P. and McHugh, M. "The Group Competitive Intensity Map", Hussey, D. E. (ed.), *International Review of Strategic Management*, Vol. 1, Wiley, Chichester, 1990.
8. Porter, M. E. *Competitive Advantage*, Free Press, New York, 1985.
9. Hussey, D. E. "A Glossary of Management Techniques", Hussey, D. E. (ed.), *International Review of Strategic Management*, Vol. 3, Wiley, Chichester, 1992.
10. Karlöff, B. Strategisk Precision, Affärsvärlden Förlag AB, Stockholm, 1991. (Note an English edition will be published by Wiley in 1993 under the title *Strategic Precision*.)
11. Gulliver, J. "How Scotland Lost Out to Back-street Hammersmith", *The Times*, 31st August 1990.
12. Fuld, L. M. *Competitor Intelligence*, Wiley, New York, 1987.

Appendix to Chapter 10
Outline Questionnaire

1. Definition of Industry

1.1. How would you define the industry in which you operate (by product and services)?

1.2. What is your definition of the relevant geographical scope of your industry? (You may find it important to analyse more than one geographical area, grouping regions with similar product life cycles, competitors or Government policies.)

1.3. Is your activity directed at a definable market segment or segments? What are these?

1.4. What is the approximate size of the market(s)?

1.5. What is the range of profits for your industry (in terms of ROCE)? Are they

above average for all British* industry ☐

average ☐

below average for all British* industry. ☐

1.6. How stable are the profits in your industry?

	Year to Year	Within a Year
Very stable	☐	☐
Stable	☐	☐
Unstable	☐	☐

2. Competition

2.1. *As the number of competitors increases, or as they become more equal in size and power there is a tendency for growing contention in the industry.*

This questionnaire was designed to facilitate analysis of an industry. It should be modified for the characteristics of the industry being studied, and is particularly useful for a company which operates in several industries. The design of the questionnaire means that it collects the information in a way that enables both industry and portfolio analysis to be undertaken. © Harbridge Consulting Group Ltd. Used with permission.

---

*Amend according to relevant geographical area.

2.1.1. List the competitors in the industry by major segment (as defined) (including your firm) with approximate market shares and position description (defined below):

Competitor   Market Share   Position Description

Position Description—use the description which best fits each firm:

Leader   a company which by virtue of its market position is likely to be followed by others in pricing.

Major   the position where no one firm is a leader, but where a number of approximately equal dominance.

Minor
Negligible

(Note: these definitions are based on those used in the Directional Policy Matrix, a portfolio analysis tool originally developed by Shell Chemicals).

2.1.2. Which word best describes the type of competition in your industry?

friendly □	gentlemanly □	polite □
bitter □	warlike □	fierce □
cut-throat □		

2.2.   *Contention increases as growth rates slow*

2.2.1. Which phase of the life cycle characterises your industry and your products?*

	Industry	Your Products
Introduction	□	□
Take-Off	□	□
Slow Down	□	□
Maturity	□	□
Decline	□	□

2.2.2. What rate of market growth (in volume terms) occurs in your industry?

% p.a.

Last five years   ....

Forecast next five years   ....

2.3.   *Rivalry increases where fixed costs are high, efficient increments to capacity are large, or external factors lead to recurring or chronic excess capacity.*

2.3.1. What is the approximate percentage of fixed costs to total costs in your industry?

....

2.3.2. What is the lead time required to increase capacity?

....

*Refer to Fig. 10.3.

2.3.3. What is your estimate of current utilisation of capacity? (Normal shifts)

%

Your industry as a whole   ....

Your firm   ....

2.3.4. Are periods of chronic excess capacity a characteristic of your industry?

....

2.3.5. Are margins maintained when capacity exceeds demand?

....

2.4   *Competition increases when the product is perishable or difficult or costly to store.*
        (Note: an air-line ticket, a consultancy service, and a banana are examples of very
        different perishable products).

2.4.1. Does your industry fall under these categories?
        Perishable   ☐
        Difficult to store ☐
        Costly to store   ☐

2.5   *Contention increases the more standardised the product and the less differentiated it is in the
        eyes of the buyer, reaching a peak as it nears commodity status.*

2.5.1. How do the buyers view the products in the industry?
        Standardised/Interchangeable   ☐
        Substitutes   ☐
        Differentiated   ☐
        Requiring a major change (e.g. engineering,formulation,
        or manufacturing process) if products changed   ☐

2.5.2. Does pricing behaviour in the industry suggest that the industry regards its products
        as standardised?

        _____

        _____

        (Note: these questions may need to be considered separately for different market
        segments).

2.6.   Competition becomes more unpredictable as firms in the industry develop different
        'personalities' or when recent entrants have different historical origins and ignore the
        'norms' of industry behaviour.*

2.6.1. How would you describe the firms in your industry?
        Club or fraternity (homogeneous interests)   ☐
        Tend to act according to the unwritten "rules" ☐
        Little common interest   ☐
        Irrational in behaviour   ☐

*Note: A similar change may occur when a chief executive changes.

2.6.2. Are the firms in the industry long established, or have there been recent entrants to the industry whose values and objectives appear to be different?

_____

_____

_____

_____

_____

2.6.3. Are there one or more "mavericks" in the industry who regularly upset the industry?

....

3. Suppliers

3.1.   *(a) Industry profits may be reduced when the bargaining power of the suppliers of the major items increases. This will happen as a supplier industry becomes less competitive.*
(b) The bargaining power of suppliers tends to reduce if the purchasing industry is highly concentrated.

3.1.1.   What is the ratio of suppliers to industry forms for each of the most important supplies?

3.1.2.   To what extent are the most important supplies:

Standardised/Interchangeable ☐

Substitutes ☐

Differentiated ☐

Tied to the industry through particular processes, plant, etc.
(e.g. if the firm changed, its supplier would have to modify ☐
its product, manufacturing process, etc.)

3.2.   *(a) Suppliers will tend to try to influence the growth of the purchasing industry when it accounts for a large proportion of the total output of the supplying industry.*
(b) The availability of competing substitute products will tend to reduce the power of suppliers and increase purchasing industry profitability.

3.2.1.   To what extent are the supplier industries dependent on the sales of your industries?

_____

_____

_____

3.3.   *Suppliers may increase their bargaining power if they can demonstrate a credible threat to integrate forward.*

3.3.1.   List any suppliers which have integrated forwards in the industry:

_____

_____

_____

(Note: backwards integration is covered in Question 3.4)

3.3.2. How does profitability in your industry compare with those in your suppliers' industries? (If higher, the threat of integration is increased, since the supplier will tend to judge the investment opportunity against his present returns).

(Note: this is not the only factor they will consider—opportunity cost of capital is also important.)

Rates of return:

Very much higher   ☐

Higher   ☐

The same   ☐

A little lower   ☐

Considerably lower   ☐

3.3.3. Is the volume of business in the hands of any one supplier sufficient to justify their operation in your industry? (That is, sales volume in relation to efficient scale of operations).

....

3.3.4. Could the supplier obtain any economies by integrating?

....

3.3.5. Consider the barriers to integration.

3.3.6. Does the industry act as a barrier to thwart suppliers' technical innovations and new products?

....

3.4. *On the other hand the purchasing industry can reduce the power of the suppliers if it can offer a credible threat to integrate backwards.*

3.4.1. List any firms in the industry which have integrated backwards.

_____

_____

_____

_____

3.4.2. Are the entry barriers to backward integration high or low?

....

4. Buyers

4.1. *The availability to increase prices is reduced when the buying industry has a low value added.*

4.1.1. How significant is the value added at each stage in the industry, e.g.

	Very High	High	Medium	Low	Very Low
Supplier					
Industry					
Buyer					

4.2.   *(a) The power of the buyer is higher the more it is dominated by powerful customers, the fewer the number of buying firms, and the greater their percentage purchases from the industry.*
(b) The power of the buyer decreases as the industry becomes more concentrated.

4.2.1. What is the percentage of industry firms to buying firms?

....

4.2.2. Is the market dominated by a small group of powerful customers?

....

4.2.3. What percentage of sales goes to each of the various categories of buyer:

Category   Industry   Your Firm

4.3.   *The power of buyers is reduced by a credible threat of forward integration by the industry: it is increased by a credible threat of backwards integration by the buyers.*

4.3.1. List any firms in the industry who have integrated forward.

_____

_____

_____

4.3.2. List any buyers who have integrated backwards.

_____

_____

_____

4.3.3. Are there any significant economic advantages in integration?

_____

_____

_____

4.3.4. Does the volume of business justify the buyer considering operation in the industry (i.e. sales volume in relation to efficient scale of operations)? Or vice versa?

Backwards by buyer   ....

Forwards by industry   ....

4.3.5. How does profitability of the buyer firms compare with that of the industry?

Higher   ☐
Same   ☐
Lower   ☐

4.4.   *As buyers become more experienced, normally as a market matures, they may exercise more influence over the profitability of suppliers.*

4.4.1. What proportion of business (by each main category of buyers), is by competitive tender?

_____

_____

_____

4.4.2. How effective are the buyers in imposing their standards on you and your competitors?

_____

_____

_____

4.4.3. What is the nature of the buying decision process in the main categories of buyers?

_____

_____

_____

4.4.4. Please describe the nature and importance of firms which may influence the buying decision, but who are not themselves buyers.

_____

_____

_____

5. New Entries: Exits

Some of the factors which make an industry attractive to new entrants have already been covered: profitability, growth, degree of competition etc. In addition there might be added a lack of entry and exit barriers.

5.1. _Entry barriers make it more difficult for an outsider to get into the industry._

5.1.1. Are economies of scale important in your industry, sufficient to ensure that new entrants have to make/set up a significant capacity at high capital cost in order to compensate?

....

5.1.2. Would vertical integration provide significant additional economies?

....

5.1.3. List any absolute cost advantages possessed by your firm and each of the major competitors.

Advantage	Competitor (Name)
Patents on products or processes	
Control of proprietary technology	
Control of raw materials	
Availability of low cost capital	
Experience	
Ownership of effective depreciated assets	

5.1.4. To what degree does each of the major competitors (including your firm) have a barrier of brand loyalty (product differentiation)?

5.1.5.   Does success in the industry require access to tied distribution networks (e.g. dealers in the motor car industry)?

Yes   ☐   No   ☐

Could a new entrant secure these?

Yes   ☐   No   ☐

5.1.6.   How would firms in the industry react to a new entrant?

5.1.7.   Do any of the following exit barriers exist in the industry?

Specialised, durable assets which have little resale value   ☐

High fixed costs associated with exit   ☐

Inter-relatedness with other businesses   ☐

6. Substitutes

6.1.   *The extent to which substitutes have been included in the analysis will depend on the definition of the industry. If current substitutes have been excluded, their industry should be subjected to an analysis similar to the foregoing.*

6.2.   What threats, if any, do you see from new substitutes?

7. Strategic Issues

What issues arise from the analysis?

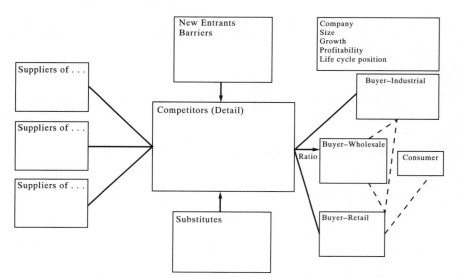

Note: This diagram should be drawn on A3 paper and used to summarise the findings from the questionnaire.

11

Analysing the UK Management
Development and Training Industry:
A Case History

Scope

Case histories of industry and competitor analysis are difficult to obtain, because of their confidential nature and because it is not always ethical to make public one's value judgements of competitors. In this chapter, I have tried to demonstrate the results of practical application of competitor analysis techniques using mainly real information. However, I have used simplified examples in some of the analytical displays, and where necessary for ethical reasons I have used fictitious exhibits, rather than disclosing my opinions of real competitors. Such exhibits have been reduced to a minimum and are included only where necessary to ensure understanding of the methods actually applied.

One of the difficulties of competitor analysis is knowing what information to obtain. The problem often varies between the extremes of having too little data for meaningful analysis and having so much that it becomes difficult to make sense of it. Once a decision has been taken on the information that is needed, the problem shifts to one of how to obtain it using legitimate and ethical methods. Finally, we reach the crunch issue of what to do with the information that we have collected.

The industry that I have chosen is one of two overlapping industries in which Harbridge Consulting Group operate. It is typical of many industries in that definition is difficult and there are hazy borders with related industries. It is also subject to certain international forces for change, although it is by no means a global industry. It is fragmented, and is unusual in having a mix of private- and public-sector competitors. Within the private sector, there are organisations that gain tax advantages from being registered as charities, although this means that they have to operate under certain rules. Among the other private-sector busi-

This chapter is a modification of an article of the same name which was published in Vol. 1, Number 4, *Journal of Strategic Change*.

nesses is a mix of one-person businesses, partnerships and limited companies. Like so many other industries, many competitors also have operations in other industries, making it difficult to interpret their results. Many aspects of our situation have echoes in other industries. It is a professional services business, although there is some competition from 'products' such as videos. Many of its characteristics would be recognised by other professional services businesses, such as solicitors, accountants and surveyors.

All the methodologies illustrated have relevance in other industries, and I have used them with clients from the whole spectrum of business activity.

The Outline Approach

Figure 11.1 shows the outline approach (this is a simplified version of Fig. 10.1), which we have been using continuously on this and other industries since the early 1980s, although some elements of our approach are even older. The analysis of information goes through four linked stages, which also helps to identify what information is required to enable meaningful analysis to take place.

All the information sources shown on the diagram have been used to a greater or lesser extent in applying these methods to various situations. In our own industry, data bases are less helpful than other sources of information, which is a reflection of the structure of the industry, the few quoted companies in the industry, the lack of published statistics and the relatively small size of most of the players.

Before going deeper into the methods that were used, I should like to explain the reasons for starting what became an increasingly detailed competitor analysis system.

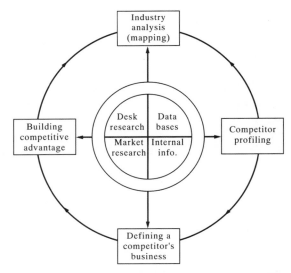

FIG. 11.1. Approach to competitor analysis. Copyright Harbridge Consulting Group Ltd. Reprinted with permission

In early 1980, we had virtually no information about our market in the United Kingdom (UK) or that of our competitors, which made strategic planning a hit or miss affair. The UK side of the firm had shown little or no growth for many years. It also followed the classic consultant's situation of basing a business on the skills of its professional staff and changing emphasis with the departure or engagement of every key employee. What we wanted to do was to position the firm in areas where we would build and sustain competitive advantage, to understand properly the pressures on the industry and to identify our real competitors from the 600 or so businesses that operate in the UK management training market. We wanted to improve our ability to plan, so that we could do at least as well as the best in growth years, and better than most in lean years. We wanted information that would enable us to speak authoritatively about all aspects of management development.

We had one additional reason, which is probably the only one that is not similar to that of any firm in any other industry contemplating competitor analysis. We needed a 'laboratory' in which we could try some of the concepts that we were developing for use with clients. What better laboratory was there than our own business, where we could be free from the restrictions of client confidentiality and develop examples that could be shared with others?

My advice to anyone starting competitor analysis is to think through the aims of the exercise first. Competitor analysis may be undertaken for many reasons and that for purely tactical purposes may take a different form from that for strategic reasons. Our intentions were mainly strategic, although as I shall show later, we did gain some tactical benefit. In addition, some types of analysis are best done as benchmark studies, rather than using the method shown here. If, for example, the need is to identify the best human resource management practice in the industry, how the best competitors are using information technology or what is being done about customer responsiveness, then a benchmark study would be a more appropriate approach.

Industry Mapping

A journey around the outer circle of Fig. 11.1 begins with what I see as the essential first step in competitor analysis: obtaining a detailed understanding of the competitive arena. To do this, we used the principles of Porter.[1] For our total strategic analysis, we set industry analysis within the context of the outside environment, as in Fig. 10.2, although for the purpose of this chapter I will not discuss environmental issues.

Our method explodes the supplier/competitor/buyer boxes of the 'five forces' model to mirror the total channel from the first link in the supply chain to the final consumer. The first task is to develop this in block diagram form, using knowledge of managers, logic and available market information. We tend to incorporate substitutes into this diagram if they are already significant or appear likely to become so. In addition, we analyse influencers of a buying action. In some industries, the influencers may do more to shape the competitive forces than the competitors themselves.

FIG. 11.2. Industry map—Management training and development

In theory, the development of such a block diagram should be easy. In practice, we find that many of our clients face difficulty, tending to draw diagrams that reflect their preconceived ideas or the elements of a channel that they use. When we began our journey towards useful competitor analysis, we found similar problems. We knew what we did and who some of our competitors were, but knew surprisingly little about buying decisions, substitute products or the overall structure of the industry. How we began to collect this information is discussed later, but the example that appears in Fig. 11.2 is the result of several analyses and is not the original.

As we began to develop our understanding, we were able to use the block diagram to record key information about the industry. Figure 11.2 gives a simplified view of our industry map. The main difference between this map and the real one is that the real map contains more competitor assessments, uses a personal system of abbreviations and includes more analysis of the buying decision.

Figures 11.3 and 11.4 show our assessment of the evolution of the market for the type of service that we provide.

These three diagrams, supported by the additional information that I have omitted for simplification or sensitivity reasons, provide the basis for a detailed strategic evaluation using Porter's[1] principles. Before I discuss a few of these findings, I should like to mention two decisions that we had to make about the arena that we were charting.

There were good reasons for studying the UK as the geographical area, and much of the market is still local to the UK. However, like most industries there is an international dimension. Recently we have explored this in more detail, in particular researching other countries in Europe and, of course, having access to information about the United States of America through our parent company. These findings have had a profound influence on our strategy, although including the detail of the analysis would expand this chapter to book length.

The second decision centred on the problem of industry definition. Figure 11.5 highlights some of the issues. The provision and delivery of management training and development services sounds a neat industry.

	1985	1989	1990	£M 1991
Open public subscription	45	60	55	40
Closed in-company	75	145	150	123
Company MBA scheme	-	4	7	7
Open/distance	10	30	33	30
Consultancy/research	26	50	55	50
	156	289	300	250

FIG. 11.3. UK market for management development and training. Copyright Harbridge Consulting Group Ltd. Reprinted with permission

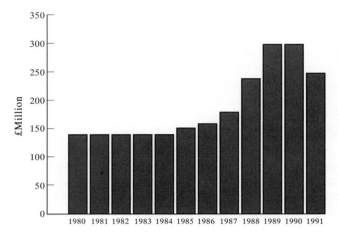

FIG. 11.4. Management training market: professional fees, etc. Copyright Harbridge Consulting Group Ltd. Reprinted with permission

However, the suppliers to it, of which a few are illustrated in the figure, are frequently engaged in related businesses. This has at least two implications: how statistical information is collated; and the gradual merging of some of the activities outside the circle with those inside it. For example, the Management Consultancies Association publishes statistics on the consultancy industry. In their figures is included a sector that covers management training. Users of these statistics might be tempted to think that this covers the output of the management training industry. But this is not so; such data excludes the activities of the other providers as not only are they not members of the association but most of them are not eligible to be members. Similarly, government frequently looks at the industry as if it was supplied only by academic institutions (which in the UK are mainly in the public sector), and often speaks of

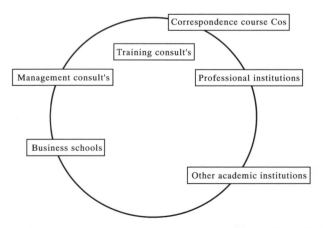

FIG. 11.5. How industries overlap in the management training and development industry. Copyright Harbridge Consulting Group Ltd. Used with permission

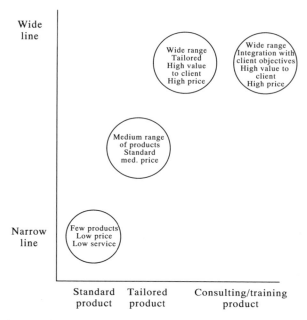

Wide
line

Narrow
line

Wide range
Tailored
High value
to client
High price

Wide range
Integration with
client objectives
High value to
client
High price

Medium range
of products
Standard
med. price

Few products
Low price
Low service

Standard   Tailored   Consulting/training
product   product   product

FIG. 11.6. Strategic groupings: a hypothetical example from the training industry. The terms low and high are relative to each other and do not imply that one is "better" than another. Copyright Harbridge Consulting Group Ltd. Reprinted with permission

total UK training when it actually means non-managerial training. The private sector holds a larger market share of the management training market than does the public sector, even before we count the in-house training activities of the 'buyers'.

The related activities of providers change the dimensions of the circle. Three examples clarify this statement:

(i) As management consultants, we frequently combine consultancy and training skills to produce a solution for clients that broadens the traditional use of training and lies both inside and outside the circle. It is indeed one of the areas of differentiation that we seek.

(ii) Academic qualifications moved into the industry when business schools began to offer tailored MBA degrees to individual companies and consortia of companies. An additional twist is that we run courses for two clients that are accredited by two different business schools towards their MBA degrees.

(iii) Distance learning has been a growth sector of the industry. Not surprisingly, some of the traditional correspondence schools have developed products that compete in the industry, and organisations such as the Open University offer their products to corporate customers, as well as to private individuals.

From what I have said, it is apparent that the boundary of the industry, even as defined, is constantly changing. It is also apparent that different views could be based quite logically on the actual boundaries of the industry. This suggests a need for careful study of some of the key competitors, including some with whom we do not compete directly, to identify the directions in which they could move and which would change the shape of the market in which we compete.

Interpreting the Industry Analysis

It would be boring to most readers if I offered a full interpretation of the industry map. What I should like to give is enough of a description of some of the findings to carry the case study along, to help later when we look at how the information was obtained and to make the value of such industry maps a little clearer. All the points that I mention are strategically important to us and have been used in formulating our own strategies.

(i) The industry is fragmented. There are numerous competitors, no one organisation has more than a 10% market share (although shares are higher in specific segments), and there are numerous buyers.

(ii) There are no universal patterns by which the buyers organise their management training activity. It is not possible to look at an organisation from the outside and predict whether management training is centralised, decentralised or a mix of both; or to identify the level at which management development decisions are taken, how much training is performed or what proportion is undertaken by the organisation's own staff.

(iii) Entry barriers to the industry in general are low, but few new entrants are able to grow into significant competitors, although an exception is when the new entrant is a spin-off from an existing competitor. Barriers are much higher in some segments than in others.

(iv) Not only do most buyers undertake a proportion of their management training with their own resources, but a number effectively become competitors by offering their services to other organisations.

(v) In addition to the sectors shown on the map, there are numerous segments. Competitors can be grouped roughly into those who offer a 'commodity' product, and those who are highly differentiated and who support their activities with proprietary approaches. For example, we do not compete with most of the 600 organisations in the UK management training market, and the number of competitors in our chosen segments usually varies between 1 and 20. The story would be very different if we were at the commodity end of the spectrum, and I suspect that we would be a much smaller firm.

(vi) There are 'switching' costs, although they are not large enough to hold a dissatisfied buyer. The nature of these costs is that only differentiated competitors are likely to benefit from them.

(vii) The product is perishable in that much of what is offered is time based. Yesterday's unused consultancy time has no resale value.

(viii) Interesting issues surround the way that most buyers make their buying decisions. Management development/training departments are controlled through budgets that measure the costs of training rather than the benefits. Not surprisingly actions follow what the system appears to demand, and most buyers would rather save £500 in the costs of an initiative (on which they are measured), than spend an extra £500 in order to gain an additional £10,000 of benefit from training (on which they are not measured).

(ix) Many relationships between competitor and client exist at the personal level, with the advantages and disadvantages that this suggests. The key for an organisation that wishes to grow is to add a parallel relationship between the consultancy and client organisations, while not destroying personal relationships.

(x) As the range of subjects and methods within management training is so great, there is always an opportunity to innovate. The cost of concept development is a growth barrier to the independent one-person business.

All this can be summed up in the statement that 600 competitors are not frightening if you can take strategic actions that result in your competing with a manageable number. The opportunities to add value are very great, and the more that this is done the greater the distance the differentiated firm can gain over the bulk of the competitors.

The purists might query whether all of these conclusions could have been read from the example of the industry map presented here. As it is abridged, some could not have been read off this map, although more can be seen from the originals that we use ourselves. However, all conclusions could have been reached through the exercise of completing the map, while the mapping process itself throws up areas where the 'facts' do not make sense, shows clearly where there is a lack of knowledge and often helps missing information to be arrived at by logical deduction.

Profiling Competitors

From what has been said so far, it is clear that we do not have to study 600 competitors in detail. Many can be grouped, as they behave in roughly the same way. Figure 11.6 shows some of our thinking on competitor groupings in this industry. This diagram could be expanded by adding the dimension of type of ownership, as public-sector organisations, for example, have very different ways of operating from those of private-sector firms.

More ideas on competitor groupings are given in McGee and Thomas,[2] McNamee[3] and Porter.[1]

Currently, we keep tabs on about 120 competitors. This includes the 20 or so that are most significant to us, a number of which have the capability of becoming more significant, and enough of the others so that we have a feel for the total situation. We do not keep information on any sole practitioner.

When we started the exercise, we had very little idea of who our competitors

Financial Results

	Group	Super Consult Ltd						Division Training				Unit			
	19XIV	19XV	19XX	19XI	19XD	19XV	19XIII	19XII	19XI	19XD	YR	YR	YR	YR	YR
Sales £M	100	91	87	80	75	65	61	50	40	15					
PDT £M	100	8	8	7	5										
PAT															
RDA															
ROS															
Prof Impl No	85	80	80	80	75										
Fees per Prof	118	114	109	107											

Product Analysis

Product	Sales				Direct Costs				Contribution				Market Share			
	19XV	19XIII	19XII	YR	YR	YR	YR	YR	YR	YR	19XIV	YR	YR			
1. Tailored £M	5	2												1%		
2. Other In Co £M	30	25	20											1%		
3. Public Courses £M	30	34	30											5%		
4.																
5.																
6.																
7.																
8.																

Marketing and Sales Activity

1. Quarterly newsletter
2. Regular exhibits
3. Regular promotional seminars
4. Monthly direct mail campaign

Sources of Competitive Advantage

SOURCES	NOTES
Infra structure	
R & D	
Logistics In	
Operations	Own printing facility
Logistics Out	Mainly use own staff for delivery
Marketing	
Sales	Specialist sales force
Services	Strong customer service orientation

Importance of Activity to Group

Super Consult is:

10% of UWS Revenue
7% of UWS Profit

Growing twice as fast as the whole group

Scope of International Operations

Total group is strong in North America, UK, Singapore. Weak in the rest of Europe and other S. East Asian countries

Key Factors

1. Own training college
2. Offers training (Management) in all European languages
3. Ties into world network
4. New CEO's in parent and SuperConsult. Watch for changes
5. Clients from bottom half of Times 1000 and similar European companies
6. Prices at high end of their sectors

Strengths	Weaknesses
1. Reputation in standardised training and open courses	1. Not well known among larger Co's who buy tailored work
2. Strong financial backing but parent Co wants dividend growth	2. Employs the wrong people for tailored work
	3. High staff turnover

Implications

Could solve all problems but corporate cash box only available for quick return prospects

Implications

Strategy may be defeated by HR issues

CSF Ratings

Factor	Comp-petitor	Own	Index
Quality Image	6	9	67
	8	6	133
Quality of Staff	6	9	67
	5	5	100
Financial Resources	6	4	200

Notes
Assess each factor 0-10 Index is
COMPETITOR SCORE
————————————
OWN SCORE

Apparent Strategy

1. Targeting tailored training market
2. Developing new products (recent advert for development personnel)
3. Will not expand UK college
4. Expected to open French college 19XV
5. Major expansion of continental client base

Organization Philosophy

Historically country companies have all reported to US parent

Recent announcements suggest a change to a more global approach

Do not use external associates employees only

Personnel Policies

Professional staff have degrees or professional qualifications. Recent adverts seek post graduate degrees.

Salaries at academic scales plus profit sharing. Some difficulty recruiting.

No equity participation. A quoted US company.

Fig. 11.7. Competitor profile: Super Consult Ltd (Subsidiary of World Consulting Services). Copyright Harbridge Consulting Group Ltd.

were. This may sound surprising to someone who is used to a typical industry structure where there are clear market leaders, but less so I suspect to someone from a similar fragmented professional services market. The steps that we took to find out will be discussed later.

It took 2–3 years from our first researches to develop profiles in the form illustrated in Fig. 11.7 . The profile shown is a fictitious example, but I have tried to make it realistic by not completing every information cell. Complete information on any competitor is very rare. What the profile shows is where the competitor gains its revenue and a series of note pads for recording strategic information, focusing on what really matters when we formulate our own strategies. Note-pad items were explained in Chapter 10.

What this profiling has done for us is to provide more discipline to our collection of information. It has given us the opportunity to deduce missing parts of the jigsaw puzzle, provided a means of storing information in an easily retrievable way and given us a series of documents that, with the industry map, allow us to survey a vast array of information painlessly when making our own plans. It has become easier for us to identify firms in the industry where collaboration is possible and to pinpoint appropriate competitors who we would recommend to clients (strange as it might seem, this happens, and if we are making a recommendation we like to be sure that we are pointing the client to the right people).

While we have by no means reached perfection in our profiling, and still tend to update our records in blitzes, rather than as a continuous process, we have been able to develop a much better understanding of our industry map through this additional work.

We have also been able to draw up some very useful generic comparisons of strengths and weaknesses between ourselves and different competitor groups (for example, business schools), while understanding the individual differences within each competitor group. In a fragmented market, it is more useful to find a strategy that builds advantages over the majority of competitors, rather than trying to beat each one singly. Products, image and philosophies that result from this exercise have to stand the test of the market.

Defining a Competitor's Business

Some of the original thinking about business definition comes from Abell,[4] who suggested plotting businesses on a three-dimensional chart showing customer functions, customer groups and alternative technologies. Many variations on these themes are possible, and indeed one could delve much deeper into the literature on segmentation to develop the ideas further.

We used simpler matrix displays, which helped to show the difference between ourselves and other organisations in a diagrammatic way. Figure 11.8 shows some of the actual charts that we made, although I have taken off the names. These made us realise the considerable difference in focus of business that we had seen as roughly comparable to ourselves. Some, although of high standing and quality, do

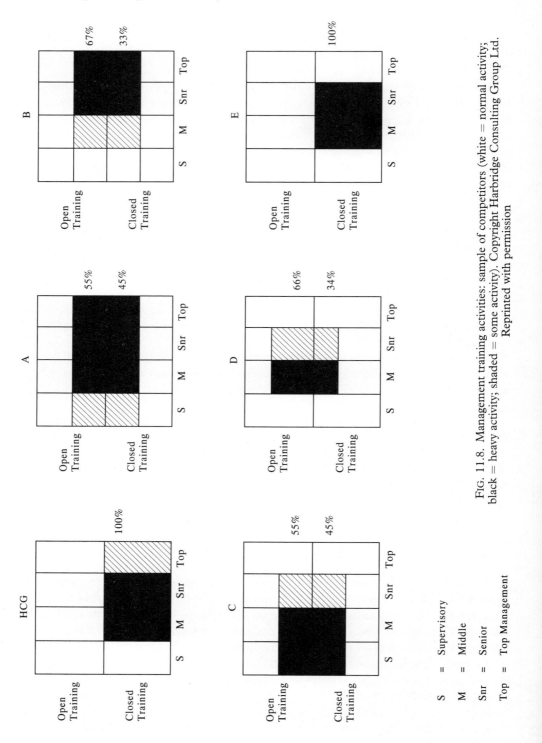

FIG. 11.8. Management training activities: sample of competitors (white = normal activity; black = heavy activity; shaded = some activity). Copyright Harbridge Consulting Group Ltd. Reprinted with permission

S   =   Supervisory

M   =   Middle

Snr =   Senior

Top =   Top Management

Date	Published information	Unpublished information
1983	Management training in UK companies	
1984	MBA and UK industry	
1985		Competitor study
1986	Tailored management education	
1986	Distance learning	
1987		Competitor information project
1988		Innovation training
1988		Management skills
1989	Consortium/Co MBAs	Management training Europe part 1
1989		Management training Europe part 2
1989		Hotel/study centres
1990		Competitor update
1991	Management training in large UK companies	
1993	Management training in medium sized UK companies	
1993	Management development in Germany	

FIG. 11.9. Primary research undertaken by us for the analysis.
("Published" means published by us.)

not really compete with us at all, although we still monitor them because they may change!

In a less fragmented industry, I would have spent further time on this more detailed type of analysis; however, the number of competitors, and their low-market shares, means that the value of going deeper than we have is questionable.

Obtaining the Information

None of this analysis would have been possible if we had been unable to obtain any information. In the beginning, the task was daunting and it would have been easy to decide that nothing could be done as the information was too sparse. In the early years, desk research yielded negligible information, because little was published at that time. This meant that we had to consider primary research if we were to obtain any information at all. Our first major competitor study was undertaken in 1985, and this set a foundation that helped us to make sense of information from other sources. After that time, there was an increase in the number of published research studies, which meant that our information became more complete.

Our first piece of research into the market was completed in 1983. This was not, at that time, intended to help us follow the competitor analysis approach described in this chapter, but was the first of a series of reports that we have carried out into management development and training to increase our knowledge of the 'state of the art' and to gain marketing information. Most of these reports are published so that they can be shared with other interested parties, and although they have contributed greatly to our understanding of buyer behaviour and awareness of changing needs and responses, they are not primarily market research reports.

In 1985, we undertook two inter-related pieces of research. We wanted to find out whether the market for our type of training was expanding. Were we getting our fair share of the growth? What were the factors that the buyers considered when choosing a supplier?

We knew many of our competitors, but did we know them all? There was a great gap between the ones that we could list and the columns of names shown in directories. Who were the competitors who might be considered to be most critical to our future? Who did the buyers think were our competitors, and who did our competitors think were their most serious rivals? We wanted to know if we were competitive in price, quality, speed of response to the client and in our overall philosophies. And we wanted to answer the same questions for each major competitor. From this, our first intention was to prepare a market-related assessment of our strengths and weaknesses, compared with those of competitors.

A sample survey was conducted by telephone of 43 buyers of our type of training service, exploring aspects of all the research objectives. We interviewed on a personal visit nine major competitors, building up our list of real competitors from information supplied by buyers and competitors. We were able to check most of the information provided by competitors from the interviews with buyers. All this research was done honestly and openly by one of our consultants.

The information from this survey provided the base from which we could build and develop on the lines already discussed, and led to immediate tactical and strategic decisions. Meanwhile, we continued to add more valuable data from our research for publication and focused some of this on areas of the industry map, which were hitherto blank. We published a report on distance learning, for example, in 1986, and another in late 1989 on consortium and company MBAs. Although not part of the published report, this survey enabled us to quantify the size of this sector of the market.

In 1987, we used an MBA student to build up the files of competitor information, which we had started to compile. This involved collecting brochures from competitors, annual reports (where available) and press cuttings. In addition, we established our first data base, using an earlier format of competitor profile. We did the usual searches at Companies' House, and probably bored the Charity Commissioners with our complaints about competitors who were registered as charities and who had not lodged their returns for several years.

Most of this activity is typical of competitor analysis generally. Three activities that yielded useful information were:

(i). Continued direct contact with competitors, including the exchange of information that would be in the annual report if we were all public limited companies. The competitor analysis system that we have built up means that there is somewhere to put the results of all these formal and informal comments, as well as information that comes to us about a competitor from elsewhere in the industry.

(ii) Obtaining feedback from clients when there is a pre-qualifying exercise or a competitive bid (whether we win or lose). This has been an invaluable source of information. On occasion, buyers have prepared an analysis of all the bidders that they have been willing to share.

(iii) Helping journalists to write about the industry and suggesting who they should approach for the collection of data for league tables. In this way, we filled several gaps in our own information, especially as a few firms who had refused to exchange information with us on the grounds of confidentiality did not have the same inhibitions when it was a question of gaining publicity.

Published information and market intelligence have become more important since 1987. Several studies have been completed, which when supplemented by our own studies have enabled us to quantify the sectors on our industry map. There is still no sound statistical base for the industry, but the combination of all of our sources means that we believe that our estimates are as accurate as they need to be for the type of decisions that have to be made.

In 1989, we reworked our competitor data base, and now store information in a form similar to that of the profiles in this article. We had hopes of creating a dynamic data base that would enable us to update the industry map automatically every time a competitor profile was updated. This is not economic at present. We have also done some concept work with an information house to develop something similar for more general use, but commercial prospects are not right.

The main conclusion that can be reached from our work is that a competitor analysis system will improve over time if continuous effort is applied, that even small pieces of information can be co-ordinated and used if there is a mechanism to handle them and that lack of published information about an industry and competitors may make analysis harder, but need not prevent it.

We have begun to extend the scope of our study to other countries in Europe and have spent more effort on identifying organisations that we can build alliances with, rather than undertaking a complete competitor analysis.

Building Competitive Advantage

None of this analysis is worthwhile unless it leads to actions. The sort of strategic and tactical actions that we took may give an indication of the benefits that readers might obtain from competitor analysis.

(i)   We identified much more clearly where we could gain differentiation, and where there were market segments where we could gain clear advantage.

(ii) As a result, one of the things that we did was to build our geographical and language capability, so that through our own resources or alliances with other organisations, we are able to run the same course for a multi-national company in every Western European language. This is especially important when the course is intended to support a European-wide strategy by the client.

(iii) We started many new initiatives to build image and awareness, including our regular publication *Management Training Update* (10 issues per year and free to management development and human resources personnel). We redesigned all our stationery and literature to achieve a common image.

(iv) A strategy was developed for operations in other countries in Europe.

(v)   Several different products and concepts were developed.

(vi) The growth of in-company MBA schemes made us seek to become better informed about what was happening, and to find ways in which our work could gain academic accreditation in certain circumstances, without in any way losing our commercial image for that of a pseudo business school.

At the tactical level, we are now able to identify more accurately those competitors who are significant for different types of assignments, and their respective strengths and weaknesses. Even when we do not know who else has been asked to bid, this helps us to plan our own proposals and presentations in a way that emphasises our advantages.

We redesigned our basic approach to proposal writing, so that our strengths, in so far as they were appropriate to the assignment, were presented in such a way as to invite the client to probe to see whether other bidders also possessed them. Our research had shown significant areas where we knew that many of the competitors likely to be asked to bid did not possess similar strengths. Almost immediately after completing our 1985 competitor study, we had opportunities to apply these tactical concepts and won two major assignments on competitive bids in quick succession. We have been fortunate in developing strong relationships with both clients, and continue to run major management training programmes for them.

Our strategy has helped us to grow faster than the market since the mid 1980s, and our concepts of industry and competitor analysis have helped us to develop these strategies. Add this to the benefits that our clients gain from similar approaches, and the value of competitor analysis becomes clear. However, it is not without cost and anyone thinking of undertaking it needs to decide whether they are looking for a one-off injection of competitor data into their strategy formulation or they wish to set up a continuing system. Both need dedication of effort, and the continuing system needs some attention to organisation and resources.

In either case, and whether the aim of competitor analysis is tactical or strategic, the only justification for the costs and effort is the action that results from the new knowledge. I hope that this case history has given some indication of the benefits, as well as a methodology, of competitor analysis and that it shows that an initial lack of competitor information can sometimes be overcome.

References

1. Porter, M. *Competitive Strategy,* Free Press, New York, 1980.
2. McGee, J. and Thomas, H. "Strategic Groups and Intra-industry Competition", Hussey, D. E. (ed.), *International Review of Strategic Management*, Vol. 3. John Wiley & Sons, Ltd., Chichester, 1992.
3. McNamee, P. "The group competitive intensity map: a means of displaying competitive position", Hussey, D. E. (ed.), *International Review of Strategic Management*, Vol. 1, John Wiley & Sons, Ltd., Chichester, 1990.
4. Abell, D. *Defining and Business*, Prentice Hall, Englewood Cliffs, New Jersey, 1980.

12

The Search for Shareholder Value

In the next chapter we will explore some concepts of objectives, which may be important both in the formulation and implementation of strategy. In order to do this topic justice we need first to explore some of the modern ideas about creating shareholder value. This is an important concept and the treatment given here will be partly about strategic concepts, and partly about ways of measurement which can be incorporated into objectives. The second part will be illustrated with some examples of how certain British companies are applying concepts of value based strategy, drawing on research conducted by my colleague Sylvia Handler[1] and published by Harbridge Consulting Group Ltd. I am grateful for permission to use this material, and indeed for the existence of the research which means that I can support a description of the theory with some examples of practice.

Some Concepts of Strategy

Supporters of value based strategy believe that the creation of value is measurable, using discounted cash flow concepts. This will be the second part of the chapter. It is a truism to say that some strategic decisions made by organisations add to the value of the shareholders' investment, while others reduce it. When Hansen bought Imperial Foods it paid £2.1 billion. Within a few months it had sold the brewing interests for £1.4 billion. Other disposals and cost reductions left Hansen with a very profitable cash generating tobacco company, after it had regained most of the purchase price from the disposals. There is no doubt that Hansen added to the value of its shareholders. There is also no doubt that on the stock market the perception was that Imperial as a whole was worth less than the sum of its parts, an example of the so called "conglomerate discount" on share prices. Decisions taken in the past by Imperial did not add as much to shareholder value as decisions taken by the acquirer. More recently another organisation with mixed interests became the subject of a hostile bid. In this case an organisation was established by various interests to mount a bid for BAT, which at that time was involved in insurance, tobacco, retailing, and various manufacturing interests. BAT split off many of its interests, effectively creating separate entities in which its shareholders could choose whether they wished to retain their investment or sell it. BAT became a two industry business, with more focus, and less suspicion that good businesses might be propping up bad ones. The bid failed.

These examples lead to the conclusion that although shareholder value is created when returns on old assets and new investments exceed the cost of capital, in a diversified organisation there has to be something that increases the overall value, so that there is synergy. In the examples given there was a reduction of value of businesses through being bound together in a group. This raises the question: how do diversified companies create value?

Figure 12.1 shows five ways in which diversified companies can affect shareholder value. The chart is derived from ideas from three sources: Goold and Campbell,[2] Porter,[3] and Buzzell and Gale.[4]

Shared resources or activities between components of a company offer one way to increase shareholder value. An example might be a distribution system which is used by all the SBUs, which because of overall size offers real economies of scale. In addition because total costs are shared among all users, the cost for each may be lower than if they all had to provide such a facility. Purchasing, research and development, and sometimes management development are other examples where value may be added by sharing. Such sharing sometimes offers increased potential for differentiation. However there are also dangers of dis-economies from sharing activities, particularly from loss of flexibility and the advantage of time through increased bureaucracy. Central purchasing and supplies gone mad has, for example, resulted in situations where a replacement light bulb could only be obtained from a central warehouse some miles away. An organisation has to sift the evidence very carefully in order to ensure that the value gained is real.

FIG. 12.1. How diversified organisations create value. Copyright Harbridge Consulting Group Ltd. Used with permission

Related to shared resources are the spill over benefits that may be gained between SBUs from activities undertaken by any one of them. This may create windfall gains for the other divisions. For example Buzzell and Gale[4] state that GE's research in turbine engines helped its aircraft engine business. GE, under Jack Welch, have periodically combined SBUs under a common sector management when it appears that there should be spill over benefits which are not being realised.

The third area on Fig. 12.1 is shared knowledge and skills. Buzzell and Gale[4] found from the analysis of the PIMS data base that clusters of businesses in similar environments have been found to out-perform clusters of dissimilar businesses. Knowledge and skills, whether technical, managerial or commercial can be passed from one business to another, thus improving performance in a way that might otherwise not have happened. Porter[3] set three criteria:

(i) The shared matter must be meaningful.
(ii) It must be in activities which are key to success.
(iii) It must give a real advantage to the receiving unit.

Buzzel and Gale found that SBUs could benefit from a shared image. A good reputation of one SBU could spin over into sister businesses. In particular bad businesses gain from association with good businesses. However this is not without penalty, because the bad business can drag down the performance of good businesses.

The final area of investigation has been touched on in Chapter 3 when we looked at the styles of planning identified by Goold and Campbell. Part of the reason for this research was to establish how the corporate centre could add value. The modern trend has been to reduce the size of the centre, and to return tasks to the businesses, eliminating duplication and delays. Some of the frustration caused by some head offices in the past is reflected in the name given by all subsidiaries of one of my clients to the person charged at head office with the tasks of evaluating capital projects. Every one outside called him the project preventer.

Trends to closeness to the customer, an appreciation of the strategic value of speed, and a need to reduce costs have led to the elimination of layers of management in businesses, and in the removal of many head office functions. The question of how each remaining function adds value to the organisation is one that should be regularly studied.

Value is too important to be left as an accidental occurrence. All the areas mentioned above have to be managed. Prahalad and Doz[5] emphasise the need to examine dependencies across different units of a global business to determine which are critical. The analysis may be very complex, with many cross dependencies. They suggest areas of cost and areas of benefit.

Costs include loss of top management focus on particular businesses, and an accompanying loss of visibility of the true results of a business. Flexibility may be reduced, and innovation may be reduced. The very need for coordination costs money at business unit and head office levels. These costs are the down-side of the positive aspects of value creation suggested in our earlier analysis.

Although many of the benefits they see from managing an interdependent global system are similar to those already discussed, their main points are listed for completeness. Shared resources bring opportunities for cost reduction and an increase in added value, technological integrity can be assured, a global infra-structure may be essential to meet global competition, there may be core technol-ogies which stretch across businesses, and size gives bargaining power with host governments.

It is easy to miscalculate the value of one activity to another. In the 1980s many British building societies and insurance companies followed each other like lemmings into the purchase of estate agents, in the belief that this would provide a good source of insurance and mortgage business. The reality was that few knew how to manage such businesses, and that the theoretical market connections did not exist to the degree expected. Consequently many divested these expensively acquired businesses, some selling back to the people they had bought from, but at a lower price. Prudential Assurance is reported to have paid £230 million for its chain of estate agents. It lost £49 million on them in 1989 alone, and in 1991 sold them for a fraction of the purchase price. Instead of adding value, the strategy reduced it.

Measuring Shareholder Value

There is some evidence that, contrary to popular opinion, the stock market is not oriented to the short term, and that capital gains are usually preferred to divi-dends. One element of evidence is that new product investments and major capital expenditures, when announced, frequently increase share price, although the short-term effect may be to reduce earnings. Investors are concerned with the increase in value of their investments over a reasonable time period. We have seen some of the ways in which multi activity companies can increase or decrease value. The problem for managements is how to develop a way of measuring value, which will enable the organisation to be run in a way that consistently increases value. The answer is a process called Value-based Strategic Management (VSM), although as we will see there are several ways of applying it.

Much of the world's experience in applying VSM comes from the USA. The Harbridge Consulting Group's research in 1991 (Handler[1]) found that there was little awareness of the approach in most UK companies, although interest was growing, and there were a number of companies who were staunch advocates. The remainder of this chapter consists of extracts from this report, including case histories which show how two companies are applying the approach. To make the extract easier to read, I have not used inverted commas. The report contains much more information, including case histories of a further five companies.

The extracts used here are not in the same order as they appear in the report, and I have omitted many sections. This suits my purpose, and I do not think I have created any distortions through this treatment. Anyone who is concerned can obtain the report.[1]

EXTRACTS FROM S. HANDLER—"VALUE-BASED STRATEGIC MANAGEMENT: A SURVEY OF UK COMPANIES"

1. Economic Value

There are a number of variations on the theme of value assessment, but all are based on an analysis of the future cash flows which will be generated. This analysis involves the discounting of future cash flow values by an appropriate cost of capital. Economic value appraises future expectations rather than current and past performance.

The limitations seen by the companies in the survey relate mainly to its practical application, for its usefulness relies heavily on making the correct assumptions and preparing the cash projections.

The advantages, it is argued, outweigh the limitations, making it the clearly favoured approach, because:

(i) It measures cash, not accounting profit, which can be distorted by accounting conventions such as those for depreciation, stock valuation and provisions.
(ii) Accounting measures concentrate on the past and the present profits, not on the future. Investors focus on future cash generation, looking for dividends and capital gains.
(iii) It considers the time value of money, unlike the other methods. It is concerned with the timing of all cash flows.
(iv) Empirical studies show that future cash flow is a better indicator for potential value creation.

2. Accounting Model

The traditional accounting model involves various standards of performance based upon reported profits:

Earnings per Share (EPS) Growth in EPS (after-tax profit attributable to ordinary shareholders divided by the number of ordinary shares) is used to measure performance and the return to shareholders. If EPS is growing, shareholder value is assumed to be enhanced.

The limitations include:

(i) The calculation of EPS is based on accounting conventions.
(ii) The time value of money is ignored.
(iii) The element of risk is ignored.

P/E Ratio The P/E ratio relates the market price per share to the earnings per share. As it is based on EPS, it suffers from the same limitations. One fallacy of this model is that it assumes that P/E multiples never change. But in fact, P/E ratios are constantly adjusting to account for changes in the 'quality' of a company's earnings in the wake of acquisitions, divestments, future investment opportunities, and changes in financial structure and accounting policies. And that adjustment makes EPS an unreliable measure of value.

Return on Capital Employed (ROCE) ROCE is calculated by relating some measure of profit to the book value of the assets as, for example:

$$\frac{\text{Operating Profit}}{\text{Capital Employed}} \times 100\%$$

The return is then compared to the company's cost of capital. If the ROCE is consistently greater, then shareholder value is considered to be created.

The limitations include:

(i) It is based on accounting profit, which may have little to do with economic value.
(ii) It ignores the future potential of the investment.
(iii) The timing of cash inflows and outflows (not the least of which is tax) is ignored, as is the residual value of the assets.
(iv) It ignores the effect of inflation on the historic cost of the assets. (Current Cost Accounting, which would counteract this limitation, is now seldom used.)

3. Techniques Used in the Value Process

A variety of factors must be considered during the value process.

The Discount Rate

The Capital Asset Pricing Model (CAPM) and the weighted average cost of capital are the methods used most frequently in calculating the cost of capital.

More than 50% of respondents used in the survey the weighted average cost of capital approach. This compares with a 1987 study of 177 major US companies which found that more than 87% of the companies' chief financial officers used a weighted average cost of capital as the basis of their discount rate calculation (Rappaport[6]).

Although it was agreed by the majority of respondents that the rate of discounting the cash flow stream should be the weighted average cost of debt and equity, it was clear that the rate may differ across business units within a group because of their relative risk exposure.

Residual and Terminal Values

Residual value is the price that the asset can be sold for at the end of its commercial life. *Terminal* value is the value of a business unit, project or asset at the end of a planning cycle, and approximates to the economic value from the end of the cycle to the end of the relevant unit's life.

The appropriate way to calculate residual or terminal value is a critical question, because it can form a substantial proportion of the total value of a business unit.

Terminal values are most frequently computed using the perpetuity approach. The rationale is that competitors will be attracted to any business which is able to generate returns above the cost of capital. This competition will drive the return

Equity-spread approach

The equity-spread approach to valuation focuses on the difference between the return on shareholders equity (the change in share price, plus dividends, divided by the initial share price) and the cost of equity (the shareholders' expectation for return, based on the element of risk). If the equity spread is positive, then shareholder value has been created; if negative, then it has been destroyed.

Share price theory assumes that the share price is influenced by a company's expected equity spread as well as its growth prospect. Managers will do best, then, to focus investment for growth in positive equity spread businesses. The technique's value is limited because it is based on accounting value, with likely distortions. It also ignores some very important sources of value, such as deferred taxes and terminal value at the end of the planning period, and it is also very sensitive to financial leverage.

Market value multiples

This approach seeks to find a business unit equivalent of the market/book multiple. This approach lends itself to simulating both the beginning and ending market values of a business unit on the basis of the book value of its assets.

To establish the multiple it is necessary to determine what are the measurable indicators or drivers of the market value. These variables (combinations of returns, growth, R & D expenditure, etc.) are given weighted values, with the help of specially developed models and databases to help predict share price based on book value.

The key advantage of this approach is that its accuracy can easily be tested with historical data. A test of a sample of 600 US firms found that value-creation estimates based on multiples of either assets or sales corresponded more closely to actual shareholder value creation than the accounting measures of ROI and EPS (Reimann[7]). One of the disadvantages of the method is that book values (the base to which the multiple is applied to predict the 'value') can be affected by many accounting factors which could distort the picture, so it does not necessarily prove a reliable base.

Economic value added approach

The economic value added approach is the product of the equity-spread (the difference between return on equity and the cost of capital) and the total capital employed in the business. The objective is to increase the economic earnings derived from the existing or projected capital bases. (Unfortunately, if the equity spread is negative, then the approach is 'economic value lost').

This approach is frequently used at the portfolio planning stage; and some companies only use it for making strategic decisions at the group level.

Positive-value and negative-value business unit approaches

These approaches are simply the opposite sides of the same coin. Like the economic value added approach, they are used to make portfolio decisions about business units, and in making acquisition and divestment decisions – adding to or growing those businesses for which economic returns exceed the cost of capital (positive net present values). Businesses with negative economic values will be restructed or eliminated, with capital diverted to positive-value business units.

The Q-ratio approach

The Q-ratio approach also focuses on economic value. Developed in the 1960s by James Tobin, the Nobel Prize winning economist, the approach calculates the relationship of the market value of a company's assets to the cost of replacing those assets in current money. This Q-ratio is, thus, a M/B multiple with the book value of assets in the denominator adjusted for the effects of inflation. The rationale is that investors adjust their expected returns for anticipated inflation when analysing alternative investments. Therefore, the true or 'real' value of a business should also reflect this inflation factor. (Reimann,[8])

FIG. 12.2. Some valuation methods

down to the cost of capital and by the end of the planning period, the business is considered to be earning only the cost of capital on its investment. Because these cash flows do not significantly change the value of the firm (Rappaport[6]) they can be treated as though they were a continuing stream. The present value of this stream or perpetuity is the annual cash flow divided by the rate of return:

$$\text{Terminal value} = \frac{\text{Annual cash flow}}{\text{Cost of capital}}$$

Portfolio Planning

The Positive/Negative Value Business Unit approach is the most favoured technique in portfolio planning. It is preferred by 70–80% of respondents, with the Equity-Spread approach used 50% of the time.

Most companies preferred two or more value analysis techniques. They used different approaches for different purposes and at different levels. For example, the Positive/Negative Value Business Unit approach is used in making divestment decisions at group level. The Equity-Spread approach is regarded as straightforward, and its message is easily spread to business unit managers. Some companies use the Market Value Multiples method for presentation only, finding that, although it encourages returns higher than the cost of equity, the result may not maximise shareholder value.

4. Implementation of VSM in UK Companies

This survey found that VSM is used mainly at the corporate or group level, although most businesses plan to drive its application down to the level of operating units. The majority of companies use acquisition to create shareholder value, and elicit the aid of consultants at all stages of development and implementation. The 1991 MORI survey estimated that 56% of top management uses economic value for specific major decisions, 33% for routine planning and control, and 30% for reporting to investors.

VSM Begins at the Top

Most value analysis takes place by a combination of resource allocation and portfolio analysis (identifying which assets or businesses to retain, sell or buy).

British Petroleum reported that it had used value analysis to divest two business units which were outside its core business. TSB has used value analysis to change the emphasis of its business after its flotation on the stock market.

Some companies have introduced a value approach which requires a particular unit to value its business at the start of the planning period, and to highlight changes during the period. Others plan to follow this lead.

Business units may also be required to use value techniques in choosing between alternative scenarios. A business unit may be required to demonstrate that it has selected the best option for implementation before funds are released. At least one company is moving towards setting targets in terms of value generation for its main activity.

Growth Through Acquisition to Create Shareholder Value

The overwhelming majority (18 out of 19 or 94%) of responding companies reported that their strategies include growth through acquisition to create or enhance shareholder value.

However, of those 18, only seven reported a successful acquisition record (success being defined as a company's ability to earn at least its cost of capital on the funds invested in the acquisition). Of those who reported success, one of the major reasons cited was acquiring companies in the same or related businesses or markets. Other reasons included the sound valuation of acquisition candidates and the ability to capitalise on synergies. Those companies who reported failure blamed diversification into businesses where they had little or no knowledge, experience, or expertise. All of these companies feel that value analysis, in the selection of acquisitions, is the best approach.

Help from Consultants and Computer Models

The majority of companies who advocate the value approach use consultants and computer models in the analysis and implementation process.

The general consensus among respondents was that the complexity of data analysis has been a major obstacle to the acceptance of VSM. One solution is to bring in one of a number of consulting firms which offer specialist VSM advice. In addition, there are a number of software products which can be extremely valuable in helping with the introduction of the value approach.

There are at least three routes for establishing data support systems:

(i) Choose one of the proprietary software products offered by consultants.
(ii) Develop the value system in co-operation with one of the consulting companies.
(iii) Create company-specific software internally to support value analysis.

Building Value into Incentive Systems

The last stage of the implementation process should be to build value into the incentive system as a means of motivation. If it is introduced too quickly or drastically it may be demotivating, especially for those who have previously been rewarded within a conventional framework.

No firms indicated the use of incentive systems which include the creation of value. However, the literature researched for the purposes of this survey suggests that the most successful VSM incentive systems are:

(i) Those which are linked to the value created in specific businesses.
(ii) Those which discourage short-term window dressing and help to ensure that managers focus on the long term.

5. Ingredients for the Success of VSM

A number of factors were discovered to be essential for the successful use of the value approach.

Acceptance at Director Level

A prime ingredient for success is the acceptance of value theory at director level. All responding companies felt that they had the full support of the chief executive and the board. Indeed, interviews with UK companies who are proponents revealed that, in the majority of cases, the move to VSM was initiated by a new senior executive from outside the company.

There was much less acceptance and understanding at the business unit level.

Understanding of Senior Management Teams

It was felt that senior management teams must understand the relationship that exists between their strategic announcements (not short-term performance results) and their share price (evidence of financial market response). Management teams, both staff and line, must also understand the benefits of shareholder value analysis, such as the linkages between it and product–market strategies. Value must be embedded in the culture of the organisation or it will not survive.

Is the Culture Right?

Having the right culture was also seen as important to the successful implementation of value at the business unit level, although there seemed to be little awareness among managers as to what that correct culture should be. It was also generally agreed that the company must evaluate the adequacy of current organisational structure and systems in integrating shareholder value analysis, and install new systems when necessary.

Value Sharing: Motivating Managers for Value Creation

One of the most important goals for the value company is finding the best way of putting value theories into practice. Rewarding managers and staff for making the the best long-term value decisions instead of just traditional short-term performance rewards becomes a perplexing, but not insurmountable problem. It is an issue, however, that must be properly resolved before any firm can truly consider itself a 'value' company.

In addition to traditional targets (which are basically related to accounting-derived turnover and/or profit return, growth in sales and/or margins, and some definition of targeted return on profit), many managers and employers are rewarded with stock options, gain-sharing and profit-sharing plans and the like. These last rewards all involve the issue of ownership, which is crucial to the development of a value compensation system—one that makes all workers partners in the process of adding to shareholder value. The idea is to reward managers for reaching or exceeding targeted performance measures that run parallel to the creation of value on an annual basis.

Training for VSM

Training for value is a cardinal rule for those in the United States who have successfully used the techniques. However, only four of the UK responding companies offer this type of training. The importance of educating managers about value is demonstrated by VSM consultants, who spend a significant amount of their time on educational work.

Summary

The consensus was that to be successful VSM must:

(i)   Have the support and dedication of the chief executive and board.
(ii) Be introduced into a receptive culture, with the appropriate organisational structure and systems.
(iii) Allow for an investment in training, and in incentives that encourage managers to emphasise a long-term and not just short-term view.

6. Limitations to the Value Approach

The practical problems involved in using the value approach are seen to be considerable. Difficulty in making accurate and relevant cash flow and discount rate projections was seen in 50% of those responding as the most significant problem.

However, some of the practical limitations relate to common misunderstandings. For example, one complaint most frequently expressed was that there is too much emphasis on the 'numbers', and not enough on strategic thinking and 'value drivers', such as sales growth, profit margins, capital investment and taxation.

Another frequently encountered limitation was that VSM was considered by most operating managers to be too technical and theoretical.

The danger of creating and reinforcing a culture where managers spend most of their time analysing and planning, and not enough time 'making it happen' was also listed as a limiting factor.

7. VSM as a Prevention Against Takeover

VSM is seen by more and more companies as a valuable weapon in the defence against unwanted takeover bids and in controlling the value gap (the difference between the market price of a firm's ordinary shares and the share value if the company were managed for the maximum share price possible at the time). If the difference between the actual and potential share price is large, it is an invitation to raiders. Managing the value gap means changing the investment community's opinion about the company's future performance. It can involve improving internal operations, adjusting the capital structure or selling some of its businesses or assets. It will most certainly mean communicating its intent to the investing community.

Hoylake's £13.4bn ($22bn) bid for BAT Industries plc in July 1989, and KKR's £15.2bn ($25bn) bid for RJR Nabisco provide two examples of takeover attempts which developed from the bidder's belief that the acquisition candidate's shares were undervalued by current investors. Concentrating on strategies designed to maximise long-term cash flows and minimise value gaps helped BAT to successfully defeat the raider. BAT's pre-Hoylake strategy was to use its cash-generating tobacco business to pay for acquisitions intended to offset the longer-term uncertainties of world tobacco sales.

The VSM process begins with a careful financial assessment of each business unit and of the level of risk inherent in alternative strategies. It strives for long-term value creation which comes from sustainable competitive advantages in the company's mix of businesses. The value analysis may, for example, help managers to determine whether to retain or discard existing activities. The simple diagram in Fig. 12.3 relates the market value of various business units to their economic value.

The size of the bubbles represents the proportionate investment in different businesses. The business units positioned to the left of the 45° line are worth more to a potential buyer than to the group and should be divested. If a significant proportion of business units are to the right of the line, it indicates that the group is undervalued by the market. Action must be taken to reduce the gap. Practical problems arise when the activities to the left and right are interconnected.

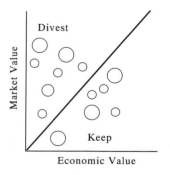

FIG. 12.3. Value decisions

To increase shareholder value, managers must identify where value is being created or destroyed and be aware of the impact of different strategies. To be effective, VSM requires the extensive involvement of those managers responsible for execution, but VSM must also be part of a balanced approach that emphasises qualitative factors, including issues such as quality and customer satisfaction.

The second part of the VSM process is implementation. This involves acceptance, commitment and understanding by line managers who need to be motivated to manage for value. For the company it means different communication and training, and incentive schemes linked to longer-term cash generation, not just short-term results.

8. Case Study: Lloyds Bank Plc

"Lloyds Bank's primary objective is to create value for its shareholders – by increase in the dividend and appreciation in the share price. This is the driving force behind our decisions and actions.... We rank each business on the basis of the shareholder value they create; each activity is viewed as a creator or destroyer of value. Businesses which consume cash and destroy value are targeted for divestment."

CEO's Report, 1989

Lloyds Bank was one of the success stories of the 1980s with a compound growth rate of 27% (on January 1981 investment with dividends reinvested), a performance not matched by any other UK bank. During 1991 its business mix enabled Lloyds to achieve a return on assets 50% higher and dividend growth 37% higher than the peer group. Its distinct structural advantages with focus on high margin, low capital intensive domestic businesses, together with its philosophy of maximising shareholder value, have made it the core bank holding of an increasing number of investment portfolios.

The group's three basic strategies, responsible for its remarkable results, reinforce its belief in what drives value for shareholders (Fig. 12.4) and its sub-targets for creating shareholder value:

(i)   To achieve a net ROE greater than 18% (Lloyds' cost of capital).
(ii) To increase the dividend payout ratio.
(iii) To maintain a strong balance sheet with equity grown from retained earnings.

The objectives and methodology of value strategy and management have been debated and agreed with the bank's senior management. The methodology is used for major strategic issues, and to a lesser extent for business unit strategies. Below this level the approach is simplified to the objective of achieving a sustainable after-tax return on equity, which will at least equal its cost of equity. Nevertheless, Lloyds believes that there is still plenty of scope for extending the full approach to lower levels within the organisation.

With the 1990 economic fluctuations out of the way, the benefits of the approach are clearly shown in the growth in shareholder value of Lloyds Bank compared with its peer group (which includes a 35%+ growth in share price

---

Value drivers in Lloyds' business

From a practitioner's point of view, Lloyds believes that identification and management of 'value drivers' should be left to the business units. Generally, though, it feels that significant number of factors drives the value to its shareholders:

• The ROE of each business unit.

• Avoiding strategic mistakes (in other words, 'getting it right the first time').

• Projecting the right image in the right market.

• Avoiding bad debts.

• Targeting customer groups prepared to pay a premium for its service.

• Quality of service to the customer: "It is cheaper to retain existing customers than to get new ones".

FIG. 12.4. Value drivers in Lloyds' business

during 1991). The philosophy of shareholder value, which was formulated and propagated by the current CEO Brian Pitman (appointed December 1983) places primary emphasis on creating distributable returns (free cash flow) for shareholders via profitable non-capital-intensive businesses.

Lloyds' Strategies for Creating Shareholder Value

Lloyds implements three basic strategies to achieve the goals stated above.
Reallocation of assets
This strategy for creating shareholder value has transformed Lloyds from a diversified international bank into a focused domestic bank. Lloyds' policy is to focus on the strengths of the market, not necessarily domestic investment versus international activities. Although it has recently disposed of some UK assets (selling its stake in Yorkshire Bank and closing its gilts and eurobond operations) and acquired others abroad (Abbey Life in Ireland and Germany), the larger proportion of its business is in the UK.

Its 62% international assets in 1981 had been reduced to 28% by the end of 1990. The significantly wider domestic net interest margins reflect a large component of consumer and small business lending funded from a base of cheap retail deposits. The international segment was wholesale in orientation, geared to low margin, euro-currency and large corporate lending. Now this is focused on international private banking in those countries where Lloyds is not a major player in the retail market.

Lloyds has moved away from low margin euro-currency lending and sold international offices in the USA, Canada and Portugal. It has also enhanced value to shareholders by recognising that growth, to compensate for declining (at the time) corporate loan margins, must come from other areas, such as increasing arrangement and lending fees, and enhancement of the personal customer base (thus Lloyds' acquisition of Abbey Life).

Lloyds estimates that its interest margin is almost 25% higher than the peer group average because of its low percentage of international assets.

Seeking selective market leadership

Lloyds' second strategic principle concerns competitive advantage. Its stated policy, which underlies its switch from international to domestic assets, is to seek selective market leadership and to avoid those markets and products where it cannot obtain a strong position. It pulled out of gilts and eurobond operations in 1987, for example, because "markets were overcrowded and we were marginal players".

High margin/low capital intensive businesses

In keeping with its policy of producing high affordable dividends (distributable returns) Lloyds has sought balance sheet growth by moving away from low margin commodity lending into risk management and fee-based services. Development of its life assurance subsidiary, Black Horse Life, began with the acquisition of a 57% stake in Abbey Life, projected to generate significant cash flow from its existing client base. This is expected to prove extremely effective in terms of capital cost regulatory requirements (cash holdback) as requirements are minimal in relation to the costs of lending under the BIS rules. Although embedded value life profits are not technically distributable, they can be included within the group's capital and so effectively free up banking-derived earnings for distribution.

Lloyds' focus on high margin areas like personal and small business lending has resulted in a higher yield on its domestic assets and stronger net interest margin than its peers.

The results of Lloyds' adherence to its strategic principles has produced amazing results since 1986 (see Fig. 12.5): its pre-tax return on assets was 185% better than peers in 1990 against 33% in 1986.

Difficulties in Implementing a Value Approach

The problems experienced by Lloyds in implementing VSM were primarily technical and involved retraining its own financial experts and those within the investing community to think of cash flow in terms of "free cash" or "affordable dividends" to shareholders rather than cash flow in the traditional sense. Lloyds' experience with the investing community was that, with a few notable exceptions, there was little awareness of, but a lot of interest in, the value techniques. Its regular meetings with analysts and fund managers has succeeded "only up to a point" in educating and convincing the investing community of the benefits of managing for value. "They [the investors] are convinced by the results, but not by the theory".

Return on earning assets			

1986	Lloyds	Barclays	NatWest	Midland
Net interest income	3.82	3.78	3.54	3.27
Other income	1.85	1.91	1.55	2.05
Costs	-3.60	-3.82	-3.25	-3.93
Subtotal	2.08	1.87	1.84	1.39
Bad debts	-0.50	-0.64	-0.52	-0.70
Investment gains	0.00	0.06	0.01	0.10
Associates	0.05	0.11	0.09	0.05
PRE TAX	1.62	1.41	1.41	0.85

Return on earning assets			

1990	Lloyds	Barclays	NatWest	Midland
Net interest income	4.29	3.07	3.34	2.74
Other income	2.84	1.97	1.88	2.45
Costs	-4.62	-3.31	-3.69	-4.00
Subtotal	2.50	1.73	1.52	1.20
Bad debts	-1.76	-1.08	-1.07	-1.17
Investment gains	0.04	0.00	-0.01	0.05
Associates	0.04	0.03	0.02	0.04
Exceptional	0.29	0.00	0.00	0.09
PRE TAX	1.11	0.67	0.47	0.02

FIG. 12.5. Comparison of Lloyds with peer groups

Lloyds feels its value strategy can be summarised as:

(i) Ensuring profitability of ongoing businesses without going to its shareholders for more capital.
(ii) Reducing investment in those parts of the business which cannot realistically expect long-term returns which exceed the cost of equity.
(iii) Increasing investment in high return businesses.

Overall, Lloyds' objective is to maximise shareholder value, which means "maximising the present value of (estimated) future affordable dividends". It does not attempt to maximise ROE but instead to take on all business which at the margin will generate 18% ROE. Lloyds believes that maximising ROE does not maximise shareholder value. Rather, it feels that success is better measured by the actual change in shareholder value over time.

When asked if it felt it would be a takeover target in the future, Lloyds' opinion was that it would not: "Management is already maximising returns for share-holders." Indeed, if the sentiments of many of the analysts surveyed are to be believed, it is a share to buy. To quote one: "Lloyds Bank represents the best combination of dividend productivity and cheapness and should be the core long-term holding in portfolios." (UBS Phillips and Drew).

9. Case Study: Dixons Group Plc

Dixons Group Plc is an international group specialising in the retail sale of consumer electronics, photographic products, domestic appliances and related services (profiled in Fig. 12.6). It trades through Dixons, Currys and Supasnaps in the UK and Silo in the USA. The Group is also engaged in property development and trading in the UK, Belgium, Germany, France, Luxembourg and Portugal through Dixons Commercial Properties International.

Dixons Group's value focus involves long-term investment to develop a mature base of operations, centred on customer satisfaction. It believes that striving for customer satisfaction will drive value across the entire business. The Group believes that the success of VSM and its benefits will depend in part on developing sales staff rewards based on customer satisfaction rather than short-term sales targets. Its considerable progress with its focus on value led in part to a 75% increase in its share price through 1991, a difficult time for retailers as many endured horrific recessionary setbacks.

The consumer electronics and domestic appliance sectors, although generally regarded as long-term growth markets, are cyclical. As a result, business is subject to considerable fluctuations in demand, which tend to be exacerbated by new product introductions and shifts in economic climate.

This had led to a number of problems:

(i) In the mid-1980s, when demand was strong and sales of new products such as VCRs, microwaves and computers were growing rapidly, Dixons made a number of investment decisions based on what turned out in the short term to

---

Profile of Dixons Group companies

Dixons. Retails consumer electronics and photographic products through high street stores.

Currys. Retails a wide range of domestic electrical products through superstores and high street stores.

SupaSnaps. Offers film processing services and photographic accessories.

Silo. Retails a wide range of consumer electronics and domestic appliances through superstores in the US.

FIG. 12.6. Profile of Dixons Group companies

be unsustainable levels of sales. Because the "brown goods" (TV, audio, video, camcorders) sector is very prone to such investment "traps", making invest-ment decisions on the basis of high short-term profitability can lead to problems in later years as demand declines, particularly when costs are also rising rapidly.

(ii)   The integration of Dixons' and Currys' logistical support and the realisation of the synergy between the two businesses was delayed because the short-term buoyancy of the market obscured the underlying problems.

(iii) Currys' competitive position was eroded because of its structure of small stores, and at the same time its cost base was high due to the location of its shops on the high street. The strategic response to the problem, the move to edge-of-town superstores, was slow to implement.

These problems were tackled in 1988 and 1989, but the solutions were poorly communicated to shareholders and analysts, and the results were not immediately apparent due to the weakness of the market and the timescale for implementation. Dixons' market share growth rate began to slow down with a simultaneous cost escalation. As a result, the share price fell sharply, and in December 1989 King-fisher made a hostile bid for Dixons Group. Although this offer was unsuccessful, it focused Dixons' management's attention on its failure to communicate with the investment community and led to a considerably better perception of the nature of the group's business, its problems and the solutions being implemented.

The group's 1990s plan for creating shareholder value is a many-faceted strategy for building long-term customer satisfaction. Dixons Group firmly believes that value in its businesses is created when long-term customer loyalty is created. This involves not only an upmarket push for Dixons and the expansion of Currys Superstores, but also the emphasis of new concepts in systems, service, merchan-dising, product improvement and innovation, and staff development and compensation.

Expansion of Currys Superstores

Currys, in shifting away from the high street to edge-of-town superstores, hopes to give customers a far better shopping experience: a large range of "white goods" (washers and dryers, refrigerators, freezers, cookers, small appliances), larger more comfortable stores with a relaxed atmosphere, longer opening hours and conve-nient parking. This move has led to improved sales, up by 11% like-for-like against a 4% reduction in its high street store sales. The group expects that Currys Superstores will account for 35% of retail space by April 1992, at least equal to Curry's High Street stores.

Upmarket Push for Dixons

Dixons' attack on margins focuses on upgrading the mix of its merchandise to achieve higher average prices. Between 1988 and 1990 Dixons saw a 24% price increase in real terms as average prices were decreasing. This meant that the volume of goods handled dropped sharply while turnover remained constant. This had a significant effect on its cost base. Retailers of white and brown goods traditionally sustain high overheads to deal with large volumes of sales (warehousing, delivery, administration, after sales service). Smaller investment in inventories has not only reduced investment in working capital, but Dixons finds itself discounting less because of obsolete and warehouse-worn merchandise.

Modernised Information Systems

The group is currently making considerable investment ($£10m$) in a sophisticated branch PC network designed to provide branches with up-to-date stock availability information as well as store profitability. It provides instant information about previously evasive issues such as discount origin, customer service history, and inventory and service parts availability. The system will eventually allow instant access to credit and repair organisations, and detailed product specification data which will give sales personnel more authority in dealing with customer enquiries.

Improved Merchandising

In addition to improved merchandising of white goods in Currys' Superstores and upgraded Dixons merchandising of brown goods the group has opened new specialist departments on a trial basis, particularly at Dixons stores. More space and a wider range of computer game hardware and software is catering to the growth of the computer game market. Other specialist departments group together low-price merchandise like films and video tapes as well as general brown goods accessories on a self-service basis.

To improve its already impressive 33% of the UK camcorder market 300 Currys High Street stores installed camcorder centres through the summer of 1991, with very encouraging results. In addition, Currys High Street stores have begun a trial (10 stores by end 1991) to reduce the space given to big white goods. Instead it sells them through an in-store catalogue centre, and focuses much more in store on small appliances. It is hoped that this move will improve its presence and market share in small appliances, while the large Currys Superstores in cheaper, cost efficient locations handle a larger than ever market share of the larger white goods.

Product Improvement and Innovation

Historically electronic goods have been made with two points in mind: ease of manufacture and number of features. "User friendliness" has until recently not been a priority. Consumer complaints range from complex and contradictory instruction booklets to $£2000$ systems that are packaged without plugs. Figure 12.7 outlines some significant Dixons initiatives guaranteed to pleasure any customer who has to install his or her own TV, stereo or VCR. In addition, with the average

---

Dixons initiatives to simplify consumer installation and engineer repair of electrical goods.

Joint customer satisfaction projects with Sony, Hitachi, Panasonic and Matsushita have been initiated to respond to calls for simpler technology.

• Circuit boards which formerly had to be soldered out now clip out, enabling repairs to be carried out in the customer's home with minimal fuss.

• Instruction booklets have large easy-to-follow diagrams with colour coding for cables and plug points, and have been rewritten to improve former badly translated Japanese and to correct contradictions.

• More care is being given to make sure that self-assembly parts are all compatible with each other.

• Design initiatives are underway for future electronic equipment which will have four or five diagnostic points built in to enable engineers to find faults quickly. 90% of engineer time is spent now in locating a fault and only 10% in fixing the fault.

• Packaging is being redesigned to make life easier for the consumer so that spending 45 minutes getting a TV out of a box may soon be a thing of the past.

FIG. 12.7. Dixons initiatives to simplify consumer installation and engineer repair of electrical goods

cost of servicing a VCR at approximately £30, eliminating an estimated 30% of unnecessary service callouts will mean significant financial benefits for Dixons as well as improving customer satisfaction.

The product innovation cycle has been quiet since 1983, the peak of the VCR boom. The expected launch in 1992 of CDI (interactive compact disk) as well as the DCC (digital compact cassette), a 16×9 picture format colour TV and high definition TV are all expected to boost the innovation cycle. And although the innovation in products is not expected to be really buoyant until 1994–1995, Dixons is projecting that its market share will continue to move upwards.

Staff Development and Compensation Programmes to Build Shareholder Value

In 1990–1991 average branch staff numbers fell by 5% in Dixons and 14% in Currys (which translated through to 12–14% increases in sales per employee). Distribution employees were also significantly reduced (16%), and branch pay increases were modest. How then does Dixons Group account for the results of a 1991 employee survey that showed a sharp drop in staff turnover and that employee perceptions of the company (and motivation to create value through retaining customer loyalty) have never been higher?

Clear career structure, trust of managers and a sharp drop in the level of customer complaints (40% drop in the 18 months to September 1991) are credited for this remarkable improvement in perception. The group's plans for developing and keeping 'value' orientated staff, as outlined in Fig. 12.8, are all based on its belief that staff give better care to customers when they have been with the company for some time, when they are better trained and when they are compensated for long-term sales, not just immediate sales which may not create customer loyalty.

Substantial Improvements to Customer Service

Dixons/Currys central service organisation, Mastercare, has improved out of all recognition. Its "same day service" really works, and engineers even call the customer directly before a visit to check on the time of appointment. With its desire to consistently deliver the best service possible, Dixons/Currys is installing in-store repair centres for quicker turn-round times for customers. The concept, which is being introduced into 30 Currys Superstores around the country, is also expected to substantially reduce the group's costs of repair while reinforcing its fundamental philosophy of building trustworthiness.

Summary

Dixons Group's concentration on building shareholder value through customer satisfaction and loyalty has captured investors' attention, as evidenced by its significantly improved share price. The message from many analysts: It is not too late to buy!

Dixons Group's plan for developing and keeping 'value' orientated staff.

1. The compensation system is based in part on commissions focused not just on sales (except for Christmas sales bonuses), but on margin improvements, add-on products, housekeeping (credit agreements, etc.) and care of stock (significant drop in lost and damaged stock in 1990-91)

2. Compensation is also linked to staff development so that those who take up offered training programmes are eligible for bonuses. Training in two key areas - product knowledge and selling skills - is carried out both in-house and through distance learning programmes, often with major input from manufacturers. Training is primarily focused on value creation, as it is directed toward solving customer problems. Training is structured with milestone targets, at which staff qualify for extra pay.

3. Staff pay is also tied to employment longevity based on Dixons Group's firm belief that loyalty for service (and presumed improved performance) must be rewarded.

FIG. 12.8. Dixons Group's plan for developing and keeping "value" orientated staff

References

1. Handler, S. *Value-based Strategic Management: A Survey of UK Companies*, Harbridge Consulting Group Ltd, London, 1991.
2. Goold, M. and Campbell, A. *Strategies and Styles*, Blackwell, Oxford, 1987.
3. Porter, M. E. "From Competitive Advantage to Corporate Strategy", *Harvard Business Review*, May/June 1987.
4. Buzzell, R. D. and Gale, B. T. *The PIMS Principles*, Free Press, New York, 1987.
5. Prahalad, C. K. and Doz, Y. *The Multinational Mission*, Free Press, New York, 1987.
6. Rappaport, A. "Stock market signals to managers", *Harvard Business Review*, November–December 1987.
7. Reimann, B. C. "Decision support software for value-based planning", *Planning Review*, March/April 1988.
8. Reimann, B. C. "Managing for the shareholders: an overview of value-based strategic management", *The Planning Forum*, Blackwell, 1987.

13

A Concept of Objectives

Some of the sense and feel of objectives will have already begun to seep through this book. It is now time to look more closely and more specifically at what is meant by "objectives", why they are required and how they might be used in management and strategic planning.

As is the case with so many aspects of management, there is a problem of semantics. "Objectives" is a word that is used with many different meanings, and, of course, has a place of its own in usage outside of the management text books. This makes it important for a close examination to be made of the definitions and views of some of the authorities on planning before any attempt is made to make a detailed analysis of the problem.

It is almost true to say that there are as many definitions of "objectives" as there are planners. It is certainly a topic that has engaged the attention of many management thinkers, and probably as much thought has been given to this as to any other single aspect of planning.

Scott[1] suggests that:

"Objectives here are the statements of planning purpose developed within any kind of business plan. They are established *within* the framework of a planning process, and they normally evolve from tentative and vague ideas to more specific declarations of purpose. Objectives, furthermore, are always present in a planning process even though they are sometimes unconsciously established."

Ansoff[2] sees objectives as:

". . . decision rules which enable management to guide and measure the firm's performance towards its purpose."

Drucker[3] maintains that a company may have a number of objectives. This viewpoint is further developed by Humble[4] into a comprehensive system of "Management by Objectives", which is capable of application at all levels in the company.

Argenti[5] takes a different view and believes that any firm has only one corporate objective:

". . . something fundamental to the nature of a company and which distinguishes it from other types of organisation: it is therefore something permanent and unalterable. It is the reason for the very existence of the company, that for which it came into being and what it is now for. It is that which, if the company fails to achieve it, the company itself fails. It is a permanent unalterable purpose, or raison d'etre." (Argenti sees the corporate objective as something distinct and separate from other types of objectives: simply as a dimension of profit.)

Many planners see a number of classifications of objectives, in particular into objectives and goals.

For example, Ackoff[6] states:

"Desired states or outcomes are objectives. Goals are objectives that are scheduled for attainment during the period planned for."

He further divides objectives into stylistic and performance, the former being desired for their own sake and defined qualitatively, and the latter "instrumentally", i.e. quantitatively. (However, it should be mentioned that some practitioners reverse the meanings of "objectives" and "goals".)

There is, too, a link between the constraints and objectives which has been discussed in some detail in Chapter 8.

Some concept of objectives is essential for the application of strategic management. The following analysis considers, firstly, the problem of the business undertaking, and ultimately the modifications to this concept which might be applicable to non-profit-making bodies, such as government departments, hospitals, charitable, and similar organisations. Later we will look at two terms which have come to the fore in recent years: Vision and Strategic Intent.

There is no doubt that Scott[1] is correct in his assertion that all organisations have objectives. They may not always be defined, and one of the first tasks of anyone undertaking corporate planning in any organisation must be to bring some clarification to the confusion—which exists in many companies—around its objectives. It is by no means infrequent for differing divisions in a company to be working to opposing objectives, or, indeed, for different people in the same division to be pulling in opposite directions. Usually this is all done in blissful ignorance, each person being certain that he is acting in the best interests of the company. Occasionally it is deliberate.

My own approach to objectives owes much to the combined weight of thought given to the subject by other writers. It has the further advantage of being tested and used in real, rather than theoretical, planning situations. Like most other planners, I see a division of the broad concept of objectives into a number of components. Those I recommend are:

(i)   The primary, or profit, objective of the business, set in advance of strategy.
(ii) The secondary, and mainly narrative objectives, again set in advance of strategy.
(iii) Goals which are time-assigned targets derived from the strategy.
(iv) Standards of performance (often identical with goals) assigned to particular individuals.

Perhaps the most important factor is that it is a concept: each of the elements bears some relation to the others.

The most vital parts of the concept are those which the company as a whole is trying to co-ordinate all its efforts to achieve. From these central and fundamental objectives should spring the purpose and role of every sector of the company and the personal objectives of individual people. Thus the concept is meaningful and capable of subdivision no matter how the company is organised. No change need be made to the principles whether they are applied to a one-man business, a conglomerate, or a multi-national undertaking. The only modifications needed are in deciding who sets which divisional (or layer of) objectives, a point which will receive attention later.

Primary or Profit Objective

The primary, or profit, objective comes directly from a consideration of the basic duty of a chief executive, which is to manage the company in such a way that it fulfils the profit obligations to all the shareholders and at the same time provides an adequate cash flow for what may be termed corporate renewal. The chief executive has full responsibility, answerable through the board to the shareholders over the means by which these aims are achieved, and subject only to the legitimate constraints which shareholders might apply, may choose the means to reach the targets.

We saw in the previous chapter that the creation of shareholder value should be a key aim of any chief executive.

No business should be operated in such a way that profit is considered unimportant (the term profit is discussed more fully later). I have heard managers speak as if a chief executive can choose between making profits or gaining turnover growth with little or no profit. The brutal fact is that, except in those increasingly rare cases where the owner and chief executive are one and the same, the chief executive does not have this choice. And even in a privately owned company lack of profits can only be tolerated for as long as the financial resources can stand it. The penalty for the chief executive who does not earn profit is elimination—either through disillusioned shareholders selling out their holdings at the first take-over offer which comes along, or because they decide to change the management, or because the company passes into bankruptcy and is closed down. Even giant companies are not immune from the effects of a disastrous cash-flow situation.

The reason for this is simple. A company that consistently fails to make profits will sooner or later cease to exist. The only factor in question is the speed at which it dies, which depends on the patience of its creditors, the size of its liquid resources, and the demands of its shareholders. We can go a step further and argue that a company that fails to make adequate profits will die either because of shareholder dissatisfaction or because the company cannot generate funds for growth and corporate renewal on which the future of every company depends.

A company that does not make an *appropriate* level of profits, and manage its affairs so that shareholder value is gained through the share price, faces the rite of being swallowed up by another, or purchased to be broken up.

A feeling for profit must be held by all managers in the organisation if the company is to be successful. A business whose individual members have no sense of profit responsibility is a depressing sight. Successful businesses tend to develop a climate in which profit is taken into account during the planning process. Any company run by managers who argue that profit does not matter to them is very sick.

One more general point should be made about profit, and this is that the philosophy is not simply one of short-term but of long-term profit growth allowing for corporate renewal, which is something better than survival. In all decisions the company's future should be given due consideration. Most companies could increase today's profit at the expense of tomorrow's: for example, by reducing advertising, abolishing research and development, cheating the customer, or innumerable similar actions. The management task is to balance the need for current profits against the need for the company to progress in the future (of course, organisations have been set up to make a "quick killing" and then close down, but these are unlikely to be interested in the concepts of management discussed here). That there is a need for current profits is also beyond doubt. The company that forgets this will perish, just as surely as the man who packs up eating at Easter and devotes all his efforts to contemplating his next Christmas dinner. Shareholders are right never to be satisfied with *Alice Through the Looking-Glass* jam—there must be some for today.

This accent on long-term considerations is not designed to lead companies into the trap of descending to platitudes. An objective such as "we intend to maximise profit over the long term" is neither meaningful nor valid. An objective in this form is of no use to any manager. "Maximum" profit depends on the individual manager's viewpoint. It will mean different things to different people, and there is no way of telling whether it (whatever it is) will be sufficient to satisfy shareholders. Maximised profit for some businesses might not be a profit at all, or might be such a small return that the correct action would be to wind up the company and give the shareholders back their assets. As it is unquantified it is impossible to carry out "gap analysis" (or any other form of mathematical exercise) to devise ways of reaching it. And as no one knows what it is, no one will know when they have got there, so the essential monitoring and controlling aspects of planning become impossible to implement. This means plans lack a cutting edge, and "planning" degenerates to a meaningless exercise which adds only costs to the company and produces no benefit. Such a phrase becomes a shelter for the inefficient. Every manager can *claim* to have maximised profit; every short-term drop can be blamed on a long-term implication.

A main difference between companies which practise effective strategic management and those which have a more traditional approach to management is that the strategic companies are not satisfied with words alone. Much more meaningful is a specific quantitative statement of *what* profit is required. The planning company will also want to tie a time-period to the profit concept. It is interested not only in what profit it requires this year; it needs to state its aims for as far ahead as it is willing to plan.

Perhaps the first step is for the company to define what it means by "profit". This must be established in accounting terms, and the definition should be used in all future plans. A company should never delude itself into believing it has achieved targets merely because it changes its chief accountant for one who has a different approach to the problems of reserves, depreciation, goodwill, and the like.

The objective should cover two dimensions of profit—quantity and efficiency. An efficiency target (e.g. return on capital employed) is not by itself a valid objective because there may be a number of different results possible which yield the same ROI%: it is possible to foresee a situation where profit may decline even though the ROI% increases. A quantity dimension by itself is a valid target, although it is much more use to the company if linked to efficiency.

Like profit, the particular efficiency rating used should be carefully defined, and the same method of calculation used for computing results as for computing the target. This does not preclude a company from using more than one efficiency ratio provided it does not get them mixed up.

The definition of the corporate profit targets over the period selected for the plan is something which required a great deal of management thought, and there are differences of approach between a parent company and its subsidiaries, and possibly between privately owned and publicly owned companies. Perhaps the best approach is to return to the basic philosophy of a shareholder's legitimate expectations. What does a shareholder expect from a company? It may be impracticable (although not impossible as Fisons have shown)[7] to ask the shareholder, who may have many expectations. One thing the shareholder would particularly like is increased earnings from the investment. Put another way this may be expressed in growth in earnings per share: this is not necessarily the same as growth in profits because the gearing effect of borrowed capital can increase earnings per share more than a proportionate increase in profits: similarly, a new share issue may reduce earnings per share although profits may rise.

Earnings per share is a concept which can be quantified, and, of course, is only a generalisation until it is quantified.

Supporters of value based strategic management, as we have seen, would take a different view of how objectives should be quantified. They would use discounted cash flow techniques to measure targets, arguing that this forces decision makers to look to the future, rather than the past. It also reconciles the economic approach to the evaluation of capital expenditures, which most large organisations take, to the overall strategies of the organisation.

A number of factors should be taken into consideration when a chief executive sets profit targets:

(i) Trends over previous years (these provide a baseline for growth).
(ii) Progress by other companies of a similar size or in the same industry.
(iii) The performance of the leading companies quoted on the Stock Exchange.
(iv) Opportunities for more profitable investment elsewhere (for instance, shareholders tend to lose interest in a company which yields them less than an equivalent investment in a bank savings account).
(v) The vision of the chief executive, and intention to give the shareholders more than they have had in the past.
(vi) The strategic need for growth to reach a size which enables the company to at least maintain its position of influence in its trade, and to provide a cash flow to generate future growth and the replacement of assets.

A reminder of the terms used

Return on investment. This is profit divided by investment and expressed as a percentage. A number of different bases are available as the measure of investment. For example, depending on the purpose of the analysis, it would be possible to use:

    Total assets
    Total assets less current liabilities
    Total assets less total liabilities (shareholders' funds)

Profit may also be taken before or after tax.

Earnings per share. The earnings attributable to ordinary shareholders (that is after deducting the earnings attributable to preference shareholders, divided by the number of ordinary shares)

Price earning ratio. This is not mentioned in the text, but is an important ratio which has an effect on objectives. It is the market price per share divided by the earnings per share.

Discounted cash flow. A method of analysis that takes into account the time value of money. It is based on the fact that a unit of money available today is worth more than that same unit at some time in the future, because of the earnings that can be gained from it. If the money is not available until some time in the future this opportunity has to be foregone. Net streams of cash for an investment or activity are forecast into the future, and discounted back to present value, using a rate of discount which may, for example, equate to the cost of capital. this gives rise to several possible measures, the two most common of which are:

    Net present value: the cumulative total of the discounted incremental cash flows. If a 10% discount rate were used, the NPV would be zero if the project equated with the standard, negative if it were below 10%, and positive if it were above it.

    Internal rate of return: the discount rate which would apply to reduce the NPV of a project to zero.

EXHIBIT 13.1. A reminder of the terms used

(vii) Rates of inflation. There should be an improvement in real terms.
(viii) Acceptable levels of risk.

The usual efficiency ratios, particularly return on capital and return on shareholders' funds, should be utilised in the study. A new chief executive who inherits a company earning a miserable 6% return on capital employed will probably have a long way to go to give shareholders the type of earnings they have a right to expect: on the other hand, he or she might consider that there is a lot of scope for improvement.

A privately owned company might adopt a different approach, although that outlined above is valid should it wish to use it. In many such companies it is possible to find out what the shareholders want, because ownership and management may be vested in the same people or there may be strong family influences. Here it may be practicable to consult the shareholders, and there may, in the family business, be other factors. A less ambitious growth target might be preferred to prevent loss of family control (either financial or through having to open the management ranks to outsiders).

Once the profit objectives have been set for the total company it is time to think about objectives for divisions and subsidiaries. Now it is possible for a subsidiary or division to calculate its own profit objectives on the lines argued above, although I believe this task should be undertaken by the Head Office subject to discussion with the division or subsidiary concerned. The reason for this is that the way in which a total company profit objective is divided up is in fact a series of strategic decisions. An objective set for subsidiary "A" reflects the parent company's decisions that that particular activity should continue in being and that a particular growth and contribution is expected from that area of business.

The proportions of the profit objective which are required from each activity area (and what is meant by this will depend on company organisation—it may be an industry grouping, a strategic business unit, a country operation, or simply something which fits in with the pattern of the subsidiaries owned by the parent) may again be divined from an amalgam of past trends, competitive activity, return on investment rates, strategic growth rates, and expectations. There should be discussion between subsidiary and head office so that objectives are agreed and accepted, but this does not alter the fact that it is a basic head office duty to set them.

It may be that, as part of a determined strategy, a particular subsidiary will run at a loss: for instance, if a new company is set up in what, for the group, is a new country. This can be reflected in the profit objectives. It is not a decision for the subsidiary alone: in fact if all subsidiaries and divisions opted to lose money, albeit for future growth, the total company would be in a sorry state. The ability of a group to accept controlled losses in certain areas depends on its ability to meet its planned profit targets by contributions from other areas. If, for properly evaluated long-term reasons, subsidiary "A" is to sacrifice profit for growth, subsidiaries "B", "C", and "D" must be able to make up the shortfall. Only the corporate centre can know what it can afford.

In many situations there may well be a conflict between sales growth and profit growth. This has another important aspect—cash flow. The value argument would imply looking at a business unit on the same lines as a capital investment, and subjecting the strategy to DCF analysis to ensure that there is an acceptable payback. If the subsidiary is a new venture this may well be done as a matter of course: if it is a new strategy for an old subsidiary this course may never even be thought of.

It is relevant to consider the profit targets of autonomous units under the concept of the primary objective. It is also relevant to realise that from the point of view of the *total* company these are not objectives at all, and in fact fit in much more closely with the definition of goals quoted earlier. From the point of view of the chief executive of the subsidiary it is a primary objective. This different viewpoint from different levels in an organisation occurs in other types of objective and will be discussed in more detail later. For the present it is enough to say that it is one of the reasons why there is confusion of thought over the topic of objectives. The fact that position does change a person's conception of an objective is part of normal life—from earth, with the naked eye, the full moon is seen as a circle: in fact it is a sphere.

Two further factors should be mentioned before the concept of secondary objectives is considered. The first is that many business groups contain subsidiaries which are not wholly owned by the group and which may have other shareholders. The duty of a chief executive is, through the board, to *all* the shareholders, and such a chief executive should play a much more important part in the setting of the primary objectives than the chief executive of a wholly owned subsidiary. The process may begin in the same way, but may be subject to a greater degree of thought and modification by the subsidiary chief executive. There is a duty to meet the legitimate demands of all the shareholders, and the chief executive should ensure that the objectives are in line with this duty.

The second is that, particularly in multi-national business, the subsidiary chief executive may be subject to government constraints which prevent acceptance of the profit objectives. These, too, cannot be ignored, and represent an additional reason—if one is needed—for consultation between the centre and subsidiaries when objectives are set.

Secondary Objectives

Profit is an important aspect of corporate objectives, but it is not the only aspect. The term secondary is chosen to describe the next group of objectives: not because they are less important to success but because they should really be defined after the profit objectives have been set.

Secondary objectives are descriptive and attempt to set out the key elements of the business of the future. Where the corporate appraisal seeks the *present* corporate identity, the secondary objectives describe the company's *future* identity. They paint a picture not of what is now, but what the company is determined to become in the future. They take the old question What business am I in? and give it a new dimension, oriented to the future rather than the present.

This type of objective, sometimes called the mission, should examine the nature and scope of the business, the geographical sphere of operation, and some of the key factors about the company which the chief executive feels are important. They may include a statement of the way the company intends to conduct its relations with its employees, customers, and society: there is a straightforward link with the chief executive's ethical viewpoint, already discussed in Chapter 7.

Some managers believe that secondary objectives are not really objectives at all, but statements of strategy that broadly describe the means that will be used to attain the profit targets. There is some justification to this opinion, but there are three arguments that can be used against it. Firstly, it does not really matter if the concept does venture into the realms of corporate strategy since none of the elements of corporate planning exist in isolation and all overlap to some degree. Secondly, this type of objective can be very useful in channelling creative thought to a desired end, and the concept can thus be justified on the grounds of expediency.

The third argument is even more compelling. Every chief executive holds a mental vision of what the company can become, regardless of the strategy chosen to reach it. There is a very real gulf between the concept the chief executive of a conglomerate might have—a willingness and ability to accept any profitable investment in any field—and that which might be held by the chief executive of a company operating in only one or two industry groups who would never, under any circumstances, consider moving too far from the fields the company understands. It may be that one day the second company would change its objectives and arrive at a broader concept of its basic purpose. As it is with a company, so it is with most individuals. As a person gains in experience and education, as family and other responsibilities increase, and as he or she gains a more realistic appreciation of strengths and weaknesses, so the concept of ultimate aims changes. There is no reason why any objective, corporate or personal, should be regarded as immutable. It need only be permanent enough to outlast the period for which plans are prepared.

Both primary and secondary objectives should be thought of as map-grid references rather than as the bull of a dart-board or shooting gallery. A map reference means that direction of travel can be changed, detours made, and the predetermined target still attained. On the other hand, a dart or bullet, once it embarks on its parabola, is committed and the action cannot be recalled or changed in any way. Objectives thought of as a map reference lead to flexibility: alternative strategies become possible and contingency planning has purpose. Objectives seen as the ''bull'' would lead to inflexible plans that would shatter at the first insurmountable obstacle.

Objectives should be set with care, since the map references should be the best one for the company. This is particularly true of the secondary objectives, as it is these which may be the most motivating and have the most impact on the total organisation. It needs no saying that the wrong map reference will lead to wrong plans which might take the company in a direction which is contrary to its real interests.

This is one reason why the secondary objectives should be defined with thought and care, and why, like the primary objectives, they are a matter requiring the attention of the chief executive. It is also fair to say at this stage that secondary objectives may change if the chief executive changes. Although the corporate appraisal should provide the factual information on which these objectives may be based, the final result is a personal interpretation by the chief executive. Thus, as with the profit target, the chief executive's thoughts, ambitions, and belief in his or her own capability make up a large part of the company's objectives.

A statement of a company's business activity should be narrow enough to focus attention on opportunities in a meaningful way, but wide enough to enable the company to identify opportunity when it sees it. Drucker[3] gives many examples of companies whose objectives were seen in too narrow a fashion, with the consequence that they embarked upon courses of action, and passed by many opportunities which they were ideally equipped to handle.

It is worth examining some examples of what this broadening of objectives has meant to certain businesses.

The UK manufacturers of various food and pharmaceutical products had many successful years when the entire reason for the existence of the company was thought of in terms of their main product: all diversification opportunities were given inadequate resources of time and money. The total accounting and management information system was geared to this one product.

This position changed with the advent of a new managing director. He defined the company's business in much broader terms, laying stress on the company's area of strength—its particular segment of the food market and its strong distribution links. Within three years the company had launched a number of new products and had many others under development. In the first year the one major product contributed virtually all the home food sales: by the third year 40% of turnover was coming from other products.

Within the company people thought of their prospects in a different light. The major product became what it should always have been, a valuable product, not *raison d'être*.

A company in the fruit and vegetable trade traditionally thought of themselves in terms of bananas, and geared their whole business to this concept. Admittedly they had certain well-developed skills in this product, but they had many problems and opportunities in common with other fresh produce wholesalers. A change in outlook led to a much wider definition of the business, still within the general area of fruit and vegetables, which in turn led to expansion and diversification in several new areas.

It is easy to state that the widening of perception was in each of these examples only a statement of the obvious, and that the opportunities would have been taken up by any good management. This would be too simple an analysis. If results in terms of profits and growth are considered, each of these companies had had "good" management, although each was facing some problems. Yet in each case it needed a change in emphasis before they could see opportunities, many of which had been available since the day the companies were incorporated. It really comes back to the problem of perception and vision. Strength of ambition is not the only factor in success, but it is very difficult to succeed without it. In a sense the secondary objectives, when combined with the profit targets, measure the strength of ambition of the company. Corporate success still requires clear judgement and good decision-making, but at least a part of the recipe for success is available.

Objectives should also be defined at various levels in the organisation. Although the objectives of each subsidiary or division should be compatible with those of the total group, they need not be identical. Few subsidiaries are in the total area of business defined by the parent, and, in any case, local conditions and local perception might make it desirable to stress certain aspects not considered by the parent as important.

Goals

Goals follow naturally on the two elements of the concept of profits so far discussed. If we may regard objectives as the map reference, we may consider goals as the landmarks and milestones that have to be passed as the traveller progresses along the chosen route. They serve exactly this purpose: to enable the company to check that it is still on course and to examine the reason why it has made any deviation.

A departure from strategy may be quite acceptable provided it is carried out with full knowledge of its effects. Alternatively, failure to achieve a goal may indicate that strategy should be changed if objectives are to be attained.

Goals can only be properly defined after strategy has been determined. They should always be expressed in quantitative terms, since they are designed as a standard of management, and it is virtually impossible to measure performance against a qualitative statement of expectations. They should also be defined against time—that is not only should they indicate what should have resulted but when it should have taken place. There is only one rule for the frequency or time intervals between goals: the usefulness of the periods selected.

In effect, a network of goals provides a form of model of the company's strategy over the whole period of the plan. The model may be as simple or as complex as the company wishes: again the criteria must be usefulness. Each goal must be purposeful and there is no value in defining targets which the company either cannot or does not intend to measure.

If goals are derived from strategy they will be compatible with each other. This is important because it is of little benefit for a company to have goals which can only be reached if other goals are sacrificed. This does not mean that a company may not apply a degree of critical targeting to all elements of its plan. For example, if inventory levels are high it may set a goal to reduce them, but this must be followed by definition of a plan to achieve that goal. In applying this element of corrective targeting the company must examine the other elements of the plan to ensure that the goals derived from these are still sensible. If, for instance, lower inventories meant poorer customer service and lower sales, these facts would have to be taken into account at the same time as the inventory goals were adjusted. The proper use of corrective targeting is, of course, during the process of developing plans and the use of goals in this way does not invalidate the contention that they are defined after strategy has been established.

The fact that goals must be capable of being measured was mentioned above. Preferred goals would be those that can be measured as a matter of routine from existing information sources, be they accounting, marketing research, or personnel records. In some cases goal-setting may indicate a need for change in the management information collected or in its manner of presentation.

Goals which can only be measured by special non-routine exercises may be worthwhile if the cost of collecting the data is less than the expected benefit. A company which includes the development and change of its corporate image as an important and essential element of strategy may define this in quantitative terms (e.g. perception levels of particular aspects) and may commission a market research study to check results against these benchmarks. Similarly, an occasional analysis of internal data might be made to provide a measurement of a goal which is not measured on any routine system.

Many different types of goals may be defined, and the possibilities suggested here are by way of example rather than recommendation. Only the company itself can know what is relevant and important to it: no textbook can provide this answer. Goals might be defined for:

—Percentage market share (by product and/or country).
—A ratio, such as return on sales.
—An absolute figure for sales.
—A minimum figure for customer complaints.
—A maximum figure for hours lost in industrial disputes.
—A labour productivity ratio.
—Total number of employees.
—A maximum employee "wastage" rate.
—A standard cost.
—A cost reduction target.
—A date by which a particular event must take place (e.g. new product launch).

Standards of Performance

The fourth aspect of objectives is a derivation from goals. While a goal is a corporate, divisional, or departmental target, a standard of performance is some-thing which is individually assigned to a named person. Sometimes the personal standard may be identical with the corporate goal: for example, a market share goal may be assigned to the product manager responsible. Sometimes the standard may be something derived from the goal: a splitting up of the corporate target into pieces for which individual people may be responsible (an example is the personal sales target given to a representative).

Performance standards may be taken from any aspect of the company's plans— the annual plan, the long-range plan, or a project plan. Frequently the standard will be a time-assigned task: Mr. Smith to complete a market survey by 1 September; Mr. Brown to negotiate a bank overdraft facility by 1 May; Dr. Stevens to develop a new product formulation by July next year; Mr. Oliver to secure the XYZ account by January next year. Such tasks may often be incorpo-rated in networks and similar documents.

The importance of personal standards is that they provide a tool for ensuring that plans are converted into things people can do—indeed, into things people are expected to do. There is thus a direct link between the tasks of the individual person and the total corporate strategy. The function and practical use of personal standards of performance will be examined in greater detail in Chapter 20, which deals with the ways of implementing plans.

In this chapter attention will also be paid to the technique of "management by objectives" (MBO) as developed by Humble[4] and its modern cousin performance management. The system of personal standards described here is a simplified variant of MBO, although its aims are narrower than those of MBO: the differ-ences will also be discussed later.

The overall concept as described here can be visualised as a network of targets, all interlinked in some way to the company's primary and secondary objectives. There are numerous levels, reaching right into the heart of the company. At an earlier point in this chapter the shifting of objectives from differing viewpoints was briefly mentioned. This should now be examined in greater detail since it applies to all the types of objectives described here.

The essence of this chapter has been to identify objectives as a target that is being pursued, and strategy as the means by which the organisation tries to achieve the objectives. Once a chief executive begins to examine objectives below the total company level he or she is beginning to deal with strategy: thus profit objectives set for a subsidiary are, in fact, an element of strategy. However, for the subsidiary chief executive these profit targets become a primary objective: only the way chosen to attain them can be called strategy. In general terms it is correct to say that within an organisation strategy set by one level in a business becomes the objective of the level beneath it. This can be illustrated very simply in Fig. 13.1.

The example is oversimplified, and in practice the company would define other objectives and elaborate its strategy in much more detail. It is very easy to visualise the example extended to cover other types of objectives and to other levels in a company. The point is that if the manager of department "O" does not produce a strategy to achieve an after tax profit of £100,000 he or she has failed, just as surely as the group chief executive who does not reach the million.

It follows that every level in the company has some delegation of freedom of decision-making from the top. (When this stops, an objective ceases to be an objective and becomes a simple instruction.) This explains why it is both possible

Level	Objective	Strategy*	
Total company	After tax profit £1 m. by 1975	Profits to come from:	
		(a) Diversification	£500,000
		(b) Subsidiary A	£230,000
		(c) Subsidiary B	£400,000
		(d) Subsidiary C	£100,000
Subsidiary A	Profit target £250,000	To concentrate effort on two departments, each marketing one product:	
		Department O	£100,000 profit
		Department P	£150,000 profit
Department O	Profit target £100,000	Develop annual turnover of £1m.	
		(a) Existing outlets	£700,000 sales
		(b) New outlets	£150,000 sales
		(c) Exports	£150,000 sales
Marketing managers	Develop export sales to £150,000 p.a. by 1975		

*The individual sources add up to more than £1 m. to allow for overheads.

Fig. 13.1. Levels of objectives and strategy

and desirable for the chief executive of subsidiary "A" to have his "strategic plan" even though the strategy is subordinate to that of the group.

What has so far been discussed is the concept as applied to the normal business undertaking. The position is different when non-profit-making or publicly owned undertakings are concerned. In organisations such as a hospital or a charity the concept of the primary objective may have little value. However, I would argue that a "cost of service" objective tied to the remainder of the overall concept is of importance. An objective of service to the community or to individual categories of people might indeed be the main *raison d'être* of the undertaking: this is no reason why a cost efficiency rating should not be valid. Where the commercial concern tries to provide its shareholders with their profit requirements, the charitable undertaking needs to give the people for whose benefit it exists the maximum service at the minimum cost. These are factors which can be defined, quantified, and used in strategic planning in a meaningful way. In my opinion an undertaking such as a large hospital requires sound commercial planning and application if the skills of doctors and nurses are to be used to the full. The criteria of decision-making may be different, but certainly exists. Commercial inefficiency merely wastes the abilities of the non-commercial worker in the hospital.

Some government undertakings have a defined task which calls upon them to make profits as well as provide a service. This particularly applies to "productive" undertakings such as—in the United Kingdom—the Post Office, the Coal Board, and the Railways. The British Post Office has, for example, the obligation to earn a predetermined return on assets (this, of course, is only half an objective, and would not fit the definition of the primary objective used earlier in this chapter).

The dilemma of publicly owned business undertakings should not be under-stressed. They are subject to direct control by government, and their objectives can alter with every change of political party. British Rail has always suffered because of the see-saw between community service objectives and short-term profit objectives. In addition, the constraints attached to the strategic freedom of the enterprise may change. Again British Rail provides an example: one government allows a diversification policy, the next states that the Railway's only area of business is to be railways. The next pursues a privatisation policy. Although outside the scope of this chapter, it is worth mentioning that Long[8] has recorded that British Rail take long-range planning very seriously and are able to extract considerable value from the process despite these difficulties. The ability of these businesses is also affected by uncertainty because of privatisation policies. Now we see you, now we don't decisions play havoc with morale and entrepreneurial ability.

Much has been said about objectives in their various shapes and forms. It would be wrong to leave the subject without some consideration of the benefits which a well-applied application of the concept will bring. The main use is the basic one: objectives enable a company to plan. The primary objective is a precursor to strategic action: how this objective is used in strategic planning—through the technique of gap analysis—will be demonstrated later.

Through their part in the strategic planning process objectives "stretch" the organisation, and help it to achieve more than may otherwise have been the case.

As the plans are devised, any failure to reach objectives causes a re-cycling of corporate thought and calls for new ideas which will enable the looked-for results to be achieved.

In addition, the total concept of objectives, from primary objective down to the lowest personal standard set, provides a motivational tool of great potential. Objectives can be made widely known in an organisation—after all, it is only the strategy which should be confidential—and can be used to stimulate the minds of men from board room to factory floor.

A measure of cohesion and co-ordination is introduced. Although, as Scott[1] has stated, all companies must have objectives (even if they are unaware of them), it is a fact that many companies have never attempted to define them in any logical way. This means that individual managers project their own desires and inter-pretations on to what they think their company should be doing. Careful attention to the definition of objectives will ensure that everyone does, indeed, get on the right tracks.

Better motivation, co-ordination, and higher levels of achievement can be expressed as a contribution to communication, which is one of the side aims of any process of formal planning. Perhaps, above all, objectives lead the company on its first steps along the path towards clarity of corporate thinking, which is a major reason why planning adds to profit.

The discussion of objectives needs to be completed by a consideration of two terms, *vision* and *strategic intent*. We met the former in Chapter 3, where it was given some attention in the context of leadership. It is a term that began to become popular in the late 1970s, and was well established by the mid-1980s. What it means for me is an expression of the longer term objectives and values of the organisation, in a way that shows what the firm is trying to achieve. The definition provided by Karlof[9] is helpful:

"*Vision*, in the sense of something seen in a dream, is the term used to describe a picture of a relatively remote future in which business has developed under the best possible conditions and in accordance with the hopes and dreams of the owner or chief executive. A vision provides a benchmark for what one hopes to achieve in business, and can be a guide to the level of ambition of strategic plan-ning ... (portion omitted) ...

"...A vision can be said to link business with corporate culture, creating a common standard of values for the individual performance of employees."

Strategic intent is a term coined by Hamel and Prahalad[10] in 1989, which has caught the imagination of some. They define this as an obsession with winning over a long period. The quote clarifies this:

"On the one hand strategic intent envisions a desired leadership position and establishes the criterion the organisation will use to chart its progress. Komatsu set out to 'encircle caterpillar'. Canon sought to 'Beat Xerox'. Honda strove to become a second Ford—and automotive pioneer. All are expressions of strategic intent.

"At the same time, strategic intent is more than simply unfettered ambition. (Many companies possess an ambitious strategic intent yet fall short of their goals). The concept also encompasses an active management process that includes: focussing the organisation's attention on the essence of winning; motivating people by communicating the value of the target; leaving room for individual and team contributions; sustaining enthusiasm by providing new operational definitions as circumstances change; and using intent consistently to guide resource allocation."

Personally I cannot see the difference between the two terms. However anyone who has studied the evolution of strategic management will have observed that many new concepts are no more than a re-expression of the old, under a catchy name. Because of the richness of the English language, it will be a long time before we run out of words and have to start recycling some of the old ones.

References

1. Scott, B. W. *Long Range Planning in American Industry*, American Management Association, 1965.
2. Ansoff, H. I. *Corporate Strategy*, McGraw-Hill, 1965.
3. Drucker, P. F. *The Practice of Management*, Heinemann, 1955.
4. Humble, J. W. *Improving Business Results*, McGraw-Hill, 1968.
5. Argenti, A. J. A. *Corporate Planning: A Practical Guide*, Allen & Unwin, 1968.
6. Ackoff, R. C. *A Concept of Corporate Planning*, Wiley Interscience, 1970.
7. Redwood, H. "The Fisons Shareholder Survey", *Long Range Planning*, April 1971.
8. Long, R. A. "Planning in British Railways", *Long Range Planning*, December 1969.
9. Karlof, B. *Business Strategy*, Macmillan, London, 1989.
10. Hamel, G. and Prahalad, C. K. "Strategic Intent", *Harvard Business Review*, May/June 1989.

14
Strategy

Some aspects of the strategic planning process have already been discussed in considerable detail. In other chapters most of the essential groundwork of the strategic plan has been worked over. At this stage in the process we may assume that the company has set its objectives, defined its social responsibility, established all the assumptions on which it will base its plan, and now fully understands its own strengths and weaknesses. All this work will, as a byproduct, have provided the company with a number of opportunities for further study.

This chapter will consider certain aspects of corporate strategy in some detail with the intention of analysing the various approaches to the formation of strategy. In later chapters attention will be focused on more detailed analysis, and eventually on the strategic plan itself.

Definitions of strategic and operating planning have already been given. Because the difference between the two activities is important, it is worth turning attention once more on these two areas. Ansoff[1] illustrates his view of the essential meaning of the terms with his well-known cow analogy. He maintains that the operating problem is concerned with getting as much performance as possible out of the company's investment in current markets—a process which he likens to "seeking the best way to milk a cow". Strategic problems are on a different level, and are concerned with allocating the firm's resources to activities which offer the largest potential return, which may not necessarily have anything in common with its current activities: "...but if our basic interest is not the cow but in the most milk we get for our investment, we must also make sure that we have the best cow money can buy." Strategic management can opt to change the cow: operating management can only attempt to be a more efficient milker.

This does not mean that strategy does not take account of current operations. Indeed it must, for the decision to remain in them is in itself a matter of strategy. Where strategic decisions encompass all the possible paths that the company might take to reach its objectives, and where the definition of what those objectives should be, is of itself a matter of strategy; operating planning is concerned only with getting the most out of what is currently being done.

253

Strategy is very much a question of a choice from the alternative paths open to the company. The number of alternatives available to any company is legion, and their identification and analysis may be a complex task. Consider, for example, the relatively simple strategic problem facing a smallholder who has set himself the task of doubling his profits over a three-year period:

(i)   Expand by buying the farm next door.
(ii) Apply more investment to the land, e.g. in the form of glasshouses or irrigation sprays.
(iii) Change the crop to another entirely different—perhaps add a cow, goat, or rear chickens.
(iv) Install another process: perhaps prepackaging fruit and vegetables or turning milk into cream.
(v)   Attention to marketing, so that a greater realisation is obtained.
(vi) Become a more efficient producer.
(vii) Sell the business and invest the capital elsewhere.

These seven alternatives can be combined into $7 \times 6 \times 5 \times 4 \times 3 \times 2 \times 1$ possible courses of action—and the best that can be said about this is that it is a lot. And this ignores the numerous alternatives hidden in the broad listings staged (buy the 50-acre farm on one side, or the 100-acre farm on the other; grow sugar-beet or potatoes or radishes).

So far the illustration makes the point that even a relatively simple business unit has a wide field from which to choose its strategy. At the other extreme, the massive multi-national, multi-divisional company will have even more possibilities (and needs special ways of considering them: see Chapters 15 and 16). Yet there is also no doubt that the illustration has also succeeded in making a relatively simple problem into a very complicated one.

This is because the evolution of strategy involves more than the writing down of possible alternatives. The steps omitted in the smallholder illustration were:

(i)   Considering the alternatives in the light of the firm's own constraints and code of ethics.
(ii) Applying the results of the corporate appraisal so that opportunities are matched to the company.
(iii) Considering those weaknesses established in the corporate appraisal which exclude some alternatives (e.g. lack of capital or skill).
(iv) Information from the environmental appraisal.
(v)   Evaluation of the alternatives themselves: some are always potentially more profitable than others.

The strategic planning process involves the identification of alternatives, the collection of information, evaluation and selection of alternatives, and, finally, the strategic decisions themselves. Much more will be said on these subjects: for the moment it is fair to assume that the applications of these stages during the process would have reduced the smallholder's problems to something he could manage—a choice between a few real opportunities.

Part of the disciplined thinking which must accompany the development of strategy is to assess the extent of the problem. One very useful and simple technique to assist in this is gap analysis. This sets out the targets the company is trying to achieve, what is expected from current operations, and what the "gap" is between expectations and requirements. Filling the gap is what strategy is about. All this can more easily be demonstrated with a simple diagram (Fig. 14.1).

The diagram measures absolute levels of profit on the vertical axis and periods of time on the horizontal axis (it could also be used to measure return on investment ratios or sales). Line A shows the progression of the company's primary, or profit, objective. This measures what the business intends to achieve.

Line D measures what the company expects to achieve from its current operations, assuming no basic strategic changes are made. In the early stages of planning, this line would probably be projected on data obtained during the corporate appraisal, possibly supplemented by more detailed forecasts in some areas. As the company moves further into the planning process it will be replaced by the projections from the operating plans. This should mean that the validity of this line should improve, although if the initial work has been carried out well the position of the revised line should not be too far away from the original.

The corporate appraisal should also provide the information on which lines B and C are prepared. Line B shows the effects of proposed profit improvement projects on profits and illustrates the extent to which line D can be moved towards line A—a partial closing of the "gap". Line B may also include profit targets to be achieved from an improvement strategy: that is, the actual means may not at this stage be known, only that the target is likely to be realistic.

One way of helping line B to be realistic is to consider line C. This is an attempt to insert the industry trend: that is, what the company would be earning if their results were based on average industry returns instead of their own individual forecast. This particular line is not always obtainable because base data is sometimes unavailable, and it is itself a forecast of trends. Nevertheless, where it can be obtained, it gives a useful perspective and aids the company in its assessment of the "improvement gap".

The gap between lines B and A is the "strategic gap". This is the area to which corporate top management must give attention, for it will only be filled if the company enters into new strategies.

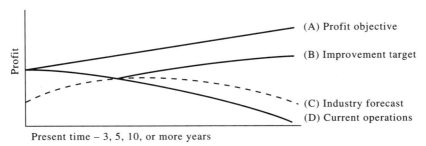

FIG. 14.1. Gap analysis

In the diagram, line D shoots rapidly downwards towards oblivion. This is by no means an inevitability, and the direction and shape of this line, and the nature of the improvement and strategic gaps, will be unique to each individual company.

The gap-analysis approach may also be used at various levels in the company—subsidiaries, divisions, or departments. The only difference is that at the lower levels the strategic gap may be a "new thinking" gap: it depends how much of the strategic task is delegated by central corporate management. In large companies it may be a great deal.

Kami[2] maintains that gap analysis can be used much more widely, and that although a simple technique it can help companies of any size. He suggests taking the analysis two stages further. Firstly, the expected results of the various programmes devised to fill the gap should also be charted so that the impact of each can be seen. As some may fail, he advocates the identification of reserve programmes: culminatively the results would then exceed the objectives, although the expectation is that not all would be implemented. His second suggestion is that control points be shown on the diagram (Fig. 14.2), to indicate the time when the company should check that it is, in fact, on course.

Gap analysis is thus used to help the organisation to "stretch" itself towards its objectives. Occasionally, closing the gap may be impossible, either because of shortage of ideas or shortage of resources. Perhaps the objective for the fifth year is achievable, but only at the expense of unacceptable losses in the early years. In these circumstances, and provided the objectives have been carefully thought out, the answer may be to re-examine the company's continued role as an independent business unit. Possibly the shareholders would be better served by a merger with another company. Alternatively, the answer may be to fire the chief executive, or the planner, or both.

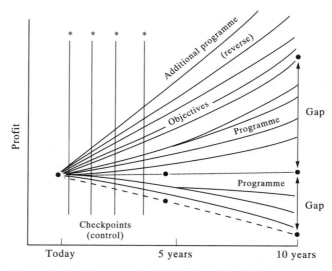

FIG. 14.2. Gap analysis with control points*. Reproduced from an article by M. Kami[2]

On the other hand, the company may find that in practice its projects considerably exceed its objectives, even after allowing for reserves. Here the company has to be very sure that all the projects are within its financial and human resources. If they are, it is in the fortunate position of being able to decide whether to change objectives and aim for a higher target, or to opt for a slower than optimum growth. The temptation to move on to a higher growth pattern is often one to be avoided, since too much growth may be as disastrous as too little.

The diagrams are designed as an aid to thought—and possibly of presentation—and it is possible, and sometimes desirable, to dispense with the drawing and analyse the figures alone. Exactly the same results can be achieved.

So far the discussion of the "gap" has provided an indication of the strategic task. Before turning to the ways in which strategy might be further identified and analysed, it is worth considering the philosophical approaches to planning defined by Ackoff.[3]

He sees three distinct philosophies which—for want of better terms—he calls "satisficing", "optimising", and "adaptivising", although in practice mixtures of the three pure forms also occur. "Satisficing" plans aim to do well, but not as well as possible, to do enough to satisfy, but not to do more than this, although it may be possible to do better. Objectives set by "satisficing" planners are always feasible—the "stretching" effect of a good system of objectives is avoided. Strategies always try to avoid conflict, and rarely involve organisational change or major variations from the past. "Satisficing" planners produce "one point" plans, i.e. their plans contain only one set of strategies and forecasts and make no provision for the possibility that things might go wrong: an artificial certainty is given to all planned actions. As it is assumed that the organisation is flexible enough to cope with the unexpected, there are seldom formal systems for monitoring and controlling the plans.

Ackoff[3] sums up "satisficing". "Not surprisingly, satisficing planning seldom produces a radical departure from the past. It usually yields conservative plans that comfortably continue most current policies, correcting only obvious deficiencies. Such planning therefore appeals to organisations that are more concerned with survival than with development and growth."

"Satisficing" planning adds little to the company's knowledge of itself or its markets. Its values to the company must be seriously questioned.

The "optimising" planner takes a completely different view of his job. He aims always to choose the best possible course of action, and relies very heavily on operational research techniques and mathematical models. He formulates all his objectives and goals in quantified terms—and tends to ignore all those which he cannot so quantify.

"This can distort the value of his work and produce justifiable discomfort in the consuming managers who must moderate quantitative results with their own qualitative judgements on important problems that have not been taken into account."[3]

The optimiser is only as good as the models he produced. Perhaps his biggest defect is that he tends to underrate the human aspect—partly because many "people" activities cannot be built into the model. Although control systems can be incorporated into the systems these tend to measure only what was foreseen when the model was built—the unforeseen is in danger of being ignored.

"Adaptivising" is accompanied by the belief that the main value in planning lies in the process and not the plans themselves. Again it is worth referring to the Harvard study by Vancil,[4] quoted in Chapter 2, and his suspicion that accuracy in forecasts might be the wrong objective of a planning system.

The adaptiviser believes that another main purpose of his plans is to prevent crises from arising—to adapt the organisation and systems so that difficulties are avoided, and so that management does not have to spend most of its time resolving the problems caused by past inadequacies and inefficiencies.

Perhaps the strongest point of the adaptiviser's platform is that he differentiates distinct types of risks in all future events. There are certain aspects which are virtual certainties (the point was made in the chapters dealing with the environment), for which the best solution is to ensure that adequate plans are made and actions committed so that the company may exploit these events. Many more events are a matter of varying degrees of probability: here the adaptiviser will prepare a series of contingency plans to cover every foreseeable possibility. (Examples have been given in a previous chapter.)

Ackoff's analysis is useful in understanding management behaviour, and it is important to know the various approaches to strategic planning as this can often help shed a new light on the way a company plans and acts. My own bias is towards adaptivising planning although, as in so many other aspects of management, there is probably no one correct answer.

But, for most of us, there is a greater interest in the identification and selection of strategic alternatives than in learning to classify our own approach to planning.

One way of analysing strategic alternatives has appeared in many books and articles—with modifications and variations—although it probably originated with the Stanford Research Institute. Variants have been used by, among others, Ansoff[5] and von Allmen.[6]

Strategic alternatives can be classified according to the matrix in Fig. 14.3.

Product \ Market	Current	New
Current	(a)	(c)
New	(b)	(d)

FIG. 14.3. Analysis of strategic alternatives

Current Products in Current Markets[(a)]

This is improving the performance of the company's existing products in the markets in which it currently trades. Much of the data for decisions in this area will come from the corporate appraisal, and the development of plans in this box of the matrix is very much the duty of operating management. The main element of corporate strategic thinking in this area is concerned with how much, how fast, and what quantity of resources should be committed to these actions. Following Ansoff's[1] image mentioned earlier in this chapter it is concerned with getting more milk out of the cow.

Actions in this area might be increasing brand share by changing any of the elements of marketing strategy—for example, sales effort, advertising, distribution channels, or the relative weightings in the marketing mix. It would also include actions which improve the profitability of current operations and thus the actions which help take the company to line B in the gap-analysis diagram.

It makes good sense for every company to fully investigate the area before moving on to the more exotic elements of corporate strategy. Although problems of the company's "risk balance" are relevant, and although the planners must ensure that the point of diminishing returns has not been reached, it is a fact that action in the area of current products and current markets is often less risky than ventures into the unknown.

New Products to Current Markets[b]

This is often a logical way to exploit particular marketing knowledge and capability possessed by the company. It is a path taken by business ever since the first business began, and is frequently accompanied by an economy of scale in marketing, distribution and sales operations. Examples of action under this segment of the strategic matrix are the supermarket which expands its activities into clothing and domestic hardware, the suit manufacturer which introduces shirts into its product range, the pharmaceutical company which adds a new cold remedy or the magazine which introduces mail-order selling to its readers. By definition these products should be handled by the same sales force, and purchased by the same consumers.

Again much of the initiative and most of the planning will be the task of operating management, though it is certainly a strategic planning task to ensure that adequate attention is given to opportunities in this area: it is ground that should be thoroughly worked over before the company attempts to work the lesser known terrain in box (d).

Current Products in New Markets[c]

This is another area where synergy can be fairly high, as development here can often bring economies of scale in production and general management. Once again it is a method of expansion which has been used from the dawn of history.

Perhaps the most obvious example which springs to mind—since so many companies do it—is to seek out new markets in other countries. There are still companies which restrict their thinking to the domestic market.

For many companies export opportunities will either already be taken up or may simply not exist at all. This does not mean that no opportunities will be available, although they may not be so obvious. In Chapter 6, which discussed forecasting, mention was made of the concept of the product life cycle. One particular reason for introducing existing products to new markets could well be to extend the product life cycle. Such an action can be important at any point on the S-curve, but may be strategically vital as the product moves into maturity, the top point of the curve associated with low growth (or actual decline) in both sales and profits. Action taken at an earlier point of the curve may, of course, help to postpone the day of maturity.

"Ovaltine" in the United Kingdom, in contrast to many other countries elsewhere in the world, is a product which has traditionally been associated with bedtime drinking. Much of the advertising of the previous years—if not decades—of both "Ovaltine" and its competitors had created the bedtime market. In 1970 a deliberate attempt was made, through the Cool-ova campaign, to create a new market—"Ovaltine", drunk in cold instead of warm milk, as an "anytime" beverage. A good try, that did not work.

This is not an isolated example of action which might be taken to create new markets. Consider the ethical pharmaceutical company which offers a range of its products, for "over-the-counter" sale in pharmacies: or, alternatively, the company selling proprietary pharmaceuticals which moves into the ethical field. Plastics manufacturers have a history of creating new markets for their products, often by attacking the position of traditional materials.

New Products for New Markets[d]

Diversification: in effect this box of the matrix can be summed up in one word. Yet this is deceptively simple, since it is potentially the most risky and dangerous path open to any company. The pitfalls are many since the ground is usually completely unknown to the exploring company. And somewhere along the path there is often a distorting mirror which reflects a powerful and glamorous image of the manager, trapping him with dreams of empire, grandeur, and glory.

Yet it can also be a rewarding path to tread. For some companies it may indeed be the only way to develop.

The way the individual firm handles the four boxes in the matrix would depend to some extent on its definition of what is a product and what is a market.

The definition of product which I like to use comes from McCarthy[7] and includes the intangible aspects of a product as well as its physical characteristics. The intangibles include those items which are offered by the company to induce consumers to buy—for example, after sales service, a guarantee, or the terms of credit it offers. The tangible aspects include, besides the obvious characteristics of shape, form, and composition, less obvious elements of packaging and branding. Thus under this definition an "own label" version would be considered a different product from the branded item, even though all other characteristics except the label were identical.

Market definition can cause similar problems, and there can be few people who have not observed with some cynical amusement the way virtually any product can be proved to be a brand leader—the only rule is to be consistent.

In practical terms there can be no universal definition of these words which is adequate for all companies. The right answer is for the company to apply definitions which suit its own purpose—the only rule is to be consistent.

One term which has been mentioned several times is synergy, the mystical force which means that the whole is greater than the sum of the two individual parts, which largely comes about because of the economies of scale which may occur in the larger unit—economies which may be in any area—management, production, physical distribution, marketing, research and development, or any other sector. In acquisition situations bitter experience has often shown that synergy is more illusory than real—but this is another story. As a generalisation synergy might be expected to be highest in box (a) and lowest in box (d).

A further generalisation can be made about synergy in diversification. It is likely to be higher in horizontal or vertical diversification than in unrelated diversification. These terms are illustrated in Fig. 14.4. Vertical diversification is integration backwards towards the raw material or forwards to the ultimate consumer. Horizontal diversification is moving towards activities on the same level in the chain, but which have common consumers or distribution channels. Unrelated diversification is moving into something which has nothing in common with the present business. Each is subject to a different pattern of risks. For example, although synergy might be high in vertical diversification, the fundamental risks to which the company is subject may not be changed: yet the amount of resources subject to those risks may be drastically increased.

Some writers suggest the preparation of a synergy chart as the next stage in the analysis. The example in Fig. 14.5 is quoted from Hargreaves.[8] A similar approach is adopted by Ansoff.[5]

During the preparation of each of these stages of analysis, preliminary screening should take place and ideas which are obviously unattractive or impracticable discarded. This is very much a commonsense approach: the main problem being to be reasonably flexible in the rejection stage, and not to kill ideas just because they are different. The ideas which are left are intensively evaluated. One of

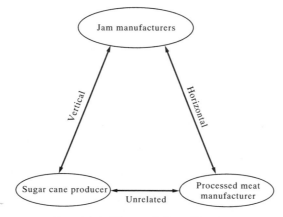

FIG. 14.4. Types of diversification

Customers	Products	Related Technology	New Technology
Existing	Existing	Wooden bedroom furniture	Metal beds
Existing	Similar	Wooden dining room furniture	Electrically operated beds
Existing	New	Wooden garden furniture	Electric blankets
Similar	Existing	Children's bedroom furniture	'Status' beds Built-in TV, etc.
Similar	Similar	Fitted cupboards	Metal kitchen cabinets
Similar	New	Wendy houses Climbing frames	Furnishing fabrics Stainless steel sinks
New	Existing	Contract sales to hotels	Bulk supply Metal school furniture
New	Similar	Wooden display units	Medical inspection couches
New	New	Coffins	Suspension filing systems
Firm Itself		Wooden mouldings Packing cases	Hinges Door fittings

FIG. 14.5. "Synergy" chart for company considering expansion/diversification. (In this case, a manufacturer of wooden bedroom furniture.) Reproduced with permission from an article by D. Hargreaves[9]

Ansoff's[5] major contributions has been his work on this evaluation process, and the suggestion of methods of selection, which take into account both the concept of synergy and an approach to the probability of success.

Quite apart from the possible financial results of alternative strategies, it is very useful to relate the alternatives to the company's own capability profile and its available skills and resources (see Chapter 9), and the particular attributes which the corporate appraisal has revealed the most strategically desirable—for example, adjustments to the company's risk balance. The object of the exercise is to select those courses of action which most effectively fill the gap between current expectations and the primary objective, which capitalise on as many of the company's strengths as possible, remove or correct its weaknesses, which comply with its objectives and constraints, and which have the highest probability of success. The main purpose of drawing up check lists and rating opportunities against them is to ensure that no important factors are overlooked.

Screening our projects, arranging them in recommended selection order, and evaluating their prospects is an important staff planning function. The final choice of strategies is not: this is a task that management should not delegate to planners. And even in the screening process the conclusions are likely to be more valid if they are worked on by the management team rather than by the planning staff alone.

There are probably three main schools of thought over the way in which the strategic net should be cast when the company begins to fish for its alternatives. The first is that it should be solely an opportunist. Full-scale selection and screening techniques as described here are not required under these circumstances: all that the company need do is to try to keep itself in the situation where opportunities come its way. Such a company is, in fact, unlikely to practise any system of formal planning, and yet is often highly successful. This carries a lesson to the planner. Every plan should leave room for the possibility that unforeseen opportunities will arise—the possibility of the "lucky break". The planning system which precludes this sort of entrepreneurial activity is likely to do its company a disservice.

The second school of thought is that the net should be thrown as wide as it will stretch in an effort to draw in every single opportunity that it is humanly possible to identify. This needs a very extensive screening and evaluation process which, for many companies, may be beyond their resources. The trend of thinking through the 1980s has been to suggest that diversification leading to the conglomerate company rarely gives the best deal to shareholders. See, for example, Porter.[9]

The third school of thought is that most chief executives are only able to work in certain industry areas and have a definite concept of the type of activity they would be prepared to take their companies into. In effect the broad field is described in the company's objectives, and it would be wasting effort to try to fish for opportunities in other areas. Even so, the size of the fishing ground may still be very extensive.

As with so many other aspects of corporate planning, the "right" answer is the one that fits the company. And as the company develops and changes so it may change its viewpoint and find another "right" answer.

Certainly the approach selected will have an influence on the identification of opportunities. This brings us to the last topic in this chapter: before alternatives can be screened, analysed, and adopted, they must be found. The very practical question of "How does a company identify new opportunities?" is one that causes concern to many managers. A few broad hints might help to put this problem in perspective.

At the outset it should be stressed that there is no substitute for individual creativity. Many of the best opportunities selected often arise simply because a creative person thought of them. Strategic planning can help by providing a framework through which these ideas can be channelled, as well as the use of particular techniques in the planning process (such as brainstorming meetings). The unexpected and unstructured "good idea" is often one of the most effective. It has been said earlier that the planning process must seek to encourage individual creativity, not to destroy it.

The logical processes of analysis described in this and other chapters should also be expected to produce a good yield of opportunities. Environmental studies, the corporate appraisal, and the attempt to analyse various possible strategic moves can produce much that is worthwhile. For the analyst there may also be much that is tedious, a statement that will be endorsed by anyone that has searched industry lists for possible acquisition candidates. Frequently the clarity with which a company is, through its planning processes, able to examine its basic problems, provides the new viewpoint that enables the solution to be found. Individual creativity may still be present in the finding of opportunities through analysis, but the advantage of an analytical process is that many opportunities can be uncovered even where individual creativity is low. A process of analysis, following predetermined concepts, starting wide and gradually narrowing down, can be rather like the net used by the trawlermen. Where the sea is rich the harvest of fish will be great—but if the wrong place is trawled the catch may be insignificant.

It would be wrong to conclude that all new opportunities are internally generated either by an "ideas" man or an analyst. Most companies will also draw much from the market place: the more marketing-oriented the company, the more effort it will make to find out what its consumers' want. In addition, some strategic alternatives may emerge from actual or anticipated moves by competitors. It is in these fields that a continuous programme of marketing research comes into its own—the continued proving of consumer requirements, and the testing of different interpretations of these should provide a flow of ideas. Some of these will lie within the strategic path determined already, although others might well take the company into new strategies.

At any point in time a company, particularly if it has invested heavily in research and development in the past, is likely to have a stream of projects ready for implementation over the next two to three years. This is today's position, and it may represent very welcome and important additions to the list of alternatives under consideration. The real problem of planning research and development is not how to make use of past ideas that have reached fruition, but how to ensure a continued flow of projects with a reasonable measure of control so that future requirements can also be met. This is a problem which will receive attention later.

The discovery of strategic alternatives is not a passive activity to be solved from behind a desk. Few planners can afford to wait for things to happen—and even fewer chief executives can afford this luxury. There is a great deal of hard work involved to be performed by the chief executive and planner or shared out among the management team. The deliberate attack on the future is by no means impossible and, indeed, is one of the aims of corporate planning.

This chapter has only made a beginning, and much more remains to be discussed on the subject of strategic planning. It is a great mountain of a subject, and all we have done so far is to establish a base camp from which to begin the assault on the summit. In subsequent chapters there will be discussion of the main groups of alternatives the company might choose, an examination of techniques of portfolio analysis, particular reference to strategic planning for multinational business, and a chapter on the practical problems of writing a strategic plan. And all this before the specialist subjects of financial and human resources strategy are reached. Let us hope that the base camp is well established, for the mountain is an Everest.

References

1. Ansoff, H. I. *Planning as a Practical Management Tool*, Corporate Planning Seminar Manual, Bradford University, May 1966.
2. Kami, M. J. "Gap Analysis—Key to Super Growth", *Long Range Planning*, June 1969.
3. Ackoff, R. C. *A Concept of Corporate Planning*, Wiley Interscience, 1970.
4. Vancil, R. F. "The Accuracy of Long Range Planning", *Harvard Business Review*, September–October 1970.
5. Ansoff, H. I. *Corporate Strategy*, McGraw-Hill, 1965.
6. von Allmen, E. *Company Planning—The Control of Corporate Destiny*, Incomtech, 1966.
7. McCarthy, E. J. *Basic Marketing: a Managerial Approach*, Unwin, 1964.
8. Hargreaves, D. "Corporate Planning: a Chairman's Guide", *Long Range Planning*, March 1969.
9. Porter, M. "From Competitive Advantage to Corporate Strategy", *Harvard Business Review*, May/June 1987.

15
Strategic Portfolio Analysis

During the 1970s there were many major contributions to corporate planning. One of the most significant was undoubtedly strategic portfolio analysis. This technique, which can be found in many different variations, helped to satisfy the emerging need for centralised decisions on key strategic issues in multinational corporations. Portfolio analysis provided a means of comparing numerous business activities in relation to each other, establishing priorities and deciding between winners and losers.

The original work is accredited to General Electric whose concept included dividing activities into *strategic business units* with like characteristics, related to the life cycles of the products. Strategic business units may be a composite of product and geographical area. It is quite possible for a product to be in a mature stage in developed countries and in a take-off phase in less developed ones. This life cycle difference could result in two strategic business units, instead of one on a more traditional product grouping.

Boston Consulting Group deserve much of the credit for developing and popularising the technique. It is this organisation's 2×2 matrix with its evocative terminology which has captured the imagination of modern business. The broadly descriptive labels attached to each box in the matrix, cash cows, dogs, stars and question marks have become part of the language of management and are quite frequently used by those who are ignorant of the underlying technique.

One axis of the Boston matrix measures growth and the other relative market share and the whole edifice is based on the assumption that these are the two major factors affecting profitability, which although it may sometimes be true is by no means a universal law. The Boston concept was linked to their theories of experience curves, which postulate a phenomenon that costs will fall by a regular percentage every time output doubles. Put together the two techniques postulate a strategy of competitive dominance and an emphasis on high market shares in high growth activities.

Much of this is open to question, and indeed is increasingly being questioned, and Boston Consulting have their critics as well as their adherents.[1,2] Competitive techniques to the Boston Consulting approach are numerous: most merely replace one axis with another factor empirically considered to be more relevant. On a broader front the Strategic Planning Institute runs a multi-company activity (PIMS) which attempts to isolate key variables from a study of actual data submitted by its member-subscribers. This service is well thought of by large companies where sufficient industry data exists on the PIMS files, and provides empirical evidence of links between factors such as growth, market share, promotional expenditure, research and development and the like, and can be used as a basis for portfolio analysis.

Hofer, in a diagram used in Hofer and Schendel,[3] suggests a different approach to portfolio analysis. His matrix has the stages of the life cycle on one axis (development, growth, shake-out, maturity to saturation, and decline), and competitive position on the other (strong, average and weak). This offers a useful way of seeing a number of corporate activities in a comparative way, without pretending to be a formula for strategic decisions. One of the weaknesses of the Boston Consulting approach is that it became a recipe for strategy: invest in stars so that they continue to shine, divest dogs, because they will do you no good, use the cash from cash cows to choose winners from the question marks (later christened by others *wildcats*) and to support the stars.

Barksdale and Harris[4] combined the Boston Consulting Matrix with a life cycle approach. This had the result of questioning whether all dogs consumed resources without delivering benefit. They pointed out that there were dogs that could be turned into useful businesses, just as there were "dodos" that had nowhere to go. Later someone else renamed the dodo "underdogs", which is rather neat. They also identified "war horses" as an additional variety of cash cow, where business was declining, but the activity would go on and on generating cash. Although the additional farmyard terminology helped expand the original thinking, the result is still strategy by formula: if it falls within a certain box on the matrix, do what the box says. This worries me, as it did many of the critics of portfolio analysis. Buzzell and Gale[5] published a summary of principles drawn from the PIMS data base. Among their conclusions, which we will revisit in more detail in a later chapter, was:

Many so-called "dog" and "question mark" businesses generate cash, while many "cash cows" are dry.

I believe that portfolio analysis is a very useful tool, that can give insights into many strategic situations. However, I prefer to use it for two main purposes. One is to look at activities within the organisation relative to each other, so that strategic issues can be surfaced. The second is to make the analysis more future oriented by looking at the likely movements across the portfolio, and the impact of actions that the company or competitors can instigate. To do this requires an approach that generates a deep understanding of the factors which really influence business success, and which can be related to other analytical approaches. This chapter will describe just such a technique, and in the following chapter a case study will be provided to give more insight into its application and interpretation.

Only one of the techniques, as far as I am aware, attempts to develop deep understanding of the factors which really influence business success. This is the directional policy matrix (DPM) developed by Shell Chemicals[6,7] and made into a three-dimensional matrix by consultants Harbridge House.[8] The DPM is a 3×3 matrix measuring on one axis the factors which influence long-term profitability in the market and, on the other, those which account for longer term competitive position. The position of a strategic business unit on each axis is determined from a weighting of numerous sub-factors. What is most significant about these is that they can be related to economic theory which explains what influences power within an industry: in fact it is of value to examine this structural analysis of industry before considering the DPM in any depth.

The Harbridge House addition is in the form of a risk matrix which, with the market success axis in common with the DPM, turns it into a three-dimensional box which can easily be modelled in clear plastic; or even more easily can be handled as a narrative qualification to the analysis of each strategic business unit or recorded on two dimensions by colour codes.

That axis of the risk matrix which is not shared with the DPM measures risk from the major environmental forces. The position on this axis is scored taking both impact and probability into account, and producing a composite score from an examination of the risks to which each strategic business unit is subject. This additional dimension is very helpful when strategic decisions are being considered, and enables top management to gain a clear insight into the main strategic issues they face.

Most general economic text books deal with market structures, and the concepts of perfect and imperfect competition. All things being equal, we would expect a company to earn higher profits the closer it come to being a monopoly; conversely, profitability might be expected to decline as the company's activities came closer to meeting the conditions of perfect competition. The difference between the two conditions is the degree of power over the supply curve, in relation to demand and the degree of freedom of the firm to set prices.

The underlying theory has been worked into a practical analysis by Porter[9] (see Chapter 10). Following his line of thought it is possible to visualise an industry in the manner described in Fig. 10.2, as five groups of interrelated forces operating within the framework of the external environment. The eight-sided figure represents one way of visualising the external environment, which has been dealt with in more detail in earlier chapters. These forces, although of the utmost significance to firms in the industry, are generally common to all competitors, although their impact will vary from firm to firm.

Readers will remember from Chapter 10 that the central box in the diagram deals with the competitors in the industry. Although there are a number of clear-cut factors which affect the degree and depths of competitive rivalry, this is also modified by the power of suppliers and buyers. The greater the power and influence of these two groups, the lower profitability tends to become in the industry. Both of these boxes should be analysed to the required depth relevant to the industry. Buyers, for example, would normally be divided into wholesalers, retailers and the consumer. For industrial products there may be further manufacturers. Relationships between each of these buyer groups will be significant in the overall examination of factors which affect profitability.

Not surprisingly the industry is also affected by the availability of close substitutes. A near monopoly position in one product may be effectively threatened by substitute products and the firm may find that this seriously affects its prospects. The question of substitutes also has to be considered in deciding on the relevant boundaries of the industry, a point which will be returned to later.

The final box deals with the possibility of completely new entrants joining the industry, and the possibility of firms leaving the industry. Ease of entry or exit is likely to affect the behaviour and profitability of firms in an industry.

Before exploring the implications of these factors for portfolio analysis, which we will deal with shortly, the analyst has to answer the question: "What is the relevant definition of the industry?" This is often easier to ask than to answer, and has dimensions of product/market characteristics and geography. The widest possible definition of products/markets would sweep all the substitutes into the competitors' box, and result in a canvas too vast for the type of picture that needs painting. On the other hand, too narrow a focus, such as one product out of a vast industry, will distort perspective. If the portion of the artist's canvas which is examined is too small, it will not be possible to draw any conclusions about the picture. These issues were discussed in Chapter 10, but are worth repeating here.

The dilemma is illustrated in Fig. 15.1, where alternative views of an industry are presented. The final decision has to be made in the light of knowledge of the industry and its markets and the purpose of the analysis. An examination of Ford might, because of its wide interests and integrated position, focus on the entire automotive industry. A manufacturer of invalid cars might gain no value from such a broad picture, and could benefit more from a study of his segment of the industry. If there is a principle, it is to start broad and to narrow down if the canvas is too big.

A related problem is one of geographical scope, illustrated in a similar way in Fig. 15.2. Here the criteria is one of normal competition and the existence of natural or artificial barriers to foreign competitors. Perspective may change over time: at one period it was possible to take a meaningful view of the UK petro-chemicals industry; now a regional Western Europe view is the minimum common sense would suggest. Again the right decision is likely to

FIG. 15.1. What market?

FIG. 15.2. What geographical market?

be broad rather than narrow, and has to be taken in the context of the specific industry.

Neither of these problems are unique to industry analysis and they recur in strategic portfolio analysis in the definition of meaningful strategic business units and strategic business areas. A workable decision is thus essential for both types of analysis, and if both are considered together it should be possible to find common definitions.

The difficulty of reaching the right solution is one of the vulnerable areas in both approaches, since the action prompted by the analysis may well be both wrong and dangerous if the answer is wrong.

There is also the danger of treating the approaches as if they resulted in a series of natural laws which automatically dictate the only possible strategy. History proves that some companies can prosper in industries that look sick, because of particular efficiencies of operation, a carefully chosen niche in the markets, or occasionally for a reason which seems to defy analysis.

One approach which is very useful is to apply industry structure analysis at the level of the strategic business unit, using the data generated as one source of information for portfolio analysis. This has the advantage of providing valuable strategic insight of a type appropriate for each level in the company. It also means that at corporate level there is no need to request a long list of data from strategic business units which is of no value to the unit providing it, nor is there a need to embark on expensive surveys duplicating data already available elsewhere in the organisation. There may of course be a need to work independently to check data or fill gaps.

The Market Prospects Axis of the Matrix

The market prospects axis consists of three groups of factors which analyse the industry as a whole. The descriptions used vary to some degree from those in the material published by Shell,[6] and include my own experience of using the approach in a number of industries and situations. The factors are compared with points of principle from industry-structure analysis so that similarities and common ground can be seen. In this comparison the debt to both Professor Mike Porter and the Shell analysts must be fully acknowledged since the analysis is built on their original work.

Directional Policy Matrix Weighting

Industry Structure Analysis

1. Market growth   4 points
(Scored on a pre-established scale which relates to the firm or industry under consideration).

1. Rivalry in an industry will tend to increase as growth rates slow, and competitors can no longer satisfy objectives from primary demand increases, and so begin to fight harder for brand share.

2. Market "quality"   4 points
2.1. Relative profitability of sector, and stability of profits.

2.1. High profitability may attract new entrants to the industry, therefore entry barriers should be carefully studied.

2.2. Are margins maintained in times of overcapacity?

2.2.1. Competition increases when fixed costs are high, incremental capital investments are large, or external factors lead to severe and often occurring excess.

2.2.2. The degree of contention in an industry will increase when the product is perishable or expensive to store.

2.3. Is the product resistant to commodity pricing behaviour?

2.3. The greater the differentiations between products, the easier will competition become.

2.4. Is the technology of the product freely available or protected?

2.4. Patent and similar protection tends to restrict new entrants to the industry. It may also increase the degree of product differentiation.

2.5. Is the market supplied by a relatively few competitors?

2.5. The profits of an industry tend to be adversely affected as competitors increase in number. This trend may be accentuated when competitors are both numerous and of similar size.

2.6. Is the market dominated by a few powerful customers?

2.6. Profits tend to be adversely affected as the power of the buyer *vis-à-vis* the industry firm increases. Particular points which affect buyer power are:
*Domination by few powerful buying firms, particularly when these take a high proportion of the output of the industry;
*When the buyer offers a credible threat of backwards integration (conversely, a credible threat of forwards integration by firms in the industry may reduce the relative power of buyers);
*When the buying firms are in a low profit industry; and

2.7. Does the buyer's final product have high added value?

2.7. *When the buying firm has low added value, and therefore little room to adjust margins.

2.8. In the case of a new product is the market likely to remain small enough not to attract competitors?

2.8. Refer to 2.5 and to "Entry barriers".

Directional Policy Matrix Weighting	Industry Structure Analysis
Directional Policy Matrix Weighting	*Industry Structure Analysis*

Directional Policy Matrix Weighting

2.9. Is the product one where a change by the buyer would mean a change in machinery or formulation?

2.10. Is the product vulnerable to substitutes?

3. Raw material and supplies
4 points

3.1. Are there any industry problems in obtaining supplies of components and raw materials?

3.2. What is the ratio of supplier firms to industry firms for each major component or material?

3.3. To what extent are substitute supplies and raw materials available?

3.4. Does the industry purchase a high proportion of the output of the supplying industry?

Industry Structure Analysis

2.9. Bargaining power of buyers is reduced (and that of the industry firm increased) when the buying firm is bound by the economic costs of changing production processes, plant, methods or obtaining new clearances from regulatory bodies.

2.10. At best substitutes put a ceiling on the prices and profits of the industry. At worst they may capture the entire market.

3.1. —

3.2. The bargaining power of suppliers (of important items) tends to increase at the cost of industry profits as the supplying industry becomes less "competitive" (that is the fewer and larger the firms in the supplying industry).

3.3. This works in the same way as 2.10, but as an advantage to the industry when substitutes are available.

3.4. When this is the case, the bargaining power of the supplier is reduced, and industry opportunity for profit increased. At the same time it may encourage suppliers to try to help the growth of the industry on which they are so dependent.
But suppliers' power is enhanced when they offer a credible threat of forward integration, and reduced when the industry offers a real threat of backwards integration.
Entry/exit barriers
Entry and exit barriers receive more emphasis in the Porter analysis, since entry barriers reduce the risk of increased competition, while exit barriers force competitors to behave more aggressively since they cannot easily realise their investment.
Entry barriers include: high capital investment; specialised high cost plant; patents; product differentiation; highly efficient producers; complex distribution networks.

My own experience is that the answers to each sub-question in the directional policy matrix need to be scored and weighted (see the next chapter), and I have found empirically that the matrix has meaning when approximately half the weighting is assigned to a combination of market growth and profitability and the remainder to those other factors which are likely to affect future profitability.

The Competitive Capability Axis

A similar comparison can be made of questions considered in the other axis of the directional policy matrix, and a further set of factors analysed in industry structure analysis. (Industry structure analysis treats these in the context of the diagram in Fig. 10.1 and not as a matrix.)

Directional Policy Matrix

1. Market position
weighting   4 points
1.1 The concept is one of leadership rather than brand share.
Scoring positions are:
Leader (4) Followed by others in pricing and usually has a pre-eminent market share.
Major producer (3) When no company is a leader, but a number are well placed.
Viable producer (2) Strong viable position but below top league.
Minor producer (1) Inadequate to support position in long run.
Others (0).

2. Production capability
weighting   4 points
2.1. Economics of production (relative to competitors).
2.2. Available capacity.
2.3. Geographical distribution of capacity.
2.4. Security of raw materials and supplies.

3. Product research and development
weighting   4 points
This is a compound question dealing with the ability of the company to support its market share in the future (R & D, technical service, product development, etc.).

Industry Structure Analysis

1.1. Competition increases (and industry profits tend to fall) as the number of competitors in an industry increases, and as they become more equal in relative size and bargaining power.
It is the relative positions which are frequently as important as the absolute.
1.2. Competition becomes more volatile as companies develop different "personalities". A newcomer to an industry will often upset the unwritten "rules" in the industry.

2. Competitive analysis would be made of each of these factors. Question 2.4 would also be considered in relation to the points on a credible threat of backward integration.

Again, when plotting positions on the competitive axis of the DPM, I have found it convenient to assign half of the total weighting to historical performance and the other half to those factors likely to affect future performance.

Portfolio Analysis in Practice

Figure 15.3 provides an example of the directional matrix completed for some hypothetical strategic business areas, and this may serve as an example of how all the other portfolio analysis techniques are applied.

Three of the boxes are labelled with words suggesting that divestment is the approximate action to consider, because of weakness in market growth and position.

Two boxes suggest cash generators. In both cases there may be need for some maintenance investment ("Proceed with care" suggests *slightly* more generous

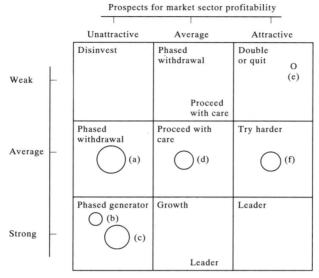

Prospects for market sector profitability

1. Size of circles proportionate to turnover
2. Strategic business units indicated by letters

FIG. 15.3. Example of DPM

investment policies), but for both the aim should be to harvest as much cash flow as possible.

Four boxes imply different approaches to growth strategies. "Leader" and "Growth" both suggest investment is worthwhile, but carry the implication that the growth box should aim for a balanced cash flow, while the leader box may be both cash hungry and supported. "Double or Quit" really says choose some of these, back them to grow, and get out if they fail. It is from this box that future "leaders" should come. The remaining box is a reminder that a little more effort might bring that leadership position.

I do not use these labels when I apply the technique, because they are statements of tendency rather than fact, at least when applied outside of the chemicals industry. It is useful to know them, but the temptation to plan by recipe should be avoided.

Now if an organisation could array all its activities, on such a matrix, it at least has a preliminary indication of what might be a sensible overall corporate strategy to each. And if each has been plotted using industry structure analysis, the positions in the matrix should be backed by carefully thought out strategic business unit strategies. Put the risk analysis behind the matrix, in a series of categories of low risk, average and high risk, and a new dimension of thought is opened up.

A number of observations should be made. Firstly, the position on the matrix is not an eternal truth. Over time, in line with product life-cycle theories one might expect a decline in prospects, a drift towards the left of the matrix. Similarly, one might postulate an increasing tendency for a decline in each position. The overall effect suggests that today's leaders may become tomorrow's cash generators, and ultimately candidates for divestment. Understanding and managing the drift is an important aspect of strategic management.

Secondly, the grids on the matrix are not finite barriers. Interpretation is very difficult when a strategic business unit falls near a boundary. A high degree of judgement in interpreting results is needed, and the techniques are certainly no black box.

Thirdly, the importance of the point made earlier about getting the strategic business area sensibly defined becomes very apparent from a glance at the matrix. A high position in a fast-growing segment might put the SBU into the leadership box if defined in segment terms. If looked at on a larger canvas this could translate to a slow growing market in which the company has a poor position, which might indicate divestment. Getting the approach right requires much searching thought, and is unlikely to be the same answer for each organisation.

Fourthly, it is easy to see that the different types of strategic positioning of the SBUs requires managers of different capabilities, personalities and skills. The entrepreneurial manager may fit the "double or quit" business, and be quite incapable of running a cash generator effectively. Managing an operation for planned divestment also calls for a different degree of talent. Some work has already been done on matching people to opportunity[10, 11] and it is a field wide open for significant academic study.

No one should imagine that this, or any other portfolio analysis technique, can solve all strategic problems. If this simplistic view could be taken, strategy would be reduced to four or five groups of decisions and life is much more complex than this. What the matrix should do is highlight *indicative* action for further investigation, and also provide a way of seeing all parts of a complex company in relation to each other—reduced to one piece of paper for those whose managements properly understand the technique. My own experience has found it to be a useful approach to take discussions back to corporate objectives and philosophical arguments on the nature and shape of company desired and, then, into the organisational and people's problems of attaining it. Thus, strategic decisions become well rounded and give attention to all the problems involved in implementation.

Portfolio analysis will not work for everyone. Businesses where market share is unimportant for success (for example, agriculture) cannot sensibly be analysed, particularly if reasons for being in them are associated with capital appreciation and tax advantages. (Products requiring regional or local markets can usually be evaluated if the geographical scope of the market is sensibly defined.)

It may also fail in an organisation with complex production inter-relationships. Give up product x may be wrong advice if in fact it is a byproduct and failure to dispose of this at the best price would alter the cost structure of product y. This is really an argument for understanding the businesses before they are plotted on the matrix, and a reinforcement for carrying out industry structure analysis as a prerequisite step.

Risk Matrix

Risk takes many forms as has been discussed in earlier chapters, and there are techniques for examining different aspects. These vary from the methods of analysing risk by discounted cash-flow methods (Hertz[12])—which will be returned to in a later chapter—to a number of ways of looking at environmental risk, which we have discussed previously.[13]

Shell[14] describes another method of looking at environmental risk, primarily on a broader front. The result is again to force consideration of the issues and to gain some awareness of danger areas for which special strategies might be necessary.

The risk matrix discussed in detail here was first described in Hussey,[8] and, as mentioned earlier in this chapter, is used to give a third dimension to portfolio analysis. It could be used as a stand-alone technique but interpretation is considerably more meaningful if it is used in the way described. Although my experience has been to apply it as part of my modified directional-policy-matrix approach, it could be altered to fit any method of portfolio analysis.

There is no need to describe the axis it holds in common with the directional policy matrix. The remaining axis is a scored position based on an assessment of the specific environmental factors that appear to be of concern; the score is arrived at by considering both the probability of occurrence and the potential impact on the organisation. Figure 15.4 provides an example of the worksheet and the scoring methods.

As with all the approaches, the real issue is in deciding which of the many environmental aspects are likely to be of concern, and which for practical purposes can be ignored. (The answer will vary with the strategic business unit and area.) The methods used to arrive at this assessment vary from backroom analysis to ways of mobilising management judgement at various levels of the organisation. Both can be useful, and it is often advantageous to combine them.

I have frequently used a questionnaire approach on an individual plus small-group discussion basis to follow the back room analysis. The questionnaire not only provides checklists which aid consideration (these are varied, because environmental issues facing, for example, a bank are not all of the same type as those of concern to an industrial company). The questionnaire carefully considers the issues in relation to the manager's view of the organisation, identifies his perception of the organisational response, compares with the way the organisation has responded in the past, and finishes by analysing detailed actions that should be taken. (See Chapter 7 for more detail.)

An advantage of the risk matrix is, like the other two approaches, that it forces thought about the issues. In addition it provides an overview of the entire organisation and one that can be related to the strategic importance of each business unit and to the importance of each to the organisation.

This last point can be covered by plotting each position on both the DPM and risk matrix by drawing circles whose size is proportional to importance. Another approach is to redraw the matrices inserting total figures for profit contributions,

(a) Individual scoring of risk is achieved by multiplying the score for probability by the score for impact, using the following scales:

Impact		*Probability*		
Extremely high	6	A certainty	100%	6
	5	Very likely	84%	5
High	4	Quite possible	67%	4
	3	As likely as not	50%	3
Relatively low	2	Probably not	33%	2
	1	Highly unlikely	16%	1
None	0	Impossible	–	0

Scoring examples
Impact extremely high and Probability a certainty: $6 \times 6 = 36$
Impact high and Probability very likely: $4 \times 5 = 20$
Impact low and Probability very likely: $1 \times 5 = 5$

(The scores derived from the environmental assessment method of chapter 7)

(b) Example of work sheet for environmental risk (hypothetical data)

	Strategic business areas		
Environmental factor	A	B	C
Inflation above 15% p.a.	$3 \times 4 = 12$	–	$6 \times 4 = 24$
Labour militancy	$6 \times 6 = 36$	$6 \times 5 = 30$	$3 \times 3 = 9$
Anti-pollution legislation	$1 \times 4 = 4$	$6 \times 6 = 36$	–
Increase in VAT	$3 \times 3 = 9$	$6 \times 6 = 36$	$3 \times 3 = 9$
Nationalization of major customer	$6 \times 6 = 36$	–	–
Social attitude–anti-profit	$4 \times 4 = 16$	$6 \times 4 = 24$	$1 \times 1 = 1$
Total score	113	126	43
Average score	18.8	31.5	10.75
Interpretation	Medium–high risk	Very high risk	Medium risk

Note: (i) Probability score can vary by SBA if the geographical area is different.

(ii) It is also possible to add scores across to see a seriousness weighting of the factor on the total company–but be careful when SBAs are in different areas, since the combined factor may then have little meaning.

FIG. 15.4. Risk matrix scoring

sales, capital employed, cash flow, etc. for the activities which fall within each box.

Figure 15.5 provides an example of the risk matrix. Figure 15.6 shows this as the third dimension of the DPM: the use of perspex blocks as illustrated makes it easy to provide a visual representation and has much appeal as a desk-top toy, although the same visual impact can be gained at lower cost by using different colours to show different levels of risk on a single plane.

Despite their defects, the portfolio-analysis techniques have taken the practice of planning several steps forward, and have much to offer the complex organisation.

FIG. 15.5. The risk matrix

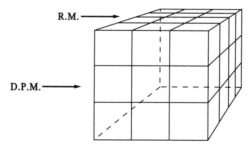

FIG. 15.6. Combined three-dimensional matrix, portfolio analysis plus risk

References

1. Thackray, J. "The Corporate Strategy Problem", *Management Today*, October 1979.
2. Marmamesh, Anderson and Harris *Harvard Business Review*, May–June 1978.
3. Hofer, C. W. and Schendel, D. *Strategy Formulation: Analytical Concepts*, West Publishing, St Paul, 1978.
4. Barksdale, H. C. and Harris, C. E. "Portfolio Analysis and the Product Life Cycle", *Long Range Planning*, Vol. 15, No. 6, 1982.
5. Buzzell, R. D. and Gale, B. T. *The PIMS Principles*, Free Press, New York, 1987.
6. Anon. *The Directional Policy Matrix: An Aid to Corporate Planning*, 2nd ed., Shell International Chemical Co, 1979.
7. Robinson, S. J. O., Hitchens, R. E. and Wade, D. P. "The Directional Policy Matrix—Tool For Strategic Planning", *Long Range Planning*, Vol. 11, No. 3, 1978.
8. Hussey, D. E. "Portfolio Analysis: Practical Experiences with the Directional Policy Matrix", *Long Range Planning*, Vol. 11, No. 4, 1978.

9. Porter, M. E. *Note on the Structural Analysis of Industries*, Harvard Business School, 1975.
10. Pappas "Corporate Planning at Du Pont", *Chemicals Engineering Process*, June 1978.
11. *Business Week* "Wanted—a Manager for Each Strategy", *Business Week*, February 25th, 1980.
12. Hertz, D. "Risk Analysis in Capital", *Harvard Business Review*, January/February 1964.
13. Newbauer, F. F. and Solomon, N. B. "A Managerial Approach to Environmental Assessment", *Long Range Planning*, April 1977.
14. Shell, Societal response matrix.

16

Portfolio Analysis in Practice

The purpose of this chapter is to illustrate the application and use of two particular methods of portfolio analysis. The first is derived from the directional policy matrix. The second is the risk matrix. Both were described in outline in the previous chapter. In order to achieve this purpose a fictional company, Good Investments Plc is described. This company has a wide spectrum of businesses. Although the company does not exist, the situation it faces does. The industries and dilemmas are all ones in which I have had experience, and Good Investments is a sort of disguised composite of consulting work with several clients. The data given about the industries and markets is also disguised, so do not be tempted to use it for a real analysis. The example is set in a normal period: in other words no recession is in progress. Also, because it had to be written at a certain time, industry prospects may have changed by the time you read this: if this is the case, please suspend disbelief in order to see how to score and plot businesses on the matrices, and how to use them. The material is adapted from a case study I wrote for Harbridge Consulting Group, and is used with permission.

Good Investments (GI): The Background

In recent years the company has not performed well, and the institutional shareholders are demanding action. They wanted a pre-tax return on capital employed of something more than 15% (which they felt was the average return in the UK), and they also wanted a profit growth target of at least 3–4% per year.

GI consisted of eight major divisions with a combined turnover of about £500 million. By far the largest division was industrial fasteners (£200 million) which was currently turning in a poor performance. During the two years of the recent recession it had made small profits, and last year produced a modest increase in profit. During this period it had invested heavily in new plant "to gain market share".

Historically this division was very significant as it was the foundation business of the group and had in the past contributed the cash which had enabled the other business to be acquired or developed. It held about 50% of its rather specialised world markets, and its current business plan was to invest several million pounds in a new look marketing campaign, and to build a new divisional headquarters office to "restore morale".

The general feeling of the GI Board was that fasteners had done so much for the firm in the past that it should now be supported in its time of need. Its competitors included a US group which had 40% of the market, but which also operated in a number of other unrelated fastener segments not touched by GI. The remaining 10% share was held by three small competitors. Everyone was aware that the fasteners market would show only very small growth in the future of not more than 1% per year.

General Hydraulics was the second largest division with £100 million turnover. It had a 10% market share of a large but declining world market, and was a poor third in the market to a German company (30%) and a US company (25%). This had always been a problem division, making profits on average only about one year in every three. It had been re-organised several times in its twelve year history. Currently the division's management were negotiating the purchase of the hydraulics interests (about 3% of market) of a diversified giant company. A purchase price of £20 million was speculated. The main benefit of the acquisition was seen as the opportunity to put more production through GI's hydraulics plant. However, the industrial relations problems and the costs of closing the other plant on acquisition had not yet been evaluated.

Pneumatics was a good cash contributing division, with products allied to defence. At £75 million turnover, which had shown no real growth over the past few years, it managed to make 15% return on capital employed and was a major cash contributor. It was estimated that it held about 60% of the UK market in its specialist application, the remainder being shared between four other British firms. The market was unlikely to grow in future, but existing contracts meant that business was secure for at least another three years.

Oil Rig Services (£40 million turnover) provided an engineering support service to the offshore petroleum industry. This was an essentially local business operating out of Aberdeen and had 45% of the market in that area. Previously high rates of growth of 10% per year had slackened to around 2%, which was the forecast rate for the foreseeable future. Expansion of market share locally was highly unlikely. If significant expansion of business was wanted the division would have to replicate its activities in other geographical locations and fight against entrenched competition.

General Engineering Contracting had a £30 million turnover. It had been very profitable but was affected badly by the recession and by technological advances which meant that to stay competitive it had to make a significant investment. It held 10% of a fragmented market where all activities tended to be restricted to the UK. Its management expected to break even unless new investment was made, in which case a 3% return on capital employed was forecast.

The rate of return (discounted cash flow basis) on the new investment was exceptionally high, and most Board members of GI felt that the £6 million modernisation programme should be approved, despite the fact that the market showed no signs of growth. The general feeling was that past heavy investment in this division had to be protected.

GI had stumbled into machine tools almost by accident, but through the personal energies of one of the main board members had built a profitable £10 million turnover business in a growth niche in the market. The division had been yielding a 20% return on capital employed. It had a respected name in the UK with a 20% market share, but did not trade in other countries. Lately new Japanese competitors had come into the market. The Board thought that the market share could be defended easily against the Japanese, and felt it appropriate that GI should have this stake in applied high technology.

Another high technology business was personal computers. The product aimed at the small business which was too small for the IBM PC, but required something more sophisticated than the home computer. In its three years of operation in the UK market the firm had grown from zero to £25 million of highly profitable turnover. Over the next three years its sales were expected to increase eightfold, and that included allowance for a fall in market share from 75 to 55%. Currently 25% return on capital employed was earned, but the business was cash hungry and continually had to invest to meet the increased production needs. A £50 million investment plan featured in the demands of the UK market and a foothold into the as yet undeveloped European market. Some board members believed that the division should only be allowed to reinvest what it earned itself, otherwise it would take away resources "earned by fasteners and needed by fasteners". There was also a feeling that the market outside the UK could wait until the British market had been dealt with.

The eighth division was GI Security which had two product areas—guarding services and security vehicle services at £10 million turnover each. The former was labour intensive and a highly fragmented market with low entry barriers. The market was static and the activity did little better than break even.

Security vehicles were profitable, and entry barriers were higher because of the investment needed for security vaults and vehicles. GI had 10% of the overall market and was number four out of six competitors. However it only operated in 20% of the population areas in the UK, and in those areas success was much higher (around 50% of the market). The market was growing at 3% per annum, but expansion of market share was related to the investment in vaults in new geographical areas.

Analysing GI

The difficulty of the situation described above is that, through conventional means, it is not easy to see the relative merits of the components of the total company. Without this relative view, it may also be difficult to decide investment priorities. Are the schemes in hand the best use of resources? We need also to look at the question of shareholder value, and whether such a wide dispersion of activity can be good for the shareholders. In a real life situation in which I was involved when Vickers and Rolls Royce Motors merged, the problem was that the company had too many businesses, and not enough funds to develop them all properly: the danger was that this could have led to poor results for all of them: for a description of this work see Stopford.[1]

Portfolio analysis can help create a strategic understanding, but the information given so far for GI is inadequate for this purpose. The analyst would have to probe deeper, and Tables 16.1 and 16.2 provide the data that will enable us to plot positions on the portfolio matrix.

The scoring rules for plotting the matrix positions are set out in Appendix 1 to this chapter. They make a boring read, but are essential for anyone who wishes to apply the method to a real situation. Tables 16.3 and 16.4 show how the rules are applied to the facts set out in the earlier exhibits. Figure 16.1 shows the matrix with the various businesses positioned: the numbers key to the numbers on the exhibits. The sizes of the circles are designed to give an impression of the relative size of sales turnover of each business (see Table 16.5). It might have been better to use net assets as a base had this information been available. Profits are another base that could have been compared, except that I do not know the best way of treating losses on such a diagram. A further method, which is sometimes useful, is to show a pie diagram proportionate to market size, with a slice representing the company's market share. An even more ambitious approach is to show the "served market", that is the segment or sector in which the company operates as a pie slice of the total market, and the market share of the served market as a further slice.

In this example the impact is meant to be visual, as a reminder of the importance of each business to GI, and there is no information to go deeper than this.

The matrix offers a better way of viewing the company. At this stage I have only plotted the present situation, and have taken statements about the geographical scope of the business at face value. Later we will question some of the assumptions, and look at the impact on positioning of some of the strategies that have been suggested. Viewing all these businesses at once, in a strategic way, on one piece of paper, makes it easier to reach decisions that are in the interests of the whole.

I have avoided attaching labels to the boxes on the matrix, because I think that this can lead to a formula approach to decisions. In real life, I would never wish to plot positions on the matrix unless I had also undertaken industry analysis, as it is very easy to misinterpret the prospects for a business. The fact that a business is doing well or badly is partly to do with markets and the structure of the industry. It may also be a result of good or bad management, and the way in which the organisation has responded to the opportunities and problems it faces.

Below I have listed the strategic actions that GI had under consideration for each business, with my provisional recommendation drawn from the analysis. They do not always agree!

TABLE 16.1. Acts and judgements: GI portfolio—market prospects

Market Factors	Industrial Fasteners	General Hydraulics	Pneumatics	Oil Rig Services	General Engineering Contracting	Machine Tools	Personal Computers	Guarding Services	Security Vehicle Services
1. Market growth	<1%	Declining	Static	2%	Static	3.5%	Over 100%	Static	3%
2. Industry profitability	125	5%	16%	20%	5%	16%	20%	3%	15%
3. Stability of margin	Modest reductions in margins	Significant margin erosion	Occasional price cutting	Occasional price cutting	No margin control	Occasional price cutting	Little or no change in margins	No margin control	Modest reductions in margins
4. Degree of product differentiation	Modest differentiation	Modest differentiation	Significantly differentiated	Modest differentiation	Standardised product	Significantly differentiated	Significantly differentiated	Commodity product	Modest differentiation
5. Ratio of industry to customer firms	1:100+	1:50	1:10	1:10	1:75	1:75	1:100+	1:100+	1:50
6. Threat of backwards integration	Unlikely but possible	Quite likely	Moderate threat	Moderate threat	Quite likely	Moderate threat	None	Serious threat (in-house services)	Unlikely but possible
7. Customer added value	Average	Average	High	Very high	Average	Average	Average	Average	Very high
8. Threat from substitutes	Some threats emerging	Under threat	Some threats emerging	None in sight	Under threat (technology)	Possible but unlikely	Some threats emerging	Some threats emerging	None in sight
9. Degree of "switching" cost protection	Low	Moderate	High	Low	None	Moderate	Very high	None	Low
10. Entry barriers	Moderate	Moderate	Fairly high	Fairly high	Moderate	Fairly high	Moderate	None	Fairly high
11. Supply difficulties	Average	Very few	Average	Very few	None	Some serious problems	Very few	Some serious problems (labour)	Very few
12. Ratio of suppliers	6:1	6:1	6:1	20:1	6:1	3:1	3:1	—	3:1
13. Threat of forward integration by supplier	Unlikely but possible	None	None	None	None	Unlikely but possible	Moderate threat	—	None
14. Degree to which supplier depends on the industry	Under 20%	20–33.3%	Under 20%	Under 20%	Under 20%	Under 20%	Under 20%	—	50–74% (vehicle)
15. Geographical area considered	World	World	UK	Local—Aberdeen	UK	UK (but should it be world?)	UK (but should it be world?)	UK	UK

TABLE 16.2. Acts and judgements: GI portfolio—market prospects

Competitive Factors	Industrial Fasteners	General Hydraulics	Pneumatics	Oil Rig Services	General Engineering Contracting	Machine Tools	Personal Computers	Guarding Services	Security Vehicle Services
1. Market position	Major	Minor	Leader	Major	Viable	Minor	Leader	Negligible	Negligible
2. Relative profitability	Same as industry	Consistently 10–20% lower	Consistently 10–20% better	Consistently 10–20% lower	Consistently 10–20% lower	Consistently 25% higher	25% higher	More than 20% lower	Consistently 10–20% higher
3. Production economics	Same	Worse than average	Better than average	Better than average	Worse than average	Better than average	Better than average	Worse than average	Better than average
4. Capacity utilisation	Above 60–80%	40–50%	Above 80%	Above 80%	50–60%	60–80%	Above 80%	50–60%	Above 80%
5. Quality of plant	Better than major competitors	Worse than major competitors	Better than competitors	Worse than competitors	Worse than major competitors	Better than major competitors	Better than major competitors	—	About the same
6. Firm's supply problems	A bit better than the industry	About the same as the industry	About the same as the industry	About the same as the industry	About the same as the industry	Average	Better than major competitors	—	About the same as the industry
7. R&D services	Almost right	Has some deficiencies	Almost right	Right for the market	Right for the market	Inadequate	Has some deficiencies	—	—
8. Technical support	Better than average	As good as relevant competition	Better than average	Better than average	Worse than average	As good as competition	A leader in this field	—	—
9. Distribution	Excellent	Average	Good	Good	Average	Average	Good	Below average	Average

TABLE 16.3.

	Weight	(1) Industrial Fasteners		(2) General Hydraulics		(3) Pneumatics		(4) Oil Rig Services		(5) General Engineering Contract		(6) Machine Tools		(7) Personal Computers		(8) Guarding Services		(9) Security Vehicle Services	
		Score	Wgtd Score	Score	Wgtd Score	Score	Wgtd Score	Score	Wgtd Score	Score	Wgtd Score	Score	Wgtd Score	Score	Wgtd Score	Score	Wgtd Score	Score	Wgtd Score
A. MARKET GROWTH	5	0	0	−1	(5)	0	0	0	0	0	0	2	10	4	20	0	0	1	5
B. MARKET QUALITY																			
—Industry profitability	8	1	8	0	0	3	24	3	24	0	0	3	24	4	32	0	0	2	16
—Stability of margin	1	2	2	1	1	3	3	3	3	0	0	3	3	4	4	0	0	2	2
—Degree of product differentiation	1	2	2	2	2	3	3	2	2	3	3	3	3	3	3	0	0	2	2
—Ratio of industry to customer firms	1	4	4	2	2	1	1	1	1	3	3	3	3	4	4	4	4	2	2
—Threat to backwards integration	1	3	3	1	1	2	2	2	2	1	1	2	2	4	4	0	0	3	3
—Customer added value	1	2	2	2	2	3	3	4	4	1	1	2	2	2	2	2	2	4	4
—Threat from substitutes	1	2	2	1	1	2	2	4	4	1	1	3	3	2	2	2	2	4	4
—Degree of switching cost protection	1	1	1	2	2	3	3	1	1	0	0	2	2	4	4	0	0	1	1
—Entry barriers	1	2	2	2	2	3	3	3	3	1	1	3	3	2	2	0	0	3	3
	÷16		26		13		44		44		10		45		57		8		37
			1.625		.813		2.75		2.75		.625		2.813		3.563		.5		2.313
	×5		8.125		4.06		13.75		13.75		3.125		14.063		17.813		2.5		11.563
C. SUPPLY POSITION																			
—Supply difficulties	1	2	2	3	3	2	2	3	3	4	4	1	1	3	3	1	1	3	3
—Ratio of supply to industry firms	1	2	2	2	2	2	2	3	3	2	2	1	1	1	1	—	—	1	1
—Threat of forward integration by supplier	1	3	3	4	4	4	4	4	4	4	4	3	3	2	2	—	—	4	4
—Degree to which supplier depends on the industry	1	4	4	3	3	4	4	4	4	4	4	4	4	4	4	—	—	1	1
	÷4		11		12		12		14		14		9		10		1		9
			2.75		3		3		3.5		3.5		2.25		2.5		.25		2.25
	×2		5.5		6		6		7		7		4.5		5		.5		4.5
TOTAL SCORE	÷4		13.625		5.06		19.75		20.75		10.125		28.563		42.81		3.0		21.063
			3.41		1.27		4.94		5.19		2.53		7.14		10.7		.75		5.27

TABLE 16.4.

	Weight	(1) Industrial Fasteners		(2) General Hydraulics		(3) Pneumatics		(4) Oil Rig Services		(5) General Engineering Contract		(6) Machine Tools		(7) Personal Computers		(8) Guarding Services		(9) Security Vehicle Services	
		Score	Wgtd Score	Score	Wgtd Score	Score	Wgtd Score	Score	Wgtd Score	Score	Wgtd Score	Score	Wgtd Score	Score	Wgtd Score	Score	Wgtd Score	Score	Wgtd Score
A. MARKET POSITION	2	3	6	1	2	4	8	3	6	2	4	1	2	4	8	0	0	0	0
B. PRODUCTION/ SUPPLY CAPABILITY																			
—Relative profitability	4	2	8	1	4	3	12	1	4	1	4	4	16	4	16	0	0	3	12
—Production economics	1	2	2	1	1	3	3	3	3	1	1	3	3	3	3	1	1	3	3
—Capacity utilisation	1	3	3	1	1	4	4	4	4	2	2	3	3	4	4	2	2	4	4
—Quality of plant (cf competition)	1	3	3	1	1	3	3	1	1	2	2	3	3	3	3	—	—	2	2
—Supply problems (cf industry)	1	3	3	2	2	2	2	2	2	2	2	2	2	3	3	—	—	2	2
	÷8		19 / 2.375		9 / 1.375		24 / 3		14 / 1.75		11 / 1.375		27 / 3.375		29 / 3.625	÷6	3 / 0.5		23 / 2.875
C. MARKET SUPPORT SERVICES																			
—R&D	1	3	3	2	2	3	3	4	4	4	4	1	1	3	3	—	—	—	—
—Technical services	1	3	3	2	2	3	3	3	3	1	1	2	2	4	4	—	—	—	—
—Distribution network	1	4	4	2	2	3	3	3	3	2	2	2	2	1	1	1	1	—	2
	÷3		10 / 3.33		6 / 2		9 / 3		10 / 3.33		7 / 2.33		5 / 1.67		8 / 2.67		1 / 1		2 / 2
TOTAL SCORE	×0.75		11.705 / 8.78		5.375 / 4.03		14 / 10.5		11.08 / 8.31		7.705 / 5.78		7.05 / 5.28		14.295 / 10.72		1.5 / 1.13		4.875 / 3.66

TABLE 16.5. Importance of GI businesses by revenue

Division	Turnover £ million	%
Fasteners	200	40
General Hydraulics	100	20
Pneumatics	75	15
Oil Rig Services	40	8
General Engineering	30	6
Machine Tools	10	2
Personal Computers	25	5
Guarding Services	10	2
Security Vehicle Services	10	2
	500	100

Interpretation Compared with Board's Investment Strategies

1. *Fasteners*

   Several million on new-look marketing campaign.
   Construction of new head office.

   Recommendation

   Operate for maximum cash, with such expenditure/investment as is necessary to maintain market share.
   The weighting of fasteners is important, and it should not be allowed to slip.
   The feeling that fasteners should be able to reinvest their own "earnings" is wrong.

2. *Hydraulics*

   Purchase of hydraulics interest of major company for £20 million.

   Recommendation

   Do not do this. Business should clearly be considered for divestment.

3. *Pneumatics*

   No investment needed. Should be a cash generator.

4. *Oil Rig Services*

   Possible replication of other activities in other areas.

   Recommendation

   May be better to run for cash. However, I would not rule out expansion subject to careful project appraisal *and* consideration against other uses of funds.

FIG. 16.1. GI plc—Basis of strategy. The numbers are keyed to Exhibits 16.3 and 16.4

5. *General Engineering*   £6 million modernisation programme.
   Recommendation   Would the investment push it into a cash generator box? Initial indications are no. In this case divestment should be considered.

6. *Machine Tools*   Defend market share against Japanese.
   Recommendation   This business has to be looked at on a wider geographical basis, and strengths and weaknesses compared with Japanese competitors. Needs a careful market appraisal, and consideration of capital needs to give most efficient production. Investment should be balanced against risks and rewards. Indications are biased against investment.

7. *Personal Computers*   £50 million investment plan which Board predisposed to reject.
   Recommendation   Depending on competitive position in key markets, this would appear to be the best opportunity for the group. Needs heavy cash support. GI should be sure they have the resources and nerve for a game that requires a speed build up of market position across a wide front.

8. *Guarding*   Little hope, unless new concept giving unique advantage can be built up. What joint resources with vehicles?

9. *Security Vehicles*   Expansion of market share needs new facilities.
   Recommendation   On the surface, not the best use of resources.

Challenging the Assumptions

If this were a real situation I should like to challenge the assumptions for two of the businesses. It is extremely unlikely that personal computers and machine tools can be viewed solely in a UK context. Both are global businesses and have global competitors. Therefore, in the long term it is unlikely that either can survive by thinking only in UK terms.

A more likely positioning is indicated by the arrows on the matrix in Fig. 16.2. On a world basis, machine tools might be seen as slightly more attractive in

Fig. 16.2. GI using revised assumptions

prospects, but the competitive positioning would shrink to the poor box. Similarly viewed on a world basis the strong personal computers competitive position would become weak.

This immediately raises questions about the possible strategy. We do not have all the information to resolve them, but can suggest a hypothesis.

Machine Tools

This is a long established industry with entrenched competitors. The UK position is not good. The question is whether it would even be feasible to move to become a world player from such a weak base. Acquisition might be a possibility, but the issue is to build a world position in a few products, rather than to own a diversity of products none of which have a world position. Someone would have to work very hard to persuade me that a viable world strategy is even possible.

Personal Computers

Here we are moving from a strong position, in a market where it is still possible to gain market share from technological innovation. The question is not so much whether a strategy is feasible, but whether Good Investments have the resources to compete on a global basis. If not, the options might be to use the business to form a joint venture with another firm, or to dispose of it. Disposal might be sale, or a business that is large enough or strong enough could be floated through the stockmarket.

The final movement on Fig. 16.2 is the hydraulics strategy proposed by the GI board. It would barely improve the position of this business on the matrix.

Looking at Risk

The analysis so far looks at only one aspect of the strategic situation. Risk Matrix enables us to add more information, and thus to gain more insight. The rules for this technique are brief, and will be described, together with an example of their application to the GI situation. In addition to scoring rules we need an assessment of the environmental factors which are important to the company. An earlier chapter dealt at length on ways of analysing and identifying the factors, so in this chapter we will assume that GI have performed this task well. Table 16.6 provides the information that will be used as the basis for plotting risk. In a real situation there might be many more factors identified, but I have kept the list short for demonstration purposes.

Scoring the RM

The market prospects axis is scored according to the DPM rules. The "degree of risk" axis requires a scoring sheet, a completed example of which is given later.

TABLE 16.6. Risk Matrix score sheet: Good Investments Plc

Major External Threat	SBU 1 I × P = S	SBU 2 I × P = S	SBU 3 I × P = S	SBU 4 I × P = S	SBU 5 I × P = S	SBU 6 I × P = S	SBU 7 I × P = S	SBU 8 I × P = S	SBU 9 I × P = S
Emergence of focused Japanese threat	5 × 1 =	5 × 1 =	5 × 1 =		5 × 1 =	6 × 6 =	6 × 4 =		
Impact of UK trade cycle	5 × 5 =	6 × 5 =	2 × 5 =	1 × 5 =	6 × 5 =	6 × 5 =	4 × 5 =	3 × 5 =	3 × 5 =
Technological obsolescence	3 × 1 =	5 × 4 =	5 × 6 =	1 × 5 =	4 × 6 =	5 × 6 =	5 × 5 =	2 × 2 =	2 × 2 =
UK unemployment continues at high rate							3 × 5 =	3 × 5 =	
Political power of peace lobby		1 × 4 =	6 × 4 =		1 × 4 =	1 × 4 =			
Instability of major customer countries	4 × 2 =	4 × 2 =			5 × 5 =		4 × 4 =		
Decline in real oil prices				5 × 5 =	1 × 5 =				
TOTAL AVERAGE PENALTIES RM SCORE									

I = Impact P = Probability S = Score

This scoring sheet lists the identified external factors and scores them for each strategic business unit, on the basis of impact and probability.

Impact and Probability are scored on the following basis:

Impact		*Probability*		
Extremely High	6	A Certainty	100%	6
	5	Very Likely	84%	5
High	4	Quite Possible	67%	4
	3	As Likely As Not	90%	3
Relatively Low	2	Probably Not	33%	2
	1	Highly Unlikely	16%	1
None	0	Impossible	—	0

To obtain a matrix score, the impact is multiplied by the probability score. The average score is calculated by dividing total score by the number of items with a positive score (e.g. ignoring zero or irrelevant items).

This first measure of risk ignores the problem of multiple risks. For example Businesses A and B may both score 15, but if A has in the make up of its score a number of factors of high impact and probability, while B is only subject to two factors altogether, this would suggest that A is the more vulnerable business.

To compensate for this penalty points are added to the average score, on the following basis:

		Add
For every factor scoring	16–20	1
	21–25	2
	26–30	3
	31–36	4

The results of the scoring are built up through three stages. Table 16.7 is a repeat of Table 16.6 with the scores calculated. It is a worksheet, but provides some valuable interpretive information in its own right. A horizontal reading illuminates the factors which have most potential impact on the whole group, which are the UK trade cycle and technological obsolescence. An overall strategic response by GI, on the assumption that it decided not to change its portfolio of businesses, might be to take action to speed up new product development in order to gain extra time to benefit from products in an era of shortening life cycles. This could well be important enough to become a corporate initiative, introducing new approaches to project management, and providing more resources for new product development. The dependence on the UK economy could lead the group to consider more expansion into other parts of the world, such as South East Asia. A later chapter will discuss global strategies in some detail, so I do not want to argue the merits or demerits of such a move here. However it is an option that emerges from the analysis so far.

Figure 16.3 plots the scores on a matrix. The distribution of results is of course different from those that we saw in the portfolio analysis because one axis of the matrix has been changed. I regard this stage as an interim step, and prefer to leave

TABLE 16.7. Risk Matrix score sheet: Good Investments Plc (as Table 16.6 with scores calculated)

Major External Threat	SBU 1 I×P=S	SBU 2 I×P=S	SBU 3 I×P=S	SBU 4 I×P=S	SBU 5 I×P=S	SBU 6 I×P=S	SBU 7 I×P=S	SBU 8 I×P=S	SBU 9 I×P=S	TOTAL
Emergence of focused Japanese threat	5×1=5	5×1=5	5×1=5		5×1=5	6×6=36	6×4=24			80
Impact of UK trade cycle	5×5=25	6×5=30	2×5=10	1×5=5	6×5=30	6×5=30	4×5=20	3×5=15	3×5=15	180
Technological obsolescence	3×1=3	5×4=20	5×6=30	1×5=5	4×6=24	5×6=30	5×5=25	2×2=4	2×2=4	145
UK unemployment continues							3×5=15	3×5=15		30
Political power of peace lobby		1×4=4	6×4=24		1×4=4	1×4=4				36
Instability of major customer countries		4×2=8			5×5=25		4×4=16			57
Decline in real prices of oil	4×2=8		5×5=25	1×5=5						20
TOTAL	41	67	69	35	93	100	100	49	19	
AVERAGE	10.25	13.4	17.25	11.67	15.50	25	20	16.3	9.5	
PENALTIES	2	4	5	2	7	10	6	3	—	
RM SCORE	12.25	17.4	22.25	13.67	22.50	35	26	19.3	9.5	

I = Impact P = Probability S = Score

FIG. 16.3. Environmental risk matrix

interpretation to the next stage, illustrated in Fig. 16.4. Here the risk matrix and the portfolio analysis are combined, and immediately a new insight is provided. Immediately we see that two businesses where we already had identified some critical strategic issues, machine tools and personal computers, numbers 6 and 9 on the chart, are also subject to high risks from environmental forces.

FIG. 16.4. Portfolio analysis showing risk

The next area of consideration from the information we have assembled is to see where the group is adding to shareholder value. At first sight it is difficult to see what it is that GI offers which is an addition to the value provided by each business unit. An earlier chapter discussed ideas about how value can be created, and the reader might wish to test GI against these. A key part of the GI strategy should be to increase shareholder value. I make this point because it illustrates that although we have gained considerable insight from the two analytical techniques, they cannot answer every strategic consideration.

The final decisions about GI's strategy should also take into account the strengths and weaknesses of the group and its components. We would want to challenge some of the internal beliefs about markets and the industry, and delve much deeper into industry and competitor analysis. I should also want to see whether there are common strands of technology across the group, and identify the core competencies of the organisation. Any further analysis should also consider "soft" aspects such as culture.

I should not, as you have guessed by now, want anyone to think that our two pieces of analysis have cracked the problem of what to do in GI. However I hope you will agree that we have gained considerable strategic insight into the group, and that GI management did not possess this insight before the analysis was completed. We have some clear ideas about decisions which would be good or bad for the group, even if we have not uncovered all the options. Any one relevant technique of analysis will show some facets of a strategic situation. I think mistakes occur when an organisation latches on to only one technique, and bases all decisions on the outcome of this. My view is that this is a dangerous fault of many managers and analysts.

In the final event the future of GI will be determined not by the analysis, but through the quality of the decisions made by management, and the creative way in which they identify responses to opportunities. Analysis helps strategic thinking: it does not replace it.

Reference

1.   Stopford, J. M. *Vickers Plc (A)*, London Business School, 1989.

Appendix to Chapter 16
Scoring Rules and Worksheets for DPM

Summary of the Score Weightings

Market Prospects Axis

Three groups of factors are considered for this axis, and are weighted to represent their importance. Weightings could vary with the type of business: the ones suggested below were worked out for manufacturing companies:

Factor Group	Weight
Market Growth	5

Here we are concerned with the underlying trend. The growth rate is assessed on historical evidence, adjusted by forecast changes, but ignoring short term "blips" caused by recession.

Market Quality	5

This examines the profitability of the activity. It is concerned with historical evidence, adjusted for factors which are likely to change that position.

Scoring considers the degree of product differentiation, ratio of industry to customer firms, whether margins are maintained in terms of overcapacity, threat of backwards integration, added value by the customer, technical position and entry barriers.

(Note: there are weighting differences for these sub-questions which are described in the scoring rules.)

Supply Position (Total Industry)	2

This looks at supply difficulties, ratio of suppliers/industry firms, the threat of forward integration and the degree of supplier dependence on the industry.

Competitive Position Axis

Three groups of factors are considered in plotting this axis. Whereas the other axis asks questions about the industry/market, this axis is concerned with only answers about the firm.

Factor Group	Weight
Market Position	2

This uses a concept of relative market position rather than an absolute share.

Production–Supply Capability	1

Consider the firm's profitability relative to the industry, the production economics of the firm, capacity utilisation, quality of productive resources and ability to source materials and supplies. Some questions in this sub-group are weighted more heavily than others.

Note: Be prepared to modify these rules to fit the particular business.

Market Support Services   1
Examines the extent to which the present market position is being supported by
research/development effort, technical support, and the distribution network.

Scoring

The scoring is organised so that the final maximum score on each axis is 12. Another
maximum figure could have been selected to avoid some of the arithmetic in scoring, and the
main reason for this choice is familiarity. Scoring rules have been adjusted from time to time as I
have used the approach in different industries and I have found it helpful to have a constant total
figure.

Note that market growth scores will be adjusted to suit the needs of each company. The
choice of midpoint for the scale is:

(a) Target rate of growth for the firm as a whole, or
(b) Average rate of growth historically achieved by the firm.

The rest of this section offers detailed scoring rules.

Directional Policy Matrix: Scoring Scales

1. Prospects for Market Profitability

1.1. Market growth
Assumption
3–4% real growth p.a. would be a reasonable target for GI. The scale should be amended if
this objective is changed.

Rate of Growth	Points
Negative	−1
0–2%	0
2–3%	1
3–4%	2
4–7%	3
Over 7%	4

Growth should be primarily the historic pattern over recent years, tempered by any known
trends for the future.

It is impossible to compare these ambitions with historic and forecast rates of GDP growth. If
this suggested a growth rate of 2–3% were more realistic, the scale should be amended. In
practice the scale is thus set up according to the realistic objectives of the company.

1.2. Profitability record
Suggested scale:

Description	R.O.C.E.	Score
Very high	Over 20%	4
High	16–20%	3
Average	15%	2
Low	10–14%	1
Poor	0–9%	0
Loss	Negative .	−1

This question attracts 21% of the total weighting for this axis of the matrix.

Note: The profitability scale can be set up from statistical data on the profitability of UK
industry, for example using ICC Business ratios data.

1.3. Margins maintained in times over capacity/low demand

	Score
Little or no change in margins	4
Occasional price cutting	3
Modest reductions in margin	2
Significant margin erosion	1
No margin control	0

1.4. Degree to which product seen as commodity or differentiated

	Score
Differentiated—seen as almost unique	4
Significantly differentiated from competitors	3
Modest differentiation	2
Standardised product	1
Commodity status	0

1.5. Ratio industry to customer firms

This considers the relative dependence of the industry on its customers.

Description	Ratio	Score
Numerous customers	1:100+	4
Many customers	1:75	3
Average	1:50	2
Few customers	1:10	1
Unity	1:1	0

An adjustment may be made to the rating when one buyer takes a major share of all purchases.

1.6. Threat of backwards integration

	Score
None	4
Unlikely but possible	3
Moderate threat	2
Quite likely	1
Serious threat	0

1.7. High/low customer added value

	Score
Very high	4
High	3
Average	2
Low	1
Very low	0

1.8. Threat from substitutes

	Score
None in sight	4
Possible but unlikely	3
Some threats emerging	2
Under threat	1
Already serious	0

1.9. Degree of "switching" cost protection

	Score
Very high—ensures continuity of business	4
High	3
Moderate	2
Low	1
None	0

1.10. Entry barriers

	Score
Very high—new entrant unlikely	4
Fairly high	3
Moderate	2
Very few	1
None	0

1.11. Supply difficulties
Does the industry in the country of operation have difficulty in obtaining raw materials, components, etc?

	Score
Very serious problems	0
Some serious problems	1
Average	2
Very few	3
None	4

1.12. Ratio of suppliers to industry firms
The question applies to the key supplies by value

		Score
+30:1	Very healthy	4
20:1	Healthy	3
6:1	Average	2
3:1	Causing concern	1
1:1 or worse	Dangerous	0

1.13. Threats of forward integration by supplier

	Score
None	4
Unlikely but possible	3
Moderate threat	2
Quite likely	1
Serious threat	0

1.14. Degree to which the supplier depends on the industry

	Score	
	If suppliers large firms	If suppliers small firms
Proportions of sales		
Over 75%	0	
50–74%	1	
33–49%	2	
20–33%	3	No
Under 20%	4	score

1.15. Overall weightings for market prospects axis

Market growth	5
Market quality	5
Supply position	2

Of this

Based on historical fact (profits and growth)	7.5 = 6.2%
Balance	4.5 = 37.5%

2. Company's Competitive Position

2.1. Market position

Rating	Key word	Description
4	Leader	A company which normally has price and technical leadership in the market place. The associated brand share will vary. For example a company with 25% share (the highest) in a field with 10 other competitors each with shares varying from 1–15% will be likely to be a leader. Another company with a 30% brand share and two major strong competitors may not be.
3	Major	The position where no one company is a leader, but 2–4% companies of similar size have major shares in the market.
2	Viable	A company with a strong stake. Usually this will be the next position when one competitor is the leader.
1	Minor	Less than adequate to support R&D and other services in the long run.
0	Negligible	Current position negligible.

This question has 50% of total weighting on this axis of the matrix.

2.2. Company's profitability relative to the industry

	Score
More than 20% higher	4
Consistently 10–20% higher	3
Same level as industry	2
Consistently 10–20% lower	1
More than 20% lower	0

2.3. Production economics

Description	Indication	Score
Excellent	Over 15% advantage	4
Better than average	5–15% advantage	3
Same	Prices roughly the same	2
Worse than average	5–15% disadvantage	1
Poor	Over 15% disadvantage	0

This question represents a judgemental effort to compare the economics of the firm with major competitors. The clue will often lie in relative prices.

2.4. Capacity utilisation

	Score
Above 80–100%	4
Above 60–80%	3
Above 50–60%	2
Above 40–50%	1
Under 40%	0

2.5. Quality of plant, etc.

To some degree this is related to production economics. It is a judgemental question about the state of productive assets and methods compared with competition.

	Score
Very much better than major competitors	4
Better than major competitors	3
About the same as major competition	2
Worse than major competitors	1
Very much worse	0

2.6. Materials/components supply problems faced by firm

	Score
Considerably better than the industry	4
A bit better than the industry	3
About the same as the industry	2
A bit worse than the industry	1
Considerably worse than the industry	0

2.7. R & D services

Does the company undertake the degree of R & D necessary to sustain its position in the market?

	Score
R & D effort right for the market	4
R & D effort almost right	3
R & D effort has some deficiencies	2
R & D effort inadequate	1
R & D effort very poor	0

2.8. Technical support

Is the company able to provide the level of technical support needed to support its position?

	Score
A leader in this field	4
Better than average	3
As good as relevant competition	2
Worse than average	1
Very poor	0

2.9. Distribution network and methods

	Score
Excellent	4
Good	3
Average	2
Below average	1
Poor	0

3.0. Weightings for competitive position axis

	Score
Weightings are distributed:	
Market position	8
Production/supply capability	4
Market support	4

Approximately 63% of total weightings are applied to the provable elements of market position and relative profitability.

17

Strategic Planning—A Second Look at the Basic Options

In Chapter 14 there was a considerable discussion of the matrix (Fig. 14.3) into which most strategic alternatives could be fitted. Within each sector of this matrix there are many actions that can be initiated, and these may be classified under a second list of headings on which discussion should now be turned. These are:

(i) Divestment.
(ii) Obtaining licences.
(iii) Granting licences.
(iv) A simple expansion approach—hiring staff
                                partnership
                                broking
                                "piggy-backing" operation
                                contract production
                                selling own services.
(v) Research and development.
(vi) Acquisition and merger.
(vii) Alliances.

Divestment

A decision to give up a particular sphere of activity may be very difficult to make. There are often emotional or prestige reasons for wishing to continue: a dislike of admitting failure, an unpleasantly high loss to be faced in one year, problems of employee morale, and, above all, a sneaking feeling that someone else might pick up the divested area and make a success of it. For a chief executive this may be like advertising personal inadequacies. If it is a major divestment, the whole of the business world will observe it and will note the results if another chief executive does succeed where the first has failed.

The decision to divest can come in varying degrees of size. The dropping of a few minor products may cause no problems at all. In another case an entire activity area may be sold without having any noticeable effect on the day-to-day operations of the company. A decision to divest the company of a complete division or subsidiary may have a much greater impact.

Divestment may be a very important strategic decision to consider. Although my opening sentences on the subject hinted that failure could be the incentive to divestment, this is only one of the many possible causes. It is possible to divest from strength as well as from weakness.

A divestment decision might well arise from a tidying-up operation after the company has made its corporate appraisal or evaluated its portfolio. Perhaps the operation, although profitable, does not fit in with the company's perception of what it should be doing. Here it may be sensible to apply the maxim of concentration of effort by attempting to withdraw from an operation which makes demands on top management time but which has no place in long-term strategic thinking.

A related divestment decision might arise because although the company might wish to remain in a business, it may be unable to afford the capital expenditures required to make that business a successful long term competitor. In these circumstances it is better to find a way to withdraw now, while the business is seen as successful, rather than waiting until it has lost competitive ground. It was this sort of circumstance that lay behind the reshaping of the Vickers portfolio over the three years following the merger with Rolls Royce Motors.

Divestment may be the result of a desire to reduce risk. An assessment may suggest that the company is unwise to rely on profits from its subsidiary in an underdeveloped country because of the high probability of political unrest. It may be prudent to divest the company of all or part of its operations in that country in order to avoid a possible problem at a later date.

As we saw in the GI example in the previous chapter, the perception of risk may be related to the perception of the strategic requirements of this business, and it may be the combination of the two that brings the divestment decision to the fore.

Shareholder value has been discussed several times, and has provided a different motivation for divestment. This may take the form of reshaping the portfolio in the way already suggested, or it may take the form of returning to the shareholders an equity stake in an activity hived off from the current ownership. Argos was hived off in this way from BAT Industries, and now has nothing to do with its former parent, although no doubt it still has a number of shareholders in common.

Divestment may be forced for legal reasons. In the USA, anti-trust legislation has compelled many large organisations to divest part of their businesses. This has long been an element of American business history. For example the break up of the great Standard Oil Company in 1911 into 38 state-centred oil companies ultimately led to a number of the mammoth world players of today. There are many more recent examples, such as ITT. Monopoly legislation is not restricted to the USA, and the legislation of the EC and its component countries has made companies divest businesses that they would rather have kept, sometimes as the condition for allowing a merger to take place. In other countries, such as Malaysia, there has been legislation that has forced the sale of a major part of the shareholding to local people. This type of legislation may be the trigger that leads an organisation to withdraw from the particular country.

The final example is where the legal background to the competitive arena makes it impossible for the company to compete on level terms with its main rival. BP sold its downstream oil interests in Canada to the state-owned oil company. Not only was Petrocan in a preferred position through many Government actions, but it became impossible for BP to expand to meet its challenge because of legislation which made it very difficult for a foreign owned company to expand by acquisition in Canada.

A divestment decision from weakness might arise in order to improve the cash-flow position. The sale of a profitable activity might be the solution to a difficulty that cannot be resolved by other means. Alternatively, an activity may be divested now in order to avoid a major capital investment foreseen in the near future. In this way a potential problem is avoided, and the more favourable time (for the vendor) may be picked for the sale.

There are many divestment strategies. The simplest is to offer the business for sale, and here the skill is to do this in a way that gains the maximum price, but does not cause a flight of customers or key staff. The need for what might be termed confidential promotion has led to specialist acquisition broking businesses. When Vickers decided to divest the diesel division they approached it in a similar way to how they might have chosen a diesel company to acquire. In other words, which companies in the world would it best complement, in terms of development, product range, and geographical coverage. This resulted in a short list of target companies who could be approached with a carefully prepared proposition showing where the benefits were. The buyer was Perkins. The probability was that this approach brought a better price, and because it was handled by the top management of the division, may have maintained management morale and kept the key people together.

Another means of divestment is the management buy-out. This has long existed, and became particularly popular during the 1980s, often leading to businesses which prospered once they had thrown off the shackles of the head office. One well known example is the purchase of the National Freight Corporation from the British Government by its management and other employees, a story which has been described by Thompson.[1]

Charterhouse in the 1970s was a combined industrial, merchant banking and financial services organisation in the UK. During the late 1970s it began to reduce its investment in the industrial holdings, and to use the funds to build the merchant banking operation, including the acquisition of another major player. The divestment strategy applied to many of the strongest companies in the port-folio was to float them on the stock market, initially retaining a significant share-holding which could be disposed of later. This was a neat way of divesting, in that it gained maximum realisation without it being necessary to find and negotiate with one particular buyer. Customer confidence was unaffected: it was after all a sign that the company had grown up, and it avoided the internal upheaval of an acquisition.

It is also worth stressing that divestment does not have to be total. It is sometimes worth removing some of the problems of risk and inability to fund growth by merging a subsidiary with that of another organisation. A stake may be retained, possibly for sale later. However there can be risks here, particularly if one partner wants to slow investment and the other to increase it. Just such a situation is described by Friedman:[2] the joint company formed in the USA from the construction equipment interests of Allis Chalmers and Fiat. Allis Chalmers wanted to reduce their stake in this business: Fiat wanted to expand. Consequently there was a clash every time Fiat called for new investment, which would in fact have increased the Allis Chalmers stake. Fiat had purchased 65% of the construction equipment from Allis Chalmers. This attempt at reducing involvement in a business led to litigation and acrimony.

In all divestment decisions attention must be given to personnel, morale throughout the whole company (nothing spreads faster than a rumour that the ship is sinking), and to the public relations aspect. The divestment plan should deal specifically with these matters.

A divestment decision is based on forecasts and assumptions in much the same way as an investment decision. The main difference is the light of publicity. The outside world rarely knows when an investment opportunity is rejected or even— except in the case of large failures—where a decision to invest proves less successful than had been hoped. Divestment is a public act and calls for a higher degree of management courage. Despite this, it is an action which should be considered when a company evaluates its future strategy, for it may be the key to greater profits.

Obtaining Licences

A decision to obtain licences may arise from a study of any of the boxes in the strategic matrix, although it is more likely to be associated with new products, whether for existing or new markets. It may be a logical decision in a situation where a licensed process can bring lower production costs for existing products or can upgrade the products so that they give a better market performance and in these situations can contribute to expansion under the two existing product boxes of the matrix.

The main drawbacks of obtaining licences are cost, continuity, security of information, legislation, and availability. A licensing agreement involves the payment of a fee, frequently on a royalty basis, over the life of the agreement. This usually means a commitment of future margins, which can cause problems if the company ever moves into a situation where these are declining.

Continuity is another problem which depends on the type of agreement, the remaining patent life (if any), and the strategies of the licensee. Unless carefully considered a licensing policy brings the risk that what has become a major product area may disappear overnight if the agreement is cancelled or lapses, there is no control by the licensee over research and development, so he may not know whether product improvements are being carried out or how vulnerable it is to technological developments by competitors.

Security of information may not always be a disadvantage, or at least any disadvantage may be more emotional than real. But a licensee must provide information to the licensor and, in many cases, must give access to the books of account, marketing plans, and production processes. This may be a disadvantage if the venture proceeds well, giving the licensor full information about the market which might tempt him into it on his own account with this or the next improved version of the product. In this way the licensee may, in effect, be carrying out the expensive market development work on behalf of another company. This information problem can become more acute when company ownerships change: what is quite sensible policy at the beginning may become much more of a problem if the licensor is acquired by a major competitor of the licensee.

Legislation may be a problem which has to be taken into account. For example, the payment of royalties may be prohibited by some governments. A change in legislation can be particularly difficult for both parties.

Perhaps the biggest problem of all is finding someone who wants to license a product or process. There are specialist agencies which can assist in bringing interested parties together, and it is possible to identify possibilities and make a direct approach to the company concerned. In many ways there may be similarities with identifying and negotiating with a suitable acquisition prospect. Success cannot be guaranteed, and the company must always remain wide awake to the unexpected opportunity.

The difficulties and problems should not be overstressed, for co-operation is possible even among the most aggressive of competitors (e.g. the licensing arrangements in the world pharmaceutical industry). There are very real benefits to a licensing agreement, and in most cases these outweigh the disadvantages. In any case many can be overcome through care in negotiating the terms of the agreement.

Firstly a company may save time by taking a licence. It may be possible to put a new product on the market within a matter of months, where by other means it might take years. The quality of the product is known already, as may be its performance in other markets, and thus the risk of delay through product failure is considerably reduced (although a licensed product may still fail in a new market). This shortening of the time-span, and the reduction of risk, can accelerate the product's ability to contribute to profits.

Licensing may further reduce risk because it provides access to a brand name which is already known if not established. This is not always the case, but it may well happen.

This strategy may also give the company access to technical knowledge and skilled personnel which would otherwise be difficult or impossible to obtain. It may give a back-up service which might be beyond the resources of the company itself.

In many cases a licence will also bring the benefit of patent protection—on the one hand, enabling the company to undertake a process which would otherwise have been denied to it, and, on the other, providing it with a shield behind which it can shelter.

A licence may also reduce competition or the possible threat of competition. This may be important if the development for which a licence is sought represents a major technological advance over the company's own product. The licence, besides securing the development for the company, ensures that the licensor does not become a threat by entering the market as a competitor.

Granting Licences

One way of extending existing products to new markets is to actively seek to grant licences to other companies. We have examined some of the reasons why it is worthwhile for a company to obtain a licence: now it is time to look at the other side of the coin to see the benefits available to the company granting the licence.

Perhaps the biggest is that it provides opportunities to profit from the product or processes without tying up working capital or carrying the risk of market development work. The licensor may also gain time—just as the licensee does, although for different reasons. To establish an effective production and distribution unit in another country may take at least a year—longer if factories have to be built and plant ordered. By granting a licence a company can often ensure that it is receiving an income from its project within a much shorter period.

A company may avoid the commitment of working capital for normal marketing and the expenditure of fixed capital. It does not have to erect overseas plants or expand domestic capacity to cope with exports. This may enable expansion beyond a company's own capital resources, and because the additional earnings are obtained for only a meagre additional working capital requirement, may dramatically improve profitability ratios.

The nature of licensing means that tariff barriers can often be jumped without subeconomic ventures being set up in high risk countries. This may be a means of expanding or a way of avoiding all loss of profits when an export market closes its borders through protective tariffs.

Few strategies are without some disadvantages, and there are points which should be considered. A licensing agreement is often vulnerable to changes in government policy, e.g. the imposition of controls which prohibit royalty payments to external companies. There may be risks in passing on technology to outsiders who may abuse the terms of the agreement. Perhaps the greatest disadvantage need not be a disadvantage if a company does its long-range planning well: licensing agreements can make it more difficult for a company to set up its own organisation in an area which has shown significant development. It therefore behoves a company to carefully plan its strategies for a particular country or product area so that the terms and conditions are matched to its ultimate ambitions.

Simple Expansion

Often in an analysis of strategic options the obvious gets forgotten. For the two boxes of the matrix dealing with existing products the best way of expanding may be the simplest way. Just do it. This is the situation when the strategy can be fulfilled from within the company's existing resources—either out of current capacity, from expanding existing factories, or from the transfer of technology to new factories and new business areas. This really is so obvious and so logical that it needs no further analysing.

In cases where technology is closely related, it may be possible for new products to be launched in this way, particularly "me-too" products which involve no creative research and development.

Where the technological threshold of an industry is low, it is also a worthwhile possibility to take the simple approach and just start the operations required. In this case the only skills needed may be brought in through the engaging of suitable employees. Thus a decision to open a chain of hotels, or hairdressing salons, or a small factory making cement blocks, could be implemented through the recruitment of people with the requisite skills, the investment of capital in the resources needed, and, as an optional extra, the use of specialist consultants to help the venture off the ground. As the technological threshold increases, often accompanied by a rise in the financial stake needed to enter the industry, the simple method of expansion becomes more difficult and more risky. But it is rarely impossible (although it may in some industries be highly dangerous) and it is the method of growth and development which originally set many of today's mammoth companies on their paths of expansion.

There are alternative ways of tackling this method of expansion. Additional skills may be obtained, or risks reduced, by joint ventures or partnership arrangements. These may provide a safer method of, for example, expanding existing products into a new overseas market, and at the same time reduce the capital resources needed to finance the operation.

Another method may be to seek to use other companies' resources to help expansion. One example of this is contract manufacture, which may be exploited as a dynamic tool, or to protect existing market interests in a country where a new protective tariff has changed the competitive position of current supply sources.

Perhaps one of the most frequent examples of using contract production to exploit new opportunities is provided by the "own label" boom in the grocery trade in Europe and the United States. Supermarkets rarely own their own production sources and use the facilities of existing manufacturers to supply the required product. Expansion of the "own label" business would have been more risky and costly without this opportunity.

A second example is provided by the tyre factory opened in Rhodesia during the 1950s. Within a few months of opening behind a protective tariff it was producing tyres for other rubber companies.

Production is not the only resource, and it is possible for a company to devise a strategy which exploits opportunities available through the marketing and distributive skills of others. Such strategies are usually medium rather than long term, and can be of great benefit to both parties. They vary from the usage of specialist brokerage firms, to what has been called "piggy-banking".

Management Today[3] reports how Canada Dry used piggy-backing to break into the grocery market sector in the United Kingdom. The company was well established in the licensed trade and, rather than set up its own sales force, decided that the best way into the grocery trade would be through a company already established in that sector. It chose Wander, manufacturers of Ovaltine to "piggy-back" it for selling, invoicing, and delivery operations.

Another area of expansion which has been successfully selected by certain companies is the sale of its essential services.

Hanan[4] points out that many companies have service areas traditionally regarded as cost centres. It is possible to visualise them as opportunity or profit centres, and to develop them as a basis for expanding business.

The British firm Marketing Advisory Services Ltd. was one of the early marketing research businesses to perceive the benefits the computer could bring to their type of activity. After a few years' experience with the IBM 1130 they found that they were in a position to offer both software and computer time to outside organisations. This occasional offering of services to companies closely associated with the business later became a profit centre in its own right with the purchase of a second IBM 1130 and the establishment of a subsidiary company Data Analysis Services Ltd.

In common with many other companies Tate & Lyle, the sugar group, looked very hard at their physical distribution operations. Here they found that they were able to offer a delivery service to selected clients for goods—including shoes, canned food and wine—which were compatible with their own products. This has now become a steadily expanding activity.

The "piggy-back" example quoted above was, for Wander, a sale of part of its own service area. In this case it profited from its selling and physical distribution systems.

Alternatives based on the profitable exploitation of essential service areas are always worth examining provided they do not divert scarce management and financial resources from options which are more important to the company's long-term strategic needs.

Research and Development

In some situations the various alternatives discussed above will provide the solution to a company's needs. Probably in many other situations they will be inadequate, and much more attention will have to be given to the remaining options, one of the most complex of which may be research and development. For many companies, research and development is an essential to survival, and at least as part of its strategy must be directed along this path. Science based, or highly technological industries, may have to accept that a commitment to research and development is part of the price they pay for being in that business area. It is almost impossible to conceive of the Hoffman La Roches, the Union Carbides, the Du Ponts or the IBMs of this world without conceding the vital part that research and development plays for each of them.

Yet it would be wrong to see all research and development as one single type of problem area. For some companies a measure of basic research is an essential; for others it is a matter of applied research only; still others do little research and their emphasis is on the word "development".

Some definition of these terms may be helpful. Basic research may be defined as research which is carried on in the search for knowledge but without specific commercial objectives: when carried out by a firm it may seek a discovery which will benefit the firm, although the discovery may not initially be tied to any particular objectives. Applied research is, on the other hand, aimed to fulfil specific objectives. Development "is concerned with the technical non-routine activities associated with translating scientific knowledge into marketable products" (Steiner[5]). An ethical pharmaceutical company, for example, might have to accept a measure of basic research if it selected a strategy of developing new basic substances: on the other hand, a generic manufacturer, producing only those ethical products which have come off patent, might only need the bare minimum of applied research. One food manufacturer might concentrate mainly on development work—for example, new products to marketing specifications based only on known technologies: another might finance a programme of basic research to produce edible protein from a petro-carbon source. The problems of planning are different for each of these research and development areas, basic research being the least predictable and reliable: probably most companies will never have to face the difficulty of trying to plan this type of research.

Research and development may be selected as the strategy for all of the boxes in the matrix. It may be the path for complete diversification or the vehicle for product improvement. It may improve the margins of an existing product through the development of a new process or a change in a formula, R & D may fulfil a current and urgent need for today's operations or may be selected as the lynch-pin of a future diversification strategy.

The strategic planning process should provide the framework for research and development planning, by:

(i) Specifying the product or business areas to which research is to be directed.
(ii) Setting priorities for research and development projects.
(iii) Assigning time targets for R & D.
(iv) Setting the cost framework in terms of both revenue and capital requirements.

Requests for research and development may emanate from operating management (for marketing, technical, or financial reasons) or may come from the studies carried out at strategic level by the top management planning group. The value of a heavy top management involvement in the setting of R & D objectives and in ensuring that these are an integral part of total company strategy has been stressed by many writers. For example:

Steiner[5] states: "...top management involvement in choosing R & D programmes is important whether or not it considers itself technically qualified."

Quinn[6] argues: "R & D planning and budgeting ... must therefore be directly tied to total corporate planning."

Rance[7] stresses: "In my experience the programme of the group R & D function must be determined through consultation at the highest possible level of executive authority in the company."

Every R & D objective should be justified: that is, an attempt should be made to show what is required, why it is required, and the benefits the project will bring. Top management, through the planning process, must also assess the priorities for R & D work. The strategic plan should provide a clear indication of the most important areas to which R & D effort should be directed: establishing this is a part of the decision process which leads a company to select R & D rather than one of the other alternatives.

Closely tied in with priorities and the strategic decision are time targets. It is important to establish whether the work required is of the type that will respond to additional resources or whether there is a natural sequence of events that cannot be speeded in any way. If R & D is unlikely to produce results in the required period of time, the company may be forced to reject it as a method of growth or it may be compelled to develop other additional strategies to fill the gap caused by the extended time required. Unfortunately, the time required for a project and its related component cost is frequently underestimated. For example, Allen and Norris[8] found that time was underestimated by 204% on average, while cost was exceeded by 46%. Once a time target has been set in the plan, every available control tool should be used to ensure that the company keeps to it (see Chapter 20).

It should also be recognised that certain types of R & D projects are subject to two forms of failure. R & D may not succeed in producing the required product or process at all. Where an improvement or cost reduction exercise is involved an R & D success may be implemented immediately. A new product, however, is subject to a second type of failure: although R & D may have met all specifications, it may still die at the marketing stage. Norwood and Smith[9] report on a study of post-marketing new drug failures in the US pharmaceutical industry over a long period. In the survey definitions, post-marketing failure rate was about 13% over the period 1958–1966. However, the authors maintain that "the pre-marketing failure rate for the pharmaceutical industry is much higher than that for all of American industry". An assessment of the pre- and post-marketing failure rate for all American industry is provided in Fig. 17.1.

In the grocery trade, studies over a period of time (eleven years USA, fourteen years UK) by Nielson indicate that even at test-market stage the failure rate is relatively high. On average some 60% of products test-marketed went national in the United States, while in the United Kingdom only 46% were launched. A study by Kraushar Andrews & Eassie Ltd.[11] showed that in the United Kingdom the average new product which reaches national distribution has only a 50% chance of

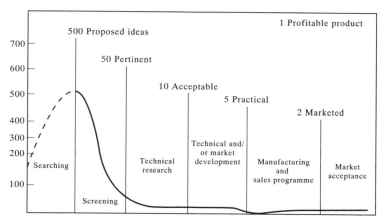

FIG. 17.1. Product evolution. From "Guides to Screening New Product Ideas", by J. L. Dooley and J. A. Ciapolla,[10] in *Management for the Smaller Company,* © 1959 American Management Association. Reproduced by permission of the publishers

surviving four years or more. New products in this context are not necessarily new in an R & D sense, but the data gives some indication of the risks involved.

Assessing the cost of a project is important for both decision and control purposes. Firstly, the amount of resources required for a new project should be compared against the cost of alternative strategies. If it is too high and too risky, the company might well have to fill the matrix by another method. In addition to the cost of an individual project the company must consider the total long-term budget for its R & D section. It may be good policy to reject an R & D strategy because to follow it would mean spending more on total R & D than the company can justify: each project may be of reasonable cost by itself, but cumulatively the position becomes strategically unsound. (Control was referred to when time was discussed.)

Steiner[5] states that there are a number of "rules" in practical use which are applied to the setting of R & D budgets.

"Establish the total R & D budget at some percentage of sales.

Try to match what competitors are doing.

Find the industry average and stick to that.

Take a past historical average for the company and increase it by an amount equal to the internal rate of growth that is set as a company objective. If, for example, the company decides to grow at 8% per year through internal product developments, then increase the budget for research and development by 8% each year.

Cost out R & D needed to meet specific product objectives and add a percentage for independent research to be determined by those doing it. Give the R & D staff what is requested if the amount is reasonable in light of the firm's financial ability. Develop in the planning process a balance among R & D and all other activities."

My own recommendation is that the amount of resources allocated for R & D should arise from the planning processes: that is, it should be a balance between the various activities of the company set at strategic level. In setting the balance the company should also take account of the cost of individual projects, so that these may not exceed the total allocation, and so that money is not allocated willy nilly when in fact it is more than adequate for all the projects that are required. For sustained R & D effort one of the main requirements is a measure of stability in budget allocations. This is an area where corporate planning can be of considerable assistance because, by tying in R & D effort to total corporate strategy, it helps the company to both identify and provide for its needs. If the plan throws doubt on the company's ability to finance the required measure of research, the best solution might well be to opt for a lower measure where there is more stability. No amount of planning can remove management judgement. Having set cost and time targets, only top management can decide whether to continue or to cut off once the limits are reached. Similarly, judgement is required in the selection of an R & D strategy, on its likely success, and on the cost effectiveness of such a strategy.

A further area of decision in the selection of an R & D strategy is whether to commission the work internally or externally. The availability of universities and specialist agencies should not be overlooked, and may provide a means of avoiding "humps" in the company's internal R & D staffing needs.

The subject of R & D may be left with a final thought on the type of R & D strategy which may be selected. Pavitt[12] classifies these into "offensive" (the intention to be first in the field with a major innovation), "defensive" (the intention to avoid mistakes by following the leaders—never being first but reacting quickly enough to be second), and "absorptive" (obtaining developments on licence and carrying out minimum R & D work to further develop them). The basic R & D approach selected would have a bearing on the choice of R & D instead of one of the other alternatives discussed in this chapter. Pavitt sums up the management implications of his strategy in Fig. 17.2.

In this discussion of R & D strategy I have left one aspect unexplored: the technology strategy of the company. This will be discussed in a later chapter.

Acquisition and Merger

A major area of strategic choice open to a company is acquisition, or its variant, merger. In many ways this strategy is too inviting, and can easily become a trap for the unwary. While the paper advantages of acquisition may be enticing, the management and human aspects—often incalculable at the early stages—may become so great that they prevent the strategy from becoming a success.

"Merger-mania" can easily run riot, and the speed with which third parties frequently make intervening bids during a battle between two companies suggests that little thought or strategic planning has entered the process. The real reason for many acquisitions may be corporate or individual pride, without attention to what is good for the company or sound for its long-term future.

Yet there may be positive and genuine benefits to an acquisition strategy: real reasons which demonstrate that this method of development can provide a sound

R & D strategy	Implications for management		
	Resource and managerial requirements	Possibilities of penetrating foreign markets	Specific problems and opportunities for European firms
Offensive	High R & D, high risk, high pay-off with success. Requires managerial flexibility and creative and perceptive science, technology and market exploration.	Relatively easy, provided that foreign demand exists.	Most difficult when US firms have strong technology/market advantages. Other advanced technologies do, however, exist and can be exploited.
Defensive	Medium R & D risk. Lower pay-off unless leader makes mistakes. Need for good knowledge of competitors, short lead times, and strong marketing capability.	Likely when lead times very short, leading firm makes mistakes, or when firm makes improvements in design or in secondary characteristics.	Best strategy when consolidating past mistakes, or when dealing with competitors with strong technology/market positions.
Absorptive	Low R & D and risk. Low pay-off, unless there exists strong advantages in man-power or material costs, or other company attributes.	Likely when market restriction clauses can be avoided, and cost advantages rapidly exploited.	More difficult as big firms prefer to invest rather than licence. Possible when firm has its own technology. Medium- and small-sized firms more likely to license than big ones.

FIG. 17.2. Research and development strategies (from an article by K. Pavitt[10])

bridge to the future, and is not necessarily a way of dissipating resources to give solid form to misty illusions of personal grandeur. It is worth studying these potential benefits, before looking at some of the practical results of merger activity, and some of the ways of ensuring that if an acquisition strategy is selected it has a good chance of being successful.

Acquisition may be used to fill every box in the expansion matrix; for example:

(i) *Existing products/existing markets.* Acquiring an extra link in the chain—backwards integration to control supplies, or forwards integration to take on a further step in the distribution process.

(ii) *Existing products/new markets.* Buying a wholesaler in a new export market, to provide an easier means of entry.

(iii) *New products/existing markets.* Acquisition of a company that can be completely integrated with present operations.

(iv) *New products/new markets.* Complete diversification through acquisition of a company in an entirely new field.

This is something of an oversimplification of the reasons for acquisition, and needs further elaboration. In fact there may be many sound arguments in favour of acquisition.

(a) Reduction of Risk

In the previous section examples were given of new product failure rates for two industries. The acquisition of a business with suitable products may provide an opportuntity for a firm to expand without carrying this risk of failure. Such a policy may be in the interests of the individual firm but will only benefit the community if the acquisition has a synergistic effect (of course, it is in the interests of the company to seek synergy).

There is also the possibility of a negative effect—for managerial and morale reasons the two companies may achieve less when put together than they would as single entities. Nevertheless, the risk to a company may still be less than one of the alternative expansion strategies, even in a situation where the cost of implementation is higher. We will look later at the research into success and failure of acquisitions.

(b) Avoidance of a Profit Slump

Acquisition may be a way of buying immediate profits, where one of the other alternatives would have caused a period of reduced earnings. Profits may increase in absolute terms, but still bring a reduction in return on investment, although this, too, may be avoided if synergy can be exploited. The way the acquisition is financed will also affect ROI.

(c) A Means of Entry into a New Area

Not all new business areas are easy for an outsider to enter. The more advanced technology and high capital industries (often the two go together) have by their very nature a measure of protection against intruders. To break in may require the injection of heavy capital resources into a business area in which the company has little experience, or the problem of somehow obtaining the necessary technical knowledge which can be difficult, costly, and with few chances of success. In these circumstances acquisition may be a very attractive strategy and may save both time and money.

(d) A Means of Obtaining Cash

Certain types of company may have a healthy cash-flow situation, large liquid reserves, and a relatively poor history of profits. Such a situation may, for example, occur with a shipping company, where positive cash-flows from depreciation on very expensive fixed assets make re-investment of the cash a difficult strategic problem. In this sort of situation, a company with a good profit record and a need for capital to exploit its many projects may find it possible to acquire the other company on a share exchange basis—in effect buying cash for paper. Such a move may be facilitated if the Stock Market has valued the companies on a yield, rather than on asset, basis. The acquiring company is left with the problem of increasing earnings so that its present shareholders are not dissatisfied—the synergy which makes this possible may be simply a use for the surplus cash.

(e) Welding Together a Fragmented Industry

Some industries are highly fragmented. This makes it difficult for any company to gain a major share of the market by any internal strategy. The only way to build up a sizeable operating unit is through a process of acquisition and rationalisation. A move of this nature may be encouraged by government as the best means of creating a healthy industry: an example of such a situation was the UK machine-tool industry during the 1960s. It is worth pointing out that although acquisition may be the only workable strategic choice within an industry, a far better option might well be to expand into a completely different field. The danger sign to be avoided is when top management begins to see itself as the crusading saviours of the industry rather than professional managers charged with the duty of looking after shareholders' interests.

(f) Removal of Competition

Example (e) above may have the effect of removing competitive products, but is not the main reason for the acquisition. On the other hand, it is possible to seek the destruction of competition through acquisition for monopolistic reasons: to gain complete control of a market in order to reduce consumer choice and increase prices. Acquisition for this reason now verges on the impossible in many developed countries because legislation exists expressly to prevent it.

(g) Opportunity for Synergy

Some aspects of synergy have already been discussed, and the synergistic effect is something which should be looked for in any acquisition situation. The main reason for an acquisition may be because the company has spotted a synergistic opportunity. Cash resources have already been discussed (they are something of a special case), but opportunities may also exist in areas of research and development, production, distribution, or marketing. The only thing to add is a plea for caution: in most merger situations, what is known about a company is only the tip of the iceberg: what lies hidden under the surface may be enough to destroy the apparent opportunity.

(h) To Obtain New Ideas

A sterile company may turn to acquisition for growth because it lacks creativity and has no ideas of its own. Unless a radical change takes place such a company is likely to find that an acquisition provides it with only a short-term opportunity.

The next phase of growth will also require ideas, and the company is no more likely to have these after the merger than it was before. In my experience many companies which turn to acquisition do so because they do not know what else to do. And this is not a very good reason.

(i) To Obtain New People

It is sometimes said that a reason for acquisition may be to obtain particular management skills. It is difficult to think of many acquisition circumstances where such a reason is sound: the services of a firm of "headhunters" may be cheaper and more effective. A possible exception may be when a company particularly wants a person who is running a small business and there the purchase price is small. The situation may be different in a true merger situation, where management of complementary skills and talents wish to come together for the benefit of both parties: again, this is a solution which is more likely in small- to medium-sized companies than in the larger businesses.

(j) Capital Cost of Growth

Acquisition may also be chosen for financial strategic reasons rather than because it is the less risky or more profitable path open to the company. A business with a poor cash flow may not have the capital to choose, for example, the R & D route, but may be able to acquire by an exchange of shares and without cash. Whether this is a good reason for acquisition depends on individual circumstances.

Whether these reasons for merger are actually achieved in practice is another matter. The well-known American study by Kitching[13] of twenty US corporations covering sixty-nine mergers showed that about one-third of the mergers were failures. Mergers were mostly likely to succeed if carried out for financial reasons and were likely to succeed if undertaken for marketing reasons. Gains from production economies or technology were found to be much less likely. The study also showed that a horizontal integration—between firms in the same industry—was most likely to be successful. Among the most important conclusions was the fact that the achievement of benefits from merger called for considerable management talent, needing both speed of action after merger and a formal and clear management information system, so that the results of merger activity was clearly and regularly reported. Failure was high in instances where head office interest in the merger was lacking. Later studies produced very similar conclusions for European mergers.[14]

Porter[15] found a very similar pattern in a more recent study. He examined the diversification records of 33 companies from 1950 to 1986. The study "... found that on average corporations divested more than half of their new acquisitions in new industries and more than 60% of their acquisitions in completely new fields. Fourteen companies left more than 70% of the acquisitions they had made in new fields. The track record in unrelated acquisitions is even worse—the average divestment rate is a startling 74%."

The study by Ansoff et al.,[16] quoted in Chapter 2, also showed that companies which planned their acquisitions were more likely to be successful than those which did not.

Perhaps the most important lessons to be learned from merger studies are that success calls for careful management planning, deliberate and speedy action to achieve the merger objectives, and control to study the results of the action. The planned approach to mergers tries to take out many of the elements of risks.

Firstly, any company considering merger should clearly identify why this particular alternative strategy is being selected above all others. If an acquisition idea cannot pass this preliminary screening it should be rejected. If there is a prima facie case for acquisition, the next stage should be the identification of the acquisition objectives. This must be a deliberate and unemotional approach, and related to the general requirements of the strategy rather than a particular acquisition candidate: moving the analysis to a specific company comes later.

The acquisition objectives should serve as the framework around which the next stage of analysis can be built—the detailed acquisition profile. Again, without a particular company in mind—for this will only cloud the judgement—the planning team should prepare a pen picture of the type of company that is required in order to fulfil the strategy. The profile should specify all the factors that are considered important—and those will vary from company to company. It is rare that the ideal acquisition candidate exists in real life, but the profile provides a standard against which all candidates may be measured. For the measurement to be really useful, it follows that great care must be exercised in drawing up the profile so that all important factors are both identified and quantified. If a particular criterion is vital this must be stressed since there is no point in making an acquisition that cannot possibly fulfil its purpose. On the other hand, other points in the profile may be desirable but not essential: this, too, should be stated.

There are many ways in which an acquisition profile may be set out, and, as in so many aspects of management, there is no one golden rule. The example given here is of what might be done rather than what must be done, and refers to a hypothetical situation where the planner can be very specific about the market in which he expects his acquisition to be operating. A more general example will be provided later.

Acquisition Profile: Marine Heating and Ventilating Company

1. Size. To cost no more than £1 m. at an initial return on capital employed of not less than 10%.
2. Products. Design and manufacture of complete environmental control systems for the shipping industry.
3. Market position. Must have at least 10% of the UK market and must have customers in more than five shipyards. Must have 25% of sales in export markets, including Norway, Holland, and Japan.
   At least 90% of sales must be in original equipment. Turnover about £1 m. per annum.

4. Technical position. Must be accepted in its industry as a leader in technical innovation. Over the past five years an average of at least 5% of annual sales must have been spent on research and development.
5. Management. Competent management at all levels is desirable. Good top management is essential, as is technical management at all levels.
6. Factories. Plant and equipment must be relatively modern (90% of plant must be under five years old).
   Factory must be located in the north-east of England. The site must have room for expansion, and it must be physically possible to treble output within three years.
7. Conditions. No company will be acquired unless it is possible to obtain all voting shares.

In some circumstances a company may wish to be more general in acquisition requirements. For example, a company wishing to expand in the food business may be willing to choose a candidate from a number of subsectors of that broad industry group (the hypothetical company above was able to be much more specific than this and to say precisely which industry and which market it wished to enter). A conglomerate company may wish to define its acquisition policy in even more general terms, being willing to consider a number of candidates from a number of industries. In this sort of situation the requirements may be much more matters of financial strategy than any particular market strategy, and the intention may be to exploit investment and financial management skills, rather than to develop any particular wing of the business. Such general profiles are still an aid to the identification of acquisition candidates, and have been used by many companies. An example is given below.

The XYZ Company intends to diversify into four new business areas, and to achieve this end will acquire suitable companies in the food industry in Europe, the United States, and North Africa.

Acquisition efforts will be concentrated on companies which have a demonstrable record of product development. The companies must have strong franchises in advertised and branded consumer food products, and must hold less than 10% of the domestic market.

Food industry investments will be selected from companies in any of the following areas:

Coffee and tea
Canned foods
Pet foods
Sweets and chocolates
Sauces, pickles, and condiments
Frozen foods

Restriction

Not more than two companies will be acquired in any one country, and not more than one will be in North Africa.

Size

The minimum size of any company by turnover will be £3 m. per annum, of which at least 75% will be domestic sales.

Profitability Criteria

No acquisition will be considered that does not offer the prospect of returning 10% on shareholders' capital within three years and after taxes. The average return on capital employed during those three years must not be less than 8%. Profits (after tax) of at least £300,000 per year must be possible.

Any acquisition in North Africa must yield 20% return on capital employed, according to the above definitions.

Ownership and Management

No company will be acquired unless at least 80% of equity can be obtained, and 100% is preferred.

The competence of management, proved by past records, and the continued availability of key people is an essential factor in any acquisition.

A great deal of thought and hard work will have been put into these first stages of the acquisition study, but this is only a beginning. The next step is to study the companies theoretically available for acquisition and to match their characteristic against the predefined acquisition profile. This statement hides what in practice may be a long and boring task: it may require an analysis of several hundred companies to arrive at two or three which are close to the profile, and even then acquisition may prove to be impossible. Much of the analysis may be at a fairly simple level, certain factors from the profile (for example, turnover range) being used to screen out the obviously unsuitable and to reduce the list to manageable proportions.

Now it may well be that no company matches very closely with the acquisition profile, and management may be called upon to decide how far they can compromise, or whether the deviations are so great that they indicate that an alternative strategy should be chosen. Each successive stage in the screening processes is likely to involve more detailed analysis work. By the time the short list is reached the company may have had to carry out original market research in order to establish some details of the companies concerned: certainly very detailed desk research will have taken place. Figure 17.3 provides an illustration of how the acquisition research might develop, although this can only be a generalised view, and there may be differences in particular situations.

The screening processes should result in a short list of companies which closely match the acquisition profile. An attempt should be made to identify the probable cost of acquiring each of these companies with the possible financial strategies that

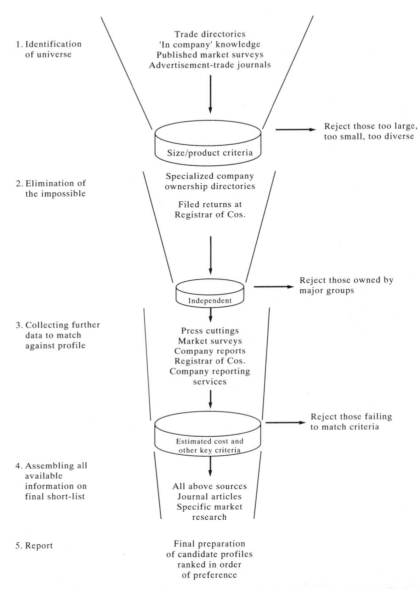

FIG. 17.3. Stages in the identification of acquisition candidates showing sources of information

might be adopted. An acquisition objective should then be developed for each candidate, showing exactly what benefits the company seeks. Much of this will be derived from the general acquisition objectives, although much may be specific to the particular candidate. From this a provisional value of the candidate *to the company* may be established. This may be higher than the valuation of the candidate on past and expected performance because of the things the company intend to do to that company once it is acquired. The final candidates may now be ranked in order of preference, putting management in a position to decide whether to proceed with the acquisition.

Until this decision is made no indication of interest will have been given to the candidates concerned, and all work should be carried out in strict confidence. After this point the company has to approach the candidate either directly or through a third party (e.g. a merchant bank) to establish whether there is any interest in selling. There are differences between the acquisition of publicly quoted and privately owned companies: with the former an offer can be sent to shareholders even if the directors of the candidate company oppose the acquisition. In a private company, where management and financial control may be in the hands of the same people, such tactics would be unlikely to succeed. In either type of company amicable discussion is preferred, since this may give the purchaser access to much more information about the candidate, enabling him to define the acquisition objectives with more precision and to value the company with more confidence.

Negotiation is outside the scope of this book, as are valuation and the many legal and taxation problems which arise from acquisition activity. Before a firm offer is made, the purchaser should be very clear on what he intends to do with the company since, as has already been stated, speed of implementation is very important once an acquisition offer has been successful.

Uncertainty about what will happen may damage morale in both companies at all levels unless action is taken with speed. In addition the expected benefits of the merger may evaporate if undue delays take place. In my opinion it is more important to move with speed, taking all necessary steps within a matter of weeks, even though this may bring the risk of a wrong decision. Change over too long a period—or rather speculation on what that change might be—can bring a psychological blight over the company. If changes are implemented quickly, people can begin to relax and accept that they are now only subject to normal business hazards rather than the abnormal ones of the acquisition situation.

The achievement of this speed of action requires careful management planning both before and after acquisition. It calls for the commitment of top management time and interest, the allocation of responsibility for merging the two companies to a specific senior manager, and the control of the implementation of the acquisition plan by a regular reporting system. Acquisition may make a great demand on managers of both companies. Problems vary from the large tasks of rationalising two factories or merging two marketing operations, to the less important but time-consuming difficulty of putting two accounting systems on to a common basis. Overall the emotional climate may be coloured by fear.

The human factors are so important in merger success that they are worth more detailed examination (see Chapter 21).

The example of Penn Central Railroad's diversification efforts provides a grim warning of where a badly managed acquisition policy may lead. Penn Central's bankruptcy in June 1971 has been described as the worst collapse in the history of modern US business. (Some observers maintain that the collapse of Penn Central can itself be traced back to the formation of the company in 1968 with the merger of two railways, Pennsylvania and New York Central.) The report on the collapse by the Interstate Commerce Commission, the body which regulates all US operations, stated—among other things—that eagerness to diversify into non-railway activities led to the investment of $309 m. into pipeline, airline, real estate, and other activities. The total return on these massive investments was only $4–7 m., and in some cases Penn Central management failed to insist on their subsidiaries paying any cash dividends.

Strategic Alliances

Joint ventures have always been with us as a strategic option. Perhaps the oil industry offers the longest historical view of the use of this approach, often forced on the companies because of the costs of developing an oilfield, or the fact that control of production or markets may be divided so that limited collaboration is desirable. During the 1980s, the joint venture option became broadened to a concept of strategic alliances. A strategic alliance may involve investment by two or more companies in a specific venture. It may be broader, and involve forms of collaboration over marketing, technology, manufacture or other factors that are to the benefit of both companies. This second form of strategic alliance is appealing, but much more difficult to manage. In an acquisition or merger the partners become one. In a joint venture it is possible to set up an organisation to fulfil the required purpose, although not always without some clashes of objective between the partners. In the other form of alliance the companies may operate through their existing structures, making it difficult for either party to control what is happening.

The drive for alliances is partly fuelled by the fact that in many industries, for example the defence industries, the number of large players who may be available for acquisition is close to zero. Companies still need to find ways of competing with global competitors who may be operating on a larger scale. Alliances offer one way of doing this, or of obtaining benefits from larger market operations without the risks or requirement for high investment. The avoidance of what may be very high levels of investment may itself be the driving force. In some situations, government controls or protective rules may make alliances the only way of getting into a particular market.

The steps in selecting alliance partners are similar to those in finding acquisition candidates. However an additional essential step is to ensure that each party is aware of the objectives of the other before any agreement is signed. If the aims of the alliance partners are not compatible, the chances are that the alliance will break up quickly. A second requirement is not to underestimate the amount of management attention needed to make an alliance work. It is worth being realistic about the expected life of an alliance, since once the objectives of the partners changes, the alliance may become unworkable. It follows that alliances that are established for a short-term purpose have more likelihood of succeeding than an alliance that pretends it is a merger.

Some Strategic Principles

The complexity of strategic decision making becomes more apparent the deeper the exploration of the subject. Even this chapter, which appeared to be self contained, and indeed was when I wrote the original in the first edition of this book, has thrown up a need to look more deeply into the strategy of technology (and I will link this later to some thoughts about manufacturing strategy), and the human issues in acquisition. To neglect the people issues would mean that we are looking at strategy and not strategic management. We have yet to explore any of the thinking about global strategy.

At this point in the exploration of strategy it is worth referring to one of the few extensive data bases from which the cause and effect of different strategies has been studied over a long period. I refer to the PIMS data base. PIMS stands for profit impact of market strategy and has been in operation since 1972. Buzzell and Gale[17] provided a useful analysis of what can be gleaned from PIMS, and at the time they wrote there were 450 corporations contributing information on a total of 3000 business units. Data is collected annually, and the length of membership varied from 2 to 10 years. Member companies came from the USA and Europe.

The top principles of strategic thinking which emerged from the analysis were:

(i) The most important single factor impacting on the performance of a business unit is quality relative to competitors. They found that superior quality often brought premium prices, and in addition could lead to market growth and an expansion of market share. The word relative is important, because competitors are unlikely to stay still. This strategy therefore requires constant action if the company is to stay in the lead.

(ii) A second finding was that there was a link between market share and profitability. Companies with highest market shares tended to have better profitability. The authors caution against interpreting this statement as a belief that high market share at any cost is a good strategy. It is not.

(iii) High investment intensity acts as a drag on profits. Profitability tends to be highest where the amount of investment is lowest. This conclusion, in my opinion, should not lead anyone to the simplistic strategy of avoiding reinvestment to gain competitive advantage, a route that could eventually lead to total failure.

(iv) Much of the conventional wisdom about "dogs" and "cows" is not borne out by the evidence. This statement was discussed when we considered portfolio analysis, and is only included here for the sake of completeness.

(v) Vertical integration is a profitable strategy in some situations but not in others. The analysis is somewhat complex, but basically shows that vertical integration decreases profitability in business with a low relative market share. Businesses with an average or high market share do best when vertical integration is high or low, but not when it is in the middle. The conclusion seems to be: avoid it if you have a low market share. If you have a stronger position only go for vertical integration if you are prepared to do it in a significant way.

(vi) Most of the strategic factors that boost return on investment will also boost long-term value.

These points are drawn from one chapter of the book by Buzzell and Gale. This point is made because there is a great deal of explanation and wisdom in the other 11 chapters, and these are worth reading.

As always, when considering any points about strategic principles, remember that there are no hard rules and absolutes. Conclusions such as the above are helpful, but have to be considered with all the other factors and issues that have been covered so far, and many that we have yet to cover. Getting a good strategy is not a matter of applying a formula.

References

1. Thompson, P. "The NFC Buy-out—A New Form of Industrial Enterprise", Taylor, B. (ed.), *Strategic Planning and the Board*, Pergamon, Oxford, 1988.
2. Friedman, A. "Fiatallis: From Marriage to Divorce", *Financial Times*, February 11th 1985.
3. Monahan, J. "How Canada Dry Mixed its Marketing", *Management Today*, November 1970.
4. Hanan, M. "Corporate Growth Through Internal Spin Outs", *Harvard Business Review*, November/December 1969.
5. Steiner, G. A. *Top Management Planning*, Macmillan, 1969.
6. Quinn, J. B. "Technological Strategies for Industrial Companies", *Management Decision*, Autumn 1968.
7. Rance, H. "Financing R & D", *Management Decision*, Autumn 1968.
8. Allen, J. M. and Norris, K. P. "Project Estimates and Outcomes in Electricity Generation Research", *Journal of Management Studies*, October 1970.
9. Norwood, G. J. and Smith, M. C. "Market Mortality of New Products in the Pharmaceutical Industry", *Journal of the American Pharmaceutical Association*, November 1971.
10. Dooley, J. L. and Ciapolla, J. A. "Guides to Screening New Product Ideas", Martin, E. (ed.), *Management for the Smaller Company*, American Management Association, 1959.
11. *New Products in the Grocery Trade*, Kraushar Andrews & Eassie Ltd., 1971.
12. Pavitt, K. "Technological Innovation in European Industry: the Need for a World Perspective", *Long Range Planning*, December 1969.
13. Kitching, J. "Why do Mergers Miscarry", *Harvard Business Review*, November/December 1967.
14. Kitching, J. *Acquisitions in Europe; Causes of Corporate Successes and Failures*, Business International, 1973 (Summary published in each June 1973 issue *Business Europe*).
15. Porter, M. E. "From Competitive Advantage to Corporate Strategy", *Harvard Business Review*, May/June 1987.
16. Ansoff, H. I., Avner, J., Brandenburg, R. G., Porter, F. E. and Radosevitch, R. "Does Planning Pay? The Effect of Planning on Success of American Firms", *Long Range Planning*, December 1970.
17. Buzzell, R. D. and Gale, B. T. *The PIMS Principles*, Free Press, New York, 1987.

18
Multi-national and Global Strategy

Once a company begins to operate outside of its own national environment, its problems of strategic choice begin to multiply (some of these complications may also occur in a company with a number of large subsidiaries).

International business has been with us for a long, long time. It arrived at the dawn of civilisation and for centuries provided the motivation for many of the acts which shaped the path of history. If wars were not fought for personal grandeur, territorial expansion, or religion, they were usually fought for trade. By the fifteenth century the international company was well established in the shape of the banking and merchant businesses which flourished in Italy.

The international company began to get larger, and during the European colonial period was frequently entrusted with the task of government, administration, defence (and we might add aggression), as well as sordid commerce. The British East India Company, the Hudson's Bay Company, the British South Africa Company—just a few of the names which can still set the imagination reeling. Some of our modern multi-national giants may be bigger, but how many can bring their private armies and navies to back up their grand strategies?

Problems of managing international business are also very old. Drucker[1] quotes the example of how the Rothschild family managed its international banking business—stationing key members of the family at the foreign courts where business was to be generated and banishing the inept members to places where there was no business.

Although many problems are old, they are still very relevant, and should be considered against the background of the different types of international business which exist today. These can be classified under four headings:

(i) The company whose only international business is trading internationally.
(ii) The company which has a high volume of export business supported by marketing companies in other countries and the occasional manufacturing subsidiary.
(iii) The trans-national company with a network of subsidiaries or associate companies in other countries, including many overseas plants.

(iv) The multi-national company that produces and markets internationally and which has a multi-national management, possibly international ownership.

The trans-national and multi-national companies polarise into two strategic types, multi-domestic and global. A multi-domestic strategy is a coordinated series of country operations, possibly grouped into regions, where strategies are designed as a response to local market conditions. The global company looks at the world as one market, and in many but not necessarily all of its strategies will act on a global basis.

Strategic management for the first two types of companies presents only a few additional problems over those faced by the national business. These arise mainly from the complications of distance, language, national cultural differences, the management of additional profit centres, and the need to take account of more than one national business environment.

It is the last two categories which are the main subject matter of this chapter, and in particular the spectrum of multi-domestic to global. What is it that drives a company to change from a strategy of having subsidiaries which respond individually to their own markets, to an organisation which in the extreme case clones an identical response to every market? And what options lie between these extremes?

Forces of Globalisation

Yip[2] argues that there are four groups of factors which are the drivers for an industry to become global: market, cost, government, and competitive.

Market

The factors here include a convergence of market requirements in different parts of the world, as life styles and tastes draw closer together. Customer organisations, who are themselves global, increasingly expect their suppliers to offer a global service. There are now more areas of the world which enjoy a relatively affluent life style. However this last point should not be over stressed, as the population in the less developed world is expected to continue to increase as a percentage of total world population.

World travel creates a requirement for the same service to be available on a global basis. Visa or American Express are good examples of markets where a world wide service is needed, and which give the companies concerned an advantage over a credit card that can only be used in the country of issue.

Demand is related to price, which in turn has connections with cost. The nature of many markets is that the market size is achieved because world requirements are compressed into a few factories, thus enabling costs to tumble through economies of scale and the experience curve effect, allowing continued price decrease in real terms. The vast increase in instant information, through the explosion of information technology has meant that facts about the markets and business environment are known quickly, enabling a fast response.

Costs

In addition to the volume effect on costs that can be achieved by a global approach, a global approach may be forced by technological change, and the trend to shorter product life cycles. World volumes may be needed in order to afford the required level of research and development, and the capital costs of new production requirements. Because of issues like this many industries have seen a concentration that would have been unnecessary 40 years ago. The number of players in the world aerospace industry has fallen as development and production costs have risen, and it is now inconceivable that any one could contemplate entering this industry on a small scale, based only on the demand from domestic airlines.

Information technology has also helped the cost factor. Computer aided design (CAD) and computer aided manufacture (CAM) enable products to be designed in any country, and instantaneously be made available in any other location. This makes it easier for manufacture to be located in areas of lowest cost, and design and development in areas of high talent. It also makes it easier for engineering teams in different countries to collaborate in the design of a new product.

Government

Recent years have seen the amalgamation of separate countries into vast trading blocks, of which the best example is the European Community. In addition to creating a larger accessible market, EC regulations have removed many non tariff barriers by setting common standards for many products. Many difficulties in reaching a standardised product, essential for true global operations, have thus fallen away.

Overall barriers to trade have been steadily reduced, despite occasional setbacks as in the 1992 GATT negotiations.

There has also been a world trend to privatise industries previously in the public sector. Thus the opportunity for global expansion in telecommunications now exists, when it was impossible in the 1970s.

Competitive

Although certain local niche strategies may sometimes be successful in an industry where most players are global, increasingly it is being realised that the rules of the game are changing, and that it is next to impossible to defeat a global player through a country by country strategy. One reason behind the demise of the British and American motor cycle industries was that the companies concerned had been driven out of their markets before they realised that the new competitors were thinking in world terms. The reason behind the success of the global strategies is partly the lower costs that can be achieved through a mixture of high volumes and standardised products, and partly because the decision base is different. In one grocery products assignment I handled in the late 1980s, my client operated on a country by country basis in most European countries. The leading competitor operated on the basis that Europe was one market. Whereas my client demanded that each country made profits, the competitor took a global view and would willingly reduce profit in a particular country to combat any attempt by the other players to increase their market share. This was always possible, as my client, in common with the other competitors, took marketing decisions piecemeal at the country level, and never mounted a coordinated attack in all countries at the same time.

While many companies have evolved into global players, there is an increasing tendency for at least some organisations to be global from start up. Jolly et al.[3] studied four companies from different countries which had a global vision from start up, and implemented that vision immediately. The companies were Logitech, a Swiss based manufacturer of desk top aids for computers, Technophone, a British firm providing hand portable telephones, Connor Peripherals, started in the USA to commercialise high performance Winchester disk drives, and Lasa, which established itself simultaneously in the USA and Europe. Lasa is also in the high technology computer related field. While a few years ago it might have been sufficient to watch the strategies of those companies that already had a presence in many countries, the signs are that we may see more global start ups in the future. The pressure to go global is therefore not only based on what can be seen today, but also on the way it might develop in the future.

Kenichi Ohmae[4] argues that for long-term success, global businesses have to have a sound position in all of the three geographic centres of the world: USA, Japan and Europe. Those that stay in only one or two of these areas are un-likely to succeed in the long run, because the volumes of production which will fall to those competitors that do penetrate the total triad will give an immense cost advantage. The argument is based on the fact that these areas contain some 600 million people in the largest and most sophisticated markets of the world.

Globalisation as a Strategic Decision

Figure 18.1 illustrates the fact that for the individual company globalisation is a strategic decision. The diagram is derived from points made by M. Cvar[5] in a 1986 study of patterns of success and failure in global competition.

The analysis suggests that there are certain characteristics in industries that become global, in that there has to be the opportunity for high levels of demand for standardised products which also give rise to economies of scale. Globalisation is not a naturally occurring state but is man made, and the triggers are the identi-fication of common segments in different countries that enable a product to be defined globally. In turn this enables supply sources to be consolidated, so that the competitive cost advantages can be gained.

The study also showed that the successful global companies had five factors in common. They had all developed a preemptive strategy, effectively becoming the agency that created the global market. All managed their companies on a global

FIG. 18.1. Global competition (From research findings by Cvar, M. R. (1986). Case studies in global competition: Patterns of success and failure. In Porter, M. E. *Competition in Global Industries*, Harvard Business School, Boston)

concept and measured their performance on this basis. It was also observed that all had higher than average R & D compared to their industry. All had demonstrated a measure of single mindedness in overcoming obstacles to globalisation.

The implication of the global dimension is that for many companies strategic thinking has to stretch beyond the country dimensions that may have been traditional in the industry. Whether the company seeks to create a global business, on the lines suggested by Cvar, or whether it chooses to let a competitor initiate this process, is a matter for the individual company. Once the industry goes global the opportunities for the company with only a local market view will certainly change, and may diminish.

Prahalad and Doz[6] suggest that the key factors in deciding how to operate are the need for integration on a global basis, contrasted with the need for local responsiveness. If these two concerns are seen as two sides of a matrix, it follows that different businesses can be positioned on the matrix and appropriate strategy decided. However the authors point to a factor which most strategists will have already observed, that the number of industries where global integration is the dominant factor increases every year. The pressures are created by customers and competitors, and it is dangerous to assume that an industry which has local responsiveness as the key factor today will remain like this in the future.

Figure 18.2 provides a diagram which was inspired by the Prahalad and Doz matrix. Exhibits 18.1 and 18.2 provide a set of questions to enable organisations to plot the industry situation, and the way their company is operating. In this diagram the need for a globally integrated approach is seen as one end of a spectrum, the

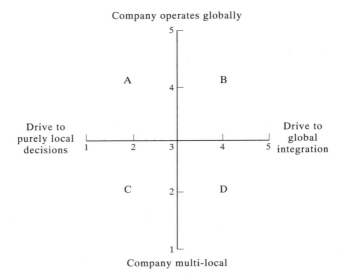

FIG. 18.2. Company fit with competitive need

other end of which is a need for a totally local response to the market. The vertical arm of the quadrant measures whether the company is operating in a global or multi local way. Quadrants B and C are on the face of it potentially appropriate company responses. Quadrant D could be appropriate if the company has been able to identify niches in each market which are defensible. However, my experience is that the statement "we are niche players" is often a rationalisation to explain the strategy, and often has no basis of fact behind it. It is hard to think that an answer which fell in quadrant A could be appropriate, and behaving globally in markets that cannot become global seems like a quick route for disaster.

I have not refined and tested Fig. 18.2 yet in real situations, as I have with most of the other methods and models I have described in this book. So far its use has been restricted to teaching the concepts of global strategy through the medium of case studies. More work is required on the questions and the scoring, but I have included it here because the line of thinking it follows is valid.

The point should be made that different degrees of "globalness" may be appropriate for different functions in the organisation. Thus design might be integrated globally, manufacture to a significant extent, while certain aspects of marketing, such as advertising might be different for each country. Once again the answer is not a formula, that can be applied to give one right answer, but management's strategic response to the circumstances as it sees them.

The Decision Making Process

Perhaps the first strategic problem a company which operates across national boundaries is called upon to solve is how far the decision making process should be decentralised. If the intention is for all strategic decisions to be made at head

Please circle one number on each scale according to the position of the industry

MARKETING AND SALES

1. Market requirements diverse	1	2	3	4	5	Market requirements homogeneous
2. Few opportunities for cross country standardisation	1	2	3	4	5	Many opportunities for cross country standardisation
3. Numerous market segments	1	2	3	4	5	Few market segments
4. Distribution channels differ by country	1	2	3	4	5	Distribution channels the same in all countries
5. Customers all local operations	1	2	3	4	5	Customers all global operations
6. Low customer pressure for world wide service	1	2	3	4	5	High customer pressure for world wide service
7. Competitors all local buying	1	2	3	4	5	Competitors all global buying
8. Numerous competitors in world	1	2	3	4	5	Few competitors in world
9. High fiscal barriers to trade	1	2	3	4	5	Low fiscal barriers to trade
10. Many non fiscal barriers	1	2	3	4	5	No non fiscal barriers

RESEARCH AND DEVELOPMENT

11. Low rate of technology change	1	2	3	4	5	High rate of technology change
12. Low level of R & D effort	1	2	3	4	5	High level of R & D effort
13. Short development time for new products	1	2	3	4	5	Long development time for new products
14. Long product life cycle	1	2	3	4	5	Short product life cycle

OPERATIONS

15. Low scale efficiencies	1	2	3	4	5	High scale efficiencies
16. Low procurement scale economy	1	2	3	4	5	High procurement scale economy
17. Flat experience curve	1	2	3	4	5	Steep experience curve
18. High transport costs as % total costs	1	2	3	4	5	Low transport costs as % total costs

Total score   _____

Average score   _____

EXHIBIT 18.1. Global/local responsiveness questionnaire

Tick the statement which most accurately describes how your company operates

		A		B		C	
Executives' focus of vision	Local view	☐	Co-ordinate but define locally	☐	One view of the world	☐
Manufacturing	Each subsidiary has its own plant	☐	Plants at country level but coordinate	☐	Few plants serving the world	☐
R & D	At country level	☐	Coordinated centres	☐	Few centres, global orientation	☐
Quality concepts	Set at country level	☐	Common principles	☐	Same everywhere	☐
Culture	Each company differs	☐	Some common features in all companies	☐	Same everywhere	☐
Decisions try to maximise profit	At local level	☐	Through synergy	☐	On world view	☐
Control systems	Local	☐	Local but internationally co-ordinated	☐	Global	☐
New product development	Local	☐	Co-ordinated local	☐	Centralised globally	☐
Marketing management	Independent, local	☐	Co-ordinated	☐	Global	☐
Area of markets	One or few countries	☐	Strong in at least one Triad region	☐	Strong in whole Triad	☐

Score 1 for each tick in column A
Score 3 for each tick in column B
Score 5 for each tick in column C

Total score   =
Average score =

EXHIBIT 18.2. Questionnaire—How does your company operate?

office, very little more need be said. My own view is that no multi-national or trans-national company of any size can prosper under this approach. However there is clearly a difference of which strategic decisions should be decentralised, depending whether the company is operating globally or multi-domestically. In either case the answer lies in a *controlled* decentralisation of decision making.

Under this concept the country chief executive would have a wide degree of freedom to operate within the strategic framework established at the centre. This requires a shared understanding and commitment to the vision, clear objectives, and strong financial control to be exercised over the sources of finance and the way in which capital is used. A wide strategic freedom should not lead to abdication by the parent company. The shared vision is always important, but even more so in the global company, because many aspects of strategy have to be pulled together centrally to reach a world view, and these cannot be left to the country chief executives. Decisions which can be taken locally should not be taken in the centre. The worst of all worlds is when a company operates a multi-domestic strategy, but determines its strategies as if it were operating a global strategy.

The reasons why the chief executive of international subsidiaries should have a large say in their own strategies are:

(i) Opportunities can best be seen by the people on the spot. The larger the group and the greater its geographical dispersion, the harder it is for opportunity to be spotted from the centre. Quite apart from remoteness from and lack of understanding of the local scene—however well informed the head office management—there is also an enormous problem in organising and handling the vast volume of market and other environmental data needed to spot opportunities from many thousands of miles away.

(ii) Motivation is better secured in each subsidiary if the local management feel that they have a say in what is to be done. Better quality managers can be recruited, including chief executives who think as chief executives and not as branch managers.

(iii) Acceptance of profit responsibility is more likely—and fairer—when local management has some freedom of manoeuvre.

(iv) Many subsidiaries may be joint ventures or have minority shareholders, and the rights of these partners should be observed.

The keyword is "controlled". Uncontrolled decentralisation will result in chaos, for any head office needs to retain certain rights.

(v) The right to override a local strategy (and change the strategic framework) if this is in total group interests. For example, a cross-licensing agreement with another company might be very beneficial and profitable on a worldwide basis, but might require the sacrifice of certain products sold by a particular subsidiary. The local chief executive would never suggest this, and, indeed, would probably never be aware of the wider opportunity.

(vi) The right to refuse to sanction a capital expenditure (where reasons are good and valid).

(vii) The right to bring some international rationalisation to marketing, research, production, procurement, and physical distribution.

It follows that there will, on occasions, be a conflict of interests between parent and subsidiary. Recognition of this fact is an important part of the strategic planning process. This problem will be discussed in greater depth, but before doing this I should like to mention one way in which the effects of conflict may be mitigated.

Within limits I have argued for chief executives of subsidiaries to be given a wide degree of freedom in local strategic planning. It is possible for the talents of these managers to be used in a much broader sense to help the chief executive of the total group to identify and select the overall strategies. Considerable benefit may be gained if there is a measure of participation in the shaping of the future of the group. Such an action may be brought about through the participation of subsidiary managers in group planning exercises, in working parties, and think-tank sessions.

All this is valuable, but none of it detracts from the ultimate responsibility of the top managements of the parent company to plan the whole business in a way which satisfies the owners.

For analytical purposes five further discussions areas have been identified for close study: conflict of interest between parent and subsidiary; selecting a multi-national strategy; multi-nationalism and third world countries; the additional risks of multi-national business; the future of multi-national business.

Conflicts of Interest: Parent and Subsidiary

One of the major problems of multi-national strategic planning is the fact that there are numerous situations where a choice has to be made: a decision which will either increase parent company profits or increase those of the subsidiary. Jacoby[7] argues that such clashes need not occur provided the parent insists that each subsidiary operates under the forces of competition. This is a view which is very difficult to accept. There are often unavoidable clashes of subsidiary and parent interest, and there can be few multi-national groups who would find it profitable to allow a complete state of *laissez-faire* among their own subsidiaries.

A conflict of profit interests may cause two other areas of difficulty, in addition to the basic strategic decision. The first is an internal problem, the company's own interpretation of its ethical and moral constraints (see Chapter 8). Many multi-nationals claim to be "good citizens" of each country in which they operate, something which is by no means as easy as it sounds. The second difficulty is one of law. It is by no means unknown for the parent of a multi-national to make a decision which would compel the board of directors of the subsidiary to commit an offence: usually a contravention of the tax or exchange control regulations through an action which effectively transfers assets or income outside of the control of that territory.

Examples of the type of decision which might well bring a conflict situation are:

(i) Various subsidiaries might operate individual plants. Others might import from neighbouring countries. A group study shows that a large geographical area could be more economically served if one centralised plant were erected. For certain subsidiaries this would mean the closure of their own plants and the consequent cessation of exports. Some subsidiaries might pay more for their goods than they did before, although total group costs are lower, because some element of profit must be returned to the subsidiary in the country which operates the plant.

Strategic decisions such as this are becoming more acute as the benefits of regional specialisation become more apparent, and as economic unions become bigger (for example the enlarged European Community).

(ii) Investment proposals from a subsidiary are turned down because more profitable or less risky projects exist elsewhere. In the eyes of the subsidiary their project may be essential for profitable growth, and may comply with all the minimum profitability criteria of the group. From their point of view there is nothing wrong with the project: from the parent's angle it is a simple question of using international resources in the best possible way.

(iii) A desire, because of wide margins in taxation rates or difficulties in repatriating profits, to make as much profit as possible in the parent country. There are many ways in which this aim can be achieved, and it is usually possible to find a legally acceptable formula: for example, abnormal profits may be built into raw material prices, there may be "contributions" to research and development, royalties, management fees, and technical aid agreements. Often these are fair: sometimes they are unfair, and the payments are out of all proportion to any benefits obtained. The authorities frequently accept the arrangements because they are unaware of the amount of profit being siphoned off (in, for example, raw material prices). A danger sign is the situation where a multi-national parent can "afford" to let a subsidiary make a loss year after year. Frequently a situation like this means that the loss is only in the books of the subsidiary: a consolidation of profits in the books of the parent would reveal a profit.

(iv) Insistence that subsidiaries purchase products from group sources even though cheaper supplies are available in the open market.

(v) Defining a trading area for a subsidiary and preventing it from seeking sales outside it: such a policy is essential for orderly international marketing, particularly with branded products which may be available in many countries. Essential though it may be, it may still reduce profit opportunity for a subsidiary.

(vi) Insistence on standards of quality which reflect group prestige and which are higher than those required by the subsidiary or the environment in which it operates. These standards may relate to factory buildings, office accommodation, plant, products, or commercial behaviour (e.g. insisting that all managers have written contracts of employment when such an approach is alien to the country).

As multi-national companies come closer to the ideal of multi-national ownership, some of these problems might fall away, since a decision on a point of conflict in favour of the parent would produce profits which accrue to investors on a wide economic front.

The strategic problems arising from such issues will, for the foreseeable future, have to be solved by chief executives operating outside of these ideal circumstances. Because the situations are more complex than simply deciding to do what gives the most *apparent* profit, there are no universal guide rules that can be applied. There are numerous considerations to be brought into the decision, many of which can only be subjective: for example, the political repercussions at home and abroad, the effect of adverse public relations on the markets of subsidiaries, and the company's internal constraints and code of ethics.

It is a fact that managers in a subsidiary are often involved in actions which, although they may not be illegal, are against the national interest of their particular country. Certainly, there is a reasonable argument that their task, like that of the management of the parent company, is to increase shareholders' value. In many circumstances this may be justification enough: often it is an oversimplification which avoids the real issues.

It is also clear that the host government of the country in which a subsidiary is based would prefer to see profits maximised locally, and would rather assets were utilised in the national interest rather than for the benefit of some other country. In Europe and North America there are fairly clear rules about what may and may not be done, and although companies sometimes find themselves in dispute with tax and exchange control authorities, there is generally an understanding of each other's viewpoint. In this environment reasonable solutions can usually be found. Both parties are also well aware of the mutual benefits of multi-nationalism, something which helps to balance the scales when they appear to be biased in a particular direction. Developing countries, particularly the emerging "Third World" countries, frequently take a different view to that of the Western World, a point which will be returned to later.

Perhaps the most difficult element of all to incorporate into the decision process is the one of management motivation. The criteria for economic decisions of this type is usually some form of accounting exercise: a quantification of expected results for each alternative. What is so often forgotten is the human motivation factor. Even when a local manager is genuinely and wholeheartedly a "group" person it can become very depressing when because of the structure of the profit routing decisions, the subsidiary apparently is unable to earn an adequate return on the capital employed under its control. After a year or two it is very easy to forget the local profit sacrificed to another area of the group and for the manager to be judged on the apparent results. If a situation is created where local managers become depressed and lose motivation (and therefore inspiration and creativity), the local results might well be much worse than the accounting exercise suggested. Management is a human activity: strategic decisions which forget this have a fair chance of being wrong.

Sometimes an adjustment can be made through the management accounting system, so that managers know what their real contribution to earnings is and are aware that they are given credit for it. If authority, responsibility, and account-ability become mixed, a situation may be created where no one can be judged by results. This may be in the interests of a poor manager: it is never beneficial for a good manager and rarely right for the company.

These problems have been discussed at some length because they are an important consideration in the strategic planning process. They are just the type of factor which is likely to be ignored by the organisation which indulges in planning but not strategic management. Any company which does overlook them does so at its peril.

Selecting a Multi-national Strategy

Rutenberg[8] makes the point that many companies have become international by "creeping incrementalism" rather than deliberate strategic choice. A soundly conceived strategy should remove most of the problems of *what* to do in *which* countries. This means that somehow the company has to arrange its affairs so that it can examine opportunities throughout the world, which should include relevant countries in which the company currently has no business. There should be a multi-national strategy into which current and projected operations are slotted. Part of this strategy turns on the setting of objectives about which there has already been much discussion (Chapter 13): certainly profit objectives for subsidiaries can only be set realistically if they are defined within the framework of an overall strategy.

It is interesting to look at the typical development pattern of a company which becomes international without giving much thought to the process. The company is hypothetical: the situation is one I have observed in life:

> The company develops a large export trade, appointing agents and applying promotion generally on a percentage of sales basis. It has considerable variety of special packs and labels, and various methods of pricing have crept in over the years. Haphazardly, after visits by export executives, agents have in some areas been replaced by the company's own marketing subsidiaries because each report appeared logical at the time. Similarly, certain markets have been singled out for abnormal promotional expenditure: but the company has not thought of how long it will take to recover this or whether exports will be able to continue if a tariff barrier is levied. Where countries have in the past imposed protective tariffs, the company has built factories "to protect its markets". Each factory has come as the result of pressure, and many are inefficient and of sub-economic size.

Now contrast this situation with a similar hypothetical company, trading in the same markets and with essentially the same problems. The difference is that this company has an international strategic framework and is therefore able to make rational decisions and to bring some order to its problems:

> The company studies each of the countries in which it has (or might possibly have) business, and classifies these into three main classes which reflect profit-ability and development potential. Advertising and promotion support is removed from the third class of market, where the company's business is small with little chance of change. The top market grouping is of countries with good development potential, and here advertising and promotion is allocated on a mission basis subject to certain long-term considerations. The middle category has provision for some market expenditure, but only sufficient to maintain the company's position: markets in this category have little expansion potential but are profitable.

An overall examination is made of the alternative merits of agents and the company's own marketing subsidiaries, and certain criteria are established. The company produces a plan to set up the type of selling operation which best suits each market, and intends to implement this over a three-year period. There is a deliberate rationalisation policy to reduce variety in packs and labels.

The company also defines its position on local manufacturing plants. It now decides the circumstances under which it will open an overseas factory (size, investment, type of pack, profitability criteria). These circumstances exist in three markets, and the company decides that it is in its long-term interests to work towards establishing plants there within the next five years. Contingency plans are developed for contract manufacture or licensing for a number of markets where a protective duty is possible but where a plant would be uneconomic.

All assessments of market development expenditure for the top grouping of countries are made in the context of the longer-term prospects of the country. Such investments are not undertaken where the risk of a protective duty being imposed is high, unless the company believes that its contingency plans are sufficient to give it a reasonable future return.

Both of these hypothetical companies are too neat to be real, but they do indicate the value of a predetermined strategy for international operations. It may seem rather too obvious that a strategy is required which conditions all actions, but it is a point which is often overlooked.

> An international company decided to concentrate most of its investment and development in Europe and the United States. In no circumstances was it prepared to invest in certain unstable countries. Nevertheless, a development plan was produced for a certain highly unstable export territory, urging a five-year period of low prices and high advertising, during which time no profit would be made. No one had considered risks of import controls, tariff barriers, or political change which could cut off exports at any time. No one had any idea what should be done if this happened apart from a determination not to open a factory. The logical decisions within the strategy were completely overlooked.

Van Dam[9] has demonstrated that it is possible—and profitable—to study countries on an international basis, so that a strategy may be developed which involves concentrating on those which appear to be reaching a stage of economic development which is "right" for the company concerned. His work follows—and adapts for business use—that of Rostow,[10] who analyses the stages of national economic growth into: the traditional society, the pre-conditions for take-off, the take-off, the drive to maturity, and the age of high mass consumption. The classification of countries into criteria developed from Rostow's five stages can be a valuable step in the identification of the areas of value to the company, so that it can decide how each should be treated from a strategic point of view.

Unless a company has an overall outline strategy for its multi-national operations it is likely to make decisions which pull it in the wrong direction.

Multi-nationalism and Third World Countries

International business is no stranger to the emerging nations. In addition to additional risks—which will be discussed later—of dealing with such nations, there are other problems which often tend to be overlooked. It is very easy for multi-national business to try to continue policies which have been found workable in dealings with the Western world. Patterns of business behaviour in countries in Europe, North America, Australasia, and southern Arica may not be identical in each country, but they have a strong similarity. A policy which works in one of these areas has a high probability of working in the others.

Yet these policies may be completely unworkable in dealings with Third World countries to the extent that some companies deliberately opt to omit these countries from their sphere of operations: others, regrettably, do not know that there is a difference.

Any generalised view which purports to cover all Third World countries is bound to be wrong in some detail when applied to a particular country. Despite the weakness of generalisations, it is worth making a few, since if they act only as a warning light as multi-national strategy is defined, they will have served a useful purpose. At the least they should make it clear that certain additional problems do exist.

Conflict of Objectives

The impossibility of being a good citizen of every country of operation has been discussed elsewhere. This fact may become an acute strategic problem in a Third World country. A business unit in an underdeveloped country tends to be smaller than a subsidiary in a more developed area although it may be large in relation to other business in that country. The perception of the headquarters of the multi-national group of its smallest subsidiaries may be vastly different from that of the host government: even more so, if the subsidiary is a member of a large, prestigious, and internationally well-known group. A mouse appears larger to a cat than to an elephant: what is insignificant to the giant is a major element of the economic diet of the small country.

Decisions which appear to be against host country interests—for example, failure to invest, failure to export, particular employment policies or dividend requirements—loom much more important in the eyes of the government of the Third World country than they would do in one of the more mature countries. This problem is made worse by the fact that the underdeveloped country may be passing through a period of nationalistic ardour, political development (or change), and may, indeed, feel that its particular needs mean that any conflicts of objectives should err on its side rather than that of the multi-national company.

Local Participation

Many Third World countries have legislation which compels a local equity participation in each foreign controlled company. Other countries may not have any legal requirements, although their decision-makers may consider that multi-national companies should take note of local aspirations for equity participation.

When a multi-national group tries to impose a concept of wholly owned subsidiaries and runs against this real feeling in the host country, resentments tend to build up. At the same time, from the multi-national point of view, joint ventures and minority shareholders make administration and control more difficult. Local directors of suitable calibre may be hard to identify.

Apart from the public relations aspects, local equity participation may be a way of reducing risks, and should not therefore be rejected by multi-national companies just because they have a general policy which acts as an internally erected barrier.

Employment

Restrictions on the employment of foreign nationals are not the sole prerogative of the Third World countries. Perhaps Switzerland is one of the most protective of countries in this respect, with vigorous controls and licensing arrangements for foreign workers. The United States has stringent immigration controls. The United Kingdom also restricts immigration, although this legislation was much more a question of slowing down the flood of Third World immigrants than any desire to protect nationals from competition for jobs. Naturally, business has to operate within the framework of these laws.

An underdeveloped country is likely not only to be more stringent in the application of such laws, but also to be extremely suspicious when it is forced to grant permits for the employment of non-nationals, and resentful that business has not "trained" locals to take the top management slots. These feelings can lead to unofficial blacklisting and "problems" put in the way of the company concerned. Even where it has the support of the government, it may be a target for the opposition, the trade union movement, or the newspapers.

An example of this comes from personal discussions I once had in a Caribbean country. I was frequently told by government and quasi-government officials of the sins of a particular company—the main "sin" being the number of labour permits it had obtained for expatriate managers. Even though each permit had been individually justified and granted, the "sin" still led to other actions and contributed to delays in dealing with the company's applications under the price control legislation.

Suspicion, Distrust, and a Different Ideology

It is a fact that many Third World countries completely and absolutely distrust multi-national companies: the larger the company the more this distrust occurs. Multi-national business is branded as an oppressor and exploiter, a stealer of the natural resources which make up a nation's heritage. This stigma is applied broadly and without regard to the merits of the case. For example, former President Nyerere of Tanzania has been reported as stating that his country should accept a slower rate of economic growth achieved through its own efforts rather than allow "exploitation" by multi-national companies of its natural resources, human talent, and finance.

The record of the Western world at both the public and private level, shows that there is much to justify this viewpoint, although it may be unfortunate for those companies whose intentions are honourable.

In addition the concept of "reasonable profit" is often not the same as in developed countries, and completely opposed to that of the company itself. There is often a feeling that economic activity should be undertaken by a company for social motives. Once a business is established it is expected to expand even though this action may not earn an adequate return: it has a "duty" to employ more and more local people.

It may be argued that this view in part springs from large companies themselves, who continually oversell to host governments the benefits their subsidiaries bring to a country's economic progress (particularly at a time when they are trying to wring protective concessions out of that government). In part it is due to the unfortunate effects of successful "blackmail" schemes through import control and protective tariffs by governments, which have led to the erection of sub-economic plants by companies as a desperate measure to protect their markets. Most of all it is due to fundamental differences between the West and the Third World countries, and in views of politics, economics, and social development.

The Size of the Multi-nationals

All these feelings are inflamed by the sheer size of some of the multi-national groups, relative to that of the smaller countries, making government officials feel resentful in the belief that the problems of their country are never understood or debated at main board level: simply because no one at that level is ever involved in them.

It is rarely company presidents or chairmen who visit underdeveloped countries, and representatives from group headquarters, although senior managers, are not always the highest level: yet they expect to meet the key ministers and officials in the country they are visiting.

The Record So Far

The situation in general terms is that the rich countries are getting richer while the poor ones appear to be standing still or, in some cases, moving backwards. Natural resources of the underdeveloped world are mainly consumed by the much smaller population living in developed countries. With this record behind them, it is not surprising that Third World countries take actions which are against the interests of individual businesses.

All these factors are important, because they must affect the company's approach to multi-national strategy. They provide an additional reason for involving the chief executives of subsidiaries in major decisions: these managers on the spot are in a much better position to see the total problem. Emphasis is given to supporting strategic decisions with other actions: for example, any company with a large stake in the underdeveloped countries should consider a detailed public affairs strategy, to ensure that its relations with centres of influence in that country are strong enough to further its interests.

The Additional Risks of Multi-national Business

Multi-national operations may bring an increased opportunity for profit: they may, as some companies claim, be an agency for international understanding and a contributor to world peace. They also bring additional challenges to a company, over and above the normal business risk that comes from all operations.

Some aspects of this have already been discussed in the chapters on environmental issues and, by implication at least, in earlier parts of this chapter. No discussion of international strategy can be complete without some further thoughts on this problem which must colour the overall decisions of the company. Even effective objectives cannot be set for subsidiaries unless some thought is given to the additional risks in each country: any decision to concentrate on particular areas of the world must have risk as part of its input.

The additional risks include those of fluctuations in exchange rates, which can completely alter the asset value of an overseas subsidiary (at least in the currency of the parent company), as well as changing the real value of profits earned and dividends paid. In addition changing exchange rates can cause accounting difficulties in the books of both parent and subsidiary: a subsidiary may be in a position of meeting all its profit targets measured in local currency, but failing miserably in the books of the parent.

Failure of a country to meet its international debts is another problem which strikes from time to time. This may mean that payment cannot be obtained for exports, or that foreign governments refuse to honour contractual arrangements. This is only matched for severity of effect by outright expropriation. Although there are international agreements covering expropriation and compensation, these are not always observed: even when compensation is given it may take many years before the matter is finalised and payment actually received.

On top of this, there are the risks that a localisation policy will force the company to withdraw key managers and skilled personnel and to replace them with untrained and untrusted local employees. Systems of licensing may close overseas markets as may penal protective duties. Stringent price-control measures may force retirement from a market, or heavy losses: often the overseas government concerned does not mind which.

The risks are not all bad ones, and there are some factors to be considered on the credit side as well.

International operations may bring taxation advantages, either by facilitating the use of tax havens or by enabling the company to obtain tax holidays from some of its overseas operations. An example of the latter is the ten-year tax holiday once given by Singapore for "pioneer" industries. (Tax is really a matter of financial planning, although it should have an impact on strategic decisions.) Tax advantages are also given by former Communist countries of central Europe.

Additional incentives are given by certain countries to encourage exports. An example is Australia, which doubles the tax allowance on certain expenses incurred in marketing exports, as well as giving other fiscal inducements. In some countries overseas debts can be insured, as through the UK ECGD scheme (subject to certain conditions).

The United Kingdom and other OECD countries also have an investment insurance scheme which covers companies for political risks as far as new capital is concerned. This makes it much easier to decide that an attractive investment in a politically unstable country really is attractive.

Financial help is also given by some governments, including the United States, to aid pre-investment studies in certain overseas countries.

Overall, multi-national business is attractive because it represents one of the best ways of getting maximum return from marketing, production, and research and development investment. Despite the abnormal risk of multi-national business, it is often less risky to extend a developed product to another market than to commit sums to research and development in new products which carry a high normal risk of failure.

The Future of Multi-national Companies

For the most part strategic decisions are looked at in two dimensions: the viewpoints of the individual country and the individual company. These dimensions are not always in sympathy with each other, and occasionally may result in outright conflict.

There are indications that in future multi-national business might also have to begin to consider yet a third dimension in its strategic planning—the world economy. The case, which is now convincingly argued by ecologists and environmentalists, is that the world be regarded as a system of finite size. Pressures on this system through population growth, urbanisation, the limitations of the world and the biosphere, the problems of industrial wastes and pollutions, and the now predictable exhaustion dates of certain natural resources (e.g. oil and natural gas) will increasingly bring the situation where the interests of an individual company although in balance with those of its host country are against the interests of the world as a whole.

The fact that a multi-national company may increase its total earnings by expanding geographically does not mean that the world economy benefits to a greater extent. Sometimes a number of competing single-country businesses would serve the world better: sometimes it may be that the venture would benefit the world most if it were not done at all. Rutenberg[8] argues that in the future the multi-national company will be forced to prove—to a much greater extent than hitherto—that there is a measure of synergy in multi-nationalism.

The conflict of the three competing dimensions can be illustrated by a simple hypothetical example. A multi-national company finds that because of the high costs of air and water pollution control its home production units become more expensive to operate. An underdeveloped country sees the industry as an economic benefit and is willing to accept less stringent pollution control measures. The factory is moved to the new country and both the company and this country feel that they are better off. But what of the world as a whole? Pollution levels are still the same: the same noxious chemicals are discharged into the air and the sea.

Although not all governments are in sympathy with the spirit of multi-nationalism (in fact even the United States senate was recently asked to approve a bill which—if passed—would effectively have smothered all American multi-national business), it is likely that the question of how far companies are to become multi-national in ownership will become increasingly important. I believe that this is a strategic decision which must receive more attention from both business and governments.

It is also likely that the underdeveloped countries, which control much of the natural resources currently consumed by the developed world, will demand a fairer share of the economic activity. Some 75% of the world's population live in these countries. It will be necessary for the multi-national countries to re-define their multi-nationalism in this context. Whether we wish it or not, the economic limitations of the world, and the pressures on world peace that failure to act will bring, will mean that some transfer of activity from the developed to the under-developed world is likely.

One of the more significant issues to come to the fore in recent years is the international control of multi-national companies (which owes something to the growth of international trade unions, many of which see the multinational company as the enemy). In 1976 OECD published a voluntary code of conduct for multi-nationals, which member governments agreed to encourage companies headquartered in their countries to adhere to. This has had may effects on individual companies reacting under government pressure. The ILO has prepared its code of conduct for multi-nationals, and the United Nations has a code in draft form. Pressure is mounting to make such codes legally binding.

Certainly the multi-national companies face more challenge and difficulty than the company which opts for single country development. But the risks are not without reward, and for many multi-national operations offer the most profitable of the strategic choices available. And many are multi-national already, and have the problem of managing their vast complexes. The path to profit is rarely an easy one, and let no one underestimate the additional challenge that may be found on the road to a multi-national strategy.

References

1. Drucker, P. F. *Managing for Results*, Heinemann, 1964.
2. Yip, G. *Total Global Strategy*, Prentice Hall, Englewood Cliffs, New Jersey, 1992.
3. Jolly, V. K., Alahuhta, M. and Jeannet, J-P. "Challenging the Incumbents: How High Technology Start Ups compete Globally", *Journal of Strategic Change* 1992.

4. Ohmae, K. *Triad Power*, Free Press, New York, 1985.
5. Cvar, M. R. "Case Studies in Global Competition: Patterns of Success and Failure", Porter, M. E. (ed.), *Competition in Global Industries*, Harvard Business School, Boston, 1986.
6. Prahalad, C. K. and Doz, Y. *The Multinational Mission*, Free Press, 1987.
7. Jacoby, N. H. "The Impact of Multi-national Corporations", *Dialogue*, Vol. 4, No. 2 (abridged from an article in the *Centre Magazine*).
8. Rutenberg, D. T. "Planning for a Multi-national Synergy", *Long Range Planning*, December 1969.
9. Van Dam, A. "Strategic Planning for Corporate Growth in Developing Countries", *Long Range Planning*, September 1969.
10. Rostow, W. W. *The Stages of Economic Growth*, Cambridge, 1964.

Note: Parts of this chapter were derived from a paper presented at a conference of the American Management Association in New York in February 1972, and subsequently published:
Hussey, D. E. "Strategic Planning in International Business", *Long Range Planning*, June 1972.

19

Technology and Manufacturing

There is a relationship between the two subjects of this chapter, since the technology will affect manufacturing. However, the organisation has to get both components right, as it is possible to have a poor strategy for technology, while planning manufacturing in a very effective manner. Similarly there may be a superb approach to technology, yet the company may not get the best out of manufacturing.

Technology

While a great deal has been published about the market and economic aspects of strategy, the literature on strategies for technology is relatively sparse. Loveridge and Pitt[1] argue that awareness of the importance of technology in strategy has been greater among managers than among writers. "So we feel confident that awareness of technological change in terms of its pervasiveness, dynamism, difficulty of managing and strategic significance is high among practitioners. In contrast, admittedly with some honourable exceptions, research-oriented writers have only recently chosen to address squarely the significance of strategic decision-making." I wish that I could share their confidence.

Early planning literature on technology concentrated on technological forecasting, a topic discussed in an earlier chapter, and of which the book by Wills[2] is fairly typical. There may be more recent books, but most that was worth saying on this subject was written during the late 1960s and 1970s. However forecasting and strategy formulation are not the same thing. Anyone who has tried to bring technology into the strategic planning process will know that there are immense difficulties in even describing different technologies in a way that is helpful.

The starting point that I should suggest is a technology audit of the organisation. I suppose that logically I should have included this in the chapter on the corporate appraisal, for this is where such an audit really fits. To do this would have made it harder to suggest an overall approach to technology.

Henry[3] offers a four step approach: the audit, assessing the strategic implications of the technology portfolio, an implementation plan, and a technology monitoring programme. This is a useful way of thinking about the topic, and the first two steps are followed here, although I have added ideas from other authorities. The last two will be discussed more generally in later chapters.

Step 1: The Audit

Henry[3] states: "A technology-asset audit focuses on determining the real or perceived value that any technology node, or its individual technology links, has in the business benefit–cost chain—from raw material acquisition, to the supply of the produce or service, to the customer". He suggests that comparisons should be made against the competitors. Several basic questions are proposed for an audit.

—"What are the basic technology assumptions in the company's current business strategy?
—"What are the basic technology assumptions in competitors' strategies?
—"Is the customer's perception of the technological qualities of the companies important?
—"What value, if any, do customers place on the technological qualities of competitors' products?
—"Is corporate R & D contributing to the improvements in the company's current technology position, or are improvements starting to take longer and cost more?
—"Are competing technologies becoming cost effective? Are competitors making gains ahead of the company?
—"How does the company manage information related to these questions?"

There is no general right way to conduct an audit, and to demonstrate this I include a list of equally sensible questions derived from an article by Ford.[4] Some of these overlap those of Henry, but most are different:

—What are the key technologies and "know-how" on which the business depends? This is a slightly different way of looking at Henry's first question.
—What sort of record does the company have in bringing home grown technology to market, and what are the reasons behind this record?
—What sort of gap is there between the technological knowledge of the company and that of its key customers?
—What is the life cycle position of each of the key technologies?
—What technologies are emerging which could affect our markets? This question harks back to the environmental assessment discussed in an earlier chapter, and is also the place where technological forecasting may be helpful.
—Where are the technological strengths and weaknesses: in product or in manufacture?

Does the company fully exploit its technologies?
Are there any unwanted technologies which could be sold or licensed to other companies?

To these questions I should add one inspired by Gluck and Foster,[5] which is to find out the phases of a development project where top management spends most of its time. The suggestion of this article is to look at the phases of development under the headings, study, design, development, production, marketing, and post marketing. Top management can exercise most influence on the final outcome if it is involved most heavily in the first two phases and early stages of the third. In many companies this is the opposite of what happens and most top management effort is put on the final three phases.

However, by this time, the major technological strategic decisions have been taken, usually by someone quite low in the organisation. It reminds me a little of a presentation I once heard by a mid level person from a city's town planning department. He declared that he alone determined the whole town planning strategy. Yes there were elected councillors, he had several managers above him, and they thought they were making the decisions. But he set all the assumptions on which the strategy was based, and no one had ever questioned them. His assumptions determined the strategies that could be followed, and eliminated many others. In technology it cannot make sense for the paths that the company will follow to be determined by people who have no responsibility for the overall vision and strategies of the firm.

We touched on another aspect of the audit in an earlier chapter, with the core competency approach of Prahalad and Hamel,[6] and I will not repeat these ideas again. However, they do have links to thinking by Abell,[7] which was not discussed earlier. Abell suggests a three dimensional matrix which classifies activities under the headings *customer function, customer groups* and *alternative technologies*. Figure 19.1 shows the shell of such a matrix. It is possible for a business to serve multiple or single customer functions, to specialise on a narrow or broad range of customer groups, or to use one or more technologies to meet those functions and the requirements of the customer groups.

This method, which pays attention to some of the questions of Henry,[3] although technology might well be defined much more broadly under the Abell approach, is very similar to many of the three dimensional methods used to examine market segmentation.

Figure 19.2 illustrates a way of trying to define and examine technologies across an organisation. This particular example is derived from an assignment of mine in an unusual organisation which was a cross between consulting engineering and process engineering, although neither term is an accurate description of the activity. In essence the business was concerned with the application of engineering principles to new applications, up to and including the installation of the proven prototype. The technical strands of a business such as this are of great importance in defining future strategy. To preserve confidentiality I have extended it to a completely different industry.

It is tempting to think that an audit of technology is only a matter for the high technology companies, and can be ignored by all others. This is true only for as long as the technology stays static. A few examples worth mentioning of where new technologies have taken over a market, and frequently led to the collapse of

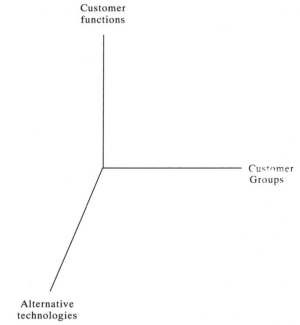

Customer
functions

Customer
Groups

Alternative
technologies

FIG. 19.1. Abell's three dimensions for business definition

Core Technologies

Markets	Products	Fats & oils	Surfactants	Emulsifiers	Skin chemistry	Flavouring
Consumer	Laundry soap	■	■	■		
	Soap flakes	■	■	■		
	Toilet soap	■	■	■	■	
	Cleaners		■	■		
	Fabric softener		■	■		
	Shampoo		■		■	
	Toothpaste		■	■		■
	Mouth wash		■			■
	Deodorant				■	
	Skin care				■	
Hotel	Toilet soap	■			■	
	Shampoo		■		■	
Laundry	Detergent		■			
	Fabric softener		■			
Industrial	Detergents		■			
	Cleaners		■	■		
	Toilet soap	■	■		■	

FIG. 19.2. Technology analysis—Generalised example, detergents industry

some or all of the traditional players are: typewriters, which have been to a great degree replaced by computers; electro-mechanical telephone exchanges, which are now an obsolete technology; home ciné cameras and projectors, which have almost completely given way to video.

Assessing the Strategic Implications of the Technology Portfolio

Henry[3] argues: "Step 2 of the Analysis is conducted with a view to ascertaining how best to leverage the company's technology assets to meet tomorrow's business objectives as defined by the strategic plan." The modest techniques already illustrated provide one basis for further strategic evaluation. Neubauer[8] suggests a technology matrix, a version of which appears in Fig. 19.3. This has *technology position* on one axis, moving from weak to strong. The other axis shows *relevance of the technology*, ranging from low for old technologies of little value to high for new technologies where many applications are possible. Strategic business units are plotted on the matrix, in much the same way as was described in Chapters 15 and 16.

I know of no rules for weighting and scoring the factors that enable the patterns to be plotted, and I have not had occasion to use the matrix myself. The factors suggested for each axis are:

Technology position	**Relevance**
Patents	Breadth of application
Licences	Speed of acceptance
Development lead times	Developmental potential
Personnel	Application in other industries
R & D budgets	Environmental acceptability

These questions would need to be applied to each technology used in the SBU, and a weighting system designed to produce a combined answer.

FIG. 19.3. Technology matrix

The suggestion is that the final matrix would be used firstly to check that current investment in technology matches the need, and that priorities are shifted to reduce investment in low relevance technologies, and increase it in business where the company needs to catch up or maintain leadership.

The suggestions I am making here can only be classed as ideas, stimulated by the technology matrix. It seems to me that the value of the matrix could be much enhanced if more attention was placed on the individual technologies, and particularly those which are common across several SBUs. This would aid consideration of cross SBU technology links and help develop synergy between the businesses. It may also prevent duplication of effort, or actions which would benefit one SBU but harm another. A set of matrices could be prepared, one for each key technology, culminating in the summary matrix suggested by Neubauer.

Neubauer makes the link between the type of portfolio analysis of Chapters 15 and 16 and the technology matrix. This could be made tighter by combining the information. The simplest method might be to colour code the SBUs on the market prospects/competitive position matrix according to their position on the technology matrix. Nine codes may be a little to much to digest, but it should be possible to reduce these to a manageable four by redrawing the grid on the matrix.

Ford[4] suggests three different types of technology strategy. Firstly there is a technology acquisition strategy. The basic routes that can be followed are those already outlined in Chapter 17 and need not be repeated here. Ford adds the caution that there is a need to examine the position on the life cycle of technologies or sub-technologies acquired. He provides a matrix, Fig. 19.4, which shows how various factors affect the decision to use internal or external sources.

There also needs to be a strategy for exploiting technology. This goes deeper than the issue of the strategic business portfolio, and includes an aggressive approach to finding other ways of gaining benefit, such as licensing others to use the technology. Again, the various ways of doing this were discussed earlier.

Finally Ford comes to the need for a strategy to manage technology, which implies making decisions on all the issues identified in the audit and portfolio analysis.

A sound technology strategy can be critical to success. Although for many industries there is often a chance to change course later to catch up, sometimes the change brought by technology is so far reaching that a company caught out of step could literally go out of business. An example of a company that had to change dramatically is STC, which until the mid 1970s was a leading manufacturer of electro-mechanical telephone exchanges. The change to electronics meant that many plants had to be closed, and many of the core skills of the company became obsolete, with a considerable impact on human resource strategies.

Technology can give organisations a competitive advantage. Certain airlines have undoubtedly gained a lasting advantage from the electronic booking systems which they had developed, which through various means gave them a better chance of being chosen than competitors. Otis Elevators has benefited from

Acquisition methods	Company's relative standing	Urgency of acquisition	Commitment/ Investment involved in acquisition	Technology life cycle position	Categories of technology
Internal R & D	High	Lowest	Highest	Earliest	Most distinctive/ critical
Joint venture		Lower		Early	Distinctive or basic
Contracted out R & D		Low		Early	Distinctive or basic
License in		High	Lowest	Later	Distinctive or basic
Non acquisition (a)	Low	High	No commit- ment/invest	All stages	External

(a) i.e. buying final product or part production from others

FIG. 19.4. Factors affecting technology acquisition decisions (from "Develop your Technology Strategy" by David Ford, *Long Range Planning*, **21**(5))

harnessing IT to its lift service operations, giving an advantage which it is difficult for a small operator to emulate. Simon Engineering changed the North American market for mobile booms for use on construction sites by developing the much smaller, lighter, more economical and more flexible *Eagle* and *Constructor* machines which gave access to awkward and high places through an entirely different lifting concept.

More frequently, the game is about avoiding competitive disadvantage, and catching up with competitors who have got ahead. The lead time for enjoying the "monopoly" benefits of something new are shrinking, which means that no company can afford to be complacent. Simon Engineering caught the industry by surprise, and gained a real advantage, some of which has remained with them. Within a comparatively short time their competitors were able to develop and market similar classes of machines, which reduced but did not eliminate the advantage gained.

Manufacturing

In the mid to late 1960s the literature on technology strategy seemed to be dominated with technological forecasting, presumably on the doubtful premise that if we can produce a good forecast, somehow strategy will follow. Manufacturing strategy was being served somewhat better, with some excellent approaches to new thinking. The lead was at that time taken by faculty at Harvard, in particular Wickham Skinner, a collection of whose landmark articles, many dating from the 1960s, appeared in 1978.[9] I find it rather sad that this excellent body of work was largely ignored, and that few companies began to treat manufacturing in a strategic way until the mid to late 1980s.

In many organisations, manufacturing was the rather boring activity that followed the marketing strategy, and was treated as operational, rather than strategic. Comparatively few companies, until the 1980s, had taken strategic decisions that related marketing and manufacturing into one coherent strategy: in other words manufacturing was treated as a sequential activity, whereas in reality there is a mutual interaction between the two. Skinner stressed the need to take a top down view of manufacturing, rather than the traditional strategy from the bottom approach. Under the traditional approach the individual engineers, industrial relations experts, information technology specialists, the production planners, and other experts may all have been very efficient. Efficiency and effectiveness are not always synonymous, and it needs management input to ensure that the right thing is done.

Modern thinking raises the significance given to manufacturing, partly because of the actions of competitors, and partly because new methods and technologies force manufacturing decisions to be more strategic. In addition to the Skinner idea of the focused factory, we now have to wrestle with CAD–CAM, JIT, flexible manufacturing, world class manufacturing, and the impact of global strategies, to name only some of the modern concepts. We will look at various aspects of manufacturing strategy, although not all will apply to all organisations or to all parts of an organisation. However, if you know what to consider, you have a better chance of getting what you need.

The Focused Factory

Skinner[9] developed the concept of the focused factory in contrast to what is still a common practice of production units which have a broad range of objectives. His argument is that unless the factory concentrates on a narrow range of manufacturing objectives it will not achieve optimum levels of effectiveness. This implies setting up factories which have only a limited number of production technologies, meet only a few market demands, do not mix long production runs with specials, only produce products that have common quality objectives, and have a limited number of manufacturing tasks. Output is impaired when conflicting production requirements are placed on the same unit. The issue is not whether the plant and machinery is capable of producing too many objectives, but whether it is economic to keep changing. In thinking of this we have to think of the learned skills of people. For example it is extremely difficult for a factory to mix aeronautical parts with commercial production, because it is not possible for the same operatives to keep changing the tolerances and quality to which they work to meet the lower specifications. The fact that the flame plating unit is capable of producing for both applications is not the relevant issue. A simple example is the production of spares for after sales support on the lines that produce the original equipment. Each interrupts the other.

He gives an example of two market requirements for furniture. One is for low prices and high volume, the other requires high fashion, high price, and limited editions. The manufacturing requirement for the former is for large lot sizes, mass production machinery, and a high proportion of lower skilled workers. Economy of scale is important, as costs will fall with volume. The latter may require fast production of new models, repeated model changes, an effective production control system to reduce lead times, and hand finishing, requiring a higher proportion of skilled workers. Mix up the two sets of production objectives in the same factory, using the same machines and work force and there is a recipe for sub optimal working.

Skinner argues that the apparent duplication of buildings and machinery caused by the separation pays back in lower costs, and better service to customers. However, where it is not feasible to have two quite separate facilities, he suggests setting up a factory within a factory: that is establishing quite separate units within the same umbrella buildings and organisation. Hussey[10] describes how the factory within a factory concept was applied by Otis Elevators in 1984. The factory at Liverpool, England, had been laid out by machine type, following a flow line principle whenever possible. It made architectural products for lifts (car, doors, door surrounds, etc.), controllers for lift operation, and machines to drive the lift. It also produced spares for all these items. Costs were high, delivery times were long and often not kept, and an extensive computer system was used to keep track of each contract, which cost £500,000 per year to run, and could not deliver the needed information.

"However, in February 1985 the managing director of Otis UK was able to give a presentation at an international conference in Singapore showing a complete turnaround in the Liverpool factory. He demonstrated how Liverpool's costs had shrunk: for example it could now produce a gearless machine 18% cheaper than Taiwan. Lead times had reduced and the proportion delivered on time had increased. This dramatic improvement was the result of considerable hard work by the Liverpool management team, implementing a major new strategy in the Liverpool factory.

"The foundation of the strategy was the breaking down of the Liverpool factory into a number of workshops, physically united, each of which could be managed as a business unit. The manager of each would be responsible for all aspects of his operations. To facilitate this the central stores were broken up, each workshop operating its own, and the white collar staff associated with each operation were moved from the office block and housed in custom built offices each adjacent to its manufacturing operation.

"This released 114,000 square feet of productive space which was separated from the rest of the factory by a brick wall, and sub-let to another organisation, Masons. (This also reduced the rates bill.)

"The workshops were organised around the major elements that make up an elevator, plus the field workshop. The elements are Machine, Architectural Products, and Controllers.

"From being a 'vendor of the last resort' the field workshop was turned into a focused activity which could be used to help salesmen gain modernisation orders; it is now frequently visited by customers, and the employees have a close association with the field activity. A fifth workshop is Consolidation and Shipping, which is the link between the other workshops and the customer. Each workshop has its own technologies.

"Service spares are no longer produced at Liverpool. This activity was transferred to be close to the service warehouse in London, removing from the premises an activity which had little in common with the remaining operations.

"There is no doubt that the focused workshop has produced significant financial improvements. Lower costs, shorter lead times and on time delivery have resulted in an increase of orders to Liverpool.

"For the first time in memory the number of indirect staff fell below the number of direct workers. Despite lower hours per unit of production, standard hours of production began to rise as orders from Otis companies overseas started flowing back to Liverpool. The field workshop began capturing work previously given to outside vendors." (Hussey[10])

The architect of the change, John Miller, summarised the reasons for the approach:

"The advantage of the focused approach was that workshops could be established from a zero base, allowing a break with past practices and the previous culture. A manufacturing resource could be created to suit the specific needs of each warehouse. Smaller focused units made it easier to use a team approach to problem solving and contributed to job flexibility. Above all, it was possible to give people something to identify with, which they could run as a business and see the results of their efforts." (quoted in Hussey[10])

The Learning Curve

Learning curves were first observed in a factory producing aircraft. Every time cumulative output doubled, there was a constant percentage fall of 20% in the unit labour cost. Thus:

> 4th plane requires 80% of the labour of the 2nd plane
> 8th plane requires 80% of the labour of the 4th plane
> 100th plane requires 80% of the labour of the 50th.

This is not the same as economy of scale, which is the fall in unit costs brought about by an increase in capacity and throughput over a given period.

Economies of scale are not cumulative in their effect. The learning curve reduction is caused by the increased skills of the labour force as more experience is gained, and has been found to apply in a variety of different industries.

A greater level of significance was given to this finding by the Boston Consulting Group, who derived the experience curve concept. "Each time the accumulated experience of manufacturing a particular product doubles, the total unit cost in real terms (i.e. in 'constant money', net of GDP inflation), can be made to decline by a characteristic percentage. The decline is normally in the region of 20–30%"

(Hedley[11]). When plotted on a logarithmic scale, the experience curve appears as a straight line.

The experience curve embraces the learning curve, but the empirical findings are that it covers all the other costs of manufacture as well. The whole organisation becomes more effective through experience measured in terms of cumulative output. The implications of this are that the strategy has to exploit the maximum potential from the experience curve. If competitors manage to obtain the predicted level of benefit, but your company does not, the competitive disadvantage may widen to a point of no recovery.

When demand is inelastic and there are other competitors it is difficult to make use of this concept, since it is probably not possible to increase output enough to gain dramatic decreases in cost. The situation changes when demand is sufficiently elastic, because here it is possible to gain volume from lower prices, and lower costs from the increased volume. If the equation can be pushed far enough it will mean that new competitors would find it almost impossible to obtain volumes large enough to be competitive. Similarly the laggards among existing competitors will become increasingly uneconomic and be shaken out.

This concept has worked well in many parts of the electronics industry, where the real decline in both prices and costs is easily observable. However it is not necessarily as simple as it sounds. For example many small producers of personal computers are able to operate as low cost producers because they are designers and assemblers, benefiting from the low costs of components which they buy in. The experience curve in these cases is more beneficial to manufacturers of chips, disk drives, and other components, than it is to the companies that market the computers themselves.

The implications of the learning curve on strategy are clear. An experience curve concept implies relatively few plants supplying global markets, standardised products, and total coordination between marketing and manufacture. When marketing reduces the real price, manufacturing must be ready to supply the increased volume. It implies careful attention to purchasing and sub contracting. Above all it implies the maintenance of quality, so that lower prices do not become associated with inferior goods. These are all features of the way in which Japanese electronics, automotive and motor cycle firms operate. The experience curve is a partial explanation of the forces that drive firms towards a global strategy, as discussed in a previous chapter.

The competitive impact of trying to compete against the machine like operations of the experience curve by traditional means is best illustrated by the British motor cycle industry. Just before the industry collapsed in 1974, the best British motor cycle factory produced 18 cycles per man year, compared to 350 in the best Japanese factories. Even though the British industry had consolidated, each marque still ran its own factory as if it were independent. No products were standardised, even at the components level. The British industry was beaten by a strategy that it never understood.

There are limits to the experience curve. The need for an elastic demand curve was mentioned earlier, and to this we might add a need for continued market growth. This probably explains the continued introduction of new models by the consumer electronics industry: without this growth could slacken, and the experience curve go into reverse. Presumably if demand falls costs will rise, prices will rise, causing a further fall in demand.

Henry Ford had never heard of the learning curve, yet he used it to good advantage with the model T Ford car. Then one day he woke up to find that nobody wanted to buy this car any more. His competitive position slumped to the bottom of the league, and the factory had to be closed for a lengthy period until a successor model could be designed and produced. This story is described at some length by Abernathy and Wayne.[12]

There is a connection between the focused factory concept and the learning curve, in that without focus it may be impossible to gain the potential benefits of the experience curve, as the experience is dissipated across other products.

Some Modern Manufacturing Concepts

Anyone considering manufacturing strategy should include in the options some of the modern concepts of manufacture. A brief description of some of them is given here. For more details refer to Hill[13] and Hayes, Wheelwright and Clark.[14]

Flexible manufacturing system (FMS), is a way of handling small batch sizes economically, giving more flexibility of production, and reducing throughput times and inventory sizes. The concept is the grouping of parts into families, with manufacture controlled by computer, using machine tools with the ability to change tools automatically. In effect small batches can be manufactured as efficiently as larger batches, which provides the opportunity to modify standard products to suit individual market needs. FMS can change strategies for global production.

Computer aided design (CAD) is the use of computers by the designer to design products on screen, and store all the critical information electronically, including all dimensions and tolerances. A library of design elements can be retained in a design data base, reducing design time for future products. Not only does CAD speed up the design process, but it makes it easier for designs to be modified and manipulated. Standardisation becomes easier, because of the access to the data base. It is also much easier to pass design information to others, inside and outside of the same building. Floppy discs are much more manageable than large blue prints.

Computer aided manufacture (CAM) takes CAD a stage further by using the computer to convert drawings and designs into manufacturing instructions. Information on tools, jigs, routing instructions and the like can be incorporated into the product data base. CAM can also produce the instructions needed to drive computer controlled manufacturing processes.

Just in time production is a system which ensures that each item is only made at the time it is required, or in the case of purchased items, delivered to the production line when needed. The system reduces inventories throughout the process, but requires careful attention to scheduling. Its adherents believe that the system prevents problems from being hidden behind inventories so that they can be dealt with. JIT offers a low technology approach, based on demand pulling requirements. However it requires some stability in demand levels, and requires considerable effort to install and make effective.

World Class Manufacturing

World class manufacturing has become an important concept since the 1980s. It requires regular benchmarking, a topic discussed in Chapter 10, although in this case the aims of the benchmarking are specifically manufacturing. Competitor performance is very important, but such benchmarking would also cover other relevant industries.

Hayes, Wheelwright and Clark[14] define world class manufacturing: "Basically, this means being better than almost every other company in your industry in at least one important aspect of manufacturing." They suggest that there are four stages of manufacturing competitiveness into one of which every company can be slotted. Stage one is "internally neutral". The role of manufacturing is simply to make what they are told to make, and the company relies on its product designs and marketing skills for its success. Under these conditions a factory is something that you have to have, but you expect it to play second place to marketing.

Stage two they call "extremely neutral". Here companies are concerned to meet the standards of costs, delivery and quality of their competitors. Such organisations tend to use the same suppliers as the bulk of the industry, to follow industry standards and to recruit manufacturing personnel from within the industry. The driving objective is to copy competitors to stay competitive.

Stage three is for manufacturing to be "internally supportive" of the rest of the company. It is not just a question of making product to competitors' standards, but of using manufacturing to enable the whole company to achieve more. Manufacturing does more than copy competitors: it tries to tailor manufacturing strategy to the competitive strategy of the company.

The final classification is stage four, described as "externally supportive". Here the company seeks to use manufacturing as a source of competitive advantage, and is not concerned with being as good as competitors but being better than them. This is true world class manufacturing, when the organisation is perpetually seeking ways to improve. The authors suggest that such organisations are the ones sought out by suppliers when they wish to develop or test new machinery. They have higher quality personnel at all levels than most of their competitors. They are able to react faster, meeting changes in the market far quicker than their competitors. Designs of new products are tied so tightly to the manufacturing process that competitors can only copy them if they invest in extensive re-tooling and major design costs. They do not recognise that they have reached an optimal state, so that effort is continually being put to improving things that others might consider to be at a state of excellence.

The philosophy that the organisation elects to follow is in itself a strategic decision, and will change how it takes every other strategic decision in manufacturing.

Strategic Decisions in Manufacturing

This chapter so far has covered a number of strategic manufacturing areas, both around the role of manufacturing in the company, and many of the options that may become the basis of the strategy.

By implication, the discussion has touched on many different types of strategic manufacturing decisions. To make sure that nothing is lost, the final part of this chapter will summarise some of the more important areas. Skinner[9] and Hayes, Wheelwright and Clark[14] both provide guidance which largely covers the same ground. However, the latter make an interesting distinction between issues which they term "bricks and mortar", which are to do with physical things, and those they term "infrastructure", which are to do with people and systems.

Bricks and Mortar

(i) The capacity that needs to be provided, and the timing of various increments of new capacity.

(ii) Location of capacity, including the number of locations. This issue becomes of critical importance for companies with global competition.

(iii) Type of facilities, and the degree of focus within each.

(iv) Production technologies, and the nature of the equipment and systems that have to be provided.

(v) Make or buy decisions for materials, systems and service.

(vi) Health, safety and environmental issues.

Infrastructure

(i) Human resource policies, covering recruitment, training, reward systems, security and skill requirements.

(ii) Communication and management policies to support the required culture.

(iii) Quality requirements and the approaches to be used to attain them.

(iv) Production planning and control systems, and equally important the philosophy that lies behind them. Companies using JIT have to operate differently from those using more traditional methods.

(v) Organisation structure and design, including such issues as layers of management, empowerment, and the role of staff functions.

(vi) Measurement and control systems.

(vii) The processes for developing new products.

This chapter should have revealed the importance of technology and manufacturing in the strategic decision making process. Although some aspects of these strategies are reactive to the corporate objectives and strategies, there are also times when they should be proactive, and help to re-shape those objectives and strategies. This is more likely to happen when companies are operating at level four, and is very unlikely for those which are on level one.

For many managers, manufacturing and technology are closed books, and are therefore ignored whenever possible. Good strategic management should not allow this to happen, and the seeds of ultimate failure are sown whenever companies opt out of giving strategic attention to these areas.

References

1. Loveridge, R. and Pitt, M. *The Strategic Management of Technological Innovation*, Wiley, Chichester, 1990.
2. Wills, G. *Technological Forecasting*, Penguin Books, Harmondsworth, 1972.
3. Henry, J. P. "Making the Technology–Strategy Connection", Hussey, D. E. (ed.), *International Review of Strategic Management*, Vol. 1, Wiley, Chichester, 1990.
4. Ford, D. "Develop Your Technology Strategy", *Long Range Planning*, Vol. 21, No. 5, October 1988.
5. Gluck, F. W. and Foster, R. N. "Managing Technological Change: A Box of Cigars for Brad", *Harvard Business Review*, September–October 1975.
6. Prahalad, C. K. and Hamel, G. "The Core Competence of the Corporation", *Harvard Business Review*, May–June 1990.
7. Abell, D. F. *Defining the Business: The Starting Point of Corporate Planning*, Prentice Hall, Englewood Cliffs, New Jersey, 1980.
8. Neubauer, F-F. *Portfolio Management*, Kluwer, Deventer, Netherlands, 1990.
9. Skinner, W. *Manufacturing in the Corporate Strategy*, Wiley, New York, 1978.
10. Hussey, D. E. *Management Training and Corporate Strategy*, Pergamon, Oxford, 1988.
11. Hedley, B. "A Fundamental Approach to Strategy Development", *Long Range Planning*, Vol. 9, No. 6, 1976.
12. Abernathy, W. J. and Wayne, K. "Limits of the learning curve", *Harvard Business Review*, pp. 109–119, September–October 1974.
13. Hill, T. *Manufacturing Strategy*, MacMillan, London, 1985.
14. Hayes, R. H., Wheelwright, S. C. and Clark, K. B. *Dynamic Manufacturing: Creating the Learning Organisation*, Free Press, New York, 1988.

20

Financial Planning

The question of financial planning has appeared on other pages of this book only to be dismissed in summary fashion with a rider stressing its importance. This is the unfortunate consequence of the need to analyse one thing at a time, and creates a measure of unreality in that in a real-life management situation many things are pursued concurrently.

Any feeling that financial strategy is something that happens after the real managers of the business have made their decisions should be rapidly dispelled. Financial plans, as documents, may appear to be the last link in the planning chain, and perhaps the final appraisal and financial strategies will be made at this point, but any major strategic decisions will have already considered financial implications: for example, an acquisition plan must be interwoven with the financial strategy since this will dictate how the plan is implemented.

Good financial management has three major aims: to keep the business solvent, to maintain sufficient liquidity for it to meet liabilities as they become due, and to ensure that in the context of these first two aims it provides the company in the most efficient way with the finance it needs for growth. A company which practises strategic management will be trying to meet these aims more effectively—a way that is future-oriented, considers more factors, is better coordinated, and which should make it possible for better financial decisions to be made. Just as strategic planning as a whole sets out to be a better way of running a business, financial planning—one of its components—sets out to be more effective in managing the finance function.

A pre-condition for good financial management, and therefore also for financial planning, is a corporate attitude of mind. Senior managers must consider cash-flow implications in all their major decisions. Every senior manager is involved in the utilisation of corporate financial resources, yet too many managers never think beyond profit (pre-tax and pre-financial charges).

Financial plans will express the company's forward plans so that they positively identify the financial needs, problems and opportunities. This is an important aspect of financial planning, but only has real value when it is overlaid by the financial strategy, which will involve the selection of the means of financing, management of surplus funds, ways of avoiding the incidence of taxation, and changes in the company's general policies. Financial strategic decisions may act as a constraint on broader, strategic thinking, drawing the investment line which the company may not overstep. It may act as a goad to stimulate further capital investment so that liquid balances are reduced, thus using money more profitably and reducing the danger of the company becoming an acquisition victim hunted for its cash.

There is a very close relationship between the financial plan and the other plans of the company, and these provide the raw material from which financial requirements can be assessed. Although most financial managers try to take a forward view of financing needs, this is very difficult where the company has no formal planning system. Corporate planning gives the opportunity for dramatically improving this view, giving greater accuracy, a more comprehensive coverage, and a method of control. Its forecasts are based on what the company intends to do rather than on trend lines constructed from past performance.

So financial planning represents (at least for the well-managed company) an improvement rather than a revolution. For the company whose financial management is weak it may well act as a revelation.

The strategic plans, discussed previously and the operating plans, which will appear later, will provide the company with an estimate of future profits under a specific and defined strategy and set of circumstances. They will also outline the capital budget needed to support and implement this strategy. Capital investment figures may sometimes be in the form of a range, rather than one definitive figure, and although this is a complication it does not cause any real problems. In reality, profit forecasts should also be seen as a range.

These plans should also provide an estimate of depreciation, an expense which, in cash-flow terms, is not a real expenditure. Specific provision should exist for calculating this in operating plans, and in plans for new activities it may be estimated directly (there is no historical depreciation in such plans, so direct calculations may be made from capital investment needs: the main complication would come from acquisitions).

In this way the financial planner is provided with some of the main parameters of his cash-flow forecasts: profits, capital expenditures, capital inflows from divestments and depreciation. The way in which he receives them gives the figures a validity which his own estimates would not possess.

The strategic and operating plans also provide information on movements in sales and purchases which enable some of the other components of the cash flow to be calculated: debtor and creditor levels and inventories. Definite decisions may be made to change present ratios: for example, to reduce credit given or cut inventories. Plans, plus existing data available to the financial manager, and certain strategic decisions in the area of finance (e.g. dividends) provide the elements from which the remaining cash-flow components may be estimated.

In the initial stages the cash-flow part of the financial plan will make assumptions about the sources of funds to provide the company with the means of financing the plan. These decisions are not automatic, and are major elements of strategy in the consideration of which there are many factors to take into account.

Changes in the sources of finance will affect, among other things, interest, dividends, and taxation. At this stage it is of value to quantify some of the alternatives. In many companies the amount of work involved in these calculations will justify some computer assistance.

The embryo plan should also be tested for sensitivity to various items of risk. A plan that will run the company into serious financial trouble if a few things go wrong should be viewed more critically than one which appears safe under most circumstances.

Cash-flow forecasts prepared in this way suffer from one major defect. They represent the expected position as at a certain time of the year. Most businesses have seasonal variations, and to ignore these can be very dangerous, particularly if the plan is produced in the troughs. A plan produced at the time of the peaks might lead the company to raise more capital than it requires.

The planned cash flow would, therefore, be of more value if it were accompanied by estimates of constant and variable capital needs. Constant capital may be defined as the fixed capital of the business plus that level of working capital which is needed to maintain operations in the slackest period of the year. It is "constant" only for that year, and may change with each year of the plan. Variable capital is that extra element of working capital which may be required over and above the constant level to finance the company at other periods of the year.

Constant and variable capital levels will have a greater gap in a business with a heavy seasonal influence. A company with no seasonal influences is likely to have little or no variable capital.

Adequate financial control can only be exercised if the company works to a regularly revised short-term cash-flow forecast based on the budgetary control process. Here, more than any other area, it is necessary to constantly study and, if necessary, re-schedule the actions shown in the plan. A postponement of a capital expenditure project can easily change the way in which finance is raised. Failure to control in the short term can lead to a loss of liquidity which sends it into insolvency.

Another schedule which should appear in the financial plan is a long-term capital budget (more will be said about short-term capital budgeting in Chapter 26 which deals with investment appraisal). This need not be a very complicated document, and should attempt to list each planned fixed capital expenditure over the period of the plan, phased by the expected year of expenditure (this may be different from the year in which the project is completed). Sometimes it may be desirable to give the figure within a range: sometimes, as a choice between two alternatives, only one of which will be accepted (Project A £500,000 *or* Project B £450,000).

This document may also be used to indicate working capital requirements from new areas of business arising from the strategic plan. Sometimes it is easier to calculate these in this way than to pick them up from ratios based on production and turnover projections. The important rules are to omit nothing and avoid double-counting.

So far this aspect of financial planning has been treated on the level of a relatively simple company. Most of the problems involved in handling the more complex (and more usual) business are matters of detail rather than of principle, and as such can easily be identified in practice. There are two practical points which deserve some additional attention.

The first is that the figures which find their way into the financial plan need not necessarily be the total of all operating plans in the company. Consolidation is not always a question of simple addition. The company that simply adds up the fore-cast capital requirements of hundreds of operating plans from all around the world is likely to end up with a borrowing requirement it can never achieve. The point will be made in more detail in Chapter 24 that the corporate planner must exercise an element of discrimination in selecting which figures of each operating plan go forward into the total corporate plan.

The second complication is in the area of international business. Because cash is not freely transferable from one country to another, cash flow projections are likely to be more use when calculated on a single country basis. A shortage of cash in Australia is not compensated by a surplus in Nigeria. At the same time, the financial plan should treat capital as a corporate rather than an individual subsidiary resource. Expenditure on inferior projects should not be allowed just because that particular country has a capital surplus. Strategy should consider the funding of one country by another where this is both legal and desirable. And, of course, local financial strategies must be approved at corporate level.

International factors in financial planning make the task much more complex: it would be wrong to overstress this, however, as the complications have to be faced by financial management in any case, and arise despite—and not because of—any efforts to plan ahead.

So far attention has been concentrated on the assembly of data to give a first indication of corporate resources and needs. This is a relatively simply task, and at this stage is little more than the analysis of other people's data. Once the work is done it is possible to return to a more interesting application of skills—financial strategy itself.

It is possible that the cash-flow projections reveal a position which can safely be adopted as the financial plan. This will come about where financial implications have been fully considered at the strategic planning stage, and where plans have been based on a careful appreciation of the company's available financial resour-ces. From the corporate planner's viewpoint this is a very pleasant state of affairs and means that he has no re-thinking to do. Unfortunately it is an unlikely possi-bility, and the most probable outcome will be a need to reconsider sources of funds and, in some cases, their application. Projects which appeared to be highly desirable may have to be postponed or rejected on financial grounds, which in turn may open a gap between primary objective and plan, which the planner thought had been safely closed.

Three other possibilities are more likely:

(i) The cash flow will reveal no difficulty in balancing sources and application of funds, but will highlight areas where financial policy is weak and requires changes, which may in turn unbalance the cash flow. For example, if the ratio of debt to equity is becoming disproportionate.

(ii) Despite projects which may be expected to achieve all profit objectives, the company has a surplus of liquid assets.

(iii) There is a shortfall of resources, which have to be made up unless planned capital expenditure is to be cut back.

Each element of the projected cash flow will have been based on either an assumption or a known financial policy, which means that it can be deliberately changed. In addition, a strategic action planned for the future may indicate a need to change policies immediately. An intention to "go public" in three years' time may be facilitated if certain financial policies are changed next year.

Setting financial policy is one of the major tasks of financial planning, and is fundamental to the company's successful use of corporate planning. No figures in the cash-flow projections are firm, no policies which cause them are immutable.

It is possible to divide the cash-flow statements into two broad groups: elements which are internally generated and elements which have to draw on the world outside. These are, perhaps, not the most accurate descriptions, but will assist further analysis.

Internally generated elements include all working capital, fixed capital expenditure, dividends, depreciation, and taxation (although this last stretches the definition somewhat).

Working Capital

There are still companies where little or no attention is given to the way in which working capital is used, although these are becoming fewer in number. Where they do exist, they are usually in the position of having a surplus of funds and reasonable profits. In companies such as this there is often "flabby" management with no top management interest in debtors or inventory levels. The need to borrow money, particularly at a time of credit squeeze or high interest rates, often forces such a business to turn its attentions inwards and economise in its use of working capital. Such an outlook may also come about with a change in mangement.

A reduction in working capital through greater efficiency has three main effects: an improvement in liquidity, a saving in (or earnings of) interest, and an improvement in return on investment ratios. Savings may be made by adjusting the length of credit period given to customers and taken from suppliers, or by reducing inventories.

No financial manager should act alone on these points, since they are also matters which concern operational management. In some circumstances precipitate action can cause more problems than it solves. Solutions may be complex and require the assistance of skilled services: as in the design of an inventory control system, a change in order-handling procedure which gets invoices out quicker, or a detailed study to cut down inventories by reducing the number of distribution depots, or standardising products so that raw material and finished stock levels may be set low.

Good management will demand that measures such as these become part of day-to-day considerations. Operating managers should be encouraged to think about working capital when planning any new decisions. In a less well-managed company opportunities for improvement should have been uncovered through the corporate appraisal.

The chances of a normally well-managed company releasing large flows of capital by changing policies which affect the use of working capital are not high, but the possibility should not be overlooked.

Fixed Capital Expenditure

Investment requirements for fixed capital can only be defined in broad terms in any long-range financial plan, but, nevertheless, these estimates may be accurate enough as a basis for financial strategy.

If it appears that finance is going to be a problem it may be necessary to re-look at these expenditures and take one of the following actions:

(a) Ration the available capital according to profitability, risk levels and strategic needs.
(b) Identify expenditures which can be postponed for a defined period without unduly upsetting overall strategy.
(c) Concentrate on investments with the earliest payback.
(d) Re-examine alternatives.

Item (d) requires some explanation. One possibility is to consider ways of implementing the project which involves less capital expenditure, or which phase the same expenditure over a longer time period. Shortage of capital may mean that new projects should be based on renting property, rather than buying; hiring assets rather than purchasing them; or even buying on hire purchase. It may suggest changing a project from one of expansion to acquisition, giving a better opportunity to purchase for paper rather than cash.

What all this indicates is a critical examination of the projects and their effects on profits, and is probably best carried out as a joint exercise between financial management and the strategic planner.

Dividends

One of the ways in which capital may be generated internally is to distribute less of the profits to shareholders. In a family business, where ownership and management are the same, it is much easier to decide on policies which restrict or reduce the distribution of profits to the owners. In this case, there is full knowledge of the reasons for the decision and an acceptance that a sacrifice now will bring greater benefits later. In small businesses such methods of financing are frequently adopted.

In a large business with many shareholders, and particularly in the case of a quoted company, there are likely to be valid reasons against financing by a reduction in dividends (except possibly where earnings have fallen). Such an action would alter the yield of the shares and cause a fall in share price on the Stock

Exchange. Existing shareholders would lose capital as well as income. This in turn could make the company more vulnerable for takeover.

A policy of holding dividends to existing levels, despite increases in earnings, is unlikely to be so upsetting, at least in the shorter term. (A continuation of the policy over a longer term could result in a situation where market price was less than break-up value, and this too might attract the eye of the hunter in the acquisition jungle.)

Dividends are by no means the only factors which cause fluctuations in share prices.

They are—subject to adequate profit performance—one of the areas over which the company has some control. It may be that other elements of the financial strategy require the maintenance of a strong share price: if it is planned to enter the acquisition field it would be more costly if any paper exchange were made on the basis of a low share price. The better deal is likely to come when the shares are strong.

In international operations there may be taxation or exchange control advantages in ensuring that subsidiaries pay a reasonable dividend, even if this causes them difficulties in financing capital expenditures. A bird in the hand from a potentially unstable country is probably worth two in the bush that may be locked in by exchange control measures, or that carry a risk of being lost through expropriation.

Depreciation

Depreciation rates may, within limits, be set by the company itself. There are variations between companies and although auditors generally protect investors against a change of depreciation rates in a way that is designed only to manipulate profits, it is possible for companies to alter their policies from time to time.

Over provision, once a sign of cautious financial management, is now generally considered much less desirable, in that its effect on profits and real asset values may make the company an attractive acquisition possibility.

The importance of depreciation in cash flow will vary from company to company, but it is often—as for example in a shipping company—one of the largest generators of cash the company has.

Taxation

Taxation cannot be evaded, although it is frequently possible to plan the affairs of the company in such a way that the burden of tax is reduced.

On an individual project basis (see Chapter 26) taxation is an important item in the appraisal process, and will influence discounted cash-flow calculations. Investment allowances against tax will be usually assumed in project analysis to be available in the year in which they are due: that is, the assumption is that other areas of the company will be earning profits so that the allowance can be set against these. One of the aims of financial strategy must be to ensure, as far as possible, that this assumption is true. The financial benefits of ensuring this can themselves lead to a particular corporate strategy: for example, a company with low profits and high allowances seeking to acquire a company with high profits that will mop up the allowances. If tax allowances cannot be taken, it may be preferable to avoid capital expenditure and lease instead.

In a multi-national group it may be possible within the constraints of the law, to choose policies which attract a lower incidence of tax. In all such groups there is some freedom of decision over where profits are made (see Chapter 18).

Under the second group of strategic decision areas there is a consideration of ways in which the company may raise finance. In broad terms these are all matters of relationships with bodies or people outside of the company itself, although within the limits of availability the decision to tap these sources is one taken by the company itself. Strategic consideration will include the basic categories of financial requirements, equity sources, and borrowing.

Categories of Finance

There are a number of ways of categorising sources of finance, and these are useful for setting the scene even though they may only influence—and not dictate—the eventual financial strategy of the undertaking.

One classification is into short, medium, and long term. A traditional, and largely outdated, view is that the type of borrowing should fit the type of need: short-term borrowing should never be used to finance the purchase of fixed assets. Certainly there is a point to be watched in defining the financial mix, since excessive reliance on short-term funds for long-term needs can put the company in a vulnerable position. The problem is one of balance, rather than doctrine, and will be returned to when gearing is discussed.

Another classification is risk, fixed assets, and working finance. Risk capital is finance which belongs to the owners of the company (either from retentions or share issues) and which the company is prepared to stand the risk of losing. Both fixed asset and working capital may, of course, be financed from risk capital. Although companies need not necessarily use separate sources for each, it is worth considering that the greater the risk attached to a venture, the more desirable it is that it is financed from equity sources. A heavy investment of loan funds in an R & D project which is unsuccessful could have a much more serious effect on the company than a similar loss of risk capital.

Equity Sources

One of the first platforms of financial strategy must be to define the extent of gearing which is acceptable to the company. Initially this will be only to set the parameters of future decisions and will lay down the maximum debt : equity ratio which will be considered acceptable.

The company's basic objectives must be considered here. Many firms now define their profit objective in terms of growth in earnings per share. Additional equity finance in many circumstances would, despite the increasing profits, cause a reduction in average earnings per share, thus preventing the company from achieving its objective. This would tend to drive business with this type of objective to loan funds rather than equity. Similarly a value based strategy approach would lead to a different mix of strategic–financial decisions.

Objectives are only one aspect of the decision. Financial strategy must also consider a number of factors varying from the state of the money market, to control, to cost of finance, as well as the ever-present need to maintain liquidity and solvency. Some of these points should be examined in more detail.

A public company, with a wide spread of ownership of its shares, is unlikely to face any direct problems from loss of control when floating an additional issue. Indirectly, the possible weakening of share price on the Stock Exchange could lead to changes. The company that has all shares concentrated into a few holdings, and which is forced to go outside its existing shareholders for the new issue, is likely to find the control problem of more importance.

Additional equity participation carries the advantage that its servicing costs are related to overall profits. If there is no profit, a dividend need not be paid (or indeed, a dividend can be withheld even when there is a profit). Interest on a loan has to be paid regardless of profits. Equity may, in some circumstances, cost more than a loan. It means giving away a share of the profits of current operations, even though the new operation for which the additional equity is required may be making a lower marginal contribution (although this may be avoided if preference shares are issued). While borrowing provides the opportunity of increasing the return on shareholder's funds, additional equity is likely to reduce that ratio, although total profits may increase.

The decision may also be affected by the current and forecast state of the money market. From the market's viewpoint there are times when it prefers equity to loan investment (or the opposite). A share issue which is unsuccessful, even if taken up by underwriters, may reflect very badly on the company's public image. In times of credit squeeze, when the pressure is to reduce loan finance, equity may be the only available source: but this is not a justification for raising long-term equity to meet short-term problems, unless the plan shows that the additional equity would in any case have to be raised in the near future.

Equity becomes of particular importance in acquisition strategy, for an exchange of paper is often a means of avoiding a cash outlay. Such moves are popular with vendors because they may solve certain personal taxation problems. In many circumstances the acquiring company may obtain liquid funds for the exchange of paper. Control may become a much more urgent problem in these circumstances since large blocks of shares in the "victim" may translate to even larger blocks in the "hunter". A combination of cash and paper may avoid this.

Sources of equity are the Stock Exchange, inter-company deals in an acquisition, or, of course, the traditional personal sources. Additionally, an injection of equity may sometimes be obtained from merchant bankers or other finance houses. In an international business, advantage may be taken of local sources of equity to finance the development of subsidiaries, although the disadvantage of such an action is usually the complication of having minority shareholders.

Many different types of equity are possible, and a company may protect its existing shareholders by issuing preference shares or shares which have voting right restrictions. These may, on the other hand, prove unattractive to the market.

Borrowings

Some of the issues associated with loan finance have been covered in the discussion on equity. One of the major issues to consider is the burden of interest which heavy borrowing will incur. In theory no money will be borrowed unless it earns more for the company than it costs. There are some problems here. Firstly, the calculations must be made on expectations—which may be wrong, either through error or a change in the basic circumstances. Companies do not always make the profits they forecast. This is really a question of acceptable risks, which must be taken into account when the plan is prepared.

Secondly, to maintain a positive cash flow, the *retained* profits on the projects for which finance is required must be greater than the interest.

Thirdly, a project may be a good investment, but may not break even for several years. During this early period the interest burden—along with other unrecovered costs—must be paid from elsewhere. This is another indication of the need to have an overall financial plan since the total picture may alter conclusions which would be drawn from a study of individual projects.

Cost is as important in considering borrowed finance as it is with equity. With borrowed funds there may be the added complication of having to choose between fixed and fluctuating rates, which requires an assessment of future interest levels before any sensible decision can be made.

Probably the most widely used source of short-term finance is the bank overdraft, which can often be the simplest and cheapest method of obtaining working capital. In times of credit squeeze this source may not be so readily available, and levels of overdraft previously negotiated may be reduced. One of the advantages of overdrafts is that levels can usually be negotiated in advance, but only taken up as required. Additional sources of finance are factoring debtors and discounting bills of exchange. The former may be an expensive and unpalatable solution. The latter is nowadays more likely to arise in companies with export business.

It is possible to obtain long-term loans from banks and finance houses of various types. In some countries there are government-backed development corporations designed to provide this type of credit. The stock market may be tapped through the issue of debentures, although success is likely to be dependent on both the standing of the company and the state of the money market. It must be remembered that debentures carry a fixed interest rate, which may present the company with a long-term disadvantage if an issue is floated at a time when interest is abnormally high. (This, of course, is a comment which applies to all fixed-interest loans.)

Long-term finance needs may also be obtained from mortgaging existing property or taking out a mortgage to buy a new property. In these cases the funds are likely to come from houses which specialise in this type of operation. A variation of using property to raise finance is sale and leaseback. This is venture capital and not a loan. Although it brings in an immediate capital sum it may be expensive (although not necessarily when looked at over a long term if in a situation of rising rents) and suffers from the further disadvantage that it reduces flexibility. Once sold in this fashion, the property is no longer available as specific or general security for other loans—and in a normal situation of rising property prices may remove from the company an asset which increases steadily in value.

Medium-term credit can be obtained from most of the sources mentioned and in addition from leasing and hire purchase.

Taxation implications must be considered in making the decision, since the effect of tax may change the real cost to the company.

The final financial strategy selected should be fully integrated and include provision for contingencies—both for failures by the company to achieve plans and failures of the proposed source of finance to be available at the expected cost. Although the company should be trying to set a long-term strategy, it must be aware that finance is an area where there may be sudden and dramatic environmental changes which can affect the comparative cost of various sources and their availability.

A good financial plan is more than projection of the application and sources of funds statement. In addition, there are few companies whose strategic decisions in the area of finance are as simple as the factors so far discussed might suggest.

One overriding strategic consideration is that the company should try to select its sources in a way that leaves it the utmost flexibility. This means, all other things being equal, that unsecured loans are preferable to secured loans, or that equity might be better than a loan which puts a charge over all the company's assets.

This flexibility question also has implications in the next point. It pays to be right in the assessment of funds needed. Often it is simpler to raise one large sum than two smaller ones, and the costs of so doing are likely to be less. If the loan requires the mortgaging of property, it may be less easy to raise a second mortgage than to obtain the whole sum on a first mortgage—a smaller loan can take away as much flexibility as a large one. On the other hand, the raising of too much finance, of either equity or loan, is expensive and strategically dangerous.

Financial strategy in multi-national operations has added complications quite apart from the legal ones. Some international companies try to arrange finance so that subsidiaries remit as much money back to the centre as is possible, and the subsidiaries themselves operate on the largest local loans they can raise. This is not solely financial in its implications, and may impinge on operations: for instance, the "loading" of raw material prices to get money back to the centre may make the subsidiary avoid certain operations which appear to be unprofitable in its own eyes, while the burden of interest payments may further decrease the company's apparent earnings.

Certainly any multi-national strategy must give consideration to national and international sources of funds, and one element which should be defined in the plan is the constraints which should be observed by subsidiary companies. The backing of the parent is often sufficient to enable the local subsidiary to obtain larger loans more easily than it would if it relied solely on its own assets.

Equity stays with the company. Loans have to be paid back (although in practice certain types of loan finance may continue almost indefinitely). Provision must be made in the plan for any refunding operations which might be necessary over the period of the plan. In some cases the intention may be to pay back the loan: in others it may be to renegotiate for a further period.

A further aspect of the plan should cover financial public relations, which may be a helpful tool in giving the company credibility, and ensuring that it is known to the financial world and the investing public. Credibility will often hold up share prices when there is an off-trend drop in profits because the explanation given is accepted. It may help the company in driving off an attack from a would-be acquirer or getting the terms of its own acquisition bids accepted.

No one should believe that financial public relations will have more than passing value unless the company is basically sound. A massive edifice cannot be erected in safety on crumbling foundations, and although a PR "front" may prop things up for a short while, it will not last for long unless backed by facts and results. Although financial public relations may be a specialist area it cannot be separated from the general public relations activities of the company. It is not possible to present two different pictures of the company without both losing credibility.

Financial plans may have to deal with surplus liquid funds as well as shortages. Strategic changes and implications of too much cash have already been discussed. If surpluses do exist, it is up to financial management to make the best use of them, and this is a requirement whether the funds available are moderate or excessive. A well-prepared plan will aid this task in two ways. The projections of capital needs will reveal the changing amount of excess funds available and, therefore, the length of time for which financial management can afford to offer when investing, and sensitivity analysis will help the assessment of the risks in tying up cash in this way. Environmental assessments will enable investments to be made against the background of an appreciation of the money market, changing interest rates, and general economic conditions.

The financial strategy of an organisation may be highly creative and innovative, and this is frequently an essential.

British Petroleum financed its Alaskan oil field, and secured a major strategic position in the USA by a brilliant move. At a time when it was financially stretched it acquired a minority holding in Sohio in exchange for Alaskan oil and other US activities. Sohio were to take over the financing of Alaskan production and had the strength to do this. As Alaskan oil began to flow BP would gain additional equity participation in Sohio in which it would eventually be the majority shareholder. As it was initially an investment, not a subsidiary, BP could not present consolidated accounts which meant that none of the Alaska financing affected its balance sheet.

Much of the company's future success will depend on the skill with which it prepares its financial strategies. It is an area which it cannot afford to neglect, and an area where failure can render useless all the effort expended by others in the organisation.

21

Strategic Planning for Human Resources

Business is a human activity (despite the fact that many actions take place in the name of business which the cynic might claim would suggest inhumanity). Although labour requirements change, clerical workers may be replaced by computers and factory workers by automation, middle managers may disappear as their organisations de-layer, there still remains a basic fact: no company can operate without people.

The two fundamental resources of any business, of whatever size and whatever nature, are people and money. And of these two, the people resource is the most complex. Money is money whether it comes from loan or equity sources: it does not need to be distinguished from any other money; one pound note has the same value as another. People on the other hand are all different. They have different physical characteristics, different temperaments, different educational levels, different personal values, different skills, and different abilities. A company, at any one time, has a requirement not for people in general, but for specific people who are able to fulfil the function for which they are needed. When it requires managers, it cannot satisfy its need by recruiting labourers: nor can a surplus of managers make up for a shortage of skilled production workers.

In addition, the resource of people is always needed in a particular place. The financial needs of a plant in Glasgow can be met from a bank account in London. The people who work in that plant can be in no other place but Glasgow. Because people are not pawns on a chess board, and have relationships and responsibilities, desires and preferences, and a life outside business, they are a relatively immobile resource.

When money is in surplus there is always a way in which it can be utilised. When the people resource of the company is in surplus it becomes a drain on profits—an unnecessary expense. Because they are human beings, there are good reasons why they should not be treated casually—indeed the social climate and legal constraints of the day may prevent this.

The people resource cannot easily be turned on and off like a tap, yet the effectiveness of the company depends on getting the balance of human resources right. This means that if a company is to be sure that it can achieve the strategies it has set itself, it must give full consideration to the human factor, and must give a priority to planning the personnel aspects of the business. This means bringing people considerations into the strategic selection and implementation process, and ensuring that a strategic orientation is given to the planning and management of the human resource function.

In Chapter 3 we looked at the relationship between strategy, structure, systems and culture, and this thinking is important when we consider a strategic approach to human resource planning. The human issues in strategy will be looked at in more depth later in the book. In this chapter the concentration will be on strategic planning for human resources, a topic which although it began to emerge in the 1960s is barely recognised, and not understood by the majority of managers and human resource specialists.

The first attention to human resource planning began in the 1960s with books on manpower planning, although most of these dealt to some degree with organisational planning. Of these McBeath,[1] Lynch[2] and Bramham[3] are a good sample. I still find these books helpful, although the philosophy behind most of them is more reactive to corporate strategy than proactive.

In the 1980s attention began to be given to the value of linking management development to corporate strategy, both to ensure that management development was more cost effective for the company by incorporating more bottom line discipline into it, and because the power of training initiatives as a way of implementing strategy was not generally recognised. Useful references here are Bolt,[5,8] Hussey[4,6] and Nilsson.[7] To the best of my knowledge these cover the two early articles, and the only three books so far published on this topic. An increasing number of articles are now appearing in planning and human resource journals.

My own work moved from strategy, through some manpower planning, to management development strategy, and on to a total strategic approach to human resource management. So far the literature on a total approach is scanty, although the idea of such an approach has crept into seminar titles. I know of some works that are being written, but at this point the only reference I can give is Salaman.[9] It will be very different when the time comes to write the next edition of this book. I expect it to become a much more important topic both in theory and practice.

A Framework for Strategic HR Management

The strategic elements of human resource management are the areas which should alter to reflect changes in the organisation's strategy, and which should also have a proactive relationship with the development of that strategy. They are all areas where the investigator should expect to find differences compared with similar activities in other organisations. These are not necessarily differences of basic concepts, but of the interpretation of those concepts so that they fit the unique needs of the company.

The strategic elements of human resources are only a portion of the work that goes on within the HR function. Behind the strategic activities stand a host of administrative and support services. The direction of these is of course shaped by corporate policy and strategy, but many more would be directly transferable from one organisation to another. For example, the policy towards recruitment may be strategic: the actual processes of recruitment may be very similar between organisations. Record keeping is an administrative task of all HR departments, not very different between organisations: what information goes on the records may be changed by the organisation's specific approach to competencies, manpower planning and management development.

Figure 21.1 sets out the framework in diagrammatic form. The heart of the model holds the vision, values, objectives and strategies of the organisation. These should drive the strategies and policies of the activities in the middle ring. As mentioned, there is a two-way influence, in that the activities in this ring can affect the corporate strategy. For example the manpower planning activity may show that the strategic assumptions behind a new strategy are fallible, in that the people needed to implement a new strategy may be unobtainable.

The inner ring activities are management development, manpower planning, succession planning, climate and culture, competency assessment, and a group of policies towards recruitment, remuneration, and industrial relations. The activities in this group may vary in their degree of strategic importance from time to time.

The outer ring shows the support activities mentioned above. These will only be dealt with in the context of the inner ring activities in this chapter.

In planning HR activities a starting point should be the corporate strategic elements at the heart of Fig. 21.1. There are a number of steps to go through which are illustrated in Fig. 21.2. Most of this diagram is self explanatory, but two steps are worth stressing.

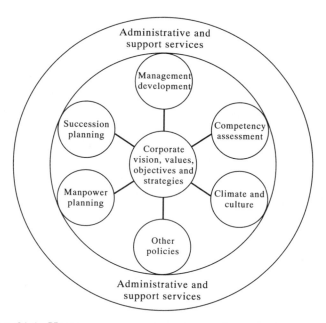

FIG. 21.1. Human resource management and corporate strategy

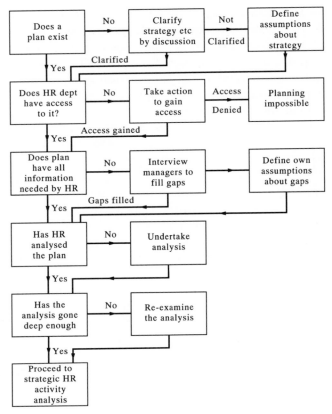

FIG. 21.2. Relating HR actions to corporate plans

(i) The figure suggests that if the HR department is not given access to the strategic information, the whole planning process should be abandoned. It also suggests that if no plan exists, and it is not possible to clarify the strategy officially, assumptions should be made. The different view taken is to do with how the HR department is perceived. If in good esteem, it is worth making assumptions to fill gaps. If not esteemed highly enough to share the plan, then assumptions would be a waste of time because someone else has the true picture, and assumptions from a source that lacks credibility would have no meaning. The implication of what I am saying here, is that no worthwhile strategic plan for HR can be prepared if the function is shut out from other strategic discussions: in addition no organisation that excludes HR can expect to produce sound strategies that are capable of being implemented.

(ii) There is a box in Fig. 21.2 which questions the depth of the analysis. This is a point born from experience and supported by Harbridge Consulting Group research, Tovey.[10] It is possible to treat a delayering and downsizing decision at two levels. The first is the obvious one, of redundancy actions, early retirement, and communication. The second is more subtle, like how do we make the organisation work now that we have delayered? This involves new management processes such as empowerment and performance management, and the training that enables both the empowered and the empowerers to understand how to make the new concept work. The research showed that very few companies were thinking at the second level. It is not surprising that the sort of motivation problems identified in Scase and Goffee[11] should be found when no action is taken to make the new organisation function.

Figure 21.3 shows how to begin to see the corporate plan in HR terms. The example is illustrative only, and the examples are deliberately kept at a simple level to show the method. Behind each tick should be a list of explanations: for example what is it that management development will have to do to support the delayering strategy?

It is worth mentioning that few strategic plans are written with HR in mind, and that very often HR thinking will not appear in those plans. There is always a need for intelligent interpretation, and it may often be necessary to take the interview route suggested in Fig. 21.2 to fill some of the gaps. An alternative to one to one interviews is to organise a meeting where senior managers are persuaded to think through the HR implications of the plans. The point is that if this type of thinking is new to the company it may be rather more ragged than the figures suggest. This is how experts earn their keep!

Strategic sources		HR areas impacted					
Type	Description	Mangmt dev.	Succession planning	Manpower planning	Competencies	Climate/ culture	Others (specify ⟶ reward
Vision	Customer responsive	✓			✓	✓	
	Global	✓			✓		
Strategies	European expansion	✓	✓	✓	✓	✓	
	New R&D unit			✓			
	Delayering	✓	✓	✓	✓	✓	✓
	Strategic alliance	✓				✓	
Values	People centred	✓	✓	✓		✓	
	Performance management	✓			✓	✓	✓
	Integrity				✓		✓
Objectives	25% PA Revenue growth	✓	✓	✓	✓	✓	✓
	Double market share	✓	✓	✓	✓	✓	✓

FIG. 21.3. Using matrix displays (illustrative only)

Relating to the External Environment

The Human Resources strategy, like other business strategies, is impacted by what is going on in the outside world. It is important that HR looks at these events and trends, as in most organisations no one else will be doing this from an HR viewpoint.

Earlier chapters suggested ways of thinking about and assessing the environment, and these will apply equally to the HR strategy. As with strategic changes, it is possible to think deeply about these issues or be superficial in looking at the HR impact. For example the changes in demography in many countries of the world are well documented. It is possible to look at these only in terms of recruitment and retention, and overlook more subtle impacts such as increased diversity in the cultural and ethnic backgrounds of the workforce in certain age groups, making it important that the organisation plans to handle this diversity in the most constructive way. At one extreme there may be a need for training in cultural diversity. At the other there may be a need to modify the work place and work place procedures to make people from minority groups feel more welcome. Laura Tovey[10] in her research found that most organisations in the UK were only planning to deal with the obvious things, and had not considered the less obvious, but potentially more important issues.

Another example is that changes in technology may bring a long term shift in the nature of jobs in a company and in the people who are competent to fill them. Amin Rajan[12] showed in his research how the financial businesses, such as insurance, were changing to require more knowledge workers where previously the overwhelming requirement had been for clerical people.

Figure 21.4 sets out a matrix for considering environmental issues from an HR perspective. This is a special adaptation of the method given in Fig. 7.2 and although the sub-headings given are illustrative, and would need to be expanded to fit the specific situation, they give a good idea of the sort of trends and issues that should be considered in an HR plan.

It is also important to consider the level of environmental turbulence and its impact from an HR view point. This concept, described in detail in Ansoff[13] and Ansoff and McDonnell[14] was summarised in an earlier chapter.

Each level of turbulence calls for different managerial characteristics, because the business has to be managed in a different way. Ansoff and McDonnell provide profiles for management skills, management climate, and management competence required for each level of turbulence.

The implications for HR management are mainly as we move from the present to the future. If the position on the scale of turbulence is changing, it may be that the nature of management in that organisation must also change. This can change succession plans, may have a training implication, and will alter other aspects such as performance management and recruitment policy.

A Strategic Approach to Management Development and Training

Now it is possible to explore the circles on the inner ring of Fig. 21.1. All will be approached in a strategic way. It is worth mentioning that this is not the way in

Assessing the impact of environmental issues on HR activities						
Broad headings	Example checklist	The important changes	Impact	Probability	Importance	How does it impact HR?
Demographic	Age structure of population					
	Migration levels					
	Size of population					
	Diversity of population					
Economic	Inflation reflation/ recession					
	Wage and salary levels					
	Taxation					
Legal	Employment law					
	H & S legal					
	EEC rules					
	Information disclosure					
Technological	IT					
	Production methods					
	Product life cycles					
Infrastructure	Educational system					
Industry/ market	Competitor employment practice					
	Industry norms					
Ecology	Environment movement					
	Pressure groups					
	'Green' attitudes					
	Smoking attitudes					
Social	Work attitudes					
	Cultural differences					
	Educational values					
Political	Likely pressures					
	Government changes					

FIG. 21.4. Assessing the impact of environmental issues on HR activities

which most organisations currently think about HR issues, although research by Harbridge Consulting Group (Kate Ascher[15] and Laura Tovey[10]) shows that an increasing number of organisations have adopted this view.

The concept for management development is shown in Fig. 21.5. The argument is that the philosophy for management development should put emphasis on corporate needs, in addition to the traditional view which looks at individual needs in the context of what the organisation is willing to spend.

In order to make this effective, those drawing up the management development plans and programmes must have an intimate knowledge of the corporate strategy, and the ability to get behind the strategy to the management development actions needed to support it. This may require the actions to survey senior managers as mentioned in the first part of this chapter, additional analysis by human resource specialists who have an appreciation of the firm's strategy as well as a knowledge of their own craft, and a large supply of common sense. Management development and training people who expect to be able to find a company book with all the answers will be disappointed. It is they who have to be proactive and write the book!

My experience suggests that once a company begins to adopt this model, it will find that it also has to change how it assesses individual needs. One possibility is

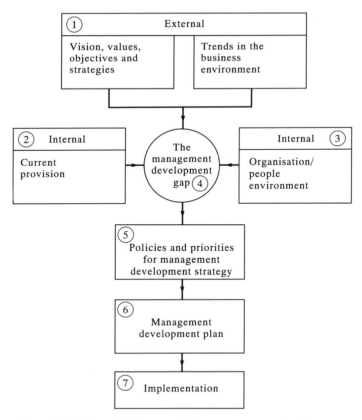

FIG. 21.5. Strategic framework for management development

the use of company relevant competencies, which can be used as a basis for assessing needs. These have value in many methods of assessment, including assessment centres. Some brief thoughts on a strategic approach to competencies will be given later. The assessment of individuals remains an important element of the mix, but a strategic view may well lead to different ways of making that assessment.

Matrices should be developed to help relate individual needs to corporate needs. Figure 21.3 provides a starting point, and the following hypothetical example shows how the corporate need for training in specific skills and knowledge might be derived from the data in this figure. Only the items listed under strategy are considered for the purposes of the example, although in reality all of the strategic sources would be covered. I make no claim that the example covers all that the organisation might require from its managers, nor that the answers would be the same for other companies following a similar strategy.

Strategy	*Corporate Management Development Need*
European expansion	Market planning
	Country cultural differences
	Working of the EC
	Managing change
	Visionary leadership
	Project appraisal
Delayering	Empowerment
	Career management
	Situational leadership
	Interpersonal communication
	Performance management
Strategic alliance	Successful alliance management
	Understanding cultural differences

Such matrices would need to be developed for various levels of management, and possibly for different areas of the organisation, and in some cases for specific jobs. It should also be clear that these matrices are a starting point. Each item needs to be looked at in more detail to specify exactly what the need is, and what sub-topics would also have to be covered.

Another box on the diagram is the audit of current management development provision. All the researches already quoted, and other studies with which I have been involved, suggest that cost benefit analysis is not a regular feature of management development management, and that there is a tendency to hold on to training programmes, and the resources which deliver them, even when there is a high level of dissatisfaction with the providers.

A framework for auditing all current management development activities, of which the majority will be training programmes, is offered in Fig. 21.6. Many organisations find it surprisingly difficult to answer these simple questions, which suggests that the management of the function has been less than professional. (A longer check-list, covering the policy issues, appears in Fig. 21.8.)

```
For each initiative

           1. Aims                        2. Results/current plan

    • Objectives                    • Number of events
                                        planned          1992
    • Corporate goal, KSF or            actual           1991
      strategy supported               actual           1990

    • Other rationale for           • Number of
      initiative                      participants      1992
                                                         1991
    • Target population                                  1990

    • How target population         • Participants as %
      identified?                     of target groups   1992
                                                          1991
    • How are people selected                             1990
      to attend
                                    • When did the initiative
                                      start

                                    • How is it resourced?

                                    • Breakdown of costs

                                    • What are the course
                                      ratings

                                    • How are the benefits
                                      measured

                                    • How has the initiative
                                      contributed to the
                                      objectives?
```

FIG. 21.6. Audit of current training provision

From the gap that emerges out of the audit, it becomes possible to define new policies and priorities for management development. This leads to another box on Fig. 21.5, the development of a management development plan. The final box is a reminder that plans have to be implemented, and to support this some guidance will be given on selecting external resources to help implement the training elements of this plan.

The integration of these various types of information in the approach shown in Fig. 21.6 allows management development to be viewed in a business oriented manner. Most organisations that work in this way change the priorities they had been following, and alter many of their approaches to development and training. It also allows more initiatives which can be tied directly to bottom line results, thereby making it easier to demonstrate the value of training to the organisation.

Figure 21.7 suggests three groups of training needs that might be defined from such a study. Without trying to be dogmatic, because the decisions will vary by company, I have indicated on the diagram possible proportions of corporate effort

Increase areas of overlap to achieve
multiple policy objectives

FIG. 21.7. Some policy issues

that should be devoted to each group. Initially I should like to discuss each circle on the diagram as if it were a watertight entity, but later will try to show how initiatives that fall in the overlap areas of the circle may enhance the value of the initiatives, by killing two or more birds with one stone.

By direct priorities I mean initiatives that contribute directly to corporate aims and objectives, such as training events designed to implement a strategy or structural change, formulate strategy, deal with an issue from the business environment, implement a policy change, change culture to enable a strategy to succeed, or provide solutions to a specific problem or issue. By their nature these needs are likely to be met by initiatives that are action oriented, have bottom line objectives, and have a high degree of urgency. In turn this affects the solutions, which may well be courses that cascade through several levels of an organisation, are entirely run in company and have a high degree of tailoring. Only if they have these characteristics can these initiatives deal with the type of issue that is identified as a direct need.

Indirect priorities may be equally important for the company, and many of the initiatives will be more long term in both their objectives, and the time over which personnel are involved in an initiative. However not all will be lengthy initiatives. Under this heading I include induction training, career development programmes, and actions to improve personal performance. I believe that the policy here should be to tie to long-term objectives where appropriate, to be very clear about the aims of and target population for the initiative. Here there may be a balance between in-company and external initiatives, and a mix of training and development actions.

Many in-company courses under this category would benefit from being tailored, but the depth of tailoring may often be less than for a course dealing with a corporate issue. The decision hangs on the learning objectives of the various components of a course or programme.

The final category are needs which are identified by individuals in discussion with their managers, but which are personal in that they do not have a high corporate priority. If people are motivated to develop themselves, there is likely to be value to the organisation in giving encouragement. What I believe is appropriate here is not company courses, but the creation of a climate of self help, and the provision of support. Under this heading I should consider giving financial support for distance learning, for example, and perhaps establishing a resource centre where self study can take place. In return for this support, I would expect individuals to give some personal time to the course of study.

Clarity emerges from such an analysis, but the benefits to the firm may be increased if deliberate attention is given to the overlap areas. For example indirect needs can be tied closer to direct needs through the use of competencies as the standard against which the developmental and remedial needs of individuals are evaluated. Competency assessment will be the next circle to be considered from Fig. 21.1.

A second way of adding value to "indirect" initiatives is to build in some of the direct issues into the longer term development programmes, through teaching materials and project work.

Another example is to use a workshop initiative to help business units to develop sound strategies, which with modification can be used later for an indirect development need, to train less senior managers in business planning.

Creative thinking can help an organisation obtain much more from management development than the three circle diagram may initially suggest, but the value of the planned approach cannot be over-stressed.

This approach does not mean that organisations should never do any training that can only be looked at as an act of faith. It is a question of balance. Just as it is poor management for the total management development strategy to be built from the bottom up, so it would be equally poor if it were to be totally built from the top down.

There should be a switch from a purely cost based decision on available options, to one of cost benefit analysis. It is common practice for training managers, for example, to take an out of pocket expenses view of training initiatives. The cost of participants' time in attending training initiatives is rarely considered, and almost nobody adds in the real economic factor, the opportunity cost of this time. As a result many current decisions on training matters are aimed at reducing the cost of the initiative, rather than increasing the benefits. This has led to many decisions which are wrong for the companies concerned.

A Different Slant to Assessing Individual Needs

It may be of interest to record that Tovey[10] found that all of her sample of large UK companies used a performance appraisal method to establish needs, and for

40% it was the only method. Only 10% used competency assessment, and assessment centres, where used, were on a selective basis (which is sensible). Other methods such as surveys and assessments by training managers were used by the 60% that did not rely solely on assessment centres.

The annual appraisal interview is a notoriously poor way of assessing development needs, as it depends on two levels of perception, the subordinate and boss, both of which could be erroneous. Greater use of the competency approach can ensure that the right questions are asked, but does not remove the bias.

I have found that bottom up assessment is particularly good at identifying needs that may have otherwise remained hidden, but I have only used this method for looking at management and interpersonal skills. On a confidential basis questionnaires are completed by the subject manager, and by at least three subordinates and/or peers. These are aggregated and the individual reports are not revealed to the subject. What is of value is the "photograph" of management behaviour, which is often different from the self perception. This method can be used in a general way, although there are also approaches which are related to researched topics, such as the management of innovation, leadership, and organisation climate.

Surveys can be a valuable periodic tool, and can be focused on the competencies that are important to the firm. We have found it useful to obtain ratings on perceived abilities and the perceived importance the person places on them. This is particularly useful in a change situation, when management sees the need for new skills, and this view of relevance is not shared by those below them.

The use of assessment centres is well known. What might be less well known is the way in which they can be designed to mirror the strategic requirements of the organisation, both in assuring the selection of the right people for a particular situation, and in identifying the strategically oriented training needs. Most experts in assessment centres come from the industrial psychology route and they give more emphasis to the individual than to the firm. Put a business orientation to assessment centre design and a very powerful tool is created. *HR Reporter*[16] shows how Pratt and Whitney used an assessment centre approach to help restore their competitive position. Their response to being pushed out of the number one position in aero engines by GE was to break down a 21,000 person operation into 52 smaller business units. Managers had to be selected and trained to operate as small business managers, a move considered necessary to respond to the changed business situation.

Conclusions

The strategic view postulated here enables management development, to add more value to the corporation, without necessarily spending more. At the same time it provides a permanent mechanism for aiding the implementation of strategies, an issue which will be discussed in more detail in a later chapter.

Figure 21.8 provides a longer checklist of questions for an audit of management development using the principles of the model in Fig. 21.5.

1. What is management development contributing to the achievement of corporate objectives?

2. Do you know whether it is helping you to gain competitive advantage?

3. How do you know?

4. What explicit connections are there between training initiatives and corporate strategy?

5. When was the management development plan last fully reviewed against the strategic needs of the company?

6. Is there a mechanism for top management involvement in such a review, for example by a regular steering group, or by periodic detailed consideration by the chief executive?

7. How are management development plans determined?

8. Do management development initiatives cascade from top to bottom of the organisation, or is all effort concentrated on one or two levels?

9. When training initiatives are designed to help implement strategies, do you start at the top of the organisation and work down?

10. How are budgets for management development activity determined?

11. Are budgets related to the corporate need, based on a clear management development and training plan, which is broken down into defined and costed projects?

12. What is your total expenditure on management development?

13. Are all elements of expense of management development under the same budgetary responsibility: or is it possible for one part of the organisation to save expense by causing increased costs to another part? (For example, by the training manager choosing a cheaper hotel in the country because this looks better against his budget, but in doing so causing much higher travel costs which fall under other budgets.)

14. Are the opportunity costs of the people attending training programmes identified and considered when planning such courses?

15. Does the control system force actions to minimise the expense of training without any consideration of whether this minimises the return on the opportunity cost?

16. How large is your training budget compared to competitors? In your home country? In other countries?

17. How does your management development effort compare with best practice in the world at large? (e.g. bench-marking yourself against the leaders)

18. When you require a global training initiative to develop a common approach across all subsidiaries, do you run the programme in the language of the company, or do you deliver a programme which keeps the integrity of the original, but makes adjustments for country cultural difference, and offers the programme in the various mother tongues of participants?

19. Do you have a clear policy difference for the different categories of need identified in Figure 21.7?

20. How are people selected to attend a programme: in relation to the corporate need, or on a 'volunteer' basis?

21. How is management development organised in your organisation?

22. Does the structure enable corporate priorities to be identified and addressed?

23. How are differences of perception, about what is of corporate importance, between different areas identified and resolved?

24. How are management development activities coordinated between corporate, divisional head offices, country offices and other organisational units of the organisation?

25. What actions are taken to ensure that management training results in changed behaviour in the job situation?

26. How do you evaluate the effectiveness of a management development initiative?

27. Do you do anything more than give a reactions questionnaire at the end of a course?

28. There are 500-600 providers of training services in the UK alone. Do you understand the differences between the various types of competitor, so that you can relate their particular competencies to your need, or have you stereotyped providers so that you automatically use business schools for senior management initiatives without evaluating whether there are other high quality providers who may be more appropriate for the task?

29. Do you insist that when an outside provider is quoting you for a tailored course that the proposal shows the effort that will be spent researching the course in the company, and developing the right amount of company relevant teaching materials? Are your tailored courses really tailored, in the sense of being unique to your organisation and its needs?

30. How long have you used all your present training suppliers?

31. Is there a mechanism so that you can judge their performance?

FIG. 21.8. Check-list of questions for an audit of management development

A Strategic Approach to Competency Assessment

The idea of defining management standards and competencies is not new, but in the UK received a new emphasis after the publication of the report into management development by Constable and McCormick.[17] This led to the formation of an organisation called the Management Charter Initiative (MCI), one of whose activities was to research and publish generic management competencies for various levels of management. So far competencies have been published for supervisory, first line and middle management (MCI[18-20]). These competencies are intended to "provide a basis against which managers may be assessed, their performance improved and their skills more effectively utilised".

Properly used, competencies have value in management development, manpower and succession planning, recruitment, and performance management.

MCI use the following headings to define competencies:

(i) *Units of Competence:* the broad descriptions of what is expected from a competent person at each level.
(ii) *Elements of Competence:* a break down of the units.
(iii) *Performance Criteria:* which specify the outcomes which have to be achieved for competent performance.
(iv) *Range Statements:* which describe the range of instances and circumstances in which the element is applied.
(v) *Evidence Specifications:* what evidence is required to show that competence is achieved.

The MCI competencies are well loved by the British Government, which likes the idea of standards that can be universally applied, and by many academic organisations, which use them as the basis for developing new educational programmes, in the belief that relevance to industry is thus assured.

While the concept of competencies has undoubted value, the generic approach has serious faults. Figure 21.9 shows in an approximate way how levels of management are affected by the strategic decisions of the firm. While the job of a supervisor may be almost entirely the same, regardless of the vision, values and strategies, it is hard to argue that senior management jobs are equally identical. In the diagram, the black area shows where generic competencies are likely to be of value: the white area where they have doubtful validity. Exact positions of the boundaries will vary by company, so the argument is not that the generic approach is never appropriate, but that how and where it is appropriate will vary considerably between organisations.

A second disadvantage of the MCI approach is that it does not set out to cover all competencies. It aims to cover the generic rather than the functional skill

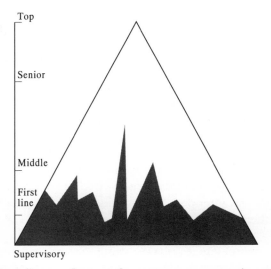

FIG. 21.9. Generalised diagram: Impact of strategy on competencies at various management levels

elements of management jobs. Even if all the generic descriptions were right for a particular organisation, the competencies would still not cover all the things that needed to be done to enable the organisation to achieve strategic success.

One example will suffice to question the value of the generic approach. Two multi-national grocery product companies face up to their markets in very different ways. One operates a global strategy, where country differences are subordinate to the overall strategy. The other works on a multi country basis, with every country operation being an ROI centre, and having a high degree of strategic freedom. The management and business skill competencies for most senior level jobs would be quite different between the companies. A successful country managing director in the global company has to operate in a different way from his competitor in the multi country company. A successful career in one company does not guarantee success in the other.

Figure 21.10 shows a more strategic approach to competency assessment. Like the strategic management development approach, to which it is related, it begins

A strategic approach to competency assessment

FIG. 21.10. A strategic approach to competency assessment. © Harbridge Consulting Group Ltd. Used with permission with a strategic review (step 1). This is fundamentally the process described earlier in this chapter. In step 2 the competencies the company requires at each level, in order to implement the strategy successfully, are defined. These are blended in step 3 with the assessment of required competencies at the level of the key jobs. There is a re-cycling loop at this point, to ensure that the individual competency assessments are properly related to the corporate needs. The most likely issue is that a change of strategy could bring a requirement for new strategic areas of competence which are not seen by those who should be affected, because either they are unaware of the strategy, or of its implications for them. The approach, with case histories illustrating different aspects of its implementation, has been fully documented by Tovey.[21]

To make sense of competencies derived by the above method requires a way of grouping competencies once they have been identified. Figure 21.11 shows a method which we have used, which is related to our research into leadership. The core of the model is flexibility, because it is believed that this is a prerequisite for success in modern competitive conditions. The inner ring consists of the individual skills and attributes each manager should have in order to perform effectively in the particular company situation. The outer ring shows the elements each manager should possess to be an effective leader in the particular company. Other ways of grouping could be used.

Figure 21.12 gives an example of the competencies that might be derived for a specific company under one of the sub-headings of the model in Fig. 21.11. Although some elements might appear in a similar exercise undertaken for a

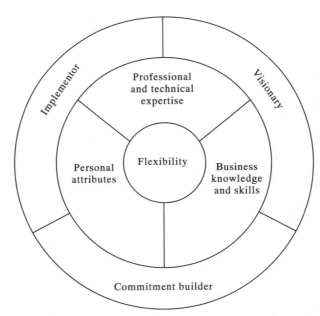

FIG. 21.11. Strategic competency profile. © Harbridge Consulting Group Ltd. Used with permission

Visionary

Conceives longer term direction for the business in the context of opportunities, competitive factors and profit requirements: causes a desired future state to be defined that is realistic, motivating and meaningful to others: shares this with conviction so that people know where they are going and what they have to do to get there.

Strategic thinking

Able to combine analytical method and mental flexibility to produce creative and realistic responses to changing business situations

• Insightful analysis
• Solution oriented questions
•Non linear mind set

Industry and market knowledge

Understands the key external factors and trends which help to shape the direction of the company and underpin the formulation of its vision and mission

• Being customer focused
• Knowing the competitors
• Understanding the external environment

Knowing the company

Understands the key internal factors and issues which enable the best operating decisions to be made for the company, its customers, and the business units and the individuals who work in them

• Strengths and weaknesses/distinctive competencies

Core values

Behaves in a way which reflects the values and beliefs of the company and is consistent with its vision and mission

• Being credible
• Showing conviction
• Display integrity
• Constancy of purpose

FIG. 21.12. Example of competencies related to one element of Fig. 21.11

different organisation, what we find is that there are differences in priorities, detail, and nuances of meaning because of the different business activities and strategies. The example company operates in only one country: additional elements would have to be introduced if it were to have a multi-national strategy. Similarly it is a single industry company. Additional competencies would be needed at the top if the company operated more broadly, perhaps competencies in portfolio management. The reference to customer focus is not because the consultants considered this to be a good thing, but because it was a key plank in the company's strategy. Similarly there is no reference to competence in value based strategy concepts, which there would be in another company which was dedicated to this concept.

Climate and Culture

There are three dimensions to the audit of corporate culture:

(i) What is the current culture?
(ii) What is the desired culture to achieve corporate success?
(iii) What should be done to change or reinforce culture?

In every day terms, organisational climate can be paraphrased as "how it feels to work around here". It is closely related to culture, and some authorities see little difference between the two. It is important because an organisation's climate has a direct impact on what that organisation can achieve. This is increasingly recognised, and some of the major re-positioning moves of large companies have been accompanied by a deliberate attempt to change the culture. Examples include the 1980s drives by Jan Carlsen of Scandinavian Airlines and Jack Welch of General Electric. Publicly announced actions in the UK include those by British Telecom and British Petroleum. It is not easy to change the culture of an organisation, unless there is a crisis situation which is widely accepted, as there are always many factors within the organisation that reinforce the historic situation. What is widely observable is that there are now many top management groups in companies who have assessed what culture they believe is necessary if their companies are to be successful over the next decade, and have issued edicts which say things such as:

Our culture will be open and honest, giving appropriate recognition to and respecting the rights of the individual. The company puts the customer first, and makes decisions as low down the organisation as it can. It is dedicated to creating an environment which encourages entrepreneurial attitudes and individual creativity.

The reality is often different!

Inside the company there is an attitude that the business would be fine if only the customers would stop complaining, no one knows what decisions are being taken at the top, there is no delegation, the people are risk averse, and every one will always try to pass decisions upwards. This example is not an exaggeration.

Figure 21.13 shows the dimensions of climate used by my firm. A critical determinant is the management practices of superior managers. The research on which this model was based, Litwin and Stringer,[22] showed that certain practices dramatically affect climate, that these can be measured objectively by taking a reading from the people who report to the manager, and that any desired changes to climate can best be achieved by persuading managers to modify their work practices in critical areas.

The clusters of practices that have been found to be critical are:

(a) Structure—clarity of roles and responsibilities.
(b) Standards—pressure to improve performances coupled with pride in doing a good job.
(c) Responsibility—the feeling of being in charge of one's own job.
(d) Recognition—the feeling of being rewarded for a job well done.
(e) Support—the feeling of trust and mutual support.
(f) Commitment—a sense of pride in belonging to the organisation.

FIG. 21.13. A model of organisation climate and performance—the determinants. © Harbridge House Inc. Used with permission

The advantage of using an objective method to audit climate is that it is easier to see what is compatible or incompatible with corporate strategy, discussion internally on what should change is focused and has more credibility, it is possible to remeasure at some future time to monitor the effect of changes, and it is possible to compare the cultures in different parts of the company.

Because virtually all ways of looking at climate or culture are proprietary or protected by copyright, it is not possible to provide a check-list for any detailed approach to measuring climate. Readers may care to refer to Handy,[23] where an alternative approach to assessing the culture of organisations is provided. This includes a questionnaire attributed to Harrison.

A Strategic Approach to Succession Planning

Succession planning may be considered as one aspect of manpower planning, and is only looked at separately because of its strong links with management development. It is also possible for an organisation to gain considerable benefit from succession planning without necessarily undertaking any other manpower planning activity.

As with all other HR activities, succession planning can be either a dynamic and powerful tool which supports the corporate strategic effort, or it can be a bureaucratic exercise which results in neat looking succession charts which do not contribute in any way.

Since our approach is strategic, succession planning should begin with a consideration of the impact of the strategies and changes in the external environment on the structure of the organisation. This by now will be a familiar approach, and much of this consideration will have already been given if the analyst has followed the order of this chapter. It is self evident that any change, or projected future change, in key jobs will affect the skills and qualities looked for in any potential successor to the present incumbent. In addition, the nature and pace of change resulting from the strategy, may bring a need for more, or different, managerial positions.

Succession planning also requires a means for identifying people with the potential to move upwards in the organisation. There are dangers if the only means of making this identification is the assessment of superior managers. The dangers include:

(i) Different perceptions across divisions: a person judged in one area not to have succession potential may in fact be better than another from a different area, judged by his or her manager to be a strong candidate.

(ii) There may be a tendency to judge that people have potential, but that they will not be ready for, say, two years. However when the exercise is repeated the following year, the same people are still seen as being two years away from being ready.

(iii) The perception of the superior manager of another person's suitability to succeed may be based on what the job is now, rather than how it will be by the time that person succeeds.

(iv) Judgements may also be biased because the candidate is compared against the manager's belief in his own capabilities. An interesting sidelight is thrown on this by Akira Ichikawa.[24] He observes that all Japanese business leaders are short people, despite the overall growth in the height of the Japanese population. However, leaders are always selected by their predecessors, and the culture means that a successor will not be appointed if he is in any way seen as superior to the present incumbent. Someone who is taller, unless he has family ties, has little hope of appointment. Western culture is somewhat different, but not so different that selection is always unaffected by using oneself as the ruler against which potential successors are measured.

A more balanced view of potential may be obtained if assessment centres are used in addition to assessment by superior manager, and if there is a review mechanism so that all potential successors are considered by a high level management group on a regular basis.

A Strategic Approach to Manpower Planning

Figure 21.14 offers one way to approach the task of preparing a manpower plan. It suggests certain steps which have to be followed in order to end up with a meaningful and comprehensive plan. And as will now be familiar to the point of becoming boring, the critical starting points are the environmental trends and the vision, values and strategies of the company. The strategy issue has been thoroughly debated, and there is no need to add anything at this point. The environ-

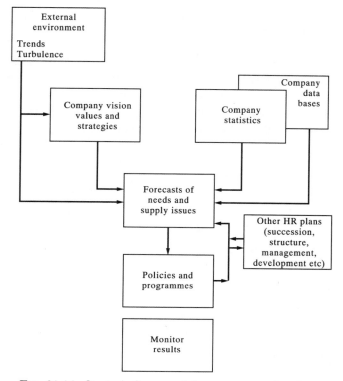

FIG. 21.14. Strategic framework for manpower planning

mental box is worth a brief mention as there are some things to consider which have not so far been dealt with at any length.

If the full audit of the environment has been undertaken carefully, most of the trends which affect manpower planning will have been picked up. Obvious trends include demographic changes, not only to population size and the age structure of that population, but also to ethnic mix at different age levels. For some businesses, the analysis may have to be undertaken at a local level for certain types of labour. Although overall there may be a surplus of a certain type of low grade labour in a country, this may be an academic fact to a company which operates in an area where there is a shortage.

The external study should also cover education and skills. Thus it may be important to understand the changes in the expected output of graduates in certain disciplines, or the speed at which the supply of a profession (for example actuaries) can be adjusted to meet expansion in national demand.

It is almost impossible to make effective use of the information covered in the environment and strategy boxes, unless there is a strong base of company statistics. If, for example, you do not know how many people there are at a particular level or function, there is not much that can be done with an assessment that implies that the company will need this particular skill to support its expansion plan. Without knowledge of the rate of labour turnover, and the reasons for people's leaving, it is impossible to begin to estimate the number of people that the company should plan to recruit.

Figure 21.15 lists some of the statistics that the organisation should be collecting.

Although in most cases the most recent information is the most important, time series can be very useful to allow the study of trends, and to examine the impact of new policies.

In addition there will be needs from time to time for additional information. Behind the regular series of statistics there should be a comprehensive data base, which allows the identification of individuals with particular attributes, and the collection of specific statistics. In addition to basic employment records, the data base might contain details of training given, particular skills (such as language capability), psychological profiles (e.g. tolerance of ambiguity, career aspirations,

---

1. Total number of employees by:

   Grades
   Business areas
   Locations
   Meaningful jobs/skills
   Sex
   Basis of employment (e.g. permanent, part time, etc.)

2. Age and length of service structure by grades, business areas, locations, meaningful jobs/skills and sex.

3. Labour turnover rates, by grades, etc: by age and by service length.

4. Productivity data by grades, business areas, location, meaningful jobs/skills and sex.

5. Potential of employees in critical jobs (see succession planning), and statistics on promotion

6. Accidents and other occupational health data, by activity, location, age etc.

7. Time lost through sickness, by grades, business areas, etc.

8. Industrial relations disputes, by grades, etc.

9. Trade union membership statistics, by union.

10. Recruiting activity and success rates, by grade, etc: number of unfilled vacancies by grade, etc.

11. Overtime statistics, by grade etc.

12. Contract and agency employees, who are substituting for full time employees.

13. Number and type of transfers across business units and across functions: across countries.

14. Number of employees by grade etc who are on secondment or temporary transfer outside of the planning unit.

FIG. 21.15. List of some of the internal statistics needed for manpower planning and particular experience (such as service in a particular country), salary grade and level, and salary history. Competencies could be used as one of the parameters for the data base.

Because all organisations are different, the planner should construct his or her own list of statistics needed. It is not untypical to find even large organisations which have trouble tracking basic statistics, such as the total number of employees each month, and sometimes two conflicting figures are passed to top management: one from the accountants, based on payroll, and the other from the personnel area. While it is possible for there to be legitimate differences in these figures (such as someone being on the payroll in the month following departure because over-time or bonus payments have to be paid), a good place to start an audit of manpower planning is the availability, timeliness and accuracy of the HR statistics.

The interpretative part of the manpower planning process is in the box where forecasts of needs, and the supply issues in meeting them, have to be drawn together. If good information is available, the main problem here is uncertainty. Even forecasts for one year ahead can be inaccurate in a turbulent environment. Those for longer periods may justify considerable sensitivity analysis, so that the impact of changes can be properly understood.

The policies and programmes which result from the forecasts may cover any or all areas of HR management. For some issues the solution may lie in training: for others it may be recruitment or remuneration. And sometimes the right solution is not an HR issue but a change in the management process of the organisation as a whole.

Other Policies

There is only one box left to consider from Fig. 21.1, and this is not looked at in detail, because what is strategic will vary from time to time. For example, remuneration may for much of the time be a purely administrative function. However it may achieve strategic importance if the remuneration policy is hindering achievement of a corporate objective, such as a bonus scheme which emphasises individual effort, whereas the required climate of the company is to emphasise team working. Here the bonus system may be driving people to behave in the wrong way.

One way to determine areas which need attention for strategic reasons is to rate what each activity does to aid the achievement of the corporate objectives. A matrix such as the following may be helpful.

Activity	Hinders 1	2	Scale Neutral 3	4	Helps 5
Recruitment					
Remuneration					
Benefits					
Welfare					
Industrial Relations					
Employee Relations					
Communication					
Pensions					
Records					

This analysis will probably need to be undertaken at various levels in the organisation. Any activities which prove to be strategically critical should then be examined using the principles used for each of the other components of the model.

Intercultural Issues

One area which should receive strategic consideration is cultural differences between countries, and the way these can affect operations. The overall trend is for the management world to become smaller, and for more organisations to mix nationals of various countries in management teams. The assumptions behind this are often that cultural differences will iron themselves out. In the days when a minority of expatriate managers spent long periods of time in other countries this may have been a reasonable assumption. The assumption is not true of most modern business situations, and particularly untrue when organisations are trying to become pan European, or truly global. Of course cultural differences do not only extend to colleague managers, but to customers, suppliers, politicians, and public servants.

Every country has stereotypes of people from other countries, and these get in the way of understanding. A stereotype is a nationally shared view of people from one country, race or religion by people of different countries, race or religions. One of the earliest psychology books I read carries an amusing chapter on stereotypes. A short example appears below:

"The English consider themselves sportsmanlike, reserved, tradition loving, conventional, and intelligent; astonishingly enough, Americans agree, adding however that the English are also sophisticated, courteous, honest, industrious, extremely nationalistic, and, I hardly dare put this down, humourless!" H. Eysenk.[25]

Now ask someone from France and someone from Spain what they think!

Stereotypes get in the way of understanding. An objective understanding of the differences aids communication and enables managers to achieve better results. For example, appraisal systems and reward systems which work well in British and US cultures, can be a total disaster in other countries. This does not mean that the objectives of those schemes cannot be achieved, but that a different vehicle would be more effective. Cultural understanding is not about trying to be like the other person, but being aware of the interaction of your culture and that person's so that you act differently, and interpret differently.

Fortunately we can get behind the stereotypes to at least some of the real differences. The leading authority is Hofstede,[26] whose Institute for Research on Intercultural Management (IRIC) continues to explore and validate intercultural differences. An alternative approach has been developed by Trompenaars.[27]

The Institute for Training in Intercultural Management (ITIM), headquartered in Holland, has links with IRIC. The five dimensions which they use to measure cultural differences between countries have been applied to almost the whole world, with the result that it is possible to study the interaction of any national culture on almost every other culture. The dimensions, taken from ITIM literature (direct quotes in inverted commas) are:

Power Distance: "extent to which the less powerful members of society accept that power is distributed unequally."

Individualism: an individualism/collectivism scale. Are the predominate attitudes to look after the interests of oneself and one's immediate family, or to look after the interests of the group to which one belongs?

Masculinity: Are the dominant values achievement and success (masculine), or caring for others and quality of life (feminine)?

Uncertainty Avoidance: "The extent to which people feel threatened by uncertainty and ambiguity and try to avoid these situations."

Confucian Dynamism: "The extent to which a society exhibits a pragmatic future-oriented perspective rather than a conventional historic or near term view."

The Strategy May Change the Required Skills and Capabilities of the Organisation's Managers

Earlier I gave the example of how a global strategy would affect the competencies required from senior managers, compared to a multi domestic strategy. Same industry, similar products, same market, but different competencies are needed because the management situation is different. However this example was only the tip of the iceberg, and all the elements of Fig. 21.1 may be impacted by strategic changes. In this discussion I am excluding the obvious acquisition of new skills the company does not possess when the strategy takes the company into new technologies or new markets. It is the less obvious that is worth stressing.

In particular I should like to draw attention to two strands of thinking. The first concerns the portfolio techniques which were discussed in Chapters 15 and 16. Pappas,[28] writing about Du Pont, argued that different management skills were required for businesses in different positions on the matrix. An unsigned article in *Business Week*[29] continued this line of thinking. The argument is that it takes different skills and approaches to manage a cash generating business than it does one selected for expansion. Similarly, managing a poor business, which may well be disposed of, is a different matter again. It is possible for a manager to have the flexibility to adjust to the situation, but it is dangerous to assume without careful checking that a successful entrepreneurial type could be equally successful in managing a business for maximum cash.

We can take this idea of situational management a stage further. In Chapter 3 the environmental turbulence concept of Ansoff was discussed. Ansoff and McDonnell[14] deal at considerable length with the position of the organisation on the scale of turbulence, and the implication this has for management competencies, organisational climate and structure. There are considerable variations in the ideal profiles they provide of managers under each of the turbulence headings, under the headings: mentality, external versus internal orientation, time orientation, model of success, risk propensity, power of general management, leadership style, problem solving, knowledge, and leadership skills.

This is not really surprising when one thinks about it, and it is easy to see how an effective manager at level 1, where the environment is repetitive, and there is more administration than entrepreneurship in the job, could be an utter failure if in a level 5 company where the environment is surpriseful and discontinuous. It helps explain many of the problems of managers in the UK's national health service, who for decades have operated at around level 1, and now find themselves at the stroke of the government's pen coping with a level 4 situation. The move to a competitive market type way of operating takes away all the previous stability. It may well be better in the end, but in the short term almost every manager is out of step, in terms of accumulated experience, success formulae, and skills to cope with the new. As outsiders looking in, we can see great needs for culture change, management training, different ways of appraising people, new recruitment policies: in fact something different has to happen in each box on Fig. 21.1.

What is equally important, and much more difficult to spot, is for each organisation to think of where it is now on the scale, and where it is likely to be in the near future. The analysis will not bring the same result for every business in a diversified company, but is likely to throw up many factors that are important for strategic HR planning.

Results of a Comprehensive HR Strategy

The benefit that comes out of a strategic review of HR activity is of course directly related to how well HR is already contributing to the strategic aims of the firm. My experience and research I have been associated with suggests that the organisations which take a strategic view of all aspects of HR management are still in the minority, at least in the UK. If this is correct, most organisations that make a serious attempt to follow the ideas set out in this chapter should obtain considerable benefits.

If every organisation followed the advice of this chapter, there would be a much greater commitment of top management to the critical HR issues, and it would be easier for HR managers to demonstrate the value of their work. Much less would be an act of faith. This seems to me to be a move towards more business oriented and professional HR management than exists in many organisations.

This has been a long chapter, but it by no means exhausts the people issues that must be considered in strategic management. We will meet a few more of them in later chapters.

References

1. McBeath, G. *Organisation and Manpower Planning*, 2nd ed., Business Books, London, 1969.
2. Lynch, J. L. *Making Manpower Effective*, Pan, London, 1968.
3. Bramham, J. *Practical Manpower Planning*, Institute of Personnel Management, London, 1978.
4. Hussey, D. E. "Implementing Corporate Strategy: Using Management Education and Training", *Long Range Planning*, Vol. 18, No. 5, 1985.

5. Bolt, J. F. "Tailor Executive Development to Strategy", *Harvard Business Review*, November/December 1985.

6. Hussey, D. E. *Management Training and Corporate Strategy*, Pergamon, Oxford, 1988.

7. Nilsson, W. P. *Achieving Strategic Goals Through Executive Development*, Addison Wesley, Reading MA, 1987.

8. Bolt, J. F. *Executive Development*, Harper Business, New York, 1989.

9. Salaman, G. *Human Resource Strategies*, Sage, London, 1992.

10. Tovey, L. *Management Training and Development in Large UK Business Organisations*, Harbridge Consulting Group Ltd., London, 1991.

11. Scase, R. and Goffee, R. *Reluctant Managers: Their Work and Lifestyles*, Unwin Hyman, London, 1989.

12. Rajan, A. *Capital People*, Industrial Society, London, 1990.

13. Ansoff, H. I. "Strategic Management in a Historical Perspective", Hussey, D. E. (ed.), *International Review of Strategic Management*, Vol. 1, No. 1, Wiley, Chichester, 1991.

14. Ansoff, H. I. and McDonnell, E. *Implanting Strategic Management*, 2nd ed., Prentice Hall, Hemel Hempstead, 1990.

15. Ascher, K. *Management Training in Large UK Business Organisations*, Harbridge House, London, 1983.

16. *HR Reporter* "Training Small Business Managers for a Big Business Atmosphere", *HR Reporter*, Vol. 3, March, Los Angeles, 1988.

17. Constable, J. and McCormick, R. *The Making of British Managers*, British Institute of Management, 1987.

18. Management Charter Initiative *Occupational Standards for Managers, Management 1 and Assessment Guidance*, London, 1991.

19. Management Charter Initiative *Occupational Standards for Managers, Management II and Assessment Guidance*, London, 1991.

20. Management Charter Initiative *Management Standards, Supervisory Management Standards*, London, 1992.

21. Tovey, L. *Competency Assessment: A Strategic Approach*, Harbridge Consulting Group Ltd., London, 1992.

22. Litwin, G. H. and Stringer, R. H. *Motivation and Organisational Climate*, Division of Research, Harvard Business School, Boston, 1968.

23. Handy, C. B. *Understanding Organisations*, 2nd ed., Penguin, London, 1981.

24. Ichikawa, A. "Leadership as a Form of Culture", Hussey, D. E. (ed.), *International Review of Strategic Management*, Vol. 5, Wiley, Chichester, 1993.

25. Eysenk, H. J. *Uses and Abuses of Psychology*, Penguin, Harmondsworth, 1953.

26. Hofstede, G. *Cultures and Organisation*, McGraw-Hill, London, 1991.

27. Trompenaars, F. *Riding the Waves of Culture*, Economist Books, London, 1993.

28. Pappas, N. "Corporate Planning at Du Pont", *Chemical Engineering Progress*, June 1978.

29. Anon. "Wanted: A Manager to Fit Each Strategy", *Business Week*, February 25 1980.

22

Preparing the Strategic Plan

Several preceding chapters have been devoted to aspects of corporate strategy and the choice between options. In an earlier chapter it was postulated that action was the end product of planning, and that plans were the intermediate product which enabled action to result. So somehow the chief executive or strategic planner, having guided the company through its decisions, has to write all this into a document that can be used as the basis for action.

For many, the preparation of strategic plans will present few difficulties. There are others who find the task of translating concepts into plans a daunting one. This chapter is designed to provide a measure of practical advice about writing a strategic plan, and is supported by a hypothetical example of what such a document might look like.

Once again it should be stressed that the principles discussed here are matters of judgement rather than dogma. There are few approaches that are definitely right or definitely wrong: the best solution is one that works in the circumstances of the company. Nevertheless, a suggested solution is often valuable as a starting point, even though the reader might then choose to approach the task in another way.

A good place to start is with the types of strategic plans that might be prepared. Some planners suggest that the strategic plan should show the broad outline strategy. Each major element should then be treated in greater detail in separate plans dealing with acquisition, diversification, divestment, and research and development.

My own approach has always been slightly different. I believe in the use of project plans for the detailed examination of a particular element of strategy. Thus there might be a project plan to launch a new product, acquire a particular company, or build a new factory. Each of these project plans is a detailed investigation, supported by full financial analysis, and designed to confirm that the conclusions drawn in the strategic plan are still valid. A project plan is always prepared on an "as required" basis and becomes self-extinguishing. It is not the same as a separate long-range plan dealing with one particular aspect of strategy.

I also believe in separating the research and development plan, because once the strategic decisions have been made the administration of the R & D department is no more a matter of strategy than the operations of a marketing department. The definition of what to research and how much to spend on it is very much strategy: the interpretation of these decisions into something that can be implemented is very much an operational task.

I also like to distinguish two other types of top-level plan which form part of the total strategic viewpoint of the company—finance and human resources.

So my approach to writing a strategic plan would be to include all the detail of the acquisition, diversification, and divestment plans, but the major strategic decisions only in the areas of research and development, finance, and manpower. Relevant elements of strategy will, as they begin to harden, be investigated in depth as projects.

There is another point about the subdivision of strategic plans which springs out of statements made earlier in this book. In Chapter 13 it was maintained that strategy and objectives change places in the eyes of different levels in the organisation. The profit objective given a subsidiary is strategy for the parent, an objective for the subsidiary. In Chapter 18 it was argued that the chief executives of subsidiaries could be given a high degree of freedom of strategic decision-making, subject to the overall strategic framework set by the parent. The nature of that freedom will vary depending on whether the company is following a global or multi-country strategy.

It follows from this that part of the strategic task is delegated—again it is stressed that the portion delegated is within a detailed framework—and that certain detailed elements of strategy will not therefore appear in the group strategic plan. Instead these will be worked up in the strategic plans of subsidiaries. In a large multi-national company it is possible to see a network of subsidiary strategic plans, each of which makes a contribution to converting the group outline framework into a defined course of action. To me this appears to be a meaningful subdivision of work.

One rather naive question which is sometimes asked is how long a strategic plan should be. The answer is that all plans should adhere to the principle of good business reports: they should be succinct, and therefore as short as possible, but should also contain all the necessary facts. A strategic plan need not include a blow-by-blow account of the boardroom debates which centred round each strategic decision. It need not necessarily list every course of action considered and rejected, although it is sometimes useful to include decision trees which summarise the main actions and chance events. Any alternatives reserved as contingency plans should be mentioned. The plan should be cross-referenced to the studies and reports which led to the conclusions.

A number of factors influence the length of a plan (quite apart from the style of the person writing it). A complex company, with geographically diverse units operating in several industries, is likely to have a longer document than a company of similar size which is based on one industry in one country. The larger the company, the longer its plan is likely to be, although this is by no means an invariable rule. The ambitious company will have more actions planned than the stagnating company of similar size. A company with major problems and planning many corrective actions may have a more complicated—and therefore longer—

plan than an organisation with few problems. Companies which hug all their decisions to the centre will end up with a fatter document than those which delegate. What goes into corporate strategic plans of a complex multi-national may be based very firmly on portfolio analysis. Important top-management issues are different from those faced by the simpler companies which are illustrated in the example at the end of this chapter.

All this is common sense, and reinforces what we know to be true. The value of a plan is measured by the quality of its content, not its weight, dimensions, or number of pages. The fact that one planner's plans appear different from those described by other companies in articles and at seminars is not significant.

Plans should be presented in a way which makes them easy to read and handle. Nothing is worse than the business document (of any kind) which physically falls to pieces whenever it is used. Plans are meant to be used. It is also a mistake to present them too well. A typeset document, with multi-colour diagrams and bound in leather, may look, smell, and feel impressive: it will also carry a false idea of permanence and authority. Plans are working documents, and those using them should feel free to write on margins, tear out pages, and scribble comments across the text.

Charts and diagrams also help understanding, and can link in to visual aids used in presenting and discussing the plan. Decision trees have already been suggested, and may be augmented by graphs and histograms. Portfolio and risk matrices are of immeasurable value for complex organisations. The key principle is to keep to what is useful and not to chart facts which have little impact on the decisions involved. The idea is not to produce a child's guide, with a picture on every page, but a usable business document.

There can be no firm rules about what items should make up the content of a strategic plan, although I should recommend that the following at least be considered.

Introduction

It is always worth allocating some space to describing the scope of the plan and its relationship with other plans. Because it is as a photograph of a situation, seen at a particular moment of time, every plan has limitations, and it is important that these should be understood by all who read and use the document.

Assumptions

Those assumptions which are important for a proper understanding of the plan should be detailed. Specific opportunities, or problems which spring from these, will appear later in the document, and some form of cross-referencing is useful. General effects of the assumptions will occur throughout the plan and will not need this treatment. In Chapter 5 it was argued that many assumptions defined and used on the way to the final plan are not essential to its interpretation and should not appear in it.

Primary Objective

A statement of the profit objectives of the company, expressed in the way that is most useful for the company. As these objectives will have been accepted by top management at an early stage in planning, there is no need to give all the reasoning which led to the particular choice of figures.

It is sometimes convenient to show in this section how the total objective has been allocated to divisions of the company, and what is the target left to be filled by completely new strategies.

Secondary Objectives and Constraints

The statements of purpose and other similar objectives should be clearly stated, as should the self-imposed constraints under which the company intends to operate. Only factors which are really meaningful to the plan should be included: again, the supporting reasoning should be omitted, as it should already be top management policy.

Strengths, Weaknesses: The Current Situation

In any military plan an appraisal of the current situation is of considerable importance. The same is true of the strategic plan, which should show the main strengths and weaknesses of the company as defined in the corporate appraisal and subsequent work.

This should not be a repetitive listing of factors which have lost their value, and "weaknesses" which have already been corrected should be excluded. The list is designed as an integral part of the plan, not a means of flattering top management by showing how much they have achieved.

The section becomes of much greater value if it is indexed to subsequent parts of the plan which make use of the information, and if the weaknesses are divided into two parts: those which are corrected by the plan and those with which the company has to live for some time to come.

Some companies like to include a narrative appraisal of the current position, emphasising problems and the events which have led to a need for action. Statements of this nature are of considerable value if somebody intends to use them: they are worth little if their only use is as padding to make the report look better.

The key to the decision to include anything in a plan is the value it has in defining, explaining, and recording the intended actions, or in their subsequent monitoring or controlling.

Statement of Expected Results

Somewhere in the plan there must be an interpretation of its meaning in terms of money, and a comparison of results with the targets and objectives set. It is often convenient to have this at this point, so that it summarises actions before the reader becomes involved in the details of strategies. If the "gap" between target and expected results is *not* closed, this is something which top management should be aware of from the beginning, as it will condition their interpretation of the plan.

The expected results should show key figures using the company's standard accounting definitions, but under main summary headings only. The figure should illustrate profits, cash flow, and the main efficiency ratios. It is always helpful to back up this summary with several previous years' history (often a chart of key figures showing the projected position and a long period of history is a key to better understanding).

It is good discipline to include a section here, comparing previous plans with actual results and the new plan. Although I always recommend completion of a strategic plan on a rolling basis, with the opportunity to update and revise annually, this does not mean that changes should be made without thought. Any changes must be made responsibly and the fact that a record is kept helps this to happen.

Risk and Sensitivity

Logically, risk and sensitivity analysis should appear at the end of the plan, since it is difficult to think coherently about the risks attached to a strategy until the strategy itself is understood. On the other hand, the statement of results lacks meaning until those reading the plan have some feel for the profitability of success or failure, and the expected impact of either of these events on the results. Although risk should have been taken into account during the strategic selection process, whatever strategies are finally selected will still carry some risks, and these must be understood by all concerned.

Really, the positioning of this section of the plan is a matter of judgement, and is not the most difficult problem the planner will have to face.

Strategies

The word "strategies" covers innumerable ways in which the meat of the plan—what the company intends to do—may be presented. Some possible ways of analysis are:

(i) By present operations, and then the appropriate choice of main headings from Chapters 14 and 17.
(ii) By strategic business unit, showing, for each, strategies in relation to new and present operations.
(iii) By strategic business areas of operation, perhaps further subdivided under one of the two systems shown above.
(iv) By order of importance to the company: often the most dramatic presentation, but confusing when operations are complex.

One of the problems in writing any plan is that narrative has to be written as a sequence of words, and in most companies even the tightest of prose will run into a number of pages. This makes it hard to see the total picture. A diagrammatic representation of the decision path—perhaps in the form of a decision tree or portfolio matrix—may mean that pages of narrative can be summarised in one diagram, giving an overview which is otherwise difficult to obtain.

"Strategy" should not only include the main actions in the fields of marketing, production, acquisition, and divestment. It should show organisational changes which result from these strategies, manpower policies, financial policies, and, where relevant, ancillary policies such as public relations. Each of these subjects may be taken up in more detail elsewhere, but where the action is an important condition to the success of the company it should have a place in the strategic plan.

Contingency Strategies

Details should be given of those strategic courses of action reserved for contingency purposes.

One point that is often overlooked in the preparation of strategic plans is that the information available at the time the plan is made will vary in quality between strategies, and between one plan and the next. It is therefore not possible for the company to write down each of its strategies with the same degree of exactitude. Some strategic paths will be crude lines on the company's map of its future; others will be painted in finite detail and every bump in the road identified and understood.

To attempt to delay the plan until all strategies can be identified with equal confidence would mean, in many companies, that no plan was ever produced. The problem is that any plan is but a static photograph of a dynamic scene.

The knowledge should not tempt the company into letting its strategy plan become vague and meaningless. Vision is required, but not wistful dreams. some evaluation should have been done, however crude, on every option that appears. It is, in my opinion, also valid to indicate areas in the plan where the company has not yet made up its mind: thus one part of the company's strategy may be to take one of two indicated paths, both of which are subject to further evaluation.

The plan may reveal an intention by the company to enter a particular industry by acquisition. Although the exact cost of this action may not be known, it is possible for the company to have ascertained that acquisition candidates are potentially available within certain limits of capital costs and returns, and that— provided this proves to be true—acquisition is a better choice of action than any other option. Thus the plan can carry the matter much further forward, although there are still some uncertainties.

The company may also, through its strategic plan, have decided to move its factory, sell the old buildings, and update its production equipment. Costs and benefits may initially be known only within broad parameters.

Other actions may have progressed much further—as these two examples will have done by the time subsequent strategic plans are prepared—and the company may have in its possession its final appraisal of its course of action.

It is pleasant to visualise a situation where plans are all neat and tidy, where things can be clearly labelled and pigeonholed, and where the strategic plan can, accordingly, be used as a handbook for a sequence of actions the effect of which is known to the last halfpenny. But we live in a real world, not a fairyland, and it is only occasionally that a company will find that its strategic plan fits so neatly into place that there is nothing to do over the next five to ten years but sit back and watch it all happen. The real world is untidy: so most strategic plans will contain some loose areas with ragged edges. And the world also has a habit of changing!

When a plan is written (and provided it appears that the actions selected are adequate to enable the company to meet its targets) this mixture of levels of detail could result in statements of this kind:

(a) The company will select three of the five courses of action identified in this plan, and will initiate one of them in each of the next three years.
(b) The company will enter the furniture industry in Australia in year two of the plan and will invest up to £1m. in this project, with the intention of breaking even in year one, and with expectations of achieving an internal rate of DCF return of 15% assessed over a fifteen-year period. Five alternative ways of achieving this result have been identified, and a selection of the most beneficial course of action will be made during year one.

In the next planning cycle the company will have completed more of its studies and be in a position to be more specific about some things. In each case the company has committed itself to a strategic course of action although it still has flexibility. It is because there are so many uncertainties that the company needs a portfolio of options: contingency plans that can be brought in at short notice to replace actions which subsequent events show are no longer valid.

No strategic action should be implemented without a final detailed examination. This is the function of the project plans discussed earlier.

In order to help bridge the gap between theory and practice an example is given of a hypothetical strategic plan. Because it is a hypothetical situation, it includes simplifications which enable the plan to be shorter than might be the case in a real situation. This is to avoid boring the reader and although slightly unreal does serve to stress what was stated earlier: that plans of any type should be as short as possible. It is also a plan for a relatively simple company where the concept of strategic business units is not really suitable.

The object of the example is to demonstrate how the document known as the strategic plan might be written. It is not intended to be a study of the actual strategies chosen: for present purposes it is not relevant whether the chief executive of the hypothetical company has chosen wisely or badly.

The example is a strategic plan for a hypothetical company—Thru-Draught Heatvent Co. Ltd.—engaged in heating and ventilating contracting. At present all profits emanate from this activity. Last year's after-tax profit was £250,000 arising from a turnover of £20m. Total capital employed is £10m. giving a return on investment of 2.5%. The company's activities are closely linked with the building trade, and are therefore subject to cyclical fluctuations. In the last five years the lowest after-tax profit was £50,000. Last year's figure is the peak for this period (although higher profits have been achieved in the past), but the current year's estimate is also £250,000.

All the equity is owned, in equal proportions, by four members of one family. More capital is available from family sources if prospects can be improved and if the risk of profit fluctuations can be reduced. Alternatively, the family is willing to consider "going public" and raising equity funds for future development through the stock market. In any case, the company currently has no loan finance.

The managing director is 45 and had held his appointment for about eighteen months. He was brought in from outside, and entered the business on the retirement from executive roles of two of the shareholders. The remaining shareholders hold the positions of production director and financial director respectively.

At the time the new managing director joined the company it was facing a number of problems. He believes that it was his efforts which led to last year's profit improvement. He caused work to begin on a corporate plan shortly after he joined the company, and after much thought, analysis, and internal discussion has now reached a point when he has a detailed five-year plan ready for presentation to the board.

This is the document that is set out on the following pages. May I plead with the purists to take the plan at face value, and not to view it as an exercise in accounting? Anyone who follows the accounting too closely is bound to find anomalies, as the figures were prepared only to give body to the example, and have no particular significance of their own.

Strategic Plan: Years 1–5: Thru-Draught Heatvent Co. Ltd.

1. Introduction

1.1.   This document presents the aims and intentions of the company, and the main strategic path that it should follow. It is an ambitious plan, but one that is achievable and realistic. It also will bring a considerable improvement over results achieved during the previous five years.

1.2.   The plan does not purport to solve all the problems of the company, and has identified many areas where further investigatory work must be carried out before firm conclusions can be reached. This work is in hand, or projected in the plan.

1.3.   Support is given to these board strategies by separate and detailed plans covering the area of finance, manpower and current operations.

2. Assumptions

2.1.   The general level of prices will increase by 8% per year in the first two years of the plan, and thereafter at 6% per year. Steel is expected to increase in price at 8% per year throughout the plan.

2.2.   The company will continue its present pattern of good industrial relations and will not itself be subject to any strikes or disruptive labour disputes.

2.3.   The government will continue to implement its announced five-year programmes for the rebuilding of obsolete hospitals and the establishment of health centres.

3. Primary Objectives

3.1.   The intention is to treble after tax profits by the fifth year of the plan.

	Last year	Current est.	Year 5
After tax profits (£000)	250	250	750
Return on capital employed (%)	2.5	2.5	5

(Note: the minimum acceptable average return on investment for new projects is 12%.)

4. Secondary Objectives and Constraints

4.1.   The company is in the business of environmental control wherever and whenever it is required. It is engaged in the operations of designing, manufacturing, and installing such systems.

4.2.   For the next five-year period the geographical area on which the company will concentrate is Europe.

4.3.   The company intends to be a "good citizen" of each country in which it operates, although it will always give preference to shareholders' interests whenever this is legally possible.

4.4.   The company will always endeavour to treat its employees fairly and to give employees the opportunity of sharing in the growth of the company.

4.5.   Obligations to customers are treated very seriously, and the company prides itself on its high standards of workmanship and quality. It is a matter of fundamental belief for the company that honesty and integrity of performance are more important to it than quick profits, and that in all areas of the company quality specifications must be observed and inferior work rejected.

5. Strengths and Weaknesses

	Strengths	*Implications*
5.1.	A reputation for quality and technical excellence.	See paragraphs 8.1 to 8.4.
5.2.	A special leadership position (55% of domestic market) in specialist heating and ventilation systems for computer rooms, laboratories, and other buildings housing sensitive equipment requiring a high degree of dust and temperature control (currently 15% of sales) split in the ratio 2 domestic to 1 export.	See paragraphs 8.1 to 8.4, 8.8.
5.3.	An established position in European export markets (10% of sales).	
5.4.	Strong technical management.	See paragraphs 8.1 to 8.4.

Weaknesses

5.5.	85% of sales related to general building activity, and consequently subject to fluctuations in volume and profits.	See section 8.
5.6.	40% of profit emanates from the 15% turnover in the specialist control area.	See section 8.
5.7.	One in every five general contracts is undertaken at breakeven, in order to secure the business.	See paragraphs 8.5 and 8.7.

5.8. All business in France (50% of export sales) has been undertaken at a loss due to over-estimation of the competitors' prices.   See paragraph 8.4.

5.9. The company, with its two UK plants, has double its required capacity without allowing for overtime working.   See paragraphs 8.5 and 8.14.

5.10. Marketing management is generally poor.   See paragraph 8.10.

5.11. Management information is rudimentary. Lack of data is a contributory reason for several bad decisions taken in the company.   See paragraph 8.12.

5.12. The company has reached a point when it must make many changes. Its profitability from current operations must be improved, and new activities must be started, both to bring profitable growth and to reduce the effect of profit fluctuations.

5.13. If the company does nothing new and merely continues to operate as at present its turnover will increase to £25m. by the last year of the plan. Profit, at its best estimate, will have declined to £200,000—or much less if the general building industry does not develop at the rate expected. This gives a "gap" of £550,000 between the profit objective and the current forecast, as well as indicating a worsening position and a declining return on investment.

5.14. The company has also to think beyond the five-year period, and must commit research and development resources to produce a new generation of environmental control equipment to meet the needs of the future.

5.15. Many decisions have to be taken, and a new pattern of risks accepted. The company is fortunate in being in a position from which it can make the necessary changes to assure its future.

6. Statement of Expected Results

	Profits (£000)					
	Current year	Year 1	Year 2	Year 3	Year 4	Year 5
Computer and speciality	207	250	350	400	450	500
General building	310	400	420	420	430	430
Licensing	—	50	150	200	250	250
Domestic air conditioning	—	(50)	(50)	50	200	250
Profit contribution	517	650	870	1070	1330	1430
Administration expenses	(100)	(130)	(150)	(160)	(170)	(180)
Profit before tax	417	520	720	910	1160	1250
Tax	167	200	280	365	465	500
Profit after tax	250	320	440	545	695	750

		Current year	Year 5
Capital employed	(£m.)	10	14
ROI	(%)	2.5	5.4

(Detailed cash-flow statements are not shown here—although essential in any plan—but an example will be found in Fig. 31.2)

Note: The simplifying assumption is made that sales and contract completions are the same.

7. Risk and Sensitivity

(Detailed sensitivity analyses are not developed here. Some examples will be found in Chapter 31.)

8. Strategies

Licensing

8.1.   The company has its main strengths in its reputation for quality, its technical skills, and its leadership position in the specialist ventilating field. One of the main areas of expansion will be the further exploitation of these strengths. There are opportunities in Europe and the specialist ventilating market is expanding at 10% per year.

8.2.   To fully exploit this opportunity and attempt to obtain a higher share of the market by the traditional methods would involve major capital expenditures (£500,000), would run at a loss for two or three years, and would have a high degree of risk.

8.3.   The alternative of licensing has therefore been chosen, and negotiations are in an advanced stage with the XYZ Company of Paris to license this company to produce for the French market. This will involve the conversion of our current business in France to the new arrangement, but as these sales have been at a loss this in itself is a means of profit improvement.

8.4.   In return for technical assistance, specifications, the use of brand names and marketing advice, and all rights in France, we will receive a royalty of $7\frac{1}{2}$% of turnover— which will yield an immediate profit of £50,000 in the first year of the plan, rising to £250,000 by year 5.

Operational improvement

8.5.   All current production activities will be rationalised into one factory. This will bring a reduced unit cost and thereby improve the profitability of all contracts.

8.6.   The personnel implications of this move are still under study, but are unlikely to be severe because of the new use that will be made of the factory which will be released in this way (see paragraph 8.14).

8.7.   A deliberate short-term reduction of general building business will be sought and no break-even contracts will be entered into. The effect of this policy on turnover is forecast as:

	Current year	Year 1	Year 2	Year 3	Year 4	Year 5
General building—domestic (£m.)	16	14	13	13.5	14	14

An immediate profit improvement of £90,000 will result from the combination of this policy and the plans outlined in paragraph 8.5.

8.8.   Domestic market concentration will be on the area of greatest strength—the specialist market. Sales forecasts are:

	Current year	Year 1	Year 2	Year 3	Year 4	Year 5
Computer and specialist— domestic (£m.)	2.0	2.25	2.5	3.0	3.5	3.5

8.9.   These forecasts will be achieved through an improved marketing approach (the subject of a separate report), and the results of a continued R & D effort. Profits from this area of our business (net of a continuing £100,000 per year expenditure on R & D) will rise from just over £200,000 this year to £500,000 by year 5.

Organisation and management

8.10.   The marketing department is being strengthened and reorganised under a product management concept. Full supporting services will also be provided. The detailed organisation is the subject of a consultant's report.

8.11.   Increased emphasis will be placed on management development to support the company's intention to expand (see consultant's report). A nucleus of young graduates will be built up, trained in the company, and thus be available for the major diversification discussed below.

8.12.   An information technology strategy will be developed next year, and the first stages of this will be implemented immediately. Training will be provided to managers and secretaries to enable an electronic environment to be operative by the end of next year.

Diversification

8.13.   Anticipated improvement in the efficiency of current operations as outlined above will enable the company to give adequate attention to a major diversification into the home air-conditioner market.

8.14.   Initial products will be based on the technology of an American firm from whom a licence has been obtained, the agreement including technical assistance. Production will be carried out in the factory released from normal production (paragraph 8.5). (Feasibility and market reports are reaching their final stages.)

8.15.   The immediate impact of this strategy will be a reduction of profits in years 1 and 2. Thereafter the project will be profitable and by year 5 will be contributing £250,000. There will be no sales in year 1, the loss in that year being due to initial expenses. Turnover will develop to:

£000			
Year 2	Year 3	Year 4	Year 5
200	500	750	800

8.16.   The project is subject to different risks from those of our present business and should therefore have a stabilising effect on profits.

Finance

8.17.   Full financial implications are developed in the Financial Plan. All requirements can be met if dividends are held to current levels and if short-term needs are met by bank overdraft (£200,000 ceiling) in years 1 and 2.

8.18.   By year 3 the success of these strategies will have been proved. At this point the shareholders may consider "going public". It is because there is doubt over this intention that earnings per share objectives have not been set.

9. Contingency Plans

(This section has not been completed since it has a relationship with risk and sensitivity and is unnecessary for demonstration purposes.)

A Note on the Example

The example was written for the first edition of this book, and although I have updated it a little, I have allowed inflation to make it an example for a much smaller company than was the original intention. Lack of information, which they recognise, means that they have not undertaken careful industry and competitor analysis. Most of us as observers might have many reservations about the particular strategies in favour. However it offers a practical example of what a plan might look like.

In doing this it takes us very neatly to the next chapter. When you are asked to evaluate a strategic plan, such as the one in the example, how do you set about it? In the final event, success is not a question of neat plans, but of sound strategies, properly implemented. In the next chapter there is some guidance on how to think critically about a plan.

23

Evaluating a Business Plan

It is not easy to review a plan that someone else has written, although many of us are required to do just that. If you prepare a plan yourself, you know the background situation, the analytical approaches applied, the gaps in the information used to formulate strategy, and you have a good grasp of all the elements of the strategy. The position may be very different when you are asked to evaluate a plan that someone else has prepared. This may happen in situations where the context is known, such as commenting on the strategic plan for your own company or of one of its divisions. It may also happen when the context is not known, such as when evaluating the plan of another SBU, or foreign subsidiary, or of another organisation in a friendly merger or joint venture situation. Professional organisations, such as banks and accountancy firms, often also frequently face situations when they have to judge plans of other organisations for various purposes. The same need often occurs with management consultants. The problem which this chapter tries to solve is how to begin.

There are at least two aspects which need consideration. The first is the quality of strategic thinking that goes into the plan: the second is the quality of the planning document—the plan—as a communication medium and an aid to implementation. Both are important, and the simple matrix in Fig. 23.1 can be used as a way of exploring their significance.

It is worth spending a little time thinking about this matrix. The preferred situation is when the strategy is sound, and the plan that describes this is clear and concise, yet comprehensive. There can be few attempts at planning that do not strive for this condition. It gives the organisation the best chance of both deciding and implementing the right things.

When the quality of the strategy is good, but the plan is poor, there is a real danger that it will not be communicated adequately. An SBU, for example, may find that the level of corporate support it expects is not forthcoming because of

Adapted from Hussey, D. E. "Evaluating a Business Plan", *Journal of Strategic Change*, March/April 1992, used with permission. (It also appeared in *Strategic Management Review*, Japan Vol. 17, No. 2, 1993.)

Quality of plan

Poor   Good

Quality of
strategy

Poor

Good

FIG. 23.1. Relationship of quality of plan to quality of strategy

misunderstandings over the strategy. At any level there may be a failure to implement if there is no clarity about what has to be done.

Perhaps the most dangerous situation is when the plan is good, and therefore convincing, but the underlying strategy is poor. This can result in the wrong things being done with considerable zeal. The quality of the document may be such that the right questions are never asked about the appropriateness of the strategy. The document looks so good and reads so well that everyone believes the strategy is sound.

The poor/poor box, which is occupied more commonly than is desirable, leads to a situation where little of the planning effort brings any benefit to the organisation. The reasons for this planning failure may be varied. It could be that the rapidity of change in the business environment is too great for traditional approaches to strategic planning to have any impact. It may be that the style of top management makes planning impossible. It may be a lack of competence in those concerned in the planning process.

In this chapter attention will be given to both aspects, but before we start I should like to draw attention to a widely observed tendency which I am sure many readers have themselves noticed about plans.

The "Laws" of Planning

Years ago I defined two laws of planning, which all written plans seemed to follow. They are as noticeable in project plans supporting requests for capital expenditure as they are in strategic plans.

(i) *In any written plan, everything comes right in the third year.* This does not mean that it will come right, only that the plan says it will. The third year is close enough to appear to have meaning, but far enough away to escape retribution. The underlying psychology is that three years is long enough for things to work out.

(ii) *The third year never comes.* My second law of planning is that the bounty of the third year is never delivered. Somehow the cornucopia expected three years ago when the plan was made is as empty in the third year as it was in the first two.

Of course things can come to pass as the plan suggests. However knowing that so many plans show two lean years followed by a time of plenty makes me want to probe very deeply into any plans which follow this pattern. This usually means exploring the information on which the plan was based, as well as studying the strategy itself.

Does It Have a Purpose?

Both of those aspects of the plan which were identified earlier should have a purpose. The most important is the strategic aspect. What objectives are the strategies trying to achieve, and is the expected outcome consistent with the aim? This does not mean that the strategy is sound or the plan good, but it indicates whether the writer believes it to be appropriate. If there are no stated objectives, and the expected results are not stated, the plan will be in a vacuum.

The purpose of the written document should also be understood. Clearly it is to describe the strategy that will achieve the objectives. Behind this is another layer of subtlety: for whom is the plan being written? The written document may well take a different form depending on its target readership, and this will affect any critical evaluation of that plan. For example, a business plan written mainly to record the strategy and communicate it within an organisation that is well aware of the background situation may need to contain much less information about the market and company situation than a plan, covering the same strategy, written to gain the support of a remote parent company. In the latter case the decision makers may have a preferred format for plan presentation, but may lack understanding of the local situation. Part of the rationale for the document may be to persuade and convince upwards, whereas in the first case the purpose was to communicate downwards. A business plan written partly with an intention of gaining support from bankers or major external investors may require a different format again. Before evaluating the quality of a plan, it is worth finding out what it is to be used for.

Testing a Strategy

Strategies may be good or bad, and even a good strategy may fail through poor implementation, or a poor one succeed because of the skill and flair of individual managers. It is useful to test strategies for basic flaws, and the following points are designed to help this process.

Is the Strategy Identified and Clearly Stated?

It is impossible to assess a strategy until the strategy is known, a point which is self evident. Yet surprisingly a very high proportion of the written plans I have seen fail this test. I have ploughed through pages of material on many occasions, and found a history lesson on the company, but have had no idea of the strategy the organisation was following. When this happens there is no plan.

Has It Considered Competitors and the Industry Structure?

Competitive positioning is a critical element of strategy. In addition the strategy should be developed with an awareness of competitors, and the moves which they are likely to make. The competitive structure of the industry will also affect the possible strategies that might be successful, which implies that the strategy should be considered in the context of the industry structure. If the strategy is to break the rules, by changing the power structure of the industry, the method should be clear from the plan. Many of the plans I have examined assume that the desired changes will happen, without there being any reason why they should. Wishful thinking is not the same as a strategy!

Does It Match the Realities of the Market?

All strategies face the test of market realism. New products will only have a chance of succeeding if they meet a requirement of the buyers. Old products will not suddenly increase their sales unless there is a reason. One of the hardest things is to persuade an organisation that has been expanding rapidly on the back of one major consumer durable that there is a saturation point and that product life cycle theories do in fact apply. Equally hard has been to convince companies to strike a note of realism when taking a successful product into a "new" country. People will not necessarily flock to buy that product just because the corporate plan says they should.

Is the Geographical Scope Appropriate?

In some industries the need for global integration is more important than the need for local responsiveness. The "globality" of the industry must be examined, and strategy tested against this. What appears to be sound on a one country basis may not be sound when the global nature of the industry is understood. And this is not a static analysis, in that global pressures affect more industries each year. In the UK I have often found that managers do not take a world view of their businesses. When I helped in implementing the merger of Vickers and Rolls Royce Motors in 1980, one of the major achievements was bringing about an understanding of the global nature of many of the markets. This led to strategies that were quite different from those previously formulated under the assumption of local businesses (see Stopford[1] for a description of this process).

Is It Consistent with Environmental Forces?

The assumptions on which the strategy is based should be stated. No strategy exists in a vacuum, and there are many environmental trends and forces that have an impact on strategy. One test is to examine the extent to which the strategy considers the outside forces.

Are the Levels of Risk Acceptable?

A strategy may look very elegant, but it may also be a disaster if it is a "bet the company" move. In testing a strategy it is important to think of the economic risks the company afford. It may also be valuable to consider whether the chief executive responsible for the strategy is willing to accept the personal risks involved. If not the strategy may be good, but is unlikely to be implemented.

Does It Enhance Shareholder Value?

Some might argue that this test should be number one. I have put it in its present position only because it is not possible to assess the impact on shareholder value until the underlying soundness of the thinking can be gauged. Increasingly companies are using value based planning approaches to measure contributions to shareholder value, effectively expressing the outcome of the plans in discounted cash flow terms. There is more to shareholder value than this. A simple example is whether synergy is gained between business units, or whether they are so competitive that they duplicate resources and miss opportunities for joint working, or shared resources. Another example is the role of a head office and whether it adds value through how it operates, or merely adds to costs.

Does It Match Corporate Competence and Resources?

In other words can it be done? A common fault is for plans to be too ambitious, to ignore existing factors, or to expect things to happen faster than the organisation can implement them. A related question is: does the plan identify and build on core competencies?

Is the Company Structure Appropriate?

Structure and strategy have to be compatible. Even sound strategies can fail if the structure is designed to fulfil a different strategy to the one chosen.

Does It Match the Company Culture?

This is a difficult question to answer, but is important. If the strategy calls on the company to act in a manner totally alien to its culture, the strategy has a high chance of failing unless the culture is changed. Scandinavian Airlines offers a good example. In the early 1980s it introduced a strategy one plank of which was customer responsiveness. The culture at the time was bureaucratic, with all decisions referred upwards. To be responsive meant driving many decisions much lower in the organisation, and to make this happen meant that the company had also a plan for a major change in company culture.

Does It Have an Appropriate Time Horizon?

The plan should be developed to cover the time period necessary to fulfil it. A strategy that ended with a major investment, with no outcomes shown for that investment would clearly be deficient. The plan should not be positioned on the salami system, with just a few slices of investment shown, disguising the fact that the real shape is a tubular sausage and not a flat circle! There may sometimes be a need to develop the strategy for a longer period than the company's planning process requires. In fact one of the problems of business units of a larger corporate entity is that often the corporate planning horizon is too long or too short for their situation.

Does the Plan Have Internal Consistency?

The final test question asks whether the plan is logical and hangs together. It may sound a trivial point to those who plan well themselves, and it is not usually the obvious that goes wrong, such as marketing planning to expand volumes without manufacturing being able to produce them. In my experience the two most common problems are quantification and people. The quantified results of a plan should be related to the strategies in the plan, but sometimes they are put together using ratios and growth factors which do not take account of the costs and rewards of the actual actions planned. The second coordination area which seems to defy logic is the changes that have to be made to structure, culture, and human resources. This section of the plan often appears to be put together without any consideration of the strategies.

The Missing Question

The discerning may feel that this list of points to look out for misses the most important, which is whether the strategy appears sound. This is of course the most critical issue, and one of the most difficult to reduce to a few sentences. Experience in strategic thinking, and knowledge of those principles that have been defined are the two most important elements. Yet experience also shows that because most of the principles are statements of tendency, rather than rigid rules, a strategy that defies the accumulated wisdom of the experts is not necessarily bad.

There is also an element of fashion in strategic thinking, which may be another way of saying that strategies have to fit the age in which they are made. In the 1970s portfolio arguments of having cash cows to fund stars, and wildcats that may become future stars would have figured in the judgements of strategy, whereas today adding shareholder value is seen as of more significance.

However there are some principles, dealt with in greater detail elsewhere in this book, that are worth repeating, even though they cannot be used slavishly.

(1) Porter[2] has codified many principles around the relative positions of the various players in different industry structures. An appropriate strategy for an industry where there is a dominant leader may be totally wrong for a fragmented industry with no entry barriers. There may even be differences between fragmented industries like the guard and patrol sector of the security industry which has little opportunity for differentiation, and few niches, and an industry like management consulting which has many opportunities for differentiation, and numerous niches. An awareness of the industry principles is an essential starting point for evaluating any strategy.

(2) Buzzell and Gale[3] drew a number of lessons from some 15 years' experience of operating the PIMS data base, which collects cause and effect data from its members to allow the derivation of strategic factors. Among other things these principles show the importance of market share, the importance of quality, and the impact of vertical integration. The danger is if anyone tries to interpret these findings blindly. Yes, higher market share is associated with higher profitability, but as the authors point, out using this to justify a strategy to move from the bottom of the share league to the top may be the road to a totally uneconomic course of action.

(3) James[4] offers some interesting thoughts on mega strategies, and draws comparisons between business and military principles. The insights here are of particular value when the strategy involves expansion into another country or market, or when considering defence against an incursion by an invader who is trying to do the same thing to you.

(4) Remember that all the evidence is that more acquisitions fail than succeed. Kitching[5–7] provides many principles derived from research in Europe and the USA, and shows the types of merger that have the highest chance of success. Porter[8] showed that the success chances of mergers and acquisitions had hardly changed since Kitching's work. The practical implication of all this is that I look very hard at any strategy which depends on acquisition, and want to see the actions that are planned to increase the chances of success. In many strategic plans acquisition is a form of cop-out, and a statement of intent to acquire replaces real thought about the situation.

All this advice is important. But in evaluating strategy we can borrow the words of the great economist Alfred Marshall.[9] "It is doubtless true that much of this work has less need of elaborate scientific methods, than of a shrewd mother-wit, of a sound sense of proportion, and of a large experience of life". He goes on to add a qualification "Natural instinct will select rapidly, and combine justly, considerations which are relevant to the issue in hand; but it will select chiefly from those which are familiar; it will seldom lead a man far below the surface, or far beyond the limits of his personal experience". Although it applied to economics, the words are equally relevant to another branch of economic activity, the formulation of strategy.

Testing a Plan for Quality

Plans are written for different purposes, and the particular purpose should be considered when the plan is evaluated. There is a wide spectrum of styles and formats that could be applied, and the suggestions below accept that there is no one right way to write up the plan.

Concise but Clear

A plan should be as brief as possible, but must communicate the strategy: a verbose plan may be less clear than a concise one, particularly if it is also poorly structured. Sometimes, it is useful to impart information that is relevant to the plan: a good plan would probably separate the information (for example, market evolution) from the strategy section, but would demonstrate that the information has been used through the way the strategy is presented. Experiences shows that lengthy narrative information sections that appear in plans often have nothing to do with the decision process in the plan. What is there should be integrated.

Use of Diagrams

One of the best ways of relating strategy to complex data is through diagrammatic displays. For example an industry "map" may show the key data about the competitive structure of the industry on one piece of paper. A portfolio diagram allows the strategic situation of various business units to be compared, again on one piece of paper. Matrix displays of any type may add clarity, compress information, and relate the strategy to the information.

Structure of the Plan

The plan must have a structure, and that structure should aid understanding. Without being dogmatic about order of presentation or content, there should be as a minimum sections on the strategic situation, internal strengths and weaknesses, vision and objectives, the chosen strategies, expected results and the action plan. It does not mean that a plan is bad if it lacks these, but it raises a line of questioning.

Too Many Actions

Corporate strategic plans are fairly broad. Plans at lower levels exchange breadth for depth. In both, a common error is to be over-optimistic about the number of new initiatives that can be implemented in a given period. All strategic actions planned must be considered against the resources of the unit, other claims on time, and should include realistic assessments of the elapsed time an action will take. A plan should not become a do-it-yourself hangman's kit.

Implementation

The final test is around implementation. Even a sound strategy can fail if attention is not given to implementation. The plan should address this, by establishing goals (milestones) to measure progress, breaking down the strategy into main action plans, and dealing with the issues which arise from this.

Issues may include involvement of those who will be required to implement, training in new skills needed to implement, communication and appropriate control mechanisms.

Summary

All of the points in this chapter can be compressed into a few sentences. The evaluator needs to:

—Understand the strategy
—Be convinced of its soundness in relation to industry structure, competitors, the market and the environment
—Be convinced that it fits the competence and resources of the organisation
—Establish that it can be implemented
—Know the purpose for which the plan is written.

References

1.   Stopford, J. M. *Vickers Plc A*, London Business School, 1989.
2.   Porter, M. E. *Competitive Strategy*, Free Press, New York, 1980.
3.   Buzzell, R. D. and Gale, B. T. *The PIMS Principles: Linking Strategy to Performance*, Free Press, New York, 1987.
4.   James, B. G. *Business Wargames*, Penguin Books, London, 1985 (originally published in 1984 by Abacus Books).
5.   Kitching, J. "Why do Mergers Miscarry?", *Harvard Business Review*, Cambridge MA, November/December 1967.
6.   Kitching, J. *Acquisitions in Europe: Causes of Corporate Success and Failure*, Business International, Geneva, 1973.
7.   Kitching, J. "Winning and Losing with European Acquisitions", *Harvard Business Review*, Cambridge MA, March/April 1974.
8.   Porter, M. E. "From Competitive Advantage to Corporate Strategy", *Harvard Business Review*, Cambridge MA, May/June 1987.
9.   Marshall, A. *Principles of Economics*, 8th ed. (my edition was published by Macmillan, London, 1956).

PART 4

Operational Planning

"He that complies against his will,
Is of his own opinion still"–

SAMUEL BUTLER, 1612–1680.

24

Operating Plans

Much has been made of the strategic decision process and the type of plans which are prepared for use at the company's highest levels. There is need for widespread participation of managers in the selection of strategy, and preceding chapters have suggested some ways of achieving this.

It is easy to argue that the strategic plan is the most important document the company possesses. From the use that top management makes of it this undoubtedly has some truth: yet it is rather like the argument that the roof garden of the millionaire's penthouse flat is more important than the foundations of lower storeys of the building. Seen in this light, the argument no longer seems so emphatically strong.

One of the foundations of a sound corporate planning process is a strong system of operational planning: that is, plans for the company's existing areas of business activity. Continuation of an area of activity is in itself a strategic decision (it must be if it is accepted that divestment is a possible alternative of strategy), and top management, with the help of the operating managers concerned, will have tried to define the place of each operational area within the overall strategic framework.

Subject only to the constraints and targets set from the top, the initial task of planning for an existing area of business activity should be completely delegated to the line managers responsible for that area. In other words, having decided the broad parameters, the chief executive should expect the line managers themselves to demonstrate what they should do with the area of business entrusted to them and how they intend to go about providing their share of the action which will attain the corporate objectives. In practice, certain additional elements of strategy may be delegated to managers, such as new products which bear a close relationship with the existing business.

One point which occasionally causes confusion is that many operational managers have dual roles. On one side they are charged with the duty of planning for their own business areas, in doing which they have a subordinate role to the total business strategy. On the other side they may, as members of the top management team, carry an important responsibility in the strategic planning process itself. This dual role—which is encountered in other aspects of management by every executive director—should not prevent the concepts of strategic and operational planning being separated.

This chapter concentrates on long-range operating plans. The questions of short-term plans, and other ways of converting long-range plans to deeds, are discussed in some detail in the future chapters. Because operating plans are a wide subject, most of the examples given here will relate to marketing and production. At the outset it should be stressed that other areas of the company may also be brought into this aspect of planning process: for example, some of the key areas which should receive attention with longer-term aspects in mind may be office accommodation, computer facilities, or a management information system. The simplification is not meant to confuse the complexities which exist in any real situation.

Most people who write about strategic planning, or who are themselves successful practitioners, agree that planning processes must have maximum involvement from managers. Planners should not attempt to do planning on behalf of operating managers and should not construe this as being any part of their duty. They have to make planning happen: they should not themselves make the plans. Pennington[1] makes the point that planners should not seek the participation of managers in preparing their own plans: the emphasis should be that managers should create the plans and the planners participate.

There are few managers who would be content to allow others to plan their actions for them. Planning is an integral part of every manager's task, and a manager is no longer managing if this element of his function is removed from his control.

One decision about the system of planning designed for the company must be which managers should be called upon to prepare a long-range plan, and how far down the line involvement in long-range planning should go. Planning responsibilities must follow organisational lines: it would be a bad system that allowed a manager to bypass a superior and submit a plan directly to the chief executive. As a general rule, the higher the managers are in the organisational pyramid the more they should be involved in the longer-term aspects of planning. Lower levels of management can contribute to idea sessions, and in a much fuller way in short-term planning.

As a guide I would suggest that in any major unit of the company the prime responsibility to prepare a long-range plan must fall on the person in charge. However, he or she should call upon all senior managers with a major responsibility for a part of that unit to contribute a long-range plan for their particular areas and to participate in discussion over the total plan of the unit. The planner—in large companies there may be separate divisional planners for each unit—should assist by helping the manager in charge to split up the planning task.

How these principles work may be seen from the simple example of a marketing manager who has as direct reports a general sales manager, four senior product managers, and a few service areas. Responsibility for preparing the marketing plan must belong to the marketing manager, yet it is good sense for senior managers to be invited to participate in setting the general policy of his department, and therefore to write long-range plans for their own activities. The general sales manager may call for thought contributions—but probably not complete plans—

from the regional managers. The senior product managers should certainly be expected to prepare their plans in conjunction with their assistants.

Unfortunately, strategic management cannot make a dramatic change to the capability of the individual manager. It can help a good manager to become more effective: but even a major increase in the effectiveness of a poor manager is unlikely to change him or her to a good manager. If a manager avoids decisions, the fact that problems are now defined in greater depth will not cause decisions to be made. The really poor manager may seize on planning as a way of avoiding action: it can be used as an excuse; a means of finding all the reasons for not doing things.

The good manager will find benefits. It will lead to better decisions, and provide a clearer knowledge of his or her part in the total company effort. A tool will have been gained which helps to motivate and control subordinates. Such a manager may need help from the planner in learning how to improve planning and use plans more effectively. Unlike the mediocre manager, he or she will benefit from this help.

The reason for stressing this is that there are still some chief executives who believe that planning will solve their management problems and will miraculously turn the dullards into intellectual giants, the sluggards into power packs of energy, and the timid into dashing front runners. Planning may force the chief executive to solve these management problems because it may isolate the weak and mediocre to an extent that they can no longer be ignored. This may force the chief executive to undertake unpleasant tasks to modify the management team, although planning will only be the means of exposure and not the reason for the action.

Any company that begins planning must expect its managers to accept a planning discipline, although this may be only a mild one. Time-tables must be observed, certain key data must be included in plans, their subordinates must be involved, assumptions must be taken into account, the planning process they use must be compatible with the total corporate approach. Most companies write up the essential elements of the system into a handbook or manual (an example is given in Chapter 29).

One of the problems in defining a system of operational planning is that it is very easy to produce a good argument which proves it is impossible. Long-range sales forecasts will be an important element of both the analysis of alternatives and the final plan. It is possible to "prove" that such forecasts must take into account the forward cost structure of the company and be related to general economic trends in the market. Cost accountants will demonstrate that forward costs can only be estimated if production output can be defined in relation to capacities and changing methods of production. And, of course, production will argue that they would welcome the opportunity to produce this data—if only someone would give them a sales forecast.

The procedures must break this circle and thus enable planning to take place. This means that essential time-lags must be allowed for in the system, so that where possible a department only begins its plans when it receives the input of key data from another department. Someone has to set assumptions so that work may proceed: for example, on the cost of goods—so that sales forecasts may be made, and price, promotion, and other strategies linked with them. Information has to be passed from one department to another, and departments whose efforts affect each other must have provision for general discussion, and co-ordination. Opportunity must be given for the final draft of plans to be reviewed to take account of changes caused by the intentions of other departments.

Production cannot, for example, complete their plan until marketing have provided data on sales—quantities, packaging, and product specifications. In turn the production plan may modify that of marketing—to meet the required level of sales may be costly, involve major capital expenditure, or occasionally be completely impossible. Unless the system provides for co-ordination and the exchange of information, plans are unlikely to be very realistic. Although the planner should assist in this co-ordinative task, the responsibility must be shared by the operating managers themselves—and even more by any general manager who has a responsibility for both an area of production and marketing.

The best service a planner can perform is to design the procedures and time-tables so that co-ordination is a matter of course and cannot be avoided, rather than regarding it as a job to be done afterwards.

It was earlier reported that other areas of the company (e.g. IT) might be required to complete operating plans. At the least an expense forecast will be required so that total profit figures may be arrived at. This takes the planner to another decision: How far should service department expenses be allocated to operating divisions? In planning terms, allocation is usually not necessary, and better long-term plans can be made if items such as office accommodation are viewed in total. However, the annual budget probably does allocate. The planner needs to decide how far incompatibilities of budget and long-range plans are acceptable, and whether any compromise is desirable in either or both.

Operating planning can be improved if each planning cycle is formally started, rather than leaving managers to their own devices. This removes any excuses for forgetfulness or failure to complete plans, and at the same time provides an opportunity for providing managers with any planning information they need to have. One good way to begin the process is to issue a letter, setting out the detailed time-table for the cycle, including the dates of any co-ordination and review meetings required, finalisation dates for plans, the names of people who should receive advance information (and when), and an official routing for the completed plans.

At the same time all managers will need to be informed of any assumptions on which plans must be based (a good planning system will have already provided an opportunity for discussion on these). Examination may be requested of specific alternative courses of action: either alternative strategies or the same strategy under different assumptions.

The letter should also provide clear guidance on the strategic policy for each division or subsidiary, which must be taken into account during the preparation of the plan. This can be issued in the form of a set of guidelines to each divisional manager, incorporating the objectives set for the division, stressing areas of weakness which must be corrected, clarifying the availability (or otherwise) of capital for the division, and generally relating the plan to the overall strategy in which it fits.

A good rule is for this letter to be issued and signed by the chief executive, as this can avoid suspicion that the planner is dictating policy, which is not a planner's function. Sometimes it may be simple to separate the guidelines from the time-tables in which case the planner will not cause problems by signing the routine instructions.

If they are planning effectively, every responsible divisonal head will reissue the start-up letter, with their own guidelines added, to each of the managers who is to contribute to the plan. This is an important step because it can avoid subordinate managers wasting their time on ideas and strategies which will ultimately be rejected. Assistance may be given by the planner in preparing these guidelines, but, again, it is important that they be issued by the person responsible and not by the planner.

The system of operational planning should cover the position of committees. Some companies set up "planning committees". These may be useful as forums of co-ordination, discussion, and review, but are dangerous if they are set up to replace the individual planning responsibilities of managers or the planner. Where adequate provision already exists in the company for discussion, special regular committees may be superfluous—although *ad hoc* working parties put together for a particular task are likely to be of considerable value.

Managers who have never before produced written plans frequently find their first plan of great difficulty. The planner can help by ensuring that the planning manual gives clear guidance, by designing the system with the problems of operating management very much in mind, and by being available to give help during the planning cycle.

There are a number of principles which can be applied to any form of plan, and managers should be made aware of these:

(i)   A plan should be concise yet long enough to give a clear understanding of what is intended. Verbosity should be discouraged. Despite the frequent claims by line management that they are short of time, many operating plans are overlong. This is a difficult dilemma for the planner. To request that the plan be rewritten is likely to cause bad feeling, and will certainly mean that even more time is spent on writing plans. A more gentle approach often results in the same mistake being made the following year. Each planner has to find an individual solution to this problem.

(ii) Every well-prepared plan has a purpose. There must be a reason for the plan. It must set out to do something. Failure to understand the purpose frequently leads to the diversion of management thought into unprofitable byways.

(iii) There is always more than one possible course of action. Good planning will identify all practicable alternatives—the decision tree technique is useful here (see Chapter 31).

(iv) The course of action chosen must be properly defined and the reason for the choice understood. Not only must the plan have a purpose, but it must show how that purpose will be attained.

(v)   Results expected from the course of action must be specified so that management can follow the logical outcome of accepting the plan and also measure progress against the plan.

(vi) If the plan is to result in deeds it must allocate responsibilities in a clear way. There must be no doubt over who is to do what task.

What items of information are included in the long-range operating plans will depend on the requirements of the company and its individual components. It will also vary depending on whether the units are businesses with a high degree of strategic freedom, or departments. A dogmatic approach, with piles of forms from corporate headquarters and giving no discretion to individual managers, is likely to be damaging. The object of the planning system is to persuade managers to consider the future and to face up to the challenge of change—it is not to constrain their thoughts along innumerable little boxes on innumerable sheets of paper.

Yet some formalisation of content is necessary. To ask managers to prepare plans without giving them any guidance is merely to increase their problems. Similarly, all financial data must follow some rules or it will not be possible to monitor the plan through the accounting system or even to judge whether results improve or decline. The company's normal accounting definitions should be used although global headings should replace unnecessary (from the planning sense) detail.

Most companies will need to include some forms—or prescribe a format for financial data, which is really the same thing. The golden rule is to keep the forms simple, and few in number, and not—as some companies do—to try to extend the annual budget into the future.

Guidance should also be given on the sort of thing which is likely to be relevant in a plan. Although I believe that every plan should have two parts, a narrative "programme" and a "budget", I believe that the keyword should be "guidance". Managers should be given freedom to write the narrative parts of the plan in their own style and fashion, and to include the essential information in the way that suits them best. At the same time the guidance should be comprehensive enough to cater for the managers who are so new to writing plans that they will follow all the suggestions in the manual as if they were edicts, given force by severe punishments for those who ignore them.

Again, the planner, working with the managers, has to decide individually what the balance is and which approach best suits his company.

All this advice is rather general. It is useful now to look at operating plans for marketing and production to suggest (with examples) how these might be completed. The guidance given here assumes that these are departments within a business unit which is also preparing a strategic plan.

Marketing Plans

Before they can make marketing plans with confidence, all marketing managers will wish to survey the background of information available to them on their products and performance in the market place. At a later stage in the proceedings they will be reviewing their strategies with the chief executive or the board. They, too, will need to have access to facts about the market, although they will not necessarily need to use them other than for reference.

Marketing planning is greatly assisted if the provision of this information is made an integral part of the planning system. It is usually better to treat the background data as an appendix to the plan, bound as a separate document, rather than trying to fit both plan and information between one set of covers.

Marketing is vitally concerned with change in the needs, desires, attitudes, and opinions of its consumers, the way in which product reaches the consumers, and what competitors are doing in the market place. This is something of a simplification of the marketing task, but it is these areas that many forecasts and assessments have to be made if marketing plans are to be more than wild hopes coupled to blind guesses.

Information on the market usually is available from many sources: published economic and demographic statistics, published market studies, specially commissioned market surveys, consumer panels, retail audits, and sales records. Many more sources are available to the dynamic marketing research department.

The co-ordination of data, of varying sources and degrees of accuracy, into a comprehensive handbook is a valuable first step in marketing planning. The discipline ensures an understanding of the available information, and identifies gaps in the dta, where assumptions must be made or additional marketing research commissioned. It is a step that can be justified for every major market (or product), although it may not be worthwhile giving such extensive treatment to minor product areas.

This is an area where I should recommend the company to prepare set formats, so that data for each product area always appears in the same order. Products of a completely different type—e.g. industrial and consumer—may need separate formats. Figure 24.1, reproduced from my earlier work,[2] provides a check-list of the information headings which might be used to develop the format.

Much of the handbook will consist of firm data abstracted from reliable sources, the compilation of which may be a relatively junior task. The handbook should be future oriented—after all, it is for use in planning rather than the control of past results—and for this reason will include certain forecasts and predictions. These, together with assumptions set to cover gaps in the data, are a more senior responsibility. At the least they must be fully accepted by the marketing manager as a reasonable basis for the plans: responsibility for the actions planned from these forecasts remains with the marketing manager.

Carefully prepared handbooks of this nature, updated at regular and frequent intervals, are invaluable for future planning. They help the marketing manager to appraise current strategies against the hard facts and expected developments of the markets. Critical examination of what is currently done is always a good starting point for doing something new. (If the strategy is still valid, there will be no need to change it.) The handbook forces the separation of hunches, informed opinion, and facts: it ensures that where facts are available the manager is aware of them, and that he or she does not guess where there is already knowledge.

From this solid base, the marketing manager is able to venture into the less than solid future.

1. GENERAL DATA
  (a) Population   age and sex
                          region
                          households
                          social class
                          urban/rural
                          working/non-working
  (b) National income   *per capita*
                          per household
                          regional differences

2. PRODUCT PROFILE (by relevant headings as in 1A)
  (a) Demography   present users
                          heavy users
                          non-users
                          competitive product users
  (b) Product image
  (c) Analysis of uses of products
  (d) Time or day of usage analysis
  (e) Frequency of usage
  (f) Frequency of purchase
  (g) Price/volume relationships
  (h) Brand shares

3. DISTRIBUTION (by relevant headings as in 1A)
  (a) Source of purchase   all users
                            heavy users
                            competitive product users
  (b) Brand shares by source of purchase
  (c) Retailer attitudes   to product
                            to company
                            to competitors
  (d) Wholesale attitudes   to product
                            to company
                            to competitors
  (e) Profitability of product retailer
                            compared with all products
                            compared with competitors
  (f) Degree of customer service
                            given for product
                            given by competitors
  (g) Retailer attitudes to trade packing
                            consumer packing

4. MARKET SIZE (by relevant headings as in 1A)
  (a) Definition of market
  (b) Size of total market   by value
                            by quantity
  (c) Market forecasts   by value
                            by quantity
  (d) Market size per pack size
  (e) Details of substitute products
  (f) Quantity and value of market by various channels of distribution

5. PRICE
  (a) Analysis of consumer prices
  (b) Analysis of trade prices

6. PROMOTION
  (a) Advertising   by media
                            by competitor
  (b) Merchandising activity
  (c) Special offer etc. activity
  (d) Response of retailers to promotions

7. MARKET SEGMENTATION

8. HISTORICAL DATA

9. PRODUCT COST DATA   by standard costs
                        by fixed and variable costs

All these headings are indicative only. A full listing can only be made after a study of the firm's particular problems. Such a list can be prepared by any competent marketing manager. There is no significance in the order in which headings appear.

FIG. 24.1. Broad indications of some possible data headings for the market background appendix

The general outline of a marketing plan might well include the following points:

(i) Marketing targets and objectives.
(ii) A sales forecast for each year of the plan (supported by back history) for each main product, or product grouping, and in both value and quantities.
(iii) The marketing strategy for the period of the plan, *in broad outline*.
(iv) Details of price movements planned for each product over the period of the plan (really an element of strategy, but of particular importance if the company is to cope with inflation).
(v) Clear definition of goals so that strategies may be monitored (e.g. future market shares).
(vi) Anticipation of problems and methods designed to deal with them.

The whole marketing programme must be conceived against the background of the market and competitive forces in that market.

One of the most difficult tasks for managers is setting strategy in outline: that is, concentrating on the longer-term elements. Plans frequently contain a great amount of information on the next special offer, this year's market research programme, and very little about the future of the product in the long-term marketing portfolio, the long-term product image that is required, or the improvements needed to enhance its performance. Getting the balance right takes a fair amount of practice: lack of it results in plans which are confused and lengthy.

It is easier to write about marketing strategy if the plan is prepared within a conceptual framework, which means breaking down the total strategy into various elements. A number of classification schemes exist and are widely used by marketing managers, and the planner need not be dogmatic in insisting that plans follow his preferred classifications. Planners will find it useful to have a preference so that they can make a constructive recommendation to managers who do not have an acceptable approach of their own.

A very useful format is the "four P's" approach suggested by McCarthy[3] which divides total marketing strategy into price, product, place, and promotion. (The example planning manual in Chapter 29 provides a fuller description of these terms.)

The company must decide at an early stage how it will treat inflation in its long-range plans (see also the previous chapters on the external environment). In a situation of inflation, price strategy is particularly difficult to plan. Some companies solve the problem by ignoring cost and price rises and making the sweeping assumption that any additional costs will be recovered from the market place. This may make it easier to put plans together, as it simplifies many of the issues. But it is not planning. Avoidance of an issue does not make it disappear: one of the reasons for planning is to help the company cope with future problems, and to pretend that one of the most complex problems of all does not exist is not a solution. In many countries it is not possible to increase prices without government permission. In any circumstances complete recovery of cost increases may take some substantial planning and thought.

In common with any operating plan there should be a section dealing with future organisation structures and people. It is important that line managers give considerable thought to these aspects of their forward plan, even though there will be an overall corporate plan dealing with human resource issues. The reasons why I believe this to be important were given in Chapter 21: that all mangers have a responsibility towards people which they should never be allowed to abdicate. Additionally, any change in marketing requirements and sales efforts may bring a need to change the numbers, types, or relationships of the people required to fulfil the plan. In turn this affects costs and profits. Many plans fail because it is assumed that the present organisation can cope with the future intentions, and the "people problem" is often not recognised until valuable time has been lost. The programme must be supported by the budget section of the plan. Exactly how this is set out, and which information headings are important, must be a matter for the individual company. Accounting definitions will vary between companies, so any general suggestions made must be subject to alteration to suit the particular company.

Nevertheless, a way of setting out the data is suggested in Figs. 24.2 and 24.3. If required an additional line can be inserted in Fig. 24.3 to show quantities by product.

The approach suggested is capable of easy modification to provide separate information for home and export sales although a company should really be thinking of individual markets, rather than an amorphous lump called "export". "Product" may be interpreted as a group of products, or widened to deal with specific pack sizes. Sales costs are shown as allocated to products, although many companies may prefer not to do this. Depreciation is shown as a notation, as it has a place in the financial plan.

Department		Five-year plan 19 –19				£000
Last year 19	Current year 19 Estimated	Five year plan				
		19	19	19	19	19
Total sales (after discounts)						
Cost of goods sold						
Gross margin						
Gross margin (% of sales)						
Direct marketing costs						
Direct marketing contribution						
Direct marketing contribution (% of sales)						
Indirect marketing costs						
Total contribution to company profit						
Notational only – depreciation						

FIG. 24.2. Summary of results

Department.............

Product.............

Five-year plan 19 – 19   £000

Product.............

	Last year 19	Current year (Est) 19	19	19	19	19	19	Last year 19	Current year (Est) 19	19	19	19	19
Sales (after discounts)													
Cost of goods sold													
Gross margin													
% of sales													
Advertising & Promotion													
Product mkg. research													
Direct selling exps:													
Sales force													
Commissions													
Other													
Physical distribution													
Other direct marketing costs													
Total direct marketing contribution													
Direct marketing contribution													
% of sales													

FIG. 24.3. Product details

The essence of the suggested forms is simplicity. Long-range budgets should be supported by a schedule of intended capital expenditures, although these are more likely to occur in a production plan (although they may be heavy in a marketing department which is responsible for physical distribution).

Example of a Format for a Long-range Marketing Plan

Note: The example shows (simplified) extracts from the marketing plan of a hypothetical company. It begins after the definition of objectives and assumptions and shows the general marketing strategy of the company, and the specific strategy for one of its products. All the "facts" were invented for the example, and the reader may assume that the budgets would quantify adequately the revenue and expenditures.

1. General Marketing Strategy

1.1. Introduction
The plan is a continuation of the strategies laid down over the past two years, leading to a reduction in the company's profit-dependence on garden ornaments, and on sales through the specialist garden shop. Garden ornaments currently produce 75% of profits (95% two years ago) and this will be reduced to 50% by year 5. Garden tools and accessories will be the company's major target over the next five years.

1.2. Garden care market
The tools and accessories sector of the market is still increasing at the rate of 30% per year and currently is worth £30m. at retail prices. Ornaments have been declining by 10% per year and the market is worth £10m. The tools and accessories sector is forecast at £45m. by year 5. Some recovery in the ornament market will enable it to reach £12m. over the same period.

There are seven main elements to the company's plan for this market:

   (i) *Brand policy.* All garden accessories and ornaments will in future be marketed under the brand name "garcare". Research shows that this brand has a significant image among consumers, suggesting quality and skilful design, which extends beyond the accessories on which it has hitherto been applied. It is a platform of the long-range plan that this strategy be continued for all *relevant* new product introductions.

  (ii) *Changing the image of garden ornaments.* The intention is to move the products away from the "small suburban" image of garden ornaments, through:

    (a) market segmentation (see (iii) below);
    (b) branding of all products and building up an image to support each product (see (iv) below and product strategies);
    (c) use of public relations to stress the value of the products to all garden lovers;
    (d) product promotion to move selected items from the garden to the home.

(iii) *Market segmentation.* New variants of products will be introduced to segment the market and will be supported by specific promotion through media which reaches the target buyer. The accessory market will be segmented into the "garden fanatic", the "garden lover", and the "keep it tidy" buyers, which research has shown to be meaningful segments.

(iv) *Promotion.* Emphasis on advertising and promotional expenditures will be on the accessory market (60%), group promotion featuring the "garcare" brand for a range of products (25%), and ornaments (15%). (Total promotional expenditure is given in the budget.)

 (v) *Sales force.* A new sales force of forty people will be formed over years 1–2 and the system of agency distribution progressively abandoned. (The distribution targets for individual products are given in the product sheets.) The main target outlet will be the "garden centre" where the company currently has no business. (See personnel section for details of organisation and manpower.)

(vi) *Supermarkets.* The private label participation in this business is worth £1m split equally between the two market areas, of which the company currently has 90% (ornaments) 1% (tools and accessories). An effort will be made to increase the tools and accessory business to 20% of the market by year 2 (see detailed programme).

(vii) *Mail order.* A mail order division will be opened in year 2 (see detailed programme and targets).

1.3. Competition

There are two main competitors in each field ....
(details omitted to simplify the example)

2. Individual Product Strategy—Garden Gnomes

2.1. Promotion

(a) 90% of advertising expenditure will be designed to change the "small garden in suburbia" image of gnomes to the broader "A gnome makes a home", stressing the aesthetic delights of gnomes in both garden and house.

(b) This will be effected through both television and press advertising (exact allocations will be made in the annual plan) over the whole period of the plan.

(c) In addition, the new branded pack will be used promotionally and carry a theme message.

(d) There will be a medium term (two years) public relations campaign with a budget of £5000 per year to stress the novel features of garden gnomes. (Detailed plan to be prepared by Mr. Brown.)

(e) Supporting expenditure by direct mail shots will promote the special gnome for special people theme (e.g. the "Zurich" gnome for persons interested in finance). This will be aimed at the Christmas trade to reduce the winter seasonal drop in sales.

2.2. Distribution

(a) No other branded gnomes are currently on the market. The company aims to increase its overall share (retail audit: value of sales) of the garden gnome market to:

	Goals				
	Years				
Current	1	2	3	4	5
25%	25%	40%	40%	45%	45%

Monitoring responsibility—Mr. Green.

(b) Brand share performance will be increased in the following areas of weakness, through tactical adjustments to local distribution, pricing and in store promotional activities.

		Goals (Retail audit—value)				
	Current	Year				
		1	2	3	4	5
Southern	10%	15%	20%	25%	30%	35%
Midlands	15%	20%	25%	30%	35%	40%
York	10%	15%	20%	25%	30%	35%

Monitoring responsibility—Mr. Green.

(c) Certain minimum penetration levels will be attained in the major outlets through own sales force activity and tactical adjustments to merchandising allowances and tailor made promotions.

		Goals (Retail audit—value)				
	Current	Year				
		1	2	3	4	5
Garden shops	75%	75%	75%	75%	75%	75%
Garden centres	—	35%	70%	75%	80%	90%
Departmental stores	5%	10%	15%	20%	20%	20%
Supermarkets	1%	25%	30%	40%	45%	50%

Monitoring responsibility—Mr. Green.

2.3. Product

(a) The range of normal garden gnomes will be rationalised from twenty-five varieties to not more than twelve, within a two-year period.

Action—Miss Smith.

(b) Up to six special "indoor" gnomes will be available in any one year for the Christmas trade.

Action—Miss Smith.

(c) All products will be packed in branded boxes with transparent display panels, twenty-four to an outer. This change to be effective during year 1.

Action—Miss Smith.

2.4. Price

(a) General retail price policy is to demonstrate the superior quality of the product through a price structure which commands a 2p premium over competitive products. This policy will be maintained.

(b) A new price structure will be designed to provide an incentive for quantity purchase and to meet requirements of supermarkets. This will be introduced in year 1.

Action—Mr. Green.

(c) Production cost increase can be held for years 1 and 2 (through the effect on unit costs of the expected increase in volume), and will rise by about 5% in year 3. New technology will be available by year 4 and should hold costs steady. Price policy will be to maintain prices for two years (unless competitors increase their prices in which case strategy will be reviewed), increase by 10% in year 3 and thereafter hold steady. Regular review of price policy is essential.

Action—Mr. Green.

2.5. Key results

		Year				
	Current	1	2	3	4	5
Sales £000	1000	1400	1675	1750	2000	2250
Advertising and promotion (£000)	75	140	168	175	140	158
Advertising and promotion as % sales	7.5	10	10	10	7	7
Direct marketing contribution (£000)	100	140	250	260	300	335
Direct marketing contribution as % sales	10	15	15	15	15	15

Production Plans

Marketing plans show what products are to be sold, changes of form and pack required for marketing purposes, and the profitability of the products. It was mentioned earlier that, during the planning process, there must be co-ordination with production.

The purpose of the production long-range plan is to show how the marketing requirements can be made available and at what cost. It should examine the capacities of the various areas of the factory, the ways in which these may be changed in the short term (e.g. overtime) and in the long term (new equipment). If the company has more than one production unit it may require a plan for the optimum sourcing of product. It should take account of technological developments, alternative methods of production, and ways of improving profitability (see also Chapter 19).

One area of difficulty in production planning is the objective the unit is to work to. If the accounting system allows the "sale" of product to the marketing department it may be possible to set a "profit" objective. For many companies production will be treated as a cost centre, and the only objectives which can be set are in terms of efficiency—either based on physical units (as with wastage factors) or a maximum standard cost which has to be beaten.

The main reason for the plan must be the profitable running of the production unit and the anticipation—and therefore avoidance—of problems. Terms used in the plan should be internally defined. Capacity calculations may require particular care: in any case it is not enough to examine theoretical annual capacity against forecast requirements, unless some consideration is also given to the pattern of requirements during the year. A product with seasonal peaks may have an average monthly surplus of capacity and yet be unable to meet marketing requirements for six months of the year.

In many instances production planning will require the examination of many options: capital investment or additional labour; overtime or new plant; higher inventories or more capacity to cope with seasonal peaks.

As with all operating plans, the production plan should pay attention to problems of organisation and people, although (as has been stated in the discussion on the marketing plan) the intention should not be to replace an overall personnel plan for the company. The chances are that the production area is the company's biggest employer of labour, it may have the most acute problems in industrial relations or wage negotiations, and it would be unrealistic to request a plan which ignored these factors.

The budget requirements of the production plan should be kept to the simplest terms. Individual product costs of production will appear in the marketing plans, so in most companies it would be superfluous to state them again in the production plan. So the production plan should show summary figures: total expenditures on each of the major raw materials, other direct costs in total for each of the major departments, and production overheads. Again depreciation should be itemised separately to assist cash-flow calculations, a point which applies to any operating plan.

Equally important is the long-range capital budget. In most cases this will deal with broad estimates, but should be designed to give a clear indication of expenditure needed to support the production plan. Each major project should be itemised.

An example is provided of how the narrative section of the long-range plan of one department in a production unit might be set out. General issues of personnel and organisation, and capital and revenue budgets are not included in the example, and would appear as part of the total plan for the unit. The example is meant to provoke thought, and is not intended to be the last word on writing an operating plan: as in almost any other aspect of corporate planning there are many "right" ways of doing the same thing.

Example of a Format for a Long-range Production Plan

Extract from the plan of a hypothetical pharmaceutical company

General Packaging Department

Objective
To package the "SIX" and "OPQ" ranges of pharmaceutical products to the defined standards to ensure compliance with government and health regulations and the quality requirements of marketing.

Production requirements (000 packs)

			Year		
	1	2	3	4	5
Hard packs	80	75	60	60	60
Strip packs	260	280	300	450	325
Auto-line packs	1000	1200	1500	1800	2000
Liquid packs (small)	500	520	550	600	700
Liquid packs (large)	200	200	220	240	250
Total packs	2040	2275	2630	3150	3335

Capacity

All calculations are based on 2000 hours production per year (250 days by 8 hours).

	Packs per year
Automatic tablet counting line	3 million
Syrup packaging (100–150 ml)	2 million
(1–21)	75 million
	Tablets per year
Strip packaging	12.5 million

Programme

(1) Manual packaging. Rationalisation of packs and products (in conjunction with marketing) is expected to steadily reduce the need for manual packaging operations. The need will remain for certain large packs containing 5000 tablets or more tablets as these cannot easily be processed by available automatic or semi-automatic methods.

Action—Rationalisation studies to be completed year 1: implemented years 2–3: Mr. Young. Working party to study ways of mechanisation or work simplification. Report end year 1: Mr. Briggs.

(2) Strip packs. The capacity of this section is estimated at equivalent to 12.5 million tablets per year. Tablet numbers to be processed are:

		Year (million tablets)			
This year	1	2	3	4	5
5.0	12.0	13.0	13.4	14.0	15.0

This suggests that capacity will be exceeded in year 2. It is not planned to order new capacity until year 3 for installation in year 4 (estimated capital cost £5000) because:

(a) This will give time for sales forecasts to be evaluated against results in view of the large increase of sales expected from as yet untried products.

(b) Requirements up to and including year 4 can be met through overtime working, although this becomes less economic in year 4 than purchasing a new machine.
(c) A new machine would double present capacity.

   Action—Check production requirements during year 1—Mr. Young. Evaluation of machine required year 3—Mr. Young.

(3) Automatic tablet packaging line. This line packages the standard range of small tablets into plastic tubes of various sizes. All tablets are currently counted semi-automatically, using King TB-4 electronic counters. Filled tubes are automatically capped, labelled and placed manually in outers. Capacity is adequate for the period of the plan, with sufficient flexibility to meet seasonal factors or unexpected increases in requirements.

Action—Working party to investigate ways of fully automating all aspects of the operating: to report in year 1—Mr. Briggs.

(4) Syrup packaging unit. Seasonal factors are such that syrup packaging capacity will be utilised 50% during the winter months and 25% during the summer. A constraint of higher utilisation is caused in the syrup manufacturing unit which has a lower capacity than the packaging plant. No new plant is required during the life of the plan.

(5) General opportunities. Surplus capacity in various sections of the packaging unit provides an opportunity for increasing revenue by taking in outside contract packaging. This possibility will be investigated (Miss Jones) during year 1, with a view to implementation towards the end of the year. (As this is an unproved opportunity, no account has been taken of it in the budget.)

General

These plans are not produced solely for the benefit of the operating manager. They are an important part of total company planning and must be integrated into the total system. This means that something must happen to them once the operating manager has completed them.

It is worth remembering that operating plans are a form of communication between managers and the chief executive. The planner must not become a blockage. The help and advice given to managers as they complete their plans, the way the planner tried to ensure that they have evaluated the logical implications of each course of action; have studied alternatives; and have taken account of the company assumptions—all these must be carried out in a way which does not destroy the plans as a communication channel.

Good planners will enjoy the confidence of line managers—although this is something which may take time to win—and will be able to help and guide them informally during the planning preparation. The borderline between help and interference is a very fine one which the planner must be careful not to cross.

Plans should be routed to the chief executive through the planner. The planner's task at this stage is to relate the plans to the outline strategy and corporate policies, to check them for completeness, and to co-ordinate them with the plans of other operating divisions. At this stage the planner may informally or formally go back to the manager on aspects of the plan.

Eventually they should be passed through to the chief executive with a note (copied to the line managers concerned) of the main issues for decision—results, areas of risk, main problems, strategic issues, and the like.

There should always be a review of plans by the chief executive and, possibly, other members of the top management team. Reviews may be held of all plans in one major meeting attended by all concerned. Alternatively, and I prefer this, they may be small meetings consisting of the chief executive, planner, the operating manager, and whatever team he wishes to bring with him. Sometimes a private meeting between chief executive and manager may be better, in which case the planner should not expect to attend as a right.

In large companies the strategic planner may have a number of divisional operating plans, all broadly accepted, to integrate into total company strategy. Some companies simply add up the profits and capital needs of all divisions and call that the plan. In my view consolidation is not as simple as that, and may require adjustment to the figures carried through for strategic planning. An example of this is with estimates of capital requirements: in operating plans these are frequently high for two years (where managers have firm projects in mind) and tail off to nothing for the rest of the plan. The planner may need to adjust these estimates.

Review may lead to modification. Once a plan has been agreed and accepted it becomes an instruction from top management to the operating manager to begin to implement, which should lead to the preparation of the tactical plans discussed in Chapter 24.

It is not a blanket authorisation to commit vast sums of capital expenditure, although it is an agreement that, provided the detailed appraisal of the expenditure indicates acceptable results, the capital will be made available. Chaos is often caused in companies where plans are accepted but no thought is given by top management to capital needs. If there is no intent to provide the necessary capital, the lubricant which makes the plan work, the plan itself must be changed.

Techniques may be used to aid the task of operational planning. Some have already been described in earlier chapters, and a number will be discussed later. Success in this type of planning is not a matter of techniques, but of the method of approach and motivation. If this goes wrong, much of the company's planning effort will be wasted. If it succeeds the company will reap many rewards.

References

1. Pennington, M. W. "Why has Planning Failed?", *Long Range Planning*, March 1972.
2. Hussey, D. E. *Introducing Corporate Planning*, Pergamon, 1971.
3. McCarthy, E. J. *Basic Marketing: A Managerial Approach*, Irwin, 1964.

25

Continuous Profit Improvement Programmes

The main part of this chapter was written for the first edition of this book, which was published in 1974. The issue in 1993 was whether it was still valid to include it, given the modern emphasis on Total Quality Management, or as it is sometimes called, Continuous Improvement. Certainly the emphasis of the schemes described here is profit improvement rather than total quality, but this does not make them invalid. The idea of teamwork on a managed basis, widespread involvement of people at many levels, and measurement have much in common with today's approaches to TQM. I believe that there are organisations which could make use of the concepts described here and which are not necessarily following a TQM route. I also know that the concepts work, as I was personally involved in one of the systems described here: the others were researched especially for the book. Perhaps it is significant that three of the four companies which are the subject of this chapter are still leaders in their fields. The fourth, Shell-Mex and BP, was a joint marketing operation which for strategic reasons was dissolved and its activities returned to its two owners.

I decided to retain the chapter and let readers judge for themselves. (Note that the figures quoted were recorded in 1973.) To complete the picture I have added a brief note about TQM at the end of the chapter.

Emphasis has been placed elsewhere on the importance of improving the profitability of current operations and treating improvement projects as a key element of corporate strategy. The appraisal of strengths and weaknesses (Chapter 9) is an important part of the planning process in the course of which a number of areas of profit improvement may be uncovered. One of the points stressed by those who advocate the use of management by objectives (Chapter 20) is the contribution the approach may make to improving the way things are done.

Every manager would unhesitatingly agree that part of the job is to try continuously to find ways of running the operations in a more profitable way, subject to the objectives and constraints of the company. This duty is present at any level of management. In addition most managers are able to call upon specialist services from within the company to help them seek this greater efficiency: operations research, works study, systems analysis, organisation and methods, process development, and many more.

The importance of increasing efficiency (or productivity, if this term is preferred) is accepted, as is the fact that it is one of the major weapons available to business to combat the problems of this modern, inflationary age.

It would be very easy to jump to the conclusion that as all this is true, it is sufficient to leave the improvement of profits on current operations to the responsible managers supported by the in-house service departments. Many companies are, indeed, content to rest the matter there. For some companies this may be the right decision, but there are many for whom it is not. The fact that management consultants, a change of managers, or an exercise such as the corporate appraisal can uncover what are often massive improvements, proves that it is wrong.

At the same time the managers in the companies in which the improvements ae found may be above average in ability and performance. It is worth spending some time to examine the reasons why profit improvements can frequently be identified even in areas controlled by even the best managers.

(i) All managers have many claims on their time. They have a problem of priorities and have to concentrate on the things which seem to them to be the most important. Frequently their priorities are right—but this leaves many things which they never get round to looking at properly.

(ii) It is a human tendency to concentrate on the obvious weaknesses. An area that is making a loss, a system which has bottlenecks, a product which no one will buy, are all problems which jump to their attention. They may not even consider looking at an area under their control which is working well and is not an obvious loss or abnormally high expense. If it works, leave it alone is the usual maxim: they will not be criticised for what works but they may lose their jobs over something that does not, even though the potential profit improvement may be higher in the first instance than in the latter.

(iii) They are judged by results, and this may narrow their objectives to what suits them rather than what the company needs.

(iv) If they are among the lower ranks, they may feel unable to question current policies and procedures. If they are senior managers, and particularly if they feel insecure, they may resent such criticism. "Maintain the *status quo*" becomes an unwritten law.

(v) Probably such managers will be concerned with a relatively narrow field of judgement. They are not in a position to stand back and take a company view because they think this would not be welcomed, and in any case they lack the necessary information about what is going on in other departments.

(vi) They tend to regard things as "done" when they have investigated them: the mental blockage set up when three years ago they thoroughly investigated and improved an area, prevents them from seeing that changes which have occurred since may mean that there is yet another opportunity for improvement.

None of these things mean that a manager is bad, and at least some of them apply to every manager.

Some companies have deliberately set out to overcome these problems by introducing a continuous process of profit improvement. The key elements of all these processes are: they are planned and an attempt is made to remove any haphazardness out of the seeking of improvements; they are participative and involve people within the organisation at all levels, yet they do not usurp the individual authority of managers; they are creative, and designed to cause a change in motivation and attitude, which outlasts the programmes themselves; they have the support of the board; there is an effective monitoring and control system to ensure implementation.

A number of companies have evolved profit improvement programmes of a permanent or semi-permanent nature. References in this chapter will be to the Operations Improvement Programme (OIP) of the giant multi-national Union Carbide, the Profit Improvement Unit (PIU) of Shell-Mex and BP, the Methods change approach of another great multi-national, Procter & Gamble, and British Oxygen's Profit Improvement Plans (PIP). Much of the material in this chapter comes from the helpful information provided by these companies.

The actual investigation and analysis processes recommended in these improvement schemes will sound familiar to anyone with experience of organisation and methods, work study, or any similar technique, and are similar to the approach recommended in this book for conducting a corporate appraisal. Shell-Mex suggest that the following questions be asked: Need the job be done at all? Can it be simplified? Is the part which must be done being done in the most economical way? Union Carbide stresses the use of the technique of value analysis.

Procter & Gamble have given an interesting twist to this basic idea, and their elimination approach, by treating these questions in a different way, succeeds in stimulating constructive thought. The steps in the elimination approach are:

(1) *Select the cost for questioning.* The principle is that an attack is made before the problems arise, any cost being open for questioning. Major costs are examined first: this has maximum impact, and often leads to the elimination of minor costs as well.

(2) *Identify the basic cause.* This is the factor which controls the elimination of the cost, for the whole effort of the approach is to strive for elimination rather than reduction. An answer is sought to the basic question: If it were not for what fact could this cost be eliminated?

(3) *Challenge the basic cause.* If there is no basic cause, the cost should be eliminated. If there is a basic cause it should be challenged by disregarding it. What would happen if the operation were not done, the material was not used, or the equipment removed? If the same or better results may be obtained by eliminating one of these factors, then that particular factor can be eliminated. The area of influence of the basic cause is determined, so that it becomes possible to see what would happen elsewhere if the cause were eliminated.

(4) *Find the key change.* If the cause cannot be disregarded, a change should be sought which will overcome the basic cause. All possible changes should be identified and listed (this is similar to one of the stages in value analysis) and should include ideas which may at first seem ridiculous. These ideas are all evaluated and from them may be chosen the key change: the cheapest feasible change which will eliminate the total cost.

It is claimed that the way in which the question is framed in step 2 forces attention on what is stopping the cost from being eliminated. Conventional questions such as Why are we doing this? identify only the obstacles to change, and cause people to defend and justify the existence of the cost. Perhaps more important than the phrasing itself is Procter & Gamble's contention that this approach is capable of universal application by any person in any area of the company, and that it is so applied. Significant benefits are also claimed by other companies employing a continuous approach to profit improvement. It is interesting to examine the various systems to see how these benefits are obtained.

Shell-Mex and BP tackled this problem by setting up their PIU to administer their programme. This was to supplement the normal and continuous programme of investigation into costs which is the responsibility of each director and general manager as a permanent process. The PIU programme was controlled by a director and was the particular concern of the chief executive. Projects for profit improvement study were agreed at board level, might be in any area of the business, and might cut across normal division lines.

Every project was studied by a team set up for the purpose, the leader usually being one of the nucleus of specialist staff that mans the unit. The other three or four members were drawn from the function or division responsible for the area being studied, and might include people from other functions. It frequently includes an accountant.

The team worked full time on its project, its members being selected for their potential contribution, other arrangements being made for the performance of their normal duties.

An unusual feature of this approach was the appointment of a senior manager from the division concerned to each project team to act as observer, to contribute positively with ideas and suggestions, to attend each meeting to become familiar with the background and arguments on which the final recommendation was based, and to see that the team had a "smooth run" in the division concerned. Observers were not released from their normal duties.

Each project team worked to a deadline, although it might work as a unit for as long as two or three months. The basic principles under which each study was to be conducted outlined the questioning nature of the approach. They stressed that the facts, estimates, and arguments must be assembled and fully discussed with the managers concerned and firm recommendations jointly agreed. The principles accepted that recommendations would cause considerable changes, and project team reports had to demonstrate both the need for changes and their benefits, show how they will be implemented, and identify problems arising from changes and the solution to those problems.

Each project report had to be accepted by the appropriate general manager and subsequently by the board. One part of each report showed the implementation programme and time-tables. Implementation was the duty of the responsible line managers. Monitoring of the actions against the implementation programme was handled by the PIU and ultimately in reports to the board.

In fact the separate PIU only operated for about two years, during which it made a considerable contribution to corporate results. Projects were completed in all areas of the company and covered a wide range of subjects: for example, distribution, hiring of warehouse facilities, the purchase of utilities (electricity, gas, water, etc.), and order handling. The approach was used in organisational studies of the public relations and advertising and purchasing departments. In two years about forty projects were covered with a saving in costs, where applicable, of at least £5m. over five years.

The organisers maintain that the formal system was stopped, i.e. the maintenance of a full-time unit, because it ran out of projects which could justify the maintenance of a full-time unit. They considered, however, that it left behind an improved motivation and understanding by all managers that they were encouraged to challenge any established procedures, however sacred, and an addiction to the team approach. Apart from considerable monetary savings there was a benefit in motivation. This has been borne out in that whilst the unit itself has been disbanded, the PIU project system continued in use in all the senses set out above for major projects.

The experience of all the companies tends to support in varying degrees the view of Procter & Gamble that while any costs are incurred at all there is something that can be eliminated. Indeed, it is a basic principle of the Procter & Gamble approach that the end is never reached. Shell-Mex and BP have, however, found that the intensity of operation of PIU needs to be varied over time.

Procter & Gamble's view is backed by a long experience which began in the United States in 1946, and, in the United Kingdom, the level of savings increased annually until in the late sixties they were running at about 4% of annual production value. Union Carbide's OIP (Fig. 25.1) started in the United States in the 1950s, but only became a corporate wide effort in 1964. British Oxygen began hesitantly in 1967; its PIP, established on a divisional rather than a corporate basis, led to a number of improvement programmes and a variety of experience.

One of the principles of Procter & Gamble's Method Change is that it is defined as a part of every manager's job that he must investigate change in his department instead of just maintaining efficiency. It was accepted that there must be management involvement in change if the natural resistance to new ideas was to be overcome and to avoid the feeling that change was imposed by staff experts. From this Procter & Gamble evolved the idea of setting up methods teams. A team was set up for each process group, led by the manager of that group, and including his or her departmental manager, and representatives from the engineering and maintenance units which serviced that group. A methods engineer services the teams

(Exhibit 1)

OPERATIONS IMPROVEMENT PROPOSAL   (To be inserted
                                          by coordinator)

Location: Date: OIP project no.

To: Submitted by:

Title:

Description:

Equipment requirements:

Estimated cost to implement: Capital $ Non-capital $
Estimated by:

Estimated savings: $ Recurring (plant)   ☐
                                 Recurring (non-plant) ☐
                                 Non-recurring   ☐

Basis for estimated savings:

To be filled out by coordinator

Coordinator's name
and department: Date acknowledged:

Reviewed by:
(Advisory Board Members)   Date reviewed:

Action: assigned to   For implementation   ☐
                                 For study   ☐
                                 For team study   ☐
                                 Rejected   ☐

Comment:

FIG. 25.1

Status of OIP Project

Project no. . . . .

Dept. & location . . . . Coordinator

Title . . . .

Assigned to . . . . Date. . . . .

Estimated savings . . . . Type savings . . . .

Estimated completion date. . . . . Est. cost of study . . . .

Team members. . . . .

Date report submitted. . . . . To. . . . . By . . . .

Proposal savings . . . .

Proposal cost to implement: Capital . . . . Non-capital . . . .

Date	Activity record
. . . .	. . . .
. . . .	. . . .
. . . .	. . . .
. . . .	. . . .
. . . .	. . . .
. . . .	. . . .
. . . .	. . . .
. . . .	. . . .
. . . .	. . . .

FIG. 25.1

MASTER INVENTORY OF PROJECTS AND STATUS

Project no.	Date proposed	Project title	Action dates					
			Completed	Accepted dates		Rejected	Rejection review
				Implementation	Study		

FIG. 25.1. Three of the forms used in Union Carbide's OIP. (Reproduced by permission of Union Carbide)

and acts as a co-ordinator. Later the approach moved out of the factory and throughout all areas of the business.

Each team is motivated through the need to achieve certain targets which had previously been jointly agreed by its members as acceptable.

Procter & Gamble put considerable effort behind their philosophy of change, recognising that little progress is possible unless managers have a belief in this method of approach and are consequently willing to devote adequate time and thought to it. Experience has proved that method change works best when large numbers of people are involved in it. It is also a philosophy which has top management conviction, and is accordingly woven into other aspects of the company's management processes, its views on organisational development, and its personnel and training policies. Procter & Gamble believe that the overall effect of their policies is to give the organisation a flexibility and enthusiasm for change. Monetary returns more than justify the 5% of his time which the average team member spends on method change.

Similar views, manifested in a different approach, can be seen in Union Carbide's OIP which is defined as "an organised effort to manage improvement on a continuing basis". The programme seeks to find problems, solve them, and make the solutions effective.

Like Procter & Gamble, Carbide work to monetary targets, starting with a corporate-wide goal, which is later extended to individual divisions and units. The target is expressed as a percentage of total annual cost.

OIP works through co-ordinators at a corporate, divisional, and unit level. It is held to be a divisional responsibility, and the link between corporate and divisional co-ordinators is one of a close co-operative working relationship and is informal. Most co-ordinators carry on with their normal job in addition to OIP duties.

A co-ordinator's task, at whatever level in the organisation, is to work with the responsible managers to establish a programme to meet the monetary goal. In some cases the manager may opt to be the co-ordinator. The co-ordinator has to spread and teach the philosophy within the unit (including the techniques), act as an administrative channel for project ideas, and exchange information through corporate headquarters with other co-ordinators.

The three basic principles behind the approach are:

(i) Involvement of personnel at all levels.
(ii) Co-ordination of effort on a corporate-wide basis.
(iii) Teamwork approach to the solution of problems.

Any employee may submit project ideas to the co-ordinator, who prepares a master list of proposals, from which an advisory board of managers from that unit adopts, recommends for further study, or rejects the idea concerned. Responsibility for individual or team action is assigned by the advisory board. Final decisions to act are the prerogative of the responsible manager so that in no way is authority usurped.

Progress of individual projects and overall progress against the monetary target are monitored by the co-ordinator and the advisory board.

One feature is the insistence that there be an OIP plan set annually for the forthcoming year.

British Oxygen was able to benefit from the experience of both Procter & Gamble and Union Carbide, and maintain that PIP should not be imposed on any division in the company. As improvement is a management responsibility it is up to each manager to decide whether to use PIP to fulfil this. Perhaps one reason for this voluntary approach is a belief—based on in-company experience—that PIP only works when the senior managers of the division can be seen to be genuinely committed to it. Lip-service to orders from corporate headquarters and without enthusiasm ensures that PIP will fail.

British Oxygen also found that teams could only be kept working effectively if an individual was given the responsibility to keep them enthusiastic. This is akin to the need Union Carbide determined for its co-ordinators.

Team work is perhaps stressed more by British Oxygen than Union Carbide. A number of teams may be set up to produce and investigate ideas, their recommendations controlled by a local review panel. Teams have been found to work better when motivated by pre-set goals.

The local review panel exists to make sure that suggested projects neither duplicate work being carried out elsewhere nor cut across long-term plans. Detailed work on a project may not proceed until it has been passed by the review panel. Once the full analysis and evaluation has been completed by the team, the project again goes for approval to the panel who, if they accept it, delegate responsibility to someone to implement it.

It is interesting to contrast the approaches to the selection of projects. Shell-Mex and BP chose their projects at board level—although it would be a mistake to assume that they took no suggestions from less senior managers. The result of this top-down approach is inevitably a concentration on major (or potentially major) cost reduction areas, and on rather broad projects. One of the practical problems that had to be overcome was the definition of the terms of reference for each project, which had to be broad enough to allow the team to cover enough of the problem to be effective, but not so broad that the investigation was impossible to complete.

The other companies have designed their schemes so that, although there is top management involvement, ideas are generated from all levels in the organisation. The effect of this is that projects, or many of them, tend to be narrower and more numerous. Although there may be some projects which produce massive savings, the majority are comparatively small in their effect. The larger projects receive a higher priority, but nevertheless the numerous small improvements are cumulatively worth a considerable amount.

The continued discovery of change areas by people from all levels in the company is possibly one reason why these schemes have not run out of projects, and can continue contributing to profits for—as Procter & Gamble claim—an indefinite period.

All of the four companies have achieved worthwhile results. Some of Shell-Mex and BP's success areas have already been mentioned. British Oxygen claim to have improved profits by £500,000 per year through PIP, and believe that the scheme has considerably improved motivation in the units that apply it.

Procter & Gamble are enthusiastic about their results, the effect of which may be best expressed in their own words, from the English company's 1964 annual report:

"The criterion for efficient manufacture and marketing must be represented by the real price the housewife pays for the goods we sell. In the past ten years while the official Retail Price Index has advanced by about a third, the average retail price of the company's main products—packaged powders for the weekly wash—has increased by only about a twentieth. During the same period our basic wage rates have increased by 69% and the performance of our products has improved. . . ."

A few of the successful Proctor & Gamble projects are illustrated in Fig. 25.2. These have been set out in a way that shows the analytical approach described earlier in this chapter.

One point worth stressing in any improvement scheme is that management has to make sure that projects are implemented. Nothing is more damaging to the programme than a belief by the proposers of projects that their work is being ignored. It is for this reason that Union Carbide insists that co-ordinators write to thank anyone who proposes an idea and keep them informed about what happens to it. Any change in methods or procedures requires a management discipline, and there is nothing more disheartening than to see a company which lacks this. If management does not intend to enforce the new rules and thus implement the changes suggested by the improvement scheme, it might as well save everybody's time.

If any general conclusions can be drawn from the experience of these companies which use continuous profit improvement schemes, it is that they are more applicable to the larger company (although the actual techniques, be they the elimination approach or conventional value analysis, are valid for any business unit). What is available to any company, regardless of size, is the profit improvement attitude. This alone is worth striving for, although it requires much more from top management than the erection of a suggestion box in the factory.

Whatever the approach chosen, the corporate planner of every company should ensure that some attention is given to profit improvement.

Extracts from Union Carbide's OIP Manual

(Reproduced with the Permission of Union Carbide)

Establishing an Inventory of Proposals for Improvement

This phase of the Operations Improvement Program is the first active or participative phase. In this phase it is desired to establish the habit of having everyone in the organization seeking actively for possible ways to improve some operation, procedure or action which is going on within the corporation. It is desired to have every single function carried out under constant scrutiny by all those who come in contact with it so that possible means for improvement can be continuously generated. The fundamental concept involved in this phase is that improving is not a one-man job; it is a job, and a very essential part of the job, of every single individual within an

Stages	Tank field at factories	Fat splitting for soap manufacture	Van loading and unloading	Buying dept. order forms
1. Select the cost for questioning.	The costs of tanks for storing oils and fats before they are processed.	The cost of oil filtration.	(a) The cost of hand-loading vans at depots. (b) The cost of unloading them at shops.	The cost of the copy order form filed in buyer's offices
2. Identify the basic cause.	The need to hold stocks in order to maintain production.	If it were not for what fact could this cost be eliminated? Filtration could be eliminated if it were not for the fact that there is dirt in the oil.	(a) The need for getting cases from the depot on to the van. (b) The need for off-loading at the other end.	The occasional need for buyers to have routine details of an order to hand.
3. Challenge the basic cause by disregarding it.	If stocks were not held what would happen? Production would stop if there were no reserves to draw on; and it would not be economical or practical to have separate small deliveries made just as and when wanted. It cannot be disregarded. In what ways can it be attacked? (a) Build the tanks under-ground and save space usage costs. (b) Stack tanks one on top of the other, save space, reduce construction and heating costs, etc. This latter has been done at Manchester factory	If the oil were not filtered, what would happen? Dirt is removed anyway in the later distillation process. The end product would therefore not be affected. Would the dirt foul the fat-splitting equipment? A careful experiment showed that the equipment was not significantly fouled. No difficulties would arise if dirt were not filtered out of the oil. Filtration was eliminated.	Do they matter? Yes, both are necessary because vans are the means of distributing goods to the shop. If they cannot be disregarded how can they be attacked? (a) Put the cases into the vans on pallets and by fork-lift truck. This cut loading time but made unloading more difficult. (b) Change the type of van by putting in side doors. This makes unloading easier because with cases stacked in columns the driver doesn't have to dig for the brands and sizes he wants at any given shop. He can get at them from three sides.	Would it matter if this copy were scrapped? Not if the majority of this part of a buyer's work could be delegated to trace clerks (who had to have a copy of each order in any case so as to be able to follow it up). One copy of the order form has been eliminated. Should a buyer need to refer to an order he can consult the trace clerk in the office just outside his own. The duties which previously necessitated his consulting the copy order are now carried out by his tracer. This means more efficiency, less filing, less paper and lower stationery costs.

FIG. 25.2.   Examples of Proctor & Gamble's method change

organization. Actually every individual in an organization has something at stake and should realize that their own wellbeing is also involved in this action.

It is desired to establish on the part of everyone the habit of taking a cold, hard, objective look at everything they do. If this is done, it is not long before the entire organization comes to the realization that a tremendous number of things that we do every day need improving. Furthermore, it is not long until the realization is reached that these things can be improved—and without too much difficulty. A large pool of possible improvement proposals is desired so that we can get the *most savings* for the *least effort* at the *lowest cost*. It is desired to establish a continuing backlog of short-, medium- and long-range projects for improvement. To keep the effort balanced and the right kind of project available for the manpower that happens to be available at any one time, such a backlog of proposals is necessary.

To maintain this backlog it is desirable to continue to add to the list as fast or faster than the items can be removed from the list by implementation.

In considering the need for a backlog of improvement proposals, consider the magnitude of various tasks. A major proposal such as a revamping of an entire plant will tie up an engineering organization for a long time. On the other hand, while this particular part of the organization is being tied up on a long-range program, the rest of the organization is doing little. Later on when the engineering group has been relieved from the pressure of the long-range program, other people are busy getting the new facility into operation, and the engineering group has a much lower work content than previously.

In the same manner, many smaller projects can be generated and implemented within the department in which they are generated, or at least with a minimum of engineering help. Other projects can perhaps be implemented by an outside organization with very little requirement for aid from the internal engineering group. Thus it takes all kinds of projects to provide a balanced work load in any organization. Perhaps the key is that a specific attainable schedule of objectives or improvement proposals acts as a definite challenge to the organizational group involved. Management must assume a key role in setting specific and not general objectives, selecting areas for major improvement, working out time schedules, priorities, assignments and allocation of manpower. Extensive thought must be given in advance to planning each year's improvement program.

The generation of an inventory of improvement proposals will result from a systematic search as well as a subconscious effort on the part of every individual in the organization. Ultimately the conscious effort becomes a subconscious habit.

Thus the first phase is considered to be the act of establishing the habit of having everyone ask searching questions about everything that he does—and then searching for the answers. This questioning process can be expedited by the use of a check list and certain questions which act as a guide in reviewing areas for possible weaknesses and opportunities to improve. In taking a cold, hard look at an operation one should examine it from the standpoint of elimination, of combining, of changing it and of simplifying it. One should examine the motion pattern used, the tools, gauges, work place and equipment, the sequence of work, the design of the product and the raw materials or partially-finished materials used in the product.

There are six very simple thought-starting questions:

WHAT?
WHY?
WHERE?
WHO?
WHEN?
HOW?

Constant use of these six thought-starter questions will establish the habit of questioning.

A more detailed listing of these questions and the thoughts which can be generated by them will be found in the following pages. These should be gone over with the staff group prior to embarking upon the initial effort to find some improvement proposals. If the trip through an operating department is made after this review, a substantial quantity of improvement possibilities can be expected.

The procedures used in formal problem-solving sessions also contribute very strongly to the ability of finding improvement possibilities. This will become readily apparent as one of these techniques—Value Analysis—is studied. This procedure is used to reach the underlying causes for waste or inefficiences and establishes the various procedures for determining the prime function and for finding more creative approaches.

General Check List for Job Improvement

Can we eliminate by:

1. Changing material
2. Changing dimensions
3. Revising design or specification
4. Standardizing operations
5. Having material packaged for better handling
6. Making instead of buying
7. Buying instead of making

Can we combine by:

1. Changing material
2. Changing dimensions
3. Changing tools or equipment
4. Proper planning of work

Can we change by:

1. Relocating machines and work areas
2. Revising operational sequence
3. Modifying design
4. Proper scheduling of work

Can we simplify by:

1. Following principles of Methods Management
2. Improving the workplace
3. Pre-positioning tools, gauges and material
4. Eliminating manual holding

TO ENSURE GIVING ADEQUATE CONSIDERATION TO ALL FACTORS BY ASKING SPECIFIC AND DETAILED QUESTIONS OF YOURSELF AND OTHERS, IT IS ESSENTIAL THAT THE FULLEST USE BE MADE OF *CHECKLISTS* IN APPLYING METHODS MANAGEMENT TECHNIQUES.

Check List for Job Improvement

All job improvements can be said to occur in one or more of the following areas:

1. Motion pattern
2. Tools, gauges, workplace and equipment
3. Sequence of work
4. Product design
5. Raw materials or supplies

Motion pattern (operator)

1. Is work properly performed? Is additional instruction needed?
2. Can he perform his work while either sitting or standing?
3. Sequence of work
4. Product design
5. Raw materials or supplies
6. Can foot devices be used? Holding jigs? Indexing fixtures?
7. Are operators using the same methods on every shift?

Tools, gauges, equipment and work area

1. Do we have the best type machine for the job? Is it in good condition?
2. Can the machine be made more automatic?
3. Is the machine running at the right speed?
4. Are the machine controls properly located? Safe?
5. Are tools and materials pre-positioned for use?
6. Can any two tools be combined?
7. Can automatic feed be used?
8. Is disposal automatic?
9. Is work properly illuminated? Ventilated? Heated?
10. Do we have the best layout?

Sequence

1. Is every activity or phase of work necessary?
2. Are all operations performed at the right time?
3. Do we have the best plant layout?
4. Are conveyors feasible?
5. Can operations be combined? Separated?
6. Could lot size be changed?

Design

1. Will a change in tolerances help?
2. Can the product be made, sold, or shipped in a more advantageous form?

Material

1. Can scrap and rejected material be reused?
2. Is it purchased in the most economical length? Size? Shape? Finish?
3. Can more processing be done by the supplier?
4. Will cheaper material meet the need? (Quality buying does not mean buying supplies, materials and so forth of a grade better than that demanded by the particular use to which they are to be put.)

DO NOT CONFINE YOURSELF TO THIS LIST. THIS PARTIAL LIST SHOULD BE EXPANDED AS YOU ACQUIRE MORE EXPERIENCE WITH THIS APPROACH. DON'T GIVE AN 'OUTSIDER' THE OPPORTUNITY OF ASKING YOU A QUESTION CONCERNING YOUR DEPARTMENT THAT YOU HAVE NOT ALREADY CONSIDERED.

Typical Questions

After applying the six thought-starter questions of WHAT, WHY, WHERE, WHO, WHEN, and HOW, we arrive at the facts concerning the method under consideration. These facts should be used in developing an improved method.

Although the questions we may ask ourselves to improve the method are infinite in number, the following are a few which may stimulate thought for possible improvements. Notice that the questions all point to either an ELIMINATION, COMBINATION, CHANGE OF SEQUENCE, or SIMPLIFICATION of the method being analyzed.

The operation

1. Can the operation be eliminated or simplified by using different material?
2. Can machine delays be reduced?
3. Are the machines or equipment close enough to each other?
4. Is the stock of the operation close enough to the machine?
5. Is the dispose position for one operation the pre-position for the following operation?
6. How much time is spent in sorting?

The part

1. Are there unnecessary variables in the material limits, production schedules, finishes, sizes or methods?
2. Can the parts be removed from the container, jig, fixture or die without difficulty?
3. Is there a satisfactory method for keeping the stock, parts, and equipment clean?
4. Is scrap reworked?
5. Is a suitable container used for collecting the scrap at the machine?
6. Is the finish suitable, too fine, or too coarse?

The material

1. Is the most economical material being used?
2. Is the material received in the most suitable form?

The machine

1. Is the machine best suited for the job?
2. Is the fullest possible use being made of the machine?
3. What is the feed limit of the machine?
4. What amount of grindings, chips, or scrap must be removed from the machine?
5. What method is used to remove grindings, chips, and scrap from the machine?
6. Is hand or foot control used for starting the machine?
7. How are the parts held in the machine?

The tool

1. Who grinds the cutting tools?
2. Is there a specified number of grinds per tool?
3. Will there be less waste if the machine is hand or machine fed?
4. Should a coolant be used? If so, how much?
5. Should the feed of the cutting tool be continuous or intermittent?
6. What type holder keeps the tool in place?
7. How are the tools maintained, inspected and distributed?
8. What is the method for replacing dull tools?
9. Can a jig or fixture be used for more than one operation or part?
10. What is the method of clamping?
11. How many pieces are clamped per clamp?
12. Should the size, weight, length, width, strength, quality or quantity of the tools be increased or decreased?
13. What is the size of the handle of the tool? Is it awkward?

The method for moving material

1. At what rate is the material supplied to a machine, group or department?
2. How many pieces are carried per container?
3. What is the number of moves per hour?

The material handling factors

1. What method is used to move a part or material to an operation?
2. Is there adequate material handling control?
3. Is the part easily removed from the container?
4. Does the number of pieces supplied to the operator at one time make for economical material handling?
5. Is the material arranged to prevent rehandling?

The operator

1. Is the operator placed on the 'right' job?
2. Is the operator consistent in his action?
3. Does the operator have excessive reaching?
4. What is the position of the part with respect to the operator?
5. Should he stand or sit to perform the operation?
6. What does the operator do while the machine is adding value to the product?

The conditions of the operation

1. Does the product design require a force fit or binding fit?
2. Is there interference or delay due to maintenance of tools, machines, stock or inspection?
3. Is the work area kept clean and orderly?

Total Quality Management (Continuous Improvement)

"Total quality management (TQM) is an approach to improving the effectiveness and flexibility of business as a whole. It is essentially a way of organising and involving the whole organisation; every department, every activity, every single person at every level." (Oakland[1]). Perhaps the main differences between TQM and the traditional view of ensuring quality through inspectors are:

(i) The drive for quality is seen as continuous. It is not just meeting a current standard, but improving on it.
(ii) Quality is not restricted to the end product, but applies to all the processes in the organisation (hence the preference for the continuous improvement label by some authorities).
(iii) Quality is a task for everybody, and is more likely to be achieved when people work in teams.
(iv) Quality is not only about whether a product lives up to its specifications: it is about all aspects including reliability, customer service, and timeliness.
(v) Quality can be seen as a chain, which stretches back to suppliers and forward to customers.

One result of a TQM approach is that many companies have changed their attitudes to suppliers, from seeing them as adversaries to working with them as partners. This means that supplier–buyer relationships become more stable, and there are joint attempts to make improvements that feed into the quality of the end product.

Modern thinking about quality owes much to Deming[2,3] and Juran,[4,5] although they are by no means the only contributors to the subject. Deming offers 14 points for management attention, which are paraphrased below.

—There must be an unchanging objective to improve both products and service.
—The whole company must adopt the new policy of constant improvement.
—Change from a policy of quality inspection to one where statistical evidence proves that quality is built in.
—Cease choosing suppliers only on the basis of price.

—Continually seek and solve quality problems.
—Provide on the job training.
—Change the emphasis of supervision from meeting numbers and quotas to quality.
—Change motivation to remove fear.
—Work across departments to break down the walls between functional and departmental chimneys.
—Eliminate all goals and slogans which try to increase productivity without attention to method.
—Remove work standards that prescribe numerical quotas.
—Take away barriers between the shop floor worker and pride in workmanship.
—Support the approach by company wide education and training.
—Establish a top management structure to make all this happen.

Juran offers 10 points, some of which overlap with those of Deming.

—Ensure that there is awareness of both the need and the opportunity for improvement.
—Set targets for improvement.
—Set up an internal organisation to reach the goals.
—Give training.
—Use a project approach to solve problems.
—Establish a process to report progress.
—Give recognition to those involved.
—Communicate the results of the process.
—Measure the results.
—Make annual improvement a norm for the company, which is incorporated into all systems and procedures.

On the surface, the Juran points have a close fit with the profit improvement philosophy discussed earlier. The main differences are that the objectives of the approach are broader, and that top management has a larger role to play. The team approach remains important, but teams may be drawn from a wider spectrum of people and may seek more cross-departmental members than might be the case with the profit improvement schemes. However if the Deming philosophy is superimposed, there is a change not only in how the improvement process works, but in the basic philosophies by which the company manages. A TQM approach, if successful, changes the culture of the organisation.

Many organisations have gone down the TQM route, particularly during the 1980s and early 1990s. Not all have found it easy to provide the significant amounts of management time needed to make such systems work. Some have found, rather like Shell-Mex and BP with the original scheme, that after a while it is difficult to keep the momentum going. As with so many ideas, it is too easy for TQM to become a management fad, that is not implemented thoroughly, and which does not receive ongoing attention from top management. When this happens the benefits are likely to be somewhat slim.

References

1. Oakland, J. S. *Total Quality Management*, Heinemann, Oxford, 1989.
2. Deming, W. E. *Quality, Productivity and Competitive Position*, MIT Center for Advanced Engineering Study, Cambridge, Mass., 1982.
3. Deming, W. E. *Out of the Crisis*, MIT Center for Advanced Engineering Study, Cambridge, Mass., 1986.
4. Juran, J. M. *Quality Control Handbook*, 3rd ed., McGraw-Hill, New York, 1979.
5. Juran, J. M. *Quality Planning and Analysis*, 2nd ed., McGraw-Hill, New York, 1979.

26

Project Planning and Appraisal

The need for project plans, as one of the ways in which a company moves its long-range plans into today's actions, was mentioned in Chapter 3. The company's strategic plans may be regarded as a snapshot of the entire company and its intentions taken at a particular moment of time. Project plans are an enlargement of one specific piece of that snapshot, which is studied with microscopic attention.

Although there should be a close link between the strategic plans and project plans—indeed, so close that they should all be regarded as part of the same system—projects may be investigated at any time of the year and are not tied to the planning cycle. Similarly, the length of time chosen for the evaluation of the project need not be related to that chosen for the strategic plans.

Ideally there should never be a need to investigate a project unless this has appeared in the long-range plans. If this policy could be maintained it would ensure that the place of the project within total corporate strategy had been established according to all the best rules. Unfortunately, real-life situations rarely occur with this degree of nicety: managers are human and will sometimes omit things from their plans; strategic planning is, in any case, a continuous process, and new opportunities may be uncovered between plans; environmental changes may cause new projects to arise.

It is because of this that no company can afford to issue a blanket edict that only capital expenditure mentioned in the plans will be authorised. To do this would mean that sometimes the company would have to act against its own interests and refuse investments for doctrinaire reasons rather than from good business sense. However, it is a good idea if top management makes known its displeasure when "surprise" projects are dropped on its table for no good reason. The degree of acceptable "surprise" depends in some measure on the company's position on the scale of environmental turbulence (see Ansoff and McDonnell.)[1]

What is needed is a sub-system in the corporate planning process which deals with projects. The components of this sub-system are: a method of short-term capital budgeting; a routine which ensures that each step in the project planning process is undertaken at the right time; rules for the appraisal of capital expenditures; and a method of control.

There is nothing particularly novel about any of these elements, and the approach outlined is followed by many companies who practise no other element of formal planning in their organisation. It is possible to develop a very efficient way of dealing with projects, which contributes much to the effective use of corporate resources, without having any form of strategic plan. The danger here is that although each project is dealt with carefully on an individual basis, it is not necessarily the action that is best for the company.

It is not possible to operate a complete process of corporate planning without treating projects effectively. This is why this important aspect of planning appears in this book, even though the methods described are not the sole prerogative of corporate planners. The fact that planners often find themselves in situations where no effective project planning system exists is justification for its inclusion.

Capital Budgeting Procedure

Long-term capital budgeting has been discussed in Chapter 20 as a component of the financial planning process. Short-term capital budgeting is much more of a control process, and aims to provide procedures for authorisation of different types of capital expenditure to budget for expenditures over, for example, a twelve-month period, to provide for management review of capital requirements and to control expenditures against budget.

Although minor capital expenditure does not require over-elaborate methods of evaluation, it does require to be justified and controlled. In a large company minor expenditures can accumulate to a significant total sum, and one which the company has to provide from its financial resources. It is very easy for any company to become undisciplined and to waste its resources.

For minor expenditures it should be sufficient for a simple system of authorities to be introduced, using a form which requests explanation but not financial evaluation. This ensures that expenditures can only take place on the approval of the responsible manager who, in any case, is held accountable for keeping within his capital budget. Thus a departmental manager may be allowed to authorise expenditure up to £10,000, and a divisional manager up to £25,000, with anything above this coming out of the "minor" category and requiring different treatment.

There may be exceptions to this rule. For example, the company may insist that these authorities apply only to items which appear in the capital budget, and that approval for anything excluded must in any case come from the board. Or an embargo may be placed on specific types of expenditure (such as new furniture), which means that power to authorise money spent on these items is restricted to certain higher levels of managers.

The system may also be used to cover revenue expenditures although exceptions will usually have to be made for certain departments: for example, advertising expenditures by a marketing department because of the size and nature of its transactions.

Operation of any system of authorisation of minor expenditures (and it should not be forgotten that for many items the difference between a revenue and a capital expenditure is a matter determined internally by the company's accountants) will be assisted if the company has standing policies. Much unnecessary expenditure can be avoided if there are firm policies laid down to cover the type of word processors which may be purchased, what functions may have micro computers, what variety of furniture may be chosen, and so on. Often the reason for capital expenditures on small items is a "want" rather than a "need", and is a desire to enhance status on the part of individuals. Such expenditures rarely contribute to corporate profits, and frequently lead to a chain reaction from other people who in turn wish to make similar expenditures.

A second category of capital expenditure, which requires slightly different treatment, is the replacement of fixed assets. Certain replacements are a routine expense for which a simplified system of authorisation may be introduced, even if the amounts are outside the "minor" expenditure limits. An example of this is the replacement of sales personnel's cars. Provided the replacement is within the policy laid down, there is little point in making the authorisation system too complex. Replacements of all types should be estimated in both the long-term plans (in global figures) and in the short-term capital budget (in detail).

Not all asset replacement situations are as simple as this. Major plant also wears out and from time to time has to be renewed. Such renewals should not be automatic, and should be fully studied well in advance of their need. Provision should be made in the appropriate plans for the financial commitment, so that the need to make capital available for this purpose is not overlooked. The time to replace plant and machinery does not always coincide with the book depreciation, so it is important that the plans reflect management thoughts rather than financial extrapolations.

Technological development and other forces may cause obsolescence long before assets are fully depreciated. From a planning point of view the most important element in a replacement decision is time. If it is left too late, a crash programme may have to be introduced to replace the item so that production is not impaired. If considered in time, it becomes possible to examine alternatives, some of which may be far reaching and also involve expenditure on additional plant. The authorisation system should ensure that these studies are carried out and the need for them identified well in advance.

Profit improvement capital expenditure is the third important area to be encountered. (Sometimes a replacement expenditure may also be profit improvement.) A general feature of this type of expenditure is usually a high return and quick payback, coupled with the difficulty of identifying individual projects on more than a short-term basis. The authorisation system should provide for speedy investigation and approval of these projects, but should not overlook the fact that the implementation of some may be accompanied by changes in the personnel area. Some companies with continuous profit improvement systems (see Chapter 25) have a quick-routing system for capital expenditure requests of an improvement nature. Except where personnel problems are involved, the strategic positioning of the unit under review, or the amount of capital is very large, there is rarely a good reason for delaying the introduction of a profit improvement measure.

In some circumstances it may make sense to increase the authorisation limits of certain managers for improvement projects. This should reduce delays. Capital budgeting should provide a lump sum for investment projects (as noted earlier, it is often impossible to forecast individual projects).

The largest amounts of capital expenditure are, in most companies, for investment and corporate development. (There may be exceptions: for example, ship replacement may for a shipping company be the main use of its capital.) The capital is required to do something new to secure growth for the company. Each development project should arise from the decisions taken in the strategic plan, and the implications of the outline project on corporate strategy should already be known. (The possible treatment of projects omitted from these plans has already been discussed.)

Major development and investment projects are the ones which require the closest and most detailed evaluation before capital is committed, and this should include network or other systems for ensuring implementation. In other words, although the decision to proceed will be largely financial, the strategic decision having already been made, the evaluation must also cover all non-financial aspects.

In most companies major authorisations of this type must be made either by the board or by a special sub-committee set up by the board. These may be exceptions where authority is delegated, within specified limits, to the board of a subsidiary.

One of the main problems in setting a system of capital budgeting is to make sensible delegations of authority to approve capital expenditure. The balance must be found that gives operating managers and chief executives of subsidiaries enough flexibility to act, and yet does not remove all control for those ultimately responsible for the well-being of the company.

It is also important that the authorisation system does not create too much "red tape" and too many bureaucratic delays. The longer the chain of approval, the greater the delays will become, and it is not unusual for subsidiaries of multi-national companies to wait several months before answers come back from the centre. Frequently the job of evaluation is done twice, which is wasteful—once by the subsidiary and once at head office. In a competitive situation no company can afford to have systems which impede its progress.

The British subsidiary of a multi-national group gave advance warning in its plans that it would have to make a major investment in a replacement boiler house. The opportunity was taken to study the possibility of relocating the plant, and after proposals were rejected by the head office (on strategic grounds) a project was prepared to request capital for the new boiler house. Six months went by before there was a word from the head office, and over a further six months the head office insisted on re-examining all the engineering alternatives. Eventually the insurance company—as had been predicted—threatened immediate withdrawal of coverage. The whole organisation went into a panic, approval was given to replace the boiler house, and the only obvious result from the delay was that the time-lag had caused costs to rise by 40%, relations with the insurance company were impaired, and many hours of engineers' time were lost.

Capital budgeting systems should regularly report actual expenditure against the budget. This requirement does not replace the need to control individual projects, a point which will be discussed in some detail later.

Project Evaluation Routine

The planning system should include a routine which ensures that all projects go through a number of defined stages, and that the right people are brought into the project at the right time—for investigation, co-ordination, approval, and implementation. Unless this is clearly defined, the company may well find that important stages are overlooked, and that decisions are made before the project has been evaluated. Such a system also improves inter-departmental communication and helps to prevent a manager from keeping his projects to himself and deliberately denying access by people from other departments who should play a part in their evaluation.

As mentioned earlier, the project planning system cuts across the strategic planning system of which it is a part. The relationship can perhaps be visualised as a series of horizontal and vertical bars. The horizontal bars are successive strategic and operating plans which are joined together by the various vertical bars of project planning. Some vertical bars may overlay several horizontal bars—occa-

FIG. 26.1. Relations of project plans to long-range plans

sionally they may be so short that they barely embrace one horizontal. This relationship is illustrated in Fig. 26.1.

There will be variations in the project planning system to suit different types of projects. The development and introduction of a new product is likely to follow a longer path than a project to install a new piece of equipment. The internal organisation of decision-taking within the company will also affect the way in which the system is organised.

Even with these qualifications, it is still useful to consider an outline of what a project planning system might look like. The example (Fig. 26.2) is of a procedure for the development of a new product, and was designed for a company in the food industry.

This example simplifies some of the problems; particular projects may need to add further stages. A decision to launch a new product may mean that the company has to extend its premises, which in turn means a detailed study of the physical and financial alternatives. The amount of work within each of the stages will vary from project to project, and may be complicated by failures at certain points which bring a need to go back to the beginning again. The system does not indicate control mechanisms. It becomes apparent from a study of this simplified system that it requires a co-ordinator. Someone must be responsible for ensuring that each step is completed, that everyone knows the part he is to play, and the date by which he has to complete.

Different types of project require different co-ordinators. In this particular example it could probably be adequately filled by the product manager responsible for the project. For other projects there may be other sensible choices: the best co-ordinator is one who has a personal interest in seeing that the project is completed to its targets of finance, physical performance, and time.

Complex projects require the assistance of co-ordinating and controlling techniques (Chapter 31). Networks are particularly valuable, the more so when it is remembered that each of the sub-stages may include a number of tasks which themselves have to be carefully planned and co-ordinated.

Rules for the Appraisal of Capital Expenditure

Certain of the stages in the system demonstrated above showed the need for appraisal of the project. Some projects may be so simple that complex appraisal techniques are unnecessary: for example, a project to reorganise the flow of paperwork in a company.

Wherever a project involves a significant expenditure of capital, the company should insist that a careful financial appraisal is made. To ensure that results are comparable between areas of the company over time (and to build in a means of monitoring and controlling) the investigation and appraisal should follow defined rules.

Many companies find it useful to set out these rules, including a description of the techniques of evaluation to be used, in a handbook or manual. Techniques of appraisal can be applied manually, although they can usually be efficiently

1. Identification of idea
   Ideas may come from many sources, including:
   (a) Inspiration
   (b) Marketing research
   (c) Brainstorming and similar "ideas" sessions
   (d) Competitive action

2. Initial prospects study
   Desk research to establish prospects for the idea, leading to definition of a preliminary product marketing concept and postulation of an ideal launch date.

   Action:
   Marketing

3. Preliminary product marketing concept
   Defining the outline concept, *possible* level of sales (within perhaps a wide range), request for research and development work.

   Action:
   Marketing

4. Definition of research and development objective
   A statement of the meaning of the product marketing concept in R & D terms, assessment of product flexibility, estimated time needed to complete task, estimated cost of research, any problems arising from priorities.

   (Note: see also Chapter 12)

   Action:
   R & D

5. Decision to proceed

   Action:
   Top management

6. Refined product marketing concept
   At a point where R & D work, and such complementary marketing research work as is possible and desirable, shows sign of success the PMC should be refined. This stage will include provisional financial data – costings, range of margins at various possible selling prices, process and investment data.

   Action:
   Marketing assisted by appropriate departments

7. Decision to proceed
   If stage 6 shows a probability of acceptable results the project may proceed without reference to top management. If failure is detected at this stage, the project should be referred to top management for a decision whether to abandon or continue.

   Action:
   Marketing or top management as appropriate

8. Feasibility study
   The project now moves into a stage when a full feasibility study is possible. The completion of this study requires the initiation and completion of work in a number of areas, such as:
   (a) Marketing research, such as concept testing
   (b) Process development
   (c) Further R & D work
   (d) Technical feasibility investment needs
   (e) Packaging development
   (f) Revised costing
   If these steps do not indicate any revision of thinking (e.g. complete rejection of the concept at the marketing research stage), it becomes possible to move to the next step.

   Action:
   Marketing
   R & D
   R & D
   Process engineering
   R & D
   Accounts

9. Marketing plan (Project) and project evaluation

   (a) Preparation of outline marketing plan, broad sales, and marketing cost estimates.
   (b) Detailed test market (or alternative) plans.
   (c) Examination of project in relation to corporate strategies.
   (d) Detailed financial appraisal, including sensitivity analysis.

   Action:

   Marketing
   Marketing
   Planning
   Planning and/or Accounts

10. Decision to proceed
    The immediate decision to be made is whether to proceed to test market. However, this will only be made if the expectations for the project still appear to be good. In practice investment decisions may have to be made at this stage, although ideally they would be deferred until stage 12.

    Action:
    Top management

11. Completion of test market: Re-evaluation
    Stage 9 should be repeated using the results of the test market and updating all forecasts.

    Action:
    As appropriate

12. Decision
    Final decision to launch or reject.

    Action:
    Top management

FIG. 26.2. Stages in project planning: a new product

computerised (package programmes are available from many sources). Computer assistance is virtually essential if any complicated sensitivity analysis is to be carried out.

The best all-round work on techniques and methods of appraisal is that of Merritt and Sykes.[2]

Project evaluation is essentially the study of and selection between alternatives. The strategic planning process should have settled the main lines of action and development, and will itself have been a choice between broad alternatives. A project narrows each of these strategic choices to a particular choice of action. Within each project there may be many different ways of achieving the project objectives, each with different profit and cash flow implications. This can be illustrated by taking as an example a project to market a new product by a company whose factory is operating to capacity. The options which should be examined might include:

   (i) Withdrawal of existing products of lower profitability to make capacity for the new product.
  (ii) Constructing a new factory for the new product.
 (iii) Extension of existing factory premises.
  (iv) (possibly) Building a new factory on a new site to house both the new and the old activity.
   (v) Having the new product manufactured by someone else.

Within the chosen alternative there is another selection of choices. How big a factory extension? What type of plant and why? Rent or buy premises, plant, and equipment? Which firm of contract manufacturers? The list is apparently endless.

Although many options may be eliminated fairly quickly and without too much difficulty, the company should aim to identify and evaluate as many as appear to be practicable solutions. It is not always the "obvious" option which provides the best answer to the problem. In any case, for financial reasons, the company may prefer to choose a solution which is not the best: it has already been demonstrated (Chapter 20) that sometimes a project with a quick payback is more expedient than one with higher profits but a slower payback. Companies sometimes have to take the course of action they can afford rather than the one they would prefer.

Mathematical analysis techniques, although essential in the evaluation, are not the only factors which should be considered. The strategic requirements of the company (particularly a need to shift into a different area of risk), the public relations effect of the company's action, or the personnel and morale problems caused by the action, are among the qualitative factors which should be given considerable weighting in the decision process. The answer does not lie only in the numbers, but in a combination of numbers and business judgement. In any event, no quantitative analyses of an expected future development can be read as if they were audited statements of past performance.

Each analysis is based on assumptions (which should be defined) and forecasts (which should be explained). Sensitivity analysis will assist in the interpretation of the figures.

The best thing a company can do to ensure that its quantitative appraisal techniques have meaning is to see that they are based on a careful and objective study of the project. Any technique is only as good as the data that goes into it, and it is fair to claim that a crude profitability measure (such as percentage Return on Investment) based on well-founded data is of more value than the most sophisticated discount cash flow (DCF) analysis of data which has been thrown together without thought.

Objectivity is easier to achieve in theory than in practice. The responsible line managers must play a part in the appraisal and evaluation of their projects if only to ensure that they have a commitment to their implementation, and so that they can accept the standards defined in the project plan as a something for which they are held accountable.

Many managers understandably find it difficult to be objective about their own projects. They are likely to see as obstacles anything that slows down or prevents their projects obtaining the required capital appropriation, and in their eyes no other project in the company could possibly be as important. Already prejudiced about the view of their project, many are not averse to taking a deliberately optimistic view of sales and profits—or to suggest unjustified changes to their forecasts should the first DCF analysis look unfavourable. Pushing through the new project in this way means that they are not wasting their effort which they personally have put into the scheme, and cannot be accused of doing nothing.

Once top management starts to exercise control through the project plan the trouble starts. This is hitting below the belt (after all, every thinking person knows that managers will try to make pessimistic forecasts which they can exceed, if they are to be judged against them). Excuses follow, reasons why the project forecasts just have to be different—the time factor, new developments, someone else's figures were wrong: who has not heard the answers before?

The best way of improving objectivity and avoiding this sort of unprofitable conflict is for all appraisals to be a matter of teamwork between operating management and staff expert. Each has to convince the other of the validity of any conclusions which may be drawn, and the final report is binding on both. From the outset, the control use of the document must be known, and specific data built into the project to facilitate this. Both sides must understand the methods of analysis: the staff expert because he has to make and interpret the calculations; the line manager because he is bound by the results. A manager's understanding may be at a different level to that of the expert. He or she need not be able to make the calculations, but must understand the principles of the technique used and the meaning of the answers.

This teamwork and understanding should be backed by an insistence that the financial calculations be supported by written project plans and, where desirable, networks or other ways of ensuring implementation. It must be very clear what action has to be put into effect to achieve the results shown in the project plan. Insistence on this type of plan will often improve the accuracy of the figures on which the analysis is based.

Before discussing the content of project plans, it is worth spending a little time thinking about the team which makes the appraisal. The reasons for a line and staff partnership have already been made clear. The combination helps to ensure objectivity, without moving into an "ivory tower" situation, where all judgements are made by a remote planning staff. On the management side, input may come from a number of different areas and departments. The staff experts would in most companies, come from a special project appraisal unit. Strong arguments can be made for attaching this to corporate planning, but these are matched by reasons of equal validity which suggest that the accounting side is the right home. The real answer is that it does not matter, the important thing being the calibre of the people employed in the unit, who should be experienced in the methods of appraisal and used to the real problems of working in close association with busy line managers.

Most companies will from time to time have projects which, when implemented, will not be the responsibility of any present operating department. In these cases the company should use the best talents it has available to form the appraisal team, which may mean drawing on a line manager even though he may have no ultimate responsibility for the project.

In many ways an outline format for a project plan will resemble an outline for a long-range plan. Information will be required under headings which have many similarities with those in the long-range plan, as it has been argued that project plans are only enlargements of part of the "photograph" which is the strategic plan, and it would therefore be surprising if there were not similarities.

The company has to decide on the time-span over which forecasts will be made and the project evaluated. Although it is possible to make useful analyses of data over a five-year period, it may often be desirable to extend this to at least ten years (the longer the period, the less the impact on DCF calculations of the theoretical treatment of the residual value of fixed assets: in a five-year calculation the need to credit these as a cash inflow in the last year has a much greater distorting effect and can lead to the wrong conclusions). Each company may choose its time-span to suit itself, but should try to apply it to all projects to facilitate comparison between different projects.

Only a generalised view can be given of the narrative contents of a project plan since there are obvious differences between projects. An investigation of a project to re-locate a factory must result in a report which bears little resemblance to a new product launch. The suggested outline refers to a marketing project with some production investment, and is not meant to be the answer to every project problem which might arise.

Assumptions

Those assumptions specific to the project should be carefully defined. This requirement includes assumptions on which sales forecasts are based.

Objectives

The purpose and aim of each project should be defined before the investigation begins, and preferably should form part of the terms of reference of the project appraisal team. A well-thought-out statement of purpose can assist the board in understanding the significance of the project when it comes up to them for decision.

The project objective should be cross-referenced to an action listed in the long-range plan. If it is additional to the long-range plan this fact should be clearly stated, with an explanation of the reasons for its omission from this plan.

Marketing

A glance back at the new product system will show some of the steps that have to be taken to arrive at a satisfactory marketing plan. It is rarely adequate for the sales forecasts used in appraisal of the project to be conjured out of the air (although it is unfortunately true that many companies throw their forecasts together in this way, as if the ball-point pen which writes them were a magic wand). Many projects may require extensive marketing research. The information background, as well as the marketing strategy and tactics, should appear in the project appraisal report. Exactly what marketing research is carried out, and how much money is invested in investigations, is a matter which each company has to decide on its merits.

A detailed marketing plan will provide cost estimates for advertising and promotion, sales force, and similar items. It will provide sales forecasts.

For practical reasons it is often useful to have only a summary marketing plan in the main report, all the detail being placed in appendices. Those finally authorising the capital expenditure are unlikely to need to read the detailed plans: they must be satisfied that they exist.

Production

The project should include a full technical assessment of the process of manufacture, the plant recommended, and the specifications of the raw materials required.

This analysis leads to forecasts of capital expenditure and of costs of production. Although few would claim that forecasting capital expenditures is easy (especially when considering the need to estimate expenditure in each year of the project), it is child's play when compared to the problem of forecasting production costs. The difficulties of making accurate assessments for new products to be produced on new plant by a new process cannot be overstated: neither can the need to put every effort into making forecasts which are reasonably accurate. To make any sensible cost assessments the project team must have an intimate knowledge of the project, and must have the experience necessary to interpret a manufacturer's rating for a new piece of equipment into what throughput will actually be obtained in practical operation. (It goes without saying that a cost assessment is easier to make when for the expansion of an existing product, of which the company has practical experience.)

Costs in projects should be looked at from a number of ways. A DCF calculation calls for assessment of the *additional* revenues and costs brought by the project, and, of course, ignores depreciation as this is a positive cash flow. (The cash leaves the organisation when the asset is purchased: annual depreciation is an attempt to match those previously incurred costs with the period in which they will produce income.) A more traditional calculation should also be made, so that the company can examine its pricing policies in relation to the full costs (and the market), and so that a study may be made of the effect on variable costs of different levels of production.

Projects may also involve additional problems, such as where to locate the new plant, or which of several plants in various countries to expand. Often the optimum solution of these problems requires extensive operations research help.

Again the detailed technical appraisal should form a sub-plan with only a summary in the main report.

Personnel

Once again the importance of that other major resource, people, comes into the limelight. Any project will fail if adequate supplies of manpower are unobtainable, and this aspect must be given close attention.

There may also be ways in which the project affects current employees, and these, too, should be studied, the problems identified, and solutions found. A project to close an old plant has an obvious and direct effect on the people working in it. An expansion of a factory may also alter the rhythm of the lives of present employees. There may be promotion opportunities, training needs, and disputes because it is believed that the working conditions in the new unit are better than those in the old, and additional pressures on employee facilities, such as canteens. All of these problems are possible: it is equally possible that none will trouble the company. Certainly some considerable time and thought should be devoted to examining the possibilities in the project planning stage.

Risk Analysis

It is good management for a company to examine the various risks to which its new project is subject and, through a sensitivity analysis, to assess the possible financial effects of the various risks. Some will spring from the assumptions made about the factors influencing the project (e.g. competitors' reactions to the new product). Others should examine risks connected with political events, fiscal changes, raw material cost changes, technological development, and like factors.

The aim is to understand the project, to be awake to particular dangers, and—if the effect of these is outside the company's limits of acceptable risk—for the board to know this. Risk analysis can lead to the abandonment or modification of apparently profitable projects.

Financial Appraisal

All the subsections of the project plan should be designed to yield quantified data which can be analysed to show the full financial effects of the action planned. This means taking account of fixed and working capital as well as profits, and implies the discipline of trying to foresee all the capital expenditures over the period studied. This is so that the shape of the whole project is known, and that top management is not asked to approve investments on a piecemeal basis. There is a great difference between authorising an expenditure of £5m., which completes the project, and allowing a similar investment which is followed by annual calls for more capital in order to "protect" the original investment. Simple examples are:

(i) The project to expand a factory this year, which can only work efficiently if accompanied by an increase in warehousing space next year.

(ii) A major overseas expansion which will not be workable unless head office also expands.

(iii) An acquisition project which requires further capital expenditures to modernise it to "protect the investment".

The board may, of course, approve only the first phase of the investment and require the rest to be re-evaluated at a later date.

Another choice to be made is whether all calculations should be taken at constant prices or allow for inflation. It is certainly true that in certain types of project, inflation—the effect of which is subject to forecasting errors—can tend to increase the apparent rates of return. On the other hand, the real world is subject to inflation, and for this reason I should argue—as I have over the total corporate plan—that the figures should try to be as close to reality as possible. In other words they should allow for the effect on costs and income of expected price changes. Again, a strong secondary reason is that monitoring and control, already difficult, becomes almost impossible if the figures are not at current prices. There is, however, considerable value in converting figures back to a real rate of return after assessing all inflation effects.

Inside the company, standards should be set below which projects would normally be considered unacceptable and automatically rejected. (Exception may be made for specific strategic reasons.) This rate does not have to be the same for all areas of the company: it may be 12% DCF rate for division A and 15% for division B, with further differences for operations in specific countries. Rates may be adjusted in relation to the position of the division in a portfolio analysis matrix (see Chapter 15). Acceptance of a standard does not imply automatic authorisations of anything that exceeds it: it is merely the entrance qualification.

Some companies have schemes which alter the rates of return predicted in a project through a reliability index. This is based on a comparison of the accuracy of performance against forecasts over the past few years. Those managers with a high rating are assumed to be able to continue thus into the future, and their projects are judged likely to be close to the figures calculated in the appraisal. Those whose record has been poor have their calculated returns reduced, which may mean that their projects are rejected.

Although I stated earlier that projects should be assessed on a marginal basis, judgement should not be based on these results alone. The reason for this is that a loss-making operation may still be loss-making, even after the addition of a capital expenditure with a very high rate of return. If the project is examined in isolation it may appear to be highly desirable. When looked at on a consolidated basis the conclusion could well be that it is throwing good money after bad. The actual techniques of project appraisal are beyond the scope of this chapter.

Financing

Each report should include recommendations on the financing of the project. For small projects there may be little to say, as they may present no problem. Larger projects may be quite different, and may, as intimated earlier, require the investigation of several options. Certainly at the final decision stage the board must know that the projects it authorised are capable of being implemented.

Monitoring and Controlling

Implementation is a keyword in planning. Top management must have a method of monitoring and controlling projects so that it can ensure that the actions are carried out, and that the results are acceptable. No one can control the future, and there are occasions when forecasts just cannot be achieved. If this happens, top management should be aware of it, and the fact that they are aware is often enough to ensure that corrective or compensating actions are implemented, which bring the results closer to the planned position. The idea should be for management to be aware of deviations either before or while they are occurring: knowledge after the event may be of educational value and help the company to avoid such mistakes in future, but it can do nothing to improve the situation.

The capital budgeting system discussed earlier is useful for overall control but insufficient for the management of individual projects. On an individual project basis the company needs to control capital expenditure, financial results, and the physical application of the resources. Top management has to be able to know that a sum authorised for the purchase of a particular piece of equipment has in fact been used for this purpose.

Capital expenditure and the way in which it is used can be controlled through networks and schedules, and a regular system of reporting. For both it is probably advisable to report at least once a month, to compare actuals with the plan, and to project the total position forward so that the new expectation may be compared with the plan. This implies the discipline of breaking down expenditure into the same periods and into very detailed stages. It is no use, for example, waiting for a building to be completed before finding out whether it has cost more than planned: construction must be broken down into timed stages, such as site preparation, foundations, and each subsequent stage completion. In this way a major deviation at an early stage will be known early in the proceedings—as will a failure to meet the time-table. (Delays in time may affect an actual DCF result as much as over-expenditure of capital.) Someone must be held responsible for co-ordinating and controlling the project and reporting to the board (on an exception basis).

The usage and expenditure of capital are relatively easy to measure (although there should be no delusions that they are simple to control), and it also becomes apparent at a very early stage if there are any major delays in implementation. The new factory which is late being built, or the new product which lags behind its planned introduction date, are factors that become obvious very quickly.

Much more difficult is to measure the overall results against the project appraisal. Every analysis will show how the capital expenditure is to generate profits, and most analyses rightly look on the marginal contribution made by the project. Sometimes the project might be for a complete new division which will be a separate accounting unit: more usually it is to do something which is fully integrated in the activity of an existing accounting unit. Sales of a new product may be easy to identify: the real effect on output and costs of improving one part of the plant may be very hard to isolate, particularly when other factors, unconnected with the expenditure, are also changing.

The basic problems are that it is unlikely that the accounting system would normally make it possible for the company to examine the results of all projects, and that in any case the figures recorded are likely to be on a total rather than a marginal basis. The implication of this is that companies should give thought to how they are going to monitor projects at the time they approve them.

If the company makes it an essential part of its system that its project appraisal unit examines progress against plan and reports on major variances at a certain period after implementation—say the first full year's trading after the initial expenditure has been completed—an incentive is provided to ensure that results are recorded in a way that facilitates comparison with the project.

It would be a mistake to insist that only those results which can be ascertained through the accounting system should be measured. In many circumstances it is useful to go one stage back and measure against non-financial standards. If a machine is supposed to produce a certain number of units per year, this can be measured. If new plant is expected to reduce the number of people employed in a unit by 10%, it becomes possible to see whether, in fact, the number of people is so reduced.

By careful thought at the outset it is possible to express most projects in terms which can be measured later. How long into the future the company continues to monitor performance against individual projects is another matter. For most projects one report is sufficient: beyond that the project should become part of the normal planning and control processes and integrated into the long-range plans and budgets.

References

1. Ansoff, A. and McDonnell, E. *Implanting Strategic Management*, 2nd ed., Prentice Hall, London, 1990.
2. Merritt, A. J. and Sykes, A. *The Finance and Analysis of Capital Projects*, Longmans, London, 1963.

27

From Plans to Actions

Action must be the end product of planning, for without action planning is a pointless and empty activity. All the benefits—of mental stimulation, careful analysis, the integration of more facts into decision making, and of the involvement and greater participation of managers in defining the future of the company—become ghostly shadows that lack substance and vanish in the harsh light of reality. No company anywhere in the world has ever added a single penny to its profits from making plans: the rewards are only realised when plans are implemented.

Figure 27.1 looks at the planning process in a different way from the models used so far. What it shows is that there are two aspects to strategic management, analytical and behavioural. So far we have looked deeply into the analytical, although with occasional forays into the behavioural. However, it is clear that when we begin to think about turning plans into action, we have to give attention to both.

Although there has been considerable research into the success and failure of planning systems, much less attention has been given to the implementation of strategy. Bomona[1] suggests that when a company finds that its strategy has not produced the right outcome, it is as likely to assume that the strategy is wrong, as it is to recognise that the problem may have been a failure to implement. This often leads to a change in a perfectly appropriate strategy, which is hardly the way to effective strategic management. When considering the implementation of strategy, we should remember that we are really looking at an aspect of something that may be much broader: the implementation of strategic change.

Observers (e.g. Ringbakk[2]) have noted that many managements fail to use their corporate plans. It is surprising that the planning systems that many companies have installed frequently end with a long-range plan, and rely on the annual budget, informal measures, and luck to convert those plans into firm actions which really happen.

Alexander[3, 4] researched the problems which American companies found when implementing strategy, and later extended this to public agencies. The ranking of the factors in each study is shown in Table 27.1. However, the important fact is

FIG. 27.1. Stages in effective preparation of a plan

not only the problems themselves, but the fact that more of them related to issues of culture, structure and human behaviour, than to analysis and formal system. In this chapter the concentration will be on the system and procedure issues necessary to implement plans, and the more complex, softer issues will be discussed in Chapter 28.

Only when plans have been turned into deeds can a company claim that its planning makes sense. Actions bring results—which may or may not be as forecast—and results give management the ability to exercise a control function and to interpose additional actions, or cancel others, if its intentions are being frustrated.

A planning system without a formal method of creating actions is likely to lead to poor quality planning. If managers cannot be held to account for failing to fulfil their plans, the plans themselves will have less validity, and will become as a knife that has lost its cutting edge, instruments that lack a point. And the chances are that the planning system itself will fail, and all the time and money invested in it will be wasted.

Moving from plans to actions and controlling against results is not an easy task

TABLE 27.1. Strategy implementation

Problems			
Problem	Order of importance		Nature
	Pvte firms	Public Orgs	Hard/soft
Implementation took longer than expected	1	1	H or S
Major unexpected problems arose during implementation	2	3	H
Inadequate coordination of implementation activities	3	6	S
Other activities distracted attention	4	4	H
Inadequate capabilities of employees	5	-	S
Inadequate training at lower levels	6	-	S
Uncontrollable external factors	7	2	H
Inadequate leadership and direction at departmental level	8	9	S
Implementation tasks not fully defined	9	-	H
Inadequate information systems to monitor	10	-	H
Employee resistance-incongruent goals	-	5	S
Lack of teamwork by key people	-	9	S
Overall goals not understood by employees	-	7	S

in any company, and may become extremely complex in large or diversified organisations. It is also an area which may meet unusually strong opposition from
managers because life for them would be easier if the implementation was left to
them on a purely informal basis. It is not possible to conceal dust under the carpet
if someone looks under the carpet every day.

The wise planner will incorporate a number of steps in the planning system.
These will be intelligent steps, which allow for the consideration of deviations
from the plan which should be made in the best interests of the company. No
manager should be expected to slavishly follow a plan to the letter, when events
or further analysis shows that the action is no longer appropriate. The plan
should be the slave of the manager: horrific results may occur when the opposite
is true.

Some of the particular steps recommended are "planning". Others are very much "control". Conceptually it is possible to distinguish between the two (e.g. the views of Anthony[5] were described in Chapter 1). In this instance, as the object is to show how a total approach may be used to bring about the implementation of plans, an overall view is taken of a complete system.

The steps may be divided into seven essential and one optional, which may be used as an alternative to one of the essential steps. They are:

Essential

(1) Conversion of long-range plans into short-range tactical plans.
(2) Assignment of tasks to individuals (standards of performance).
(3) Budgetary control.
(4) Monitoring performance against plan.
(5) Monitoring assumptions.
(6) Updating and reconsideration of plans as required.
(7) Yearly report on planning activity.

Optional

Management by objectives.

Tactical Plans

No complex organisation can easily implement the usual type of long-range plan because there are many key actions which are not defined in detail and which are not broken down into tasks that can be assigned to a particular person. The long-range plan of the company, covering periods of perhaps up to fifteen years (though more usually five), needs to have elements lifted out of it and examined in depth. Perhaps the only sound way of doing this is to prepare tactical plans which will be further developed into tasks for individuals and linked with the company's budgetary control processes.

There are two main types of tactical plans, each of which fulfils a specific need: short-term operating plans and project plans.

The short-term operating plan is an expansion of part of the long-range plan. The period of time it covers may be chosen on an arbitrary basis, although there is a strong argument for choosing a year: basically "year 1" of the long-range plan, together with such actions as have to be committed in "year 1", in order to bring about the results required in subsequent years. A year is a reasonable period of time to handle in detail, and has the added advantage that it can be closely linked with the annual budget. Thus the annual operating plan and the budget become two sides of the same coin, and together provide documentation that is capable of tight management control.

Project plans, on the other hand, have a time-span that is dictated by the implementation time of the project itself. It may be shorter than a year (as in certain profit improvement plans) or may extend considerably beyond this (as in the construction of a new building). For detailed evaluation purposes the financial implications of a project plan may be studied for much further ahead than the long-range plan itself: for control and implementation the emphasis is on the short period. The plans cover what their title suggests—projects—which may be of any nature whatsoever: installation of a computer, construction of a building, marketing of a new product, development of a new technology. Networks are of particular value in controlling and implementing project plans.

These particular tactical plans were discussed in detail in the previous chapter.

The annual operating plans are organised around functional areas (whereas the project plans may—and usually will—involve many different functions). Each operating plan will also embrace, perhaps only by cross-referencing, the projects in which the functional area has an interest.

Annual operating plans should always be seen in context of the longer period. They are not isolated documents and should be fully integrated in the process which leads to the production of the company's longer-range plans. Amongst the most important constraints on the preparation of the annual operating plans is that they must translate to the immediate future the strategies of the longer term: they should never be used as a means of introducing additional strategies unless the long-range plan is also modified at the same time.

There should be no surprises in the annual plan: there may, nevertheless, be a considerable amount of detailed work. Fullest effectiveness is reached when the annual operating plan is seen as the raw material of the budget: in this way the budget becomes closely integrated with the long-range plan, reflects the intentions of that plan. More will be said on this later in this chapter.

For corporate control purposes, annual operating plans should be prepared for each area where there is a long-range operating plan. What these areas are is something which comes from the shape and size of the company itself, but which may in the simplest terms be considered as the main functional areas of the company. In most companies this will be an oversimplification, but it requires little imagination to consider the various possibilities—and in any case some of these have been discussed in previous chapters.

Long-range operating plans are best prepared with a wide degree of management participation. The annual operating plans offer an opportunity of gaining even more participation, through the involvement of numerous levels of management. The part of a regional sales manager may be used as an example to illustrate the different approaches. A manager at this level is unlikely to play any part in writing a long-range plan, although he or she may contribute to the plan of the division through group discussion. Little benefit may be obtained from demanding a five- or ten-year plan from a manager in this position in the organisation chart. On the other hand, it may be of considerable value to ask such a manager to define a planned course of action for the forthcoming year, even though the plan may consist of only one or two pages.

In an article I[6] described how Fyffes Group Ltd. had extended their annual operating plans to cover their fifty branch managers. The existence of a plan of action for each branch (a branch had responsibilities for banana ripening, local purchasing, physical distribution, sales, certain marketing decisions, and cash collection) proved to be a sound way of translating the divisional long-range operating plan into an effective tool of management.

Lower level plans need never be seen beyond divisional management, and are certainly not the type of document which should go through to corporate head-quarters and the chief executive. The corporate planner will have little direct interest in them except to ensure that they are prepared, or if giving specific help to a divisional manager to improve planning right down the line.

Plans at this level must be prepared within the context of very detailed policy guidelines and targets issued by the divisional manager, and drawn from divisional plans. In this way it is possible to be sure that the plans will be compatible with the agreed long-range plan for the division. In effect this is delegating part of the planning tasks to subordinates in much the same way as he or she has received part of the chief executive's task. What the divisional manager receives from the more junior managers is a detailed programme for the performance of certain elements of the overall plan: these submissions have a parallel with his or her own submissions to the chief executive which are within the framework of the strategic plan. As in the day-to-day function of management, there are many more constraints at the lower levels, and the lower the level the more constraints are imposed.

Annual operating plans of this type give the divisional manager a tool for controlling development and progress, assist in motivating managers, and help to spread the formal approach to planning throughout the organisation. This may stimulate new ideas, and certainly will ensure that junior managers become fully aware of corporate policy, as it affects the division, because this has to be defined before they can plan their contribution. Tasks and actions which are identified and accepted by junior managers have more chance of being fulfilled. Managers at the lower levels are individualists, just as much as their seniors, and the more they exercise their own individualistic creativity, the more satisfied they are likely to be.

The annual operating plans which are used at the corporate level are those of the units or areas which contributed to the long-range plan. There should be an annual plan for each long-range operating plan. Top management should take a careful interest in these documents because they show how the strategies detailed in the long-range plan are to be carried out.

It makes sense for the annual plans to cover the same general headings used in the long-range plan but treating the subject in a different way. The object is not to repeat what has already been said but to change the broad statements of policy and intent into an itemised programme for action.

The long-range marketing plan would discuss the place of a particular product in the marketing plan, its positioning in the market, the general image of the product, and the way it is to change. The annual plan, within this broad strategy, gets down to detail and should become a blueprint for the year's activity, capable of implementation even if the managers concerned leave the company for any reason. Advertising will be looked at in terms of detailed campaigns, media schedules, and supporting promotional activity. The example of the planning manual in Chapter 28 shows some of the information headings which should be considered.

The quality of annual operating plans can be improved by careful attention to procedure. A comprehensive time-table should be issued by the planner, so that all understand the part they have to play, and the date by which their contributions must be received. (The time-table should be related to that for the annual budget in view of the close association of this with the operating plan.) It is frequently wise for the instruction to begin preparing the annual operating plan to go out under the signature of the chief executive, who may add any additional policy guidelines and planning assumptions which should be taken into account. For the most part, these should come from the long-range plans.

Each operating plan should be scrutinised by the planner, to check that it is compatible with the long-range plan. It should be reviewed by top management at the same time as the budget.

Assignment of Tasks to Individuals

One of the most important components of any annual operating plan is the list of goals and personal standards of performance (reference Chapter 13). These give the company the ability to measure performance against the plan.

The financial effects of the annual plan will be reflected in the budget and controlled through the time-proven processes of budgetary control. This by itself will not ensure that the company is working to its plan, since budgets can be made to come right for the wrong reasons, and many essential actions cannot be measured through the budget.

Quantified goals and the assignment of tasks to particular people provide the company with a means of controlling all the aspects of the plan: a point which will be discussed in more detail later.

One of the tasks of the planner in the scrutiny of the annual operating plan should be to ensure that managers have converted all generalised statements of strategy into specific action steps. It is also necessary to ensure that actions which must be committed next year in order to make possible the plan for future years are also correctly identified and listed.

In a practical situation it is very easy for key actions essential to the long-range plan to be "lost", and for the company not to discover this until too late. The administrative task involved in preventing this is complex—but not difficult—and must be rated as an important part of the corporate planning process.

All personal standards of performance should be grouped by organisational responsibilities so that control can be exercised through normal management reporting lines. It also follows that the person who is expected to perform the task must be properly informed about it: an obvious requirement but one that is often overlooked.

Budgetary Control

The process of budgeting and budgetary control will be familiar to every reader of this book and needs no description. What is less well known is the relationship of the budget with the long-range planning procedures of the company. Mention has already been made in this chapter of this link, and it is now time to explore it in greater detail.

It is true to say that many managers confuse planning and budgeting. There are also many who consider that ruling a few more columns and extending a budget for five years ahead turns it into a plan. Yet although planning and budgeting are different, and are carried out for separate purposes, they have a close relationship.

I like to think of the annual budget as the quantification in financial terms of the annual operating plan, which itself derives—as we have seen—from the long-range plans. In this way the budget defines the expected effects of a planned course of action, tied in with longer-term strategies, and expected to achieve certain profit targets.

The long-range plan provides a standard for judgement of the budget: for strategic actions through the annual operating plan and, equally important, the profit targets which the budget should achieve. In the long-range plan the company identified the results that each major unit should achieve.

A budget that has no relationship with any long-term plan tends to be a shallow document. The actions allowed for may, or may not, be in the long-term interests of the company. Similarly, it is more difficult to be sure that the results of the budget are what the company ought to be aiming at.

The annual budget goes into much more detail than the long-range plan—it has to, as it is a control document and must provide control information for many responsibility centres split down to all meaningful items of expense and income. Postage may be a very important item in the budget but of no interest as an isolated expenditure in the long-range plan. Because of this difference of detail, and also because there is a time-lag between the completion of the long-range plan and the commencement of the budget, there are likely to be some differences in the figures. I believe this is inevitable.

However, the availability of the narrative description of the budget (annual operating plan) and the predetermined profit targets give top management sound criteria against which the budget can be compared. Areas of shortfall can be identified, and it is possible for annual operating plans and budgets to be referred back if they are inadequate. As divisional managers have already committed themselves in a general way to the long-term strategies and profit objectives, it is not unfair to expect them to sort out any differences.

At this point the annual operating plan and budget should be read together. Any significant change in budget should cause a re-examination of the annual plan, which in turn may put a question mark against a particular long-term strategy.

Eventually budget, annual operating plans, and long-range plans should be reconciled.

The budget is, of course, broken down into time periods. Monitoring results against budget, considering the effects of these on the chances of hitting targets, and identifying action areas to bring a straying company back on course are well known aspects of a budgetary control procedure. At any reporting period during the year the company should have a latest estimate of expected results.

The budget, from the beginning of the new year, becomes a way in which information on the results of long-term strategies begins to come back to top management. It provides an early warning system to allow management to begin to re-examine the validity of its strategies. Some discretion is needed in relating short-term results to long-term strategies, and deviations either way do not necessarily mean that the plan is wrong. On the other hand, it is often possible to see the validity of a new strategy at a very early stage.

There may be three main reasons for a deviation between budget and results—wrong implementation, wrong assumption, or an erroneous expectation of results (i.e. a wrong forecast). None of these necessarily mean that the plan is wrong: for example, a deviation from the expected sales because of abnormal weather conditions will rarely be a reason for altering all strategies. The combination of planning and budgeting makes it easier to identify which of the three causes of deviation actually applies (they may occur in combination), thus making it easier for management to decide what needs to be done.

Monitoring Performance

The goals and standards of performance (including tasks which have to be completed) set during the process of preparing the annual operating plan are there for a purpose. Because they are defined and assigned they can be monitored. The planner should consider a way of doing this when he designs the company's planning procedure.

Before studying ways in which this might be done it is worth thinking about the reasons for monitoring. Certainly it is not to ensure that all planned actions are carried out regardless of their present validity. Earlier in this chapter it was stated that the plan should be the slave of the manager, and not the other way round. In the first century BC Pubilius Syrius stated: "It is a bad plan that admits to no modification." The words are just as true today.

The fact that it may be desirable to change a planned course of action is not a licence for neglect. Managers are expected to fulfil all plans which are still appropriate and to substitute modified plans where plans are inappropriate. The important element is deliberate decision and evaluation and understanding of the implications of the change: it is not action by default. It is not an offence to change, but it is an offence for managers not to know that they have changed.

There are some actions which should be referred back to the chief executive before a final decision is taken. No company can have a situation where a major strategic action is changed because an individual manager prefers something different. But most of the tasks and performance standards measure aspects of the plans which lie within the competence and responsibility of the manager implementing them.

Monitoring these standards should give top management an opportunity to see the effect on the overall plan of failure and changes. A situation where actions rarely proceed according to plan may indicate lack of planning ability, or fast changing circumstances which are difficult to forecast. Lack of attention to plans in the first place is something that can be improved in time—provided the lesson is learned. Fast-changing circumstances may suggest that more attention should be given to contingency plans or that an attempt should be made to improve forecasting ability.

However good the company is at planning, events will change from time to time. The wise planner will accept this, and will devote efforts to ensuring that implementation changes are made responsibly and with intelligence. The planner will also identify the key goals and standards of performance. Many can be altered without any major effect on the company's overall strategic plan, particularly where an alternative action is substituted. A few are fundamental, and the planner must be aware of these.

The planner has a number of factors to consider when designing a monitoring procedure.

(a) How far is it possible to use existing organs for review and discussion which already exist in the company (e.g., committees)?
(b) How far can the process of monitoring be delegated to line management?
(c) Whether reporting should be on a total or exception basis.
(d) The frequency of the monitoring procedure.
(e) Whether the feedback procedure should be formal or informal, written, or verbal.
(f) How far the management information system has to be changed so that it regularly provides data needed to measure progress.

One simple procedure is to list all the objectives—used here in the sense of personal standards of performance—classified by organisational units and completion dates. A series of preplanned review meetings is established and the lists of objectives arranged so that all are reviewed on the meeting following the due date of completion. The lists become the basic agenda for the meeting, while additional columns on these lists can be filled in to provide the minutes.

Figure 27.2 provides an example of the format. If the objective has been achieved no further time need be spent on it (if the financial results turn out other than as forecast they will be picked up through the budgetary control system). Where it has not been achieved it becomes necessary for the responsible manager to account for his actions, state why he has failed, and assess the implications of failure. The review meeting may assist in examining the implications and helping the manager to define what should now be done.

					If not achieved, complete this section			
Date due	Person responsible	Description of objective	Source of objective	If achieved tick	Actual results attained	Reason for failure	Implications of failure	Action taken

FIG. 27.2. Example of a review sheet for personal standards of performance

Any actions which are re-scheduled are entered on to the appropriate agenda sheet for control at a future meeting. Careful organisation of the meetings can mean that they can be graded by seniority, so that each manager is effectively reporting upwards through the review meeting. It is also possible to add other key objectives which might be set during the course of the year, and to monitor these at the same time.

Heads of subsidiaries or major divisions report to the corporate management on an exception basis. They control their areas of responsibility through the system, and are in turn accountable to a higher level for achieving what their tactical plans and budget have promised.

This procedure works very well. In companies which already have a committee system it has the advantage of considerably reducing the length of the meeting, simplifying the minutes, and focusing attention on the important issues. It is a flexible system that can easily be fitted into any organisational need. It provides an opportunity for all managers who are affected by a failure in implementation to be aware of this. The system works mainly on an exception basis. Above all, it is simple to administer, requires little paper work, yet ensuring that nothing is neglected or allowed to go by default. Responsibility is firmly pinned to a particular individual from start to finish.

An alternative procedure is for the planner to abstract the list of items on a regular basis and for a letter to be sent to the relevant operating managers asking them to report on progress and explain the failures. Items which are known to have been implemented may be excluded. In addition to the regular reporting, a check should be kept on items of major significance on an *ad hoc* basis. If this system is used it is often valuable for the letters to be signed by the chief executive, thus stressing that it is top management which is most concerned with the plan's progress and making managers realise that it is the boss—and not the planner—who is going to be upset by a failure.

This procedure is more cumbersome than the first, and makes it harder to introduce exception reporting. It also raises the possibility that managers may feel that the planner is playing an unfortunate disciplinary role: something which they might resent. Certainly the planner cannot disguise the part played in the control procedure. Much ill feeling can be avoided if the planner sets out to be helpful to managers, reminding them of actions which he or she knows have been overlooked so that they have an opportunity to perform or explain the failure before they receive the letter from the top.

In any organisation there may be managers who consistently fail to implement. It is up to the chief executive to deal with them—not the planner. Failure to enforce some of the discipline will endanger all the company's planning effort. If no one appears to really care about implementation, the whole process of monitoring becomes an empty administrative exercise, and the plans themselves are debased.

The monitoring of capital expenditure appraisals, another important aspect of the control system, was discussed in the previous chapter.

Monitoring Assumptions

The fact that all plans are based on assumptions, and the importance of these in trying to bring the company to terms with its environment, are things which have been stressed several times in this book.

One important aspect of the control of plans is to continue to study and assess environmental trends so that the company may know whether its assumptions are still correct. If there are fundamental changes they may suggest that the plan should be reconsidered or altered. A computer model of the company can be of considerable help in examining the effect of these changes (see Chapter 31).

A company which is planning well will have contingency plans ready to implement in the event of a failure of key assumptions. Any company, including those who have neglected the preparation of contingency plans, should ensure that it becomes aware of major changes.

The organisation of a system to monitor assumptions need be little more than an extension of the company's continuous assessment of the environment. This may be carried out in a central planning department by the company's economic section or through its market research unit. The exact assignment of duties must depend on the company itself: the principle of this aspect of control is the same for every company.

Updating and Reconsideration of Plans as Required

Most companies are likely to prepare their long-range plans on a rolling basis with the opportunity to review annually. There are companies which expect a five-year plan to last them five years without amendment, but they are in the minority and certainly will not be following the advice of this book.

The need for flexible planning has also been stressed frequently, as has the fact that plans may have to be changed from time to time. Even the annual revision of strategies is an arbitrarily chosen period of time, and the events which bring the need for a change in plan cannot be guaranteed to occur at these chosen intervals. Something major is just as likely to happen on the day of publication.

When a fundamental change occurs it may be necessary to update a part or all of the plan outside of the normal planning cycle—a task made easier where the company has contingency plans and/or a computer based corporate model. Recognition of the need to amend the long-range plan is not an indication of failure by the planner: indeed, it is possible to claim it is a success. The ability to identify something that is going wrong before it happens, and the flexibility to react speedily to external influences are factors which all chief executives should seek in their approach to planning. There can be no doubt that a certain amount of replanning may be essential between planning cycles, nor is there likely to be much difficulty (assuming an effective control system) in identifying the circumstances when this is advisable.

Some planners recommend a regular updating of the financial results of the long-range plan rather than the *ad hoc* response to circumstances outlined above. A regular revision of all expected results for the whole of the period of the long-range plan is made as a matter of routine at quarterly or six-month intervals, under the theory that such a revision forces managers to correct for the multitude of developments which might otherwise have been ignored until the start of the next planning cycle, and at the same time forces the managers to see their plans as a dynamic document which they have to use. The concept is that such measures will provide top management with a clear idea of what the company is to achieve over the five-year period (or whatever time-span is used in the company's plan) rather like the "latest forecast" column which may be compared with the annual budget under a normal control system.

The great danger is that such a system can easily become empty, mechanistic, and bureaucratic. Usually nobody takes any notice of the data generated (often this is the fate it deserves), and there is a great danger that the company will slip into a system of extended budgeting rather than real planning. It is also very difficult for participants to be fully objective, and the expected results of the next few years tend to be unduly influenced by yesterday's sale, last week's strike, or the indigestion which started after lunch. The theoretical benefit of constant updating is that the manager, through being kept aware of his long-range plan, will make all decisions against the longer-term strategy. The practical result is at best usually a meaningless chore and, at worst, can be dangerous for the company. Where the complete processes of preparing a long-range plan demand several days thinking time from a manager, much evaluation, and spirited discussion, the partial regular revision is likely to be a ten-minute exercise.

Yearly Report on Planning Activity

The combination of the measures outlined so far will provide a motive force to drive the company to implement its plans. There is yet another step which should be taken as a means of measuring progress and as a tool to assist in the overall improvement of the company's planning ability. This is an annual progress report by the planner to the chief executive (to which specific managers may be invited to contribute) which should include:

(i)   A comparison of progress of the company against the long-range plans, including a note of revisions to plan which may have been made from time to time.

(ii) An analysis of the progress of the past year, its successes and failures and the reasons for variances.

(iii) The implications of the past year on future plans.

(iv) Ways in which the planning procedures may be improved.

Naturally the first item suggested above will have little value in the first year, but will build up into a useful dossier of planned results and performance. Much can be learned from this about the company's planning and forecasting ability.

The second section is not intended to be a repetition of the final report of results against budget, as there is little sense in duplicating work that has already been done. The planning report should analyse performance against all key goals and concentrate on the reasons for deviations: failure by managers to fulfil key tasks, over-ambitious targets, pessimistic forecasting, and lack of attention to assumptions. There may be some minor overlaps with the budget reports but basically the planner is seeking to draw planning lessons for the company so that it is possible to help managers to improve their planning and so that it is easier to move to the next stage of assessing the implications of the past year on future plans. Needless to say, the report is easier to write when things have gone well than when the company has had a bad year.

One of the most difficult problems is to assess how far a short-term reversal justifies a revision of strategy. Because so much depends on current profits—including the survival of the top management team—a shortfall creates an emotionally charged atmosphere with the danger that managers will deduce a trend from what has happened, haphazardly change long-term plans, and proceed to short-term cost-reduction methods which are not always in the company's interests. It may not be an easy situation, but it is always one which an objective analysis by the planner can help the company to act sensibly.

Logically there is no reason why any company should not encounter bad years from time to time. Acceptance of the logic does not, unfortunately, make the problem much easier when it actually occurs.

The planner should be just as objective in the assessments when the company has had a good year. Often this is accompanied by a wave of optimism which has as little foundation, in fact, as the pessimism which surrounds a bad year.

At any time the planner should be thinking of ways of improving the planning procedures, either through changes to the system, the introduction of refinements, or the use of new techniques. The planner's annual report should, against the background of the company's ability to plan, suggest actions that should be taken to do the job better. Planning is a dynamic process, and the company can easily outgrow its methods if it is not careful.

The planner's report should, although submitted to the chief executive, be designed for use by the company. It should be made available for all senior managers, and opportunity should be created for discussion on its assessments and recommendations.

It has to be accepted that a report of this nature may sometimes be critical of certain managers or divisions. While adverse criticism is rarely enjoyed by those singled out for mention, it is sometimes essential for progress. In this case the planner should take the manager concerned into his confidence before submitting the report, discuss the matter fully, and provide the opportunity for the manager to make any comments. Relations between managers and planner are likely to be better when everything is open than if there is a suspicion that any points made about them are done behind their backs. In any case, the planner in this report should concentrate on the results and should make no comments about abilities or skills.

The combination of all seven of the stages discussed in this chapter can make a very important contribution to the company's ability to implement and use its plans, to be more aware of what is happening to it, and to generally improve its planning expertise. My own experience suggests that together the stages make a powerful tool which is adequate for most companies: a tool which has sufficient flexibility to allow for modification to suit the needs of individual companies.

There is another approach which can replace some of the methods suggested here, and which is used effectively by many organisations: management by objectives.

Management by Objectives (MBO)

Much has been written on MBO—one of the most useful books is that of Humble[7]—and the brief résumé given here cannot do full justice to the subject. However, it can identify the main elements of MBO to show how these can fit into a total corporate planning process.

MBO really starts where the process of defining corporate and divisional objectives finishes (see Chapter 13). There have been instances of MBO being successfully introduced into companies which do not have any defined objectives or formal approach to planning, but this is not the recommendation of most of those who developed the system.

One of the first steps is what Humble[7] calls a key results analysis. This is an assessment worked out between each manager and his or her superior, identifying the key results which the manager must achieve to be successful in the job. From these are quantified standards of performance, a method of measuring results and identification of problems which have to be overcome.

Perhaps the biggest difference between this and the systems already described in this book is that MBO deals with all aspects of a manager's job, and can be used right down the organisation to managers whose direct influence on the implementation of the plan may be hard to see. The method described earlier in this chapter is designed to deal only with actions which arise out of the corporate plans, and is therefore applied only to managers whose link with those plans can be clearly identified. MBO is intended to be much more comprehensive than the other method: and being more comprehensive means that it takes much more effort to apply. Most practitioners recommend the appointment of MBO advisers to install and maintain the process.

Figure 27.3 provides an example of one key task for each of three functions. Exponents of MBO normally expect to identify about eight tasks, or key result areas, for each manager.

The manager is invited to set out in the key results analysis his or her own ideas for improving personal effectiveness and that of the company. These improvement plans are, in conjunction with the key tasks and control requirements, discussed between the manager and his superior, and firm improvement plans drawn up from them.

Control information goes to both the manager and his superior at frequent intervals, and is discussed between them. The idea is that such discussion will identify individual strengths and weaknesses, and areas where further training should be given. Figure 27.4 shows the link between MBO and the personal development of individual managers.

The complete process of MBO is shown in Fig. 27.5 which illustrates the relationship of individual performance with that of the unit in which the manager works.

The strength of MBO is that it is a participatory process in which the manager and his superior are both fully involved. Because it is a process which demands joint participation it can fail if senior managers do not fully contribute to it. It also leads to a much greater understanding by each manager of what his superior expects from him, what the important elements of his job really are, and how far he needs to change in order to be able to perform them in a satisfactory manner. The key idea is obtaining more enthusiasm and better motivation in a controlled atmosphere which descends directly from the corporate objectives and plans.

Its weakness is that it is not something to be entered into lightly, and demands a great deal of senior management attention. A simpler method of controlling plans may be made fully effective in a much faster time: but this is all it will do. It will not, like MBO, embrace all managers, nor will it be connected with training and other aspects of personal planning.

The company has to decide for itself which of the methods of control it will apply. The company which puts in no control mechanism will find it very difficult to bridge that wide gulf between planning and action.

MBO has many behavioural aspects, and many consider that it has been overtaken by more recent concepts of empowerment.

Key task	Performance standard	Control data	Suggestions for improvement
E.g. of a key task for a Production Manager Use of resources. To ensure that the most effective use is made of available resources	Labour: When average waiting time never exceeds 0.5% in any month. When ratio of direct to indirect labour does not exceed 4.0. When labour turnover, including staff, does not exceed 15% p.a. When pay performance is 95%.	Returns from wages office. Quarterly check on personnel records. Quarterly check on personnel records. Returns from wages office	
	Machines: Average machine utilisation never falls below 75%. No machine is utilised for less than 85% of its time.	No control information available at present. No control information available at present.	This information must be produced.
	Floor space: When not less than 90% of available factory floor area is utilised for production.	Annual check on floor area by works engineer.	
	Stocks: When the money utilised in providing stocks never exceeds the specified figure.	Monthly accounts.	These figures are based only on past experience; suggest a project be carried out to determine optimum figures
E.g. of a key task for an Area Sales Manager To establish with each customer the stock levels he should hold so that delivery times can be kept economic with minimum risk of stock-out.	Following delivery times are acceptable to customers and met: |	90% Orders within	97% Orders within
Cat. A	7 days	14 days
Cat. B	4 days	7 days
Sp. Accts.	7 days	14 days		(1) Outstanding orders analysis (2) Customer complaints	If we are to meet even these generous delivery times reliably, either depot stocks of some items will have to be increased or lead times from the factory reduced. I suggest an OR investigation of optimum stock levels.
E.g. of a key task for a Research Manager To recognise competitors' technological strategy and to advise M.D. when objectives should be modified.	Company's marketing and operating programmes never require "crash" changes due to failure to recognise competitors' technological strategy.	No record needed. Any such occurrence will be recognised by all.	Our methods of collecting news of competitors' technological strategy need improving. (See improvement plan for first half of 1966.)

FIG. 27.3. Key results analysis. (Reproduced by courtesy of Urwick Orr & Partners Ltd.) This analysis includes a summary of the *Main Purpose of Job; Position in Organisation; Scope of Job; Personal Activities;* and *Limits of Authority.* The heart of the analysis is the *Key Tasks* section

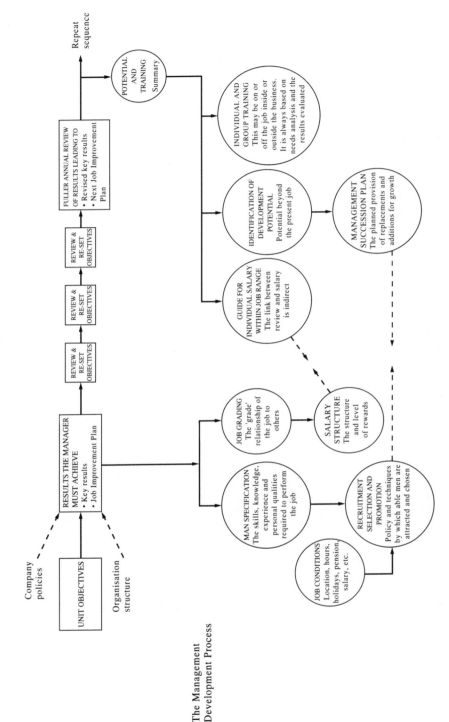

The Management
Development Process

FIG. 27.4. Improving management performance. (Reproduced by courtesy of Urwick Orr & Partners Ltd.)

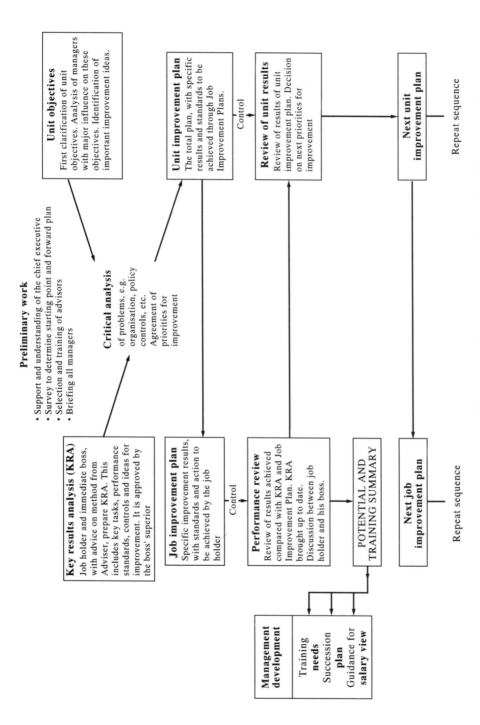

FIG. 27.5. Typical launching sequence for MBO. (Reproduced by courtesy of Urwick Orr & Partners Ltd.)

References

1. Bomona, "Making Your Marketing Strategy Work", *Harvard Business Review*, March/April 1984.
2. Ringbakk, K. A. "Why Planning Fails", *European Business*, Spring 1971.
3. Alexander, L. D. "Successfully Implementing Strategic Decisions", *Long Range Planning*, Vol. 18, No. 3, 1985.
4. Alexander, L. D. "Strategy Implementation: Nature of the Problem", Hussey, D. E. (ed.), *International Review of Strategic Management*, Vol. 2, No. 1, Wiley, Chichester, 1991.
5. Anthony, R. N. *Planning and Control Systems: A Framework for Analysis*, Harvard, 1965.
6. Hussey, D. E. "Corporate Planning at Fyffes Group", *Long Range Planning*, September 1969.
7. Humble, J. W. *Improving Business Results*, McGraw-Hill, 1967.

28

Management of Change

In the previous chapter we looked at some of the behavioural issues in implementing plans, but concentrated mainly on the systems rather than the people. Change is going on all the time, and not always as the result of a predetermined strategy, which is why I have given a somewhat broader title to this chapter. However, the subject matter is critical to the successful implementation of strategic decisions.

Figure 28.1 shows a typical change sequence. Something triggers off a need for change. It may be the result of a considered strategy, or of a reaction to something that happens outside of the business. Whatever it is, change is unlikely to happen until someone has recognised the trigger event. Since we live in the real world, it is worth stressing that the trigger event is often not a major change in circumstances, but the arrival of a new chief executive whose perception is different from that of his or her predecessors. We saw this in the Lloyds Bank example in Chapter 12, where the trigger was not a new strategy, but realisation that looking at issues in a different way would lead to innumerable new strategies. We saw it in Chapter 10, where one of the danger points in competitor analysis is when there is a change of top management. Empirically we see it in examples of major transformational

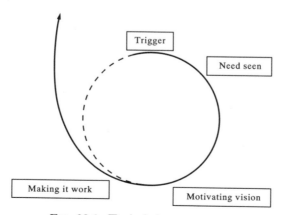

FIG. 28.1. Typical change sequence

509

change, such as British Petroleum, GE, and British Telecom. In each of these companies, change is associated with a particular chief executive, who recognised triggers that others might have missed.

A trigger event can take place, but will only cause change if the need is seen. Thus many organisations miss the signals. Ansoff might well argue that companies which are managing in a style inappropriate to their level of environmental turbulence would probably miss the signals, or react in an inappropriate way (see Ansoff[1]).

Chapter 3 discussed the idea of leadership and vision, and as we will see these are important ingredients in the management of change. In Fig. 28.1 the reminder is that unless the perceived need is translated into a new vision of what has to be done, change is unlikely to occur. The really hard work starts in the next box on the diagram, making it work. The future course of the company depends on how well each stage of this model is carried out. In the diagram, the thick line symbolises success and movement to a new and appropriate future. The dotted line implies that although much energy is expended, nothing much happens, and the company ends up in the same place from which it started. Not shown, but also possible is the end state being considerably worse than the present, either because the wrong strategy is implemented, or the right strategy is not implemented.

Different Circumstances of Change

Before proceeding further, we should consider a variety of different change circumstances. My thinking here owes a considerable debt to Stace and Dunphy,[2] who pointed out that there are both different types of change, and different change strategies that can be successful.

Figure 28.2 uses some of their ideas. It draws attention to two fundamentally different types of change, incremental which moves in a series of small steps, some of which may be hardly noticeable, and transformational where the change may be vast and fundamental. This is related to the situation in the company, the degree of support for the change from the key players. Stace and Dunphy provide a spectrum of styles:

—collaborative
—consultative
—directive
—coercive.

Box A shows incremental change where there is a high degree of support from the key people. The change may be known, as in a marketing plan which involves the launch of a new related product, or it may be unknown in the sense that the aims are clear, but empowered teams or individuals are determining the actions that are to be implemented, as in a continuous improvement process. Under the circumstances of box A, the most appropriate style is likely to be collaborative or consultative. This does not mean that leadership is unnecessary (see Chapter 3), but that there is likely to be minimal resistance to, and possibly even enthusiasm

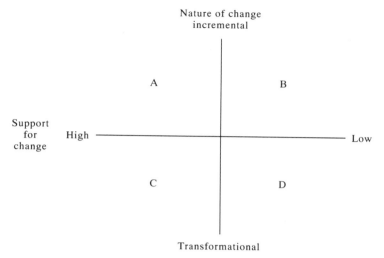

FIG. 28.2. Types of change and the degree of support for change. Based on the ideas of Stace and Dunphy[2]

for, change. Because the gap between where the organisation is now and the next step is not too vast, there may be little fear of the effects of change. Continuous improvement and total quality management processes are an excellent example of collaborative incremental change in action. Teams are empowered, but coordinated, and ideally are drawn from across the organisation to avoid a "functional chimney" view. The philosophy under which the teams work is shared, and there is continuous measurement of progress. Under this concept the amount of change attained may be very great, although each action is one step on a journey without end. The continuous improvement concept will only work when there is support through the organisation, widespread involvement at all levels, and adequate training of everyone who is touched by the process. It also requires much top management time.

In box B there is an incremental change without the support of the key people. The assessment here is whether support can be gained in a reasonable time, in which case a consultative approach could be appropriate, or whether to use directive means which may involve making people take certain actions. A mix of both is possible. Directive methods do not necessarily imply that commitment by those involved is not achievable. Although attitudes to a large degree affect behaviour, and logic suggests that the right thing to do to build commitment is to change attitudes first, the evidence is that in many situations a change of behaviour can bring about a change in attitudes. In fact there are situations when behaviour is not in line with an attitude: for example a number of smokers may now hold an attitude that smoking is not a good thing, but they may still smoke.

Box C moves to transformational change. Stace and Dunphy use the term charismatic change to describe this box. Support may be there because of the charisma of the person leading the change, and a willingness by all to accept that the vision painted of the new future is the right one, because of faith in the qualities of the leader, or it may be because the logic of the situation is apparent: the company faces insolvency unless urgent action is taken. Collaborative or consultative styles would be appropriate here, provided there is enough time to apply them. The greater the shared perception of urgency, the more likely are people to be willing to follow a directive style without this causing any negative effects.

Transformational change which implies hard actions, like restructuring an entire business, closing down loss-making divisions, or expanding into a new geographical area is usually easier for people to relate to, even if they are numbered among the losers, than accompanying changes in culture. It is hard to see how culture can be related to the new vision, without some flexing of styles between directive and consultative. Previous chapters have mentioned how Scandinavian Airlines went through a major change of strategy and culture during the 1980s, moving from a system driven to an empowered, customer responsive organisation. Much of the change was achieved through communication and consultative methods. At times the style was much more directive, as for example when key managers were asked to leave and replaced by others with empathy for the change.

Box D represents the toughest situation of all. The change may be massive, but is not supported by many people. Much of the literature focuses on the need to build the required level of support in the organisation. Figure 28.3 adds a layer of detail to the leadership model which was explored in Chapter 3, and offers some sub-headings under which essential management practices are grouped. Under vision, we now have the tasks related to formulating a vision of the desired state, and implementing that vision. Under commitment we have tasks which firstly build a shared commitment, and secondly sustain that commitment. Under management, we have issues of managing performance and managing change itself. There are other models and approaches, but most have a strong behavioural element.

FIG. 28.3. Expanded leadership model. Copyright Harbridge Consulting Group Ltd. Used with permission

There are of course strong arguments for managing change in a way that gains the support of the people in the organisation. However, it is not the only model, and again I am grateful to Stace and Dunphy[2] for drawing attention to the coercive approach, where change is steam rollered through by the top person and anyone who does not go along with it is, in a manner of speaking, squashed flat. One example is the way Murdoch changed the way his newspapers were produced, in the teeth of ferocious opposition by the print unions. The change was imposed, and everything that needed to be done to drive the change through was done. It did not matter if at the end there was a complete change of employees, as the ultimate vision of a cost effective production process was all that mattered. The power of the union over the manning levels and methods of production was broken for ever, and few would argue that the industry as a whole is not better for it. But there is no doubt that the methods used were totally coercive. Lewis[3] provides a detailed research study of coercive transformation in an Australian college, where change was achieved through "short sharp bursts of activity, that is by discontinuous change". The model mirrored the freeze–unfreeze–freeze approach of Lewin,[4] and although attempts were made to supplement the coercive change strategy with other methods, these failed because of luck of trust. All the new objectives were achieved and sustained over a lengthy period, and the change was achieved quickly at each unfreezing stage. The downside was a long-term situation of demoralised staff, with a gulf of trust and understanding between academic staff and management.

A steam roller approach fits the personal style of some managers, and is therefore something that they may feel comfortable with. However if we are trying to make a rational choice of the appropriate method to achieve change, we should exclude this factor (a preference does not necessarily mean that the approach is appropriate) and consider when transformational change might best be achieved by draconian means. I suggest the following circumstances for consideration:

(i)   When the change has to be completed at maximum speed and there is no realistic alternative.

(ii) When consensus is impossible under any circumstances, which was probably the case in the Murdoch newspaper example.

(iii) When the price that has to be paid in employee motivation, resignations, loss of trust, and complete lack of shared vision and commitment is seen as less important than a fast result, or of little importance at all.

Some Examples of Transformational Change

Most major transformational change will follow a mix of styles, and in some way following the thinking if not the letter of the leadership model. It is about creating, defining and building commitment to a new vision, and supporting this with the management effort that enables it to work. The two examples that will be mentioned are of British Telecom and British Petroleum, and in both cases the information has been drawn from published sources.

British Telecom

The vision of British Telecom is to become the most successful world-wide telecommunications group. The trigger for changes was a mix of external pressures and internal constraints which by 1990 had reached a point where the chief executive felt that action had to be taken. External pressures included the pace of technological change, with a 30% per annum fall in the costs of telecommunications as new technologies became available. The complexity of the telecommunications industry had increased, to the point when it was difficult to see the joins with other industries, such as computers. The degree of turbulence in the environment had increased dramatically. Internally there was a mis-match of the organisation and its old public utility culture with the vision and the external world. Managers' perceptions were not always appropriate, and the culture was introspective and controlling, rather than outward looking and proactive.

The desired change included a need to alter the culture of the organisation. Before the change strategy was implemented the culture was prescriptive, with individuals being expected to conform to requirements. The desired change was to a culture that enabled individuals to excel, with the company providing the support that made this possible. At the same time there was a need to reduce the number of jobs and, partly to reduce costs and partly to enable the organisation to be more customer responsive, this included a new structure which would remove nine layers of management.

On 26th March 1990 the chairman addressed the top 300 managers, they were told that the organisation would change over the next 12 months, and that all 36,000 managers would take on new jobs. They were informed that there would be fewer jobs, and that the new organisation would be in place by 1st April 1991. One purpose of the change arose from a TQM initiative which had begun in 1985, which was to gain more customer focus by using culture change that included values that addressed the customer. A team was set up to implement the changes.

After 4 months organisational design had become an industry in its own right, many of those involved in this new "industry" were demonstrating the behaviours that the new design was intended to remove, such as the withholding of information, arbitrary decision making and a growth in bureaucracy. This led to a measure of cynicism in the organisation. A survey was made, which showed that actions were at odds with the vision, help was needed if managers were to behave differently, the whole process had made people more inward looking, and individuals were seeking sustained and continuous leadership from the board.

One result of this survey was the introduction of a 2.5 day leadership programme. By 1st April 1991, 600 managers had been through the programme, with a heavy involvement of the chairman. The balance of managers had seen a video presentation, with a board member present to answer questions. By March 1992 there was a widespread recognition that the business was more turbulent, that most senior managers had been operating operationally rather than strategically, and a level of awareness had been developed among many people to enable them to participate in translating the group strategy to action.

Much of this change process was highly visible, because of the high profile of the company. The need for communication and effort to build shared values is clear from what happened, as is the need to train people to enable them to play the right part in the changed situation. Also clear is the length of time needed to change values in a long-established organisation.

British Petroleum

It is not possible to have a higher profile in a change process than to invite a journalist to sit in and write about the board meetings where the change strategy is decided. This is what BP did, with decisions being taken over several meetings in the presence of a *Financial Times* journalist.

BPs change strategy was the result of a very detailed analysis involving many people. In July 1989, the chairman designate, Robert Horton, commissioned "Project 1990", a major internal study which had the aim of showing how to reduce complexity in the organisation, to re-design the head office organisation, and to re-position the company in approach and style for the 1990s. The project team consulted widely inside and outside of BP, undertaking over 500 interviews and processing some 4000 questionnaires.

The implementation on the culture change began in 1990, when Horton was appointed chairman. Its objective was to achieve the BP vision through the people, within a simple, supportive organisation. The process followed a number of principles.

(i)   The need for change was analysed in a way that took information from many people, as described above.
(ii) Considerable effort was given to inspiring enthusiasm for change, involving communication of various types, and including explanations of the need for change.
(iii) The emphasis was on building an organisation for the future, and the structure chosen was unusual enough to be exciting.
(iv) Top management drove the change process, and provided adequate resources for implementation.
(v)   There was widespread involvement of everyone in the change process, including a major educational initiative.
(vi) Processes were developed to support the change, including the identification of the competencies needed for employees working under the new culture.
(vii) There was continuous review of the change process.

Of course things did not always go smoothly, and a major problem was an increase in environmental turbulence at the time the change process started. The UK moved into recession in 1990, and the oil industry worldwide found oil prices declining. This meant that certain strategies for disposing of non-core businesses became more urgent, and more costs had to be taken out of the company. This meant that in addition to the planned changes leading to a smaller head office and more putting out of work to third parties, there were other factors which meant that many people had to leave the company. Change was thus implemented against a background of budgetary pressure, terminations and early retirements. Part way through the process the chief executive left the company. However, the strength of the change process was that culture has changed in the direction desired, despite all the additional complications and individual uncertainties.

Change and People

One popular myth is that people resist change. Like all myths, there are some elements of truth in the statement, but we could also argue that many people welcome change. The fact is that our daily lives take place in an environment where change of one sort or another is a normal state. What may make people react adversely to change is:

(i) lack of understanding of the need for change
(ii) belief that the change proposed is not appropriate
(iii) failure to appreciate the urgency behind a planned change
(iv) concern that the change will have an adverse personal impact
(v) failure to appreciate the many small actions needed to implement a major change.

The leadership model discussed earlier deals with how to overcome some of these problems. There is an additional concept which may help to explain why people sometimes appear to resist change, even though they may agree with its objectives. This is the concept of the psychological, the unwritten part of the relationship between employer and employee. It embraces the expectations of both parties, and because it is internal to the parties, and could never be made totally explicit (partly because some components only become critical when they are threatened), it may be difficult to deal with. Let me give an example. A managing director of a subsidiary may have reported direct to the main board, and may have felt that the relationship with the board is a critical part of the job, giving prestige, a feeling that there is an influence on main board strategies, and regular contact with the top people. The structure changes, and the managing director now reports to a regional office, which also determines many aspects of broad strategy. The job title, salary, and subordinate relationships have not changed, but what has been lost is something that the incumbent felt was an important part of the job. The psychological contract has changed, and this change may be enough to make the managing director resist the change. Resistance may take many forms. It may be passive, in that there is apparent acceptance, but the excitement has gone out of the job, levels of effort reduced, and there may be a few telephone calls to executive search consultants. It may be very aggressive, with active opposition of the new order, and even sabotage. Resistance may take the form of working to rules, and no longer doing more than is demanded by the new procedures.

The important point in considering change management is that psychological contracts exist at all levels. One argument for consultation during a change process is that it provides the opportunity for the expectations to be clear, and for issues to surface before they become problems. Later in this chapter there will be some discussion of empowerment, but it is worth remembering that the introduction of a process of empowerment is likely to break the psychological contacts of both empowerers and "empowerees", and may be reinforced by uncertainty of both about how they should work under the new concept. Such changes are more likely to be successful if accompanied by counselling and training, as well as the changing of company processes and systems that do not reinforce the concept. Just issuing a policy statement that the organisation follows the principles of empowerment is unlikely to bring about any effective change.

Figure 28.4 draws heavily on some ideas by Alexander,[5] one of the few people who has undertaken research into the implementation of strategic plans. It suggests that there may be two factors which work either together or against each other to contribute to successful implementation: agreement with the change and the degree of effort put in by key implementors. It is possible to have low effort combined with an agreement with the change. This may be because the implementers are preoccupied with normal work, and do not give the time to the change, it may be because they do not understand the role that has to be played by them, or think that it is someone else's job. It may also be that the psychological contract gets in the way. Alexander calls this tokenism, and it is important for those trying to cause change to develop approaches to overcome it.

The second low effort box is when there is little or no acceptance of the change, either because the need is not seen, or because the strategy is believed to be wrong. This can cause outright rejection, cynicism ("We've heard that one before", "Open communication with that lot upstairs!", or "I'll believe that if it happens"). Good communication, with clear explanation of the need to change may change this situation, although there will always be a problem if the rejection is justified, and the change is inappropriate!

The ideal box is where both dimensions are high, and the key implementors take on the task of inspiring others and driving the change forward. The final box may

| | | Effort by key implementors | |
		Low	High
Agreement with the change	High	• Too busy • Not my responsibility	• Inspire others • Let's get on with it
	Low	• Rejection • Cynicism	• Trust the board • Best of a bad job

FIG. 28.4. Typical responses to strategic change. Inspired by Alexander[5]

lead to successful change, but can indicate a problem. "I don't agree with it, but I expect the board is right" as a response may help the change forward, but is unlikely to lead to many creative inputs from the implementors. Making the best of a bad job conceals disagreements that would be better in the open.

All the boxes in this diagram reinforce the value of the leadership model in Fig. 28.3.

Getting Managers to Plan the Implementation of Strategy

We saw in the last chapter that there are many things which may prevent a strategy from being implemented, and in particular we were able to look at the top problems identified in Alexander's research.[5] One of the practical issues which I find is that many managers have little experience of planning the implementation of strategies, particularly strategies that are transformational. It is at this stage when we have to move from the broad statements of intent, to the detail of what particular people must do. We touched on this in the last chapter in a system sense. However, just planning the actions that people have to undertake is not the whole story. It may not be enough to agree that a particular action has to happen, and we may also have to ensure that the people who have to carry out the action have the skills and knowledge to do it well.

Figure 28.5 is an example of a method I have found useful in strategy workshops to get managers discussing and identifying the mix of hard and soft issues that should be considered. It takes a number of negative statements from Alexander's research, and turns them into positive things that have to be done. Sixteen items appear on the list. It would be possible to add more, and this may be desirable if there are particular situations in the company that should be considered. All managers in the workshop are asked to rank 10 of the 16 items. The scoring method is designed to make it easy for all the questionnaires to be aggregated, so that a top 10 for the whole group can emerge. After ranking, they are asked to assess the degree of difficulty they see in dealing with each issue. When producing a total difficulty score for all people on the workshop, it is worth remembering that the appropriate average is of the people who have ranked the factor, not of the number who have completed the questionnaire.

The value of the approach is that it helps managers to consider the hard and soft issues in the context of what they have to do. This means that there is a norm (the total picture drawn from all questionnaires) with which individuals can compare their answers, which provides a rich ground for discussion. Unless all the managers are from the same function and business unit and are facing the same change, there should be differences between the answers. The facilitator also has a secret weapon. If no one appreciates the importance of what are clearly critical factors, it is always possible to force a discussion by comparing their answers with the overall results of Alexander's research. The differences between the research results and this questionnaire are in timing. The questionnaire tries to anticipate what must be considered, so that ways of doing this can be constructed. The research looked back at what went wrong in implementing strategies.

	Factor	Rank up to 10 factors in order of concern to you (10 = highest 1 = lowest)*	Rate your chosen factors on difficulty to overcome (1 = easy 5 = very hard)
1.	Defining key implementation task and activities in enough detail		
2.	Foreseeing all the issues and problems that should be tackled		
3.	Preventing day to day operations from distracting implementation		
4.	Ensuring that major changes in the business environment do not block implementation		
5.	Ensuring understanding by your managers of the strategy		
6.	Creating a shared vision at all levels of management		
7.	Ensuring that managers possess the knowledge and capabilities needed to implement		
8.	Ensuring that other employees have the skills and capabilities to implement		
9.	Dealing with the situation when the new strategy is not compatible with manager's personal goals		
10.	Ensuring that there are enough resources to implement		
11.	Setting an achievable time scale		
12.	Setting a system so that implementation may be monitored and controlled		
13.	Ensuring that senior managers have the time to implement		
14.	Communicating the implementation plan to the right people		
15.	Overcoming employee resistance to implementation		
16.	Dealing with the fear that change can provoke		

Please add any other factors that you think should be in your top 10.
* Score the most important factor 10. The second most important 9, etc.

FIG. 28.5. Factors to consider in implementation

Management Training and Strategic Change

In Chapter 21 the case was argued for a more strategic view of management training and management development. The value of using training as a key part of a change process cannot be over stressed, although to be successful may involve throwing out some preconceived ideas about the design and delivery of training courses.

In Chapter 21 the types of situation where training could contribute to strategic change were listed briefly. In a little more detail they are:

Strategy Formulation

The right programmes can be used to challenge the assumptions to which current plans are based, or to examine strategic options.

Strategy Implementation

An appropriate initiative can be used to enable an understanding of the strategy to be gained in the broad terms, and in its impact on an individual and his or her job. Commitment can be built as people discover the reason for the strategy, and decide for themselves that it makes sense. Implications of the strategy can be explored and converted into personal action plans. Appropriate training can be given to correct deficiencies in the skills or knowledge of those who are involved in implementing the change.

Policy Implementation

A change in policy, such as a decision to put more effort behind competitor analysis can often be effectively implemented with the aid of training programmes, which can build commitment to the policy and ensure that people are both able and willing to implement it.

Corporate Culture

Training may be a major tool in creating a culture or changing a culture. In turn this will help ensure that strategies and culture are compatible.

Environmental Change

Significant changes in the business environment may provide threats or opportunities. Appropriate training initiatives can help the organisation identify and deal with major changes.

Solving Problems

Training programmes may also be designed to solve particular problems, such as how to increase market share, or improve profitability. The mechanism is similar to the other categories shown, and among other things is based on shared understanding, involvement, and the enhancement of skills needed to deal with the situation.

A glance back at the factors in Fig. 28.5 will reveal that many would be partly solved had the power of management training been used to help implement.

A training initiative does not have to be positioned as training. It may be logged as work, since it may deal totally with real issues, and the educational element may be hidden. An example is the questionnaire discussed above. A good facilitator could bring out the importance of the issues and their consequences in the context of developing an action plan for implementing a strategy.

As can be seen from the example a training initiative can be used to develop knowledge and skills the lack of which would frustrate implementation, it can be part of the communication process, and it can provide a collaborative approach, either in the formulation of strategy itself, or more frequently in defining the detailed implementation issues. It can build commitment to the change.

I argued that some preconceived ideas may have to be discarded. The first is that we are not talking about a routine programme. The initiative has to be specifically designed, and totally tailored to meet the needs of the company. If issues are included, the materials for the programme must be developed to include those issues. Such a programme cannot be lifted off the shelf, and must be specially designed for the company, which means that it may be more expensive than a routine training initiative. Few internal training staff have the experience and capability to design initiatives of this type, which by their nature stretch across many functional skills, and require a different approach to a standard training course. Even in companies that normally staff all training events from internal sources, there is a need for the services of external, uninvolved, senior consultants to make the concept work. In many companies, the training function lacks the credibility to perform the task, even if it possesses the skills.

It is indicative that in both of the transformational case histories given earlier, training was used as a means of facilitating change. Many of the problems that do occur would be removed if more organisations chose this route, and supported it with an adequate budget.

Empowerment

The final topic of this chapter is to turn attention to modern concepts of empowerment. In doing this I have drawn on an unpublished paper by Phil Lowe[6] of Harbridge Consulting Group, who has helped me to appreciate the difference between the modern concept of empowerment, and the long established issue of delegation. It is something more than old wisdom dressed in new clothes.

Of course it is possible to argue that empowerment as a concept has been around a long time, even though it may not have found its full place in management. The earliest writing I have found on this, also incidentally about what is probably the first recorded management consulting assignment, is found in the Bible, Exodus, Chapter 18, verses 13 to 27.

Moses' father in law watched him judging and counselling the people in the ways of God, and noted that the process lasted from morning to evening, exhausted Moses and tied up most of the people. I pick up the story at verse 17.

17.   And Moses father in law said unto him, The thing thou doest is not good.
18.   Thou will surely wear away, both thou, and this people that is with thee: for this thing is too heavy for thee: thou art not able to perform it alone.

19.   Hearken now unto my voice, I will give the counsel, and God shall be with thee. Be thou for the people to Godward, that thou mayest bring the causes unto God.

20.   And thou shalt teach them ordinances and laws, and thou shalt shew them the way wherein they must walk, and the work that they must do.

21.   Moreover thou shalt provide out of all the people able men, such as fear God, men of truth, hating covetousness; and place such over them, to be rulers of thousands and rulers of hundreds, rulers of fifties and rulers of tens:

22.   And let them judge the people at all seasons: and it shall be that every great matter they shall bring unto thee, but every small matter they shall judge: so shall it be easier for thyself, and they shall bear the burden with thee.

23.   If thou shalt do this thing, and God command thee so, then thou shalt be able to endure, and all this people shall also go to their place in peace.

24.   So Moses hearkened to the voice of his father in law, and did all that he had said.

25.   And Moses chose able men out of all Israel, and made them heads over the people, rulers of thousands, rulers of hundreds, rulers of fifties and rulers of tens.

26.   And they judged the people at all seasons: the hard cases they brought unto Moses, but every small matter they judged themselves.

27.   And Moses let his father in law depart: and he went his way into his own land.

History does not record the size of the consultancy fee, but in this extract we see aspects of training, competencies, structure, definitions of responsibilities, limits of authority, and delegation. Had the advice been given now, no doubt there would have been some de-layering! In true consultant's style, Jethro the father in law also painted the benefits to Moses of following the advice. Unusually he seems to have stayed around to see it implemented.

Empowerment is defined by Lowe[6] as:

"A process by which individual employees are given the autonomy, motivation and skills necessary to perform their jobs in a way which provides them with a sense of ownership and fulfilment while achieving shared organisational goals."

An empowered organisation is more responsive, in that people closest to the source of problems are able to deal with them, it gives flexibility in managing change, and is essential if organisations are to function once layers are torn out of the structure. Reaching a state of empowerment is difficult, because it challenges many things that the managed and managers had taken for granted. Managers, for example need to see their roles as facilitators, coaches and sponsors, where historically many have been organisers of others, and supervisors. To make this change, and those managed may find it as difficult as do those who manage them, requires the alignment of company systems and processes to the new concept, considerable training, and counselling over a period to ensure that managers actually apply the new concept.

An empowered organisation should provide individuals with:

(i) A sense of purpose and a commitment to company goals.

(ii) Recognition of individual achievements, and continuous feed back on performance.

(iii) Training where it is needed.

(iv) Autonomy to perform their jobs in a way that suits them, providing it is consistent with organisational goals and values.

It means that all employees are able to see the results of their work, accept responsibility for their own performance, feel that they have an identity in the organisation, are able to have a say in things which affect their work, and share a commitment to continuous improvement.

TQM is a driver towards empowerment, as is much of the modern thinking on manufacturing. The pressure for improved customer responsiveness is another driver, for adequate responsiveness can only occur when those close to the customer are empowered to make most of the decisions about issues that affect the customer.

Summary

What perhaps separates strategic management from strategic planning is perhaps this emphasis on the totality of strategic change. Planning strategy is not easy, but the difficulties are as nothing compared to managing a process of strategic change. If strategies are not implemented they are a waste of time, and as we have seen implementation calls for a variety of different skills, not all of which may be possessed by the average manager. Today's manager cannot rely on miracles, as Moses is reputed to have done, and few have father in laws who can give such sensible advice. There we have to find other ways of coping, and I would put leadership and the management of change very high in the list of competencies which managers at all levels should possess.

References

1. Ansoff, H. I. *Implanting Strategic Management*, 2nd ed., Prentice-Hall, London, 1990.
2. Stace, D. A. and Dunphy, D. C. "Translating Business Strategies into Action: Managing Strategic Change", *Journal of Strategic Change*, Vol. 1, No. 4, July/August, 1992.
3. Lewis, D. "Power-based Organisational Change in an Australian Tertiary College", *Journal of Strategic Change* Vol. 2.6, December 1993.
4. Lewin, K. *Field Theory in Social Science*, Harper and Row, New York, 1951.
5. Alexander, L. D. "Strategy Implementation: Nature of the Problem", Hussey, D. E. (ed.), *International Review of Strategic Management*, Wiley, Chichester, 1991.
6. Lowe, P. "The Background to Empowerment", Harbridge Consulting Group, London (unpublished working paper, 1993).

PART 5

Introducing Planning to an Organisation

"Immortality is to labor at an eternal task"—
ERNEST RENAN, *L'Avenir de la Science*, 1890.

29

Introducing Strategic Management

Throughout this book the aim has been to present strategic management at both a conceptual and a practical level. In order to make sense the practical implications have been restricted to the particular aspect of planning which was under discussion. It is now time to leave the discussion of individual components and to look again at the complete process. The next chapters are very much a continuation of the first three, which also examined corporate planning from a wholistic viewpoint.

This and the following chapters deal solely with practicalities. In this chapter are presented some thoughts on the problem of introducing strategic management into an organisation. Some problems will still remain, and these will be discussed in the next chapter, which draws heavily on the published surveys of planning in practice. This will be followed by a discussion of some of the techniques that may be used in corporate planning and which, although they may have appeared in passing in earlier chapters, have not been dealt with at any length.

I think it is true to say that many attempts at introducing corporate planning have been doomed to fail from the outset simply because too little forethought was given to what was really involved. A technique such as marketing research, a new forecasting method, or discounted cash flow can be applied to a company at will in as large or small a dose as desired. We saw in Chapter 1 that strategic management is not a technique but a complete way of running a business. The application of corporate planning is not like taking a patent elixir in casual doses, but is a strict regimen that transforms the patient and which can do harm if administered haphazardly.

Strategic management in any company should begin with a decision. The only person who can take this decision is the chief executive, who must reach the conclusion that this is the way in which he or she wishes to manage the company. Ideally at this stage the top management team should share this enthusiasm. The chief executive's enthusiasm must also infect others with the same feeling. The decision to implement planning should not be taken lightly.

The first problem the chief executive will encounter following the decision is how to implement it. If the company is of any significant size, the probability is that it will need some full-time professional help in the person of a corporate planner. Smaller companies may need this assistance but may not be able to afford the services of a full-time person: for them there is another solution—the use of part-time specialists. At the start-up stage it is possible for a chief executive to use a firm of management consultants, although this solution is usually only economic in the short term, and a more permanent arrangement is needed once the problems of introduction have been overcome.

The best solution of all, if it is workable, is for the chief executive to be the planner. This will only work where he or she is fully conversant with all aspects of the corporate planning process and if it has been possible to delegate enough of the other work to allow adequate time for planning matters. Unfortunately, the nature of top management being as it is, these circumstances rarely apply. In many ways this is a pity because maximum enthusiasm would be generated in a situation where the chief executive was so obviously deeply involved in the process.

Part-time professional planners are a solution which has been rarely applied. For many small companies the specialist need is probably for only three to four days attendance a month, and could be achieved by the appointment of a suitable non-executive director to the board (or, more exactly, a part-time executive director). From the point of view of the specialist planner the ability to work for a number of non-competing companies makes this an interesting and economic proposition. The company gains expertise from someone with a continuous involvement in the business: this, too, can be an economic concept. There are one or two firms of consultants who specialise in this type of service. I believe that it is a concept which will become increasingly important in the future.

Much of the impact of strategic management throughout the world still depends on the professional corporate planner. Few effective planning processes have been installed without the skilled services offered by this type of manager.

The chief executive who decides a corporate planner is needed is faced with another choice. Should someone be recruited from inside the organisation or brought in from outside? Each possibility has advantages. The person from inside may know the business well and already command the respect of senior managers. On the disadvantage side he or she may know nothing about strategic management. This disadvantage may be removed if there is sufficient time to learn about the subject before being turned loose on the company. Too often, planners appointed in this way are expected to do the impossible—to become experts overnight. A person appointed from within should always be a manager "who cannot be spared": anyone who can be easily spared is unlikely to hold the good opinions of colleagues. It is unfortunate, too, that planning positions filled in this way are often pitched too low: the temptation to do this is much stronger where the chief executive can virtually force anyone from the company into the new job.

An outside skilled planner should bring particular benefits through expertise. He or she will be unfamiliar with the specific company (although not necessarily the industry), but this problem can be overstressed. A good corporate planner can learn the key areas of the company very quickly and should have a consultant type skill for adapting to new situations. Above all, the person should be expected to know what to do in the new job.

It is very easy for those inside a company to overstress the time it takes to learn the business. A line manager who has spent an entire business life learning the craft from the shop floor upwards is likely to believe that no one can understand the dynamics of the business without following a similar career pattern. This is just not true, and confuses two different types of knowledge. A production manager in the iron and steel industry needs to have an encyclopedic knowledge of how to make iron and steel. The corporate planner does not have to be able to make the product: but has to understand what makes the business tick.

The chief executive must, however he or she decides to recruit the planner, set the position at the right level of seniority. The person chosen should be able to walk on equal terms with the senior management of that company, and should be a member of the board or management executive committee—or whatever the senior organ of management is in that company. This immediately answers the question of how much a planner should be paid. Salary (and status) should be within the band applicable to the most senior managers in that company. The planner need not be the highest paid nor need be regarded as the most senior of the group: but must be within that group.

The reasons for this are sensible and straightforward. The planner and the chief executive, to be a successful combination, have to develop a level of rapport that is much greater than that of other managers. In many ways the planner is only an extension of the chief executive: it is only possible to function in this way if there is mutual support and confidence. Without it, the planning function will wither and die, like a plant whose roots have been severed. If the gulf of seniority and standing is too wide, the required relationship will never develop. No good planner is a "yes" man (or woman) and no good chief executive will want anything but a self-confident individual in this particular function. Criticism of an idea or decision of the chief executive is often a delicate task: it may well become impossible if the planner is positioned as a keen, middle-management type rather than a high-level executive.

Similarly, relations with other managers are conditioned by seniority. Few managers like to meet opposition to, and criticism of, their ideas and decisions: yet in a planning situation this need may arise from time to time. Such moves by a management peer are tolerable. If the planner is not seen as an equal, many of the actions he or she must take to do the job properly will do nothing more than erect a barrier of resentment which will effectively close the way to a process of strategic management. The chief executive, too, can be put in an impossible position when forced to arbitrate between two managers of highly disproportionate seniority. Arbitration between equals is carried out in a much less emotionally charged atmosphere and, because of the dynamics of the situation, the need for such intervention to settle disagreements is something that rarely arises.

Managers are human. In any circumstances there may be some hostile feelings to the idea of an additional person who will hold the confidence of the chief executive. If the planner is too junior this can well change to bitter jealousy, coupled with the fear that the planner is a "whispering Rasputin" who is really only out to get their jobs. If already an equal, many of the fears will not occur: the planner has a job as good as theirs already, and has no incentive to work against their interests.

From the foregoing it is clear that much of the success of strategic management in an enterprise will depend on the personality and ability of the person selected to be the corporate planner. If this person's behaviour and attributes antagonise managers continuously it will not be possible to succeed at the job whatever the person's paper qualifications and however distinguished the record. Planners also need to be respected by those in the company for their skills as a planner and as a manager. Corporate planners have been called "specialists in general management". It is very easy to move from broad statements of this nature to long lists of the disciplines and personal traits which should characterise the good corporate planner. Unfortunately such an approach would do nothing more than resemble the lists of the personal attributes of leaders, and the qualities of leadership, which were produced by the early industrial psychologists. One is left with the impression of a saint-like creature, barely human, the identification of whom would defy the efforts of the most skilled and efficient of management "headhunters". There is no single person who exists who fulfils the requirements of the "ideal" planner. But there are many people who are excellent corporate planners.

Before any real consideration can be given to the selection of a planner, it is necessary to give some thought to the real nature of the job. There are at least two levels of planning in any organisation: strategic (the duty of the chief executive and the top management team) and operational (the duty of line managers). The corporate planning function has to be able to operate at both levels, which really means that there are two closely integrated but very different planning requirements. At all times it is worth remembering the maxim that the real planners in any company are the managers. The job of the planner is to help make planning happen; to co-ordinate all planning efforts; to help the company more clearly see the issues that affect its future and the alternative paths it may take to systemise planning procedures in the company, including control methods; to analyse and evaluate various issues; to draw the plans together. It is no part of the planner's job to replace any manager's duty to perform the planning elements of management.

In a previous publication[1] I outlined a generalised job description for a corporate planner. This is reproduced in Fig. 29.1, and although there will be variations between companies I believe that it still includes the main functions of the job and the requirements of the person.

Title: Corporate Planner
Reports to: Chief Executive
Purpose: To assist top management to plan the future of the company in an orderly and
              systematic way.

Principal Responsibilities

1. Introducing a system of formal long- and short-range planning covering all areas of the organisation.
2. Assisting management in the definition of objectives and goals.
3. Identifying long-term internal and external factors and their potential effect on the company.
4. Assisting the Chief Executive in the development of strategies to achieve corporate objectives.
5. Analysing and making recommendations on alternative courses of action, including capital investment, acquisitions, divestment, and expansion.
6. Ensuring that the future implications of all decisions are taken into consideration.
7. Appraising corporate strengths and weaknesses.
8. Advising all management levels on planning matters.
9. Writing strategic plans to reflect the decisions of the Chief Executive: co-ordinating the plans of line managers.
10. Monitoring plans and the assumptions on which they are based so that the Chief Executive can control progress.
11. Maintaining a manual to describe the planning system and to specify the part each person has to play in that system.
12. Initiating special studies and research appertaining to the future of the company. (Where available, working through appropriate departments within the organisation.)
13. Training management in planning principles and methods.
14. Applying appropriate techniques to the solution of problems.

Qualifications:
> Should be qualified to degree standard in an appropriate discipline, but should not be a narrow specialist. A wide range of disciplines are suitable, e.g. economics, business administration, market research, mathematics, statistics, marketing.

Experience:
> Should have experience of corporate planning principles and methods, and ability in some management techniques (ability in *all* techniques is virtually impossible). Appropriate techniques and concepts include:

DCF	Decision theory	Strategic portfolio analysis
Risk analysis	Marketing research	Organisational development
Network analysis	Forecasting	Competitor Analysis

> Should also be thoroughly experienced in management theory and philosophy. Must be able to express his thoughts fluently both verbally and in writing.
> Must have integrity in his approach and must not be afraid to make recommendations that may be unpopular.
> Must be able to communicate with all levels in the organisation.

Age:
> Not younger than 30.
> An example of an actual specification is shown in Fig 29.2

FIG. 29.1. Job description of a corporate planner

HEAD OF CORPORATE PLANNING

Province:
The introduction, development, and maintenance of a system of corporate planning in the group which is sufficiently comprehensive and all-embracing to be capable of achieving the full potential benefits of such a system.

Responsibilities:

1. To be responsible to the group managing director and to work within the authority laid down by him.
2. To keep abreast of developments in the external environment (political/economic, social, technological, competitive) and to make periodic written reviews on it, exercising judgement with regard to possible future trends and developments.
3. To ensure that due emphasis is placed on the need for change within the group to reflect developments in the external environment, particularly on the technological and competitive fronts; to accept the entrepreneurial role of being alert to new opportunities for the group in the widest sense; to assist in the evaluation of such opportunities as are considered by the managing director to be worthy of study.
4. To initiate and actively progress corporate planning procedures throughout the group.
5. To provide an advisory service to subsidiary companies and group functional management to aid them in executing their own planning responsibilities. (Such assistance will not of course relieve them of these responsibilities.)
6. To assist in the creation of a climate positively favourable to planning by a continuing informal educational campaign and through participation in formal training courses and contribution to house journals.
7. To co-ordinate the group's planning activity, monitoring its progress in relation to an approved time-table.
8. To integrate plans prepared by subsidiary companies and group functional management in such a way that a corporate plan is produced which is realistic and which properly reflects group aims.
9. To carry out other assignments of a co-ordinating nature in order to progress matters which may have been held up because of pressure of work elsewhere – as approved by the group managing director.
10. To recruit and maintain a multi-discipline staff (at present limited to three people) who will be able to make their main contribution through their specialisation but will also assist in the general aims of the function.
11. To maintain discipline and morale within the function; to appraise the performance of staff and recommend salary increases as appropriate; to assist in the development of staff and make recommendations to group personnel with regard to their promotion.
12. To keep abreast of developments in corporate planning and in business management generally through reading, contact with other companies and attendance/participation in outside courses.

Approved   *Group M.D.*
Agreed   *Head of C.P.*

FIG. 29.2. Example of an actual job specification from a British industrial company

The organisation of the planning function is another matter that requires careful thought and consideration. There may be a great temptation to establish a large centralised planning department in order to ensure the mix of disciplines which go to make up the "ideal" (and non-existent) planner. This may be reinforced by a common belief that the worth of a manager is measured by the number of direct reports: thus empire building is seen as a way of increasing the status of the manager.

Whatever the temptation, a large planning department is something to be avoided. As a general principle it may be said that the employment of every additional person in the planning department is a relative degree of failure, something to be undertaken only when it is so essential that no other answer is possible. This is a good principle for all chief executives or planning managers to keep at the back of their minds but there are further guidelines which might be suggested.

Decentralisation of Planning

In the larger companies, particularly those with major operating subsidiaries, multi-national operations, or particularly complex or diverse activities, it may be impossible for one person to fulfil the total planning role. This problem is unlikely to be solved by building up massive central planning staff who attempt to do everything. A much better approach is to put divisional planning managers in the major divisions or subsidiaries of the company, reporting to the chief executive of that division, or subsidiary, with a functional relationship to the central planning manager. For such divisional appointments, the same basic principles apply on the selection and seniority of the person concerned. It is particularly important that the divisional planner be associated with the divisional management.

Avoidance of Duplication

There is a great temptation to set up duplicate services in a planning department. Special studies, the analysis of projects, the quantification of plans, and the application of OR techniques to planning problems are all activities which make a heavy demand on specialist services. Certainly many projects can be completed more quickly if the planner has a dedicated team of accountants, market researchers, and similar people.

Yet this can be a great danger. Studies might be completed at a faster rate, but they are more likely to be accepted if they have been carried out in participation with others. Accountants who deal in plans are likely to find themselves at loggerheads with their colleagues in budgeting departments. A more practical solution is to approach the process of planning with the firm intention of involving as many of the company's employees in the system as is humanly possible. This means that existing services should be expected to contribute to planning activity, and the need for rival teams of specialists is avoided. Just as managers are the company's real planners, so their specialists are the support staff of planning.

The effect of this principle will be to keep down the size of the planning department.

Confirm that Planning is the Right Umbrella for New Services

Existing functions in the company will not always have the specialists that corporate planning requires, and in many cases there will be a need to employ support staff. The fact that a corporate planner has identified the need is not of itself a good reason why the specialists must of necessity report to that function. Each situation should be examined on its merits.

Use Working Parties where Possible

Often implementation of corporate strategy brings a requirement for additional staff in the planning department. A decision to acquire another company may bring an immense burden of essential work. This may carry a need to increase the number of central planning staff. Again, there is an alternative which is frequently better: to set up special working parties of people drawn from other areas of the company.

A maxim to consider at all times is that the larger the planning staff, the harder it will be to obtain the full involvement and participation of managers. For this reason a less obvious way of getting things done is frequently to be preferred if it brings the opportunity of drawing the company as a whole much more into the process. Strategic management should be something which is part of the company concerned: it is not something clever which stands aloof and separate from the main stream of company life.

It is worth mentioning one solution to the function of planner which has been used in some companies: no planning staff are permanent and the position of planner is held for a temporary period by each senior line manager in turn. Carson[2] reports:

"Baker Perkins has adopted an effective approach to solving this problem of who acts as corporate planner. It rotates the job among its line managers. The spell in planning is thought to be useful for the managers. Installing a new planner every three years keeps the planning process fresh and responsive to changing needs. The risk is some loss of technical expertise during each man's initial learning period in planning.

"But this very lack of expertise ensures that planning in the company never becomes a remote activity for some staff experts, unfamiliar with the day-to-day realities of managing the company. With line executives taking their turn as planner, the planning naturally remains part of the process of managing."

A method of achieving a similar rotation of planners and "doers" was argued by Ross[3] in 1962, who suggested that, despite the administrative complications of such an approach, it could have considerable benefit as a means of integrating long-range plans with operations "so that each activity reinforces the other". One of the main reasons for the scheme is that its originator believes that it taps the "large reservoir of experience of men at the lower management level".

So far in this chapter it has been taken as datum that the planner should report to the chief executive. In practice, other solutions are employed, and planning is frequently "delegated" to the top financial manager, who then has the planner responsible to him. Although in planning many solutions may be found to work, my personal belief is that the planner should be regarded as an extension of the chief executive and can therefore report to no other person.

Many attempts at introducing planning fail because of the approach taken in the initial stages. One of the difficulties of writing about the things that need to be done at this time is that the importance of the various steps will vary between companies. Similarly, the length of time a particular step takes will also vary, which may mean that compromises have to be made if the work is to follow any form of time-table. Sometimes it is more convenient to change the order in which certain steps are taken. The whole point is to come to the problem with an open mind. This does not mean that the planner should not have any idea of how to proceed, for if the problem is approached without expertise it is likely to lead to a mess.

Figure 29.3 shows in network form an approach to the problem of introducing planning into an organisation. Though subject to all the factors mentioned above, it provides a generalised framework which is capable of amendment to suit the particular set of circumsances.

(i) Familiarisation

This period is required whether a planner is recruited from inside or outside the company. In the first situation it is the time needed for the "insider" to gain knowledge of corporate planning, and may last several months. In the case of the "outsider" it is a shorter period, of perhaps two weeks, to get to know the broad scope of the company, the key people involved, and the geography of the company and its buildings. Firstly, the planner should establish the culture of the company and its organisational style, so that planning solutions fit. There is a need to ensure that the planner and the chief executive hold similar views of the objectives of the planning initiative. Failure to do this can lead to an impossible situation later as philosophies clash.

It is during this period that the chief executive should begin to exercise a very important function—controlling the introduction. The planner should be required to produce some form of implementation plan—perhaps in the form of a network as in this example—which should be presented and discussed at a board meeting or whatever other organ is the company's main committee of policy and control. In this way the chief executive becomes familiar with what the planner is doing, and demonstrates a personal involvement to the senior managers.

Regular progress reports and, where necessary, the updating and amending of the implementation plan should be a part of the system of control which the chief executive uses. This may seem very elementary, but it is a fact that many planners have taken an over-long time to get corporate planning off the ground, because there was neither pressure nor interest from the top.

After the familiarisation period is over, the planner begins four tasks which may be carried out concurrently, yet which have a close relationship with each other.

(ii) Begin appraisal of strengths and weaknesses

This really is a natural development of the familiarisation period. As shown on the network, it is very much an initial period collecting available data, and planning the approach to the corporate appraisal, and rapidly reaches a stage where the task subdivides into three.

(iii) Environmental appraisal

Appraising the external environment of the company is a task which begins in

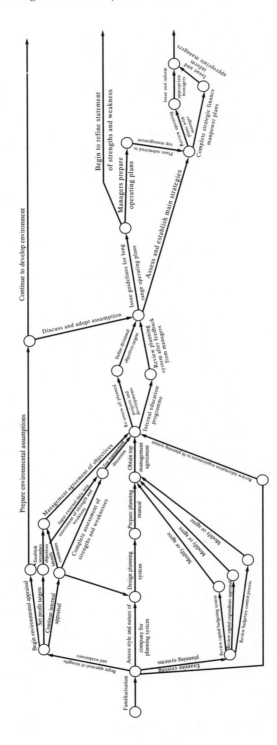

FIG. 29.3. Network of main events on introduction of corporate long-range planning

parallel with the internal appraisal. Relevant data is input into the overall assessment of strengths and weaknesses at an early stage. At a later point in time planning assumptions are defined as the basis for plans. The main task of monitoring and assessing the external environment is continuous and outlives the network itself.

(iv) Set profit targets

After the first stages of the corporate appraisal (assessment of strengths and weaknesses) have begun, including the study of past results and trends, it becomes possible to establish the profit targets or primary objectives. This is desirable even at this early stage because it helps to provide the company with a framework for the other on-going tasks. Although not shown on the network, it is implied that these first objectives may be revised at a later stage (provision is made for them to be agreed by management).

(v) Establish secondary objectives

The identification of the company's statement of purpose is a logical evolution from the profit objectives, although I believe that these cannot be defined until the company has nearly completed its assessment of strengths and weaknesses.

(vi) Continuation of internal appraisal

The continuation of the assessment of strengths and weaknesses moves simultaneously with the start of the environmental appraisal, and leads naturally to the completion of this assessment, with the full integration of all relevant external data, and a detailed top management discussion. (It is, of course, possible for management to discuss objectives at the same meeting.) The word discussion implies, in this concept, acceptance, rejection, amendment, and—most important—action, for as has already been seen the appraisal is a key stage in the development of any plan.

(vii) Identify constraints

During the appraisal of strengths and weaknesses the planner should reach a point when it is possible to help top management identify any self-imposed constraints which they wish to apply to the running of their business. This definition forms part of the total package of objectives which has already been discussed.

(viii) Examine management information available

One of the initial tasks of introduction is to examine the management information available and to take a close look at the management information system. Management information is necessary as an input to the corporate appraisal, although the emphasis here is the selection and usage of relevant data. The examination shown on the network is much more concerned with the suitability of current information for long-range planning needs.

It follows that the system may either be adequate, or may require revision. In the latter event consideration should be given to amending the system so that it provides a better fit with the total approach to planning. The network suggests that this be done at a relatively early stage: however, in a practical situation it must be accepted that the complete reshaping of a management information system could take much longer than the network suggests, although the objectives of the system could be specified at this early stage.

(ix) Examine existing planning systems

There can be no company in the world that has no current systems which fulfil at least a part of its planning requirements. It is always good practice to make maximum use of whatever currently exists, and to make as few changes as possible. In some cases it may be that some systems are inadequate or non-existent: for example, there are still companies which do not have any formal methods of appraising capital expenditure projects. The end product must be a compatibility of these particular systems with the total approach to planning which is finally adopted.

The network shows three such systems—capital budgeting, capital expenditure, and budgetary control—but there may be others which should also be examined. Other possibilities are standing policies, personnel administration, and manpower planning procedures.

(x) Assess style and nature of company for planning system

The planner has to be familiar with the company, the philosophies of management in that company, its current organisation and reporting relationships, and various other factors which help to see the company in terms of a planning system. Much of this assessment can be developed from work that has to be carried out for the corporate appraisal. It is a time for reconsidering views formed during the familiarisation phase.

(xi) Establish if major strategic or organisational changes are needed

This is an essential spin-off task from the corporate appraisal, and must be completed before the planning system is designed. The line on the network envelops what may in some companies be a very complex series of investigations and decisions.

Problems in this area are critical to the future success of planning, and may act as a bottleneck which prevents further development. The situation will vary from company to company, and many planners may find that there are no problems to face.

In many planning situations the decision to begin strategic management arises from a change in top management or a realisation that the company faces severe difficulties. It may be that an outline strategy has to be prepared by top management before a process of strategic management is extended to the total company. This strategy may call for profit improvement measures, the re-organisation of operating units, and even the closure or divestment of certain operations. Planning will lose credibility if these major changes are made later in the introductory process. A manager who is told to start devising plans for a business area one day and is made redundant the next is unlikely to have a feeling of confidence in the planning process: neither will his old colleagues who remain with the business.

Other situations may arise where although there are no drastic strategic upheavals, organisational relationships are poorly defined or inadequate for planning purposes. There are still companies which move towards strategic management from a point where one of the basic things they lack is an organisation chart. No adequate total planning system can be designed unless it is related to a clear management structure. Again this particular situation may prevent further development until it is resolved.

(xii) Design planning system

Once the above problems have been removed, the planner can design the system of planning which the company will use. Implicit in this statement is the need to work very closely with key managers so that the system fits the business, ties in with its existing time-tables (year end, budgetary meetings, and seasonal factors), and is something that converts the textbook concepts into a process unique to the particular company.

(xiii) Prepare planning manual

It is logical that the complete system should be written up into a planning manual and subsequently accepted by top management as a description of the process that company will use. The manual itself is an important document, and one of the agents for training the whole company in corporate planning, and because of this will be discussed in more detail later in this chapter. However, the approach to the manual and the way it is used internally must be compatible with the style of the company.

(xiv) Reassess all planned projects and developments

Introducing a process of planning into a company would be much easier if the company would close down for six months. This, of course, is an impossibility, and one of the challenges the planner faces is how to organise planning in a dynamic situation. In a way it is like a stunt man who has to jump on to a moving vehicle. At first this main task is to keep his footing and gain a position in that vehicle: at this point he can do nothing to change its momentum. Later, he is able to alter the speed of the vehicle or to make it change direction.

In all companies there are projects which are underway, and which it would be inadvisable to postpone during the first stages of introduction, although any major projects which were incompatible with the company's outline strategy would have come to light when this was examined.

The company has now reached a point on the network when objectives are set, strengths and weaknesses defined, and major anomalies corrected. A reassessment of on-going development projects is in order at this stage, with the possibility of postponing those which do not, in the light of all the new information, appear right for the company.

(xv) Define divisional objectives and targets

One of the hardest tasks is splitting up the total company objectives between divisions. This is an important prerequisite of any form of divisional planning, and is linked to all the investigatory work which the company has already carried out.

(xvi) Internal education programme

In many companies managers have to be helped to plan more effectively, and this is a key task for the planner. The system of planning has to be explained to managers throughout the organisation, and the right frame of mind created in all those who will participate. This line on the network summarises a number of actions and these will be discussed in some detail later in this chapter.

It is reasonable to expect that detailed discussions of the system throughout the organisation might suggest areas of improvement which should be incorporated. If it is seen as a participative system, the opinions and recommendations of managers should be welcomed.

(xvii) Issue guidelines for long-range operating plans

The company has now reached a point in time when it is ready to prepare its first long-range plans. The actions divide into strategic and operational planning, the link between the two being the guidelines, which incorporate objectives, environmental assumptions, strategic constraints or intents (often provisional at this stage), and the detailed planning time-table.

(xviii) Managers prepare operating plans

Long-range operational plans are prepared by managers, submitted to top management, discussed and debated, and themselves provide part of the input of the strategic planning process. At the same time the information generated leads to refinements of the statements of strengths and weaknesses, a process which outlives the network and continues into the next planning cycle.

(xix) Assess and establish main strategies

The main strategic choices, on which some work has already been carried out, are made, and re-examined in the light of the operating plans. The strategic plan and its associate financial and personnel (manpower) plans are drawn up. Simultaneously operational plans are reviewed in depth with line management.

(xx) Issue plans

All plans are issued to the appropriate managers and become instructions to begin implementation.

The network is of necessity compressed, and could be enlarged for a particular situation. The time-span covered will vary with the complexity and nature of the company, and has been found by many investigators to take up to three years to complete in full, although some divisions of the company may be involved earlier than this. My own experience suggests that the company need not wait this long, and can be in possession of its first valid set of plans within twelve to fifteen months of start-up. This target is much more likely to succeed if the whole approach is tightly planned and controlled, as in the example, and if the company from the top down gives planning a reasonable degree of priority. The fact that much of the work causes an involvement of managers from an early stage is one factor which assists a reasonably speedy movement to a complete process of planning.

In the review the importance of an educational programme was stressed. For practical purposes the word "educational" is emotively bad and any planners who announce that they are employed to "educate" their fellow managers are doomed to failure. Perhaps a much better approach is to stress the need for managers throughout the company to fully understand both the principles of planning and the process being applied in their company.

This may be a great stumbling block in the way of the innocent corporate planner. Many of the concepts of corporate planning are alien to what many managers have been taught. In any company there are variations in the age, ability, function, and educational attainments of managers, and they can by no means be regarded as a homogenous group. Many managers will regard the task of management as an exciting science, and will keep up to date with the latest developments (including strategic management): others will lack the time or inclination to ever read a book or journal on a management subject. Many would go so far as to argue against the view that management can be studied, believing it is something that is inborn and instinctive (and they will not be reading this book).

Much of the task of changing the outlook of the management falls on the chief executive. It is impossible to avoid this. By personal example the chief executive must demonstrate the value of strategic management: by actions and attitudes the chief executive must motivate managers to the extent that they are willing to attempt to play their full part in the planning process. The chief executive who opts not to employ a corporate planner must bear all the burden of this personally.

Where there is a planner the burden is eased, for the corporate planner should do much to ensure that fellow managers become familiar with the essence of corporate planning. This requires a high quality of leadership by the planner who has no power to *make* managers follow the paths indicated, but may help them perceive the paths and wish to follow them of their own volition.

Like the chief executive, the planner has to prove the point by personal example in day-to-day conduct. Insincerity quickly becomes apparent, and managers will soon have the measure of someone who does not practise what is preached.

The planner must be able to communicate with the managers, must talk in terms they can understand, and must be knowledgeable enough about their functions to be able to appreciate their problems and what they are saying. Communication is one of the most difficult areas of management. It is important that the planner never speaks over the heads of managers—which means never sheltering behind the jargon of the techniques or position as an "expert". Similarly, the planner must never be condescending and speak down to managers.

The methods which a planner should consider using to fulfil the task of showing the path include:

Personal Discussion

One of the most effective methods of moulding opinion is still discussion on a personal basis, talking over with managers points of planning detail in relation to their own problems and getting to know them as individuals. This begins during the familiarisation period, and gains in intensity as the planner becomes more deeply involved in the company's business and helps managers in the preparation of their own plans.

Planning Manual

A manual, which clearly defines the system of planning and shows how each part of the system fits into the whole is a very important tool. The reasons for this are that a concise record of the process, besides protecting the company's investment in planning, is important if managers are to understand their own part in it. The manual may be a vehicle for general planning concepts, and may form the basis of subsequent methods of planning development. A well constructed manual will also save managers their most precious commodity—time. It will remove from them the task of thinking out the problems of setting out a plan and leave them free to face the more important task of considering decisions.

Internal Planning Conferences and Courses

I am a great believer in the value of holding internal conferences and courses to explain to managers what is involved in corporate planning, to describe the overall process being used in the company, to highlight the reasons for introducing planning in that company, and to demonstrate to each manager that he has a part to play. A course gives opportunity to improve planning skills at the individual level.

Conferences and courses may be held at various levels in the organisation, and senior management should be dealt with separately although, apart from this, it is often a good idea to deliberately mix up seniority, departments, and functions. The content may be varied to suit the audience, as may the length of the conference.

One useful conference format is to use an outside speaker to talk on the concept and general principles, and to follow this with a presentation from the planner on these principles as applied to the company. Where possible the chief executive, or an appropriate deputy, should participate by providing a brief speech of encouragement and policy. It is vital that the chief executive plays a major part in the conference for senior managers.

Each conference should provide for adequate discussion time, and should be designed to encourage and stimulate discussion. To achieve this means limiting the numbers attending to between 20 and 30, and if necessary repeating the performance several times in order to accommodate everybody.

Conferences are often improved if they are designed by professionals. This is even more true of courses where amateurism can impede learning. The ideal course would have between 15 and 20 people attending, and would be based on participative learning methods. Case-study approaches and real planning projects can be very valuable for teaching business strategy, analysis, the use of techniques, the problems of change, and the nature of planning systems (to list but a few examples). Provided they are professionally prepared, it is often valuable to write cases based on company experience to demonstrate the relevance of the concepts. There are organisations, such as Harbridge House, which can help planning efforts to become effective.

Attendance at Outside Seminars

Every planner has biases which are built into the approach to strategic management. There are usually other ideas and concepts which because of this bias are not presented to managers. Yet a virile planning system requires the development of the company's approach to planning by the managers themselves. If they are herded along one path alone, they may never have the opportunity of extracting benefit from some of the opposing planning ideas. Realisation that planning is a live subject, and that real contributions can be made to methodology by managers at all levels is important both for planners and the company in general. The planner should not be positioned as the high priest who alone holds the key to the revelations of the gods.

This problem can be solved by asking selected managers to attend external seminars on strategic management. Those on offer are usually useful in exposing participants to new ideas, but should not be seen as a substitute for education.

All these approaches are of limited use unless backed by the total involvement of the company in strategic management. Training and development of any kind is best when of a continuous nature closely related with day-to-day activities and duties. Thus the best training in planning comes from using this method of management consistently, with the chief executive and planner both acting as guides to smooth the way.

The planning manual has been mentioned on several occasions in this chapter. This is a document that may be prepared in any one of a number of different ways and which should be designed to suit the particular and individual needs of the company.

It is always easier to think constructively about something if a concrete example is provided, even though the example is meant to show one solution and is not given as dogma. For this reason, the rest of this chapter will be devoted to an example of a planning manual. The company is assumed (to reduce the size of the example) to be a relatively simple operation with four main divisions: marketing, production, research and development, and finance/accounts. In Ansoff terms it is operating at around a turbulence level 3.

Because the example is designed for adaptation it is complete in all but two particulars. The omissions are suggested forms for use in planning, which have been given as exhibits in previous chapters, and the descriptions of certain techniques which are optional rather than essential. This attempt at comprehensiveness means that the example repeats points made elsewhere in the book: this is unavoidable. Those whose fear this will be tedious may jump ahead to the next chapter and reserve the example for future reference.

References

1. Hussey, D. E. *Introducing Corporate Planning*, Pergamon, 2nd edition, 1979.
2. Carson, I. "The Big Leap in Corporate Planning", *International Management*, April 1972.
3. Ross, D. J. "For LRP—Rotating Planners and Doers", *Harvard Business Review*, January–February 1962.
4. Drucker, P. F. *Managing for Results*, Heinemann, 1964.
5. Hussey, D. E. "Corporate Planning: Some Problems and Benefits", *The Accountant*, 30 September 1971.

Appendix to Chapter 29

Example of a Corporate Planning Manual

XYZ Company Limited January xxxx

Note: Terms like Corporate Planning have not been updated from the first edition of this book (they are of course still valid). Neither have I tried to build in concepts such as competitor analysis. This manual is essentially a description of the planning process and the example does not go deeper than this.

Contents

Introduction

This manual outlines the procedures and methods the company is using to plan its development. None of the instructions set out in the manual should be interpreted as being rigid and inflexible: any part of the system will be reviewed at the request of any manager, and it is intended that the whole process will be moulded to suit the changing needs of a developing company.

Corporate planning is not a narrow technique. It is a way of managing a business. It stretches throughout the organisation, involving to a greater or lesser extent every manager in the company. No one can opt out, for the failure of any one department to respond can endanger the whole system.

The manual provides in Section I a brief theoretical background to corporate planning. The first article is optional reading, but the other pages of Section I should not be neglected, as they contain important general information which is not repeated elsewhere in the text.

Section II provides detailed instructions which show how corporate planning will work for the company.

Throughout the process all of us must guard against the temptation to allow our planning activity to degenerate to form-filling. The emphasis must be on careful thought about the future rather than the creation of elegant documents. The plans described in this manual are a means, not an end.

The company will achieve maximum benefit when planning becomes a part of day-to-day management; when all sectors of the company work towards predetermined objectives; when every action taken is accompanied by a full recognition of the effect it will have on the company's future; when the company continually challenges the *status quo*, and always seeks more profitable ways of doing things.

From plans must spring action. Planning without action is an empty exercise.

Drucker[4] sums up what planning is really about:

> "But tomorrow always arrives. It is always different. And then even the mightiest Company is in trouble if it has not worked on the future. It will have lost distinction and leadership—all that will remain is big company overheads. It will neither control nor understand what is happening. Not having dared to take the risk of making the new happen, it perforce took the much greater risk of being surprised by what did happen. And this is the risk that even the largest and richest company cannot afford and that even the smallest business need not run."

Section 1: The Background to Formal Planning

Corporate Planning: Some Problems and Benefits[5]

I.1. Corporate planning rose to the fore in the United Kingdom in the late 1960s and remains the "in thing" for "with it" managements. Unfortunately, like all fashionable management approaches it has frequently been misunderstood and often implemented in a way which can only lead to disappointment or total failure.

I.2. Many managing directors still introduce it for the wrong reasons, perhaps because they have just heard a good lecture on it, read an article, or met someone who is an enthusiast.

I.3. Too often the job of corporate planner is thrown to an inadequate managaer: perhaps one who is close to retirement or who lacks the basic knowledge of the elements of planning. With a complete misunderstanding of the processes of planning it is still too common for a chief executive to insist that the planning function does not take up his time by reporting to him.

I.4. This is not meant to be a general criticism of all companies undertaking corporate planning. There are a number that do it very well.

I.5. What I am trying to do is to dispel any illusions that corporate planning is something that can be carried out for trite reasons, something entered into lightly with inadequate thought, or something superimposed on a top management outlook that is completely alien to it.

I.6. I do not believe that any chief executive should be bludgeoned by emotive oratory into accepting corporate planning. The planned approach is part of a complete style of management, and will therefore change the company which uses it. The decision to adopt corporate planning should only come after full understanding has been reached of all the implications (the truly autocratic chief executive should never use it). I also do not believe that only those businesses which use corporate planning can be successful. All the facts point to the conclusion that success can come to many styles of management.

I.7. I do believe that the company which is ready for corporate planning and which introduces it carefully and sensibly will improve its results.

I.8. By "corporate planning" I mean a formal and complete approach to both short- and long-term planning. I do not suggest that companies which do not do corporate planning do not plan: this would be patently untrue. All businesses plan: it is just that some can do it better than others.

I.9. Long-range planning without a built-in means of action and control tends to be something of an academic exercise. It is for this reason that I think of corporate planning as a complete management process of which the long-range plan is but a part.

Management participation

I.10. Corporate planning—that is, a formal process of planning—is in effect one way to run a business. The principles of planning, including a commitment to objectivity, are applied throughout the company in its day-to-day actions.

I.11. Many planning systems go awry because they do not provide for sufficient management participation. Where plans are written and devised by staff planners as a sort of "ivory tower" exercise, they will rarely succeed. However good they are, however sensible and logical, they will still run up against a basic problem—human nature. No good manager likes having his thinking done for him.

I.12. It is my belief that the best plans come about when they draw on the thoughts of managers throughout the organisation. Each senior manager should be responsible for producing his own plan, but should draw his subordinates into the process. Thus a marketing manager would probably ask his product managers and sales managers to prepare certain parts of his plan.

I.13. Plans produced by line managers can be entitled operating plans. It is, of course, important that they are not produced in a vacuum. The instruction from the chief executive should be much more than a simple exhortation to go away and prepare a plan. He should give much more guidance than this, including:

(a) a statement of key objectives and targets;
(b) the basic assumptions to be taken into consideration during the preparation of plans;
(c) strategic guidelines which the manager should observe when planning.

I.14. In a truly participative company the managers preparing plans will have had some opportunity to debate and contribute to each of the items above. They will not, therefore, be autocratic announcements, although sometimes the guidelines may run contrary to the wishes of a particular manager.

Strategic plans

I.15. The operating plans are not the most important part of a formal planning system, although they are vital to its success. The key document is the strategic plan. This is the master plan for the whole company and is the plan of the chief executive and his top management team. It will embrace in broad terms the actions described in detail in individual operating plans, and in addition will show the actions that have to be taken over and above those falling under the responsibility of a line manager.

I.16. A strategic plan will rarely be just the sum of all operating plans. Usually there will be a difference between this and the company's long-range objectives. Part of the task of the strategic plan is to devise means of closing this gap.

I.17. This particular function of formal corporate planning shows one of its main differences from the traditional approach. Corporate planning works to pre-set objectives. In other words, a decision is made by top management of what the company should achieve (e.g. in terms of profits, return on investment, and sales growth). The company then works out how to get there (and usually will calculate several alternative means). Traditional methods of management tend to be less precise in their approach to achieving better performance.

I.18. The strategic planning function has another important role. It is through its strategic decisions that a company can change direction, speed its growth in certain areas, slow down in others, or broaden the basis of its operations. The strategic plan shows the chief executive's reaction to threats and opportunities perceived in the external environment—the world in which the company operates, but over which he has little or no control. It also shows his plans to correct weaknesses or build on the strengths revealed from studies of the company itself (frequently described as the corporate appraisal).

I.19. A continuing study of the environment, to guide the company in its future actions, is an important part of the planning processes. Similarly, there is a continual introspective study, peering inwards at the company's operations and subjecting these to self-criticism. From the first activity come many opportunities for expansion (and some for divestment); from the second come ways of improving the profitability of current operations as well as revelation of its own pattern of new opportunities.

I.20. A good strategic plan is always backed by two other master plans which are inextricably bound up with the actions the company wishes to take—the financial plan and the personnel plan. These two documents examine the two major resources the company needs to achieve anything—money and people. Shortage of either of these resources can cause the company to modify its strategic plans and can be a constraint against development. On the other hand, a surplus of either might stimulate the company to develop more ambitious plans.

Role of the planner

I.21. Most companies which practise the planned approach to management have at least one professional corporate planner on their payroll. Many have large planning departments, and I believe that some have departments which are much too large.

I.22. Planning is part of the task of the chief executive, and indeed of every manager in the company. In my opinion it is a task which can never be delegated. The professional planner should never be engaged to do the thinking for either the chief executive or other managers.

I.23. What can be delegated is the task of co-ordinating the plans of various sectors of the company, the investigation and analysis of opportunities, the study of environmental factors and their possible effect on the company, the guiding of managers so that they become better at planning, the designing of a system of planning for the company, and many other tasks connected with planning; but not the decision-making function.

I.24. In the larger companies these tasks would consume more time than the chief executive has available to be able to do them more effectively. It is this lack of time which creates the need for the corporate planner. The planner does not take any power away from the chief executive; rather, he acts as an extension of the chief executive. The basic task of motivating the other managers to follow this particular method of management still falls on the chief executive—this is why planning fails when he does not believe in it or when he does not understand it.

I.25. Having said this, I may now stress the fact that a good planner can contribute a lot to the success of corporate planning in his company: a bad planner can make it fail.

I.26. The number of planners employed by a company should be very small: the best number to aim for is one (although it may be sensible to allow the chief executives of major subsidiaries, particularly those operating in other countries, to have planners of their own). Ideally, the "planning department" of the company should consist of all other managers and the planner. Where additional staff are required for special exercises, they should be drawn on a task force basis from other departments. On no account should functions (such as market research, OR, or project evaluation) which already exist in the company be duplicated in the planning department.

I.27. Unfortunately, there are still many managers who measure their position in the company by the number of people they directly control. This tendency requires to be checked particularly in the planning area, since management involvement and participation in planning tend to reduce as the planning department gets larger.

Reasons for planning

I.28. Quite a long description has been given of corporate planning, and few reasons why anyone should do it at all have been mentioned. Obviously, there is no point in anyone undertaking corporate planning unless it brings benefits, and no chief executive should commit his company to a difficult and time-consuming procedure unless he has a fair idea of what he will get out of it.

I.29. Before examining the reasons for corporate planning in greater detail I should like to stress one more point. The fact that a company has plans which stretch some time into the future does not mean that it can in any way foretell the future. It will be right more often than it would otherwise be because it takes into account more factors; its greatest power is not clairvoyance but flexibility and speed of reaction.

I.30. The application of logic to a business situation enables us to identify the effect on the company of a certain future event: we can prepare a plan that will achieve our objectives if our basic assumption is correct. A good plan will also contain a number of contingency or alternative plans so that, if the assumption is wrong, it becomes possible to abandon the course of action rapidly and to start equally rapidly on a new course. The need for a monitoring and controlling system, to ensure that plans are carried out and do still represent the best course of action, is self-evident.

I.31. The benefits that a company may expect from corporate planning include:

(1) *Improved ability to cope with change.* A feature of modern life is the amount of change with which managers have to come to terms, but perhaps the biggest problem managers now have to face is not the extent of change but the rapidity with which it occurs. Corporate planning cannot prevent change happening—in fact it does not seek to do this. It can help managers throughout the company to have a greater awareness of the incidence of change, can build this into its plans, and can give the company a greater chance of taking advantage of the opportunities (and avoiding the threats) that change brings.

(2) *Encouraging innovative thought and creativity.* A good planning system should provide ways of stimulating innovative thought and encouraging the individual creativity of managers. It seeks to encourage flair and to co-ordinate it to a common purpose.

It is possible for so-called long-range planning systems to be nothing more than a form-filling exercise aimed at producing an extrapolative budget. This is not corporate planning. A good planning process will provide avenues for individual participation, will throw up more ideas about the company and its environment, will encourage an atmosphere of frankness and corporate self-criticism, and will stimulate managers to achieve more.

(3) *Better appreciation of the logical outcome of a course of action.* A company may not always be clever enough to select the best strategy, but it should always be able to calculate the logical outcome of its strategy.

(4) *Motivation.* To achieve the best results, individual people have to be motivated—after all a company, however powerful and important, is really only a collection of people. Corporate planning motivates because it defines and makes known what the company is trying to achieve. It thus provides all the company with a common purpose.

(5) *Co-ordination and control of complex activities.* Top management has a tool which not only co-ordinates all activities of the company but which provides them with a way of controlling that company. Better co-ordination leads to better motivation and it avoids costly mistakes. Each sector of the company has a greater awareness of what is going on elsewhere, and is forced to work closely with other sectors which have a bearing on its results.

(6) *Definition of objectives.* The company never loses sight of what it is trying to achieve although it may change its method of approach. Plans should have flexibility. A company should regard its objectives as a map-grid reference rather than the bull on a dart-board.

The only way to the bull is the trajectory of the dart: once committed, the action is irrevocable. On the other hand, there are innumerable ways of reaching the map-grid reference: if there are obstacles in the way a straight line might not be the quickest method. Actions can be changed (if noticed in time), and it is still possible to reach the map reference.

Some difficulties and problems

I.32. One of the main shortcomings of any summary description of a management process is that everything appears so easy. Although one or two problem areas have been mentioned—in particular the need for backing and belief from the chief executive—the account still reads as a simple series of logical steps.

I.33. It is my belief that many of the problems arise from a lack of skill by chief executives in applying the planned approach to their companies, failure to understand the principles behind planning (and how it changes the way a company is managed), and not identifying the unique character of every company.

I.34. Managers throughout the company must be made aware of the effect corporate planning will have on the company in general and them in particular. Those that need it must be shown how to improve their own planning ability. This is a vital area to success, although the amount of effort that needs to be devoted in this area will vary from company to company.

I.36. Inevitably there will be some casualties among senior managers. Those that do not believe in this style of management will, if they cannot get it changed, tend to leave the company. Most, despite enormous variations in skill, experience, qualifications, and ability between one manager and another, will not only be able to cope with the new methods, but will find them exciting and stimulating. A few will find the need to work to targets, and to define and commit themselves to a course of action, a traumatic and uncomfortable experience.

I.37. Planning may fail because it is implemented badly, because some of the basic steps are omitted (e.g. many companies have never carried out any objective appraisal of company strengths and weaknesses), because the planner is of low calibre or of too low a standing, or because the chief executive is not a good manager or makes the wrong approach to planning.

I.38. This list of problems and difficulties could be extended; however, enough has been written to demonstrate that the installation of corporate planning in a company involves costs as well as benefits. In nearly all cases it is possible for the benefits to exceed the costs—there are only a few situations when it is impossible for corporate planning to pay off.

I.39. Whether the company achieves all the potential benefit for a reasonable cost depends on the way it implements planning. The rewards are there; unfortunately, many fail to achieve them.

Note: This is a reproduction of an article published in the *Accountant*. Reprints of this or similar articles could be used by planners who do not wish to write their own papers.

Marketing Planning

I.40. No one will question will question the importance of marketing to the company's success or the need to bring as much attention and care as possible to the task of marketing planning.

I.41. A conceptual framework for marketing planning is set out below. This is a marketing oriented approach, and provides a way in which managers can study their own marketing problems. No attempt is made to impose this framework on managers, for it is appreciated that there are innumerable ways of analysing marketing strategy: however, it is stressed that all plans should be completed within a logical framework of one kind or another. As with all other aspects of planning the criteria must be serious thought and consideration of alternatives rather than the blind following of headings.

I.42. The suggested approach is illustrated in the diagram (Example 1). The inner circle represents the consumer, whose desires and needs affect all decisions, and who should be considered when alternatives are evaluated. Naturally, the profit motive remains paramount and all alternatives must be judged by this yardstick. One aspect of marketing planning is to identify the consumer's wishes (the use of marketing information in the planning process is discussed in Part 2 of each subsequent section).

I.43. The outer ring represents the environment and the factors which are outside the control of the individual manager (although some may be modified in the long term). This environment cannot be ignored, and must be considered in the decision process (see paragraphs II.13 to II.32). The manager should identify the effect of these before he makes his plans.

I.44. The middle ring shows the controllable areas—the elements of a manager's marketing strategy. Four headings only have been used in the diagram (Example 1), and these cover all parts of the marketing mix.

I.45. To some extent each of the elements of strategy is an alternative to the other elements: for example, one may increase sales by decreasing price, or by gaining a wider distribution, or by advertising. This point does not need to be laboured. What is important is the realisation that the identification and consideration of alternatives is a major aspect of the planning task.

I.46. In detail, the elements of strategy are:

Product: This heading covers all decisions relating to the product, e.g. physical appearance, taste, grading, branding, and packaging. In addition it includes the intangibles attached to a product, such as guarantees of quality and after sales service.

Place. The term "place" can be defined as a distribution policy. Decisions here would cover the proportion of business to be put through the different channels (e.g. key accounts), or how to widen (or narrow) the variety of channels used. It would also cover the physical distribution function.

Promotion: This would include all the promotion options—advertising, public relations, point of sale material, competitions, special offers, etc.

I.47. *Price:* The fourth element of strategy is price, and of course this may be used to give

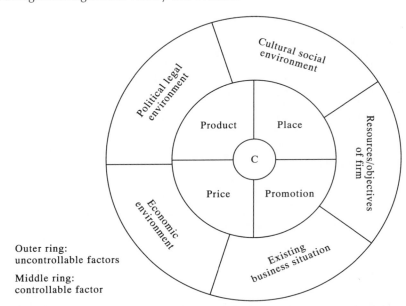

Outer ring:
uncontrollable factors

Middle ring:
controllable factor

EXAMPLE 1. Marketing strategy. (Reproduced with permission from *Basic Marketing: a Managerial Approach* by E. Jerome McCarthy, 3rd ed., Homewood, Ill.: Richard D. Irwin Inc.)

effect to some of the other elements: for example, price may be used as a tool to increase average order size as a way of reducing physical distribution costs.

I.48. An important area of decision not shown in the diagram (Example 1) is market segmentation. The identification of market segments, and the design of specific strategies to appeal to these, is an important part of market planning.

I.49. The product life-cycle concept is also important in market planning:

(a) in forecasting;
(b) to enable an action to be planned which will change the shape of the life-cycle curve;
(c) to enable strategic decisions to be taken to extend the product life-cycle.

I.50. Above all, market planning is designed to produce a stimulating programme of new ideas, to become a true innovatory process, and to encourage flair and entrepreneurial development. It should lead to creative thought, to a questioning of existing strategies, and to the exploration of new products and new concepts.

Objectives

I.51. Objectives play a key part in corporate planning. There are several different types of objectives. In essence these enable a simple model to be made of the company as it will be in the future, so that strategies may be devised that will enable the company to achieve its targets, and so that monitoring and control procedures may be instituted to ensure that the strategies are proving effective.

I.52. Company objectives are made up of the following elements:

—long-range profit targets;
—a narrative description of the company's answer to the question: What business *should* we be in?;
—goals—a network of quantified targets which will have to be met if the company's strategies are to be considered successful: for example, brand shares, sales growth, distribution penetration levels, liquidity ratios, ROI, etc.

I.53. A similar pattern of objectives should be created for each department which is completing long-range plans. These must, of course, be compatible with the company objectives, but may be wider in some aspects than the objectives for the whole company.

I.54. Certain parts of the departmental, etc., objectives will be set by the chief executive: particularly profit and turnover targets. Managers will be able to discuss these and suggest changes if a particular target is unattainable or unrealistic. Once a target has been accepted, it is up to the manager concerned to devise—for that sector of the company entrusted to his control—the means to reach it.

I.55. The third area of objectives is in the setting of personal standards of performance for individuals. In its crudest form, such a standard may be no more than a time-table under which a named person may have to fulfil certain obligations by a pre-decided date. A more sophisticated form would provide quantitative targets for the performance of certain key tasks. In its widest form this moves into a system of "Management by Objectives"—a method of management which not only sets standards and measures performance but is linked with training, management development, and regular reviews of individual abilities and performances.

Note: Similar sections may also be included to cover other simple techniques used in the planning process, e.g. gap analysis, decision trees, discounted cash flow, and the company's corporate computer model (if it has one).

Section II: Detailed Procedures

The Total Formal Planning System

II.1 Formal planning at the XYZ Company Ltd. consists of a number of components:

(a) Five-year long-range plans.
(b) Annual operating plan (linked to budget).
(c) Project plans.
(d) Monitoring and controlling process.
(e) Contingency plans.

II.2. The long-range plans are completed in the first half of each year and cover the five-year period from the next calendar year (e.g. the 19X1–19X5 plan will be completed during the first half of 19X0). All the alternatives should be re-examined in the light of environmental trends, the corporate objective, and the company's strengths and weaknesses, and the plan rolled forward by another year. In this way it will always cover five years. The long-range plan deals with the broader issues and principles facing the company, viewed against the background of a changing environment, and including an active search for better ways of doing things.

II.3. Annual operating plans are completed during the last quarter of the year and describe the strategy which will cause the results planned in the next year's budget. The function of the annual plan is to examine the first year of the long-range plan and to plan this in detail. The background of the long-term aims and strategies must always be kept in mind.

II.4. Project plans are an objective study of an individual project. Formal planning principles apply, but the studies (which may be for a capital investment or a particular product) are made on an *ad hoc* basis. Long-range and annual plans show in broad outline which projects are to be studied. A project plan is the detailed evaluation of a strategy: it has the advantage of being able to bridge the artificial division of the calendar year.

II.5. The end result of any plans must be action: a monitoring and controlling process is an important part of the planning system. So that plans can be controlled, all data should be presented in such a way that it is possible to compare the plan with actual results. Every effort must be made to quantify data. Planned completion dates should be given for the various elements of a plan (see also Objectives, Section I, Paragraph I.51). Unless there is a method of comparing plans with results, planning will tend to become an exercise divorced from reality.

II.6. Where possible, contingency plans will be developed so that a course of action is available for strategies that fail, or assumptions that prove incorrect.

Cost Centres and Profit Centres

II.7. In order to attain that important spirit of profit motivation it is necessary to clarify who is regarded as responsible for earning the components of profit. In the first place, every manager in the company shares this responsibility.

II.8. This statement is not specific enough for planning and control purposes. To help us operate efficiently the company should be conceived as a collection of profit and cost centres. A department or section which does not bring in direct revenue should be regarded as a cost centre. Perhaps the best example is the duty of production who make their contribution by producing the requirements of marketing at as low a cost as possible: success is measured against ability to beat the standard cost targets.

II.9. A department which brings in revenue—e.g. marketing—is a profit centre (although it may have other cost centres under its control). Success is measured in the ability to meet the profit targets.

The Long-range Planning System

II.10. The long-range planning system is made up of the following plans:

(a) *Strategic plan*
The master plan showing the objectives and the basic long-range strategies of the company, identifying action arising from the assessment of the company's strengths and weaknesses, and the events in the external environment.

Responsibility: chief executive.

(b) *Operating plans*
The plans for each of the present departments of the company.

Responsibility: appropriate managers as designated in this Manual.

(c) *Financial plan*
The ways in which the company plans to obtain the financial resources necessary to implement its planned course of action.

Responsibility: financial director and chief executive.

(d) *Personnel plan*
The ways in which the company plans to develop its human resources to meet its future.

Responsibility: personnel manager.

Co-ordination

II.11. The planning manager has a particular responsibility for co-ordinating plans and helping those involved in the planning process to make their plans compatible with those of other areas. The planning time-table will contain a number of methods to improve co-ordination, and a particular feature will be a meeting to ensure that all areas of the company are using the same sales forecasts, and that all the implications of these are fully understood. The various committees also have a co-ordinative role, and should be used during the planning process.

Assistance from Planning Manager

II.12. The planning manager is available to help managers in the preparation of their plans, and in particular to assist in the identification of alternatives. He will not write plans for other managers, although he will help them to write their plans, if required. All managers have a responsibility to bring about an improvement in the company's planning ability.

Assumptions

II.13. Our knowledge of the future is imperfect, and in many cases plans will have to be based on assumptions. A variation in assumptions will frequently result in modification of the plan (an effect which should be considered as part of the analysis of risk and sensitivity—see paragraph II.21).

II.14. Part of the reason for corporate planning springs from the fact that a company is affected by what goes on in the world outside, and therefore should try to consider the environment in its plans. Assumptions about environmental factors can only be developed intelligently after a study of these factors.

II.15. Well-defined assumptions enable a discipline to be brought to plans. It is important that everybody uses the same basic assumptions in making their plans, otherwise the results will be unco-ordinated, and it will be impossible to calculate the effect of an alteration in circumstances at a later date, causing a change in assumptions.

II.16. There will be two main types of assumptions. The first will deal with situations which are specific to the company but over which the company has little or no control (e.g. failure of new plant to arrive on time, the absence of strikes at the factory). The second type of assumption deals with environmental trends and issues which, if correct, will affect the company and possibly the whole industry (examples: population changes, taxation rates, or government policy towards industry).

II.17. The planning manager will draft for the chief executive a list of assumptions for the first type of problem, and these will be issued at the beginning of each planning cycle.

II.18. In the second type of assumption, management, planning, and market research all have a role to play. Market research will identify trends from those environmental factors where past statistics or marketing data provide a guide to the future (examples: population projections, structure of retail trade). All managers should consider those factors where the outcome deduced is much more a matter of judgement. The planning manager has the particular duty of identifying these factors for the chief executive and, where appropriate with the help of others with specialised skills, coming to a conclusion about the factor.

II.19. Both types of environmental factor should be discussed at a planning meeting attended by appropriate managers, the potential importance of the factor to the company identified, and agreement reached on the planning assumption to be used. The assumptions will include provisional forward costs for all products.

II.20. In addition to the corporate assumptions, individual managers may have to make assumptions on a departmental basis. These should be clearly defined and stated in the plans.

Risks Analysis and Sensitivity

II.21. It is important for the management of the company to have a measure of the vulnerability of the planned profits to chance events. The company cannot foretell the future with any certainty. It is therefore good management to try to identify the elements of uncertainty in any plan.

II.22. First it should be accepted that no forecasts are likely to be completely accurate. In a separate section of their plan covering risks and sensitivity, managers should re-examine their sales forecasts and provide an estimate of the band of turnover (above and below the forecast) which they feel they can be 90% certain of achieving. This should be done on a product basis, although low volume products may be grouped, and is required for the first and last year of the plan only.

II.23. There are occasions where a wrong assumption may seriously affect profits (favourably or unfavourably). Each manager should try to identify these, quantifying the effect on turnover and profits.

II.24. To make the analysis meaningful the "betting odds" should be shown against each element of risk analysis in the form of a percentage probability (based on management judgement) of the event happening in:

(a) One year out of the five.
(b) Two years out of the five.
(c) Three years out of the five.
(d) Four years out of the five.
(e) All years.

No attempt need be made to predict the actual year in which variance may take place unless this is particularly obvious.

II.25. An overall summary should be given which, after taking all the elements of risk into consideration, represents the following effect on profits:

(a) The percentage probability of reaching targets.
(b) The probability of being 10% up.
(c) The probability of being 10% down.

This estimate should be set out in the way described in paragraph II.24 above.

II.26. Those preparing plans should view the main risks and sensitive areas as a challenge, and should prepare risk avoidance strategies as part of the plan. A simple example is the development of a contingency plan to be applied if a particular event happens.

II.27. Risk and sensitivity will also be considered on a total company basis by the planning manager.

Background Information

II.28. Sensible planning is difficult without a basis of fact. All managers have the duty of ensuring that they obtain such necessary facts as are reasonably available to enable them to make valid plans (where facts are unavailable assumptions will take their place: see paragraph II.13).

II.29. Market information may be very complex and, to ensure that all who make or interpret the plans have an adequate background of data, plans should include summaries of the main facts available on key markets.

II.30. It is a matter for the marketing manager's discretion whether the facts are included in the text of the plan or published as a separate appendix.

II.31. The document should include market forecasts for each product group covering the five years of the plan. These forecasts are an essential first step to the preparation of sales forecasts under different strategies, and should be available before the start of each planning cycle: that is, by 1 January each year.

II.32. Discussions should be held between the forecasting department and product managers before the forecasts are made, so that format and content can be agreed. The final forecasts should also be agreed with marketing.

Policy Guidelines

II.33. Guidelines will be issued by the chief executive to each departmental manager at the beginning of every planning cycle. These guidelines will show the minimum targets for each department and will outline any relevant policy matters.

II.34. At the same time a detailed time-table will be issued, showing completion dates for each stage of the planning process.

The Strategic Plan

II.35. This plan outlines those elements of corporate policy which show how, why, when, where, and how fast the company intends to change in the future. It is not simply the sum of operating plans and will include additional strategies, or may adjust the financial results of those plans proposed by departmental managers to take account of additional factors, or particular risks.

II.36. The planning manager will draw up the plan in accordance with the directions and wishes of the chief executive.

II.37. The plan will include:

(a) Corporate objectives.
(b) Corporate profit goals and performance ratios.
(c) Strategic decisions in the fields of:
    (i) Present business operations.
    (ii) Improvement of profitability of present operations.
    (iii) Ways of correcting internal weaknesses and deficiencies of the company.
    (iv) Expansion, diversification, and acquisition.
    (v) Company organisation.
(d) The expected financial results of plans.

Departmental Operating Plans

II.38. The operating plan deals with the established sectors of the company.

II.39. Each plan will consist of two parts—the programme (a narrative description of the action planned) and a budget (which shows the financial results expected from this action). The exhibits provided with the detailed instructions show the way in which financial data is to be presented (included under appropriate chapters elsewhere in this book).

II.40. In long-range plans it is desirable to avoid giving an impression of spurious accuracy. Financial calculations are, for this reason, required under summary headings only, and are to be to the nearest £000.

II.41. Plans for entry into new ventures, acquisitions, and mergers should only be treated as part of the operating plan when the manager has been given a specific mandate by the chief executive to include them. (In this context, new ventures should not be taken to include new or modified products, the development of which can properly be regarded as a function of an existing area of business.)

II.42. Each operating plan should be completed with the participation of managers at various levels in the department. The final versions should be passed to the planning manager, who will check them for consistency and co-ordination and who will pass them to the chief executive.

II.43. The chief executive will review each plan with the departmental manager who completed it, and such other managers as may be appropriate.

II.44. Requirements for each area of the business are given in detail in the following sections:

II.45. Marketing.

II.46. Production.

II.47. Research and Development.

II.48. Accounts and Administration.

II.49. Personnel Plan.

II.50. Financial Plan.

Marketing

II.45. The marketing director carries the ultimate responsibility for this plan, although other managers—particularly product managers—should contribute to it.

(i) Programme

Separate consideration must be given:

—Each main product group (although minor products may, if considered desirable, be classed under a general heading).
—Home and export sales.

(a) *Objectives and goals:* The long-range objectives and goals of the department should be stated. The rest of the programme will show how the department intends to meet these targets.

(b) *Assumptions:* All assumptions *additional* to those of the total company must be listed.

(c) *Marketing programme:* This section should be completed against the background of the market and competitive activity, and should deal with the broad principles of strategy, rather than the finer points of detail. It should take into account Government controls and influence in the industry. The accent should be on the solution of anticipated problems, and the continued development of new concepts and new ideas.

The programme could be developed in two parts, one dealing with general strategy and the total approach, the other with each product.

The programme must include the following information:

—Targets and objectives for each product.
—An outline of marketing strategies for the five-year period of the plan *with due consideration of alternatives*, reference paragraph I.46. Note the strategic elements include physical distribution policy.
—A sales forecast for each of the five years of the plan for every major product area (refer to exhibits). *Forecasts must be supported by the marketing strategy.* The sales forecast becomes a key element of the plans of production, and R & D, and must therefore be sent to these departments some time in advance of the main plan. Forecasts are required both in value and quantity (including pack).
—An outline time-table for the development and launching of new products (to be co-ordinated with the plans of R & D).
—A plan for the organisation and development of the sales force.
—An assessment of price movements over the five years.
—Recognition and analysis of anticipated problems, and the methods of dealing with these.
—A plan for marketing innovation, for testing and evaluating new marketing concepts and ideas.
—An assessment of the department's strengths and weaknesses.

(d) *Personnel programme:* This will include policy areas within the competence of the marketing manager, and will include training, remuneration, redundancy and redeployment. It must also cover the additional personnel requirements needed to support the other programmes. These should be detailed as follows:

(1) Numbers and types (by skills and management levels) of personnel required.
(2) Dates when required.

Forecasts should also be given of expected wastage through resignation, retirement and dismissal.

The purpose of this section is to assist in the development of a company personnel plan.

(e) *Organisation programme:* An organisation chart is required for the first year of the plan, and for every year in the future where a change in organisation is projected.

(ii) Budget

This must show the financial results of the planned courses of action—sales, costs, and profits.

A risk analysis should be made (see paragraph II.21).

An estimate must be made of:

(a) new fixed capital;
(b) replacement capital;
(c) additional working capital required for each of the five years.

Production

II.46. This plan is the responsibility of the production director.

Detailed production plans can only be prepared in the light of the sales forecasts. *Production should not take the responsibility for producing the basic forecasts, making pack mix estimates, or converting value forecasts into quantity forecasts.*

(i) Programme

Separate consideration must be given to each key production activity of the factory.

(a) *Objectives and goals:* The long-range objectives and goals of the department must be stated (the goals should include standard costs for each product). The rest of the programme will show how the department intends to meet these targets.
(b) *Assumptions:* All assumptions additional to those of the total company must be listed.
(c) *Technical programme:* This should cover the following points:
    (i) Planned capacity (specifying number of working days, number of shifts, and seasonal problems).
    (ii) Facilities, capacity, including warehouse, office requirements, etc.
    (iii) Strategy to ensure that the plant is able to produce the requirements of the marketing department (taking seasonal requirements into account).
    (iv) Inventory control levels for raw and packaging materials and finished stocks.
    (v) Identification of unprofitable activities and products.
    (vi) Ways of utilising surplus capacity.
    (vii) Plans for improving, extending or rebuilding various plant and facilities: approximate capital costs and effects on profits must be detailed and the data presented in such a way that management can distinguish the results of using or not using capital in this way.
(d) *Improvement programme:* The ways in which the department intends to achieve higher levels of productivity—for example:
    (i) labour utilisation;
    (ii) application for labour saving plant;
    (iii) application of new technology;
    (iv) management.
(e) *Personnel programme:* This will include policy areas within the competence of the director, and will include training, remuneration, redundancy and re-deployment. It must also cover the additional personnel requirements needed to support the other programmes. These should be detailed as follows:
    (1) Numbers and types (by skills and management levels) of personnel required.
    (2) Dates when required.
    Forecasts should also be given of expected wastage through resignation, retirement and dismissal.
    The emphasis should be on identifying expected problems in the field of personnel and human relations, and solving them before they become acute.
    The purpose of this section is to assist in the development of a company personnel plan.
(f) *Organisation programme:* An organisation chart is required for the first year of the plan, and for every year in the future where a change in organisation is projected.

(ii) Budget

This must show the financial results of the planned course of action, detailing costs under broad headings. Standard costs should be provided for each product.

An estimate must be made of capital requirements for each of the five years, with a brief description of the project.

A risk analysis should be made.

Research and development

II.47. This plan should be completed by the R & D director.

The R & D programme can only be completed as the marketing and production areas become aware of the services they will need from the department and after strategic decisions have been made by top management on new research projects. It is important that projects be co-ordinated with requirements.

(i) Programme

(a) *Activities programme:*

—The identification of research and development projects, and the setting of project objectives.
—Setting project priorities.
—Allocation of resources to projects.

(b) *Personnel programme:* This will include those policy decision areas within the competence of the director, and will include training, remuneration, redundancy and redeployment. It must also cover the additional personnel requirements needed to support the other programmes. These should be detailed as follows:

(1) Numbers and types (by skills and management levels) of personnel required.
(2) Dates when required.

Forecasts should also be given of expected wastage through resignation, retirements and dismissals.

The purpose of this section is to provide basic data to help the personnel manager to prepare the company personnel plan.

(c) *Organisation programme:* An organisation chart is required for the first year of the plan and for every year in the future where a change in organisation is projected.

(ii) Budget

This must show the financial results—costs—of the planned courses of action.

An estimate should be provided for requirements of (a) new and (b) replacement fixed capital for each year of the plan.

Accounts and administration

II.48. This plan takes a different format from the others in that it shows how the various departments under the control of the financial director will develop to meet the needs of the rest of the company.

Most of the plan will be concerned with personnel and organisational problems, although specific attention should be paid to office accommodation, IT, and management information systems.

(i) Programme

(a) *General:* Treatment of specific problems, the analysis of alternative solutions, and the selection of a course of action.
(b) *Personnel programme:* This will include those policy decision areas within the competence of the director and will include training, remuneration, redundancy, and redeployment. It must also cover the additional personnel requirements needed to support the other programmes. These should be detailed as follows:

(1) Numbers and types (by skills and levels) or personnel required (categories as agreed with the personnel manager).
(2) Dates when required.

Emphasis should be on identifying expected problems in the field of personnel and human relations, and solving them before they become acute.

(c) *Organisation programme:* An organisation chart is required for the first year of the plan and for every year in the future where a change in organisation is projected.

(ii) Budget

This should provide cost estimates for each of the areas under the control of the director.

The estimates should not allocate charges to other departments but should look at the figures on a total basis.

An estimate should be made of capital requirements for each of the five years with a broad description of the projects.

Personnel plan

II.49. The responsibility for preparing the personnel plan falls on the personnel manager although every manager has a duty to consider the personnel problems of his own business area when preparing his own plans. The plan should include:

—Objectives and goals.
—Assumptions additional to company assumptions.
—Manpower forecasts by categories, taking into account retirement, dismissal, resignation, and new posts.
—Management succession.
—Management development: general training and education.
—Salary and remuneration.
—Recruitment policies.
—Labour relations and trade unions.
—Welfare and benefits.
—A budget for the five-year period showing the cost of administering the department, and the resources needed to effect the planned course of action.

A major function of the plan is to define problems in the personnel field and to provide policies for their solution.

Financial plan

II.50. This plan is initially the responsibility of the financial director, and is completed after the operating plans have been prepared. It is, of course, a matter of top management strategy. It includes:

—Five-year cash flow statement.
—Income forecasts from non-operating sources, e.g. rents, interest.
—Forecasts of interest payable.
—Financial policy.
—Alternative methods of financing the plans.
—Recommended method of financing the plans.

Standardisation of Typing and Layout

II.51. The following rules should be applied so that a uniform document can be prepared with a minimum of re-typing.

(1) Typists should be encouraged to make adequate use of space: careful attention must be given to setting out.
(2) All typing to have $1\frac{1}{2}$-line spacing.
(3) All pages to have $\frac{3}{4}$ inch margin on each side.
(4) The main heading to be the *name* of the department only, in the centre of the page, in capitals, and underlined.
(5) Section headings to be in capitals and underlined, and to appear on the left-hand side of the page.
(6) Any sub-headings to be in small letters and underlined, and to appear on the left-hand side of the page.
(7) Reproduction should be on white A4 paper, although A3 may be used for extra large tables.

(8) Twenty copies of each plan are required.
(9) Pages should be numbered in the top centre of each page, and the numbers should include the departmental prefix (e.g. 1:1, 1:2, 1:3, 1:4).

Prefixed are:
Strategic	1
Personnel	2
Financial	3
Marketing	4
Production	5
Research and Development	6
Accounts and Administration	7

Annual operating plans

II.52. Annual operating plans have a close link with the budget. It makes sense to regard the budget as the financial expression of the course of action planned.

II.53. The budget becomes the tool of management control: it provides one means of measuring whether or not the annual plan is proving effective.

II.54. Budgetary control processes, although they should be seen as part of an overall system of planning, are an accounting responsibility and will always be administered by the chief accountant and his department.

II.55. Responsibility for completing the annual operating plan is as set out for the long-range plan—with heads of departments being responsible for their own plans, and the planning manager fulfilling his role of adviser and co-ordinator.

II.56. The annual plan should be regarded as a very close look at the first year of the long-range plan. This does not mean that the figures quoted for this period in the long-range plan will always be *identical* with those obtained after the more detailed study. Planning is seldom as exact as this, and, of course, as the annual plan is prepared some months after the long-range plan, we have the opportunity of re-examining our forecasts in the light of the further developments which have taken place.

II.57. The format of the annual plan should follow the broad headings set out under "Programmes" in the description of the long-range planning system, but each heading should be treated in greater detail. (All references to five-year forecasts should be treated as referring to the coming year only.)

II.58. Marketing headings could, for example, be expanded in the following way:

(a) Product
   (i) Product standards (formulation, appearance, etc.).
   (ii) Packaging—consumer (appearance, methods, labels, etc.).
   (iii) Brand.
   (iv) Quality, etc., guarantees.
   (v) Unit size.
   (vi) Image.
   (vii) Usage.
   (viii) Trade packaging.

(b) Place (distribution)
   (i) Retail outlets.
   (ii) Wholesalers/agents.
   (iii) Catering/industrial.
   (iv) Physical distribution.
   (v) Customer service.
   (vi) Trade credit.

(c) Promotion
   (i) Press advertising.
   (ii) TV advertising.
   (iii) Other advertising.
   (iv) Public relations.
   (v) Sampling.
   (vi) Merchandising.
   (vii) Special offers, competitions, etc.

(d) Price
  (i)   Price structures.
  (ii) Bonusing/discounting.
  (iii) Trade promotion discounts.
  (iv) Differential price structures.

II.59. It is essential that alternative courses of action be explored and studied. The annual plan brings the opportunity of studying a number of aspects which can only be treated in outline in the long-range plan.

II.60. Typing and layout should be as in paragraph II.52.

II.61. Every annual plan should include an improvement programme which each department or division uses as a deliberate means of seeking better and more profitable ways of doing things. The improvement programme should identify areas which require investigation, but which may have potential for greater efficiency. Examples are the changing of packaging, the more effective use of stationery, or the initiation of action which will reduce labour costs. Obviously, there will be no need to define items which require no investigation, as these will be implemented as a matter of course. Items which do require detailed study should be listed under the following headings:

Department..............................

Project	Estimated profit improvement	Date for completion of study	Name of person assigned to project	Name of depts. from whom support required

II.62. Every plan should be accompanied by a time-table which assigns actions (other than those already listed in the improvement strategy) to named individuals, with the required completion date. This time-table is used in the monitoring and control processes described below.

Monitoring and Controlling

II.63. The only valid reason for preparing plans is to ensure that profitable action occurs. A planning system that has no built-in check to ensure the conversion of short- and long-range plans to a course of action is unlikely to achieve its purpose. This section describes the way in which results will be measured and reported to managements so that the necessary controlling or correcting action may be taken.

II.64. The budget will be measured through the normal processes of control established by the chief accountant.

II.65. The action time-tables should be monitored through the appropriate departmental committees. If, for an acceptable reason, an action cannot be completed to time, it must be re-scheduled. What is important is that nothing is lost by default.

II.66. After the close of every year the planning manager will make a review of the company's progress towards its objectives.

II.67. Deviations from plans and targets will be analysed, so that the reasons for changes are understood, and that the chief executive is able to see clearly where changes to strategy have to be made.

30

Why Planning Sometimes Fails

Several times in this book it has been stressed that planning can fail because of the way it is introduced or managed in a particular company. The last chapter set out to give positive advice on the way the introduction of planning might be handled. This chapter attempts to look at the problem from a different way—to diagnose failure areas and warn against them.

Much of the material of this chapter comes from personal experiences, backed by numerous discussions with individual planners who were facing some of the difficulties that will be mentioned. It is reinforced by the writings of others, particularly those who have carried out original surveys. One leading work on this is still that of Warren,[1] which cannot be too highly recommended, but the research of George Steiner[2] has added much at a practical level. Steiner's list of pitfalls in planning is invaluable.

It should be noted that this topic was a subject for research in the 1960s and 1970s. More recent research, much of which has been quoted elsewhere, is concerned with strategy formulation and implementation. Because the research on which this chapter draws is from an earlier period it uses terms of the time to describe planning. I have not updated these to modern times. The conclusions are still valid.

Behaviour of the Chief Executive

It has always been stressed that planning will fail if the chief executive does not believe in it, or does not understand it, and accordingly shows a lack of interest in the process. It is sad that chief executives still introduce planning for the wrong reason. Irving[3] discovered two companies out of his sample of twenty-seven who admitted introducing corporate planning because it was "fashionable". Ringbakk[4] found in a survey in America that 40% of respondents had difficulty in getting top management support for corporate planning.

Irving[3] also found that planners did not experience internal political difficulties where there was strong leadership and participation by the chief executive. As corporate planning is a complete way of running a business it is not something about which a chief executive can be neutral. Those who are not for it are against it: they cannot sit on a fence and still remain chief executive.

Unfortunately, belief and understanding are not necessarily both present at the same time. If a chief executive is to truly benefit from corporate planning, he must understand the processes which are involved. He must be as expert in corporate planning—although not necessarily in all the detailed techniques—as his planner.

Pennington[5] makes the point that the type of involvement required from a chief executive is selective. He must come in at key points, and not allow himself to be swamped with so much detail that he neglects other aspects of his work. On the other hand, under-involvement "robs planning of its impact on operations".

Success in applying planning as a process of management can usually be ascribed to a relatively simple fact. Managers throughout the company realise, from the words and actions of the chief executive, that this is the way he or she intends to run his business, and that anyone who does not like it can vote with his feet.

Actions and words must fit together. There is no instrument as sensitive as a company in the detection of insincerity. Success will not come simply through top management utterances. The chief executive who cannot be seen to be taking the medicine he prescribes for others will soon find himself with a planning failure on his hands. Ringbakk[6] observes: "In many companies lip service has been paid to planning. Although management at the top has in words recognised the importance and desirability of formal planning, the necessary action and involvement have not resulted."

Acceptance by Management

Carson[7] quotes Ken Lander, then a senior partner with consultants Urwick Orr & Partners Ltd., as saying: "It takes about two years for line managers to kill a planner through passive resistance."

Ringbakk[4] found that in more than half of the businesses in his survey the major problem was getting operating managers to accept planning as part of their job. In a much earlier assessment Wrapp[8] stated that the most serious obstacle to planning "... is the subtle, but occasionally open, opposition of some executives which appears in the early stages of development".

Warren's[1] survey supports these views, and maintains that managers too often "... dilute the efforts of those who seek to remove the obstacles to effective long-range planning". He suggests that the introduction of planning is always accompanied by a "wait and see" attitude by line managers, and their eventual support depends on the *real* backing that is given by the chief executive.

There are many reasons for opposition by line managers, including preoccupation with day-to-day tasks, systems of payment which are related to current results, and the high turnover in managers, which means that they are not around long enough to live out their long-range plans. A new person, close to the top, as a planner must be, threatens existing power structures, and may also be seen as a barrier to future progress by the managers themselves.

My view is that there need be no situation of armed hostility between planner and managers, and the steps outlined in the preceding chapter will do much to ensure that relations begin and remain on the right track. Nevertheless, the motivation of managers to use a process of corporate planning is very much a task that falls on the shoulders of the chief executive, and which depends for its success on his behaviour.

Planning will certainly fail if it does not gain a wide level of support throughout the company.

Allowing Some Managers to Opt Out

A process of corporate planning must be total. No one manager or division can be allowed to opt out of the planning system. This applies to the deed as well as the word, for commitment must be complete and must not be just a question of paying lip-service to the idea.

This does not mean that the introduction of planning may not be phased. It is quite logical, in a large company, to begin planning in one or two areas and gradually extend over the whole company. But no manager must be allowed the right of deciding that planning is not for him once his area has been brought into the planning process.

Failure by the chief executive to enforce this rule will be like glazing a cracked china cup. Sooner or later the fault will come to the surface and ruin all the work that has been done since.

Confusion about Corporate Planning and its Meaning

Warren[1] makes the point that corporate planning is often confused with one of its elements. Some managers think they are enthusiastic supporters of planning, but really do not understand what it is about. It is common for managers to confuse it with forecasting, budgeting or computer models.

Ringbakk[6] states:

"Much planning today consists of extending budgeting. In the average firm this has meant planning starting with today and going five years into the future. The concern has largely been with the financial and quantitative results with which one is concerned in one year budgeting. However the underlying causal factors which determine the financial rules often have not been adequately covered. More fundamental qualitative thinking is required. What appears to be needed most urgently is strategic planning."

Lack of understanding often leads the entire company to expect miracles. Problems do not disappear just because the company has a corporate planner, and although immediate benefits may result (from, for example, the corporate appraisal), most must by definition be of a longer-term nature. von Allmen[9] stresses this point:

"Again, many companies decide that some formal corporate planning will give them a 'shot in the arm', when a little reflection would indicate that the start up investment of time and energy will result in just the opposite. More sinister, the launching of a major effort into corporate planning is often the signal of a panic reaction to impending serious problems which are already in so advanced a stage that only some outside miracle could successfully intervene.''

Time and again it is stressed by writers on planning that it must be seen as part of the total process of management. Time and again companies ignore this advice, and try to establish planning as an operation which is additional and isolated from the total management system.

Any of these misunderstandings can—and usually do—lead to the complete failure of corporate planning, however well intentioned the original motives might be.

The Planner and Current Activities

Some companies who employ planners give them terms of reference which effectively prevent them from taking any interest in day-to-day activities. They can do what they like—so long as they do not "rock the boat" or upset the line managers.

No good planner will think for a fellow manager nor will he tell him how to run his business. But any plans made, and any systems devised, must be firmly rooted in the present activities of the company. Control of plans can only be carried out if the elements of the plans come down to things people are actually going to do.

It is impossible for any planning system to work if it is isolated from line managers. Plans made in a vacuum are likely to remain plans—and never be converted to actions.

The corporate planner has a rightful place in the top management committee of the company. Failure to give him or her this place is another step on the road to the ruin of corporate planning in that company.

The Planner Must Accept the Limitations of his Role

Much has been said about the role of the planner and what the function should be in an organisation. It is important for the planner to understand—and accept— that, despite its importance, it is a role which has definite limitations.

The planner does not magically become the company's chief decision-maker or the arbiter of its alternative policies. It is not a planner's function to foist personal pet strategies on the company or to see the role as one to be set above fellow managers. Any touch of arrogance, any impression that the planner is an overlord, will bring the planning efforts crashing down.

The planner who believes that the whole future of the company lies under his or her sole charge is doomed to failure.

All senior staff functions are difficult, and the planning function is the most difficult of all. The temptations to the planner to overstep the boundaries are very real.

von Allmen[9] mentions the "high frustration tolerance level" which planners must have, as the ". . . commonest experience of the planner is high risk of failure with ultimate partial success".

The Avoidance of Ivory Tower Planning

If the planner understands and accepts this role, there is little risk of introducing an "ivory tower" type of planning. Too often, companies expect planning departments to produce plans: too often planners see their jobs in these terms.

Perrin[10] states bluntly: "No ivory tower theorist—however brilliant—will ever be successful."

Ringbakk[1] argues from his survey that active management participation is essential at corporate and divisional levels: "It can be argued, that this is the most fundamental condition which must be met since staff planners alone cannot do the planning."

In a different forum[6] he gives the fact that "management at different levels in the organisation has not properly engaged in or contributed to the planning activities" as a main reason for the failure of planning in some companies.

A planning system which does not involve operating management will collapse and fail. It may appear deceptively quicker for a planner to write operating plans, and—out of a desire to avoid paper work—line managers may initially urge that this be done. Later, line management disengages itself, claiming that the plans have nothing to do with it and are a staff matter: so no one implements them, no one has any accountability for them. A good planning system will involve every manager to an extent which will vary with function and seniority. It is not something which is reserved solely for divisional heads and chief executives. Not all managers will write long-range plans—but most should be allowed to contribute to the process.

Plans are Not Used

Perhaps the saddest problem area of all is that of the management which fails to operate by its plans. This may occur either because of the faults of management itself or because the planner neglects to build in any form of monitoring and control activity into the planning system.

What so often happens is that the company produces a set of impressive documents which involves a hectic period of corporate activity. The plans disappear into a series of filing cabinets, and are then lost for twelve months until the process starts again. Nothing is able to lose the confidence and enthusiasm of managers more quickly than the feeling that they are competing in an annual game of bluff and the writing of fairy stories, where the prize for all is a cloak of invisibility to ensure that no one actually does anything with the plans.

Smalter[11] states: "The success of corporate planning is not measured by the production of impressive looking books titled 'five-year plan—company confidential'. Any aspiring plan will not happen merely because it is neatly documented. It is still very necessary to *make it happen*."

The neglect of a follow up and control system as part of the planning procedure can lead directly to its downfall. Planners can design the control procedures but only management can ensure that they are implemented. Unfortunately, many planners design no control mechanisms, and even when they do exist many managements fail to use them effectively.

The changing of a plan is not the same as neglecting a plan. Every manager has, from time to time, to deviate from a planned course of action. A consciously decided deviation made against the background of a firm is vastly different from a complete failure to use the plan at all.

Failure by top management to use the plan is something which is another manifestation of the first failure area discussed in this chapter, and is a reflection of a lack of understanding by the chief executive of what planning really is.

The Planner is of Too Low a Calibre

The planner contributes to the success or failure of the company's planning effort, and many statements have already been made about this difficult role, and the type of person who should fill it.

Success in any job depends on the abilities of the person who holds it, and there are many functions in any form of organisation which bring success, mediocrity, or failure by the way in which the person holding the function fulfils the duties. The functions where personal failure can cause a company-wide effect are comparatively few in number. One of these is certainly the corporate planner.

An inferior person can, despite the best of intentions, frustrate the planning efforts of the company, and in some cases will make it difficult or impossible for an effective process of planning ever to be applied in the company (this is quite apart from poor strategic decisions which may be made).

Irving[13] maintains:

"Because of the unusual nature of the planner's role, and the rare combination of qualities required for its performance, the personal attributes of the planner are one of the most important determinants of the development of planning in any organisation. People with the required personal qualities are difficult to find and therefore expensive and either of these factors can result in lower calibre appointments."

The importance of the planner is stressed in Warren's[1] work and that of many other serious writers on the subject.

Despite all this excellent advice, many companies still rush down the road to planning failure by appointing the wrong person. Advertisements still appear which show that the recruiting companies see the planner as a low-level co-ordinator. Other companies see the position as a convenient resting place for a loyal senior executive, close to retirement, who has to be side-tracked.

Any chief executive who appoints the wrong calibre person (except in the occasional circumstance where there is a mis-assessment) is revealing a lack of knowledge of what planning is about. Frequently the key advisers in the company will recommend a lower calibre appointment than should be made in order to preserve their own vested interests. In general, managers like to take action which keeps the number of their equals as low as possible.

I would advance as a hypothesis for a future research programme that planning fails in a company as much from too low a calibre person being appointed as planning manager, as for any other cause. It is sad to see chief executives who are prepared to endanger all the investment of time and money the company is to make in planning for the sake of a quick or cheap appointment.

Planning Through a Committee

Committees and other forums for group meetings may often be used to great advantage in a company's planning processes. Elsewhere examples have been given of their use in setting assumptions and monitoring plans, to mention but two valid and worthwhile functions they can perform.

What I personally believe is impossible, and a contributory factor to planning failure, is the use of committees to replace a corporate planner. Any group with the special title "planning committee" tends to be a danger sign (I believe that committees which are used should not be special to planning but should be part of the total management process in that company). Where the committee is the only organ the company has of creating and co-ordinating planning, the risk of failure rises to a very high level indeed.

By all means create forums for the involvement and participation of managers in planning, and develop these as a key element of the company's approach to corporate planning. But these should always be a tool of the planning system, not the method by which planning is introduced.

In any case, it is generally a good rule to have as few committees as possible.

Confusion of Strategic and Operational Planning

The problem of confusing techniques of planning with planning itself has been discussed, as has the need to involve managers at all levels. Companies which manage to get these points in focus often miss another, and are blind to the differences between the two major but related types of planning.

This leads to difficulties in deciding who should be involved in what, in defining the planning system, in writing the plans, and in organising the flow of planning information.

Strategic planning is, as we have seen, very different from operational planning. It is sometimes useful, but not always desirable, to involve "grass roots" managers in the writing of the strategic plan (though often valuable to devise ways that enable ideas to come from all levels of management into strategic thinking).

"Involvement" in terms of strategic planning means the full participation of the top management team in the production of the strategic plan. This one might term as essential involvement for long-term planning success. Optionally, lower level managers may also participate either because they have skills and knowledge on which the company should draw, or because the motivational value of such involvement is very high. This optional involvement may be selective both as to the choice of managers who are invited to participate and the extent to which they are involved. It is not always desirable for a company's total strategic plan to be known too widely in the company—particularly where there is a major acquisition strategy—although it may be valuable for selected aspects to be published.

For operational plans "involvement" is different. Here I believe the principle should be that the head of each operational area must be responsible for his own plan, and should certainly enable all of his senior managers and as many of his more junior managers as the circumstances indicate, to play a part in the planning process.

Failure to understand the essential difference between the two types of planning leads to confusion. It prevents planning from becoming a properly integrated part of the company's overall management system. It also leads to the production of inadequate plans which do not cover the needs of the organisation and become rapidly unusable.

Insufficient Care Given to the Format of Plans

There are two great temptations to avoid in the preparation of plans and in the design of the planning system. One is the temptation to produce a mountain of paper in long-winded documents which are designed on the basis of what somebody thinks a plan should look like rather than what the organisation really needs. The second is to place too much emphasis on forms, so that the process of planning is viewed much in the same way as the annual completion of an income tax return.

Every organisation is unique, and must decide for itself what essential data its plans must include. In addition the requirements of detail will vary through the different levels of the organisation. A divisional manager will, for example, need more control data and information in his operating plans than he should send to corporate headquarters. Some form of "pyramiding" is essential, together with the insistence that executives are only required to read those parts of plans which are valid and useful to them.

It is very easy for a planning system to become nothing but an empty, and vast, generator of scrap paper. Over-elaboration should be avoided at all costs, and simplicity should be the design keynote.

An over-elaboration of forms brings a different state of mind. A planning system which is nearly all forms is usually nothing more than an extended budgeting operation. Some forms may be required, but again they should be simple in concept and few in number.

A plan should be written to do a job—not to demonstrate the cleverness of the person who prepared it.

The Problem of Over-sophistication in Planning Systems

The planning system should not be too sophisticated for the company it is serving. A company which lacks elementary basic management tools, such as market research, management information systems, or adequate budgetary control, is not ready for a planning process that is too complex.

Many planners try to use advanced planning techniques immediately (such as complex computer models of the company) and design systems which depend on these. They force the company into something it is not yet ready to handle.

Similarly there is a temptation to make planning as complex as possible in an attempt to produce a perfect plan. Frequently it is better practice to simplify, to hold the more complex areas back until the company gains in experience of planning. It is better to produce a less than perfect plan than to delay the preparation of plans for some years until the company can cope with the sophistications of the system or to force the company along paths it cannot understand.

This list of problem areas, when read in relation to the rest of this book, has a parallel with the type of instruction book which frequently comes with motor-cars, washing machines, or other complex domestic appliances. Each part of the car is described in some detail, and the buyer is shown what it is, what it does, and what he should do. Nevertheless, at the end of the booklet there is a check-list of faults. If the engine does not start check (a) the ignition is switched on, (b) there is petrol in the car, (c) the plug leads are connected—and so it goes on.

Often the check-list enables the driver to take swift corrective action. It prevents him from calling a mechanic when all that is wrong is that he has not turned on the ignition.

This list of failure areas is presented with something of the same purpose in mind. It is needed because we live in a real world where opinions are often in twilight shades of grey rather than the jet black and brilliant white of the textbooks.

In the first problem area mention was made of the need for a chief executive to understand planning. Unfortunately this is not a simple yes/no area. There are, in addition, degrees of understanding. Thus a chief executive may have a strong feeling for what the topic is all about but still have areas where his understanding is deficient.

Alternatively, he may have been in disagreement with a statement made or argument advanced in a previous chapter of this book. His disagreement may be partial, qualified, or absolute.

The check-list provides an opportunity for a reconsideration to be made of the importance of the issue. Often what goes wrong with the introduction of planning is just one of these very simple areas discussed in this chapter—as simple as turning the ignition key, and as stultifying on all progression if the action is omitted. If it prevents him from calling in an expert to correct it, the list will have had as much value as the handbook which avoids finding a mechanic for such simple problems.

These questions should be asked to gauge the effectiveness of
a planning process. If the response is frequently a 'no', the
chances are that the process is failing and needs to take account
of some of the principles discussed in this chapter and elsewhere

- Is top management committed to the concept of corporate planning
  through deed as well as word?

- Are strategic actions, particularly the major ones, based on the plan?

- Are plans seriously reviewed and discussed up the hierarchy?

- Does management as a whole become widely involved in the planning
  process?

- Is management involvement wider than the narrow line of functional
  responsibility of the individual manager?

- Is there a top-down strategic input to plans (e.g. are the plans anything
  more than a consolidation of individual submissions)?

- Are external environmental issues studied seriously and integrated into
  the plan?

- Is management performance measured at least partly on the basis of the
  corporate plan?

- Does the planning process link up with budgetary control, performance
  standards, personnel appraisal schemes and management development
  programmes?

- Would the main competitors be grateful to receive a copy of the
  corporate plan? (Many are so useless that even competitors can gain
  nothing from them)

- Is it those managers who are good planners who get promoted?

- Are corporate plans normally completed on time?

- Is there a monitoring and control mechanism attached to the planning
  process?

- Is the management style compatible with a management process which
  requires participation?

- Is the Director of Planning a high calibre person?

- Does the Planning Department have a good, co-operative working
  relationship with finance and accounts?

EXHIBIT 30.1. Testing an existing planning process. (© Harbridge Consulting Group Ltd, 1991.
Used with permission)

Although few people would throw away a car that will not start, it is unfortunately true that many companies will discard their investment in corporate planning when this fails to fire. And it is doubly unfortunate when the cause of failure
is preventable and often as trivial as the neglected ignition key.

References

1. Warren, K. E. *Long Range Planning: The Executive Viewpoint*, Prentice-Hall, 1966.
2. Steiner, G. *Pitfalls in Comprehensive Long Range Planning*, Planning Executives Institute, 1972.
3. Irving, P. Corporate planning in practice: a study of the development of planning in major United Kingdom companies, M.Sc. dissertation, University of Bradford, 1970.
4. Ringbakk, K. A. "Organised Planning in Major US Companies", *Long Range Planning*, December 1969.
5. Pennington, M. W. "Why Has Planning Failed?" *Long Range Planning*, March 1972.
6. Ringbakk, K. A. "Why Planning Fails", *European Business*, Spring 1971.
7. Carson, I. "The Big Leap in Corporate Planning", *International Management*, April 1972.
8. Wrapp, H. E. "Organisation for Long Range Planning", *Harvard Business Review*, January–February 1957.
9. von Allmen, E. "Setting up Corporate Planning", *Long Range Planning*, September 1969.
10. Perrin, H. F. R. "Long Range Planning: the Concept and the Need", *Long Range Planning*, September 1968.
11. Smalter, D. J. "Anatomy of a Long Range Plan", *Long Range Planning*, March 1969.

31
Planning—Tools, Techniques and Linkages

One of the difficulties of trying to put a logical structure into a book is that there are often important matters which fall outside the chosen structure. This chapter deals with a number of these. Either they are matters which themselves link with the process of strategic management, such as computer models and knowledge based systems, or they are tools and techniques which could have fitted in several places, but would have changed the flow of thought. Decision trees are an example. This chapter could be viewed as a description of miscellaneous important issues. Because of this it does not have the narrative flow of the previous 30 chapters.

The ability of an organisation to manage strategically is not dependent on techniques. Nevertheless, throughout the book I have illustrated many techniques and tools which can be a powerful aid to strategic thinking. However I always have a concern that in many organisations the technique comes to dominate the process. This is more likely to happen when the technique is related to computers, because the ability to process complex numbers gives a feeling that the output has to be true. One comment I read once sticks in my mind: the advent of the personal computer and spreadsheets has put the power to bankrupt the company much lower down in the organisation. Errors look so authoritative! More seriously, when considering the use of techniques discussed earlier, and the content of this chapter, it is worth quoting Ohmae[1] "My message.... is that successful business strategies result not from rigorous analysis but from a particular state of mind. In what I call the mind of the strategist, insight and a consequent drive for achievment, often amounting to a sense of mission, fuel a thought process which is basically creative and intuitive rather than rational. Strategists do not reject analysis. Indeed they can hardly do without it. But they use it only to stimulate the creative process, to test the ideas that emerge, to work out their strategic implications, or to ensure successful implementation of high-potential 'wild' ideas that might otherwise never be implemented properly. Great strategies, like great works of art or great scientific discoveries, call for technical mastery in the working out but originate in insights that are beyond the reach of conscious thought."

This puts this chapter in a context, and I think is consistent with what I have said about other aspects of analysis as the book progressed. The topics left to cover are computer based planning models, knowledge based systems, models for project appraisal (including discounted cash flow and the analysis of risk), decision trees, networks, segmentation techniques, and some thoughts on management information systems.

Computer Based Planning Models

The dream of the early planners is now realisable. This was to have available a dynamic model of the company which correctly represents every function of that company, and which may be used to explore the full financial effect of strategic options and "what if" questions. In the 1960s and 1970s this was achievable with expensive models using main frame computers. In the 1980s the expansion of personal computers and spreadsheets put models within the reach of just about every company, although it is still sensible for many of us to buy models rather than to build them.

McNamee[2] argues for a hierarchical approach in the development of models for strategic management. He quotes various surveys that suggest that the personal computer is not used for corporate strategic modelling as often as might be desirable, which he ascribes to the failure of strategic planners, functional managers and computer modellers to fuse their skills into "a synergistic methodology which cause strategic modelling to be an integrated element in the process and practice of strategic management". Traditionally the choice of scientific method for modelling has fallen between the reductionist and the holistic. Under the former, the organisation is reduced to its fundamental building blocks, and mechanisms are sought through which they interact. McNamee believes that this approach fails to recognise the synergies from shared resources and shared knowledge, nor does it encompass the hierarchical nature of strategic planning.

The holistic approach implies that modelling can only take place when a company wide view is taken, which may be appropriate for small organisations, but ignores the normal practice of dividing businesses into strategic business units. The hierarchical approach he recommends combines both approaches. He has built and uses a number of models, which enable a view to be taken of the outcome of strategies, and which also facilitate a great deal of micro analysis of the components.

Models such as this remove a great deal of drudgery from the planning task, and enable a speedier reaction to changed circumstances. This is why they were the dream of all planners in the days when they could be attained by only a few.

Even a relatively simple corporate plan for a small one-product company brings a great volume of calculation work. Think back to the chapters on strategy and the fact that one of the things every corporate plan should do is evaluate and choose between various alternatives. Just to quantify the plan under one set of assumptions may be very time-consuming.

The trouble with most manually calculated planning systems is that, working as they must do to a time schedule, they provide the company with little opportunity to correct for adverse circumstances. If the plan does not come out "right" first time, it usually has to be amended by crude panic methods which may give a correct representation in total but which lack precisions in the detailed parts of the plan.

About a week before the board are due to consider the plan the chief executive will, typically, have some second thoughts. There may be dissatisfaction with the expected results or a wish to know what would happen if path A or path B were chosen instead. Typically the chief executive is either told he or she cannot have the figures in time, or a rush job is put in hand which frays the tempers and risks inaccuracy through human error.

Time does not permit a thorough investigation of the numerous "what if?" questions which are possible. What if this assumption were changed, or the sales forecasts were higher (or lower), or if this method of financing were chosen instead of that one? Management may be given some sensitivity data when they are asked to accept the plan, but without a model this is rarely sufficient, and plans frequently have to be accepted as if they were a print-out of past results: that is, there is only one figure for each item, giving it a suggestion of spurious accuracy.

Quick reaction to changes in circumstances which indicate a need to re-look at the figures presented in the plan becomes difficult, simply because *quick* calculation of the figures is difficult. Manpower allocated to work on the plan at the right time in the planning cycle has returned to other jobs and can only with considerable upheaval be re-drafted to do a crash updating.

A mechanical system which alleviates all these difficulties can thus be seen as something which is very desirable to both the corporate planner and top management. Such a system also gives managers the facility of testing out the effects of their ideas before they commit themselves to plans, it assists in contingency planning, and it gives the planner the opportunity to quantify the effects of assumptions and to advise managers of these effects before they start planning. Knowledge of the company's expected internal inflation rate for each product over the next few years—that is, the combined effect of all individual assumptions for cost changes on production costs—can help marketing managers to forecast sales on a more realistic basis.

Such a quick response system makes it easier to run the company through the plan. At any management meeting it becomes possible to obtain immediate answers to questions addressed to the model. If required a computer may be set up in the board room.

One of the first things to be identified is what the company wants from its model. Defining the parameters is a very important step, for it will not only affect the cost but the way in which the model can be used in future. The parameters will also help the company decide whether it has to build the model completely from its own resources or whether it can use a commercially available package.

Many planners have turned away from corporate models which seek to optimise. These models set up a specific criteria for what is the best solution and an algorithm (which provides step by step instructions under which the model proceeds with its calculations). The optimum criteria may be to minimise costs or maximise profits, and the model will select which of the various alternatives comes closest to doing this. Most optimising models make use of linear programming: other techniques are available.

Boulden[3] states:

"The early optimising models developed by the operations research groups have been largely discarded (with the notable exception of the oil companies) because (1) the policy decisions prove too complex to define in optimising terms; (2) the organisation was continually changing so that the models were no longer appropriate; (3) operating managers could not understand the models."

Many planners believe that the search for the one best answer is an impracticality for corporate planning problems, and that an optimising model is therefore an expensive impracticality.

It is because of this that the simulation approach has come into favour. This enables various strategic alternatives to be evaluated on a case study approach. It does not find the one best answer, but if enough "cases" are run many come very close to doing this. Simulation models have the additional advantage of being easier to build, easier for managers to understand, and take relatively little computing time. Alternatives are evaluated on the model by making changes to the data in the model: in the same way alternative planning assumptions may be examined and the effect of failures to meet forecasts studied. The consideration of various possible forecasts and different assumptions is essentially a form of sensitivity analysis, which helps management to understand the risks to which their decisions are subjected.

Thus a simulation model might be used to evaluate four alternative strategies and the effect on these of five sensitivity factors. In theory this means running twenty cases on the model: in practice this is not always necessary as intelligent interpretation of a number of "what if?" questions will give the planner an indication of where the answer to certain other questions must lie.

Case study models may be built up from a series of modules—or sub-models. The advantages of these are that refinement or alteration of a module is possible without affecting the whole model; it is possible to study and evaluate "what if?" questions on a module without printing out the whole model, enabling a preliminary study of marketing strategies (e.g. before looking at the effects of those strategies on cash flow). It also means that the model builder can concentrate on priorities, building the most important modules first, and later returning to build the modules for the less important areas. None of this destroys the logic of the model.

A simulation model may be deterministic or stochastic (probabilistic). The former treats only one set of conditions at a time, printing out the results of those sets of conditions. However, it has the facility of being able to print out cases dealing with any number of sets of conditions, the only restrictions being common sense, cost, and time. A stochastic model can cope with a range of possibilities and enables several to be specified for each case studied. The type of simulation model selected will naturally have a bearing on the cost of developing it and how it is used.

The model may contain no forecasting mechanism in itself except in so far as one related forecast may be calculated from another: for example, the input of a sales forecast may, through the relationships built into the model, calculate forecasts for raw materials and other production costs, debtors' levels, and the like. Obviously its accuracy depends on the accuracy of the relationships defined in the model, and some of the "what if?" questions may be designed to explore changes in these.

In other applications a more complex model may be desirable which incorporates a forecasting ability. For this, regression models may be used which use regression analysis to establish the relationships between various series of data and use these for the basis of statistical projections into the future.

Before exploring the uses of these models in greater detail it is as well to return to the problem of how a company may set about installing one. It is possible—and for certain types of business may, indeed, be desirable—for the company to build a model from within its own resources (assuming, of course, that it is willing to hire the appropriate specialists). This may bring it exactly what it wants, but it may be some time before it has a usable package.

Alternatively, the company may decide to use one of the various software packages available from outside companies which, with minimal modification, may be made to meet its needs. Some are so flexible that they enable what is virtually a custom-designed model to be built for each company.

It should also be noted that some of the software on offer is suitable for financial planning only: that is, they allow manipulation of sales and margins but do not permit detailed study of production costs or individual markets.

The diversity of models that it is possible to build, or which are available ready-built, leads to one very important principle. The company should clearly define the objectives of the model before it sets out to obtain it. Too broad a specification will result in increased costs of building, training, and operation: too narrow a specification may mean that the model can do neither what the company wants it to do nor can it easily be extended or modified. Where all the company needs is a financial planning model, it may be unnecessary to build one that does more than this: if only ten variables are significant to the company, it may be an expensive luxury having a model that will cope with a hundred.

As with all things, the final solution should be achieved by studying the costs in relation to the benefits.

Both the examples below appeared in earlier editions of this book and are of models on main frame computers. Virtually the same results can now be achieved on personal computers. Despite the difference in hardware and software, the exhibits provide a useful indication of the output of models.

A detailed example is given of a financial planning model and this may be contrasted with the subsequent example of a problem solved on a corporate-planning model. The financial planning model is FPS, a system offered by merchant bankers Baring Brothers & Co. Ltd., through whose courtesy the example is provided.

Figure 31.1 shows the role of this model in the evaluation of the financial effects of alternative corporate strategies. Figures 31.2 and 31.3 demonstrate the types of print-out which may be obtained to show the effects of a particular strategy, while Fig. 31.4 gives an example of the type of sensitivity analysis which may be carried out. The model has flexibility and can be made to fit the accounting system of most companies. It is simple to operate and can remove much of the drudgery of numerous financial calculations. It has its main value in broad-brush top-level calculations, and its main detail lies in the area of alternative financial strategies and their effect on cash flow.

FIG. 31.1. Role of the FPS model in the evaluation of strategy. (Reproduced by courtesy of Baring Brothers & Co. Ltd.)

Example Group limited Illustrative projections Income statements Pounds 000s	Year 0	0 + 1	0 + 2	0 + 3	0 + 4	0 + 5
1. Sales	65172	70910	77150	80310	84750	89140
2. Direct materials	33556	37582	40504	42163	44494	46799
3. Direct labour	11651	13827	15430	14456	15255	16045
4. Manufact overheads	3947	4184	4435	4701	4983	5282
10. Depreciation*	5117	5647	6269	6597	6970	7360
13. Cost of goods sold	54271	61243	66638	67916	71702	75486
14. Gross profit	10901	9667	10512	12394	13048	13654
20. Selling expense	1273	1385	1507	1569	1655	1741
21. Admin expense	1541	1618	1699	1784	1873	1967
22. R & D	675	734	799	832	876	923
24. Operating profit	7412	5930	6507	8210	8642	9023
33. Investment income	824	824	824	824	824	824
36. Royalties	312	339	369	384	406	427
47. Interest payable	1612	1499	2166	2275	1938	1717
48. Pretax profit	6312	4915	4796	6374	7122	7703
50. Tax	2197	1636	1589	2220	2519	2752
54. Net profit	4115	3279	3207	4154	4603	4951
60. Minority interests	215	170	167	216	239	257
61. Exceptional items	200	100	-197	0	0	0
92. Disposals - P/L	0	50	-45	0	0	0
62. Preference dividend	40	40	40	40	40	40
63. Earnings	4060	3218	2758	3698	4323	4654
65. Ordinary dividend	2710	2710	2710	2710	2860	3042
66. Retentions	1350	508	48	1188	1463	1612
11. * Depn plant etc.	4920	5452	6072	6400	6758	7133
12. * Depn land & building	197	197	197	197	212	227

Income Statements

FIG. 31.2. Example of FPS output. Income statements. (Reproduced by courtesy of Baring Brothers & Co. Ltd.)

The second example is supplied by Robin Ramm & Partners and the University Computing Centre, and is one of usage of a model built under the FEP (financial evaluation programme) system. The application illustrated is a modification of an actual case and is concerned with a typical strategic decision which arises in multi-national operations—which of two factories (located in different countries) should supply certain new products to the trading companies in six countries. In the case in question there were six new products.

Estimates of competitive pressure in the future suggested that prices could be forced down to a third below the forecast levels within five years. On the credit side an improvement in process yields, due to increased technological skills, was possible.

Example Group limited Illustrative projections Sources and Uses of Funds Pounds 000s		Sources and Uses				
	Yr 0	0 + 1	0 + 2	0 + 3	0 + 4	0 + 5
1. Retentions	1350	508	48	1188	1463	1612
2. Depreciation	5117	5649	6869	6597	6970	7360
4. Creditors	829	1294	857	312	219	914
5. Accrued tax & divs	0	-642	-55	723	424	340
8. Fixed asset disposals	0	200	300	0	0	0
9. Provisions etc	40	85	100	-100	-100	-100
10. Long debt & other cap	100	79	3078	100	-1889	257
11. Ord cap & other reserves	0	0	0	0	2000	0
13. Total sources	7436	7173	10598	6620	9067	10364
14. Stock	1282	1714	1333	1878	-627	935
15. Debtors	1198	846	920	466	655	648
19. Capital expenditure	5903	9725	12000	5250	7000	5750
25. Total uses	8383	12285	14253	7594	7028	7332
22. Opening cash	549	512	-4600	-8255	-7030	-4990
23. Net cash movement	-37	-5112	-3655	1226	2039	3051
24. Closing cash	512	-4600	-8255	-7030	-4990	-1939

FIG. 31.3. Example of FPS output. Sources and uses. (Reproduced by courtesy of Baring Brothers & Co. Ltd.)

The cases examined by the model were:

A. *Base case.* Examination of the project at the "most likely" levels for all forecasts and based on complete manufacture in country A.
B. *Sensitivity test 1.* Re-examination of the base case allowing for price erosion reaching 30% by the fifth year.
C. *Sensitivity test 2.* Repeat of test 1 but taking account of increased process yields.
D. *Sensitivity test 3.* Repeat of test 1 but on the basis of manufacture in country B.

Management needed to know whether the project to manufacture in country A was viable on the "most likely" forecasts, how critical was pricing, what could be gained from a yield improvement programme and what were the economic levels of cost of such a programme, and what, if any, improvement would there be if production were all carried out in country B?

Some of the variables which had to be included in the model were:

Sales volumes   Inventory policy
Selling prices   Credit policy
Sales support costs   Payments policy
Development costs   Financing policy
Process yields   Manufacturing times/unit

	Sensitivity Analysis				
Current values	Yr 0 + 1	0 + 2	0 + 3	0 + 4	0 + 5
1. Sales	70910	77150	60310	64750	70910
151. Deficit funds	1100	4755	3530	1490	1100
24. E.P.S. II (excl excpt 1tm)	0.143	0.140	0.181	0.190	0.143
-5.00% change in sales					
151. Deficit funds	1391	5502	4931	3690	1391
151. % change	26.48	15.70	39.72	147.6	26.48
24. E.P.S. II (excl excpt 1tm)	0.120	0.114	0.151	0.159	0.120
24. % change	-16.04	-18.64	-16.66	-16.04	-16.04
-10.00% change in sales					
151. Deficit funds	1682	6249	6333	1682	1682
151. % change	52.95	31.41	79.43	52.95	52.95
24. E.P.S. II (excl excpt 1tm)	0.097	0.066	0.121	0.097	0.097
24. % change	-32.08	-36.92	-33.33	-32.08	-32.08
Current values					
3. Direct labour	13827	15430	14456	13827	13827
151. Deficit funds	1100	4755	3530	1100	1100
24. E.P.S. II (excl excpt 1tm)	0.143	0.140	0.181	0.143	0.143
3.00% change in direct labour					
151. Deficit funds	1553	5549	4626	1553	1553
151. % change	41.20	16.71	31.08	41.20	41.20
24. E.P.S. II (excl excpt 1tm)	0.131	0.126	0.168	0.131	0.131
24. % change	-8.068	-9.840	-7.570	-8.068	-8.068
6.00% change in direct labour					
151. Deficit funds	2006	6344	5723	2006	2006
151. % change	82.41	33.41	62.15	82.41	82.41
24. E.P.S. II (excl excpt 1tm)	0.120	0.154	0.154	0.120	0.120
24. % change	-16.14	-19.68	-15.14	-16.14	-16.14

Fig. 31.4. Sensitivity analysis. (Reproduced by courtesy of Baring Brothers & Co. Ltd.)

Capital investments
Depreciation policy (tax and book)
Investment incentives
Tax regulations
Tariff barriers
Transfer pricing
Engineering support costs

Labour rates
Cost of component materials
Manufacturing overheads
Quality control costs
Administrative expenses
Profit-sharing policy
Repair and maintenance costs

Extracts from the computer print-out appear in Figs. 31.5 and 31.6. From these certain conclusions were drawn (while a study of the supporting reports from the model enabled an explanation to be derived of the reasons for the differences). Note that the original dates have been retained. It was of course a forecast not a historical report:

($000's)

	Cash flow and D C F	D C F rate	1969	1970	1976
Base case	T C F (INT)	86.619	-790.779	-1007.261	-487.967
	Net present values				
	T C F (INT)	10.000	-790.779	-1706.470	8594.192

	Cash flow and D C F	D C F rate	1969	1970	1976
Test 1 30% lower selling prices by 1975	T C F (INT)	54.831	-790.779	-1007.261	71.556
	Net present values				
	T C F (INT)	10.000	-790.779	-1706.470	3939.888

	Cash flow and D C F	D C F rate	1969	1970	1976
Test 2 Lower prices and improved yields	T C F (INT)	57.897	-790.779	-1007.261	71.556
	Net present values				
	T C F (INT)	10.000	-790.779	-1706.470	4347.716

	Cash flow and D C F	D C F rate	1969	1970	1976
Test 3 Lower prices and manufacture in UK	T C F (INT)	68.602	-790.814	-1145.605	-768.388
	Net present values				
	T C F (INT)	10.000	-790.814	-1832.273	5016.943

FIG. 31.5. Extract from computer output. Rate of return tables for each case. (Reproduced by courtesy of Robin Ramm & Partners Ltd.)

Cash flow
Profit and loss AC
Expense analysis
Purchase analysis
Stocks

Sales analysis		1969	1970	1971	1972
Quantities sold					
Product A	K units	0	25	75	150
Product B	K units	3	80	230	300
Product C	K units	0	15	80	100
Product D	K units	1	30	100	125
Product E	K units	0	10	50	100
Product F	K units	1	40	150	250
At a price of					
Product A	$ each	0.00	1.50	1.40	1.40
Product B	$ each	2.20	2.00	1.80	1.60
Product C	$ each	0.00	2.40	2.20	2.10
Product D	$ each	4.10	4.00	3.80	3.80
Product E	$ each	0.00	4.40	4.00	3.60
Product F	$ each	2.10	2.00	1.70	1.70
Total revenue					
Sales revenue		13	477	1530	2160

FIG. 31.6. Computer output. Example of secondary output tables produced for each case. (Reproduced by courtesy of Robin Ramm & Partners Ltd.)

(a) The project at a DCF rate of return of 86% is viable in comparison with the cost of capital of 10%.

(b) The project is highly sensitive to price erosion and a 30% fall by 1975 will reduce the rate of return from 86% to 54%. The corresponding fall in net present value is $4654,000, hence it would be worthwhile introducing a design improvement programme to prevent the price erosion if the cost of this will have present value less than this amount.

(c) By a similar logic, process-yield improvement is worth attempting providing the programme will have a present value of less than $408,000.

(d) The economic "trade-offs" between tax rates, labour rates, investment allowances, interest rates, freight costs, and duty payable in this study are such as to give an advantage of $1077,000 present value to UK manufacture.

The computing time for the study was recorded as forty seconds for the base study and fifty seconds in total for the sensitivity tests.

Discounted cash flow is now almost universally accepted as the most appropriate technique for the appraisal of capital expenditures. Those who wish to study DCF in some detail are again referred to Merritt and Sykes.[4]

In its simplest terms DCF may be described as an attempt to take into account the time value of money on the basis that £1 this year is worth more than £1 next year (because of the interest that can be earned with it). Thus if interest is at 10%, £1 would be worth only £0.909 if it were not received until next year, or if not received until the year after £0.826. The reduced value of the £1 is comparative to the project only and has nothing to do with inflation.

DCF has three main measures of performance. One is the "net present value" at the end of the project—that is it cumulates the cash flows of each year of the project (discounted at the chosen rate), providing a simple one-figure measure of results for comparison between projects.

The next measure is number of years before pay-back (which may also be taken at undiscounted figures).

The third is the internal rate of return (sometimes known as DCF yield). This calculates the theoretical interest rate which, if used, would produce a net present value of nil. Again, this produces a simple one-figure measure which enables straight comparison between projects. In some analyses dual-rate DCF is more appropriate. This discounts earnings and borrowings at "different" rates.

No single measure gives the correct answer. As was mentioned in Chapter 20 on financial planning, sometimes a company may prefer the project which has the earlier pay-off rather than the one with the best internal rate of return.

DCF of course, deals in cash flows rather than book profit. It looks at projects on a marginal basis and includes capital expenditures as outflows (but does not treat depreciation as an outflow as the money remains with the company). It is capable of manipulation—as, for example, the number of years over which projects are evaluated and the treatment of the residual value of assets still remaining in the company. Occasionally the simple approach described here has to be replaced by more complex methods (such as dual rate discounted cash flow). And it requires more analysis and evaluation than some of the traditional methods of project appraisal. On the other side, it is more realistic than the older methods, and provides a much better basis of comparison for alternatives or between one project and another. It also gives a starting point for further analyses, which aid the examination of risk and uncertainty.

A number of models are readily available for the evaluation of projects by DCF either as standard software or on a time-sharing basis. These models may be much simpler than the corporate models discussed earlier, which represent the whole company. The main advantages of the DCF models are that they remove the chore of tedious calculations and enable more risk and sensitivity analysis to be undertaken.

Figure 31.7 shows the logical relationships of the factors in a project evaluation. This figure could have been used to facilitate manual calculation: in fact it was the basis of a model for a new food product which enabled a complex sensitivity analysis to be undertaken. The model was built using the ICL PROSPER package—a system designed for use by accountants and planners with a programming language suitable for this aim. (The case from which the figure is

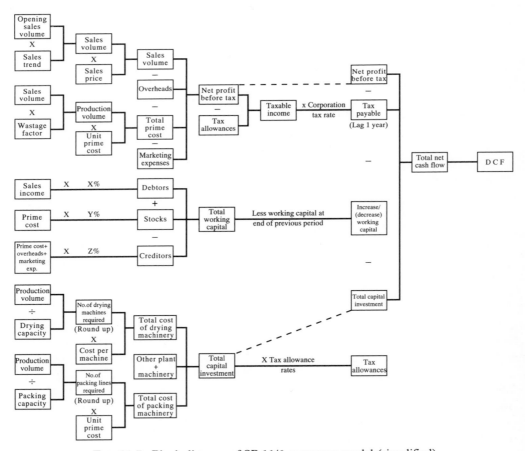

FIG. 31.7. Block diagram of SP 11/6 computer model (simplified)

taken is more fully described in Brown and Hussey.[5]) This particular project is a fond memory, in that those of us working on it felt that we were pioneering. The fact that every change of data in the model, or every run of "what if" questions took a morning out of the office to visit the computer bureau was just the price we paid for progress. It was not just that we were harnessing massive computer power to the solution of our planning problem, but we were also able to make extensive use of decision trees in a real situation (see later). Today we could do the whole exercise using a commercial spread sheet programme on our own personal computers. This does not destroy the value of the exhibits as an example of the outputs of such computer applications.

An illustration of two print-outs from another ICL package PROP is reproduced in Fig. 31.8. This shows the end product of a project analysis, using dual rate DCF.

I.C.L. Prop (1) Plant expansion - brand X, Assumptions - no in/deflation of cost/prices

Grant 20%, annual all, 20%, reducing balance for 5 years, corporation tax 40%

Year	Period	Capital investment	Other capital	Investment grant	Initial allowance	Annual allowance	Revenue Income	Revenue Costs	Revenue Profit	Tax on Profit	Net cash flow
0	3	-10000.0	0.0	0.0	0.0	0.0	0.0	-500.0	-500.0	0.0	-10500.0
	4	-2000.0	0.0	0.0	0.0	0.0	3000.0	-1000.0	2000.0	0.0	0.0
1	1	0.0	0.0	0.0	0.0	0.0	2500.0	-1000.0	1500.0	0.0	1500.0
	2	0.0	0.0	0.0	0.0	0.0	2000.0	-1000.0	1000.0	0.0	1000.0
	3	0.0	0.0	0.0	0.0	640.0	3000.0	-1000.0	2000.0	-600.0	2040.0
	4	0.0	0.0	0.0	0.0	0.0	2500.0	-1000.0	1500.0	0.0	1500.0
2	1	0.0	0.0	2000.0	0.0	0.0	2500.0	-1000.0	1500.0	0.0	3500.0
	2	0.0	0.0	0.0	0.0	0.0	2000.0	-1000.0	1000.0	0.0	1000.0
	3	0.0	0.0	0.0	0.0	512.0	3000.0	-1000.0	2000.0	-2400.0	112.0
	4	0.0	0.0	0.0	0.0	0.0	2500.0	-1500.0	1000.0	0.0	1000.0
3	1	0.0	0.0	0.0	0.0	0.0	2000.0	-1500.0	500.0	0.0	500.0
	2	0.0	0.0	0.0	0.0	0.0	2000.0	-1500.0	500.0	0.0	500.0
	3	0.0	0.0	0.0	0.0	409.0	2500.0	-1500.0	1000.0	-2200.0	-790.4
	4	0.0	0.0	0.0	0.0	0.0	2500.0	-2000.0	500.0	0.0	500.0
4	1	0.0	0.0	0.0	0.0	0.0	0.0	0.0	0.0	0.0	0.0
	2	0.0	0.0	0.0	0.0	0.0	0.0	0.0	0.0	0.0	0.0
	3	0.0	0.0	0.0	0.0	327.0	0.0	0.0	0.0	-1000.0	-672.0
	4	0.0	0.0	0.0	0.0	0.0	0.0	0.0	0.0	0.0	0.0
5	1	0.0	800.0	0.0	0.0	0.0	0.0	0.0	0.0	0.0	800.0
	2	0.0	0.0	0.0	0.0	0.0	0.0	0.0	0.0	0.0	0.0
	3	0.0	0.0	0.0	0.0	1310.7	0.0	0.0	0.0	0.0	1310.0
	4	0.0	0.0	0.0	0.0	0.0	0.0	0.0	0.0	0.0	0.0
6	1	0.0	0.0	0.0	0.0	0.0	0.0	0.0	0.0	0.0	0.0
	2	0.0	0.0	0.0	0.0	0.0	0.0	0.0	0.0	0.0	0.0
	3	0.0	0.0	0.0	0.0	-320.0	0.0	0.0	0.0	0.0	-320.0

I.C.L. Prop (2) Plant expansion - brand X, Assumptions - no in/deflation of cost/prices

Grant 20%, annual all, 20%, reducing balance for 5 years, corporation tax 40%

D.C.F. Yield rate of return - 17,1886% paying per annum, accurate to within 0.00001, 5.0000% earning rate

D.C.F. Net present value of project - 1702,1 at 7,0000% paying and 5,0000% earning rates per annum

D.C.F. Net present value of project - 1765,4 at 7,0000% paying and 4,0000% earning rates per annum

D.C.F. Net present value of project - 1634,0 at 8,0000% paying and 4,0000% earning rates per annum

Payback period - 1 year 3 periods

Average annual rate of return - 4.14%

FIG. 31.8. Example of ICL PROP output. (Reproduced by courtesy of International Computers Ltd.)

Models come into their own when the company begins to study the problem of uncertainty. One simple way of doing this is for a number of DCF evaluations to be made to test the risks to which the project is subject: in other words, sensitivity analysis. This may mean looking at the effect on results of different sales or cost forecasts, changes in price, changes in manufacturing process, or in the timing of the investments. Some of these analyses are in fact necessary for the proper evaluation of and choice between the options open to the company: others are prudent, so that the company can gauge how close they stand to disaster if certain possible events occur. Even a simple project may suggest a need to evaluate three or four alternatives and perhaps three sensitivity cases—which could be as much as twelve sets of DCF calculations for one project. If dual rate DCF analysis is made, even more calculations are needed. All this is possible by manual means, but tedious.

Figure 31.9 illustrates a technique of risk analysis (also using PROP) which is simply not practicable by manual methods. Using Monte Carlo techniques, the model makes numerous calculations, each of which yields one DCF rate of return for each variable. By random selection various possible values for variables are

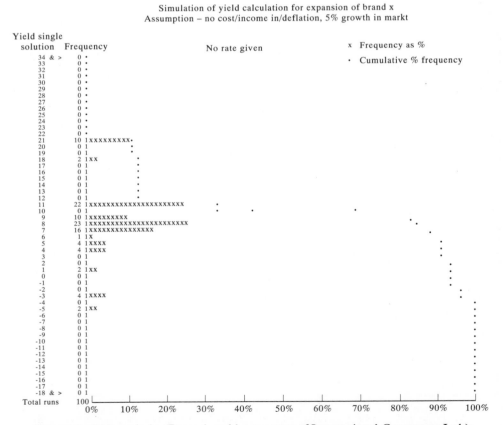

FIG. 31.9. Risk analysis. (Reproduced by courtesy of International Computers Ltd.)

substituted for the base figures, and used to produce a DCF analysis. The process is repeated many times so that a frequency distribution of possible DCF rates is built up. From this it is possible to calculate the statistical probability of each rate's occurrence. Figures 31.10 and 31.11 (for a hypothetical project) show how a simple chart can be derived from an analysis of this nature. This chart may be used to read off the probability of occurrence of each rate of return. The frequency diagram itself is useful for direct reference as it has a shape which can be compared with that of other projects.

Many mathematicians argue that it is invalid to derive probability percentages from the frequency diagram, although as many will argue for the use of the techniques.

Decision Trees

Both corporate and project evaluation models may be used to some benefit in conjunction with the decision tree technique. This is a diagrammatic method for showing alternative decisions and the probable effect of chance events on those decisions. The technique has two main advantages. The first is that it represents a logical progression of thought, and helps the analyst to identify factors which might otherwise have been overlooked. It is often useful to use decision trees in conjunction with a model, using the trees to assess what alternatives and sensi-

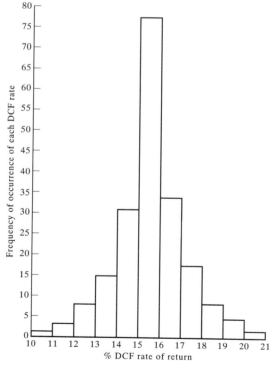

FIG. 31.10. Risk analysis. Frequency distribution of DCF rates

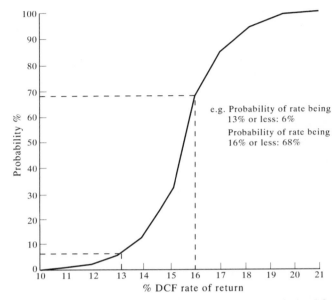

FIG. 31.11. Risk that rate of return is less than the figure stated (derived from Fig. 23.10)

tivity tests to evaluate, and using the model to quantify the results of these assessments.

Equally important, the technique is one of communication. It enables possibilities and their effects to be reduced to one sheet of paper (albeit a large sheet) in a way which is ideal for presentation and discussion at management meeting. A very complex situation can be reduced, without too many frills, to its simplest elements.

The technique is easiest to explain if first used in connection with a very simple situation where in reality it would not be applied, because there is no advantage in so using it. Once the concept has been explained, a more complicated example taken from a real case will be shown.

In its simplest terms the techniques may be used to analyse the alternatives facing the founders of a new professional society in planning their inaugural meeting and having very little idea of how many people were likely to attend.

The alternative preparations which could be made, and the effect on these of the chance event of audience size, are shown as follows:

Alternative	Event	Result
Hire small hall	Less than 100 people attend	Room just right for audience: Success
	More than 100 people attend	Not all will be able to get in: stigma of bad planning
Hire large hall	Less than 100 people attend	Unnecessary expense incurred: audience appears lost; meeting a failure
	More than 100 people attend	Room just right: meeting a success

Figure 31.12 shows the same data in the form of a decision tree. Although this particular problem can be just as easily perceived and understood from the table, it is not hard to see a situation where the list is so long that the mind can only take it in with difficulty. It is this sort of case where the technique comes into its own, and

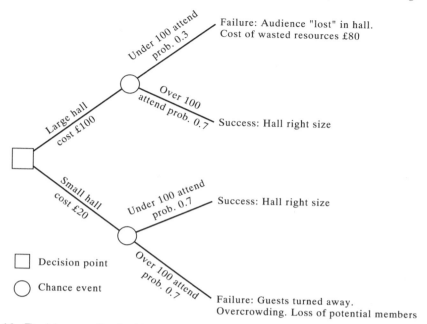

FIG. 31.12. Decision tree for the hiring of a hall for the inaugural meeting of a new professional society at which an unknown number of people will attend (hypothetical data)

Fig. 31.13 provides an example (taken from the previously quoted case history by Brown and Hussey[5]).

The main alternatives and chance events were in this example quantified with the aid of the PROSPER model (shown in diagram form in Fig. 31.7). Another refinement would have been useful—the inclusion of probabilities for the chance events.

The question of probability is a very important one in all planning situations, although there is rarely a precise method of calculating it. Nevertheless, it is good practice to request those making forecasts to put "betting odds" on them. If statistical confidence limits are possible, this is even better. This leads on to another problem. In putting together a total corporate plan the company may be dealing with numerous projects, forecasts, and assumptions, all of which carry different probabilities of being correct. Skilled judgement may enable individual betting odds to be placed on these in a manner which is helpful and useful.

Once a probability has been established and the monetary consequences calculated it becomes possible to calculate an expected monetary value (EMV) for each stage of the decision tree. This is the monetary outcome multiplied by the probability, and gives a form of index which is useful when selecting a path through the decision tree.

In its total plan top management is really interested in more than the probabilities of an individual project. It needs to know the combined probability of being on target when all factors are taken into account. If the problem is seen through the eyes of a large multi-national group, the scope of the dilemma can be easily spotted.

In theory the Monte Carlo techniques mentioned earlier would enable a frequency distribution of all possible results to be computed. With the mathematical validity of this technique in doubt for a project, it becomes very hard to recommend it for a total corporate plan.

The only other solution I know is, again, judgement: hardly satisfactory, but better than nothing.

Those who wish to explore decision-tree techniques in greater detail are referred to Moore[6] and Magee.[7,8]

Knowledge-based Systems

Knowledge-based systems (KBS) are one of the new tools available to business, with a number of applications which are directly applicable to strategic planning. KBS is a major subject in its own right, and in this chapter I can do little more than describe what it is, and provide some examples of existing systems and their use. The definition of knowledge-based systems is that of Mockler and Dologite.[9] The book from which it comes has nearly 800 pages, which goes some way to showing the complexity of the topic.

"A knowledge-based system is a computer system that attempts to replicate specific human expert intelligence activities. Human experts make decisions and recommendations, such as to whom to give bank loans or what steps to take to fix a turbine malfunction, and perform tasks, such as adjusting temperature controls in a manufacturing plant. They also assist and train others to perform tasks and make decisions. Knowledge-based systems can do these intelligent activities. Typically, knowledge-based systems enable users with a problem to consult the computer system as they would an expert human advisor.

"Like a human expert, such a computer system can extract additional information by asking questions related to the problem during a consultation. It can also answer questions asked by a user about why certain information is needed. It can make recommendations regarding the problem or make a decision at the end of the consultation, and can explain the reasoning steps used to reach its conclusions. In some situations, it can analyse a problem and take corrective action directly."

KBS is a branch of artificial intelligence. It can be linked with knowledge data bases to produce expert systems. Such systems have been developed and applied across a wide field of human endeavour. Mockler[10] provides a description and software for several prototype knowledge-based systems, including developing an overall strategy for a company, introducing a new product, make or buy decisions, capital allocation to investments, strategy for a new foreign market. I tried the first strategy system, which is based on industry principles, on the consulting business which I manage, and received generic strategy advice which had to be right, as it told us to follow the strategy we had already determined from our own analyses!

A system is available which may be of interest to anyone wishing to take the Ansoff concept of environmental turbulence to detailed practical application. ANSPLAN can be obtained from Ansoff Associates in San Diego, and enables managers to assess the turbulence level, and helps them arrive at appropriate responses.

The detailed example I have chosen to illustrate the potential of KBS is EXMAR, which stands for Expert System for Market Planning. I first came across this because one of my clients was part of the initial group of British companies that piloted the development. All information about EXMAR was provided by Hugh Wilson, who has been involved with it from the beginning, and Professor Malcolm McDonald. Their help, and permission to quote from their papers, and to reproduce printouts from the system is acknowledged, along with Cranfield School of Management where they are both based. The system uses a portfolio approach similar to the directional policy matrix which was described in Chapters 15 and 16, although the scoring rules may be somewhat different. EXMAR does more than apply portfolio analysis.

The version described here is still in prototype, although it had at the time of writing (1993) been used with over 30 companies.

"The system guides the manager through a logical process covering definition of business unit objectives, the marketing audit, assessment of future trends, and definition of marketing objectives and strategies.

"The system prompts for information to ensure important aspects are considered, offers advice at key stages, and takes the leg work out of the use of marketing tools and techniques. Tools supported include SWOT analysis, gap analysis and a variety of market matrices, which draw on an integrated data model of the business which is built up as the plan progresses. The system is highly interactive and graphical, enabling implications of possible courses of action to be explored readily. The result is a better strategic marketing plan, and equally importantly a better understanding of the business. It can be used at any level of organisation, from corporate to product group."[11]

The use and benefits of EXMAR can readily be seen by anyone who has read the earlier chapters, where the techniques illustrated were described in depth. Figures 31.14 to 31.22 show what the system does, and are self explanatory. Further information can be found in McDonald and Wilson.[12, 13]

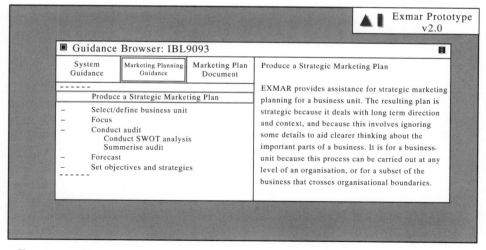

FIG. 31.14. Exmar guidance browser. (Reproduced by permission of Hugh Wilson and Cranfield School of Management)

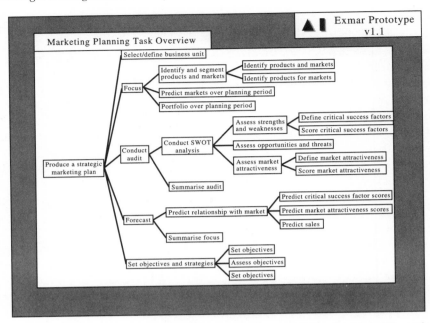

FIG. 31.15. Guiding the user through a logical process for marketing planning. (Reproduced by permission of Hugh Wilson and Cranfield School of Management)

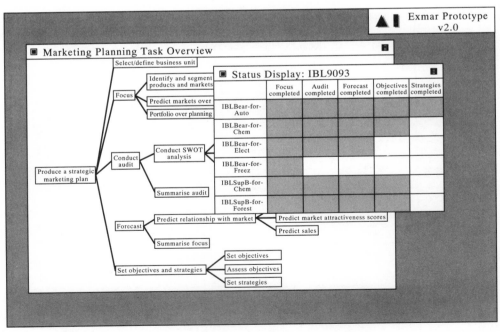

FIG. 31.16. Feedback is given on what tasks have been completed. (Reproduced by permission of Hugh Wilson and Cranfield School of Management)

FIG. 31.17. System advice is given to avoid common pitfalls. (Reproduced by permission of Hugh Wilson and Cranfield School of Management)

Networks

Decision trees are sometimes confused with networks (critical path analysis, p.e.r.t., etc.). There is a superficial resemblance to the two types of diagram. Where a decision tree tries to chart decisions, a network shows tasks in a logical order of progression.

FIG. 31.18. Graphical display showing current and forecast positions. Information behind the matrix brought to the screen. (Reproduced by permission of Hugh Wilson and Cranfield School of Management)

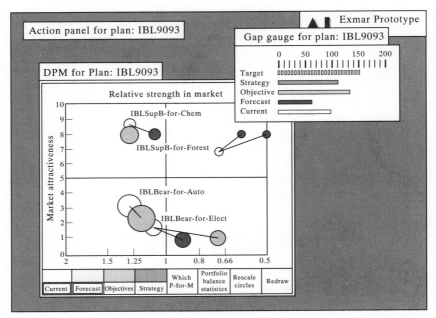

FIG. 31.19. One form of gap analysis. (Reproduced by permission of Hugh Wilson and Cranfield School of Management)

A decision tree will also try to maintain an order in the things it shows, and will show how one set of decisions follows another and how each is affected by chance events.

The network is not really interested in decisions. It looks at tasks which have to be done. A decision to clean a window might result in a number of tasks, many of which are consequential on the completion of earlier tasks:

—Prepare materials (this could be further broken down).
—Put water on cloth.
—Wash window.
—Wipe off water.
—Polish.
—Check for smears.
—Remove smears as necessary.

In a simple situation like this there is, again, little point in using clever techniques. Most business problems are very different and may involve the co-ordination of the work of many people. Some of this is key work in that until it is completed other tasks may not even be started (a roof cannot be built until the walls of the building are erected: these in turn depend on the completion of foundations, which follow ground preparation).

Some tasks are sequential; others may be carried out in parallel. Establishing which is which enables the company to see where it must put additional units of effort if it wishes to complete the project quicker or where delayed tasks are critical to completion on time.

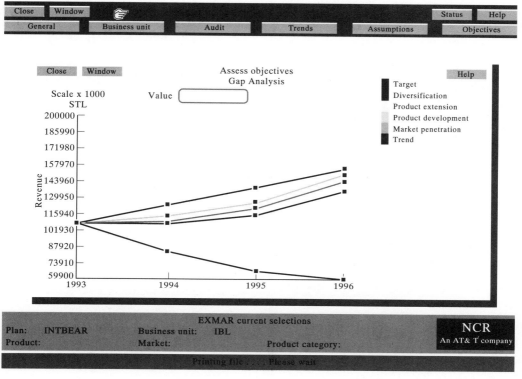

FIG. 31.20. Gap analysis. (Reproduced by permission of Hugh Wilson and Cranfield School of Management)

In their simplest form networks may be used merely to identify tasks and show their relationships with each other—as in Fig. 29.3. A more usual use is to relate them to time and/or cost and to use them to study how the project may be completed at a faster rate, and to make sure that all actions are properly co-ordinated and controlled. To do this it is necessary to establish the "critical path": that is, finding the path through the various tasks which enables all tasks to be completed in the shortest possible time. Computer assistance will often be needed to enable this to be done speedily and efficiently.

A general introduction to networks can be found in the works of many authors, e.g. Moore.[6] A more detailed study is offered by McLaren and Buesnel,[14] who present what is virtually a manual in the construction and use of networks.

It would be wrong to think of networks only in terms of production or technical projects. They may be successfully used in planning office work (such as the preparation of the annual budget) or marketing, and may be particularly useful in new product development. Dusenburg[15] presents a case history of the application of the critical path method for new product introductions in the Diamond Alkali Company in the United States. Other examples of this application will be found in McLaren and Buesnel.[14]

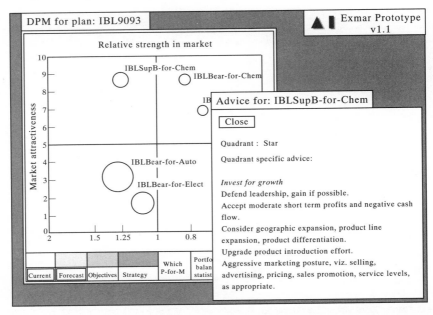

FIG. 31.21. Strategic advice by quadrant. (Reproduced by permission of Hugh Wilson and Cranfield School of Management)

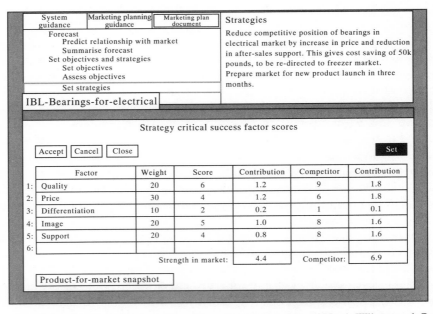

FIG. 31.22. Critical success factors. (Reproduced by permission of Hugh Wilson and Cranfield School of Management)

Management Information Systems

One of the subjects on which much has been written though little has been said, is management information. This, of course, is a deliberately cynical view which is unfair to many writers who have made genuine contributions to the subject.

The problem is the difference between what is theoretically possible and what can be done in practical terms. In theory it is possible to visualise a computerised data bank in which every scrap of management information available to the company, whether internally or externally generated, may be stored, and thence transferred to the corporate planning models and control functions, or be available for *ad hoc* use at the various levels in the organisation. Such concepts normally sort out the data by level of detail and length of time required, on the basis that information for strategic decisions must cover a longer time period but in much less detail than information required for day-to-day operational control.

Such dream systems, because of cost or human difficulties, are rarely if ever attained. One reason for this is that the perfect system will have to store information to cover all eventualities, much of which will never be used. As it is, Boulden[3] points out that a planning system normally involves only 10% of the management information available, and also that the time-scale for introducing management information systems (MIS) is much longer than that for planning systems. In addition planning partly sets the parameters of information.

The problems of establishing a total corporate-wide MIS system are still very great, while those of linking this with planning models are even greater. Nevertheless, good planning does demand information, and this is an area which should receive some attention from the corporate planner.

Information is required for two distinct needs in a corporate planning system. The first is for the purpose of making plans (in which there are many stages, as has been demonstrated in earlier pages). The second is in the area of control. Much has been said in the appropriate chapters of this book about monitoring and controlling performance against plans of all types—and these actions are only possible if the company has a means of generating the information which tells it whether or not it is proceeding to plan.

The following table from Kashyap[16] gives an indication of some of the main types of information required for the first planning need—preparing plans.

Comprehensive though this table is, it provides only a summary of needs. A little conjecture about the needs of any particular company in relation to the chapters of this book dealing with the steps itemised by Kashyap[16] indicates the great volume of data needed.

The information requirement often becomes particularly noticeable when the company moves into the area of model building. The construction of any model calls for more detailed and precise information about the company than perhaps would have been needed for a simpler manual system.

For control purposes information is needed in various degrees of detail to meet the needs of managers of various levels. Every objective or target set should be designed so that it can be monitored—which means that the information system should be

TABLE 31.1. Information for planning. From Kashyap[16]

Steps in corporate planning	Problem definition	Type of information required
1. Environmental research and analysis	What's ahead? * User needs * Competition * Technology * Economy *Regulatory problems	Industrial and market information Competitive intelligence Technological forecasts National and international economic trends Political and social trends and forecasts
2. Position audit	Where do we stand? * Resources * Capacities * Profit source * Investment * Market share	Internal information Industry information Internal information Financial information Market information
3. Identification of attributes	Company's strengths and weaknesses – Internal evaluation * Products * Resources – External evaluation * Competitors * Market standing * Vulnerability	Internal and market information Competitive intelligence Market information Market and technological information
4. Proposed objectives	What to do? Why?	Past performance (internal information) Environmental information Position audit Company's strengths and weaknesses
5. Formulation and evaluation of corporate strategy	What means to adopt?	Objectives Current forecast of future performance Industry potential analysis Estimate of resources Competitive characteristics
6. Development of strategic and action plan	Implementation of corporate strategy	Strategic decisions Detailed internal information Detailed market information

able to provide the required data. Sometimes the cost of doing this may be so great that it is more appropriate to modify the way in which the objective is expressed.

In many companies the flow of information is not as well organised as it might be, and, organisationally, responsibility for storing and reporting is split among a number of managers with very little appreciation of real need.

Often information systems print out too much data. A manager who requires one line of information may be forced to scan a multi-page computer printout. The more selective an information system becomes in its output, the more it is likely to cost. Which is one of the reasons why the concept of a total integrated MIS and planning system to which all senior managers are linked by terminal must remain a dream for most of us.

The planner may have this dream, but there is also practical attention which he may find it worth while to give to the information systems in the company. Some reorganisation may be desirable, and the objectives of the system clearly defined. Even without major changes of concept, some overhaul of both input and output may be required.

Often the key to good planning and good control lies in the information system. The company may face a need to find that key and then show its managers how to use it.

Many planners may find that the most effective way of improving planning and control in their companies is to give attention to the collection, discrimination, and utilisation of management information.

Segmentation Analysis

The last set of concepts to which I should like to refer deal with the analysis of market segments. This is not meant to be a book on marketing, but one aspect of strategy formulation may include the identification of segments, selection of target markets, and the positioning of the company in relation to these. In an earlier chapter I referred briefly to Abell[17] and his argument that strategic identity comes from the selection made by an organisation from the segments open to it, using the three dimensions of customer groups, customer usage, and technology. Although his work is useful, I find it difficult to see why those three dimensions are any more strategic than a host of others that could be chosen. Geographical location of customers is, for example, an equally strategic dimension, and when we looked at global strategy in an earlier chapter we saw some of the strategic implications of this.

Segmentation is the first stage of the analytical process, and follows the fact that markets are not made up of homogenous buyers. Every market can be looked at in a variety of ways, grouping buyers into various sub groups who share some common characteristics. These may, in consumer goods be related to consumer characteristics, such as geography, demography or psychographics; or to customer responses to the product, such as usage, frequency of usage, attitudes, and benefits. In industrial products we may add size of business, nature of business, organisational structure, buyer experience, and buying policies to this list. Neither list is complete.

Matrix analysis can be useful. Although three dimensional matrices are possible, they are difficult to draw and use. My preference is for a two-dimensional matrix, on which colours or symbols can be used to show the effect of other factors, on the style of the risk matrix discussed in an earlier chapter. A series of such matrices can bring enlightenment. However the reality is that in consumer and industrial markets we are dealing with a complex inter-relationship of factors. Figure 31.23, which by no means deals with all the factors that might be present, shows how segmentation can be taken to further levels of resolution. For simplicity, I have only followed one path through the model, although in reality each box has similar extensions.

Figure 31.23 is rooted in reality, in that it deals with the market for management training. It may be that all stages of the model are not equally important. For example, the industry of the buyer will not in all cases be an important strategic marketing issue, since it may not affect the buyers' requirements or decision.

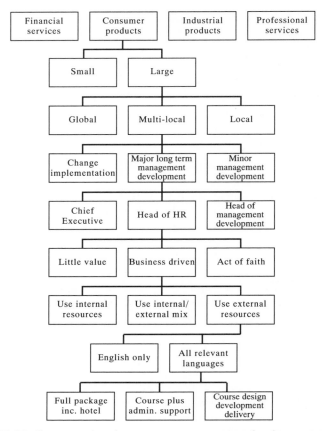

FIG. 31.23. Segmentation: in company management development market

Although it may be possible to draw up hypotheses using a series of headings such as those in the figure, research is needed to identify what is really important. Research can also help quantify the size of each segment. Size estimation becomes much more difficult as we move to more detailed levels of analysis, and in many markets is not particularly easy even at the higher levels. Frequently, at this stage, the analyst is forced to make indicative statements, such as large, medium, small, and negligible, because greater accuracy is either impossible or the costs of obtaining it outweigh the benefits.

Once the analysis has been carried out it becomes possible to profile the important segments. Examples drawn from my own work on the management training industry are:

Change Master

The use of a highly tailored course to implement change, such as strategy implementation, or making a new structure effective. It is usually bought with the strong involvement of the chief executive. The product requires multi-functional skills. The buyer will be a medium to large sized client, with a considerable degree of buying experience. Medium to large assignment sizes and projects with a defined objective and length.

Expert Ring Master

The buyer is a management development manager, usually senior, who has designed a programme and requires various outside resources to deliver one part of it. Several different suppliers may be involved in a one week programme. Likely to be a large organisation, with high calibre human resource professionals. Modest sized projects, on an as needed basis: may repeat.

Inexpert Ring Master

A real circus act, with numerous performers in a badly conceived programme, little or no briefing to suppliers, purchase decision based on price. Attempts to be an expert ring master but lacks resources and capability. Buyer is management development or training manager, company may be of almost any size. Very small projects, often no repeat business.

Multi-national, Multi-language

Has a need to run the same course across all countries, possibly as a Change Master, but recognises that the training has to be delivered in the appropriate local language. Large organisations, sophisticated buyers, some centralisation of decision making, operates in several countries with a critical mass of people in more than one country. Large projects which may span several years.

These profiles do not describe the whole market. Whether they are attractive depends on the skills, resources and abilities of the supplier. It is the stage of deciding which ones offer the best opportunities which is the process of target marketing. Factors here would include the size of the segment, the acquisition costs of gaining business, the costs of meeting the requirements of the segment, price levels (which in our example are related to the number of competitors and the degree of differentiation that can be achieved), and the business objectives of the supplier. In the example profiles, the number of competitors in each of the illustrative segments varies from 2 to 600 (I am not going to tell you which is which), just one of the points of importance in deciding target markets.

Positioning is in effect the process of determining a mini marketing strategy for the chosen segments. It covers all elements of the marketing mix, although one major difference may be the need to coordinate actions across the whole company, and to forego an attractive segment if successful operation there would have an adverse impact on other company activities. There may be strategic ways round issues. For example, in the management development consultancy example it could be difficult to mass market a packaged product, and to establish a reputation as a highly differentiated provider of tailored programmes, because the advertising needed for the former would affect the image of the latter. A strategic way round this is to establish separate businesses, each with a different focus and image.

Detailed treatment of segmentation is given in most good marketing books, of which Kotler[18] is an excellent example.

References

1. Ohmae, K. *The Mind of the Strategist*, Penguin Books, Harmondsworth, 1983.
2. McNamee, P. "Modelling the Strategic Management Process', Hussey, D. E. (ed.) *International Review of Strategic Management*, Vol. 2, No. 1, Wiley, Chichester, 1991.
3. Boulden, J. B. "Computerised Corporate Planning", *Long Range Planning*, June 1971.
4. Merritt, A. J. and Sykes A. *The Finance and Analysis of Capital Projects*, Longmans, London, 1963.
5. Brown, C. C. and Hussey, D. E. "Corporate Planning: A Case Study in New Product Planning and Marketing", Baynes, P. (ed.) *Case Studies in Corporate Planning*, Pitman, London, 1973.
6. Moore, P. G. *Basic Operational Research*, Pitman, London, 1968.
7. Magee, J. F. "Decision Trees for Decision Making", *Harvard Business Review*, July/August 1964.
8. Magee, J. F. "How to Use Decision Trees in Capital Investment", *Harvard Business Review*, July/August 1964.
9. Mockler, R. J. and Dologite, D. G. *Knowledge-Based Systems: An Introduction to Expert Systems*, MacMillan, New York, 1992.
10. Mockler, R. J. *Strategic Management*, Idea Group Publishing, Harrisburg, USA, 1993.
11. Anon, *Research Review*, Issue 5, Cranfield School of Management, March 1992.
12. McDonald, M. H. B. and Wilson, H. N. "State of the Art Developments in Expert Systems and Strategic Marketing Planning", *British Journal of Management*, Vol. 1, 1990.
13. McDonald, M. H. B. and Wilson, H. N. "Why Apply Software to Marketing Strategy? Mapping the Sources of Competitive Advantage", McDonald, M. H. B., Hewson, W. and Wilson, H. N. (eds.), *Emerging Information Strategies*, HCG Publications, Olney, Bucks, 1993.
14. McClaren, K. G. and Buesnel, E. L. *Network Analysis in Project Work*, Cassell, London, 1969.
15. Dusenburg, W. "CPM For New Product Introductions", *Harvard Business Review*, July/August 1967.
16. Kashyap, R. N. "Management Information Systems for Corporate Planning and Control", *Long Range Planning*, June 1972.
17. Abell, D. F. *Defining the Business*, Prentice-Hall, Englewood Cliffs, New Jersey, USA, 1980.
18. Kotler, P. *Marketing Management*, 6th ed., Prentice-Hall, Englewood Cliffs, New Jersey, USA, 1988.

32

Strategic Management to Strategic Change?

Strategic management has made great strides since it emerged as a topic under its old name of long range planning. We now have better techniques of strategic analysis, and new concepts of strategy formulation, and we understand more about the behavioural aspects of managing strategically. It is perhaps of interest to try to speculate where the subject might be heading.

In trying to forecast its future I should like to steal from some of my editorials from the early issues of the *Journal of Strategic Change*, and from material that Igor Ansoff wrote to mark the launch of this journal in early 1992.

I have always been an admirer of elephants, and once lived in a country where they roam wild. There is something that I find appealing about these majestic animals, and I have in the past used them to illustrate some of the issues around strategic change.

Despite this, I was unprepared for the brief report which appeared in the *Daily Telegraph* of 22nd May 1992. "Rider trapped for 2 days on mad elephant". Naturally I read on. The story was about an Indian elephant rider who, it said, was trapped on the back of an elephant while it ran amok for 200 miles before it could be tranquilized and he could be rescued. It was in a state of sexual frenzy, known as a must (what else could it be called!). However the mahout did not suffer from hunger, as he grabbed fruit that had been tied to trees for him along the elephant's route. This implies some careful planning and forecasting, in order to predict the route correctly, and needed a high degree of accuracy. An inch too far to the left or right, and the poor mahout would have gone hungry, with food just out of reach. I do not think that the story was a left-over from April 1st, although from the tone of the article I think the *Telegraph* were keeping their options open.

From observation over many years, I believe that many organisations follow a strategic path in a somewhat similar fashion to this elephant, stimulated by something, and charging off down a path without thinking about the implications. Quick response, of which the hanging down of food for the mahout is a simile, saves some of the problems from becoming disasters. Somehow we do not seem to learn as much as we should from past experience. To my knowledge there has been at least one major study of the failure rate in acquisitions at roughly ten yearly intervals. The conclusions in the 1970s, 1980s and more recently 1993 had one thing in common. The failure rate was around 50%. Either something continually goes wrong in the pre-merger strategy, or we are still struggling to learn how to implement the strategies which are so perfect on paper.

The headlong rush of the maddened elephant reminded me of a cartoon sequence I devised some years ago for a lecture about the difficulty of making change happen in organisations. The first picture showed a number of bowler hatted, pinstriped city gents trying to make a reluctant elephant move, pushing and prodding with their umbrellas: it dealt with the difficulty of getting any willingness to change at all. The second slide showed the same characters trying to restrain an elephant that was charging off in the wrong direction. I now know that it was suffering from a must! This was to illustrate the difficulty of ensuring that the right change was implemented. There were other cartoons in the sequence, which ended with a suggestion that the wrong strategy could result in the organisation becoming a white elephant.

My own company, Harbridge Consulting Group, has had encounters with elephants, both of the varieties illustrated in the cartoons and the real thing. A few years ago, two of my colleagues were running a course in Zambia. The hotel, in a game park, consisted of a series of low buildings with verandahs which were used for breakout groups. Into the hotel compound strolled a bull elephant with one broken tusk. Whether the students by that time had learnt much about strategic change was doubtful, although they demonstrated that they needed no coaching in how to beat a fast tactical withdrawal in the face of changed prospects. The elephant was not undergoing a must, and among our corporate souvenirs is a photograph of the animal attentively studying the flip chart. We have had no reports that he has applied the learning he gained within his own community!

The elephant theme has been used by others, including the mind blowing image of teaching elephants to dance, although this probably owes more to Rudyard Kipling than to Rosabeth Moss Kantor.

My belief is that the next decade of advances in strategic management will be much more about managing strategic change than formulating strategy. Indeed one could see the term strategic change becoming the new byword for the next phase of strategic management.

Strategic emphasis has, over time, been moving to a greater emphasis on implementation. I think the future will bring a greater merging of formulation skills with those of organisational behaviour and change management. Put another way, successful change comes about through a blend of the hard and soft disciplines, the analytical and the behavioural. Neglect of one in favour of the other is likely to lead to actions which do not yield the desired results.

Trends in management rarely appear from nowhere, and the emphasis I see on strategic change is a logical step in the evolution of strategic management. Nevertheless, it does challenge the traditional boundaries between functions, and requires a closer binding of many functions which have traditionally been regarded as independent. This does not mean that planners have to report to organisational development people, or that human resources in some way comes under planning.

It does mean that traditional views of roles have to change, and that each should be seen as a non-watertight element of an overall task that has to be conceived as an entity.

Igor Ansoff can fairly be described as the father of strategic management, first exposing the concept of strategic planning and later leading the thinking that developed this to the concept of strategic management. In a letter to me about the new journal, he observed:

"The role of the corporate planner ... is already obsolete, both in theory and practice, and the journal could contribute to the concept of the strategic change manager ... who combines four disciplinary perspectives: analytic, psychological, sociological and political."

While the title of corporate planner—or the many other variations on this theme—may live on, the role in successful organisations is much as Igor describes it. Similarly, organisational development can no longer be a staff activity whose efforts are unrelated to the corporate objectives and strategy, while those organisations which give little thought to organisational behaviour must find mechanisms to bring these skills into the change process. The same argument can be made for many of the activities of the human resource function, such as management development. Overall there is a need for leadership and management of a high order, activities which cannot be separated from strategic decision making or organisational development. The real issue for all players is how to manage strategic change in an era of increasing turbulence. While there are many structural solutions, the most important step is the realisation of the mutual interdependence of all these players, if successful change is to take place.

The turbulence in the business environment is a driver of change, and leads to what might be called a situational approach to strategic management. In particular I refer to the recent thinking by Igor Ansoff which appears elsewhere in this book. However, the events which change the business prospects also change the expectations and attitudes of the people we employ. The future of strategic management, which I see as strategic change, will also be a future which takes far more account of the economic value of human resources. I foresee far more emphasis on approaches and techniques to address this issue than has been the case in the past, and I would hope for a kit bag of tools which matches the range of choice now available for dealing with other aspects of strategy.

I should like to leave the last new thought with Igor Ansoff[1]: "... important as they are, unidisciplinary perspectives of a multidisciplinary problem do not automatically add up to a solution of the total problem. This fact is amply supported by the voluminous literature in cybernetics, general systems theory and sociology.

"The second reason is that I cannot think of any really important problem in today's society and its organisations whose solution is not vitally dependent on intimate contemporaneous interplay of the whole range of 'hard' and 'soft' sciences." (The extract refers to the role he sees for the journal, and the omissions do not distort his intentions.)

If I try to summarise this chapter, it is to say that strategic management will move to a new dimension of strategic change management in intent if not in name.

More emphasis will be placed on methods that provide a better strategic insight into human resource management; leadership and management of a much higher order will be required; and a more situational approach to strategic management will become the norm, in order to relate to the degree of environmental turbulence faced by the particular organisation.

This should ensure that there is much more to write about when I come to the next edition of this book!

Reference

1.   Ansoff, H. I. "Welcome to the Journal of Strategic Change", *Journal of Strategic Change*, Vol. 1, No. 1, January/February 1992.

33

Recommended Reading and Sources of Information

This chapter is designed to lead to further information. It consists of a list of general resource guides, details of planning societies, details of strategy journals, and a selected reading list of books on the subject of strategic management. All the lists are selective, but should if they are followed up take the reader to just about every aspect of strategic management. If you pass the list of recommended books to anyone else, do not forget to write in this book!

General Resource Guides

Glossaries and Dictionaries

Hussey, D. E. "Glossary of Management Techniques", Hussey, D. E. (ed.), *International Review of Strategic Management*, Vol. 3, Wiley, Chichester, 1992.

A 29-page alphabetical description of the main analytical techniques and their uses. They are cross referenced, to make it easier to identify alternative and related techniques. References are given for each technique to books and articles containing fuller descriptions.

Karlof, B. *Business Strategy: A Guide to Concepts and Models*, MacMillan, London, 1989.

This is broader in coverage, in that it includes descriptions of a number of concepts (for example, culture). However it does not describe all the techniques. The book was originally produced for use by the airline SAS, and might be expected to reflect their needs rather than the needs of business at large.

Kempner, T. *The Penguin Management Handbook*, 4th ed., Penguin Books, Harmondsworth, 1987.

There is probably a later edition than this, as the book is regularly revised. Although not strictly planning, it covers many subjects that are relevant to the subject. It makes a useful supplement to the more specific references given above.

Reference Books

Lom, C. *International Business Strategy Resource Book*, Strategic Direction Publishers, Zurich, 1990.

Lom, C. *International Technology Strategy Resource Book*, Strategic Direction Publishers, Zurich, 1990.

These books are similar in concept, and include an editorial selection, a world wide list of specialist management consultants, and details of some public training programmes. There are also some very brief bibliographies.

Mockler, R. J. *Strategic Management: A Research guide with Comprehensive Bibliographies*, The Planning Forum, Oxford, Ohio, 1993.

This guide is desk top published to enable frequent and speedy revisions. This first edition had better US than UK coverage, but the author is working on improving the book, and it is likely that subsequent editions will be even more comprehensive, and even longer. It is really a book of lists. Contents cover books and monographs in print and available in the USA, articles, dissertations, case studies, video/audio cassettes, journals and periodicals, professional associations, strategy consultants, conferences and programmes, strategic computer information systems and software. There is also guidance on accessing and using on-line data bases.

Planning Societies

There are strategic management societies in most countries. The Strategic Management Society and Society for Competitor Intelligence Professionals are global organisations, although the links in the latter society between Europe and the USA are loose. Several of the European societies are also linked through the umbrella organisation EPLAF, which may be contacted through the Society of Strategic Planning in the UK.

The Society of Competitor Intelligence Professionals in Europe is at PO Box 6500, 6401 JH Heerlen, The Netherlands, Tel. 31 45 782809, Fax 31 45 740432.

Not all societies have permanent secretariats, so there is some danger that the addresses below may have changed as officers of the society have changed or moved jobs. Most European addresses can be confirmed through EPLAF, if the information given here proves to have been overtaken by time.

In the list below the UK and USA, which have several societies, are given specific entries. All other societies which I have been able to trace are listed in country order. I apologise for any omissions.

UK

The Society of Strategic Planning has operated in the UK since the 1960s, and is the leading society for practitioners. It is affiliated to other societies in Europe and the USA. 17, Portland Place, London, W1N 3AF, Tel 44 71 636 7737, Fax 44 71 323 1692.

Society of Competitor Intelligence Professionals in Europe is a specialist group founded in 1990. It is linked to a similarly named group in the USA. The British branch may be contacted through Mike Meurisse, PO Box 204, Bracknell, Berkshire, RG12 1FG.

The Strategic Management Society "brings together the worlds of reflective practice and thoughtful scholarship". The address given is for the US, but it operates world wide, and has a UK operation. Contact Dan Schendel, Krannert Center, Purdue University, West Lafayette, IN 47907, USA. Its official journal is published in the UK.

USA

Society for Competitor Intelligence Professionals. The society exists to establish and promote competitive intelligence as a profession, provide for the professional development of its members, advocate high ethical standards for the profession, and advance the interest of its members. Its executive director is at 818, 18th Street, NW Suite 225, Washington DC 20006, USA. Tel 1 202 223 5885.

Strategic Management Society. This "brings together the worlds of reflective practice and thoughtful scholarship". Contact Dan Schendel, Krannert Center, Purdue University, West Lafayette, IN 47907, USA. Its official journal is published in the UK.

The Planning Forum, 5500 College Corner Pike, PO Box 70, Oxford, Ohio. Tel 1 513 523 4185, Fax 1 513 523 7539.

World Future Society, 7910 Woodmont Avenue, Suite 450, Bethseda, Maryland 20814, USA. Tel 1 301 656 8274, Fax 1 301 951 0394.

Other

Belgium. Strategic and Corporate Europlanners Society, Boite Postale, No 17, Bruxelles 42, B1040 Bruxelles. Tel 32 2 516 34 69.

Canada. The Planning Forum, *see entry under USA*.

Czechoslovakia. SSRIP (SSMIE), Trzste 20, 118 43, Prague 1. Tel 422 539708, Fax 422 539708.

France. AFPLANE, 9–11 Avenue Franklin-Roosevelt, 75008, Paris. Tel 33 1 42 25 87 74, Fax 33 1 42 25 95 37.

Germany. AGPLAN, Neckarstr. 5, D 4040 Neuss 21. Tel 49 2137 33 63, Fax 49 2137 45 70.

Hungary. MVST, 10A Zsigmond Vilnos utca, 1121 Budapest. Tel 361 1860 508, Fax 361 1731 232.

Italy. AIPA and Management, Piazzale Morandi 2, 20121 Milan. Tel 39 2 79 54 91, Fax 39 2 78 42 36.

Japan. Japan Strategic Management Society, Professor Gen-Ichi Nakamura, 3–4–604 Shimomeguro, Meguro-Ku, Tokyo 153. Tel 81 3 3710 4175, Fax 81 3 3760 4632.

Mexico. The Planning Forum, *see entry under USA*.

Netherlands. Strategie VSB. Neuhuyskade 40, 2596 XL, The Hague, PO Box 90730, 2509 LS The Hague. Tel 31 70 3180270, Fax 31 70 32449263.

New Zealand. New Zealand Strategic Management Society Inc, 99B Hadfield Street, Mariners Cove, Berkenhead, PO Box 2347, Auckland. Tel 64 9 483 2484, Fax 64 9 483 2484.

Singapore. Strategic Management Group, Singapore Institute of Management, Management House, 41, Namly Avenue, Singapore 1026. Tel 65 468 8866, Fax 65 469 1559.

Switzerland. SEPP, Centre Universitaire, BFSH 1, CH-1015 Lausanne. Tel 41 021 23 61 15, Fax 41 021 312 4407.

UK Planning Journals

Business Strategy Review, London Business School by Oxford University Press, Oxford (Editors, Paul Geroski and Patrick Barwise).

International Review of Strategic Management, Wiley, Chichester (Editor, David Hussey). An annual book sold on subscription.

Long Range Planning, Pergamon, Oxford (Editor, Bernard Taylor).

The Journal of Strategic Management, Wiley, Chichester (Editor, Dan Schendel).

Strategic Direction, MCB Publications, Bradford (Editor, Eric Sandelands).

The Journal of Strategic Change, Wiley, Chichester (Editor, David Hussey).

US Planning Journals

Competitive Intelligence Review, Society of Competitive Intelligence Professionals, Washington, DC, USA.

Planning Review, The Planning Forum, Oxford, Ohio, USA.

Selected Bibliography

The books listed certainly are not the only ones available on the subject. The Mockler resource book listed above has 75 pages of planning books, and this includes very few British books, and none from other countries. My task here is to give some pointers to further reading. I have therefore only described books which I have read.

General Books

Ansoff, I. A. and McDonnell, E. *Implanting Strategic Management*, 2nd ed., Prentice Hall, London, 1990. This is a unique book, in that it follows the scale of turbulence approach to planning described earlier. The reader will find a great deal about this concept, but will not find very much outside of it.

Hussey, D. E. *Introducing Corporate Planning: Guide to Strategic Management*, 4th ed., Pergamon, Oxford, 1991. A well established work which offers a concise introduction to the strategic management process. It includes chapters on the main techniques of analysis, and covers the behavioural issues as well as the analytical. Written primarily for managers.

McNamee, P. *Management Accounting: Strategic Planning and Marketing*, Heinemann/CIMA, London, 1988. Despite the suggestion of the title, which was not chosen by the author, this is a book about strategic management. It was written for the CIMA examinations, hence the title. The book gives a good coverage of the main concepts. The author is a Professor at Ulster University, and has done much to develop the concepts of strategic management.

Mockler, R. J. *Strategic Management: An Integrative Context Specific Process*, Idea Group Publishing, Harrisburg, USA, 1993. This book is lengthy because it includes a number of teaching case studies, which are of value to those teaching strategy, and may be interesting to the general reader. The book includes a computer disc, containing expert systems for general use, and some spread sheet applications for use with the case studies.

Steiner, G. A. *Top Management Planning*, Macmillan, New York, 1969. This book is old, and probably out of print. I have included it because it contains much that is still valid, despite the advances made in the subject since it was published. Also I wanted to record the real contribution that George Steiner, one of the earlier writers and researchers, has made to the subject.

Analysis

Abell, D. F. *Defining the Business*, Prentice-Hall, Englewood Cliffs, 1980. This book contains a few useful ideas, most of which could have been expressed in one chapter. However it is worth reading for those ideas of strategic segmentation, on the dimensions of customer function, customer group, and alternative technologies.

Ansoff, H. I. *Corporate Strategy*, McGraw Hill, New York, 1965. This was the first book on analysis, and is a must for every student. It is not easy to read, but still contains useful insights. Worth reading, if only to see where so many other authors got their ideas!

Buzzell, R. D. and Gale, B. T. *The PIMS Principles*, Free Press, New York. This is a valuable book in that it is one of a very small number of studies that draw strategic lessons from hard data.

Campbell, A. and Luchs, K. S. (eds.) *Strategic Synergy*, Butterworth-Heinemann, Oxford. A book of readings on synergy, many from published sources, but some not previously available.

Chandler, J. and Cockle, P. *Techniques of Scenario Planning*, McGraw-Hill, Maidenhead, 1982. As its title suggests this is a specialist book dealing with the approach to scenario planning used at that time by Reed. The reader should be aware that there are significant differences in this approach and that practised by other organisations such as Shell.

Dyson, R. G. (ed.) *Strategic Planning Models and Analytical Techniques*, Wiley, Chichester, 1990. A collection of readings on analytical approaches.

Hofer, C. W. and Schendel, D. *Strategy Formulation: Analytical Concepts*, Wiley, St Paul, Minnesota, 1978. This is one of my favourite books, perhaps because it was the first that I had come across that attempted to make sense of some of the techniques of planning. It deals particularly with portfolio analysis, but is not restricted to this. Useful in that it separates approaches for use at corporate level from those at business unit level.

Hussey, D. E. (ed.) *International Review of Strategic Management*, Volume 3, Wiley, Chichester, 1992. The main theme of this edition of this book is strategy analysis and formulation, some 170 pages of its content being on this theme. It includes papers by a number of authors.

McNamee, P. *Tools and Techniques of Strategic Management*, Pergamon, Oxford, 1985. A wider range of techniques is covered than the Hofer and Schendel book, with good descriptions of applications.

Neubauer, F-F. *Portfolio Analysis*, Kluwer, Dewenter, Holland, 1990. Fred Neubauer is a professor at IMD in Switzerland, and the book is a translation from the German original. It offers good coverage of a variety of portfolio analysis techniques, including their application to technology strategy. It does not deal with other methods of analysis.

Ohmae, K. *The Mind of the Strategist*, Penguin Books, Harmondsworth, 1983. The author is head of McKinsey in Japan, and although providing much analytical insight, takes the view that creative thinking is the essential ingredient to sound strategies. An excellent book.

Stewart, G. Bennett. *The Quest for Value*, Harper Business, New York, 1990. The author is a senior partner of Stern Stewart, a consultancy that specialises in value based strategy. The book gives extensive coverage of the subject, with numerous cameos and examples. Highly recommended.

Global Strategy

Freedman, N. J. (ed.) *Strategic Management in Major Multi-National Companies*, Pergamon, Oxford, 1991. A book of reprints of relevant articles from *Long Range Planning*.

Ohmae, K. *The Borderless World*, Harper Collins, New York, 1990. A thought provoking book on the new logic of the global market place. It also contains valuable thinking on the successful operation of strategic alliances.

Porter, M. E. (ed.) *Competition in Global Industries*, Harvard Business School, Boston, USA, 1986. This book has some excellent contributions, as well as many that I did not find useful. I found the paper by Cvar of particular value.

Prahalad, C. K. and Doz, Y. L. *The Multinational Mission*, Free Press, New York, 1987. This book deals in a comprehensive way with the analysis and development of global strategies, and contains many useful ideas. It was one of the first books published on this emerging and important area of strategic management, and contains much original thinking.

Yip, G. *Total Global Strategy*, Prentice Hall, Englewood Cliffs, NJ, 1992. Yip is the other recognised authority on global strategies. His book is very practical, and carries a detailed examination of the drivers for global strategy.

Competitor/Industry Analysis

Hussey, D. E. (ed.) *International Review of Strategic Management*, Volume 1, Wiley, Chichester, 1990. The main theme of this edition of this annual book is devoted to gaining competitive advantage, some 186 pages of its content being on this theme. It includes papers by a number of authors.

James, B. *Business Wargames*, Penguin Books, Harmondsworth, 1985. Unfortunately this book is out of print. It relates competitive strategy to military strategy, with numerous examples. It is complementary to the other books mentioned, and is more about possible competitive strategies than analysis or information gathering.

McGonagle, J. J. and Vella, C. *Outsmarting the Competition*, McGraw-Hill, London, 1993. A book for the beginner, which deals with sources of information rather than ways of analysing it. Written around US sources, and modified for UK sources, leaving it something of each.

Porter, M. E. *Competitive Strategy*, Free Press, New York, 1980. This is the book that made the author's reputation, and is excellent on industry analysis, which might be termed the competitive arena. It is a book about drawing conclusions from data, rather than how to obtain it, and is essential reading for anyone seriously contemplating industry analysis.

Porter, M. E. *Competitive Advantage*, Free Press, New York, 1985. This book continues the process of competitive analysis, and introduces the concept of value chains. I am not yet convinced that anyone except Michael Porter understands value chains, although a number of people I have met claim to have applied the concept.

Stanat, R. *The Intelligent Corporation*, Amacom, New York, 1990. I have included this book because it is the only one I know of that deals with setting up an information system to enable competitor analysis to take place. It is not as easy to read as most of the other books I have chosen, but contains useful information.

Manufacturing Strategy

Hayes, R. H., Wheelwright, S. C. and Clark, K. B. *Dynamic Manufacturing*, Free Press, New York, 1988. A comprehensive background to the issues that should be considered in manufacturing strategy, including world class manufacturing.

Hill, T. *Manufacturing Strategy*, MacMillan, London, 1985. A good treatment of strategic issues for manufacturing.

Skinner, W. *Manufacturing in the Corporate Strategy*, Wiley, New York, 1978. Skinner was one of the pioneers of the strategic approach to manufacturing, particularly his concept of the focused factory. Many of the chapters in this book had originally been published in the *Harvard Business Review*.

Information Systems Strategy

Collins, A. (ed.) *Planning for Information as a Corporate Resource*, Pergamon, Oxford, 1990. A book of reprints of relevant articles from *Long Range Planning*.

Tozer, E. E. *Planning for Effective Business Information Systems*, Pergamon, Oxford, 1988. A practical approach to the planning of information systems.

Ward, J., Griffiths, P. and Whitmore, P. *Strategic Planning for Information Systems*, Wiley, Chichester, 1990. Covers many aspects of the use of information, and its strategic management.

Human Resources

Hussey, D. E. and Langham, M. J. *Corporate Planning: The Human Factor*, Pergamon, Oxford, 1979. This was one of the first books to link the analytical and behavioural aspect of strategic planning. Perhaps because the thinking was new, the book has not been a best seller. Supplies from the original printing have only just been exhausted, and the book is out of print.

Hussey, D. E. *Management Training and Corporate Strategy*, Pergamon, Oxford, 1988. Shows how management training can be used to implement strategy, and argues for a more strategic view of management training. Based on a series of original research studies. Further development of this thinking will be found in volumes 2 and 4 of *International Review of Strategic Management* (see earlier).

Nilsson, W. P. *Achieving Strategic Goals Through Executive Development*, Addison Wesley, Reading, MA, 1987. Follows a similar intent to the Hussey book, but gives the subject a different treatment. Because all the books on this concept were written at around the same time, and are original contributions, there is as yet no book which draws together all the thinking.

Rothwell, S. (ed.) *Strategic Planning for Human Resources*, Pergamon, Oxford, 1991. A volume in the Best of Long Range Planning series, which contains an introduction by the editor and 15 articles reproduced from *Long Range Planning*.

Strategy Implementation and Change Management

Galbraith, J. R. and Nathanson, D. A. *Strategy Implementation: The Role of Structure and Process*, West, St Paul, 1978. I hope that this book is still obtainable, as it gives an excellent coverage of the links between strategy and structure, and was one of the first books to attempt to deal thoroughly with issues of strategy implementation. Highly recommended.

Hofstede, G. *Culture and Organisations*, McGraw-Hill, London, 1991. Deals with intercultural differences, and may show you why what works in one country is a flop in another.

Hussey, D. E. (ed.) *International Review of Strategic Management*, Volume 2, Wiley, Chichester, 1991. The main theme of this edition of this book is implementation, some 100 pages of its content being on this theme. It includes papers by a number of authors.

Hussey, D. E. (ed.) *International Review of Strategic Management*, Volume 4, Wiley, Chichester, 1993. The main theme of this book is leadership and vision, with contributions from a number of leading authorities.

Tichy, N. M. and Dervanna, M. A. *The Transformational Leader*, Wiley, New York, 1990. A study of the type of leadership that enables companies to travel down new paths.

Irons, K. (ed.) *Turning Strategy into Action*, Pergamon, Oxford, 1991. A book of reprints of relevant articles from *Long Range Planning*.

The Business Environment (Mainly a UK Bias)

Barham, K. and Rassam, C. *Shaping the Corporate Future*, Unwin Hyman, London, 1989. A good insight into the mega trends which are affecting all businesses. Based on original research.

Heller, R. *The State of Industry*, BBC Books, London, 1987. Useful information about the state of British industry, seen through the eyes of chief executives of major companies. Most were not too happy even in those boom years, and saw major problems in maintaining a competitive position.

Scase, R. and Goffee, R. *Reluctant Managers*, Unwin Hyman, London, 1989. Original research into prevailing attitudes and concerns among British managers.

Taylor, C. *A New Order of Nations*, Strategic Studies Institute, US Army War college, Carlisle Barracks, USA, 1992. A forecast of world population and development.

Weiner, M. J. *English Culture and the Decline of the Industrial Spirit, 1850–1980*, Cambridge University Press, Cambridge, 1981. A study of the causes of the business attitudes of the UK. Very helpful in improving understanding.

INDEX